The Idea of Israel in Second Temple Judaism

In this book, Jason A. Staples proposes a new paradigm for how the biblical concept of Israel developed in Early Judaism and how that concept impacted Jewish apocalyptic hopes for restoration after the Babylonian Exile. Challenging conventional assumptions about Israelite identity in antiquity, his argument is based on a close analysis of a vast corpus of biblical and other early Jewish literature and material evidence. Staples demonstrates that continued hopes for Israel's restoration in the context of diaspora and imperial domination remained central to Jewish conceptions of Israelite identity throughout the final centuries before Christianity and even into the early part of the Common Era. He also shows that Israelite identity was more diverse in antiquity than is typically appreciated in modern scholarship. His book lays the groundwork for a better understanding of the so-called "parting of the ways" between Judaism and Christianity and how earliest Christianity itself grew out of hopes for Israel's restoration.

Jason A. Staples is Assistant Teaching Professor in the Department of Philosophy and Religious Studies at North Carolina State University. He is a 2008 recipient of at the Jacob K. Javits Fellowship and the author of numerous articles on ancient Judaism and early Christianity.

The Idea of Israel in Second Temple Judaism

A New Theory of People, Exile, and Israelite Identity

JASON A. STAPLES

North Carolina State University, Raleigh

CAMBRIDGE
UNIVERSITY PRESS

CAMBRIDGE
UNIVERSITY PRESS

University Printing House, Cambridge CB2 8BS, United Kingdom

One Liberty Plaza, 20th Floor, New York, NY 10006, USA

477 Williamstown Road, Port Melbourne, VIC 3207, Australia

314–321, 3rd Floor, Plot 3, Splendor Forum, Jasola District Centre,
New Delhi – 110025, India

103 Penang Road, #05-06/07, Visioncrest Commercial, Singapore 238467

Cambridge University Press is part of the University of Cambridge.

It furthers the University's mission by disseminating knowledge in the pursuit of
education, learning, and research at the highest international levels of excellence.

www.cambridge.org
Information on this title: www.cambridge.org/9781108842860
DOI: 10.1017/9781108906524

First published 2021
Reprinted 2022

Printed in the United Kingdom by TJ Books Limited, Padstow Cornwall

A catalogue record for this publication is available from the British Library.

ISBN 978-1-108-84286-0 Hardback

Cambridge University Press has no responsibility for the persistence or accuracy
of URLs for external or third-party internet websites referred to in this publication
and does not guarantee that any content on such websites is, or will remain,
accurate or appropriate.

To my parents, Mark and Brenda

מתהלך בתמו צדיק
אשרי בניו אחריו

The righteous walk in integrity
How blessed is the son who follows them!

(Prov 20:7)

Contents

Tables

Preface

The present work is the product of nearly two decades of thought and research and has changed in scope and detail over that time period. I first started thinking seriously about the concept of Israel and its connection to restoration eschatology in William L. Lyons' "Hebrew Bible Prophets" course at Florida State University in the spring of 2003. That was a unique class, with three students proceeding to PhD programs in the field shortly thereafter, and we drank deeply of the prophets all semester. My term paper focused on the new covenant passage in Jeremiah 31:31–34 (LXX 38:31–34), which quickly raised the problem of how to understand "Israel," since that prophecy (along with several others in Jeremiah) promises the restoration and reunification of "the house of Israel and the house of Judah," language that specifically distinguishes the southern kingdom from the northern kingdom, the latter of which had not existed for over a century by the time Jeremiah began to prophesy.

That this prophecy would specifically include the restoration of an Israel that no longer existed in Jeremiah's own day was striking, if for no other reason than that the language of the passage presumes that Judah still lacked an exclusive claim to the Israelite covenant. But what struck me most of all was how familiar I already was with the new covenant prophecy and many other prophetic passages about the restoration of "Israel" from the New Testament, where their application seemed quite different from what I was seeing in their original literary contexts. This led to a much more extensive investigation of the concept of Israel and its variegated development after the Babylonian Exile. The present work is the result of that investigation.

The more I studied, the more the consequences of the fragmentation and siloing of many of the subfields covered in this study became evident. I repeatedly found studies of individual texts or corpora that arrived at similar conclusions to those on other texts or corpora, each study presenting its case as an outlier or exception, seemingly unaware of similar work being done in a related subfield. The number of exceptions soon grew to the point that it became apparent that several foundational assumptions about the concept of Israel in the wider field of Second Temple studies needed to be reexamined. This study aims to do just that, taking a synthetic approach reaching across multiple subfields to reassess those foundations and thus to see important aspects of each subfield more clearly.

In the process, the reader may be confronted at times with a bit of a forest and trees problem, as the larger arguments of this book (the forest) require detailed examinations of specific trees, though obviously with less depth than would be afforded by a specific study of any individual tree. In some respects, this book really involves two forests – the concept of Israel and the relationship of that concept to restoration eschatology. Since any attempt to provide a coherent account of the concept of Israel must also address the overlapping terms "Jew" (*Ioudaios/Yehudi*), and "Hebrew" (*Hebraios*), the first part of the book investigates the relationship of these terms to one another, putting forward a new paradigm for these terms and their respective domains in the Second Temple period. Part II focuses primarily on the narrative construction of the concept of Israel among Jews and others in the Second Temple period and how biblical eschatological perspectives are related to that concept, further reinforcing the model offered in Part I. The third part of the book builds on and tests the theses of the first two parts across a broad corpus of early Jewish literature, paying particular attention to the correlation between eschatological perspectives within specific texts and how Israel is portrayed (or not) in these texts. The Introduction and Chapters 1, 2, and 6 take a broader view in order to critique important assumptions typically embedded in studies of the specific bodies of evidence covered in the book. Otherwise, each chapter deals with a specific literary corpus – biblical narratives of Israel and Judah, the Latter Prophets, Ezra-Nehemiah, 1 and 2 Maccabees, Josephus, Philo of Alexandria, the Dead Sea Scrolls, and other Second Temple literature – arguing that each participates in the larger discourse about Israel by constructing the concept of Israel (and, by extension, the other related terms) in a specific way.

Each of these individual pieces is important for the larger argument of this book, though no single chapter or specific argument is itself determinative. As such, I have tried to make each individual unit worthy of close study in itself, though each chapter ultimately serves as evidence for the big-picture theses about the concept of Israel and restoration eschatology in Second Temple Judaism. The reader who is most interested in the larger theses of the book will therefore have to work through hundreds of pages of detailed discussions of specific cases, since the larger paradigm I am proposing rests on the cumulative persuasiveness of the various pieces of the puzzle and how they fit together. On the other hand, those more interested in my treatment of a specific text or corpus will need to consider the relationship of those specific parts to the comprehensive aims of the book as a whole.[1]

Put simply, this book has two specific aims. The first is to demonstrate the insufficiency of the current paradigms for understanding the concept of "Israel" and its relationship to the related categories and concepts of "Jews" (that is, *Ioudaioi* or *Yehudim*) and "Hebrews" presumed in most studies of early Judaism and early Christianity, offering a new paradigm for understanding these concepts and their relationships throughout the Second Temple period. Secondly, this book argues for a particular relationship between "Israel" language – and the concept of Israel more broadly – and eschatological expectations that appear across a broad range of early Jewish literature. Along the way, there will be a number of subtheses with respect to individual texts or corpora, but ultimately all of these serve to support the ultimate aim of the project: the establishment of a new perspective on Israel as a concept in the Second Temple period.

It should also be noted that since this book covers such a broad corpus of material and challenges several foundational assumptions across several generations of scholarship in multiple subfields, each of which involves its own (often extensive) specialized bibliography, I found it necessary to compress or omit summaries or discussions of prior secondary scholarship for the sake of brevity and readability. I have therefore limited the engagement with prior scholarly work to what seemed necessary to the argument as a whole. At an editorial level, I have translated all substantive foreign-language quotes into English. For longer block quotes, I have provided the original language quotations in corresponding footnotes when that seemed warranted. I have translated the ancient

---

[1] Cf. the similar caveats in E. P. Sanders, *Paul and Palestinian Judaism: A Comparison of Patterns of Religion* (Philadelphia: Fortress, 1977), xii.

source material into English, though in some instances I have also included specific phrases from the original languages to draw the reader's attention to particular verbal elements. All translations of ancient materials are my own except where noted. I have also chosen to transliterate frequently used terms (e.g., *Ioudaios, Yehudi, apoikia*) in the body text to make the book more easily accessible to those readers lacking facility in ancient languages. (Note: italics will mark when *diaspora* is a transliteration of the Greek noun rather than the English term.) Transliterations are based on the standards set forth in the second edition of the *SBL Handbook of Style*. All textual searches were conducted using the relevant modules of *Accordance Bible Software 13* (2019) and verified by hand except where otherwise noted.

This book grew out of the first portion of my PhD dissertation at the University of North Carolina at Chapel Hill, where I was supported by a Jacob K. Javits Fellowship and a Thomas S. and Helen Borda Royster Dissertation Fellowship, the latter in conjunction with the Royster Society of Fellows. Most of this project was written while in visiting faculty positions in the Department of Religious Studies at Wake Forest, the Department of Sociology and Divinity School at Duke, and the Department of Philosophy and Religious Studies at NC State, and I am grateful to my colleagues in those departments for their support.

As grateful as I am to have had institutional support, I am far more grateful to those scholars who have tolerated my obsession with this subject and have generously read and critiqued early versions of this research and/or discussed my theories for so many years. I am especially indebted to my *Doktorvater*, Bart Ehrman, without whose support this project would never have been completed. His incisive mind, passion for clear writing and communication, and especially his generosity and good humor have exemplified what it means to be an advisor, educator, and scholar. Anathea Portier-Young provided exceptionally detailed comments and corrections of an earlier version of this work, many of which rescued me from embarrassing gaffes and for which I am extremely grateful. David Lambert, Zlatko Pleše, Ross Wagner, and Jodi Magness read and critiqued earlier stages of this work and were valuable conversation partners throughout the process. Paula Fredriksen also provided helpful comments on early material, and her generosity and encouragement have meant a great deal. Bill Lyons not only was important in the nascent stages of the project but also has continued to provide encouragement and helpful feedback for nearly two decades. I am also deeply grateful to David Levenson for his tireless training and mentorship while

I was at Florida State, without which I would have been unlikely to pursue this path, and for his continued friendship and assistance on numerous occasions, particularly his suggestions in the Josephus material. I am also indebted to Eibert Tigchelaar and Matthew Goff, each of whom provided early guidance on the Dead Sea Scrolls and apocalyptic works. In addition, James Crenshaw, Joel Marcus, Richard Hays, Shannon Burkes, Randall Styers, Nicole Kelly, John Marincola, and Svetla Slaveva-Griffin were all generous teachers who influenced this project either directly or indirectly.

Others have been valuable conversation partners at various stages of what must have seemed like an unending project. Among these, I am especially indebted to Sonya Cronin, Stephen Carlson, Benjamin L. White, Jason Combs, T. J. Lang, Nathan Eubank, Mark Goodacre, Matthew Gray, Scott Hahn, Michael Barber, Mark Nanos, Douglas Campbell, Tim Cupery, Lauren Leve, Andrew Aghapour, Leif Tornquist, Fr. Gregory (Joshua) Edwards, and Jim Hayes. Early versions of what became portions of the book were delivered as conference papers at various sections of the AAR/SBL Annual Meeting and SECSOR over the past fifteen years; I am grateful for the incisive questions and comments of too many to list from those meetings. Two anonymous readers for Cambridge University Press truly understood the project and provided helpful critiques that improved the final product. I am also grateful for the patience and steady guidance of Beatrice Rehl, Eilidh Burrett, and the full Cambridge University Press team. The many deficiencies that remain in this work are of course my own.

This book would never have been completed without the support and many sacrifices of my family. The constant encouragement and support of my sister and brother-in-law, Stephanie and Erik Rostad, have truly strengthened weak hands and helped to steady feeble knees. Thanks also to Alan, Debbie, Natalie, Holly, Dillon, and Carly Brown for welcoming me into their family and for all their encouragement through this project. Words cannot express my debt of gratitude to Kari, my γνήσιος σύζυγος, whose love and devotion have been a constant source of strength as we have together endured flood, fire, multiple surgeries, graduate school, medical school, and parenthood. Kari has been patient beyond measure when my work has been all-consuming, has shown unusual interest in my scholarly obsessions, and has selflessly lifted me up when my spirits have been low.

Finally, this book is dedicated to my parents, Mark and Brenda Staples, who were my first Bible teachers and trained me to question everything, no matter how firmly established or widely believed, turning over every stone in the quest for truth. My mother taught me to read at an early age and instilled in me a love of learning that has never diminished, while the seeds for the paradigm proposed in this book were sown by my father as we puzzled through difficult texts together in my youth, so it is truly the case that this project was only possible because I am standing on their shoulders.

Abbreviations

Abbreviations of ancient texts follow *The SBL Handbook of Style*, 2nd ed. (Atlanta: SBL Press, 2014).

AB	Anchor Bible
ABRL	Anchor Bible Reference Library
ACEBT	*Amsterdamse Cahiers voor Exegese en Bijbelse Theologie*
Aeg	*Aegyptus*
AGJU	Arbeiten zur Geschichte des antiken Judentums und des Urchristentums
AJSR	*Association for Jewish Studies Review*
AnBib	Analecta Biblica
ANRW	*Aufstieg und Niedergang der römischen Welt: Geschichte und Kultur Roms im Spiegel der neueren Forschung.* Part 2, *Principat.* Edited by Hildegard Temporini and Wolfgang Haase. Berlin: de Gruyter, 1972–
ATANT	Abhandlungen zur Theologie des Alten und Neuen Testaments
ATD	Das Alte Testament Deutsch
BA	*The Biblical Archaeologist*
BAR	*Biblical Archaeology Review*
BASOR	*Bulletin of the American Schools of Oriental Research*
BBET	Beiträge zur biblischen Exegese und Theologie
BBR	*Bulletin for Biblical Research*
BCH	*Bulletin de correspondance hellénique*

BDAG	Bauer, Danker, Arndt, and Gingrich = Danker, Frederick W., Walter Bauer, W. F. Arndt, F. W. Gingrich. *A Greek–English Lexicon on the New Testament and Other Early Christian Literature*. 3rd rev. ed. Chicago: University of Chicago Press, 2000
BEATAJ	Beiträge zur Erforschung des Alten Testaments und des Antiken Judentums
BETL	Bibliotheca Ephemeridum Theologicarum Lovaniensium
Bib	*Biblica*
BibInt	*Biblical Interpretation*
BJS	Brown Judaic Studies
BLS	Bible and Literature Series
BTB	*Biblical Theology Bulletin*
BWANT	Beiträge zur Wissenschaft vom Alten und Neuen Testament
BZAW	Beihefte zur Zeitschrift für die Alttestamentliche Wissenschaft
CBQMS	Catholic Biblical Quarterly Monograph Series
CEJL	Commentaries on Early Jewish Literature
CH	*Church History*
CHANE	Culture and History of the Ancient Near East
CJAS	Christianity and Judaism in Antiquity Series
ConBNT	Coniectanea Biblica: New Testament Series
ConBOT	Coniectanea Biblica: Old Testament Series
CRINT	Compendia Rerum Iudicarum ad Novum Testamentum
CSSCA	Cambridge Studies in Social and Cultural Anthropology
CurBR	*Currents in Biblical Research*
DCLS	Deuterocanonical and Cognate Literature Series
DJD	Discoveries in the Judaean Desert
DJG	*Dictionary of Jesus and the Gospels*. Edited by Joel B. Green, Jeannine, K. Brown, and Nicholas Perrin. 2nd ed. IVP Bible Dictionary Series. Downers Grove, IL: InterVarsity Press, 2013
DSD	*Dead Sea Discoveries*
EDEJ	*The Eerdmans Dictionary of Early Judaism*. Edited by John J. Collins and Daniel C. Harlow. Grand Rapids: Eerdmans, 2010

EDNT	*Exegetical Dictionary of the New Testament.* Edited by Horst Balz and Gerhard Schneider. Translated by James W. Thompson and John W. Mendendorp. 3 vols. Grand Rapids: Eerdmans, 1981
EDSS	*Encyclopedia of the Dead Sea Scrolls.* Edited by Lawrence H. Schiffmann and James C. VanderKam. 2 vols. New York: Oxford University Press, 2000
EJL	Early Judaism and Its Literature
EKKNT	Evangelisch-katholischer Kommentar zum Neuen Testament
EncJud	*Encyclopedia Judaica.* Edited by Cecil Roth and Geoffrey Wigoder. 16 vols. New York: MacMillan, 1971–1972
ErIsr	*Eretz-Israel*
EvQ	*Evangelical Quarterly*
EvT	*Evangelische Theologie*
ExpTim	*Expository Times*
FAT	Forschungen zum Alten Testament
FBE	Forum for Bibelsk Eksegese
FRLANT	Forschungen zur Religion und Literatur des Alten und Neuen Testaments
FZPhTh	*Freiburger Zeitschrift für Philosophie und Theologie*
GAP	Guides to the Apocrypha and Pseudepigrapha
GTA	Göttinger theologischer Arbeiten
HAT	Handbuch zum Alten Testament
HCS	Hellenistic Culture and Society
HdO	Handbuch der Orientalistik
HDR	Harvard Dissertations in Religion
Hen	*Henoch*
Hermeneia	Hermeneia: A Critical and Historical Commentary on the Bible
HeyJ	*Heythrop Journal*
HOS	Handbook of Oriental Studies
HR	*History of Religions*
HS	*Hebrew Studies*
HSM	Harvard Semitic Monographs
HTR	*Harvard Theological Review*
HUCA	*Hebrew Union College Annual*
ICC	International Critical Commentary
IEJ	*Israel Exploration Journal*

Imm	*Immanuel*
Int	*Interpretation*
IVPBDS	IVP Bible Dictionary Series
JAAR	*Journal of the American Academy of Religion*
JAJ	*Journal of Ancient Judaism*
JAJSup	Journal of Ancient Judaism Supplement
JBL	*Journal of Biblical Literature*
JEOL	*Jaarbericht van het Vooraziatisch-Egyptisch Gezelschap (Genootschap) Ex oriente lux*
JETS	*Journal of the Evangelical Theological Society*
JHebS	*Journal of Hebrew Scriptures*
JJS	*Journal of Jewish Studies*
JNES	*Journal of Near Eastern Studies*
JQR	*Jewish Quarterly Review*
JR	*Journal of Religion*
JSHJ	*Journal for the Study of the Historical Jesus*
JSJ	*Journal for the Study of Judaism*
JSJSup	Supplements to the Journal for the Study of Judaism
JSNT	*Journal for the Study of the New Testament*
JSNTSup	Journal for the Study of the New Testament Supplement Series
JSOT	*Journal for the Study of the Old Testament*
JSP	*Journal for the Study of the Pseudepigrapha*
JSPSup	Journal for the Study of the Pseudepigrapha Supplement Series
JSS	*Journal of Semitic Studies*
JSSR	*Journal for the Scientific Study of Religion*
JTS	*Journal of Theological Studies*
Jud	*Judaica*
LHBOTS	Library of Hebrew Bible/Old Testament Studies
LNTS	Library of New Testament Studies
LSJ	Liddell, Scott, Jones = Liddell, Henry George, Robert Scott, Henry Stuart Jones, and Roderick McKenzie. *A Greek–English Lexicon.* 9th ed. With revised and expanded Supplement. Oxford: Oxford University Press, 1996
LSTS	Library of Second Temple Studies
MnemosyneSup	Mnemosyne, Supplements
MQSHR	McGill-Queen's Studies in the History of Religion
NEchtB	Neue Echter Bibel

NedTT	*Nederlands Theologisch Tijdschrift*
Neot	*Neotestamentica*
NICNT	New International Commentary on the New Testament
NovT	*Novum Testamentum*
NovTSup	Supplements to Novum Testamentum
NTOA	Novum Testamentum et Orbis Antiquus
NTS	*New Testament Studies*
OTL	Old Testament Library
OTP	*Old Testament Pseudepigrapha*. Edited by James H. Charlesworth. 2 vols. New York: Doubleday, 1983, 1985
OtSt	*Oudtestamentische Studiën*
PFES	Publications of the Finnish Exegetical Society
POuT	De Prediking van het Oude Testament
PRSt	*Perspectives in Religious Studies*
PS	Patristica Sorbonensia
PSJCO	Princeton Symposium on Judaism and Christian Origins
PT	Playing the Texts
PTSDSSP	Princeton Theological Seminary Dead Sea Scrolls Project
RB	*Revue biblique*
RBL	*Review of Biblical Literature*
RelSRev	*Religious Studies Review*
RevQ	*Revue de Qumran*
RivB	*Rivista biblica italiana*
RTR	*Reformed Theological Review*
SAAB	*State Archives of Assyria Bulletin*
SAAS	State Archives of Assyria Studies
SBET	*Scottish Bulletin of Evangelical Theology*
SBLMS	Society of Biblical Literature Monograph Series
SBLTT	Society of Biblical Literature Texts and Translations
SBTS	Sources for Biblical and Theological Studies
SchwLect	Schweich Lectures of the British Academy
SCJ	Studies in Christianity and Judaism
ScotCS	Scottish Classical Studies
Sem	*Semitica*
SemeiaSt	Semeia Studies
SFSHJ	South Florida Studies in the History of Judaism

SIM	Studies in Intermediality
SJC	Studies in Jewish Civilization
SJOT	*Scandinavian Journal of the Old Testament*
SNTSMS	Society of New Testament Studies Monograph Series
SO	Symbolae Osloensis
SP	Sacra Pagina
SPhilo	*Studia Philonica*
SPhiloA	*Studia Philonica Annual*
STDJ	Studies on the Texts of the Desert of Judah
StPB	Studia Post-biblica
SUNT	Studien zur Umwelt des Neuen Testaments
SVTP	Studia in Veteris Testamenti Pseudepigrapha
SymS	Symposium Series
TA	*Tel Aviv*
TANZ	Texte und Arbeiten zum neutestamentlichen Zeitalter
TBT	*The Bible Today*
TDNT	*Theological Dictionary of the New Testament*. Edited by Gerhard Kittel and Gerhard Friedrich. Translated by Geoffrey W. Bromiley. 10 vols. Grand Rapids: Eerdmans, 1964–1976
TJ	*Trinity Journal*
Transeu	*Transeuphratène*
TS	Texts and Studies
TSAJ	Texte und Studien zum Antiken Judentum
TThSt	Trierer theologische Studien
TUGAL	Texte und Untersuchungen zur Geschichte der altchristlichen Literatur
TWNT	*Theologisches Wörterbuch zum Neuen Testament*. Edited by Gerhard Kittel and Gerhard Friedrich, eds. 10 vols. Stuttgart: Kohlhammer, 1933–1979
TynBul	*Tyndale Bulletin*
USFISFJC	University of South Florida International Studies in Formative Judaism and Christianity
VC	*Vigiliae Christianae*
VCSup	Supplements to Vigiliae Christianae
VT	*Vetus Testamentum*
VTSup	Supplements to Vetus Testamentum
WBC	Word Biblical Commentary

WD	*Wort und Dienst*
WUNT	Wissenschaftliche Untersuchungen zum Neuen Testament
ZAW	*Zeitschrift für die alttestamentliche Wissenschaft*
ZNW	*Zeitschrift für die neutestamentliche Wissenschaft*

Introduction

Investigating the Idea of Israel

Jacob will no longer be your name but Israel, because you have contended with God and with humans and have overcome.

(Gen 32:29)

The name "Israel" is bestowed upon the patriarch Jacob in the book of Genesis after a nocturnal fight with a mysterious figure, who explains this new name by connecting it with a verb meaning to struggle or fight (שרה), resulting in a word that means either "El (God) fights" or "fights with God."[1] The name therefore serves as a description of the patriarch's character as well as an honorary title and a theological statement. This name then passed to the heirs of the patriarch, becoming the covenantal name of the people of YHWH, the inheritors of the divine promises to Abraham, Isaac, and Jacob/Israel. True to its origin, this name has been characterized by conflict and contention over its legacy – and who is its rightful heir – ever since Genesis was penned.

This book is an exploration of that conflict, examining how the concept of Israel was developed, appropriated, and contested in the period roughly between the destruction of Jerusalem by the Babylonians in 587/586 BCE and its destruction by the Romans in 70 CE. This concept is central to the development of Judaism and eventually Christianity, each of which claimed "Israel" for itself over and against its rivals, yet few ideas have proven as complex and elusive. The Mishnah, for example, says "All Israel has a part in the world to come" (m. Sanh. 10:1) but then immediately provides a list of exceptions that set the boundaries of Israel,

---

[1] Gordon J. Wenham, *Genesis 16–50*, WBC 2 (Grand Rapids: Zondervan, 1994), 297.

including Sadducees, Epicureans, those who pronounce the Name, and more (10:1–6). Similarly, a century and a half earlier, the apostle Paul declares "All Israel will be saved" (Rom 11:26) but precedes this statement with the puzzling declaration that "not all from Israel are Israel" (Rom 9:6). This juxtaposition has frustrated interpreters both modern and ancient, as Origen of Caesarea complains, "Who the 'all Israel' are who will be saved ... only God knows, along with his only begotten and perhaps any who are his friends."[2] Many modern interpreters have concluded that when Paul says Israel, he means "empirical" or "ethnic Israel,"[3] but this only begs the question rather than solving the problem, as ethnicity is neither empirical nor self-evident and is inconsistently defined and handled across scholarship.[4]

Granted, prior to the dissolution of the nation-states of Israel and Judah, Israel could be rather straightforwardly defined in national and cultic terms. To be an Israelite was defined by kinship ties and

---

[2] *CER* 4:304. For summaries of the modern discussions, see Christopher Zoccali, "'And so all Israel will be saved': Competing Interpretations of Romans 11.26 in Pauline Scholarship," *JSNT* 30.3 (2008): 289–318; Christopher Zoccali, *Whom God Has Called: The Relationship of Church and Israel in Pauline Interpretation, 1920 to the Present* (Eugene: Pickwick, 2010); Jason A. Staples, "What Do the Gentiles Have to Do with 'All Israel'? A Fresh Look at Romans 11:25–27," *JBL* 130.2 (2011): 371–90.

[3] E.g., Pablo T. Gadenz, *Called from the Jews and from the Gentiles: Pauline Ecclesiology in Romans 9–11*, WUNT 267 (Tübingen: Mohr Siebeck, 2009), 277; Susan Grove Eastman, "Israel and the Mercy of God: A Re-reading of Galatians 6.16 and Romans 9–11," *NTS* 56.3 (2010): 367–95 (368–69); Hans Hübner, *Gottes Ich und Israel: Zum Schriftgebrauch des Paulus in Römer 9–11* (Göttingen: Vandenhoeck & Ruprecht, 1984), 20; Douglas J. Moo, *The Epistle to the Romans*, NICNT (Grand Rapids: Eerdmans, 1996), 721; Robert Jewett, *Romans: A Commentary*, Hermeneia 66 (Minneapolis: Fortress, 2007), 701; James D. G. Dunn, *Romans 9–16*, WBC 38B (Nashville: Nelson, 1988), 681–82; Charles E. B. Cranfield, *A Critical and Exegetical Commentary on the Epistle to the Romans*, 2 vols. ICC (Edinburgh: T&T Clark, 1979), 576–77.

[4] See Ronald Cohen, "Ethnicity: Problem and Focus in Anthropology," *Annual Review of Anthropology.* 7.1 (1978): 379–403; Anthony D. Smith, *The Ethnic Origins of Nations* (Oxford: Blackwell, 1986), 22–30; Jonathan M. Hall, *Ethnic Identity in Greek Antiquity* (Cambridge: Cambridge University Press, 1997), 17–33; Jonathan M. Hall, *Hellenicity: Between Ethnicity and Culture* (Chicago: University of Chicago Press, 2002), 1–29; Rogers Brubaker, "Ethnicity without Groups," *European Journal of Sociology* 43.2 (2002): 163–89; Rogers Brubaker, *Ethnicity without Groups* (Cambridge: Harvard University Press, 2004); Rogers Brubaker, "Ethnicity, Race, and Nationalism," *Annual Review of Sociology* 35 (2009): 21–42. For a discussion of how ethnicity and religion (and their relationship) have been variously defined among scholars discussing Jewish and Christian identities in antiquity, see David M. Miller, "Ethnicity, Religion and the Meaning of *Ioudaios* in Ancient 'Judaism,'" *CurBR* 12.2 (2014): 216–65 (234–42).

participation in the traditional cultus and polity of Israel.[5] But after large portions of Israel were dispossessed of their ancestral land and deported to other regions by imperial powers, the question of who or what constitutes Israel became a much more complex and difficult matter and a source of conflict among those who laid claim to the legacy of Israel. The Jewish groups who returned from exile under the Persians, for example, declared that the people they found living in the territory of Israel upon their return were not in fact Israelites. Disputes between those who sacrificed to YHWH at Mount Gerizim and partisans of the Jerusalem temple persisted throughout the Second Temple period. The sectarian community behind the Dead Sea Scrolls regarded both as illegitimate and looked forward to the ultimate redemption of Israel and the disgrace and destruction of their opponents, both Jews and non-Jews. One can only imagine what the sectarians might have thought of the temple of YHWH at Elephantine. All, however, looked back to the preexilic nation-states of Israel and Judah to establish their ethnic heritage, though not everyone agreed on who else fit within that heritage.

The boundaries of Israel have been contested territory since the end of the Israelite monarchies, and any understanding of early Judaism or the development of Christianity ultimately depends on our ability to map that conceptual territory. This is not as simple a task as it may seem at first glance, as recent scholarship and new evidence – particularly recent discoveries pertaining to the Samaritans – have prompted a reevaluation of old consensus positions regarding the meaning of "Israel" in the larger context of the Second Temple period, with Steve Mason, for example, declaring Israel "a term that merits further exploration across the board."[6] This book undertakes that exploration, aiming to provide a semantic and historical account of the concept of Israel through an analysis of how the concept was shaped and contested throughout the period of inquiry. To this end, this study employs a combination of synchronic and diachronic analysis, examining how the concept of Israel is constructed and employed in individual cases while also evaluating how each of these cases participates in a larger traditional discourse,

---

[5] See Shemaryahu Talmon, "The Emergence of Jewish Sectarianism in the Early Second Temple Period," in *Ancient Israelite Religion: Essays in Honor of Frank Moore Cross*, eds. Patrick D. Miller, Paul D. Hanson, and S. Dean McBride (Philadelphia: Fortress, 1987), 587–616 (592).

[6] Steve Mason, "Jews, Judaeans, Judaizing, Judaism: Problems of Categorization in Ancient History," *JSJ* 38 (2007): 457–512 (490 n. 72).

reshaping the concept and applying it to new contexts.[7] This approach presumes that tradition is both malleable, always involving performative dimensions, and restrictive, delimiting the range of possibilities for participants in the discourse. The aim is therefore not to establish a discrete, stable entity or a specific, single meaning of the word "Israel" but rather to assess the range of possible interpretations when a person referred to "Israel" or "Israelites" in the Second Temple period in light of the traditional narrative substructure of the concept that could assumed by participants in the discourse and how the concept was developed and contested throughout the Second Temple period.

NARRATIVES OF ISRAEL, SOCIAL MEMORY, AND TRADITION IN TRANSITION

Daniel Boyarin has suggested that such a task requires going "back to the very beginnings of the history of Israel after the return from the Babylonian Exile as narrated, in particular, in the book of Ezra,"[8] but I maintain that starting *after* the Babylonian Exile is still too late, since Ezra-Nehemiah already presupposes a dominant conceptual framework and vocabulary of Israel.[9] To understand that framework, we must go

---

[7] Several other recent studies have engaged in similar surveys of a diachronic range of texts to write histories of specific concepts, including Adi Ophir and Ishay Rosen-Zvi, *Goy: Israel's Multiple Others and the Birth of the Gentile* (Oxford: Oxford University Press, 2018); David A. Lambert, *How Repentance Became Biblical: Judaism, Christianity, and the Interpretation of Scripture* (New York: Oxford University Press, 2016); Jonathan Klawans, *Impurity and Sin in Ancient Judaism* (Oxford: Oxford University Press, 2004); Christine E. Hayes, *Gentile Impurities and Jewish Identities* (Oxford University Press, 2002); Jon D. Levenson, *Resurrection and the Restoration of Israel: The Ultimate Victory of the God of Life* (New Haven: Yale University Press, 2006).

[8] Daniel Boyarin, "The IOUDAIOI in John and the Prehistory of Judaism," in *Pauline Conversations in Context: Essays in Honor of Calvin J. Roetzel*, eds. Janice Capel Anderson, Philip Sellew, and Claudia Setzer, JSNTSup 221 (London: Sheffield Academic, 2002), 216–39 (222–23). Boyarin also draws an important distinction between "looking for the degrees of separation backward and not forward," that is, looking to understand debates and negotiations concerning Israel as they already existed before the rise of Christianity "and not forward towards a split between church and 'synagogue'" – or, for the purposes of this study, between the church and "the Jews" ("The IOUDAIOI in John," 228).

[9] Dalit Rom-Shiloni, "From Ezekiel to Ezra-Nehemiah: Shifts of Group Identities within Babylonian Exilic Ideology," in *Judah and the Judeans in the Achaemenid Period: Negotiating Identity in an International Context*, eds. Oded Lipschits, Gary N. Knoppers, and Manfred Oeming (Winona Lake: Eisenbrauns, 2011), 127–51 (129–30): "Ezra-Nehemiah does not mark the beginning of the internal polemic in Yehud; this book rather carries on and transforms a long-lived polemic initiated [at least

back even further to the biblical narratives of Israel that establish a discourse about Israelite status and heritage already presumed in the disputes of Ezra-Nehemiah. These biblical stories, particularly the Primary History of Genesis–2 Kings, served as a sort of "ethnic charter" for communities for which they became foundational.[10] That is, by constructing a "biblical Israel," the biblical authors, editors, and compilers were able to create a mythic common past and a descriptive lexicon for a present people upon which later communities could build their own identities in continuity with that storied past.[11]

Just as E. P. Sanders explains that "it is the fundamental nature of the covenant conception which largely accounts for the relative scarcity of appearances of the term 'covenant' in Rabbinic literature,"[12] the Israel constructed in the biblical narratives became a "basic concept" that could be assumed by later communities, providing the framework for the more frequently cited prophetic and legal material.[13] Indeed, even the

---

as early as] in the early sixth century BCE." Gary N. Knoppers, *Jews and Samaritans: The Origins and History of Their Early Relations* (New York: Oxford University Press, 2013), 12: "the struggles depicted in Ezra-Nehemiah testify to internal Judean debates about identity, ethnicity, and nationality. The very definition of 'Israel' becomes a contested topic in a world in which a number of communities, whether more narrowly or broadly defined, claim to continue the legacy of the descendants of Jacob."

[10] On Genesis–2 Kings as an ethnic charter, cf. Andrew Tobolowsky, *The Sons of Jacob and the Sons of Herakles*, FAT 96 (Tübingen: Mohr Siebeck, 2017), building especially on the work of Jonathan M. Hall, "Ethnic Identity in Greek Antiquity," *Cambridge Archaeological Journal* 8.2 (1998): 265–83; G. Carter Bentley, "Ethnicity and Practice," *Comparative Studies in Society and History* 29.1 (1987): 24–55; Brubaker, *Ethnicity without Groups*; Brubaker, "Ethnicity, Race, and Nationalism"; Pierre Bourdieu, *Outline of a Theory of Practice*, trans. Richard Nice, CSSCA (Cambridge: Cambridge University Press, 1977); Pierre Bourdieu, "Identity and Representation: Elements for a Critical Reflection on the Idea of Region," in *Language and Symbolic Power* (Cambridge: Harvard University Press, 1991), 220–28. See also E. Theodore Mullen, *Narrative History and Ethnic Boundaries: The Deuteronomistic Historian and the Creation of Israelite National Identity*, SemeiaSt (Atlanta: Scholars Press, 1993), 46.

[11] This use of the term "biblical Israel" borrows from Philip R. Davies, *In Search of "Ancient Israel": A Study in Biblical Origins*, 2nd ed., JSOTSup 148 (Sheffield: Sheffield Academic, 1992), which distinguishes between "historical Israel" (the ancient confederacy/kingdom of that name), "biblical Israel" (the Israel of the biblical texts, shaped as it was by authors and redactors), and "ancient Israel" (a modern scholarly construct variously combining the prior two).

[12] Sanders, *Paul and Palestinian Judaism*, 420–21.

[13] "Once a concept has been placed within a historical context, it becomes possible to call it a 'basic concept' [*Grundbegriffe*] if and when all contesting strata and parties find it indispensable to expressing their distinctive experiences, interests, and party-political programs. Basic concepts come to dominate usage because at a given juncture, they register those minimal commonalities without which no experience is possible, and

covenantal framework itself is derived in large measure from the biblical narratives, which establish Israel as the chosen people of YHWH and heirs to the promises to Abraham. The concepts delivered through these stories were unavoidably in the air for those socialized into this environment. Only after immersing in this shared narrative world and rhetorical framework can one begin to understand the discourse of those who later constructed their own identities using that common capital, including a shared vocabulary shaped by those foundational narratives.[14] That is, we must engage in what Meir Sternberg calls "a historical reconstruction that delimits what the writer could have meant against the background of the linguistic knowledge that, even in artful manipulation, he must have taken for granted."[15]

That narrative context can be understood as a form of social memory which, transmitted through authoritative texts and commemorative rituals (e.g., Passover), provides the frame or background against which present events are seen and the lens through which they are interpreted.[16] In addition, this process does not operate without bounds but always applies and appropriates inherited cultural capital, which provides the primordial substance from which present communities and individuals can be shaped.[17] Although collective memory and foundational myths

without which there could be neither conflict nor consensus" (Reinhart Koselleck, "Introduction and Prefaces to the Geschichtliche Grundbegriffe," *Contributions to the History of Concepts* 6.1 [2011]: 1–37 [32]). As such, a basic concept "combines both diverse historical experiences and a multiplicity of meanings" and therefore requires interpretation rather than mere definition. Melvin Richter and Michaela Richter, "Introduction: Translation of Reinhart Koselleck's 'Krise' in Geschichtliche Grundbegriffe," *JHI* 67.2 (2006): 343–56 (345); cf. Koselleck, "Introduction and Prefaces," 20.

[14] Cf. Nathan Thiel, "'Israel' and 'Jew' as Markers of Jewish Identity in Antiquity: The Problems of Insider/Outsider Classification," *JSJ* 45.1 (2014): 80–99 (92–99).

[15] Meir Sternberg, *The Poetics of Biblical Narrative: Ideological Literature and the Drama of Reading* (Bloomington: Indiana University Press, 1985), 11–12.

[16] Cf. Barry Schwartz, "Memory as a Cultural System: Abraham Lincoln in World War II," *American Sociological Review* 61 (1996): 908–27 (910–11); Barry Schwartz, "Social Change and Collective Memory: The Democratization of George Washington," *American Sociological Review* 56 (1991): 221–36; Barry Schwartz, "The Social Context of Commemoration: A Study in Collective Memory," *Social Forces* 61.2 (1982): 374–402; Jeffrey K. Olick and Joyce Robbins, "Social Memory Studies: From 'Collective Memory' to the Historical Sociology of Mnemonic Practices," *Annual Review of Sociology* (1998): 105–40, esp. 383. For an introductory resource on social memory, sometimes also called "collective memory," see Ritva Williams, "BTB Readers' Guide: Social Memory," *BTB* 41.4 (2011): 189–200.

[17] By "cultural capital," I mean a "quantum of social force," as put forth in Pierre Bourdieu, "The Practice of Reflexive Sociology (The Paris Workshop)," in *An Invitation to*

can be altered and shaped in various ways, the "earliest construction of a historical object limits the range of things subsequent generations can do with it."[18] In this way, the present is always constrained and defined by the remembered past as it fits within a given socially mediated narrative framework, even (or perhaps especially) when individuals are not "fully aware of or articulate about the details and variants of the historical narratives that shape their lives."[19] In other words, a received "narrative substructure" and the rhetorical and descriptive lexicon encoded within it serves as the inherited *habitus* that shapes the culture and individuals, but the participants in that culture reshape and modify that *habitus* to serve new purposes.[20] Stephen Grosby reminds us that accepting a tradition carries several consequences:

One is that, through acceptance, traditions are consequently subject to constant change – this much is obvious from the history of ancient Israel, e.g., the reinterpretation of the previously local traditions of the different Judges within the framework of "all Israel," and the relatively late amalgamation of local ancestors into a common genealogy of "all Israel." However beliefs which make up traditions not only change, they also generate change; they actively transform the present, e.g., the development of the belief in a "people" of "all Israel" to whom and only to whom the law applies, or the messianic restoration of the Davidic kingdom.[21]

Shared narratives thus not only shape communities and individuals but also provide the conceptual framework and vocabulary for any discourse among those who share that common *mythos*, specifying cause-and-effect relationships and defining what is significant and what is not.[22] The

Reflexive Sociology, eds. Pierre Bourdieu and Loïc J. C. Wacquant (1992), 216–60 (229–30).

[18] Schwartz, "Social Change," 232.

[19] Christian Smith, "Living Narratives," in *Moral Believing Animals: Human Personhood and Culture* (London: Oxford University Press, 2003), 63–94 (72).

[20] Using the language of Pierre Bourdieu, "Social Space and Symbolic Power," *Sociological Theory* 7.1 (1989): 14–25; Bourdieu, *Theory of Practice*.

[21] Steven Elliott Grosby, *Biblical Ideas of Nationality: Ancient and Modern* (Winona Lake: Eisenbrauns, 2002), 45.

[22] Cf. Alasdair MacIntyre, *After Virtue* (Notre Dame: University of Notre Dame Press, 1981), 204–25; Smith, "Living Narratives"; Douglas Ezzy, "Theorizing Narrative Identity," *Sociological Quarterly* 39.2 (1998): 239–52; Jerome Brunner, "Life as Narrative," *Social Research* 54.1 (1987): 11–32; Peter L. Berger, *The Sacred Canopy: Elements of a Sociological Theory of Religion* (Garden City: Doubleday, 1967), 3–28; William J. Grassie, "Entangled Narratives: Competing Visions of the Good Life," *Sri Lanka Journal of the Humanities* 34.1–2 (2008): 143–66 (143); Paul Ricoeur, *Time and Narrative*, trans. Kathleen McLaughlin and David Pellauer, 3 vols. (Chicago: University

impact of such stories' rhetoric is, for those to whom they are foundational, inescapable, but these stories also provide the substance for new
social and cultural construction in each generation. Moreover, where a
normative body of tradition is accepted, the shared rhetorical conventions
and descriptive lexicon in that received corpus allows for a high degree of
intertextuality that may be incoherent to outsiders.[23] Contemporary
Internet and media culture, for example, is notoriously intertextual and
metareferential, constantly and self-consciously echoing and alluding to
"canonical" or normative material, the knowledge of which is expected to
be shared by at least some fellow insiders in the audience.[24] But if one
does not share the knowledge of the source material, much of what is
being said between the lines is easily missed. The communicative patterns
in ancient debates over the heritage of Israel are similarly intertextual,
fluently appropriating and reshaping phrases, concepts, and narrative

of Chicago Press). Recognition of the centrality of narrative to human action and identity
goes back at least to Plato's *Republic* 2.377c; 3.414e–15c.

[23] Cf. Francis Watson, *Paul and the Hermeneutics of Faith* (London: T&T Clark, 2004), 5,
514. The term "intertextuality" is variously defined. In a poststructuralist context,
"intertextuality" is used to denote the notion of text as infinite and never objective or
singular, as in Julia Kristeva, *Revolution in Poetic Language* (New York: Columbia
University Press, 1984), 60. But the term is also used to denote "the notion of *a strong
form of intertextuality* to denote instances … of a reference, implicit or explicit, to
another distinct text or body of texts" (Wolfgang Funk, *The Literature of
Reconstruction: Authentic Fiction in the New Millennium* [London: Bloomsbury,
2015], 103). This is the sense in which the term tends to be used in biblical studies and
is the sense in which I am using it. See also Graham Allen, *Intertextuality*, 2nd ed., The
New Critical Idiom (London: Routledge, 2011).

[24] "Metareference" has been defined as "a special, transmedial form of usually non-
accidental self-reference produced by signs or sign configurations which are (felt to be)
located on a logically higher level, a 'metalevel,' within an artifact or performance; this
self-reference, which can extend from this artifact to the entire system of the media, forms
or implies a statement about an object-level, namely on (aspects of) the medium/system
referred to" (Werner Wolf, "Metareference across Media: The Concept, its Transmedial
Potentials and Problems, Main Forms and Functions," in *Metareference across Media:
Theory and Case Studies*, ed. Werner Wolf, SIM [Amsterdam: Rodopi, 2009], 1–85 [31];
see also Werner Wolf, ed., *The Metareferential Turn in Contemporary Arts and Media:
Forms, Functions, Attempts at Explanation*, SIM [Amsterdam: Rodopi, 2011]). This
works both at a macro level, such as with Internet memes and allusions to or
reapplications of classic lines or scenes of cinema or television in other works, and on a
subcultural level, as in the numerous "Easter eggs" scattered throughout notoriously self-
referential cinematic "comic book universes." Cf. Kevin Flynn, *The Digital Frontier:
Mapping the Other Universe* (Los Angeles: Quotable Publishing, 1985). For Paul and
other early Jews, biblical or prophetic material is understood to be located on a logically
higher "metalevel," so self-referential use of such material falls under the category
of metareference.

elements from the (biblically dominated) narrative world in which they lived and argued.[25] Wolfgang Funk has noted how such metareferential practice serves a "reconstructive" function, as the new participants in the discourse renegotiate and reshape their discourse and their narrative world.[26] In the same way, the later appropriations of biblical and other inherited Jewish traditions serve the same reconstructive function, applying inherited capital to reconstruct new, renegotiated boundaries.

The biblical narratives thus established Israel as a basic concept that could be assumed, contested, and reinterpreted – but not ignored – by those who used the term "Israel" in later periods.[27] As Jacob Neusner explains, "the doctrine of what is 'Israel' and who is Israel, as worked out over [more than] seven hundred years, forms the critical component that held the whole system together."[28] Later figures like Paul or Judah ha-Nasi constructed their own interpretations of Israel's narrative, but they were themselves unavoidably shaped – and their interpretations limited – by this narrative as they had received it from prior generations, largely mediated through the Jewish Scriptures and prior interpretations thereof.[29] The multigenerational discourse concerning Israelite status is therefore rooted in the biblical texts, which provide the cultural, rhetorical, and idiomatic grammar for the controversies of later periods.[30] Consequently, the varying conceptions of Israel represented in the Second

---

[25] Cf. Richard B. Hays, *Echoes of Scripture in the Letters of Paul* (New Haven: Yale University Press, 1989), 157–58; Watson, *Hermeneutics of Faith*, 3. See also James M. Scott, "Paul's Use of Deuteronomic Tradition," *JBL* 112.4 (1993): 645–65.

[26] See Funk, *The Literature of Reconstruction*. Funk's language of reconstruction is itself intertextual, playing on Derrida's notion of "deconstruction" or *différance* (cf. Funk, *The Literature of Reconstruction*, 4–6).

[27] Richter and Richter, "Introduction," 345–46: "Basic concepts become indispensable to any formulation of the most urgent issues of a given time. They are, moreover, inherently controversial and contested, especially so in times of crisis, when the semantic struggle for definitions of social and political position becomes particularly acute."

[28] Jacob Neusner, *Judaism and Its Social Metaphors: Israel in the History of Jewish Thought* (Cambridge: Cambridge University Press, 1989), 14.

[29] Cf. Neusner's observation that the early rabbis "created, but they were also created by, Rabbi Jeremiah, among other prophets" (*In the Aftermath of Catastrophe: Founding Judaism 70 to 640*, MQSHR [Montreal: McGill-Queen's University Press, 2009], 121).

[30] On the implications of the development of scripture and ultimately canon in the Second Temple period and various modes of interpretation, see Shaye J. D. Cohen, *From the Maccabees to the Mishnah* (Philadelphia: Westminster, 1987), 184–204. For myth "as a class of *social argumentation*" through which humans "construct, authorize, and contest their social identities," see Russell T. McCutcheon, "Myth," in *A Modest Proposal on Method: Essaying the Study of Religion*, Supplements to Method and Theory in the Study of Religion 2 (Leiden: Brill, 2014), 52–71 (63).

Temple period are so dependent on the basic concept of Israel mediated
through biblical narratives and their accompanying interpretive traditions
that this earlier material – which provides their "narrative substructure" –
must be examined first.[31]

In this context, it is important to remember that ancient readers did not
read biblical texts like modern critical scholars but instead read them as a
unified narrative reporting the truth about the past, looking to the biblical
narratives to understand their own place in the cosmos. Thus, as always,
the constructed past, the *remembered* past, is more important for shaping
the present than the *actual historical events* of the past. As such, this book
does not attempt to reconstruct the empirical history underlying the
biblical narratives or to establish an inherent, transcendent ideal definition of Israel from the past but rather aims to show how the texts
construct a biblical Israel that provided the foundation for later communities and then how ancient readers built upon that concept, depending
upon and limited by the rhetorical conventions and descriptive lexicon
bestowed by the biblical framework. Nevertheless, our reconstructions of
that framework must be verified by examining how later readers inter-
acted with and interpreted these foundational traditions, meaning this
study must engage in the recursive process of examining both the foundational texts and how those texts were understood by later interpreters,[32]
thereby revealing both continuities and discontinuities within the larger
tradition.[33]

---

[31] For the concept of "Israel" as first developed in biblical literature as a "social metaphor"
central to the development of subsequent Judaism(s), see Neusner, *Judaism and Its Social
Metaphors*. For the concept of the Hebrew Bible/Old Testament serving as a critical
component of a traditional "substructure" for later authors further developing the
tradition for a new context, see especially Richard B. Hays, *The Faith of Jesus Christ:
The Narrative Substructure of Galatians 3:1–4:11*, rev. ed. (Grand Rapids: Eerdmans,
2002). Cf. also C. H. Dodd, *According to the Scriptures: The Sub-Structure of New
Testament Theology* (London: Collins, 1965). More generally, Koselleck reminds us that
a basic "concept combines in itself an abundance of meanings. Thus a concept may be
clear, but it must be ambiguous. It bundles together the richness of historical experience
and the sum of theoretical and practical lessons drawn from it in such a way that their
relationship can be established and properly understood only through a concept"
(Koselleck, "Introduction and Prefaces," 20).

[32] Thus Ricoeur explains that once around the circle is insufficient; rather, the circle must be
traversed repeatedly, allowing the text an active role in refiguring our understanding for
the next trip around the circle. See Paul Ricoeur, *Interpretation Theory: Discourse and
the Surplus of Meaning* (Fort Worth: Texas Christian University Press, 1976), 86–95;
Hans-Georg Gadamer, *Truth and Method* (London: Continuum, 2004).

[33] Cf. Lambert, *How Repentance Became Biblical*, 8–9.

This recursive process is reflected in the structure of this book, which is divided into three parts, each of which has its own focus while also depending to some degree on the others. Part I begins the study by demonstrating the inadequacy of the present paradigms – and proposing a new one – for understanding the terms Israel, Jew (*Ioudaios/Yehudi*), and Hebrew (*Hebraios*), focusing primarily on data from Josephus (Chapter 1) and the problem of Samaritan origins (Chapter 2). Starting from the problems and potential solutions discussed in the prior section, Part II analyzes the construction and development of the concept of Israel in biblical literature, paying particular attention to how Israel is rhetorically situated in biblical narratives of preexilic Israel (Chapter 3), the Latter Prophets (Chapter 4), and narratives set in the land after the Babylonian Exile (Chapter 5). This section further undergirds the paradigm proposed in Part I by showing that although there are many differences and discontinuities across the tradition, the concept of Israel is closely linked to "Restoration eschatology" (in its many forms) throughout biblical literature,[34] which helps explain the distinctions observed in Josephus in the first part of the study. Part III then tests the conclusions of the first two parts across a broad corpus of early Jewish literature, first arguing for the continued influence of restoration eschatology in the diaspora (Chapter 6) and then attempting to survey every extant pre-Christian text relevant to the development and application of the concept of Israel in the Second Temple period (Chapters 7–11).[35] The book concludes (Chapter 12) with a summary of the various continuities and discontinuities observed throughout the study and conclusions that can be drawn with respect to the range of interpretations available for "Israel" in the Second Temple period.

EXCURSUS: ANCIENT JEWS OR JUDAEANS?

Before concluding this introduction, it is necessary to address the controversial matter of how to render ancient terms such as the Hebrew *Yehudi*,

---

[34] For an explanation of the terminology of "restoration eschatology," see pp. 95–98.
[35] Since this book is concerned with establishing the parameters of the discourse concerning the concept of Israel prior to the advent of Christianity, which significantly complicates that discourse, it does not substantively address material from the New Testament that falls within the Second Temple period, though such material will occasionally draw a stray mention.

Aramaic *Yehuda'i*, Greek *Ioudaios*, or Latin *Iudaeus* into English, as
many scholars in recent years have argued that "Judaean" is a better
rendering of these terms than the more traditional translation "Jew."[36] It
is worth taking a moment to consider this debate, as it relates closely to
the thesis of the book as a whole. The preference for "Judaean" arose
largely because of concerns about anti-Judaism in the New Testament,
particularly in the Gospel of John, which often identifies the opponents of
Jesus simply as "the *Ioudaioi*" (e.g., 5:16–18, 7:1; 10:31–33), effectively
differentiating this group as an "other" from the perspective of the reader.
Translating *Ioudaios* with the familiar word "Jew" therefore potentially
encourages modern audiences to associate John's negative portrayal of
the *Ioudaioi* with modern Jews.[37] One solution, popularized by Malcolm
Lowe's influential 1976 article, has been to read *Ioudaios* as primarily a
geographical label in John – that is, as referring to inhabitants of Judaea,
in accordance with what Lowe calls "the Palestinian use of Ἰουδαῖος to
distinguish Judeans from Galileans, etc."[38] John's *Ioudaioi* therefore
refers to a specific subgroup of Jews – those specifically from Judaea –
and should therefore be rendered with "Judaean" rather than "Jew." To
do otherwise is to "provide a constant excuse for antisemitism whose
further existence cannot be permitted."[39] Others have since extended this
judgment well beyond the Gospel of John to include all uses of *Ioudaios*
and other ancient cognates such as *Yehudi* in ancient literature until some
point of transition at which (ethnic/geographic) Judaeans became (religious) Jews, though the timing of this alleged transition differs widely.[40]

---

[36] E.g., Mason, "Jews, Judaeans"; Philip F. Esler, *Conflict and Identity in Romans: The
Social Setting of Paul's Letter* (Minneapolis: Fortress, 2003), 68; BDAG, s.v. "Ἰουδαῖος,"
478–79, 478; John H. Elliot, "Jesus the Israelite Was Neither a 'Jew' Nor a 'Christian':
On Correcting Misleading Nomenclature," *JSHJ* 5.2 (2007): 119–54. This movement has
been growing in influence; the new Brill translations of Josephus edited by Mason, for
example, consistently translate Ioudaios with "Judaean."

[37] For example, Sonya S. Cronin has persuasively demonstrated how theological concerns
influenced the work of Raymond Brown in this respect (*Raymond Brown, "The Jews,"
and the Gospel of John: From Apologia to Apology*, LNTS 504 [London: T&T Clark,
2015], 23–38, 154–86).

[38] Malcolm Lowe, "Who Were the IOYΔAIOI?," *NovT* 18.2 (1976): 101–30 (130). Lowe's
conclusion was anticipated by John Henry Bernard, *A Critical and Exegetical
Commentary on the Gospel according to St. John*, 2 vols. ICC (T&T Clark, 1928),
34–35 and Karl Bornhäuser, *Das Johannesevangelium, eine Missionsschrift für Israel*
(Gütersloh: 1928), 140.

[39] Lowe, "Who Were the IOYΔAIOI," 130.

[40] To take just two examples, Shaye Cohen suggests the transition happened in "the second
or early first century [BCE]" (*The Beginnings of Jewishness: Boundaries, Varieties,
Uncertainties* [Berkeley: University of California Press, 1999], 109), while Steve Mason

Advocates of this position have gone so far as to suggest that "translating Ἰουδαῖοι as 'Jews' is not only intellectually indefensible ... but also morally questionable."[41] Unfortunately, this simple solution comes with its own potential negative consequences. Amy-Jill Levine explains:

> The Jew is replaced with the Judean, and thus we have a *Judenrein* ('Jew free') text, a text purified of Jews. Complementing this erasure, scholars then proclaim that Jesus is neither Jew nor even Judean, but Galilean ... Once Jesus is not a Jew or a Judean, but a Galilean, it is also an easy step to make him an Aryan. So much for the elimination of anti-Semitism by means of changing vocabulary.[42]

These concerns are well-founded, as illustrated by the work of Walter Grundmann, a Nazi Party member and leader of "The Institute for the Study and Eradication of Jewish Influence from German Church Life,"[43] who argued that Jesus was not a Jew because "Judaism" (*Judentum*) had been confined to Judaea, the region around Jerusalem, while Galilee was not populated by Jews but by Aryans who had been transplanted to the land by the Assyrians and were only later forcibly converted to Judaism under the Hasmoneans.[44] Grundmann's arguments anticipate several

---

suggests "Jew" and "Judaism" should be avoided until Late Antiquity ("Jews, Judaeans," 457). Cf. Cynthia M. Baker, *Jew* (Rutgers University Press, 2017), 20.

[41] Esler, *Conflict and Identity*, 68; cf. also Fredrick Danker's unusually prescriptive comment in BDAG, s.v. "Ἰουδαῖος," 478–79. See also the analysis in Baker, *Jew*, 22–24.

[42] Amy-Jill Levine, *The Misunderstood Jew: The Church and the Scandal of the Jewish Jesus* (San Francisco: HarperOne, 2006), 160, 165.

[43] See Susannah Heschel, "Nazifying Christian Theology: Walter Grundmann and the Institute for the Study and Eradication of Jewish Influence on German Church Life," *CH* 63.4 (1994): 587–605; Peter Osten-Sacken, "Walter Grundmann – Nationalsozialist, Kirchenmann und Theologe: Mit einem Ausblick auf die Zeit nach 1945," in *Das missbrauchte Evangelium: Studien zu Theorie und Praxis der Thüringer Deutschen Christen*, ed. Peter Osten-Sacken (Berlin: Institut Kirche und Judentum, 2002), 280–312; Peter M. Head, "The Nazi Quest for an Aryan Jesus," *JSHJ* 2.1 (2004): 55–89 (70–89).

[44] Walter Grundmann, *Jesus der Galiläer und das Judentum* (Leipzig: Wigand, 1940); Walter Grundmann, *Die 28 Thesen der sächsischen Volkskirche erläutert*, Schriften der Deutschen Christen (Dresden: Deutsch-christlicher, 1934). Grundmann also embraced the idea that Jesus was in fact fathered by a Roman soldier (an Aryan, of course), embracing previous polemics against the virgin birth for its racial implications. Thus Grundmann argues Jesus was born of an Aryan mother and father. Cf. Susannah Heschel, *The Aryan Jesus: Christian Theologians and the Bible in Nazi Germany* (Princeton: Princeton University Press, 2008), 154–65; Hans Dieter Betz, "Wellhausen's Dictum 'Jesus was not a Christian, but a Jew' in Light of Present Scholarship," *St* 45.2 (1991): 83–110; David M. Miller, "The Meaning of *Ioudaios* and Its Relationship to Other Group Labels in Ancient 'Judaism,'" *CurBR* 9.1 (2010): 98–126 (110). Subsequent studies have shown Grundmann's argument about the non-Jewish composition of Galilee to be aberrant. See Mark A. Chancey, *The Myth of a Gentile Galilee* (Cambridge:

recent studies, as similar distinctions between Galileans and *Ioudaioi* have once again gained currency in recent years.

Richard Horsley, for example, argues that the Galileans were not *Ioudaioi*, which he renders "Judaeans,"[45] but were instead descended from the remnants of the northern tribes remaining after the Assyrian campaigns of the eighth century BCE and – as Grundmann also argued – forcibly brought under Judaean rule only in the Hasmonean period.[46] But it is Bruce Malina's efforts in this area, however, that have especially validated Levine's concerns. On the basis of the discredited Khazar theory, which claims that most modern Jews are ethnically unrelated to ancient *Ioudaioi*,[47] Malina argues that in contrast to the modern religiously oriented term "Jew," *Ioudaios* refers to someone "situated geographically [in Judaea] ... organically related to and rooted in a place, with its distinctive environs, air, and water."[48] It is difficult to read such a statement without immediately thinking of nineteenth- and early twentieth-century discourses criticizing the Jews as lacking appropriate ethnic (*völkisch*) ties to a distinct political and geographic place.[49] In

Cambridge University Press, 2002); Jonathan L. Reed, *Archaeology and the Galilean Jesus: A Re-examination of the Evidence* (Harrisburg: Trinity Press International, 2002), 23–61; Eric M. Meyers, "Galilean Regionalism as a Factor in Historical Reconstruction," *BASOR* 220/221 (1976): 93–101; Eric M. Meyers, "The Cultural Setting of Galilee: The Case of Regionalism and Early Judaism," *ANRW* 19.1 (1979): 686–702.

[45] Cf. Richard A. Horsley, *Galilee: History, Politics, People* (Valley Forge: Trinity Press International, 1995), 13.

[46] Horsley, *Galilee*, esp. 1–61.

[47] Bruce J. Malina and John J. Pilch, *Social-science Commentary on the Book of Revelation* (Minneapolis: Fortress Press), 64. See James G. Crossley, "What a Difference a Translation Makes! An Ideological Analysis of the *Ioudaios* Debate," *Marginalia Review of Books*, http://marginalia.lareviewofbooks.org/difference-translation-makes-ideological-analysis-ioudaios-debate-james-crossley. It must be emphasized here that the Khazar theory has been repeatedly discredited by genetic studies of various Jewish populations and any scholarly model based on it (including Malina's) is not only to be rejected but repudiated. See Gil Atzmon et al., "Abraham's Children in the Genome Era: Major Jewish Diaspora Populations Comprise Distinct Genetic Clusters with Shared Middle Eastern Ancestry," *American Journal of Human Genetics* 86.6 (2010): 850–59; Robert Myles and James G. Crossley, "Biblical Scholarship, Jews and Israel: On Bruce Malina, Conspiracy Theories and Ideological Contradictions," *BibleInterp*, www.bibleinterp.com/opeds/myl368013.shtml.

[48] Malina and Pilch, *Social-science Commentary on the Book of Revelation*, 65.

[49] On the sense and importance of *Volk* and *völkisch* in this context, see David M. Miller, "Ethnicity Comes of Age: An Overview of Twentieth-Century Terms for *Ioudaios*," *CurBR* 10 (2012): 293–311 (297–99); James E. McNutt, "A Very Damning Truth: Walter Grundmann, Adolf Schlatter, and Susannah Heschel's The Aryan Jesus," *HTR* 105.3 (2012): 280–301 (8).

contrast to Malina's overt anti-Judaism, Horsley explains that his project aims to replace the idea that Jesus opposed "Judaism," which allegedly did not yet exist in Jesus' day, with a supposedly more robust idea of Jesus the Galilean opposing the southern Judaeans who had imposed their hegemony upon the Galileans.[50] Similarly, though not tying the distinction to northern Israelite ancestry, Daniel Boyarin distinguishes between the Galileans, only ambivalently connected to the temple-state based in Jerusalem, and the *Ioudaioi*, whom he defines as "an originally geographically based group maintaining a certain pietistic version of Israelite religion."[51] Inasmuch as these approaches result in a "non-Jewish Jesus," they remain troublesome with respect to the problem of anti-Judaism,[52] but the bigger problem is that the geographical rendering of *Ioudaios*, including the Judaean/Galilean distinction, also does not adequately represent the ancient evidence.

The most obvious counterevidence, as Lowe and Boyarin acknowledge, is that Galileans – including Jesus himself – are also called *Ioudaioi* in the Gospel of John (4:9; 6:41, 52; 19:19),[53] and *Ioudaios* is regularly used outside the Gospel of John to refer to people not only from Galilee but also from across the diaspora. The epigraphic evidence from the diaspora is also especially problematic. There are, Margaret Williams explains, "no hard epigraphic examples of *Ioudaios* meaning 'person (not necessarily Jewish) from Judaea'"; instead, when it occurs in ancient Mediterranean inscriptions, *Ioudaios* "simply refers to Jews wherever found and whatever their geographical origin."[54] Interestingly, Josephus specifically argues against the misconception that

---

[50] Horsley, *Galilee*, 1–15.

[51] Boyarin, "The IOUDAIOI in John," 237. Cornelis Bennema, "The Identity and Composition of OI IOYΔAIOI in the Gospel of John," *TynBul* 60.2 (2009): 239–63 (262), follows Boyarin's reading of Ioudaioi in John as strict "Torah- and temple-loyalists."

[52] April D. DeConick, "Jesus the Israelite?," *Forbidden Gospels Blog*, http://aprildeconick .com/forbiddengospels/2007/09/jesus-israelite.html.

[53] Cf. John Ashton, *Understanding the Fourth Gospel* (Oxford: Oxford University Press, 1993), 133; Boyarin, "The IOUDAIOI in John," 221–22 n. 20.

[54] Margaret H. Williams, "The Meaning and Function of *Ioudaios* in Graeco-Roman Inscriptions," *ZPE* (1997): 249–62 (252), *contra* the claim of A. Thomas Kraabel, "The Roman Diaspora: Six Questionable Assumptions," *JJS* 33.1–2 (1982): 445–64 (455), for which he provides no corroborating evidence (as observed by Williams, 251). Williams also shows that there is no evidence that the term ever denotes pagan sympathizers with Judaism, as suggested by Ross Shepard Kraemer, "On the Meaning of the Term Jew in Greco-Roman Inscriptions," *HTR* 82.1 (1989): 35–53 (49). See Williams, "Meaning and Function," 252–53.

Ioudaios was originally or primarily a geographic term,[55] reporting and rebutting stories that the *Ioudaioi* were the worst of the Egyptians driven out of their own land into Judaea, from which they took their name (*Ag. Ap.* 1.227–303),[56] as well as Aristotle's belief (through Clearchus) that the *Ioudaioi* were Indian philosophers "called Calami by the Indians and *Ioudaioi* by the Syrians, for they took their name from Judaea, the place they inhabit" (*Ag. Ap.* 1.179).[57] Instead, Josephus explains, Judaea got its name from the *Ioudaioi* rather than the reverse (*Ant.* 11.173),[58] and geography is therefore not a necessary or inherent component of what it means to be a *Ioudaios* – an important distinction for *Ioudaioi* in the diaspora who sought to retain their own customs rather than adopting those of their present lands.[59]

The argument for preferring "Judaean" has consequently shifted from a geographical basis to the claim that the word "Judaean" better represents the ethnic sense of the ancient terms without the imposition of the anachronistic modern category of religion allegedly implied by the word

---

[55] The term *Ioudaios* itself is a loanword derived from the Hebrew *Yehudi* and Aramaic *Yehuda'i*. Since Greek does not have a consonant equivalent to *hey*, the first two vowel sounds are joined at the beginning of the word without an intervening consonant, but the word was pronounced with the initial vowel distinct from the following diphthong (ye-oo-DAI-os), rather than as typically pronounced by most modern native English speaking readers today (you-DAI-os), thus the occasional form Ἐιουδαῖος. See Walter Gutbrod, "Ἰουδαῖος, Ἰσραήλ, Ἑβραῖος in Greek Hellenistic Literature," *TDNT* 3: 369–75 (369 n. 81). Given that *Ioudaios* is a loanword, it is peculiar that Esler, *Conflict and Identity*, 58–60, spends so much time on "The Territorial Dimension to Greek Names for Ethnic Groups," and bases his argument for "Judaeans" in large part on the fact that "among the Greeks it was the practice to name ethnic groups in relation to the territory in which they originated" (63).

[56] Cf. Lowe, "Who Were the ΙΟΥΔΑΙΟΙ," 105–06.

[57] For similar pagan polemical claims regarding the origin of the Jews, see Strabo, *Geography* 16.34–6 and Origen's report of Celsus' views in *Contra Celsum* 3.5. Remarkably, Lowe uses these very gentile reports as evidence "that the geographical senses of Ἰουδαῖοι … formed the *primary* meaning of the term in New Testament times" ("Who Were the ΙΟΥΔΑΙΟΙ," 105–06; followed in this respect by Esler, *Conflict and Identity*, 58–60, 63–64).

[58] Peter J. Tomson, "The Names Israel and Jew in Ancient Judaism and in the New Testament," *Bijdragen: Tijdschrift voor filosophie en theologie* 47 (1986): 120–40, 266 (124), rightly summarizes Josephus' report: "the name Jews … derives from the tribal, and later territorial, name Judah."

[59] Cf. John Ashton, "The Identity and Function of The Ἰουδαῖοι in the Fourth Gospel," *NovT* 27.1 (1985): 40–75 (46); Sean Freyne, "Behind the Names: Samaritans, Ioudaioi, Galileans," in *Text and Artifact in the Religions of Mediterranean Antiquity: Essays in Honour of Peter Richardson(9)*, eds. Stephen G. Wilson and Michel Desjardins, SCJ 9 (Waterloo: Wilfrid Laurier University Press, 2000), 389–401 (395).

"Jew."[60] But this attempt to distinguish between religion and ethnicity is itself anachronistic, as these categories were not disentangled from one another in antiquity. That is, the category of "Ethnicity" as distinct from "religious" qualities is no less modern than the category of religion.[61] To be a part of an *ethnos* meant (and still presumes!) observing cultural and cultic practices. The Roman historian Dio Cassius, for example, explicitly states, "I do not know the origin of this name [*Ioudaios*], but it is applied to all men, even foreigners, who follow their customs. This race is found even among Romans."[62] Similarly, Josephus reports that when the Roman proconsul Lucius Lentulus granted special privileges to Roman citizens in Ephesus who were *Ioudaioi*, he defined that group as "those who appear to me to have and do the sacred things of the Jews" (*Ant.* 14.234; cf. 14.228, 237, 240).[63] In the ancient world, Paula Fredriksen observes, "gods really did run in the blood. Put differently: cult, as enacted and as imagined, defined ethnicity."[64] This was especially true

[60] E.g., Cohen, *Beginnings of Jewishness*, 70; Cynthia M. Baker, "A 'Jew' by Any Other Name," *JAJ* 2 (2011): 153–80 (125); Mason, "Jews, Judaeans," 457; Esler, *Conflict and Identity*, 68; Elliot, "Jesus the Israelite," 133.

[61] Michael L. Satlow, "Jew or Judaean?," in *"The One Who Sows Bountifully": Essays in Honor of Stanley K. Stowers*, eds. Caroline Johnson Hodge et al., BJS 356 (Providence: Brown Judaic Studies, 2014), 165–75 (165–76); Miller, "Ethnicity, Religion," 239–40; Ashton, "Identity and Function," 45–46.

[62] Dio Cassius 37.17.1. See Menahem Stern, ed., *Greek and Latin Authors on Jews and Judaism, Vol 2: From Tacitus to Simplicius* (Jerusalem: Israel Academy of Sciences and Humanities, 1980), #406. Other Roman authors regard *superstitio* to be the distinctive characteristic of the Ioudaioi (e.g., Cicero, *Flac.* 28.67; Quintilian, *Inst.* 3.7.21; Tacitus, *Hist.* 5.4.1, 5.7.2, 13.1). Thus Daniel Boyarin and Jonathan Boyarin, "Diaspora: Generation and the Ground of Jewish Identity," *Critical Inquiry* 19 (1993): 693–725 (694 n. 2), concludes: "We see from this quotation that race once had much suppler and more complex connections with genealogy, cultural praxis, and identity than it has in our parlance."

[63] On these laws, see Miriam Pucci Ben Zeev, *Jewish Rights in the Roman World: The Greek and Roman Documents Quoted by Josephus Flavius*, TSAJ 74 (Tübingen: Mohr Siebeck, 1998), 150–91. Christiane Saulnier, "Lois romaines sur les Juifs selon Flavius Josèphe," *RB* 88.2 (1981): 161–98 (168–69). Cf. also Shaye J. D. Cohen, "'Those Who Say They are Jews and Are Not': How Do You Know a Jew in Antiquity When You See One," in *Diasporas in Antiquity*, eds. Shaye J. D. Cohen and Ernst S. Frerichs (1993), 1–45 (31). Cf. also Freyne, "Behind the Names," 396.

[64] Paula Fredriksen, "Compassion is to Purity as Fish is to Bicycle and Other Reflections on Constructions of 'Judaism' in Current Work on the Historical Jesus," in *Apocalypticism, Anti-Semitism and the Historical Jesus: Subtexts in Criticism*, eds. John S. Kloppenborg and John W. Marshall, JSNTSup 275 (London: T&T Clark, 2005), 55–67 (57); cf. also Lowe, "Who Were the ΙΟΥΔΑΙΟΙ," 107, and the limitations noted by Seth Schwartz, "How Many Judaisms Were There? A Critique of Neusner and Smith on Definition and Mason and Boyarin on Categorization," *JAJ* 2.2 (2011): 208–38 (234).

of ancient *Ioudaioi*, who were distinctive as an *ethnos* precisely because of cultural elements – that is, their sacred ancestral laws – that would be categorized as "religious" today,[65] and whose corporate identity was "much more conspicuously and obviously religious in nature ... than that of any other national or ethnic group in the Mediterranean world and the Near East."[66]

The evidence simply does not support any attempt to distinguish the ethnic and religious aspects of Israel or Jewishness in this period,[67] and any attempt to differentiate between these categories with respect to the Greek term *Ioudaios* and its ancient cognates is therefore even more anachronistic than the word "Jew." The ancient languages simply lack separate words for the ethnic, cultural, geographical, or religious aspects of being a *Ioudaios* or *Yehudi*, making any efforts to distinguish between such categories in these ancient sources untenable.[68] In contrast to the ambiguity inherent in the ancient terms, "Judaean" artificially and anachronistically limits the meaning to a geographical sense, leading

---

[65] Cohen, "Those Who Say," 32; Boyarin, "The IOUDAIOI in John," 221; Daniel R. Schwartz, "Yannai and Pella, Josephus and Circumcision," *DSD* 18.3 (2011): 339–59 (235); Daniel R. Schwartz, "Judeans, Jews, and their Neighbors," in *Between Cooperation and Hostility: Multiple Identities in Ancient Judaism and the Interaction with Foreign Powers*, eds. Thomas Römer and Jakob Wöhrle, JAJSup 11 (Göttingen: Vandenhoeck & Ruprecht, 2013), 13–32; Lawrence M. Wills, "Jew, Judean, Judaism in the Ancient Period: An Alternative Argument," *JAJ* 7.2 (2016): 169–93 (175–76); Yuval Shahar, "Imperial Religious Unification Policy and Its Decisive Consequences: Diocletian, the Jews and the Samaritans," in *Romans, Barbarians, and the Transformation of the Roman World: Cultural Interaction and the Creation of Identity in Late Antiquity*, eds. Ralph W. Mathisen and Danuta Shanzer (Farnham: Ashgate, 2011), 109–19 (110).

[66] Schwartz, "How Many Judaisms," 238; cf. also John J. Collins, *Between Athens and Jerusalem: Jewish Identity in the Hellenistic Diaspora*, 2nd ed. (Grand Rapids: Eerdmans, 2000), 19; Benjamin Isaac, "Ethnic Groups in Judaea under Roman Rule," in *The Near East under Roman Rule*, eds. Aryeh Kasher and Aharon Oppenheimer (Brill, 1998), 257–67 (260).

[67] Cf. Jacob Neusner, "Was Rabbinic Judaism Really 'Ethnic'? A Theological Comparison between Christianity and the So-Called Particularist Religion of Israel," *CBQ* 57.2 (1995): 281–305; Jacob Neusner, "The Premise of Paul's Ethnic Israel," in *Children of the Flesh, Children of the Promise: A Rabbi Talks with Paul* (Cleveland: Pilgrim, 1995), 1–20 (4–5).

[68] "Such a usage, if established, would indeed be singular: it would be like using the word 'Poles' to *distinguish* the inhabitants of Poland from Poles living abroad ... One would need, surely, separate words (poles apart) for natives and expatriates, which is what we do not have" (Ashton, "Identity and Function," 55). Cf. Baker, "A 'Jew' by Any Other Name," 155–56; Wills, "Jew, Judean, Judaism," 171; Annette Yoshiko Reed, "*Ioudaios* Before and After 'Religion,'" *Marginalia Review of Books* (2014), http://marginalia .lareviewofbooks.org/ioudaios-religion-annette-yoshiko-reed/.

to inevitable misunderstandings.[69] In this light, I agree with Cynthia Baker's conclusion that, "As a stand-in for 'ethnic group,' its [Judaean's] ability to clarify is matched only by its potential for obfuscation and misrepresentation."[70]

Fortunately, English does have a term as pregnant with ambiguity as *Ioudaios*: the term "Jew," which applies with equal accuracy to a medieval Ashkenazi rabbi, a first-generation convert to the Jewish religion, or Adam Sandler (but not, as Sandler emphatically reminds us, to O. J. Simpson).[71] The English word "Jew" is an ethnic term as much as it is a religious one,[72] and any attempt to limit its meaning to the latter ultimately derives from Christian polemical categorizations.[73] Indeed, the assumption that modern "Jewishness" is necessarily and fundamentally religious is misguided, ignoring the numerous modern Jews who embrace an ethnic or cultural Jewishness but do not hold to anything resembling Jewish theology.[74] "Atheist, secularist, post-Zionist Jews of globalized postmodernity" are no less Jews despite not embracing traditional Jewish theology.[75] If anything, the ancient people seem to have been more characterized by religion than a large percentage of their modern descendants.[76] There was no transition from "Judaean" ethnicity to "Jewish" religion; instead, Jewishness was both religious and ethnic in antiquity and remains so today.[77]

---

[69] For a humorous account of one such misunderstanding, see Daniel R. Schwartz, "'Judaean' or 'Jew,'" in *Jewish Identity in the Greco-Roman World: Jüdische Identität in der griechish-römischen Welt*, eds. Jörg Frey and Stephanie Gripentrog (Leiden: Brill, 2007), 3–27 (3–6).

[70] Baker, "A 'Jew' by Any Other Name," 178.

[71] Adam Sandler, "The Chanukah Song," *Saturday Night Live* (Studio City: NBC, 1994).

[72] Schwartz, "Judaean," 8. Cf. also Reed, "*Ioudaios.*"

[73] Baker, "A 'Jew' by Any Other Name," 177.

[74] As of 2013, approximately 22 percent of American Jews identify as Jewish on ethnic or cultural grounds but describe themselves as having no religion. For this data, see Alan Cooperman et al., "A Portrait of Jewish Americans: Findings from a Pew Research Center Survey of US Jews," (Washington, DC: Pew Research Center, 2013). For further discussion of Jewishness in the modern world, see Zvi Y. Gitelman, *Religion or Ethnicity? Jewish Identities in Evolution* (New Brunswick: Rutgers University Press, 2009).

[75] Baker, "A 'Jew' by Any Other Name," 174.

[76] As observed by DeConick, "Jesus the Israelite?"

[77] Schwartz, "Yannai and Pella," 230–31; *pace* Shaye J. D. Cohen, "Ioudaios: 'Judaean' and 'Jew' in Susanna, First Maccabees, and Second Maccabees," in *Geschichte – Tradition – Reflexion: Festschrift für Martin Hengel zum 70. Geburtstag*, eds. H. Cancik, H. Lichtenberger, and P. Schäfer, 1 (Tübingen: Mohr Siebeck, 1996), 211–20 (209).

I therefore find "Judaean" more problematic than "Jew" as a translation for *Ioudaios* in that it translates a richly polyvalent Greek word with
a much more limited English word, leading to a loss of nuance and
inevitably to misunderstanding. Where possible, ambiguity is best
rendered with analogous ambiguity, so despite the potential problems
inherent in using such a familiar modern term for an ancient one, "Jew"
(or perhaps "Jewish person," given the adjectival form of *Ioudaios*)
remains in my view the best translation for ancient terms such as
Ioudaios, *Yehudi*, or *Iudaeus* and should be preferred over "Judaean."
As such, I will default to "Jew" when translating the relevant ancient
terms, though I will also use transliterations where that seems
more appropriate.

IOUDAIOI VS. IOUDAIOI?

Nevertheless, the Jew/Judaean debate does arise from – and helps further
reveal – difficulties caused by how texts like the Gospel of John employ
terms and concepts like Israel/Israelite and *Ioudaios*. Boyarin is, in my
view, correct when he says that the key to understanding John's complex
portrayal of the *Ioudaioi* "is to understand that the *Ioudaioi* in John does
not mean what we mean by 'Jews' today, that is to say, it is not coextensive with 'Israelite' in its extension, but some subset of the
Israelites."[78] But because Boyarin still assumes "ancient Israelite" is
equivalent to "modern Jew,"[79] he means a subset of *Jews*, specifically
the subset who are "members of the particularist and purity-oriented
community in and around Jerusalem."[80] Boyarin therefore comes to the
remarkable conclusion that the Galileans are "obviously 'Jews'
(=Israelites), but not *Ioudaioi*."[81]

But there is no way to distinguish between Jews and Judaeans
(=*Ioudaioi*) in Greek; if Galileans are Jews, they are also *Ioudaioi*, which
John confirms by explicitly labeling Galileans, including Jesus, *Ioudaioi*

---

[78] Boyarin, "The IOUDAIOI in John," 221.
[79] Boyarin, "The IOUDAIOI in John," 221.
[80] Boyarin, "The IOUDAIOI in John," 235; similarly, Wills, "Jew, Judean, Judaism," 192.
[81] Boyarin, "The IOUDAIOI in John," 236. Lowe makes a similar mistake in suggesting
that one particular instance of the word "Galileans" in Julian's "Against the Galileans" –
although obviously referring to Christians elsewhere – refers to "'real' Galileans, i.e. Jews
who, living in Galilee, were careful to distinguish between themselves and Judaeans"
("ΙΟΥΔΑΙΟΙ of the Apocrypha: A Fresh Approach to the Gospels of James, Pseudo-
Thomas, Peter, and Nicodemus," *NovT* 23.1 [1981]: 56–90 [89–90]).

(4:9; 6:41, 52; 19:19).[82] Boyarin is therefore correct to express "skepticism that this idea is applicable to Paul's use of the terms,"[83] but neither is it applicable to the Gospel of John. Indeed, a distinction between *Ioudaioi* (=Jews) and *Ioudaioi* (=pietistic, Jerusalem-centered Jews) is untenable. The solution, however, emerges after a closer investigation of the one thing that Boyarin and others throughout this discussion have consistently left unexamined: the equivalence of Israel and the Jews.[84] This equivalence has long been presumed rather than argued and warrants a more thorough analysis.[85] It is to that task that we now turn.

[82] Boyarin, "The IOUDAIOI in John," 221–22 n. 20.

[83] Private conversation reported in Gadenz, *Called from the Jews and from the Gentiles*, 74 n. 271.

[84] As shown in Christopher Blumhofer's excellent *The Gospel of John and the Future of Israel*, SNTSMS (Cambridge University Press, 2020), which largely builds on the paradigm presented in this book and was also heavily influenced by Boyarin.

[85] Cf. Martina Böhm, "Wer gehörte in hellenistisch-römischer Zeit zu 'Israel'? Historische Voraussetzungen für eine veränderte Perspektiv auf neutestamentliche Texte," in *Die Samaritaner und die Bibel: Historische und literarische Wechselwirkungen zwischen biblischen und samaritanischen Traditionen = The Samaritans and the Bible: Historical and Literary Interactions Between Biblical and Samaritan Traditions*, eds. Jörg Frey, Ursula Schattner-Rieser, and Konrad Schmid, SJ 70 (Berlin: de Gruyter, 2012), 181–202 (182).

PART I

ISRAEL'S DISPUTED BIRTHRIGHT

I

Jews and Israelites in Antiquity

The Need for a New Paradigm

The errors of a theory are rarely found in what it asserts explicitly; they hide in what it ignores or tacitly assumes.

Daniel Kahneman[1]

The presumption that, after the Babylonian Exile, the term "Israel" is synonymous with "the Jews" (that is, the people known in Greek as *Ioudaioi* and Hebrew as *Yehudim*) is so strong that it has gone unquestioned in numerous detailed studies on the semantic ranges of the respective terms.[2] Indeed, few scholarly presumptions are so deeply rooted, as countless scholarly articles and books use these terms interchangeably, often alternating between them for stylistic reasons, regardless of the historical period under investigation.[3] The two terms, however, are not

---

[1] Daniel Kahneman, *Thinking, Fast and Slow* (New York: Farrar, Straus and Giroux, 2011), 274–75.

[2] For example, Peter Tomson opens his survey article by referring to the two terms as "alternative appellations" ("Names," 120). Similarly, Graham Harvey assumes that "[*Hebraios*] was already an accepted gentilic synonymous with ἰσραήλ or Ἰουδαῖος" (*The True Israel: Uses of the Names Jew, Hebrew, and Israel in Ancient Jewish and Early Christian Literature*, AGJU 35 [Leiden: Brill, 1996], 117, cf. also 40).

[3] E.g., Niels Peter Lemche, "The Understanding of Community in the Old Testament and in the Dead Sea Scrolls," in *Qumran between the Old and New Testaments*, eds. Frederick H. Cryer and Thomas L. Thompson, JSOTSup 290 (Sheffield: Sheffield Academic, 1998), 181–93 (188): "Biblical Israel is founded on the Torah ... presented to the Jews [*sic*] by God on Mount Sinai." "According to the Deuteronomistic History ... the Israelites of pre-exilic times were not really Jews [*sic*], as they almost never fulfilled the requirement of the Covenant and the Law" (189). See also Notger Slenczka, "Römer 9–11 und die Frage nach der Identität Israels," in *Between Gospel and Election: Explorations in the Interpretation of Romans 9–11*, eds. Florian Wilk, J. Ross Wagner, and Frank Schleritt, WUNT 257 (Tübingen: Mohr Siebeck, 2010), 463–78 (474–76); Pamela Barmash, "At the Nexus of

evenly distributed across early Jewish literature or other ancient evidence. The apostle Paul, for example, uses the term "Israel" and cognates thirteen times in Romans 9–11 but only six times in the rest of the seven undisputed letters, where *Ioudaios* appears twenty-six times. Even so, interpreters have emphasized that when Paul says "Israel," he means "ethnic Israel" – that is, the Jews, since the latter is presumed to be synonymous with the former.[4] Nevertheless, the abrupt shift in terminology in Romans 9–11 and similarly uneven distribution in Josephus, Philo, and other early Jewish corpora has led to numerous studies attempting to explain why these functionally equivalent terms tend to appear in different contexts. For nearly a century, this discussion has been shaped by Karl G. Kuhn's 1938 *TWNT* article on the terms Israel, Jew, and Hebrew, where Kuhn proposes an insider/outsider model to account for the uneven distribution of the terms in extant evidence:

ישראל is the name which the people uses for itself, whereas יהודים-Ἰουδαῖοι is the non-Jewish name for it. Thus ישראל always emphasises the religious aspect, namely, that "we are God's chosen people," whereas Ἰουδαῖος may acquire on

---

History and Memory: The Ten Lost Tribes," *AJSR* 29.2 (2005): 207–36 (233); Louis H. Feldman, "The Concept of Exile in Josephus," in *Exile: Old Testament, Jewish, and Christian Conceptions*, ed. James M. Scott, JSJSup 56 (Leiden and New York: Brill, 1997), 145–72 (162); Alexander A. Di Lella, "Wisdom of Ben Sira," *The Anchor Yale Bible Dictionary* 6:931–44 (937); Jonathan A. Goldstein, "How the Authors of 1 and 2 Maccabees Treated the 'Messianic' Promises," in *Judaisms and their Messiahs at the Turn of the Christian Era*, eds. Jacob Neusner, William Scott Green, and Ernest S. Frerichs (Cambridge: Cambridge University Press, 1988), 69–96 (69, 84); Lowe, "Who Were the ΙΟΥΔΑΙΟΙ," 103; Renée Bloch, "Israélite, juif, hébreu," *Cahiers Sioniens* 5 (1951): 11–31 (17–21).

[4] E.g., Michael Bachmann, "Verus Israel: Ein Vorschlag zu einer 'mengentheoretischen' Neubeschreibung der betreffenden paulinischen Terminologie," *NTS* 48.4 (2002): 500–12 (510), "the term 'Israel' (and accordingly 'Israelite') … is used by the apostle – at least beyond Gal 6.16 – exclusively for real Jews [*wirkliche Juden*] and never for non-Jews, never in the "figurative" sense." Gadenz, *Called from the Jews and from the Gentiles*, 277: "'all Israel' refers to ethnic Israel. Indeed, Paul has up to this point used the term 'Israel' to refer to ethnic Israel (or some part of it)." Ulrich Wilckens, *Der Brief an der Römer*, EKKNT VI/1 (Neukirchen-Vluyn: Neukirchener Verlag, 1980), 187–88: "Paul means the Jews, but throughout chapters 9–11, he almost without exception avoids the previously used word Ἰουδαῖοι … To them comes the honorary name "Israelites" as a self designation." Moo, *Romans*, 159: "By Paul's day, 'Jew' had become a common designation of anyone who belonged to the people of Israel." Cf. also Carl R. Holladay, "Paul and His Predecessors in the Diaspora: Some Reflections on Ethnic Identity in the Fragmentary Hellenistic Jewish Authors," in *Early Christianity and Classical Culture: Comparative Studies in Honor of Abraham J. Malherbe*, eds. John T. Fitzgerald, Thomas H. Olbricht, and L. Michael White, NovTSup 110 (Leiden: Brill, 2003), 429–60 (453); Hübner, *Gottes Ich und Israel*, 20.

the lips of non-Jews a disrespectful and even contemptuous sound, though this is not usual, since Ἰουδαῖος is used quite freely without any disparagement.[5]

Kuhn argues that since "Palestinian Judaism" (represented by 1 Maccabees and Rabbinic literature) was less impacted by outside factors, texts in that category prefer the term "Israel" and use *Ioudaios* only as an accommodation to outsider or diaspora use of that term, such as when reporting the speech of non-Jews or in diplomatic or official documents.[6] In contrast, because "Hellenistic Jews" had accommodated to the outsider nomenclature used by their gentile neighbors, they were accustomed to using *Ioudaios* as the default self-referential label in everyday speech, though Kuhn explains that they still preferred Israel "in prayers and biblical or liturgical expressions" due to that term's connections to Scripture and the covenant.[7] The frequency of *Ioudaios* in Philo, Josephus, Acts, and the Gospel of John can thus be explained as accommodating to "a usage which is fitting when addressing non-Jews."[8]

---

[5] Karl Georg Kuhn, "Ἰσραήλ, Ἰουδαῖος, Ἑβραῖος in Jewish Literature after the OT," *TDNT* 3:359–69 (360). Although he here concedes the contemptuous use of the term is "not usual," he later refers to "the common Ἰουδαῖος, which may often be used in a derogatory or even contemptuous sense" and "the depreciatory element that clings so easily to Ἰουδαῖος" (367–68). ET of Karl Georg Kuhn, "Ἰσραήλ, Ἰουδαῖος, Ἑβραῖος in der nachalttestamentlichen jüdischen Literatur," *TWNT* 3:360–70.

[6] Remarkably, Solomon Zeitlin, "The Names Hebrew, Jew and Israel: A Historical Study," *JQR* 43.4 (1953): 365–79 (368–71), comes to the opposite conclusion, arguing that Judaean/Jew was the typical term used by inhabitants of Judaea, while "the Jews in other countries, Babylonia, Syria, and Antioch, however, did not call themselves Jews. They were called Israelis and Hebrews" (370). Zeitlin argues that Jew/Judaean/Judaism take on a religious sense, while "the name Israel or Hebrew never became associated with the religion" (376), thus making "Israel" the best option for the name of the modern state (377–79). Zeitlin's argument is obviously influenced by modern terminology and political concerns, but the same was no less true of Kuhn. In any case, Zeitlin's argument, which features several salient points despite his modern concerns, has been largely ignored, while Kuhn's paradigm has dominated the field.

[7] Kuhn, "Ἰουδαῖος κτλ," *TDNT* 3:360. The distinction between "Hellenistic" and "Palestinian" Judaism is obviously problematic now that the latter is understood to have been Hellenized from an early period. Cf. John M. G. Barclay, *Jews in the Mediterranean Diaspora: From Alexander to Trajan (323 BCE–117 CE)* (Berkeley: University of California Press, 1996), 6; Tessa Rajak, *The Jewish Dialogue with Greece and Rome: Studies in Cultural and Social Interaction*, AGJU 48 (Leiden: Brill, 2002), 3–133; John J. Collins and Gregory E. Sterling, eds., Hellenism in the Land of Israel, CJAS (Notre Dame: University of Notre Dame Press, 2001); Fergus Millar, *The Roman Near East, 31 BC–AD 337* (Cambridge: Harvard University Press, 1995); Martin Hengel, *Judaism and Hellenism: Studies in their Encounter in Palestine during the Early Hellenistic Period*, trans. John Bowden (London: SCM, 1974).

[8] Gutbrod, "Ἰουδαῖος κτλ," *TDNT* 3:377.

Walter Gutbrod's companion article on the use of the terms in the New Testament builds upon Kuhn's model, arguing that the Synoptic Gospels conform to the Palestinian pattern, explaining the exceptions as copyist glosses or as addressed to the non-Jewish audience of the Gospels.[9]

Kuhn's insider/outsider model has proven so influential as to be baldly repeated, often without citation, in numerous subsequent studies,[10] with some even using the model to distinguish between sources in the Gospels,[11] or to assess the implied audience of a text or even a chapter.[12] John Elliot has gone so far as to argue that "Jesus was not a Ἰουδαῖος," nor should "Jew" be used at all in this period in light of the "insider" preference for "Israelite," which is shown by "incontrovertible evidence."[13] Even those who have recognized problems with Kuhn's paradigm have tended to make small corrections rather than calling the model itself into question. David Goodblatt, for instance, has attempted to replace Kuhn's geographical categories with linguistic ones, explaining, "I take [Kuhn] to mean that authors writing in Hebrew evidenced a clear preference for the ethnonym 'Israel,' while Jews writing in Greek tended to use *Ioudaioi*."[14] That is, those writing in "outsider" tongues (including both Aramaic and Greek) prefer the "outsider" term *Ioudaios*, while those writing in the "insider" tongue of

---

[9] Gutbrod, "Ἰουδαῖος κτλ," *TDNT* 3:376–78. Lowe, "ΙΟΥΔΑΙΟΙ of the Apocrypha," 59, similarly argues that the earliest apocryphal gospels' use of Israel is suggestive of especially early dates before this "Palestinian" usage had died out.

[10] E.g., Bloch, "Israélite, juif, hébreu," 17–21; *EDNT*, s.v. "Ἰουδαῖος," 193–97 (194); Lowe, "ΙΟΥΔΑΙΟΙ of the Apocrypha," 56–57; Lowe, "Who Were the ΙΟΥΔΑΙΟΙ," 104–07; Cranfield, *Romans*, 460–61; Wilckens, *Römer II*, 187–88; James D. G. Dunn, "Who Did Paul Think He Was? A Study of Jewish–Christian Identity," *NTS* 45.2 (1999): 174–93 (187–88); Brendan Byrne, *Romans*, SP 6 (Collegeville: Liturgical Press, 1996), 287; Jewett, *Romans*, 562; Gadenz, *Called from the Jews and from the Gentiles*, 64–67. I also must confess to having approvingly cited the insider/outsider argument of Elliot, "Jesus the Israelite," in "All Israel," 378 n. 36, which I now recognize as an error.

[11] Tomson, "Names," 280–82. Cf. the critique in Miller, "Group Labels," 103–06.

[12] Elliot, "Jesus the Israelite," 145; cf. also the similar arguments in Dunn, *Romans 9–16*, 526; Tomson, "Names," 288. Elliot does not explain how to make sense of the second-person address to Gentiles in Rom 11:17–25 in light of this claim. See the critiques of Miller, "Group Labels," 105.

[13] Elliot, "Jesus the Israelite," 125, 147–48.

[14] David Goodblatt, "'The Israelites Who Reside in Judah' (Judith 4:1): On the Conflicted Identities of the Hasmonean State," in *Jewish Identities in Antiquity: Studies in Memory of Menahem Stern*, eds. Lee I. Levine and Daniel R. Schwartz, TSAJ 130 (Tübingen: Mohr Siebeck, 2009), 74–89 (75). Goodblatt here reports the raw numbers, which initially appear to favor his case, but the data are not clean enough to speak for themselves, especially in texts that use both terms like 1 Maccabees and Ezra-Nehemiah. To get better explanations for how these terms are used, a closer look at each case is necessary – hence the need for much of the present project.

Hebrew use the insider term "Israel."[15] Goodblatt confesses, however, that the frequent use of *Yehudi* (יהדי) in the Hebrew sections of Daniel, Ezra-Nehemiah, and Esther are problematic for this model. Nevertheless, he suggests that, despite their Hebrew composition, these can be explained as accommodating to "outsider" official Persian designations rather than the insider language that would otherwise be expected of Hebrew documents.[16] But since all three are written to an insider audience, it is unclear why these texts would accommodate to outsider language in this way.

More recently, Lawrence Wills has attempted to salvage the model by explaining that these exceptional cases demonstrate that in the shadow of imperial colonization Jews eventually appropriated the outsider term to serve as a "more assertive, even emotive term of identity" relative to the "default Israel/Israelite," suggesting "there is a postcolonial history of this term that is yet to be written."[17] The use of *Ioudaios* by insiders thereby serves as another example of how "people often internalize and invert the aspersions of others, transforming them into affirmations."[18]

THE DARK ORIGINS OF THE INSIDER/OUTSIDER PARADIGM

The problem is that, contrary to Kuhn's oft-repeated claim (for which Kuhn himself does not list an example), there is no evidence that *Ioudaios* was ever a term of aspersion in pre-Christian antiquity.[19] Instead, the first known instances of *Yehudi* occur not in outsider contexts but rather as ordinary descriptors for people from the kingdom of Judah in Jeremiah (eight passages), 2 Kings (two), and 1 Chronicles (one).[20] Remarkably,

---

[15] Goodblatt's argument was anticipated in this respect by Jehoshua M. Grintz, "Hebrew as the Spoken and Written Language in the Last Days of the Second Temple," *JBL* 79.1 (1960): 32–47 (34–35).

[16] Goodblatt, "Israelites Who Reside in Judah," 77. But as he later observes, "Certainly anything in Hebrew was written by, and only accessible to, insiders. Who else knew Hebrew?" (Goodblatt, "Israelites Who Reside in Judah," 87). That being the case, the existence of Hebrew texts (such as Daniel or Esther) that prefer Judah/Jew language is a bigger problem for the insider/outsider paradigm than Goodblatt or others seem to acknowledge.

[17] Wills, "Jew, Judean, Judaism," 178, 169.

[18] Wills, "Jew, Judean, Judaism," 180.

[19] Cohen, *Beginnings of Jewishness*, 71 n. 5. For his part, Kuhn does anticipate this objection, protesting, "But it is plainly attested already in Jewish lit" (Kuhn, "Ἰουδαῖος κτλ," *TDNT* 3:368 n. 72), again citing no examples.

[20] Jer 32:12; 34:9; 38:19; 40:11–12, 15; 41:3; 43:9; 44:1; 52:28, 30; 2 Kgs 16:6; 25:25; 1 Chr 4:18. Cf. Wills, "Jew, Judean, Judaism," 180–81.

rather than questioning the "outsider" origins of the term on this basis, Wills instead argues that the crisis of the exile and the term's role "in boundary-related contexts" led to the term being employed as such to construct "a stronger sense of identity."[21] (One is left to wonder which identity terms do not function in boundary-related contexts.) The closest Wills gets to providing an example of the term being used "in a disparaging way by opponents"[22] is to read special emotive qualities into passages like Daniel 3:8, "Certain Chaldeans came forward and made accusations against the Jews," of which Wills claims, "one senses that it is not simply a descriptive or cognitive use of language; it is also assertive, emotive."[23] But such a judgment begs the question; one senses nothing of the sort unless one first presumes that the term had a disparaging nuance, and this instance instead seems to be a straightforward means of communicating the group against which accusations were made. Any claim to especially emotive affect must be proved rather than simply asserted. Similarly, the fact that the enemies of the returnees in Ezra-Nehemiah call them *Yehudim* (e.g., Ezra 4:12, Neh 4:1) does not suggest a negative nuance,[24] as the returnees repeatedly use the same term of themselves in these passages. Without the a priori assumption that "Jew" inherently carries a negative valence, the more plausible explanation is simply that *Ioudaios/Yehudi* was simply assumed within the text to be the default ethnonym used by both insiders and outsiders.

Although the negative valence of *Ioudaios* is unattested in antiquity, Kuhn's insider/outsider paradigm does describe the situation in 1930s Germany and Europe as a whole with remarkable accuracy. Given the hostility toward *Juden* among Christians who nevertheless associated the term "Israel" with the biblical chosen people, German Jewish communities understandably preferred the latter term, typically calling themselves the *israelitische Gemeinde* (Israelite community), while outsiders who wished to be respectful toward the Jews also tended to employ the term *Israeliten*.[25] More importantly, both Kuhn and his *Doktorvater*

---

[21] Wills, "Jew, Judean, Judaism," 180, 182.
[22] Wills, "Jew, Judean, Judaism," 182.
[23] Wills, "Jew, Judean, Judaism," 185–86.
[24] Wills, "Jew, Judean, Judaism," 182.
[25] Friedrich von Hellwald, "Zur Characteristik des jüdischen Volkes," *Das Ausland* 45.26 (1872): 901–06 (902), provides a signal example of how differently these terms were treated in prewar Germany: "Progressive education will eventually overcome prejudice against Israelites who merely profess different beliefs, but not antipathy towards the ethnically different Jew" ("fortschreitende Bildung wohl schliesslich zur Ueberwindung

Gerhard Kittel, the general editor of the early volumes of the *TWNT*, were Nazi Party members and anti-Semites themselves. Kittel's Nazi allegiances and anti-Semitic opinions are well documented, as he joined the Nazi Party (NSDAP) and published an anti-Semitic tractate, *Die Judenfrage*, in 1933 – the same year the first volume of the *TWNT* was published.[26] But Kuhn outdid his mentor with his enthusiasm for the Nazi Party and virulent anti-Semitism,[27] joining the NSDAP in 1932, a year before Kittel.[28]

---

des Vorurtheils gegen den andersgläubigen Israeliten, nicht aber gegen den ethnisch verschidenen Juden führen wird"). Cf. also Schwartz, "Judaean," 19–20; Maurice Casey, "Some Anti-Semitic Assumptions in the 'Theological Dictionary of the New Testament,'" *NovT* 41.3 (1999): 280–91 (283); Baker, *Jew*, 3–7, 47–96.

[26] On Kittel, see Géza Vermès, "Jewish Studies and New Testament Interpretation," in *Jesus and the World of Judaism* (London: SCM, 1983), 58–73, esp. 64–66 dealing with Gerhard W. Kittel, *Die Judenfrage* (Stuttgart: Kohlhammer, 1933); Heschel, *Aryan Jesus* esp. 187–89. Cf. also J. S. Vos, "Antijudaismus/Antisemitismus im Theologischen Wörterbuch zum Neuen Testament," *NedTT* 38 (1984): 89–110 (89–110); Max Weinreich, *Hitler's Professors: The Part of Scholarship in Germany's Crimes against the Jewish People*, 2nd ed. (New Haven: Yale University Press, 1999).

[27] On Kuhn's career and anti-Semitism, see Gerhard Lindemann, "Theological Research about Judaism in Different Political Contexts: The Example of Karl Georg Kuhn," *Kirchliche Zeitgeschichte* (2004): 331–38, which includes English summaries of many of Kuhn's anti-Semitic statements between 1933 and 1945; Gerd Theissen, *Neutestamentliche Wissenschaft vor und nach 1945: Karl Georg Kuhn und Günther Bornkamm*, Schriften der Philosophisch-historischen Klasse der Heidelberger Akademie der Wissenschaften (Heidelberg: Universitätsverlag, 2009), which provides the most thorough survey of Kuhn's career; Alan E. Steinweis, *Studying the Jew: Scholarly Antisemitism in Nazi Germany* (Cambridge: Harvard University Press, 2008), 76–91, which summarizes Kuhn's anti-Semitic work and emphasizes the subtlety of Kuhn's argumentation; Jörg Frey, "Qumran Research and Biblical Scholarship in Germany," in *The Dead Sea Scrolls in Scholarly Perspective: A History of Research*, ed. Devorah Dimant, STDJ 99 (Leiden: Brill, 2012), 529–64, which examines both Kuhn's prewar anti-Semitism and his postwar work on the Dead Sea Scrolls; Horst Junginger, "Das Bild des Juden in der nationalsozialistischen Judenforschung," in *Die kulturelle Seite des Antisemitismus: Zwischen Aufklärung und Shoah*, ed. Andrea Hoffmann, Studien & Materialien des Ludwig-Uhland-Instituts der Universität Tübingen (Tübingen: Tübinger Vereinigung für Volkskunde, 2006), 171–220; Casey, "Anti-Semitic Assumptions," 282–86, which focuses on the impact of Kuhn's views on his work in the *TWNT/TDNT*; and the more apologetic treatment by Kuhn's former student, Gert Jeremias, "Karl Georg Kuhn (1906–1976)," in *Neutestamentliche Wissenschaft nach 1945: Hauptvertreter der deutschsprachigen Exegese in der Darstellung ihrer Schüler*, eds. Cilliers Breytenbach and Rudolf Hoppe (Neukirchen-Vluyn: Neukirchener Verlag, 2008), 297–312.

[28] Kuhn requested NSDAP membership on March 19, 1932, and became a member on September 1 of that year (Nr. 1340672). Cf. Bundesarchiv Berlin, ehemaliges BDC, NSDAP-Mitgliederkartei; cited in Lindemann, "Theological Research about Judaism," 331 n. 2. Kuhn later claimed that he joined the party as a reaction to the breakup of his

Shortly after joining the party, Kuhn lent his authority as a scholar of ancient Judaism and Jewish texts to the cause, delivering a speech on April 1, 1933, at an event in the Tübingen marketplace advocating the boycott of Jewish businesses.[29] A year later he was appointed a lecturer (*dozent*) in oriental languages and history at Tübingen, delivering his inaugural lecture on "The spread of Jewry in the ancient world," a subject to which he would frequently return.[30] In a postwar book review, M. A. Beek fondly recalls studying Rabbinic texts with Kuhn at this time:

> Reading this booklet reminded me of an idyllic time in the summer semester of 1934 when Dr. Kuhn was still a private *dozent* at the University of Tübingen. At that time, he wore an SA uniform with an "Honorary Dagger [*Ehrendolch*] with Dedication" clinking at his side because he was among the first thousand people in the SA.[31]

This bears repeating: not only was Kuhn among the first thousand to join the Nazi paramilitary *Sturmabteilung* (Storm Detachment), he further demonstrated his enthusiasm for the cause by delivering his lectures on Judaism while wearing an SA uniform and *Ehrendolch* (honorary dagger) complete with inscription of Nazi comradeship. Together with Kittel, Kuhn was one of fifteen appointees to the Forschungsabteilung Judenfrage (Research Department for the Jewish Problem) established by the Nazis in the spring of 1936 under the auspices of staunch anti-Semite Walter Frank's Reichsinstitut für Geschichte des neuen Deutschlands (Reich Institute for the History of the New Germany),[32] which published the journal *Forschungen zur Judenfrage* (*Research on the Jewish Problem*), advertised with the slogan, "German Science in the Fight

---

engagement after his former fiancée had joined the Communist party, an apologetic also put forward by Kuhn's student Jeremias in his posthumous biography of his teacher, "Karl Georg Kuhn," 301. See also Steinweis, *Studying the Jew*, 88; and the more extensive discussion in Theissen, *Neutestamentliche Wissenschaft*, 19–21. Given the extent of his pre-1945 anti-Semitic scholarship, Kuhn's explanation seems disingenuous to say the least.

[29] Lindemann, "Theological Research about Judaism," 331–32; Theissen, *Neutestamentliche Wissenschaft*, 19–21; Frey, "Qumran Research," 542.

[30] The first part of the speech is published as Karl Georg Kuhn, "Die inneren Voraussetzungen der jüdischen Ausbreitung," *Deutsche Theologie* 2 (1935): 9–17.

[31] M. A. Beek, review of *Achtzehngebet und Vaterunser und der Reim*, by Karl Georg Kuhn, *Vox Theologica* 21 (1950): 21–22 (21–22), recalling "de idyllische tijd toen Dr Kuhn nog privaat-docent was aan de Universiteit van Tübingen in het zomersemester van 1934. Hij droeg toen een S.A. uniform en aan zijn zijde rinkelde een 'Ehrendolch mit Widmung' omdat hij behoorde tot de eerste duizend S.A. lieden."

[32] Casey, "Anti-Semitic Assumptions," 283. For a full history of the Reichsinstitut and a biography of its founder, see Helmut Heiber, *Walter Frank und sein Reichsinstitut für Geschichte des neuen Deutschlands* (Stuttgart: Deutsche Verlags-Anstalt, 1966).

against World Judaism!"[33] Kuhn contributed several scholarly articles on the so-called *Judenfrage* in the service of the ideology of the Reichsinstitut, including three in the *Forschungen zur Judenfrage*.[34] Kuhn's *TWNT* article on the terms Israel, *Ioudaios*, and *Hebraios* was published in 1938. That same year, less than a month after the November 9, 1938, "Kristallnacht" pogrom,[35] Kuhn gave an address at the fourth annual conference of the Reichsinstitut in Berlin and shortly thereafter delivered a second lecture before an overflow audience of an estimated 2,500 at the University of Berlin.[36] These lectures were quickly revised and published as a booklet for a popular audience, entitled *Die Judenfrage als weltgeschichtliches Problem* (*The Jewish Question as a World History Problem*).[37] After first emphasizing the importance of Semitics (*Semitistik*) as a discipline for the careful study of the *Judenfrage*, Kuhn describes what an awful problem the *Judenfrage* has been for the world, claiming that all Jews have been engaged in a *völkisch* struggle against other peoples. The booklet then triumphantly concludes that Judaism is "reaping what it has sown for almost 150 years,"[38] praising the Führer for finally creating the conditions for a solution (*Lösung*) for the *Judenfrage*.[39]

---

[33] German: "Deutsche Wissenschaft im Kampf gegen das Weltjudentum!" See Vos, "Antijudaismus/Antisemitismus," 90. On the *Forschungen zur Judenfrage*, see Reinhard Markner, "Forschungen zur Judenfrage: A Notorious Journal and Some of Its Contributors," *European Journal of Jewish Studies* 1.2 (2007): 395–415.

[34] E.g., Karl Georg Kuhn, "Die Entstehung des talmudischen Denkens," *Forschungen zur Judenfrage* 1 (1937): 63–80; Karl Georg Kuhn, "Weltjudentum in der Antike," *Forschungen zur Judenfrage* 2 (1937): 9–29, 64; Karl Georg Kuhn, "Ursprung und Wesen der talmudischen Einstellung zum Nichtjuden," *Forschungen zur Judenfrage* 3 (1938): 199–234; Karl Georg Kuhn, "Der Talmud, das Gesetzbuch der Juden: Einführende Bemerkungen," in *Zur Geschichte und rechtlichen Stellung der Juden in Stadt und Universität Tübingen: Aus den Jahresbänden der wissenschaftlichen Akademie des NSD-Dozentenbundes/Wissenschaftliche Akademie Tübingen des NSD-Dozentenbundes 1 (1937–1939)*, ed. Thomas Miller (Tübingen: Mohr Siebeck, 1941), 226–33.

[35] Frey, "Qumran Research," 543.

[36] Anon., "Die Gedenkakrobatik Des Talmuds," *Völkischer Beobachter* (Berlin: 1939 Jan 21): 5. Cf. Steinweis, *Studying the Jew*, 85.

[37] Karl Georg Kuhn, *Die Judenfrage als weltgeschichtliches Problem*, Schriften des Reichsinstituts für Geschichte des neuen Deutschlands (Hamburg: Hanseatische Verlagsanstalt, 1939).

[38] Kuhn, *Die Judenfrage*, 46: "Was das Judentum seit einigen Jahren erlebt – nicht nur in Deutschland, sondern weithin in der Welt –, ist nichts anderes, als daß es jezt erntet, was es in seiner großen Mehrheit nun bald 150 Jahre hindurch gesät hat."

[39] Kuhn, *Die Judenfrage*, 47; For additional quotations from the booklet in English translation, see Lindemann, "Theological Research about Judaism," 335–37. Cf. also Steinweis, *Studying the Jew*, 85–86; Casey, "Anti-Semitic Assumptions," 285. This was the only anti-Semitic publication Kuhn later renounced in Karl Georg Kuhn, "Die

Remarkably, Kuhn's reputation was rapidly rehabilitated after the war, owing largely to the supposed "purely objective-scientific attitude" and "solid study of the sources" evident in his publications.[40] "In comparison to the vulgar antisemitism that was so common in the Third Reich," Alan Steinweis observes, "Kuhn's writings seemed moderate and reasonable."[41] Beek, for example, after his fond recollection of Kuhn lecturing in Nazi uniform, is at pains to clarify, "The dagger and the uniform never hindered Dr. Kuhn's lectures on Rabbinic texts. I have never been able to question his scientific purity on this point."[42] J. S. Vos echoes Beek in declaring that Kuhn's *TWNT* articles are free from the taint of anti-Semitism:

Kuhn wrote 12 articles for the TWNT, 10 of them in Vols. 1–4. In these articles, I have found no trace of anti-Semitism or even of exegetical anti-Judaism. ... Beek's judgment on Kuhn's scientific integrity is confirmed in particular in such a crucial article as Ἰσραήλ, Ἰουδαῖος, Ἑβραῖος in Volume 3.[43]

Schriftrollen vom Toten Meer: Zum heutigen Stand ihrer Veröffentlichung," *EvT* 11.1–6 (1951): 72–75 (73 n. 4): "For my part, I say in this context that I regret that I wrote, "The Jewish Question as a World Historical Problem," Hamburg: Hanseatische Verlagsanstalt, 1939 (51 pages), and I revoke it in all forms. I regret that at that time, I was so blind not to see that the path of Hitler's Jewish policy was in the abyss of horror and that it was unstoppable. Only such blindness made it possible for me to write such a thing at that time" ["Ich für meine Person sage in diesem Zusammenhang, daß ich es bedaure, die Schrift: Die Judenfrage als weltgeschichtliches Problem. Hanseatische Verlagsanstalt Hamburg 1939, 51 Seiten, geschrieben zu haben und daß ich sie in aller Form widerrufe. Ich bedaure, daß ich damals so blind war, nicht zu sehen, daß der Weg der Hitlerschen Judenpolitik in den Abgrund des Grauens ging und daß er unaufhaltsam war. Nur solche Blindheit machte es möglich, daß ich die Schrift damals schrieb"]. Kuhn remarkably continued to defend his other prewar work on *Weltjudentum* and the *Judenfrage*, including his *Forschungen* articles, as historically accurate and academically legitimate in a letter written in the late 1960s. See Theissen, *Neutestamentliche Wissenschaft*, 138–43; Rolf Seeliger, ed., *Braune Universität: Deutsche Hochschullehrer gestern und heute; Dokumentation mit Stellungnahmen* (München: Seeliger, 1968), 53–55.

[40] See Steinweis, *Studying the Jew*, 89.

[41] Steinweis, *Studying the Jew*, 89.

[42] Beek, review of *Achtzehngebet und Vaterunser und der Reim* (by Kuhn), 22: "De dolk en de uniform hebben Dr. Kuhn nooit gehinderd bij de lektuur rabbijnse texten. Zijn wetenschappelijke zuiverheid heb ik op dit punt nooit in twijfel kunnen trekken." Jeremias and others of Kuhn's students similarly claimed that Kuhn's courses had not been anti-Semitic but rather emphasized politically neutral and objective scholarship, but as Steinweis points out, this claim "is very difficult to believe in light of the pronounced antisemitic content of Kuhn's contemporaneously published articles on the same subjects" (Steinweis, *Studying the Jew*, 79).

[43] Vos, "Antijudaismus/Antisemitismus," 94: "Für das ThW schrieb Kuhn 12 Artikel, 10 davon in Bd. I–IV. In diesen Artikeln habe ich keine Spur von Antisemitismus oder auch nur von exegetischem Antijudaismus finden können. ... Beeks Urteil über Kuhns

But these credulous declarations ignore that even Kuhn's overtly anti-Semitic work was characterized by a subtlety and scholarly sophistication lacking among many of his predecessors and contemporaries, with the anti-Semitism couched in careful scholarly analysis. Steinweis explains:

> Kuhn's antisemitic writings of the Nazi era tapped into the basic methodology of earlier anti-Talmudists. ... But Kuhn was very conscious of his academic credentials and did what he could to distance himself from the more vulgar anti-Talmudic polemics. Never once did he cite Eisenmenger, Rohling, or Fritsch. He relied instead on academically respected sources, such as the Strack-Billerbeck commentary, and on Jewish texts themselves. Kuhn's assault on the Talmud was a good deal more complex and sophisticated than that of his more popularly oriented predecessors. ... Its antisemitism lay mainly in its skewed, caricatured representation of rabbinic Judaism.[44]

Kuhn's commitment to sophisticated scholarship in pursuit of anti-Semitic aims can be seen in his review of Hermann Schroer's *Blut und Geld im Judentum*, which he attacks not for its anti-Semitism (which he acknowledges but does not condemn) but for being amateurish and thereby discrediting "our science in the new Germany,"[45] recommending another work on the subject for its "clear ideological front against Jewish subterfuge."[46] As noted by Steinweis,

> When Kuhn had published this review in 1937, his main purpose had been to protect the intellectual respectability of scholarly antisemitism. ... [O]ver a decade later, Kuhn and his defenders disingenuously, and successfully, invoked the review as evidence of his lack of antisemitism altogether.[47]

In light of Kuhn's capacity for and commitment to subtlety, the declarations of Beek and Vos – not to mention Tomson's casual reassurance that "The anti-Semitism inherent in the Nazi sympathies of Kuhn and especially of the main editor, G. Kittel ... is not reflected here" – seem naïve at best.[48] Indeed, after his own investigation of Kuhn's articles, Jörg Frey concedes,

wissenschaftliche Lauterkeit bestätigt sich namentlich bei einem so entscheidenden Artikel wie Ἰσραήλ, Ἰουδαῖος, Ἑβραῖος im 3. Band."

[44] Steinweis, *Studying the Jew*, 79, 82–83.

[45] Karl Georg Kuhn, review of *Blut und Geld im Judentum*, by Hermann Schroer, *Historische Zeitschrift* 156 (1937): 313–16 (315): "unsere Wissenschaft im neuen Deutschland."

[46] Kuhn, review of *Blut und Geld im Judentum* (by Schroer), 316: "klare weltanschauliche Frontstellung gegen jüdische Verschleierung."

[47] Steinweis, *Studying the Jew*, 89.

[48] Tomson, "Names," 121. See also the denial that Kuhn's background impacted his conclusions in Goodblatt, "Israelites Who Reside in Judah," 86–89.

Although the language in some articles (e.g. in *TWNT* 3:360 on Ἰσραήλ and Ἰουδαῖος) is similar to that of contemporary anti-Semitic writings, there is only a very subtle devaluation of Judaism, in marked contrast with Kuhn's writings in the context of his research on the "Jewish Question."[49]

A very subtle devaluation is nonetheless a devaluation, and such subtlety is precisely what should be expected from such a careful scholar as Kuhn, who emphasized the importance of relying on original source material to make one's anti-Semitic arguments or insinuations. Moreover, in his assessment of Kuhn's work on *Weltjudentum* (World Judaism) for the *Forschungen zur Judenfrage*, Reinhart Markner notes another tendency especially relevant to this discussion, judging that "Kuhn was deliberately blurring the dividing lines between the ancient and the modern world."[50] Unfortunately, Kuhn's thorough and careful treatment of the data makes his *TWNT* article and its insider/outsider paradigm all the more pernicious, as the error lies below the surface, assumed and not argued.[51]

In this light, it is difficult to read Kuhn's statements about "the depreciatory element that clings so easily to Ἰουδαῖος" as anything but an indication of the pernicious assumptions at the very root of his insider/outsider model.[52] Indeed, such a claim goes beyond similarities of language with contemporary anti-Semitic writings or even subtle devaluations of Judaism but instead involves much more foundational concerns. As Maurice Casey explains, Kuhn's assessment of the ancient evidence was shaped by the anti-Semitic assumptions he took for granted:

It is this cultural context in which Kuhn produced his *interpretation* of the fact that the word "Jew" is missing from some Jewish documents of our period which use the term "Israel." It is, and this fact does require explanation, but taking over Kuhn's anachronistic and menacing life-stance will not help us. ... It should also have been obvious that nothing justifies retrojecting Kuhn's anti-semitic convictions. When the term "Jew" is used in Jewish documents of our period, it is used

---

[49] Frey, "Qumran Research," 542 n. 65.

[50] Markner, "Forschungen zur Judenfrage," 403, referencing Kuhn, "Die Entstehung" and Kuhn, "Die inneren Voraussetzungen."

[51] "What is dangerous about [the *TDNT*] is the frames of reference from which its contributors came in: they were learned men who did not make factual errors which we can all spot. The mildest contributors to the early volumes had German Christian prejudices: the most menacing were Nazis. ... It follows that this dictionary should be used only with the utmost care. Students should be warned of this hidden menace, and all readers should consult it only with their critical wits sharpened to the highest degree" (Casey, "Anti-Semitic Assumptions," 291).

[52] Kuhn, "Ἰουδαῖος κτλ," *TDNT* 3:367–68. Cf. Miller, "Ethnicity," 297.

favourably, or neutrally, and some of the favourable uses indicate that the authors of some documents were very happy with it. Conjectures about its absence from other documents may not override this evidence. There are no documents extant in which Jewish people reject the term "Jew" or regard "the Jews" as an external and hostile group.[53]

Faced with the empirical fact that "Israelite" and *Ioudaios/Yehudi* are used differently throughout the period he was surveying, Kuhn naturally turned to his immediate context for an explanation, assuming that *Ioudaios* was analogous to the German *Jude* – complete with the potentially derogatory outsider nuance – and constructing a model in which (just like *Israeliten/Juden*) Israelite/*Ioudaios* are synonymous but distinguished by insider/outsider preferences. In keeping with the tendency to conflate the ancient and modern worlds displayed in his work on *Weltjudentum*, Kuhn thus explains the difference between "Israelite" and *Ioudaios* by *superimposing the idiom of Nazi Germany upon antiquity*. Remarkably, perhaps owing to what Kahneman calls "theory-induced blindness," this paradigm has remained the default explanation for the use of these terms in antiquity, with some arguing that the anti-Semitic assumptions at its root should be overlooked.[54] Goodblatt, for example, protests,

The claim that Jews were aware that the name *Ioudaios/Ioudaioi* sometimes – but by no means always – was used disparagingly by gentiles is only marginally relevant to Kuhn's main point. He invokes this claim to help explain the preference for the ethnonym "Israel." Even if Kuhn's suggested explanation were completely mistaken, that would not change the fact of the preference – assuming we can establish that fact.[55]

But that fact cannot be so easily established. It is indeed an empirical fact that the two terms tend to occur in different texts and contexts, as is the tendency (with several important exceptions) of "Israel" to appear more often in Hebrew literature than that written in Greek. But it is an

---

[53] Casey, "Anti-Semitic Assumptions," 285–86.

[54] On "theory-induced blindness," see Kahneman, *Thinking, Fast and Slow*, 274–77, esp. 277: "once you have accepted a theory and used it as a tool in your thinking, it is extraordinarily difficult to notice its flaws. If you come upon an observation that does not seem to fit the model, you assume that there must be a perfectly good explanation that you are somehow missing. You give the theory the benefit of the doubt, trusting the community of experts who have accepted it."

[55] Goodblatt, "Israelites Who Reside in Judah," 88–89.

interpretation of those empirical facts to conclude that one term was therefore *preferred* over the other – a conclusion that depends on one term being viewed as more positively weighted than the other. One could just as easily start from Hasmonean evidence and coinage and then pair that data with a broad swath of literature (including Esther, Daniel, and the majority of Jewish literature written in Greek) to conclude that *Ioudaios/Yehudi* was the "preferred" term. An interpretation based on preference rather than some other nuance or difference between the terms is therefore questionable at best.

Inasmuch as he continues to presume "preference" for "Israel" among insiders, Goodblatt's evaluations continue to rely upon the very assumptions upon which Kuhn's paradigm is built; Goodblatt has simply been unable to escape the established paradigm sufficiently to assess its foundations. Moreover, Kuhn's claim about *Ioudaios* having a "depreciatory element" is by no means marginal to the larger theory as Goodblatt suggests but is instead foundational to the entire paradigm. What distinguishes outsider nomenclature from favored insider nomenclature is that outsider labels by definition involve calling group members something other than the label(s) they use of themselves. The alleged derogatory nuance of *Ioudaios* provides the reason that the outsider term is not favored – otherwise one is merely dealing with *alternative* nomenclature rather than an insider/outsider distinction.

Interestingly, whereas Goodblatt concedes that Kuhn may have been wrong about the disparaging use of *Ioudaios* and argues that this claim is inessential to the model, Wills doubles down on Kuhn's claim and reproaches Casey for lacking the "modern and postmodern theoretical ... toolkit of methods" necessary to understand how outsider terms can be transformed from aspersions into affirmations, noting that "what seemed like a negative to Casey would seem typical if not mildly heroic in postmodern identity theory."[56] The problem is that in his rush to theorize, Wills has overlooked the need for evidence that the relevant term was in fact used in a derogatory manner. It bears repeating: neither Kuhn, nor Wills, nor anyone else has provided any evidence that the label *Ioudaios* (or cognates) was ever used disparagingly in this period, and appealing to the fact that "a number of excellent scholars, both Jewish and non-Jewish have begun with the observation that *Yehudi* represented an outsiders' term" does not count as evidence.[57] This is not a matter of

---

[56] Wills, "Jew, Judean, Judaism," 180.
[57] Wills, "Jew, Judean, Judaism," 180.

Casey having been theoretically underequipped; it is instead a matter of the absence of data from which one could draw the theoretical conclusions Wills advocates.

Unfortunately, Kuhn's thorough and careful treatment of the data has made it more difficult for later interpreters to notice the pernicious anti-Semitic assumptions lying below the surface of his explanation of those data. Consequently, Kuhn's paradigm has been taken for granted by scholars of this period for nearly a century – an example of what Casey calls "the widespread and unfortunate habit of repeating the words of dead professors, regardless of truth or falsehood."[58] Remarkably, some recent scholars have even attempted to employ Kuhn's insider/outsider model in the fight against anti-Judaism, apparently oblivious to how that paradigm reads the anti-Semitic assumptions of Nazi Germany into the ancient world in ways unsupported by the ancient evidence itself. Elliot, for example, depends upon Kuhn's paradigm to stake the claim that "Jesus was not a Jew," a conclusion unfortunately anticipated – though surely with different goals in mind – over half a century earlier by Nazi scholars such as Walter Grundmann.[59]

NOT ENOUGH FINGERS TO PLUG THE DAM

It is not enough, however, merely to point out Kuhn's problematic priors; one could conceivably be an anti-Semite, even a Nazi, and arrive at an accurate scholarly model. But even without accounting for its toxic Nazi-era foundations and the misguided assumption of a negative nuance to the word "Jew," the insider/outsider model itself is deeply flawed and inadequately accounts for the ancient data. It must be acknowledged, however, that the insider/outsider model would not have remained persuasive

---

[58] Casey, "Anti-Semitic Assumptions," 281.
[59] Elliot, "Jesus the Israelite"; Cf. also Boyarin, "The IOUDAIOI in John," 235–36. Grundmann, *Jesus der Galiläer*; Grundmann, *Die 28 Thesen*. Grundmann also embraced the idea that Jesus was in fact fathered by a Roman soldier (an Aryan, of course), embracing previous polemics against the virgin birth for its racial implications. Grundmann thus argues Jesus was born of an Aryan mother and father. Cf. Heschel, *Aryan Jesus*, 154–65; Betz, "Wellhausen's Dictum"; Miller, "Group Labels," 110. Subsequent studies have shown Grundmann's argument about the non-Jewish composition of Galilee to be aberrant. See Chancey, *Myth*; Reed, *Archaeology and the Galilean Jesus*, 23–61; Meyers, "Galilean Regionalism"; Eric M. Meyers, "The Cultural Setting of Galilee: The Case of Regionalism and Early Judaism," *ANRW* 19.1: 686–702. For more on Grundmann, see Heschel, "Nazifying Christian Theology"; Osten-Sacken, "Walter Grundmann"; Head, "Nazi Quest," 70–89.

to so many for so long if it entirely lacked explanatory power relative to the unequal distribution of the terms within and between texts. It cannot be denied that whereas both terms occur frequently in "insider" contexts, "Israel" is almost never used by an outsider to refer to a Jew in the extant literary or epigraphic record. It is also true that "Israel" occurs regularly in prayers and other contexts Kuhn identifies as "religious," while *Ioudaios* almost never occurs in such contexts – note, for example, the frequency of the phrase "God of Israel," while "God of the *Ioudaioi*" is vanishingly rare outside anachronistic modern scholarship.[60] But there are simply too many exceptions and theoretical problems inherent in the model for it to be tenable.[61]

First of all, the theory inadequately accounts for asymmetries between written word and spoken language, effectively treating ancient texts as transcripts.[62] It is dubious at best to assume that extant early Jewish literature – nearly all of which is insider material directed to insiders – consistently manages to convey an outsider's perspective whenever an outsider is speaking.[63] Moreover, it strains credulity to suggest that Josephus, for example, imagined his audience changing near the midpoint of his *Jewish Antiquities*. The insider/outsider model also requires marginalizing the bulk of Jewish literature written in Greek or Aramaic as "outsider" literature despite these texts plainly being written for Jewish audiences. Drawing such a linguistic division between insiders and outsiders also runs into particular difficulties accounting for multilingual Jews like Josephus, who presumably would have had recourse to use both terms in either language. Jews speaking in any tongue would have been influenced by biblical language either way, a point to which we will return below.[64]

Even more problematically, the closest thing we have to transcripts of insider communication – letters and inscriptions – consistently do the opposite of what the insider/outsider model would predict, treating *Ioudaios/Yehudi* as the default ethnonym used by insiders as well as

---

[60] Saul Kaatz, *Die mündliche Lehre und ihr Dogma* (Leipzig: Kaufmann, 1923), 43; Zeitlin, "Hebrew, Jew and Israel," 366–67; Kuhn, "Ἰουδαῖος κτλ," *TDNT* 3:360. The closest examples in early Jewish literature are found in *Ant.* 18.286, where *Ioudaios* is the object of the participle rather than of God, and in Rom 3:29, where Paul argues that God is not "the God of Jews alone."

[61] As also noted by Thiel, "'Israel' and 'Jew' as Markers," 82–83.

[62] Thiel, "'Israel' and 'Jew' as Markers," 89–90.

[63] Harvey, *True Israel*, 7. *Pace* Tomson, "Names," 123.

[64] Miller, "Group Labels," 108.

outsiders. For example, the second-century BCE Jewish papyri from Herakleopolis, Egypt, certainly qualify as insider communication, with most of the fragments appealing to leaders of the Jewish *politeuma* for resolution of an internal quarrel.[65] On the basis of the insider/outsider model, "Israelite" would be expected as the standard internal self-identifier, but the papyri go in exactly the opposite direction. "Throughout the papyri," Nathan Thiel observes, "Ἰουδαῖος/Ἰουδαία is the standard ethnic self-identifier, as is evident already from many of the greetings."[66] The Jews in Elephantine similarly self-identify with the default Aramaic *Yehuda'i*,[67] not to mention the residents of the Neo-Babylonian and Persian-era "town of Judah" (Al Yahudu) near Borsippa in Babylonia known from recently deciphered cuneiform tablets.[68] There

---

[65] Thiel, "'Israel' and 'Jew' as Markers," 86–87. See also Sylvie Honigman, "'Politeumata' and Ethnicity in Ptolemaic and Roman Egypt," *Ancient Society* 33 (2003): 61–102. The papyri themselves are collected in James M. S. Cowey and Klaus Maresch, *Urkunden des Politeuma der Juden von Herakleopolis (144/3–133/2 v. Chr.)(P. Polit. Iud.)* (Wiesbaden: Westdeutscher Verlag, 2001).

[66] Thiel, "'Israel' and 'Jew' as Markers," 86–87.

[67] Cf. Bob Becking, "Yehudite Identity in Elephantine," in *Judah and the Judeans in the Achaemenid Period: Negotiating Identity in an International Context*, eds. Oded Lipschits, Gary N. Knoppers, and Manfred Oeming (Winona Lake: Eisenbrauns, 2011), 403–19; Hélène Lozachmeur et al., *La collection Clermont-Ganneau: Ostraca, épigraphes sur jarre, étiquettes de bois*, 2 vols. Mémoires de l'Académie des inscriptions et belles-lettres (Paris: Boccard, 2006), nos. 135cv2, 182, xii; André Lemaire, "Judean Identity in Elephantine: Everyday Life according to the Ostraca," in *Judah and the Judeans in the Achaemenid Period: Negotiating Identity in an International Context*, eds. Oded Lipschits, Gary N. Knoppers, and Manfred Oeming (Winona Lake: Eisenbrauns, 2011), 365–74 (367–68); Mark W. Hamilton, "Who Was a Jew? Jewish Ethnicity during the Achaemenid Period," *RestQ* 37.2 (1995): 102–17 (105–11).

[68] Cf. Francis Joannès and André Lemaire, "Trois tablettes cunéiformes à onomastique ouest-sémitique (collection Sh. Moussaïeff) (Pls. I–II)," *Transeu* (1999): 17–34; David S. Vanderhooft, "New Evidence Pertaining to the Transition from Neo-Babylonian to Achaemenid Administration in Palestine," in *Yahwism after the Exile: Perspectives on Israelite Religion in the Persian Era*, eds. Rainer Albertz and Bob Becking (Assen: Van Gorcum, 2003), 219–35; Laurie E. Pearce, "New Evidence for Judeans in Babylonia," in *Judah and the Judeans in the Persian Period*, eds. Oded Lipschits, Gary N. Knoppers, and Manfred Oeming (Winona Lake: Eisenbrauns, 2006), 399–411; Laurie E. Pearce, "'Judean': A Special Status in Neo-Babylonian and Achemenid Babylonia?," in *Judah and the Judeans in the Achaemenid Period: Negotiating Identity in an International Context*, eds. Oded Lipschits, Gary N. Knoppers, and Manfred Oeming (Winona Lake: Eisenbrauns, 2011), 267–77 (269–72); Kathleen Abraham, "West Semitic and Judean Brides in Cuneiform Sources from the Sixth Century BCE: New Evidence from a Marriage Contract from Āl-Yahudu," *AfO* (2005): 198–219; Kathleen Abraham, "An Inheritance Division among Judeans in Babylonia from the Early Persian Period," in *New Seals and Inscriptions: Hebrew, Idumean, and Cuneiform*, ed. Meir Lubetski, HBM 7 (Sheffield: Sheffield Phoenix, 2007), 148–82.

is also no epigraphical evidence from the Graeco-Roman period that *Ioudaios* functions as a term of outside identity.[69]

Perhaps the most problematic counterevidence for the insider/outsider model or its linguistic iteration is a supposed anomaly noted by Kuhn himself: official Hasmonean documents (as reported in 1 Maccabees) and coinage indicate that the Hasmonean state was officially called "Judah" and its people "Jews" (*Yehudim*/*Ioudaioi*).[70] It is noteworthy that this choice of nomenclature contrasts sharply with the first and second Jewish revolts against the Romans, each of which adopted "Israel" terminology.[71] Goodblatt confesses his puzzlement on this point:

Whatever the reason, the Hasmoneans did not restore the state called "Israel." Instead they created a "Greater Judah." ... Unfortunately, a convincing explanation of Hasmonean usage still eludes me. Perhaps this reaffirmation of the anomaly's existence will encourage others to investigate it further.[72]

To explain this anomaly, Kuhn argues that official state communications are inherently "outsider" in nature since they presume an international context, but this is hardly persuasive for internal memos and similar communications, particularly given the epistolary evidence from Herakleopolis and elsewhere. More ingenious interpreters such as Tomson and Malcolm Lowe have managed to convert these many exceptions into source-critical tools, thus explaining away counterevidence while simultaneously using it to reinforce the conclusions assumed at the start.[73] But such creative modifications are little more than futile attempts to plug the holes of a leaky dam; there are simply too many exceptions to maintain the insider/outsider model.[74] Unfortunately, even

---

[69] Williams, "Meaning and Function," 249. See also Zeitlin, "Hebrew, Jew and Israel," 369; Boyarin, "The IOUDAIOI in John," 227.

[70] Kuhn, "Ἰουδαῖος κτλ," *TDNT* 3:361.

[71] Cf. David Goodblatt, *Elements of Ancient Jewish Nationalism* (Cambridge: Cambridge University Press, 2006), 136–37; David Goodblatt, "Varieties of Identity in Late Second Temple Judah (200 BCE–135 CE)," in *Jewish Identity and Politics between the Maccabees and Bar Kokhba: Groups, Normativity, and Rituals*, ed. Benedikt Eckhardt (Leiden: Brill, 2011), 11–27 (17–18).

[72] Goodblatt, "Israelites Who Reside in Judah," 84, 86. For additional discussion on this point, including a significantly more detailed analysis of the names of ancient Jewish states, a discussion his later publications assume, see David Goodblatt, "From Judeans to Israel: Names of Jewish States in Antiquity," *JSJ* 29.1 (1998): 1–36; cf. also Goodblatt, "Varieties of Identity," 14. For further discussion and explanation of this anomaly, see the section on 1 Maccabees in Chapter 5.

[73] Tomson, "Names," 280–82; Lowe, "IOΥΔΑΙOI of the Apocrypha."

[74] As convincingly demonstrated in Thiel, "'Israel' and 'Jew' as Markers," 80.

those who have pointed out flaws in Kuhn's hypothesis – and even the few who have entirely rejected his model – have not yet proposed an alternative theory that more adequately accounts for the data, so it has simply remained easier for most to attempt to patch (or ignore) those holes while making efforts to distance from the anti-Semitic assumptions upon which that paradigm is built. But it is high time to transition to a new model that better holds water.

ISRAELITES, HEBREWS, AND JEWS IN JOSEPHUS

The corpus of the first-century Jewish historian Flavius Josephus provides an excellent starting point for a deeper investigation of the relationship between the terms "Jew" and "Israelite."[75] Rather than treating these terms as equivalent, Josephus differentiates between them with striking consistency, even going out of his way to correct another historian's conflation of the terms in Book 7 of his *Jewish Antiquities*, where he first quotes an account from Nicolaus of Damascus about ancient wars between the Syrians and those Nicolaus calls the *Ioudaioi*:

> But the third [Hadad] was the most powerful of them all and was willing to avenge the defeat his forefather had received; so he made an expedition against the Jews (*Ioudaioi*), and laid waste the city which is now called Samaria. (*Ant.* 7.102)

Nicolaus – like many modern scholars – applies the national and ethnic labels more familiar in his own day to the distant past, referencing Hadad's conquest of Samaria as "an expedition against the Jews," but Josephus' next statement is what makes this passage noteworthy. Rather

---

[75] The bibliography on Josephus is enormous. For a more comprehensive bibliography than could be provided here, see Louis H. Feldman, "Flavius Josephus Revisited: The Man, His Writings, and His Significance," *ANRW* 21.2: 763–862 and Louis H. Feldman, "A Selective Critical Bibliography of Josephus," in *Josephus, the Bible, and History*, eds. Louis H. Feldman and Gohei Hata (Detroit: Wayne State University Press, 1989), 330–448. On Josephus in general, the first avenue of research is now the online Project on Ancient Cultural Engagement (PACE) led by Steve Mason at http://pace-ancient .mcmaster.ca/york/york/index.htm, which includes online digital copies of both Greek and English editions of Josephus along with commentaries (including the recent Brill translation/commentary series edited by Mason), annotated bibliographies, and numerous other scholarly resources. The standard critical edition of Josephus is Benedictus Niese, *Flavii Iosephi Opera* (Berlin: Weidmann, 1888), which is also available through the PACE website; the translations throughout are based on Niese's text unless otherwise noted. For more on the text of Josephus, see Tommaso Leoni, "The Text of Josephus's Works: An Overview," *JSJ* 40.2 (2009): 149–84.

than retaining Nicolaus' equation of the Jews and Samarians, Josephus promptly corrects Nicolaus' nomenclature:

This is that Hadad who made the expedition against Samaria in the reign of Ahab, *king of Israel*, concerning whom we will speak in due place after this [my emphasis]. (*Ant.* 7.103)

In contrast to Nicolaus, who apparently did not distinguish between the northern Israelite kings and those of Judah, Josephus consistently differentiates between these terms throughout his corpus. It should come as no surprise that Josephus uses *Ioudaios* as the default term for his people, with that term appearing approximately 1,188 times in the Josephan corpus. But remarkably, despite its widespread use elsewhere in the corpus, that term appears only twenty-six times in the first ten books of the *Antiquities*.[76] The terms Israel and Israelite, on the other hand, appear 188 times in the first eleven books of the *Antiquities* – precisely

---

[76] Josephus' preference for *Ioudaios* when referring to contemporary history has been noted previously; e.g., *EDNT*, s.v. "Ἰσραηλίτης," 204–05 (205). Of the twenty-five occasions in the first ten books, four refer to the Jews of Josephus' day (1.4; 1.6; 1.214; 9.291 [×2]), seven refer specifically to the southern kingdom (9.245; 10.87; 10.169; 10.182; 10.186; 10.222; 10.265), one explains why the Jews were originally called Hebrews (1.146), and three are quotations from other historians (1.95; 1.240; 7.103). Four are ambiguous, though they seem to represent those from Judah: 6.30 (land belonging to "the Jews" in the territory of Judah); 6.324 ("south of the Jews"); 7.72 ("David, king of the Jews"); 8.163 (Ezion-Geber once belonged to the Jews). Only six times does Josephus use it in a sense akin to "Israelites" (4.11; 6.26; 6.40; 6.68; 6.96; 6.97; the concentration of these instances in Book 6 is intriguing but cannot be explored here). Niese's text includes two additional instances that are likely secondary. In 6.98, the "of the Jews" (τῶν Ἰουδαίων) reading preferred by Niese only occurs in MS O and is likely secondary to the "of the Hebrews" (τῶν Ἑβραίων) reading (cf. 6.327, 344) occurring in other Greek MSS and the Latin translations. Similarly, in 8.25, the τοὺς Ἰουδαίους reading is found only in RO, likely secondary to the τοὺς ἰδίους found in the other Greek codices. MS M also has "of Jews" (Ἰουδαίων) in 10.155, though the other MSS and Niese have "of Hebrews" (Ἑβραίων). Two instances of *Ioudaikos* also appear in the first ten books, at 1.203 ("Jewish War"; Ἰουδαϊκὸν πόλεμον) and 5.271 ("tribe of Judah"; φυλῆς ὦν Ἰουδαϊκῆς). (Thanks to David Levenson for his help with the textual evidence in Josephus.) Paul Spilsbury, *The Image of the Jew in Flavius Josephus' Paraphrase of the Bible*, TSAJ 69 (Tübingen: Mohr Siebeck, 1998), 37, observes (before arguing for the contrary), "On the strength of this evidence it might be argued that the first five books of the *Antiquities* are not dealing with the "Jews" at all (the reference in Book 4 is obviously an anachronism), and that even in the next five books the word is evidence of the author's terminological inexactitude. ... Only in the post-exilic period is the term properly used." It should be noted that although *Ioudaios* is anachronistic when applied to ancient Israel, it is not entirely incorrect (especially when one intends, as does Josephus, to emphasize the continuity of ancient Israel with modern Jews), since Judah was part of Israel. For the purpose of this study, what matters is that Josephus consistently refrains from equating post-exilic "Jews" with "Israel," reserving that moniker for the northern tribes or all twelve tribes as a collective.

where *Ioudaios* rarely appears – and then nowhere else in the Josephan corpus.[77] Similarly, only two of the 297 appearances of the related term "Hebrew" in *Antiquities* occur after Book 11.[78] A graphical representation of Josephus' use of Israel/Israelite, *Ioudaios*, and Hebrew is striking (see Figure 1).

Upon close examination, *Hebraios* is Josephus' primary term for the biblical ancestors of the *Ioudaioi*, occurring 258 times with reference to these ancient ancestors. Over half (143) of these uses occur in the first four books of *Antiquities*, which focus on the period prior to the conquest of Canaan; "Israelite" occurs only twenty-two times in these sections, while *Ioudaios* appears only once in Books 2–5. "Israelite" appears more frequently after the entry into the land, after which it appears mostly interchangeable with "Hebrew," though in the era of the divided kingdoms, *Hebraios* refers to the whole people (e.g., *Ant.* 9.182; 10.72, 183), while "Israelite" often refers specifically to those of the northern kingdom (e.g., 7.103; 8.224, 286, 298, 306, 311, 314). Josephus therefore prefers Israel terminology in the monarchical period of Israel but not before or after that time, while *Ioudaios* is almost exclusively used after Israel and Hebrew no longer appear (see Table 1).

It would of course be absurd to conclude that this terminological shift is because Josephus wrote the first eleven books of *Antiquities* to an insider audience but the rest of his corpus for outsiders. Instead, Josephus not only shifts from Israelite to *Ioudaios* at a specific point in his history but also gives a specific explanation for why he does so:

From the time they went up from Babylon they were called by this name [*Ioudaios*] after the tribe of Judah. As the tribe was the prominent one to come from those parts, both the people themselves and the country have taken their name from it. (*Ant.*11.173)[79]

Josephus' explanation is straightforward: Judah/Judaea was the homeland of the southern kingdom of Judah, and the returnees from Babylon

---

[77] Of these, Israel (as opposed to Israelite) occurs only twice, in the first and fourth books.

[78] *Ant.* 14.255 ("Abraham, who was the father of all the Hebrews"); 18.228 ("in the Hebrew language").

[79] *Prōtos* is best taken in the sense of "most important" here rather than "first" in a temporal sense, *pace* Lowe, "Who Were the ΙΟΥΔΑΙΟΙ," 106, who reads "Judah was the first tribe to return from exile," and Josephus, *Jewish Antiquities, Volume VI*, trans. Ralph Marcus, LCL 489 (Cambridge: Harvard University Press, 1937), 399, "the first to come to those parts." Neither the biblical accounts nor Josephus' account give any indication that the tribe of Judah preceded the other tribes in returning to the land; rather, it was the dominant, prominent tribe of those that returned. As is often the case in translation, the problem here is not so much with the Greek, but with the English distinction between "first [in importance]," for which English speakers often use another term, and "first [in a series]."

Chapters

Sum of Israel*,sum of Hebraios and sum of Ioudaios for each Chapters.

Israel* | Hebraios | Ioudaios

Ant.1 Ant.2 Ant.3 Ant.4 Ant.5 Ant.6 Ant.7 Ant.8 Ant.9 Ant.10 Ant.11 Ant.12 Ant.13 Ant.14 Ant.15 Ant.16 Ant.17 Ant.18 Ant.19 Ant.20 Ap.1 Ap.2 Life War 1 War 2 War 3 War 4 War 5 War 6 War 7

Figure 1 Jews, Israelites, and Hebrews in Josephus

Table 1 *Israelites,* Ioudaioi, *and Hebrews in Josephus*

	Israel+	Per 1,000	*Ioudaios*	Per 1,000	Hebrew	Per 1,000
Ant. 1	1	0.07	6	0.40	14	0.93
2	7	0.47	0	0.00	54	3.63
3	1	0.07	0	0.00	41	2.96
4	13	0.92	1	0.07	34	2.42
5	46	3.11	0	0.00	34	2.30
6	7	0.38	8	0.44	41	2.24
7	13	0.68	2	0.11	38	2.02
8	23	1.14	2	0.10	23	1.14
9	55	4.18	2	0.15	6	0.46
10	8	0.65	6	0.49	7	0.57
11	14	1.02	90	6.55	3	0.22
12–20	0	0.00	530	3.85	2	0.01
War	0	0.00	468	3.73	5	0.04
Life	0	0.00	24	1.52	0	0.00
Ag. Ap.	0	0.00	51	2.48	1	0.05

returned to this land of *Judah*.[80] Remarkably, Josephus' lucid explanation of this shift in terminology has typically received only passing attention from those attempting to explain the relationship between *Ioudaios* and Israelite, and even those who have recognized its importance have tended either to misconstrue or ignore its meaning.[81] Esler, for example,

[80] *Pace* Goodblatt, "Israelites Who Reside in Judah," 82, who notes that "Josephus consistently uses the ethnonym 'Israel' when covering what for him was the biblical period (that is, up until the fall of the Persian Empire to Alexander of Macedonia)," Josephus actually discontinues the use of Israel well before the fall of Persia, with the shift coinciding instead with the return from Babylon, which, as he explains, did not include the whole of Israel.

[81] This Josephan passage and explanation is completely ignored in Goodblatt, "Judeans to Israel"; Goodblatt, "Israelites Who Reside in Judah"; Stephen G. Wilson, "'Jew' and Related Terms in the Ancient World," *SR* 33 (2004): 157–71; and (remarkably, given Mason's expertise in Josephus) in Mason, "Jews, Judaeans." Others cite or quote the passage but do not seem to recognize its full significance. For example, Lowe, "Who Were the IOYΔAIOI," 106, mentions it briefly in a summary of how Josephus uses the term but does not explore its significance. Robert Murray mentions it "as a starting point" but then never returns to it in Robert Murray, "Jews, Hebrews, and Christians: Some Needed Distinctions," *NovT* 24.3 (1982): 194–208 (198). Elliot likewise briefly mentions the passage but only in passing, on the way to explaining that *Ioudaios* was in fact a geographical label ("Jesus the Israelite," 130). One exception who does recognize Josephus' basic point here is Zeitlin, "Hebrew, Jew and Israel," 368. Interestingly, this passage receives significantly more attention from scholars of the Hebrew Bible, who tend

recognizes the change in nomenclature at this point but ignores Josephus' explanation, concluding that the change is the result of the "link between the name of the people and its homeland containing the capital city and the temple of their God," apparently forgetting that "Israel" was also the name of the traditional homeland and offering no explanation for why that name for the land was not adopted after the return from Babylon.[82] Tomson, on the other hand, recognizes and approves Josephus' explanation,[83] but then promptly ignores Josephus' distinction between the terms, asserting that Israelite and *Ioudaios* are "two synonymous names which indicate the same people," missing the larger point of Josephus' explanation and the significance of Josephus' shift in terminology.[84] Paul Spilsbury similarly notes Josephus' distinction and explanation before dismissing them in practice, concluding, "Close examination of how these three terms are used reveals that they are, to a large degree, interchangeable for Josephus," despite the fact that "Israelites" never occurs after Book 11, unlike what one would expect if the terms were truly interchangeable.[85] To his credit, David Miller rightly points to *Ant.* 11.173 as the key to understanding the shift in nomenclature, but he mistakes Josephus' explanation as an "insistence that the name for the people changed," not recognizing that the reason Josephus gives for the shift in nomenclature is that the two terms are not in fact coextensive.[86]

Part of the problem is that even those recognizing the importance of *Ant.* 11.173 have tended to overlook its connection with two earlier statements that set up the transition and further clarify the reason for the shift in

---

to be more careful to distinguish between "ancient Israel" and "Judaism," the latter of which is considered to have arisen after the return from Babylon. Unfortunately, however, this distinction has been too often used to distinguish between the "living" religion of ancient Israel and post-exilic Judaism's supposed focus on the "dead letter." The full implication of the continued distinction between "Israel" and "the Jews" in the post-exilic period is nevertheless usually missed even by scholars of the Hebrew Bible, who typically regard the *Yehudim* simply to have appropriated the other term. These points will be addressed more fully in Chapter 3.

[82] Esler, *Conflict and Identity*, 64.

[83] "Roughly, Josephus is right" (Tomson, "Names," 124).

[84] Tomson, "Names," 126.

[85] Spilsbury, *Image of the Jew*, 36–38 (38). He then cites a series of examples of overlap, mostly between "Israelites" and "Hebrews," concluding with the observation, "All three terms are used in direct address: Israelites: 3.189; Hebrews: 3.84; Jews: 11.69," ignoring that the last of these is after the exile and that "Israelites" never appears again after Book 11, as one would expect if the terms were truly interchangeable.

[86] Miller, "Group Labels," 102–03, followed by Jennifer Eyl, "'I Myself Am an Israelite': Paul, Authenticity and Authority," *JSNT* 40.2 (2017): 148–68 (149).

terminology. First, Josephus explains that the return from exile had been limited to the southern tribes: "After Cyrus announced this to the Israelites, the rulers of the two tribes of Judah and Benjamin, with the Levites and priests, went in haste to Jerusalem" (*Ant.* 11.8). This passage marks a key transition in Josephus' account, as Cyrus addresses the "Israelites," but only those from Judah, Benjamin, and Levi return.[87] A careful reader of Josephus' account of Israel to this point should be asking why only three tribes responded to Cyrus' decree, yet scholars have consistently missed the important transition here, likely owing to the prima facie assumption that "Israelites" is synonymous with "Jews." Spilsbury, for example, points to this passage as evidence that the terms are interchangeable, claiming, "Here this term [Israel] refers specifically to the two tribes who returned from exile."[88] But a more careful reading shows that Josephus here distinguishes between the Israelites, a term that to this point in the *Antiquities* has referred only to the northern tribes or the twelve-tribe totality, and those who actually heeded Cyrus' words – only those from the tribes of Judah, Benjamin, and Levi.

Lest anyone object that this is too subtle a reading of the passage, Josephus clarifies his meaning only a few paragraphs later, answering the question of what happened to the other tribes:

When these *Ioudaioi* learned of the king's piety towards God, and his kindness towards Ezra, they loved [him] most dearly, and many took up their possessions and went to Babylon, desiring to go down to Jerusalem. But the whole [ὁ πᾶς] people of Israel remained in that land; so it came about that only two tribes came to Asia and Europe and are subject to the Romans. But the ten tribes are beyond Euphrates until now and are a boundless multitude, not to be estimated by numbers. (*Ant.* 11.132–33)

So, according to Josephus, the reason *they* came to be called *Ioudaioi* was that they were the part associated with the southern kingdom of Judah, while the bulk of Israel (πᾶς λαὸς τῶν Ἰσραηλιτῶν) remained in exile in immense numbers.[89] Josephus does not shift his nomenclature because "the name for

---

[87] Josephus' distinction in limiting the return actually mirrors his source material in Ezra-Nehemiah, which similarly emphasizes the incomplete nature of the return after Cyrus' decree to "whoever is among you of all his people," with only the three southern tribes returning in any significant numbers. See Chapter 5.

[88] Spilsbury, *Image of the Jew*, 40 n. 129.

[89] Remarkably, even this passage seems to have been too subtle for most modern interpreters. For example, Barmash, "Nexus," 233, despite the focus of her article on the northern tribes, somehow misses the distinction Josephus makes between *Ioudaioi* and Israelites here, saying, "Josephus explains the existence of two populations of Jews [*sic*], one under Roman rule and the other under Parthian rule, by telling that the Babylonian Jews returned with Ezra while only some of the Jews [*sic*] in Media

the people changed,"[90] as Miller and others have suggested, but because the *people in view* changed, with the scope narrowing from the larger twelve-tribe body of Israelites to a more limited group identified with the dominant southern tribe of Judah. This is a critical point and bears repeating: *Josephus uses a different name because the group in view is different.* This fully explains why he completely drops the term "Israelites" shortly after this passage: for Josephus, the *Ioudaioi* are only a *subset* of Israel, and until the rest of Israel is again in view, "Israelites" is the wrong term for the limited portion of Israel represented by the term *Ioudaioi*.

Josephus' distinction between the terms therefore goes back to the biblical accounts about the division between the northern and southern Israelite kingdoms and their respective exiles. This accounts for the full pattern of Josephus' use of these terms, as even in the few instances where the terms do appear to be interchangeable, the equivalence only works in one direction.[91] That is, before the divided kingdom (i.e., when the full people are in view), Josephus can be more flexible with his terminology, especially where he wishes to emphasize the connection between ancient Israel and contemporary *Ioudaioi*, and in such rare cases he employs *Ioudaios* in place of "Israelites" – though always referring to activity in the southern territory.[92] But the reverse is never true, as after the division of the kingdoms, Josephus is strikingly consistent in using "Israel" or "Israelite" only for the northern tribes.[93]

After the return from Babylon, that term is therefore no longer appropriate, since Josephus explains that the northern tribes did not return with

---

returned at that time (*Antiquities*, xi, 131–33). He describes the Jews [sic] 'beyond the Euphrates' as numbering countless multitudes." In fairness, Barmash does acknowledge that "Josephus assumes that the population of Jews [sic] 'beyond the Euphrates' consists of the descendents of the northerners" (233) but nevertheless misses the larger point in this passage. Note also the similar mistake by James M. Scott, "Philo and the Restoration of Israel," in *Society of Biblical Literature 1995 Seminar Papers*, ed. Eugene H. Lovering Jr. (Atlanta: Scholars Press, 1996), 553–75 (561 n. 47), who refers to this passage as about "the Jewish nation," again neglecting the distinction in terminology Josephus makes.

[90] Miller, "Group Labels," 102–03.

[91] Cf. Spilsbury, *Image of the Jew*, 38–40.

[92] Spilsbury is right to point out that Josephus' concern is to show the origins of the *Ioudaioi* and that "he regarded his description of these ancient people as fully relevant to the 'Jews' of his own day" (Spilsbury, *Image of the Jew*, 37–40, quote from 40). But continuity between ancient Hebrews/Israelites and contemporary Jews does not equate all three terms or groups. In this case, Josephus explains that the *Ioudaioi* descended from the Hebrews/Israelites (thus Jewish history includes the history of ancient Israel), but the Jews are only a portion of those descended from Israel, which remains a larger group.

[93] Spilsbury, *Image of the Jew*, 40.

the three southern tribes, which is why he transitions to *Ioudaios* at this point in his narrative. Josephus not only carefully manages his use of "Israelites" in connection to the division between the kingdoms and their respective exiles, he explicitly explains the centrality of these events to his history:

Such was the end of the nation of the Hebrews, as it has been passed down to us, having twice gone beyond the Euphrates, for the people of the ten tribes were carried out of Samaria by the Assyrians in the days of king Hoshea, after which the people of the two tribes that remained after Jerusalem was taken were deported by Nebuchadnezzar, the king of Babylon and Chaldea. Shalmaneser deported the Israelites out of their country, and replaced them with the nation of the Cutheans, who had formerly belonged to the inner parts of Persia and Media, but were then called Samaritans, taking the name of the country to which they were deported. But the king of Babylon, who brought out the two tribes [Judah and Benjamin], placed no other nation in their country, so all Judaea and Jerusalem – and the temple – was a wilderness for seventy years. But the entire time from the captivity of the Israelites to the carrying away of the two tribes came to one hundred and thirty years, six months, and ten days. (*Ant.* 10.183–85)

Josephus here summarizes the "end of the nation of the Hebrews," which includes both the "end that overtook the Israelites" (*Ant.* 9.281) and the subsequent exile of "the two tribes" by the king of Babylon,[94] thus providing an excellent example of how he distinguishes between all three terms. The term "Hebrew" will be addressed in more detail in the next chapter, but it is worth noting that here it provides a way to represent both kingdoms as a whole while reserving "Israelites" to refer specifically to those from the northern kingdom.[95]

A NEW MODEL: JEWS AS A SUBSET OF ISRAEL

In contrast to models based on insider/outsider, linguistic, or emotive contexts for otherwise synonymous terms, Josephus treats the term "Jew" as though it refers to a subset of people within Israel. That is, at least for Josephus, although Jews are Israelites, some Israelites cannot

---

[94] See Chapter 7 for more analysis of Josephus' account of the destruction and deportation of the northern kingdom in *Ant.* 9.277–82.

[95] See D. R. G. Beattie and Philip R. Davies, "What Does Hebrew Mean?," *JSS* 56.1 (2011): 71–83 (77), "It is perhaps worth considering that the term was used at a certain period to designate a community or population that included both Israelites and Judaeans, who to outsiders did not form a single identifiable people, a term that Israelites or Jews could apply to themselves, but also apply to others."

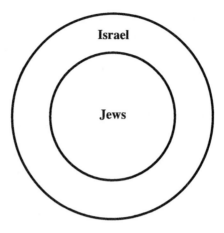

Figure 2 Jews as part of Israel

rightly be called Jews. Instead, *Ioudaios* is a *term denoting a person descended from the southern kingdom of Judah or otherwise incorporated into that ethno-religious group*. In its broader sense, the term not only includes those specifically from the tribe of Judah but includes at least Levites and Benjaminites, as persons distinctly identified with these tribes were included among the returnees from the southern kingdom of Judah to the Persian province of Yehud after the Babylonian Exile. And as with all ancient ethnonyms, to be a *Ioudaios* also includes cultural and social practices, many of which would be categorized as "religious" today.

In contrast, Josephus treats "Israelite" as a more comprehensive term, including but not limited to *Ioudaioi*. Josephus believes that the bulk of Israel never returned from exile, with non-Jewish Israelites who had been deported by the Assyrians remaining "beyond the Euphrates" and not under the power of Rome. Consequently, Josephus transitions to the term *Ioudaios* rather than "Israelite" in the Persian period, reserving Israel/Israelite language for the northern tribes or the twelve-tribe people as a whole and thus using those terms only when referring to the past people or to the future time when "the two tribes" (τὰς δύο φυλὰς) are reunited with the entire people of Israel (ὁ πᾶς λαὸς τῶν Ἰσραηλιτῶν).[96] Thus rather than being synonymous, the evidence from Josephus suggests the

---

[96] See Chapter 7 for more on this eschatological element in Josephus.

relationship between these terms is *partitive*, with Jews a subset of the larger category of Israel (see Figure 2).[97]

As will be shown throughout the remainder of this study, Josephus' use of these terms is not idiosyncratic but rather accords with the way they were used across a wide range of literature and other evidence. The next chapter looks at an important reason the distinction between the two terms persisted throughout the Second Temple period.

---

[97] Talmon came to similar conclusions but did not take his insights to their full conclusion in his construction of a three-tier model to explain the perspectives of Ezra-Nehemiah and later Jewish sectarians in which a "credal-national" identity formed the "inner-group," while an "in-group" involved national identification but not credal. In my model, Josephus would understand "Israel" as the "in-group," but "Jews" are the "inner-group." See Talmon, "Emergence of Jewish Sectarianism," 599.

2

The Other Israelites

Samaritans, Hebrews, and Non-Jewish Israel

This often unexplained but tacitly presupposed equation "empirical Israel = Judaism" is based on the adoption of certain parts of biblical historiography, especially the so-called historical work.

Martina Böhm[1]

That Josephus treats the Jews as a subset of Israel rather than as synonymous with Israel has largely been ignored due to the theory-induced blindness produced by the widespread presumption that "Jew" and "Israelite" are equivalent. That is not to say, however, that Josephus' explanation of his transition from the term "Israelites" to "the Jews" has gone entirely unnoticed in the history of scholarship. But rather than this transition being the consequence of focusing on a smaller group within the whole, it has instead been understood as denoting a transition of other aspects of the same people. Specifically, Josephus' explanation of his terminological shift was among the primary reasons Wilhelm de Wette began two centuries ago to distinguish post-exilic *Judentum* from preexilic *Hebraismus*, a distinction preserved by Julius Wellhausen and thereby

---

[1] Böhm, "Wer gehörte," 181, 182: "In der neutestamentlichen Exegese wird weithin davon ausgegangen, dass das in den Evangelien, in der Apostelgeschichte und in den Paulusbriefen erwähnte empirische Gottesvolk "Israel" und die zu ihm gehörenden "Israeliten" in hellenistisch-römischer Zeit identisch waren mit dem "Judentum," auch wenn dieses in der Zeit des Zweiten Tempels als ausgesprochen vielschichtig beschrieben werden muss. ... Diese häufig gar nicht explizierte, sondern unausgesprochen vorausgesetzte Gleichung 'empirisches Israel = Judentum' fußt auf der Übernahme bestimmter Teile der biblischen Historiographie, vor allem des so genannten dtr Geschichtswerks."

retaining significant influence in studies of Judaism and the Hebrew Bible to this day.[2]

Unfortunately, this distinction was tied to a pejorative picture in which the vibrant, prophetic "Hebraic" religion and people of ancient Israel devolved into the post-exilic (that is, post-Ezra) *Judentum* allegedly characterized by a dead, rigid legalism. In this model, Israelites became Jews when they lost their *völkisch* ties of ethnic and political unity,[3] which were especially emphasized in increasingly nationalistic pre-World War II German theology,[4] with the old prophetic spirit having degenerated into priestly legalism. Wellhausen's evolutionary model further distinguished between the *Judentum* of the early post-exilic period and the *Judaismus* of the last two centuries BCE,[5] giving rise to the problematic terms *Spätjudentum* and "Late Judaism," implying that legitimate Judaism as an heir to ancient Israel ended with the birth of Christianity.[6] Mainstream scholarship has thankfully moved away from

---

[2] W. M. L. de Wette, *Biblische Dogmatik des Alten und Neuen Testaments oder kritische Darstellung der Religionslehre des Hebraismus, des Judentums und des Urchristentums*, 3rd ed. (Berlin: Realschulbuchhandlung, 1813); Julius Wellhausen, *Prolegomena to the History of Israel*, trans. J. S. Black and A. Menzies (Edinburgh: Black, 1885), 404–10; cf. Rolf Rendtorff, "The Image of Post-Exilic Israel in German Bible Scholarship from Wellhausen to von Rad," in *"Sha'arei Talmon": Studies in Bible, Qumran, and the Ancient Near East Presented to Shemaryahu Talmon*, eds. M. Fishbane, Emanuel Tov, and W. W. Fields (Winona Lake: Eisenbrauns, 1992), 165–73; Klaus Koch, "Ezra and the Origins of Judaism," *JSS* 19 (1974): 173–97 (173–75).

[3] Cf. James S. Pasto, "H. M. L. De Wette and the Invention of Post-Exilic Judaism: Political Historiography and Christian Allegory in Nineteenth-Century German Biblical Scholarship," in *Jews, Antiquity, and the Nineteenth-Century Imagination*, eds. Hayim Lapin and Dale B. Martin, Studies and Texts in Jewish History and Culture (College Park: University Press of Maryland, 2003), 33–52 (34–35, 45–51); Koch, "Ezra," 173–74. George W. E. Nickelsburg and Robert A. Kraft, "Introduction: The Modern Study of Early Judaism," in *Early Judaism and Its Modern Interpreters*, eds. Robert A. Kraft and George W. E. Nickelsburg (Minneapolis: Fortress, 1986), 1–29 (10–11); James S. Pasto, "When the End Is the Beginning? Or When the Biblical Past Is the Political Present: Some Thoughts on Ancient Israel, 'Post-Exilic Judaism,' and the Politics of Biblical Scholarship," *SJOT* 12.2 (1998): 157–202. For a signal twentieth-century example of Ezra marking the beginning of legalistic *Spätjudentum*, see Kuhn, "Die Entstehung," 64–66.

[4] For example, note the centrality of commitment to one's *Volk* in the theology of Adolf Schlatter, as shown in McNutt, "Damning Truth," 8.

[5] Julius Wellhausen, "Israel und das Judentum," in *Prolegomena zur Geschichte Israels* (Berlin: Reimer, 1886), 370–431; Julius Wellhausen, "Das Gesetz," in *Israelitische und jüdische Geschichte* (Berlin: Reimer, 1958), 177–87. There have been other attempts to further subdivide the transition from "Hebraism" and "Judaism," such as the idea of Lothar Perlitt, *Deuteronomium-Studien* (Tübingen: Mohr Siebeck, 1994), 247–60 that "Deuteronomism" was a transitional stage between the two.

[6] For more on these problematic terms and the somewhat less problematic replacement "early Judaism," see Nickelsburg and Kraft, "Early Judaism," 1–26 and the material cited there. For the importance of the division between early *Hebraismus* from *Spätjudentum*

such anti-Jewish perspectives, though there is no denying that the communities and institutions of ancient Israel and Judah were significantly different from those of the Jews in the Persian and Graeco-Roman periods.[7]

Nevertheless, even the typical distinction between pre- and post-exilic periods leaves aside the fact that the period of transformation between ancient Israel and "post-exilic" communities was not a single massive event (*"the* exile") but a multi-century period involving numerous deportations and migrations,[8] as Ingrid Hjelm explains:

While several exiles and population displacements occurred in Palestine since the Assyrian encroachments in the region from the mid eighth century BCE and reiterated by Babylonian and Persian as well as Ptolemaic rulers, only one exile

within German anti-Semitic theology, see Anders Gerdmar, *Roots of Theological Anti-Semitism: German Biblical Interpretation and the Jews, from Herder and Semler to Kittel and Bultmann*, Studies in Jewish History and Culture 20 (Leiden: Brill, 2009), esp. 147–160, 183–88.

[7] As noted by Pasto, "Invention of Post-Exilic Judaism," 35, "we must distinguish between de Wette's literary analysis of the Old Testament and the narrative in which he expressed this analysis." On the lack of continuity between earlier Israel and Judah and the time after their respective demises, see Niels Peter Lemche, *The Israelites in History and Tradition* (London: SPCK, 1998), 84–85; Thomas L. Thompson, *The Mythic Past: Biblical Archaeology and the Myth of Israel* (London: Basic Books, 1999), 210–25, 254–56. See, however, the critiques of Pasto, "When the End Is the Beginning." One especially notable difference in the material record is the apparent absence of non-Yahwistic cultic figurines or related artifacts from the Second Temple period in both Judah and Samaria, whereas such figurines are plentiful in the Iron Age evidence. See Ephraim Stern, "What Happened to the Cult Figurines? Israelite Religion Purified after the Exile," *BAR* 15.4 (1989): 22–29, 53; Ephraim Stern, *The Assyrian, Babylonian, and Persian Periods, 732–332 BCE*, ABRL (New York: Doubleday, 2001), 479, 488; Ephraim Stern, "The Religious Revolution in Persian-Period Judah," in *Judah and the Judeans in the Persian Period*, eds. Oded Lipschits and Manfred Oeming (Winona Lake: Eisenbrauns, 2006), 199–205; Othmar Keel and Christoph Uehlinger, *Gods, Goddesses, and Images* (Minneapolis: Fortress, 1998), 385–91.

[8] Thus the terms "preexilic" and "post-exilic" (and the periodization of history they represent) are imprecise at best and inaccurate at worst, implying a much cleaner and more distinct transition than the historical reality. See the critiques of Robert P. Carroll, "Exile! What Exile? Deportation and the Discourses of Diaspora," in *Leading Captivity Captive: "The Exile" as History and Ideology*, ed. Lester Grabbe (Sheffield: Sheffield Academic, 1998), 62–79 (69–79); Philip R. Davies, "Exile? What Exile? Whose Exile?," in *Leading Captivity Captive: "The Exile" as History and Ideology*, ed. Lester Grabbe (Sheffield: Sheffield Academic, 1998), 128–38 (132–38), to the effect that to use such terminology is to privilege the mythical world created by the biblical writers for whom the Babylonian Exile takes special importance. For further criticism of the use of the term "exile" and the related term "diaspora," see Jörn Kiefer, *Exil und Diaspora: Begrifflichkeit und Deutungen im antiken Judentum und in der hebräischen Bibel*, Arbeiten zur Bibel und ihrer Geschichte (Berlin: Evangelische Verlagsanstalt, 2005), 25–106, esp. 42–47. Although Kiefer is correct that these terms are problematic, the paradigms they represent are unavoidable in the literature, so this study will not avoid their use.

has aroused scholarly interest, namely that from Jerusalem in 587 BCE. While several returns occurred throughout these centuries, the return to Jerusalem under Cyrus has been the subject of investigation. In this picture, the Babylonian exile was the interim, from which Jerusalem rose to take on leadership anew and supplant the people who had remained in the land(s).[9]

Accordingly, the Assyrian deportations of Israel are widely ignored in studies of early Judaism, New Testament, or Christian origins,[10] owing largely to a prevailing presumption that northern Israel was so thoroughly destroyed and scattered by the Assyrians that Judah was the sole remnant of Israel.[11] John Collins summarizes this consensus view as follows:

In biblical tradition, "Israel" is the union of tribes descended from the twelve sons of Jacob. For a period of some two hundred years it had a narrower connotation, referring to the northern kingdom of Israel as opposed to the southern kingdom of Judah. After the fall of the Northern Kingdom, however, the Judeans laid claim to the heritage of all Israel.[12]

---

[9] Ingrid Hjelm, "Changing Paradigms: Judaean and Samarian Histories in Light of Recent Research," in *Historie og Konstruktion: Festskrift til Niels Peter Lemche i anledning af 60 års fødselsdagen den 6. September 2005*, eds. Mogens Müller, Thomas L. Thompson, and Niels Peter Lemche (Copenhagen: Museum Tusculanum, 2005), 161–79 (161).

[10] E.g., J. Julius Scott, *Jewish Backgrounds of the New Testament* (Grand Rapids: Baker Books, 2000), 107: "The first [significant event in the formation of the Jewish world] was the destruction of the Jewish state by the Babylonians in 586 bc"; Stephen Westerholm, "Whence 'The Torah' of Second Temple Judaism," in *Law in Religious Communities in the Roman Period*, eds. Peter Richardson and Stephen Westerholm (Waterloo: Wilfrid Laurier University Press, 1991), 19–43 (31): "With the fall of Jerusalem to the Babylonians, the old 12-tribe association came to its effective end." Cf. James M. Scott, "Exile and Restoration," *DJG*, 251–58 (252); Brant Pitre, *Jesus, the Tribulation, and the End of the Exile: Restoration Eschatology and the Origin of the Atonement*, JSOTSup 37 (Grand Rapids: Baker Academic, 2005), 38, "[T]he significance of the ongoing nature of the Assyrian exile is repeatedly ignored by most scholars, including [N. T.] Wright and both the defenders and critics of his exilic hypothesis."

[11] E.g., William J. Dumbrell, "Malachi and the Ezra-Nehemiah Reforms," *RTR* 35.2 (1976): 42–52 (44): "[E]mpirical [Northern] Israel had long since vanished and was hardly reflected in the very small post-exilic temple state. But the prophetic vitality of the theological ideal is inextinguishable. The address in fact illustrates the bold transference to the rump-state by the post-exilic prophets of the prophetic ideal." Cf. Gerhard von Rad, "Israel, Judah, and Hebrews in the Old Testament," *TDNT* 3: 357–59, 357–58; Kuhn, "Ἰουδαῖος κτλ," *TDNT* 3: 359.

[12] John J. Collins, "The Construction of Israel in the Sectarian Rule Books," in *Judaism in Late Antiquity: Theory of Israel (Pt. 5 Vol. 1)*, eds. Alan J Avery-Peck, Jacob Neusner, and Bruce D. Chilton (Leiden: Brill, 2001), 25–42 (25). Cf. also Rad, "Israel," *TDNT* 3: 357–58; Philip R. Davies, *The Origins of Biblical Israel*, LHBOTS 485 (London: T&T Clark, 2007), 100; Bloch, "Israélite, juif, hébreu," 16. See also the discussions in Lester L. Grabbe, "Israel's Historical Reality after the Exile," in *The Crisis of Israelite Religion: Transformation of Religious Tradition in Exilic and Post-exilic Times*, eds. Bob Becking and Marjo Christina Annette Korpel (Leiden: Brill, 1999), 9–32 (esp. 12–14, 30–31).

According to this narrative, based mostly on a particular reading of anti-northern polemics in 2 Kings, the sacking of Samaria marks the point after which "Israel" – the ethnonym previously claimed by the northern kingdom over and against southern Judah – becomes redefined and narrowed to the Judahites, such that the terms "Israelite" and "Jew" became effectively synonymous in the post-exilic period.[13] Recent scholarship, however, has begun to reveal problems with this tidy narrative. As we have already noted, the Hasmoneans called their kingdom "Judah" rather than "Israel," and the extant epistolary and epigraphic evidence suggests that insider communication among Jews defaulted to "Jew" rather than "Israelite" even in that later period. Rather than Judah straightforwardly becoming Israel, Israelite status and the concept of Israel itself remained in flux and the subject of competition far longer than has been appreciated in most modern scholarship.

THE OTHER ISRAELITES: SAMARIANS/SAMARITANS

The most obvious problem with the widely assumed narrative is the continued presence of a competing Israel throughout the Second Temple period and beyond: the Samarians/Samaritans,[14] who claimed descent

---

[13] E.g., Moo, *Romans*, 561 n. 30: "Ἰουδαῖος (Heb. יהודי) originally denoted a person of the tribe of Judah, or of the southern kingdom generally. But after the Exile, when Judah was all that was left of historical Israel, the name was applied to any member of the Israelite nation." Cf. also Kuhn, "Ἰουδαῖος κτλ," *TDNT* 3: 359.

[14] A note on nomenclature is in order at this point, as "Samaritan" is an outsider term largely shunned by this group, who prefer to call themselves Israelites, Samarians, or שמרים ("guardians" [of the Torah]). See Knoppers, *Jews and Samaritans*, 15–16. Moreover, as pointed out by Jan Dušek, *Aramaic and Hebrew Inscriptions from Mt. Gerizim and Samaria between Antiochus III and Antiochus IV Epiphanes*, CHANE (Leiden: Brill, 2012), 71, "Samaritan" technically refers to a citizen of the third-century BCE Seleucid province of *Samaritēs* without regard to whether those citizens were Yahwists. There is also the danger of anachronism since the term "Samaritan" also refers to a modern people embracing the Samaritan Pentateuch and the special sanctity and centrality of Mt. Gerizim, while much of the period under investigation in this study pre-dates the full development of what might be called classical Samaritanism. In this respect, the term shares similar problems with "Christian" or "Jew." Nevertheless, I will avoid the terms "proto-Samaritan" or "pre-Samaritan" to circumvent "the erroneous assumption that Yhwh worship was a relatively late development or arrival in Samaria" (Knoppers, *Jews and Samaritans*, 17), and will use "Samaritan," in keeping with the typical use of the latter term in the New Testament and most modern secondary literature. As for the distinction sometimes made between "Samarians" and "Samaritans," Etienne Nodet rightly points out that "if . . . the Samaritans were [derived from] ancient Israelites, such a distinction [between Samarian and Samaritan] becomes useless" ("Israelites,

from the northern Israelite tribes of Joseph (Ephraim and Manasseh), worshiped YHWH, observed the Torah, and had their cultic center on Mt. Gerizim rather than in Jerusalem.[15] These claimants to Israelite status and heritage were decidedly not Jews–indeed, as a famous passage in the Gospel of John informs the reader, "*Ioudaioi* do not have common dealings with Samaritans" (John 4:9),[16] a statement that would be incoherent if Samaritans were considered Jews or a subset of the *Ioudaioi*.[17] Nor is the Gospel writer's explanation a late development or an idiosyncratic distinction. On the contrary, two inscriptions from Delos dating to the last two or three centuries BCE refer to "the Israelites in Delos who make offerings to

Samaritans, Temples, Jews," in *Samaria, Samarians, Samaritans: Studies on Bible, History and Linguistics*, ed. József Zsengellér, SJ 66 [Berlin: de Gruyter, 2011], 121–71 [123]). For further resources on the Samaritans in general, see Ingrid Hjelm, "Mt. Gerizim and Samaritans in Recent Research," in *Samaritans: Past and Present: Current Studies*, eds. Menachem Mor and Fredrick V. Reiterer, SJ 53 (Berlin: de Gruyter, 2010), 25–41; Alan D. Crown and Reinhard Pummer, *A Bibliography of the Samaritans: Revised, Expanded and Annotated*, ATLA Bibliography (Lanham: Scarecrow Press, 2005); József Zsengellér, ed., *Samaria, Samarians, Samaritans: Studies on Bible, History and Linguistics*, SJ 66 (Berlin: de Gruyter, 2011); Ingrid Hjelm, "What Do Samaritans and Jews Have in Common? Recent Trends in Samaritan Studies," *CurBR* 3.1 (2004): 9–59; Ingrid Hjelm, *The Samaritans and Early Judaism: A Literary Analysis*, JSOTSup 303 (Sheffield: Sheffield Academic, 2000); Alan D. Crown, ed., *The Samaritans* (Tübingen: Mohr Siebeck, 1989); Ferdinand Dexinger and Reinhard Pummer, eds., *Die Samaritaner*, WF 604 (Darmstadt: Wissenschäftliche Buchgesellschaft, 1992); Alan D. Crown, Reinhard Pummer, and Abraham Tal, eds., *A Companion to Samaritan Studies* (Tübingen: Mohr Siebeck, 1993).

[15] Böhm, "Wer gehörte," 183.

[16] Although a few early witnesses (most notably א* D it) lack this explanation, it is unlikely to have been a secondary addition, and in any case the rest of the passage presumes the distinction. David Daube, "Jesus and the Samaritan Woman: The Meaning of συγχράομαι," *JBL* 69.2 (1950): 137–47 and Richard J. Coggins, *Samaritans and Jews: The Origins of Samaritanism Reconsidered*, WUNT 111 (Atlanta: John Knox, 1975), 139 render συγχράομαι "use together," meaning Jews and Samaritans do not share common vessels.

[17] See Morton Smith, "The Gentiles in Judaism 125 BCE–CE 66," in *Cambridge History of Judaism, III: The Early Roman Period*, eds. William Horbury, W. D. Davies, and John Sturdy (Cambridge: Cambridge University Press, 1999), 192–249 (246). For more analysis of Samaritan terminology and topography in the New Testament, see Martina Böhm, *Samarien und die Samaritai bei Lukas: eine Studie zum religionshistorischen und traditionsgeschichtlichen Hintergrund der lukanischen Samarientexte und zu deren topographischer Verhaftung*, WUNT 111 (Tübingen: Mohr Siebeck, 1999); Jürgen Zangenberg, *Samareia: Antike Quellen zur Geschichte und Kultur der Samaritaner in deutscher Übersetzung* (Tübingen: Francke, 1994); Jürgen Zangenberg, *Frühes Christentum in Samarien: topographische und traditionsgeschichtliche Studien zu den Samarientexten im Johannesevangelium*, TANZ (Tübingen: Francke, 1998); Andreas Lindemann, "Samaria und die Samaritaner im Neuen Testament," *WD* 22 (1993): 51–76.

holy Argarizim," further demonstrating that the Samaritans (who also had their own separate synagogue at Delos) identified as "Israelites" rather than *Ioudaioi* well before the Common Era.[18] Indeed, the presence of the Samaritans helps explain why "Jew" was the default label for Jews in this period and why the Hasmoneans called their kingdom "Judah": another group already laid claim to the name Israel. Lester Grabbe explains:

> [I]n the external references to peoples and kingdoms of Palestine, there is no evidence that "Israel" ever refers to Judah or the Judahites; rather "Judah," "Jews," and similar designations are always used, at least until the Christian era. The only group referred to as "Israelite" in Greco-Roman sources in the pre-Christian period is the Samaritan community associated with Mt Gerizim.[19]

Unfortunately, thanks to a widespread scholarly acceptance of Jewish polemics dismissing Samaritan claims to be heirs of the northern Israelites, the scholarly habit of treating "Judaism" as synonymous with "Yahwism" and thereby assuming that "Israelite" is equivalent to "Jew" has obscured a more complex picture in which the Jews are not the only Yahwistic group claiming a share in the heritage of ancient Israel. Thus until recently most scholars have regarded the Samaritans not as a distinct people but rather as a derivative of Judaism having arisen sometime between the fifth and first centuries BCE.[20] Frank Moore Cross, for

---

[18] See Philippe Bruneau, "Les Israélites de Délos et la juiverie délienne," *BCH* 106.1 (1982): 465–504; A. Thomas Kraabel, "New Evidence of the Samaritan Diaspora Has Been Found on Delos," *BA* 47.1 (1984): 44–46; L. Michael White, "The Delos Synagogue Revisited: Recent Fieldwork in the Graeco-Roman Diaspora," *HTR* 80.2 (1987): 133–60. Boyarin, "The IOUDAIOI in John," 231, rightly recognizes that "such Israelites would obviously not have been Ioudaioi." Similarly, see also Grabbe, "Israel's Historical Reality," 12–13. *Pace* Goodblatt, "Varieties of Identity," 18 n. 14, who attempts to salvage the insider/outsider model despite these data by asserting, "The Samaritans qualify as insiders," ignoring that *Ioudaioi* would be inappropriate nomenclature for those claiming northern descent.

[19] Grabbe, "Israel's Historical Reality," 13. Similarly, Zeitlin, "Hebrew, Jew and Israel," 369: "We never find the term Israel denoting the people of Judaea, in the entire tannaitic literature of the time of the Second Commonwealth. The term Israel was used only in contrast to the priests and Levites."

[20] This view goes at least as far back as James Alan Montgomery, *The Samaritans, the Earliest Jewish Sect: Their History, Theology and Literature* (Eugene: Wipf & Stock, 2006 [reprint; original 1907]). Other important studies treating the Samaritans as a Jewish sect include Cohen, *Maccabees to the Mishnah*; Lester L. Grabbe, *The Roman Period* (Minneapolis: Fortress, 1992); Uriel Rappaport, "Reflections on the Origins of the Samaritans," in *Studies in Geography and History in Honour of Yehoshua Ben-Arieh*, eds. I. Bartal and E. Reiner (Jerusalem: Magnes, 1999), 10–19; Böhm, *Samarien und die Samaritai*, 63–64, 84; Alan D. Crown, "Another Look at Samaritan Origins," in *New Samaritan Studies of the Société d'Études Samaritaines III–IV: Essays in Honour of G. D.*

example, concludes, "Samaritanism in the form that we find it in the Roman Age and later is not a survival of old Israelite religion, pure or syncretistic, but rather is essentially a sectarian form of Judaism."[21]

The question of Samaritan origins has been reopened in recent years, however, as the supposition that the northern Israelites vanished and were replaced by foreign transplants who eventually came to worship YHWH has been recognized as Jewish polemic rather than historical reality.[22] Instead, it is now widely acknowledged that both the biblical record and the material evidence indicate that although many Israelites were deported (particularly from the northern Transjordan and Galilee) and others seem to have fled south to Judah,[23] many northerners survived the

---

Sixdenier, eds. Alan D. Crown and Lucy Davey, Studies in Judaica 5 (Sydney: Mandelbaum, 1995), 133–55; Alan D. Crown, "Redating the Schism between the Judaeans and the Samaritans," *JQR* 82.1–2 (1991): 17–50.

[21] Frank Moore Cross, "Samaria and Jerusalem in the Era of Restoration," in *From Epic to Canon: History and Literature in Ancient Israel* (Baltimore: Johns Hopkins University Press, 2000), 173–202 (175).

[22] For recent discussions on the debates concerning the problem of Samaritan origins, see Reinhard Pummer, "Samaritanism: A Jewish Sect or an Independent Form of Yahwism?," in *Samaritans: Past and Present: Current Studies*, eds. Menachem Mor and Fredrick V. Reiterer, SJ 53 (Berlin: de Gruyter, 2010), 1–24; Stefan Schorch, "The Construction of Samari(t)an Identity from the Inside and from the Outside," in *Between Cooperation and Hostility: Multiple Identities in Ancient Judaism and the Interaction with Foreign Powers*, eds. Rainer Albertz and Jakob Wöhrle, JAJSup 11 (Göttingen: Vandenhoeck & Ruprecht, 2013), 135–49; Hjelm, *Samaritans and Early Judaism*, 13–75. Cf. also Bob Becking, "Do the Earliest Samaritan Inscriptions Already Indicate a Parting of the Ways?," in *Judah and the Judaeans in the Fourth Century BCE*, eds. Oded Lipschits, Gary N. Knoppers, and Rainer Albertz (Winona Lake: Eisenbrauns, 2007), 213–22; Ferdinand Dexinger, "Limits of Tolerance in Judaism: The Samaritan Example," in *Judaism, Jewish and Christian Self-Definition*, ed. E. P. Sanders, 2 (London: SCM, 1981), 88–114; Ferdinand Dexinger, "Der Ursprung der Samaritaner im Spiegel der frühen Quellen," in *Die Samaritaner*, eds. Ferdinand Dexinger and Reinhard Pummer, WF 604 (Darmstadt: Wissenschäftliche Buchgesellschaft, 1992), 67–140; Coggins, *Samaritans and Jews*.

[23] See Israel Finkelstein, *The Forgotten Kingdom: The Archaeology and History of Northern Israel*, Ancient Near East Monographs (Atlanta: Society of Biblical Literature, 2013), 153–55; Israel Finkelstein and Neil Asher Silberman, "Temple and Dynasty: Hezekiah, the Remaking of Judah and the Rise of the Pan-Israelite Ideology," *JSOT* 30.3 (2006): 259–85; Davies, *In Search of "Ancient Israel,"* 69–70; Barmash, "Nexus." Nadav Na'aman, "When and How Did Jerusalem Become a Great City? The Rise of Jerusalem as Judah's Premier City in the Eighth-Seventh Centuries BCE," *BASOR* 347 (2007): 21–56, however, cautions that the number of northern refugees fleeing to Judah was likely not as large as often assumed. Moreover, Sennacherib's later invasion of Judah would surely have had a significant impact on those who did flee south. On Sennacherib's invasions of Judah, see Kiefer, *Exil und Diaspora*, 64–67, though he does not mention the impact this process would have had on any northern refugees. The settlement of Israelite groups in Judah in the wake of the northern kingdom's destruction may have brought

Assyrian onslaught and remained in the land, particularly in the central regions of Ephraim and Manasseh.[24] And although the kingdom of Israel ceased to exist and the Assyrians did import other peoples into the region, there is no indication of a dramatic shift in material culture in the Samarian hill country, suggesting that "of those who resided in the district of Samerina and Magiddu ... the clear majority were [still] Israelites."[25] Perhaps as a result, the region around Samaria seems to have recovered more quickly from the Assyrian campaigns than Judah did from either the Assyrian or Babylonian invasions. Indeed, whereas much of Judah experienced massive destruction and depopulation during the Babylonian conquests of 598 and 587/86 BCE,[26] the northern region

much of the northern biblical material with it, engendering a pan-Israelite sentiment in Judah (Finkelstein, *Forgotten Kingdom*, 155).

[24] See the measured discussion of both the "maximalist" and "minimalist" perspectives in Gary N. Knoppers, "In Search of Post-Exilic Israel: Samaria after the Fall of the Northern Kingdom," in *In Search of Pre-Exilic Israel*, ed. John Day, JSOTSup 406 (London: T&T Clark, 2004), 150–80 (153–60). On the population and demographics of Palestine in these periods, see Magen Broshi and Israel Finkelstein, "The Population of Palestine in Iron Age II," *BASOR* (1992): 47–60; Israel Finkelstein, "The Archaeology of the Days of Manasseh," in *Scripture and Other Artifacts: Essays on the Bible and Archaeology in Honor of Philip J. King*, eds. Michael D. Coogan, J. Cheryl Exum, and Lawrence E. Stager (Louisville: Westminster John Knox, 1994), 169–87; Adam Zertal, "The Province of Samaria (Assyrian Samerina) in the Late Iron Age (Iron Age III)," in *Judah and the Judeans in the Neo-Babylonian Period*, eds. Oded Lipschits and Joseph Blenkinsopp (Winona Lake: Eisenbrauns, 2003), 377–412; Adam Zertal, "The Pahwah of Samaria (Northern Israel) during the Persian Period. Types of Settlement, Economy, History and New Discoveries," *Transeu* 3 (1990): 9–30. On the Assyrian deportations and resettlements of the land, see Nadav Na'aman, "Population Changes in Palestine Following Assyrian Deportations," *TA* 20.1 (1993): 104–24; Nadav Na'aman and Ran Zadok, "Assyrian Deportations to the Province of Samerina in the Light of Two Cuneiform Tablets from Tel Hadid," *TA* 27.2 (2000): 159–88; Bustenay Oded, "II Kings 17: Between History and Polemic," *Jewish History* 2.2 (1987): 37–50; Bustenay Oded, "Observations on Methods of Assyrian Rule in Transjordania after the Palestinian Campaign of Tiglath-Pileser III," *JNES* 29.3 (1970): 177–86; Bustenay Oded, *Mass Deportations and Deportees in the Neo-Assyrian Empire* (Wiesbaden: Reichert, 1979); K. Lawson Younger, "The Deportations of the Israelites," *JBL* 117.2 (1998): 201–27; Gershon Galil, "Israelite Exiles in Media: A New Look at ND 2443+," *VT* 59.1 (2009): 71–79.

[25] Knoppers, *Jews and Samaritans*, 42.

[26] See J. Maxwell Miller and John H. Hayes, *A History of Ancient Israel and Judah* (Philadelphia: Westminster, 1986), 460–97. That said, the land of Judah was not entirely emptied, either. On the so-called "myth of the empty land" and its ideological underpinnings (serving a purpose similar to the myth of the northern land filled with foreigners), see Robert P. Carroll, "The Myth of the Empty Land," in *Ideological Criticism of Biblical Texts*, eds. David Jobling and Tina Pippin, Semeia 59 (Atlanta: Scholars Press, 1992), 79–93; Hans M. Barstad, *The Myth of the Empty Land: A Study in*

seems not to have undergone significant destruction in this period.[27] Instead, Samaria continued to grow, becoming "a force to be reckoned with in the southern Levant ... larger, more populous, and wealthier than its neighbor to the immediate south."[28]

It is therefore most likely that the post-exilic Samarians/Samaritans were primarily comprised of the remnant of the Israelites and other indigenous peoples remaining in the land after the Assyrian conquests of the eighth century BCE, though the peoples imported by the Assyrians were almost certainly incorporated among the natives over time as well.[29]

the *History and Archaeology of Judah during the "Exilic" Period*, SO 28 (Oslo: Scandinavian University Press, 1996); Joseph Blenkinsopp, "The Bible, Archaeology and Politics; Or the Empty Land Revisited," *JSOT* 27.2 (2002): 169–87; Hans M. Barstad, "After the 'Myth of the Empty Land': Major Challenges in the Study of Neo-Babylonian Judah," in *Judah and the Judeans in the Neo-Babylonian Period*, eds. Oded Lipschits and Joseph Blenkinsopp (Winona Lake: Eisenbrauns, 2003), 3–20; Bustenay Oded, "Where Is the 'Myth of the Empty Land' to Be Found? History Versus Myth," in *Judah and the Judeans in the Neo-Babylonian Period*, eds. Oded Lipschits and Joseph Blenkinsopp (Winona Lake: Eisenbrauns, 2003), 55–74; Jill A. Middlemas, "Going beyond the Myth of the Empty Land: A Reassessment," in *Exile and Restoration Revisited: Essays on the Babylonian and Persian Periods in Memory of Peter R. Ackroyd*, eds. Gary N. Knoppers, Lester L. Grabbe, and Dierdre N. Fulton, LSTS 73 (London: T&T Clark, 2009), 174–94. See also Eric M. Meyers, "Exile and Restoration in Light of Recent Archaeology and Demographic Studies," in *Exile and Restoration Revisited: Essays on the Babylonian and Persian Period in Memory of Peter R. Ackroyd*, eds. Gary N. Knoppers, Lester L. Grabbe, and Dierdre N. Fulton, LSTS 73 (London: T&T Clark, 2009), 166–73.

[27] Knoppers, *Jews and Samaritans*, 107–08; Gary N. Knoppers, "Revisiting the Samarian Question in the Persian Period," in *Judah and the Judeans in the Persian Period*, eds. Oded Lipschits and Manfred Oeming (Winona Lake: Eisenbrauns, 2006), 265–90.

[28] Knoppers, *Jews and Samaritans*, 2. See also Ingrid Hjelm, *Jerusalem's Rise to Sovereignty: Zion and Gerizim in Competition*, JSOTSup 404 (London: T&T Clark, 2004), 165–66; Ingrid Hjelm, "Samaritans: History and Tradition in Relationship to Jews, Christians and Muslims: Problems in Writing a Monograph," in *Samaria, Samarians, Samaritans: Studies on Bible, History and Linguistics*, ed. József Zsengellér, SJ 66 (Berlin: de Gruyter, 2011), 173–84 (178–81).

[29] Yitzhak Magen, "The Dating of the First Phase of the Samaritan Temple on Mount Gerizim in Light of the Archaeological Evidence," in *Judah and the Judeans in the Fourth Century BCE*, eds. Oded Lipschits, Gary N. Knoppers, and Rainer Albertz (Winona Lake: Eisenbrauns, 2007), 157–211 (187): "During the Persian period, there were two provinces in these areas: Samaria and Judea. The former was composed of the Israelite remnant and the peoples brought by the Assyrians. The majority of Benjamin and Judah, on the other hand, were sent into exile in Babylonia." Although it is likely that the Assyrians initially settled outsiders in the land in separate enclaves to serve as Assyrian outposts on the frontier, as suggested by Mario Liverani, "The Ideology of the Assyrian Empire," in *Power and Propaganda: A Symposium on Ancient Empires*, ed. Mogens Trolle Larsen (Copenhagen: Akademisk, 1979), 297–317; Mario Liverani, "The Growth of the Assyrian Empire in the Habur/Middle Euphrates Area: A New Paradigm," *SAAB*

Moreover, epigraphic and iconographic evidence and the prevalence of names featuring the theophoric Yah/Yahu attest to a continuous Yahwism in the region of Samaria/Shechem from the ninth through the fifth century BCE,[30] and archaeological evidence from Mt. Gerizim has indicated that a Yahwistic cult center existed in that place at least as early as the mid-fifth century BCE.[31] Thus although the Samaritan cultus was surely influenced by that of Judah to the south, Samaritan Yahwism was not merely a derivative of Judaism but was itself a continuation of an earlier Israelite legacy and surely exercised its own influence on later Jewish tradition and cultus.[32] Upon the return of Jews from Babylon, there appear to have been a few pan-Israelite attempts to unite this northern remnant with the Jewish returnees,[33] leading to a common Torah, very similar cultic practices, and perhaps to the inclusion of many northern traditions in the Jewish Bible.[34] But such union ultimately proved unsustainable, especially after the destruction of the temple on Mt. Gerizim by John Hyrcanus I, and the distinction between Jews and Samaritans persisted and indeed deepened with the advent of the

---

2.2 (1988): 81–98; and Zertal, "The Province of Samaria," 404, I find it implausible that these newcomers were not eventually absorbed by the natives of the land.

[30] See the discussion in Hjelm, *Jerusalem's Rise*, 169–71.

[31] On the archaeology of Mt. Gerizim, see Joseph Naveh and Yitzhak Magen, "Aramaic and Hebrew Inscriptions of the Second Century BCE at Mount Gerizim," *Atiqot* 32 (1997): 9–17; Yitzhak Magen, "Mt. Gerizim – A Temple City," *Qad* 33.2 (2000): 74–118; Yitzhak Magen, Haggai Misgav, and Levana Tsfania, eds., *The Aramaic, Hebrew and Samaritan Inscriptions*, Judea and Samaria Publications (Jerusalem: Israel Antiquities Authority, 2004); Magen, "The Dating of the First Phase"; Menachem Mor, "The Israelites, Samaritans, Temples, Jews and the Samaritan Governors – Again," in *Samaria, Samarians, Samaritans: Studies on Bible, History and Linguistics*, ed. József Zsengellér, SJ 66 (Berlin: de Gruyter, 2011), 89–108.

[32] Hjelm, "Samaritans: History and Tradition," 181: "We simply have to look for other scenarios and most likely for models of cooperation between Samaritans and Jews." On Nehemiah's difficulties with respect to the ties and divisions between the *Yehudim* and others claiming Israelite heritage, see Gary N. Knoppers, "Nehemiah and Sanballat: The Enemy Without or Within?," in *Judah and the Judeans in the Fourth Century BCE*, eds. Oded Lipschits, Gary N. Knoppers, and Rainer Albertz (Winona Lake: Eisenbrauns, 2007), 305–31.

[33] The movement led by Ezra may have been one example; see Chapter 5.

[34] See Stefan Schorch, "The Samaritan Version of Deuteronomy and the Origin of Deuteronomy," in *Samaria, Samarians, Samaritans: Studies on Bible, History and Linguistics*, ed. József Zsengellér, SJ 66 (Berlin: de Gruyter, 2011), 23–37; Etienne Nodet, *A Search for the Origins of Judaism: From Joshua to the Mishnah*, trans. E. Growley, JSOTSup 348 (Sheffield: Sheffield Academic, 1997); Nodet, "Building of the Samaritan Temple."

Common Era. The Samaritans were thus closely related to but distinct from the Jews, with both groups claiming to be Israelites.

Nevertheless, although their descent (largely) from ancient Israel is now widely acknowledged, the fact that the Samaritans claimed to be Israelites and shared common traditions with their neighbors to the south, not to mention Jews of the diaspora, has led many scholars still to treat the Samaritans as a derivative of "Judaism," assuming that the Samaritans had been Jews before breaking away from the Jewish mainstream. The debate therefore still tends to center on when that final schism, after which one can speak of "Samaritans" and "Jews" as distinct groups, took place. Stefan Schorch, for example, argues:

> Up to a certain point, the pre-Samaritans referred to and were regarded as part of a social, religious and ethnic framework that was common to Second Temple Judaism in general. From that point onward, however, the Samaritans became an independent group, and not just the population of Samaria but Samaritans proper, insofar as they defined themselves apart from Judaism in general within the boundaries of their own framework.[35]

Thus Schorch argues that although the Samarian population derived largely from preexilic Israel, this population should be regarded as Jews prior to a particular moment of schism, after which the two distinct communities formed. But this view assumes that any Yahwist or Torah-based community in the post-exilic period is properly called "Jewish," a presumption that, as Hjelm points out, relies on a "misleading application of the term 'Jewish'" and prima facie favors Jewish perspectives and Jewish primacy.[36]

This problem is even more evident in Alan David Crown's warning that we should be "wary of using the terms 'Samaritans' and 'Jews'; rather we should speak of Samaritans and Judaeans, inasmuch as others saw the Samaritans as a variety of Jews, hence a Jewish sect."[37] On this basis, Crown argues that before the third century CE, "especially [in] the first century, the Samaritans were Jews."[38] But there is in fact no evidence

---

[35] Schorch, "Construction of Samari(t)an Identity," 136.

[36] Hjelm, "Samaritans and Jews," 25 (cf. also 46). Ironically, Hjelm herself could be said to have fallen prey to similarly imprecise language in her analysis of Josephus' perspective in Hjelm, *Samaritans and Early Judaism*, 226–30.

[37] Crown, "Redating the Schism," 19.

[38] Crown, "Redating the Schism," 50. Similarly, Ferdinand Dexinger, "Samaritan Origins and the Qumran Texts," *Annals of the New York Academy of Sciences* 722.1 (1994): 231–49 (237): "The structure of the Samaritan Pentateuch is, generally speaking, represented in Qumran textually as well as graphically. This clearly identifies the Samaritans simply as a Jewish group of the pluriform Judaism of that age. As long as this unity was felt and was ideologically possible we should call this specific Jewish group Proto-Samaritans, and only after the overstressing of separating doctrines such as the

that anyone in this period – whether the Samaritans or others – saw the Samaritans as a variety of Jews. Indeed, Crown assumes what he aims to prove, as the evidence he cites does not call the Samaritans "Jews" but rather refers to them as "Israelites." Yet again, the assumed equation of "Israelites" and "Jews" lays at the root of the problem, forcing Crown to locate the difference between Samaritans and Jews in an alleged distinction between Judaeans and Jews, understanding the latter as a religious term roughly equivalent to "Yahwist." But again, this latter distinction is anachronistic, as there could be no ancient distinction between "Judaean" and "Jew" since both words translate the same term, and such divisions between religion and ethnicity would have been incoherent in a context in which the two were so closely intertwined.

Crown's imprecision is by no means unusual. Feldman, for example, claims, "The Samaritans themselves, according to their *Sefer Ha-Yamim*, insist that they are the direct descendants of the Joseph tribes, Ephraim and Menasseh, and that they are, in fact, the true Jews."[39] But neither the *Sefer Ha-Yamim* nor any other Samaritan literature claims that the Samaritans are "the true Jews" but rather that they are true *Israelites*. Feldman simply presumes that the latter claim is equivalent to the former, as he does when addressing evidence from the Jewish side in the same article, even making the remarkable statement that, "the fact that, according to the latter [Judah Ha-Nasi], a Samaritan is *like* a non-Jew indicates that he is really a Jew."[40] But Feldman has once again glossed over the language of the passage, presuming the equivalence of the terms; the passage in question (t. Ter. 4:12, 14) does not say "Jew" (*Yehudi*) or "non-Jew" but rather "like a [member of] Israel" (כישראל) and "like a foreigner" (כנכרי). Moreover, Feldman's logic does not follow, as the debate in this passage centers on the premise that Samaritans are *neither* Israelites nor foreigners but an ambiguous other requiring special consideration.

The imprecision displayed by Feldman here is typical throughout scholarly literature, with repeated proofs of the Samaritans' "Jewish" status consistently

---

exclusivity of the Garizim should we call them Samaritans." Cf. also Rappaport, "Reflections," 16–17.

[39] Louis H. Feldman, "Josephus' Attitude toward the Samaritans: A Study in Ambivalence," in *Jewish Sects, Religious Movements, and Political Parties: Proceedings of the Third Annual Symposium of the Philip M. and Ethel Klutznick Chair in Jewish Civilization Held on Sunday–Monday, October 14–15, 1990*, ed. Menachem Mor, SJC (Omaha: Creighton University Press, 1992), 23–45 (31).

[40] Feldman, "Josephus' Attitude toward the Samaritans," 32.

based on glossing "Israelite" as "Jew."[41] Several commentators, for example, incorrectly assume that the Jews in Elephantine had approached the Samaritan authorities as though the latter were Jews, whereas they nowhere refer to those of Samaria by this term.[42] And while Morton Smith is correct that Ben Sira had no name for the Shechemites, whom he hated (Sir 50:26), it is a mistake to conclude from this that Ben Sira considers them Jews, as he instead declares that they are "not even a people" (50:25).[43] The closest thing to an exception to this rule is found in 4 Bar. 8, which says Samaria was built by those who had intermarried with the Babylonians (cf. 2 Kgs 17:24, 30) and were therefore barred from Jerusalem. But even this passage does not suggest the Samaritans are Jews but rather the result of the intermarriage of "the people" and the Babylonians. Put simply, Second Temple period sources consistently categorize the Samaritans as non-Jews, albeit non-Jews with a claim to Israelite heritage.

SAMARITANS IN JOSEPHUS

The Josephan corpus provides important evidence to reinforce this conclusion. Josephus acknowledges that Samaritans claimed to be Israelites – a claim he deems illegitimate – but emphasizes that they were not, nor claimed to be, Jews. Instead, relying on the polemical narrative of 2 Kings 17, he explains that the Samaritans were "deported into Samaria ... out of the country called Chothous, which is a country of Persia" and that they learned to worship the almighty God from the priests of the Israelites sent back into

---

[41] E.g., Lawrence H. Schiffman, "The Samaritans in Tannaitic Halakhah," *JQR* 75.4 (1985): 323–50 (323); Ophir and Rosen-Zvi, *Goy*, 186.

[42] See the discussion in Hjelm, "Samaritans and Jews," 25. On the appeal of those at Elephantine to the Jerusalem and Samaritan authorities, see Bezalel Porten and Ada Yardeni, eds., *Textbook of Aramaic Documents from Ancient Egypt*, 4 vols. (Winona Lake: Eisenbrauns, 1986), 4.5–4.10; Bezalel Porten, *Archives from Elephantine* (Berkeley: University of California Press, 1968), 278–98; Becking, "Yehudite Identity."

[43] Morton Smith, *Palestinian Parties and Politics That Shaped the Old Testament* (New York: Columbia University Press, 1971), 189. *Contra* Schorch, "Construction of Samari(t)an Identity," 137, the Greek version of the passage does not say the Shechemites are "a subgroup of the Samarian people," though it does substitute the Samarians for the Idumaeans, nor does the change imply that the Shechemites were once regarded as part of the Jewish people, as the assertion that they are "not even a people" strongly indicates otherwise. Smith further suggests that 2 Maccabees 5:22–23 and 6:1–2 indicate that "Antiochus Epiphanes evidently considered the Shechemites and the Jews to be one religious group, and this opinion was shared by Jason of Cyrene," but each passage clearly distinguishes between the groups centered at Jerusalem and Gerizim (with separate governors set up for each), which suggests otherwise.

the land by the Assyrians to stop a plague (*Ant.* 9.288). As such, Josephus is at pains to emphasize that they are by no means *Ioudaioi*:

And when they see the *Ioudaioi* well off, they call themselves their relatives, as though descended from Joseph, and have family ties with them by that means. But whenever they see them falling into bad circumstances, they say they owe nothing to them, and that they [the *Ioudaioi*] have no right to their kindness or kindred relations. Rather, they declare that they are sojourners from other countries. But of these we shall have a more seasonable opportunity to discourse hereafter. (*Ant.* 9.288–91)

That opportunity comes in Book 11, when the Samaritans petition Alexander the Great, requesting the same benefits Alexander has conferred upon the *Ioudaioi*:[44]

The Samaritans, whose capital city was then at Shechem (a city located at Mount Gerizim, and inhabited by apostates of the nation of the *Ioudaioi*), seeing that Alexander had greatly honored the *Ioudaioi* in this way, determined to profess themselves *Ioudaioi* [αὐτοὺς Ἰουδαίους ὁμολογεῖν]; for such is the nature of the Samaritans, as we have already elsewhere stated, that when the *Ioudaioi* are in adversity they deny they are related to them (and then they confess the truth) but when they perceive that some good fortune has befallen them, they rush to have communion with them, saying that they are related to them and derive their genealogy from the posterity of Joseph, Ephraim, and Manasseh.
(*Ant.* 11.340–41)

On first glance, this passage appears to identify the Samaritans as (apostate) *Ioudaioi* and suggest that Samaritans "claimed to be Jews," which would obviously be problematic, not least because it would contradict what Josephus has already stated.[45] Noting the oddity here, Goodblatt explains, "this seems like a polemical exaggeration. Presumably the Samaritans simply noted that both they and the Judeans were of Israelite origin."[46] This can not only be presumed, it is precisely what happens just a few lines later, where the Samaritans deny that they are *Ioudaioi* but claim common descent with the *Ioudaioi*, calling themselves *Hebraioi* instead:

---

[44] For more on Alexander and the Samaritans, see Reinhard Pummer, "Alexander und die Samaritaner nach Josephus und nach samaritanischen Quellen," in *Die Samaritaner und die Bibel: Historische und literarische Wechselwirkungen zwischen biblischen und samaritanischen Traditionen = The Samaritans and the Bible: Historical and Literary Interactions Between Biblical and Samaritan Traditions*, eds. Jörg Frey, Ursula Schattner-Rieser, and Konrad Schmid, SJ 70 (Berlin: de Gruyter, 2012), 157–80.

[45] Cf. Murray, "Jews, Hebrews," 189; Harvey, *True Israel*, 110.

[46] Goodblatt, "Varieties of Identity," 18 n. 14.

And when they petitioned for him to remit the tribute of the seventh year to them, because they did not now sow then, he inquired who they were to make such a petition. When they said that they were Hebrews but were called Sidonians, living at Shechem, he asked them again whether they were *Ioudaioi*. *When they said they were not Ioudaioi*, he said, "It was to the *Ioudaioi* that I granted that privilege. Nevertheless, when I return, and have been thoroughly instructed by you of this matter, I will do what seems right." And in this manner, he took leave of the Shechemites [my emphasis]. (*Ant.* 11.343–44, 346–47)

Though aiming to obtain the same privileges as the Jews by appealing to their shared history, language, and culture, Josephus' Samaritans therefore declare that although they are "Hebrews," they are not Jews. Remarkably, in a signal example of just how sticky the presumed equation of Jews, Israelites, and Hebrews has been in modern scholarship, Feldman recognizes that these Samaritans "denied that they were Jews" but ignores this fact in his next sentence, which begins, "A hint that the Samaritans are Jews but rebellious in their views ..."[47]

In any case, these passages from Book 11 also allude to Josephus' earlier (9.288–91) explanation of Samaritan (Cuthean) origins, where Josephus has made it clear that the Samaritans are not *Ioudaioi*, nor are they descended from the *Ioudaioi*,[48] and rely upon the reader's familiarity with that (polemical) history to assess the Samaritans' claims. Indeed, the Samaritans here do exactly what Josephus earlier explained was their practice, aiming to share the Jews' benefits whenever possible, though even then they do not claim to be *Ioudaioi* but rather "Hebrews" descended from Joseph. Of course, those assuming Israelites and *Ioudaioi* are synonymous naturally miss the distinction between the Samaritans claiming descent from Joseph and identifying as *Ioudaioi*, who were not putatively descended from Joseph but Judah.[49] As for the statement that

---

[47] Feldman, "Josephus' Attitude toward the Samaritans," 36.

[48] Josephus' account of a debate between *Ioudaioi* and Samaritans in Alexandria in *Ant.* 13.74–79 further reinforces the distinctions made here.

[49] E.g., Spilsbury, *Image of the Jew*, 39 n. 126: "It should be noted, however, that the distinction [between 'Hebrews' and 'Jews'] is one which Josephus himself categorically rejects (through the narrative agency of Alexander). He also nowhere else betrays any knowledge of such a distinction." *Pace* Spilsbury, Alexander *upholds* rather than rejects the Samaritans' distinction between "Hebrews" and "Jews"; what he rejects is their request to receive the benefits of the *Ioudaioi* despite not being *Ioudaioi*. In addition, as the remainder of this section demonstrates, Josephus maintains the distinction between Samaritan *Hebraioi* and *Ioudaioi* (who may or may not be *Hebraioi*) throughout his literary corpus. Spilsbury is correct in protesting a strong distinction between *Ioudaioi* and *Hebraioi* as though they were antagonistic terms, but he is mistaken in treating them as fundamentally synonymous.

Shechem is inhabited by "apostates from the nation of the *Ioudaioi*" (*Ant.* 11.340), the answer is provided at the end of the same passage, where Josephus clarifies his first comment:

Now when Alexander was dead, the government was parted among his successors; but the temple upon Mount Gerizim remained; and if anyone were accused by those of Jerusalem of having eaten things common, or of having broken the Sabbath, or of any other crime of the like nature, he fled away to the Shechemites and said that he was accused unjustly. (*Ant.* 11.346–47)

Josephus clarifies that the "apostates from the nation of the *Ioudaioi*" flee to the Shechemites, who are distinguished from the *Ioudaioi* fleeing to them and ultimately living among them.[50] Josephus thus does *not* say (as some have asserted) that Samaritans themselves are "apostate *Ioudaioi*" or that they abandoned "true Judaism" for another type of Judaism.[51] Indeed, when recounting a debate before Ptolemy between representatives of the respective communities (*Ant.* 13.74–79), he refers to "Alexandrian *Ioudaioi*" and "Samaritans," not "Samarian *Ioudaioi*." Josephus does regard Samaritans as apostates or impostors (or some combination of both) but of *Israel* not of the *Ioudaioi*,[52] and he takes great pains to clarify that neither the *Ioudaioi* nor the Samaritans themselves identify the Samaritans as *Ioudaioi*.[53]

One final example further illustrates this point. In his account of John Hyrcanus' conquest of the Samaritans and Idumaeans, Josephus says that

---

[50] Cf. Ophir and Rosen-Zvi, *Goy*, 190.

[51] E.g., Feldman, "Josephus' Attitude toward the Samaritans," 34–39 (esp. 36), despite his recognition that Josephus generally portrays the Samaritans as distinct from the Jews. Feldman's confusion seems mostly to owe to his assumption that those who worshiped YHWH were obviously Jews (34–35). See also the similar lack of precision in, for example, Dexinger, "Samaritan Origins," 237; Rappaport, "Reflections," 16–17; Reinhard Pummer, *The Samaritans* (Grand Rapids: Eerdmans, 2016), 125.

[52] This does not, however, support the argument of Murray, "Jews, Hebrews," 199, that "Hebrews" should be understood in opposition to "Jews," with the former group understood as "those who were hostile to Jerusalem and the temple might appropriately be called 'Hebrews', though a qualifier such as 'dissenting' is probably needed." Murray suggests that the Samaritans, the Dead Sea Scroll sect, and the community behind the New Testament book of Hebrews could all fit in this category but provides no real evidence for such an application of the term. Instead, an understanding of the term as essentially linguistic, which he refers to as a "disadvantage" (199) for his theory, explains the data fully without having to ignore the many times in which the term is applied to Jerusalem-supporting *Ioudaioi*.

[53] "They were viewed by him as faithful Hebrews and yet as non-Judean. Thus, they were not viewed as a sect of the Jews in the same sense that Pharisees were, but were placed by Josephus under the more inclusive label Hebrews" (Ernest Boyd Whaley, "Samaria and the Samaritans in Josephus's 'Antiquities' 1–11" [PhD diss., Emory University, 1989], i).

Hyrcanus "permitted the Idumaeans to stay in their country if they would be circumcised and consent to use the laws of the *Ioudaioi*. ... And they have been *Ioudaioi* ever since" (*Ant.* 13.257–58). But of the Samaritans he makes no such statement; unlike the Idumaeans, they never became *Ioudaioi* but rather remained "the nation of the Cutheans" (13.255). The Samaritans themselves obviously differed with Josephus' overall explanation of their origins, regarding themselves as legitimate descendants of Israel. But his anti-Samaritan biases notwithstanding, Josephus does appear to be correct in this respect: Samaritans neither regarded themselves nor were they regarded by others as *Ioudaioi*, though they could properly be called Hebrews and claimed to be Israelites, illustrating the subtle differences between these three terms in this period.[54]

HEBREW: NEITHER JEW NOR ISRAELITE

That Samaritans could also be called "Hebrews" (*Hebraioi*) without being Jews warrants further discussion.[55] According to Kuhn,

---

[54] For more on Josephus' attitudes toward and portrayals of the Samaritans, see Magnar Kartveit, "Josephus on the Samaritans – His Tendenz and Purpose," in *Samaria, Samarians, Samaritans: Studies on Bible, History and Linguistics*, ed. József Zsengellér, SJ 66 (Berlin: de Gruyter, 2011), 109–20; Reinhard Pummer, *The Samaritans in Flavius Josephus*, TSAJ 129 (Tübingen: Mohr Siebeck, 2009); Ingrid Hjelm, "The Samaritans in Josephus' Jewish 'History,'" in *Proceedings of the Fifth International Congress of the Société d'Études Samaritaines: Helsinki, August 1–4, 2000: Studies in Memory of Ferdinand Dexinger*, eds. Haseeb Shehadeh, Habib Tawa, and Reinhard Pummer (Paris: Geuthner, 2006), 27–39; Hjelm, *Samaritans and Early Judaism*, 183–238; Timothy Thornton, "Anti-Samaritan Exegesis Reflected in Josephus' Retelling of Deuteronomy, Joshua, and Judges," *JTS* 47.1 (1996): 125–30; Feldman, "Josephus' Attitude toward the Samaritans"; Richard J. Coggins, "The Samaritans in Josephus," in *Josephus, Judaism and Christianity*, eds. Louis H. Feldman and Gohei Hata (Leiden: Brill, 1987), 257–73; Rita Egger, *Josephus Flavius und die Samaritaner: eine terminologische Untersuchung zur Identitätsklärung der Samaritäner*, NTOA 4 (Göttingen: Presses Universitaires Fribourg, 1986); Whaley, "Samaria and the Samaritans."

[55] There is significant debate about the origins of the term "Hebrew," with some identifying the term as deriving from the cognate *'apirû* or *ḫabiru* appearing in the fourteenth-century BCE Amarna Letters. From that connection, "Hebrew" is supposed to have been a term denoting a specific legal-social status (an auxiliary or servant class of some sort) rather than an ethnic group. Miller, "Ethnicity," 299, summarizes Gerhard von Rad's influential conclusion to this effect in the *TDNT*: "According to Von Rad, the term 'Hebrew' is completely different from 'Israel' and 'Judah' because *Habiru* (עברי) was originally a designation for a legal-social status; the peoples the term encompassed were not an ethnic unity (*ethnische Einheit*) like the Mesopotamians and Egyptians. Von Rad maintained that 'Hebrew' eventually took on a broader meaning as a more-or-less derogatory term for Israel, and that late biblical usage at least prepares for the use of

Ἑβραῖος becomes the more dignified, select and polite term as compared with the common Ἰουδαῖος, which may often be used in a derogatory or even contemptuous sense. Ἑβραῖος is thus used to denote Jewish nationality or religion in passages which wish to avoid the depreciatory element that clings so easily to Ἰουδαῖος. It is supposed to carry with it the very opposite nuance of high esteem and respect.[56]

Kuhn credits this supposed nuance of respect to the archaic and biblical flavor of "Hebrew" as opposed to its (allegedly) so easily derogatory counterpart.[57] Kuhn does, however, acknowledge that Hebrew often has a linguistic sense,[58] and Gutbrod's companion essay on the term in pagan or Hellenistic Jewish contexts concludes,

We may thus conclude that Ἑβραῖος is either used historically or to denote Palestinian nationality or language, especially when Jews are called Ἑβραῖοι in contradistinction from other Jews.[59]

Remarkably, Gutbrod seems to have forgotten this conclusion in his entry on this term in the New Testament, where he says, "we cannot be primarily guided by a linguistic understanding of Ἑβραῖος," citing Cadbury's claim, "The word (Ἑβραῖος) is not commonly used elsewhere

/

'Hebrew' as a designation for ethnicity (*eine ethnische Zugehörigkeit*)." Cf. Rad, "Israel," 3:357–59. This has remained a popular view, though it has recently begun to lose support for a variety of reasons. Daniel E. Fleming, for example, has suggested the early *'apirû* were broad range herders with limited ties to specific towns or cities (*The Legacy of Israel in Judah's Bible: History, Politics, and the Reinscribing of Tradition* [Cambridge: Cambridge University Press, 2012], 258–71), while Beattie and Davies, "Hebrew," 82, offer the intriguing suggestion that the term arose as "an abbreviated name for someone from 'Beyond the River' or 'Trans-Euphrates', a 'Transite' – in Aramaic עבראי." In much of their article, Beattie and Davies largely anticipate the argument of this chapter in advocating a linguistic meaning for "Hebrew" (meaning Aramaic) in the Second Temple Period, but these conclusions were arrived at independently and using a different angle of investigation. In any case, as noted by Harvey, *True Israel*, 5, the origins of the term and its ties to social or legal status are not relevant to the late Second Temple Period and will therefore not be addressed in depth here.

56   Kuhn, "Ἰουδαῖος κτλ," *TDNT* 3: 367–68.

57   Kuhn, "Ἰουδαῖος κτλ," *TDNT* 3: 367–69. As with his distinction between *Ioudaios* and Israel, this view of *Hebraios* corresponds with the contemporary German view of "Hebraism" (i.e. biblical Israel) as a living precursor of Christianity while "Judaism" was but a post-exilic husk of this previously living religion. See Pasto, "Invention of Post-Exilic Judaism," 49–51; James S. Pasto, "Who Owns the Jewish Past? Judaism, Judaisms, and the Writing of Jewish History" (PhD diss., Cornell University, 1999), 53–57; and the beginning of Chapter 3.

58   Kuhn, "Ἰουδαῖος κτλ," *TDNT* 3: 365–67. Although suggesting they may have been attempting to avoid the allegedly contemptuous connotation of *Ioudaios*, Kuhn even concedes that the inscriptions that use *Hebraios* more likely refer to Semitic speakers or those otherwise closely connected with "Palestinian traits" (369–70).

59   Walter Gutbrod, "Ἰουδαῖος κτλ," *TDNT* 3: 369–75, 375.

in a linguistic sense."[60] Similarly, although listing a second meaning as a "Hebrew-/Aramaic-speaking Israelite in contrast to a Gk.-speaking Israelite," the primary meaning listed in BDAG is simply an "ethnic name for an Israelite,"[61] which others (particularly interpreters of Paul's claim to be a "Hebrew") have then interpreted as representing a "pure-blood Jew."[62] A thorough review of the evidence before the second century CE, however, shows that the primary meaning of "Hebrew" is very plainly linguistic throughout the period. Indeed, almost without exception, the term either refers to ancient, biblical Hebrews (who could be assumed to have spoken Hebrew or Aramaic) or to modern speakers of a Semitic tongue.

Hebraios in Josephus

As discussed in the first chapter, Josephus regularly uses the term *Hebraios* when speaking of the preexilic period. In explaining its origin, Josephus follows Genesis in tying it to the primordial patriarch Heber, from whom Abraham was descended, explaining, "Sala was the son of Arphaxad, and his son was Heber, from whom they originally called the *Ioudaioi* Hebrews (*Hebraioi*)" (*Ant.* 1.146). Josephus therefore clearly identifies the *Hebraioi* with the *Ioudaioi*, although like with "Israel" the equation only moves in one direction: *Ioudaioi* are descended from the *Hebraioi*, but Josephus does not say all *Hebraioi* are *Ioudaioi*.[63]

---

[60] Gutbrod, "Ἰουδαῖος κτλ," *TDNT* 3: 390, citing Henry J. Cadbury, "The Hellenists," in *The Beginnings of Christianity (Part I)*, eds. F. J. Foakes Jackson and Kirsopp Lake, 5 (London: MacMillan, 1933), 59–73 (65). Largely on the basis of that assertion (which this chapter will demonstrate is empirically false), Cadbury argued that the "Hellenists" of Acts 6:1 were in fact gentiles, a novel view that is almost certainly wrong. See Charles F. D. Moule, "Once More, Who Were the Hellenists?," *ExpTim* 70.4 (1959): 100–2 and the discussion of Acts 6:1 below.

[61] Frederick W. Danker et al., *A Greek–English Lexicon on the New Testament and Other Early Christian Literature*, 3rd rev. ed. (Chicago: University of Chicago Press, 2000), 269–70.

[62] C. K. Barrett, *The Second Epistle to the Corinthians*, Black's New Testament Commentaries (London: Black, 1973), 293, citing Bauer and the *TWNT*, asserts, "[Hebrew] is used in two senses. The primary one (clearly used in Phil. iii. 5), is that of pure-blooded Jew; only secondarily (as at Acts vi. 1), do considerations such as language (Hebrew-speaking over against Greek-speaking) arise." See the discussion of Paul's use of the term below.

[63] Spilsbury, *Image of the Jew*, 37, "Here the concern is clearly to show who the Ἰουδαῖοι originally were, namely, the Hebrews," misses the distinction here. As with "Israel," it is

Unlike "Israelite," Josephus does not restrict *Hebraios* to the ancient biblical people but does apply the term (albeit rarely) to his contemporaries and others from the post-exilic period. These occasions reveal a clear pattern: of the forty-four cases where Josephus uses the term not in reference to the ancient biblical people,[64] thirty-eight have a clear linguistic sense (e.g. "called by the Hebrews,"[65] "in the Hebrew tongue,"[66] "a measure of the Hebrews"),[67] while the other six uses occur in an ambiguous context where the clear nuance is more difficult to pin down.[68] As we have already seen, one of these six involves the Samaritans identifying themselves as Hebrews but not *Ioudaioi* (*Ant.* 11:343–44). The other five ambiguous uses of *Hebraios* in the Josephan corpus appear to refer to *Ioudaioi*, with three of the five specifically referring to *Ioudaioi* living in Judaea.[69] So, in Josephus, when its meaning can be clearly discerned, *Hebraios* has three possible referents: (1) ancient (biblical) ancestors of the *Ioudaioi*, (2) Samaritans, (3) *Ioudaioi* from the "Hebrew nation" or living in Judaea/Syria. The commonality between all these groups is language; all three groups are all Semitic (Hebrew/Aramaic) speakers or readers as opposed to Greek speakers/readers.[70] Based on these data, it appears that, at least in Josephus, *Hebraios* functions as a national linguistic term analogous to *Hellēnē*, referencing the native tongue of the

---

      not merely that the name for the people has changed; the people who can be called by each term are not identical.

[64] Not including a variant reading of *J.W.* 1.3 in which Josephus refers to himself as "born a Hebrew" (γένει Ἑβραῖος). Since Josephus was himself a Semitic speaker, this variant is not especially relevant for the thesis of this chapter. The verb *hebraizō* (*J.W.* 6.96), meaning to speak Hebrew, and the verb *Hebraides* (*Ant.* 2.226), referring to Hebrew women in the time of the Exodus, each appear once.

[65] *Ant.* 1.80. See also *Ant.* 1.117, 128, 204, 258; 2.3, 311; 3.32, 138, 144, 201, 252, 282; 4.84; 8.61; 11.148, 286.

[66] *Ant.* 1.33, Other examples: *Ant.* 1.34, 36, 81, 333; 2.278; 3.291; 5.121, 201, 323, 336 ("Hebrew dialect"); 6.22, 302; 7.58 ("Hebrew language"); 9.290; 18.228. Cf. also 10.218 ("translate the Hebrew books") and *Ag. Ap.* 1.167 ("translated from Hebrew").

[67] *Ant.* 3.142, 234; cf. also 3.195.

[68] *Ant.* 3.247, 317; 4.308; 11.343; *J.W.* 4.159; 5.443.

[69] *Ant.* 4.308; *J.W.* 4.159, 5.443. The other two ambiguous uses are *Ant.* 3.247, 3.317.

[70] Tomson, "Names," 128, arrives at a similar conclusion. On the languages spoken in Judaea during this period, see Philip S. Alexander, "How Did the Rabbis Learn Hebrew?," in *Hebrew Study from Ezra to Ben-Yehuda*, ed. William Horbury (Edinburgh: T&T Clark, 1999), 71–89; Angel Sáenz-Badillos, *A History of the Hebrew Language* (Cambridge: Cambridge University Press, 1993); Joseph A. Fitzmyer, "The Languages of Palestine in the First Century AD," *CBQ* 32 (1970): 501–31; Chaim Rabin, "Hebrew and Aramaic in the First Century," in *The Jewish People in the First Century(2)*, eds. Menahem Stern and Shmuel Safrai, CRINT 2 (Amsterdam: Assen, 1976), 1007–39.

"Hebrew nation" and those associated with it, and when used of contemporary people(s), the term refers to those *Ioudaioi* or Samaritans still living in Palestine and thus Semitic speakers or readers.

Hebraios in Other Early Jewish Sources

The data outside Josephus also support this conclusion. Philo, for example, uses "Hebrew" fifty-nine times, of which thirty-six refer to biblical people group (nearly all in the Exodus story),[71] twenty-two have a linguistic referent (e.g. "in the native language of the Hebrews"),[72] and one provides an etymological explanation of the word "Hebrew" itself.[73] The only people Philo calls "Hebrews" after the Conquest are those who came from Jerusalem to translate the Torah into Greek for Ptolemy Philadelphus (*Mos.* 2.32), which as David Runia concludes, "probably indicates that they were speakers of Hebrew."[74] Philo also twice uses *Hebraikos*, each time referring to the Hebrew language.[75] Notably, Philo – who was a Greek speaker apparently lacking facility with Hebrew or Aramaic – never refers to himself as a *Hebraios*.[76] To summarize, in Philo, the word *Hebraios* refers exclusively to Hebrew (or Aramaic) speakers or readers.[77]

Likewise, the three occurrences of the word in 2 Maccabees (7:31; 11:13; 15:37) are in contexts differentiating Hebrews from Greek-speaking foreigners, while the eight occasions of the term (and cognates) in 4 Maccabees likewise refer either directly to the language (*Hebraidi*, 12:7; 16:15) or to faithful *Ioudaioi* being persecuted for continuing to embrace "the Hebrew way of life" (τὴν Ἑβραίων πολιτείαν, 17:9; cf. 4:11; 5:2; 8:2; 9:6; 9:18), as opposed to the Hellenism being forced upon them by Antiochus. Again, the connection with the language (and its ties to the ancient tradition) is central

---

[71] *Migr.* 20; *Heir* 128; *Fug.* 168; *Mut.* 117; *Abr.* 251; *Ios.* 42, 50, 104, 203; *Mos.* 1.15, 105, 143, 144, 145, 146, 147, 179, 180, 216, 218, 243, 252, 263, 276, 278, 284, 288, 289, 295, 305, 311; 2.32; *Virt.* 34, 35; *QE* 1, 2.2.

[72] *Plant.* 169; *Sobr.* 45; *Conf.* 68, 129, 130; *Migr.* 13; *Congr.* 37, 40, 42; *Mut.* 71, *Somn.* 1.58; 2.250; *Abr.* 17, 27, 28, 57; *Ios.* 28; *Decal.* 159; *Spec.* 2.41, 86, 145; *Virt.* 34.

[73] *Migr.* 20.

[74] David T. Runia, "Philonic Nomenclature," *SPhiloA* 6 (1994): 1–27 (15). Cf. Harvey, *True Israel*, 123.

[75] *Mos.* 1.218, 285.

[76] Harvey, *True Israel*, 124; cf. also Runia, "Philonic Nomenclature," 15. For an overview of the debate over whether Philo knew Hebrew, see Valentin Nikiprowetzky, *Le commentaire de l'Écriture chez Philon d'Alexandrie: Son caractère et sa portée; Observations philologiques*, ALGHJ 11 (Leiden: Brill, 1977), 50–96.

[77] Cf. Harvey, *True Israel*, 124.

to the context in which the term is being used. The single use of "Hebrew" in Ben Sira (1:20) likewise refers to the language.

The term similarly refers to the language or the people who speak or read the language (typically in the patriarchal period) in other early Jewish literature as well. A Hebrew fragment of T. Naphtali refers to "seventy languages" being taught to the "seventy families," while "the holy language, the Hebrew language" is passed down from Shem and Eber to Abraham (8:6).[78] The Testament of Joseph uses the term four times, all in reference to the patriarch, his land, or his God.[79] The Testament of Solomon uses the term twice, each of "the language of the Hebrews" (T. Sol. 6:8; 14:7). The Letter of Aristeas talks of *Ioudaioi* translating the Torah from the "Hebraic" ('Εβραϊκός) characters and language into Greek (3, 30, 38) – again cognates of *Hebraios* specifically refer to language.[80]

The book of Jubilees uses the term five times, including the core statement, "The angel that speaks to Moses, said to him: 'I taught Abraham the Hebrew tongue, which from the beginning of creation all lands spoke'" (Jub. 12:26), after which Abraham spends six months studying books in Hebrew.[81] Again the meaning of the word throughout Jubilees centers on the language – perhaps even suggesting that the patriarchs were *Hebraioi* because they spoke Hebrew, the primeval language, the language of the Torah, as suggested by Harvey: "If the idea that Abram and Joseph spoke 'Hebrew' depends on the passages where they are named "Hebrews" then the identification of name and language was well established before the writing of Jubilees."[82]

Harvey therefore rightly rejects Mary Gray's suggestion that "writers in the last two centuries BC may have adopted the name "Hebrews" for the Jews and their language because of an archaizing tendency and the

---

[78] Robert Henry Charles, *The Testaments of the Twelve Patriarchs* (London: Black, 1908), Appendix 2, 243; cf. Harvey, *True Israel*, 117.

[79] T. Joseph, 12:2, 3; 13:1, 3.

[80] Sandra Gambetti has recently argued that the Aristeas refers not only to translation into Greek but also to transcription from (Palaeo-) Hebrew characters used by Samaritans to a form of Aramaic block characters used in Judaea as a necessary step before the translation itself. See "When Syrian Politics Arrived in Egypt: 2nd Century BCE Egyptian Yahwism and the Vorlage of the LXX," in *Alexandria: Hub of the Hellenistic World*, eds. Jörg Frey, Benjamin Schliesser, and Tobias Nicklas, WUNT (Tübingen: Mohr Siebeck, 2020), 1–43 (34–43).

[81] Cf. Harvey, *True Israel*, 116.

[82] Harvey, *True Israel*, 116.

desire to be called by the title of the first patriarch."[83] If anything, *Hebraioi* is likely the more ancient term, associated with the language of the people, while *Ioudaioi* is the relative latecomer on the scene, used after the Babylonian Exile to refer to those from the kingdom of Judah. This connection of the language with the Torah and the ancestral traditions of the *Ioudaioi* suggests that those who continued to speak Hebrew – especially in the diaspora – did so because they were especially traditional or conservative towards their heritage.[84]

If *Hebraios* refers to Hebrew (or Aramaic) speakers or readers, one would expect to find the term only rarely used in contexts exclusively involving Hebrew/Aramaic speakers, since it would not function to differentiate parties. This is precisely what we find among the Dead Sea Scrolls, where the term is completely absent. Given the extent of the corpus, the complete lack of the term in the scrolls is significant and, as Harvey observes, "cannot be dismissed as accidental loss."[85] One letter from someone with the name Soumaios found at Nahal Hever, however, mentions that it is written *Hellēnisti* (in Greek) because "a [des]ire has not be[en] found to w[ri]te in Hebrew" (*Hebraisti*),[86] with cognates of "Hebrew" again referring to the language. The same pattern emerges in rabbinic literature also, where the term has a solely linguistic sense.[87]

Hebraios in the New Testament

The linguistic sense of the term persists in the New Testament as well. The one time Acts uses *Hebraios* (6:1), it occurs in parallel with *Hellēnistēs*, distinguishing between the Greek-speaking members of the church and those speaking a Semitic tongue.[88] Acts 9:29 intimates that this distinction between "Hebrews" and "Hellenists" existed not only among the followers

---

[83] Harvey, *True Israel*, 116–17. Cf. Mary F. Gray, "The Habiru-Hebrew Problem in the Light of the Source Material Available at Present," *HUCA* 29 (1958): 135–97.

[84] Cf. p. 81; Harvey, *True Israel*, 146, 270–71.

[85] Harvey, *True Israel*, 120.

[86] Baruch Lifshitz, "Papyrus grecs du désert du Juda," *Aeg* 42 (1962): 240–56; cf. Joseph A. Fitzmyer, *A Wandering Aramean: Collected Aramaic Essays*, SBLMS 25 (Chico: Scholars Press, 1979), 35–36; Harvey, *True Israel*, 121.

[87] As observed by Tomson, "Names," 128.

[88] Joseph A. Fitzmyer, "New Testament Kyrios and Maranatha and Their Aramaic Background," in *To Advance the Gospel: New Testament Studies*, ed. Joseph A. Fitzmyer (Grand Rapids: Eerdmans, 1998), 218–35 (123); Moule, "Who Were the Hellenists"; Beattie and Davies, "Hebrew," 73.

of Jesus in the region, but also among the other Jews. Acts also uses the adjective *Hebrais* three times (21:40; 22:2; 26:14), each referencing some-one speaking "in the Hebrew [Aramaic?] dialect." Similarly, *Hebraisti* appears in five times in the Gospel of John (5:2; 19:13, 17, 20; 20:16) and Revelation twice (9:11; 16:16), each with reference to the language. This accords with the conclusion of Derek Beatty and Philip Davies:

> [*Hebraios*] is clearly not the same as Israelite. . . . Hebrew in the New Testament mostly designates a language . . . it designates a member of a *linguistic* community or population. A Hebrew, we maintain, is a speaker of the language that is called Hebrew in the New Testament, namely Aramaic.[89]

Finally, Paul uses *Hebraios* on two occasions (2 Cor 11:22; Phil 3:5), each time as a way of establishing his authority relative to competing teachers and apostles. What Paul means in these cases has long been a matter of dispute,[90] but on the basis of the data from the other literature under consideration, the most natural interpretation of Paul's statements is that he is claiming facility in Aramaic/Hebrew. In this context, Paul's claim to be a "Hebrew of Hebrews" (Ἑβραῖος ἐξ Ἑβραίων) is especially intriguing, as Paul claims not only to be a Semitic speaker, but a *native* speaker born to parents who spoke a Semitic language.[91]

Because of confusion on this point, many interpreters have misinter-preted "Hebrew of Hebrews" as a superlative, as though the phrase indicated "that there was no non-Jewish blood in his veins,"[92] that he was somehow connected to Palestine,[93] or that he was in some other way among the "elite of his race,"[94] "a Jew's Jew."[95] On the contrary, in both

---

[89] Beattie and Davies, "Hebrew," 73.

[90] See, e.g., the discussions in J. B. Lightfoot, *Saint Paul's Epistle to the Philippians* (London: Macmillan, 1903), 147; Gutbrod, "Ἰουδαῖος κτλ," *TDNT* 3: 390; Barrett, *Second Corinthians*, 293; Gerald F. Hawthorne and Ralph P. Martin, *Philippians*, WBC 43 (Waco: Word, 2004), 185.

[91] Beattie and Davies, "Hebrew," 73: "There is no reason to suppose [Hebrew] has a different meaning in Paul's words than in any other New Testament passage. He is therefore designating himself to the Philippians as an Aramaic speaker from an Aramaic-speaking family." For other examples of the ἐκ + genitive construction as referring to birth or descent in Paul, cf. Rom 1:3; 9:6; Gal 4:4. See also Edgar J. Goodspeed, *Problems of New Testament Translation* (Chicago: University of Chicago Press, 1945), 175–76; Hawthorne and Martin, *Philippians*, 185.

[92] Hawthorne and Martin, *Philippians*, 185.

[93] E.g., Willem Cornelis van Unnik, *Tarsus or Jerusalem? The City of Paul's Youth*, trans. G. Ogg (London: Epworth, 1962), 46–47.

[94] Hawthorne and Martin, *Philippians*, 185.

[95] Andrew S. Jacobs, "A Jew's Jew: Paul and the Early Christian Problem of Jewish Origins," *JR* 86.2 (2006): 258–86 (263). Jacobs argues that although the ἐξ

passages, Paul indicates his ancestry and birth heritage through other terms. But by claiming to be a Hebrew, Paul claims that he can read the Torah in its original language (and speak in Jesus' native tongue) just like his opponents, giving him no less authority as an interpreter of Torah than they possessed.

Some previous arguments against understanding Paul's *Hebraios* as a claim about the language have pointed to epigraphic data to argue that *Hebraios* must be a synonym with *Ioudaios* without reference to language.[96] Harvey, for example, argues that since "other synagogue inscriptions have the names of geographical regions, family groups, and sectarian or political groups," those inscriptions (like at Corinth and Rome) that witness a "synagogue of the Hebrews" are unlikely to refer to language.[97] On the contrary, inasmuch as the inscriptions themselves do not clearly define the term, it is methodologically backwards to use them to judge the meaning of the term in literary texts that provide more context from which to construe meaning than do the inscriptions. That is, these inscriptions should be read in light of the combined witness of the other, less ambiguous textual evidence of the period, which suggests that the term "Hebrew" was consistently used of Semitic speakers.[98]

Secondly, even without recourse to literary evidence, given that the other synagogues used whatever label most distinguished them from other *Ioudaioi*, it is hard to imagine that the inscriptions referencing "Hebrews"

---

construction more typically refers to descent, "the genitive might also indicate a superlative, on analogy with the Hebrew superlative (viz., "song of songs," "Lord of Lords") reproduced in the Septuagint (ᾆσμα ᾀσμάτων, κύριος τῶν κυρίων)" (n. 25). Cf. also Morna D. Hooker, *From Adam to Christ: Essays on Paul* (Eugene: Wipf & Stock, 2008), 2, 164; Dunn, "Who Did Paul Think He Was?," 186. But Jacobs' examples of the superlative genitive lack the telltale ἐκ/ἐξ and are thus not applicable.

[96] Moule, "Who Were the Hellenists," 100, notes that another common objection to a linguistic sense is that Paul was clearly a Greek speaker, observing that this objection oddly ignores the probability that Paul was claiming multilingual facility. See, for example, Marcel Simon, *St. Stephen and the Hellenists in the Primitive Church* (London: Longmans, Green, 1958), 10.

[97] Harvey, *True Israel*, 131, following Barrett, *Second Corinthians*, 293. Harvey here refers to a Corinthian inscription where ΑΓΩΓΗΒΡ can be reconstructed as συναγωγή Ἑβραίων ("synagogue of the Hebrews") and a comparable inscription from a very early synagogue in Rome (dated as early as the time of Pompey). The Corinthian inscription is currently dated to somewhere between 170 CE and the early post-Constantinian period. For discussion of this inscription, see Richard E. Oster, "Use, Misuse and Neglect of Archaeological Evidence in Some Modern Works on 1Corinthians (1Cor 7,1–5; 8,10; 11,2–16; 12,14–26)," ZNW 83.1–2 (1992): 52–73 (55–58). Cf. also Benjamin Dean Meritt, ed., *Greek Inscriptions, 1896–1927* (Cambridge: Harvard University Press, 1931), 79. For a discussion of the Roman evidence, see Harry Joshua Leon, *The Jews of Ancient Rome* (Peabody: Hendrickson, 1995).

[98] As properly done in this case by Gutbrod, "Ἰουδαῖος κτλ," *TDNT* 3: 274.

were not also referencing the distinctive aspect of the synagogue, and it is difficult to imagine what that would be if not language – especially given the literary evidence of how the word tended to have precisely that function in the literature of this period.[99] It therefore appears most probable that these "synagogues of the Hebrews" were indeed distinguished by the fact that they remained synagogues of Semitic speakers/readers, with the scriptures read in Hebrew rather than Greek. These inscriptions are not evidence against the possibility that Paul claims facility in Hebrew; on the contrary, they are evidence that some conservative *Ioudaioi* continued to use Hebrew in the diaspora, a fact that should surprise no one.[100]

CONCLUSIONS: HEBREWS AND NON-JEWISH ISRAELITES

On the basis of the textual evidence that for Greek speakers of the Second Temple period, it can thus be concluded that *Hebraios*, while largely coextensive with *Ioudaios* or Israelite, is not synonymous with either term but rather serves as a descriptor for those associated with the traditional tongue of the "Hebrew nation."[101] When not referring to biblical figures,

---

[99] On the Roman "Synagogue of the Hebrews" as opposed to a "Synagogue of the Vernaculars" (perhaps speaking Latin), see Peter Richardson, "Augustan-era Synagogues in Rome," in *Judaism and Christianity in First-Century Rome*, eds. Karl Donfried and Peter Richardson (Grand Rapids: 1998), 17–29 (20).

[100] This of course does not prove that Paul actually had facility in Hebrew (or Aramaic), only that he *claimed* to have such facility. I see little reason to question the veracity of his claim, but absent other evidence, it remains just that – a claim. For an argument that Paul's language betrays a "trend of thought [that] is sometimes Aramaic," see Willem Cornelis van Unnik, "Aramaisms in Paul," in *Sparsa Collecta: The Collected Essays of W. C. van Unnik: Part One: Evangelia, Paulina, Acta*, eds. William Foxwell Albright and C. S. Mann, NovTSup 29 (Leiden: Brill, 1973), 129–43 (142).

[101] Beattie and Davies, "Hebrew," 81. It is worth noting that some slippage would be expected with such a term in much the same way a modern term like "Hispanic," which more properly refers to a Spanish speaker, is sometimes used to refer to someone who does not in fact speak Spanish but descends from Spanish speakers. A second-generation individual in a new country, for example, may not be much of a Spanish speaker but would still often be identified as "Hispanic." Similarly, "Hebrew" appears to serve the purpose of distinguishing Semitic speakers but almost certainly came to be used in some cases to mark those *associated with* Semitic speakers, even if the figures being labeled did not themselves speak a Semitic tongue. Eventually, as noted by Beattie and Davies, "the adjective Hebrew became, in European languages, a surrogate for Jewish," likely because Jewish communities typically retained their Semitic-speaking and reading roots (Beattie and Davies, "Hebrew," 73–74). But this was not until after our period, "Nevertheless, Hebrew did not become synonymous with Jew until later and then, as we have argued, through the agency of Greek speakers, predominantly if not exclusively Christian" (Beattie and Davies, "Hebrew," 81).

this term was most typically used of those *Ioudaioi* who remained Semitic speakers, typically those living in Palestine.[102] Not all Jews were Hebrews, as most *Ioudaioi* in the diaspora were *Hellēnes* rather than *Hebraioi*. Likewise, not all Hebrews were Jews, as the Samaritans in the land are an example of the former but not the latter.

Since it required effort to retain one's ancestral language where Greek was the lingua franca, Hebrews in the diaspora would typically have been cultural conservatives,[103] that is, especially pious and less assimilated *Ioudaioi* or Samaritans,[104] holding more tightly to all aspects of their ancestral identity than Hellenic *Ioudaioi* and marking themselves by continued adherence to the "holy tongue" (cf. Jubilees 12:26) of their ancestors.[105] Some indications of the importance pious *Yehudim* placed on retaining faculty in Hebrew (or, as it is called in this case "*Yehudit*") can be seen as early as Ezra-Nehemiah (esp. Neh 13:24),[106] and the fact that the bulk of the Dead Sea Scrolls and the Mishnah were written in Hebrew further supports the connection between continued use of the sacred tongue and cultural/religious traditionalists. Moving beyond the period under discussion, this linguistic meaning seems to have persisted among Rabbinic writings, though later gentile Christians appear to have begun using the term as a synonym for Jew, even when the person in question (such as Philo or Stephen) had not been a Semitic speaker.[107] This does not, however, invalidate the linguistic sense the term had

---

[102] *Pace* Harvey, *True Israel*, 270.

[103] Harvey is therefore correct in his observation that "'Hebrew' was conventionally associated with traditionalism or conservatism" (Harvey, *True Israel*, 146), although he does not seem to recognize the mechanism for this association in the word's consistent meaning of Hebrew/Aramaic speaker.

[104] John Barclay is of course correct that the level of acculturation with respect to Jews knowing Greek does not necessarily match levels of assimilation to Greek culture (*Jews in the Mediterranean Diaspora*, 92–102, esp. 96). But when the question is turned the other way around – whether or not Hellenistic Jews retain and continue to use their own distinctive language – there can be little doubt that continued use of the "holy tongue" certainly suggests a higher level of identification with the group and less assimilation to the wider Greek culture.

[105] William M. Schniedewind, "Aramaic, the Death of Written Hebrew, and Language Shift in the Persian Period," in *Margins of Writing, Origins of Cultures (2)*, ed. Seth L. Sanders (Chicago: University of Chicago Press, 2006), 137–47 (144).

[106] Interestingly, although *Hebraios* is a linguistic term in the Second Temple period, it is not a linguistic term in the Hebrew Bible, instead serving as an ethnonym or in the laws pertaining to slaves. What we now call the Hebrew language, the Hebrew Bible calls *Yehudit* (2 Kgs 18:26, 28; Isa 36:11, 13; Neh 13:24; 2 Chr 32:18). See Beattie and Davies, "Hebrew," 75–77.

[107] E.g., Eusebius, *Hist. Eccl.* 2.4.2.

previously carried; indeed, it is more likely that Eusebius and his contemporaries imagined the Jews of the past to be like the Hebrew-speaking Jews of their own day.[108]

Moreover, the evidence is overwhelming that despite sharing a common heritage, the same national deity, and a cultus closely related to that of the Jews, neither the Jews nor the Samaritans themselves regarded the Samaritans as Jews (that is, *Ioudaioi* or *Yehudim*). Rather, as Grabbe puts it, "They were not 'Jews' but 'Israelites,' while the Jews are nowhere called 'Israelites' at this time according to presently available sources."[109] And by the same token, although Jews also obviously regarded themselves as Israelites, they were distinct from the Israelites associated with Mt. Gerizim, who – at least in an international context – seem to have been more closely identified with the term "Israel" than were the *Ioudaioi*.

Treating the Samaritans as a sect of Judaism has therefore always been a non sequitur, akin to treating Canada as part of the United States or Presbyterianism as part of the Church of England. Glossing Yahwism with Judaism and equating Jews and Israelites erases the diversity of the period by uncritically adopting Jewish polemics against other Yahwists as legitimate.[110] To put it bluntly, equating "Israelite" with "Jew" is a theological position rather than an accurate historical or sociological reconstruction of the situation in the Second Temple period. But these terms are not interchangeable in the Second Temple Period precisely because not all Yahwists or Israelites were Jews. Blindness to this fact has led to great difficulties categorizing the Samaritans and understanding

---

[108] Beattie and Davies, "Hebrew," 82.

[109] Grabbe, "Israel's Historical Reality," 12. Inasmuch as the Roman province of Judea included Samaria and Idoumea (Josephus, *Ant.* 17.317), it is uncertain whether the Romans would have always carefully distinguished between Samaritans and Jews, as Samaritans living in the province of Judea could presumably have been regarded as *Iudaei* by the Romans at least in the provincial sense. This possibility is strengthened by the fact that no extant Roman law prior to 404 CE refers directly to the Samaritans. Thus the official texts that refer to taxes being levied from the *Iudaei/Ioudaioi* in Judaea would presumably include all the various people groups in the province of Judaea, including Samaritans. Nevertheless, at least one contemporary Roman shows awareness of the difference between the two, as Tacitus explains that the local Roman authorities in the first century CE used the enmity between the Jews and Samaritans for their own ends (Tacitus, *Ann.* 12.54). Origen also claims that although the Jews were permitted to circumcise, it was illegal for the Samaritans to do so (*Contra Celsum* 2.13; cf. *Comm. in Matt.* 17.29–30). See Shahar, "Imperial Religious Unification Policy," 114–15.

[110] Cf. Böhm, "Wer gehörte," 181–83. See Chapter 5 for more details on such polemics.

how they fit in the world of early Judaism. The solution is surprisingly simple: rather than presuming that all Yahwists who call themselves Israelites in the post-exilic period fall under the umbrella of "Judaism" or, worse, pushing such anachronistic language into the preexilic period, both Judaism and Samaritanism should be regarded as sects of a more broadly imagined "Israelism."[111]

---

[111] Cf. James Richard Linville, *Israel in the Book of Kings: The Past as a Project of Social Identity*, JSOTSup 272 (Sheffield: Sheffield Academic, 1998), 28 n. 28. Similarly, Benjamin Tsedaka concludes, "Both traditions grew up from the common ground of the ancient Israelite religion. It is not the 'Jewish religion' nor the 'Samaritan religion' posed before us, but a 'Jewish tradition' and a 'Samaritan tradition,' both daughters of the Israelite religion" ("Samaritanism-Judaism or Another Religion?," in *Jewish Sects, Religious Movements, and Political Parties: Proceedings of the Third Annual Symposium of the Philip M. and Ethel Klutznick Chair in Jewish Civilization Held on Sunday–Monday, October 14–15, 1990*, ed. Menachem Mor, SJC [Omaha: Creighton University Press, 1990], 47–51 [51]). See also Böhm, "Wer gehörte"; Jean-Daniel Macchi, *Les Samaritains: Histoire d'une légende, Israël et la province de Samarie*, 30 (Geneva: Labor et Fides, 1994), 43; Jean-Daniel Macchi, *Israël et ses tribus selon Genèse 49*, OBO 171 (Freiburg: Universitätsverlag, 1999), 241; Gary N. Knoppers, "What Has Mt. Zion to Do with Mt. Gerizim?," *SR* 34 (2005): 307–36; Gary N. Knoppers, "Mt. Gerizim and Mt. Zion: A Study in the Early History of the Samaritans and Jews," *SR* 34.3–4 (2005): 309–37; Gary N. Knoppers, "Cutheans or Children of Jacob? The Issue of Samaritan Origins in 2 Kings 17," in *Reflection and Refraction: Studies in Biblical Historiography in Honour of A. Graeme Auld*, eds. Robert Rezetko, Timothy Henry Lim, and W Brian Aucker, VTSup 113 (Leiden: Brill, 2007), 223–40; Anders Runesson, *The Origins of the Synagogue: A Socio-Historical Study*, ConBNT 37 (Stockholm: Lund University Press, 2001), 394 n. 497; James D. Purvis, "The Samaritans," in *The Hellenistic Period*, eds. W. D. Davies and Louis Finkelstein (Cambridge: Cambridge University Press, 1989), 591–613 (591); David Ravens, *Luke and the Restoration of Israel*, JSNTSup 119 (Sheffield: Sheffield Academic, 1995), 73–76. It may be objected that the term "Israelism" never appears in the primary texts, but etic descriptions need not match the self-designations of groups. The term "Yahwism," for example, does not appear in ancient sources, but that term is no less useful a descriptor because of that fact. Marc Zvi Brettler has recently proposed another option, arguing that despite the anachronism involved, the terms "Jews" and "Judaism" should be used to describe even the earliest preexilic Israelites as a way to emphasize the continuity of "Israelite religion" and "Judaism." See Marc Zvi Brettler, "Judaism in the Hebrew Bible? The Transition from Ancient Israelite Religion to Judaism," *CBQ* 61.3 (1999): 429–47. But this approach erases any sense of diversity in the development of various forms of Yahwism from the heritage of ancient Israel, most notably the Samaritans, and as such represents a step in the wrong direction if applied too broadly in the preexilic period. That said, retrojecting "Jew" to those specifically from the kingdom of Judah has some merit, emphasizing the distinctiveness of the southerners and the continuities between those from Judah prior to the Babylonian Exile and Jews afterwards. See also the critiques of Baker, "A 'Jew' by Any Other Name."

PART II

RESTORATION ESCHATOLOGY AND THE CONSTRUCTION OF BIBLICAL ISRAEL

3

Judah's Bible and the Narrative Construction of Biblical Israel

If the Hebrew Bible is about anything, it is about "Israel": its history, culture, cult, ethics.[1]

Philip Davies

During and after the exile(s), the biblical authors looked back at the warnings of the prophets and edited, compiled, and composed what became a collection of authoritative literature about the past and future of Israel.[2] This collection and redaction of the legal, prophetic, poetic, and historical literature that eventually comprised the Hebrew Bible has served to define and shape the idea of Israel ever since. As the earliest layer, the Torah served to define Israel for both Jews and Samaritans, though each group supplemented that foundation with additional scriptures that further shaped their respective communities and traditions. Notably, the default reading of the Hebrew Bible in modern scholarship has long presumed that since any remnant of northern Israelites had allegedly long since disappeared, the biblical writers and editors were therefore free to appropriate the term "Israel" and equate it with the Judahites/Jews in their construction of biblical Israel. That is to say, Judah became Israel.[3]

---

[1] Davies, *Origins*, 2. Cf. J. Gordon McConville, "Narrative and Meaning in the Books of Kings," *Bib* 70 (1989): 31–49 (34); Linville, *Israel in the Book of Kings*, 37; Hugh G. M. Williamson, *Israel in the Books of Chronicles* (Cambridge: Cambridge University Press, 1977).

[2] On exile and its role in the formation of Jewish and Christian scripture, see James A. Sanders, "The Exile and Canon Formation," in *Exile: Old Testament, Jewish and Christian Conceptions*, ed. James M. Scott, JSJSup 56 (Leiden: Brill, 1997), 7–37.

[3] For a strong critique of this narrative, see Gary N. Knoppers, "Did Jacob Become Judah? The Configuration of Israel's Restoration in Deutero-Isaiah," in *Samaria, Samarians,*

But we have already observed that the continued presence of Samaritans – and their claim to northern Israelite heritage – makes it implausible that the legacy of northern Israel had passed out of the frame of consciousness of the biblical writers and editors such that the term "Israel" could be so easily transferred exclusively to the Jews during and after the exile. Nevertheless, the default reading of the Hebrew Bible as a whole continues to be that the biblical narratives and prophetic material serve to claim the heritage of past Israel exclusively for the *Yehudim*, understood as the sole remnant of Israel after the Babylonian Exile. Collins succinctly summarizes this perspective:

> After the fall of the Northern Kingdom, however, the Judeans laid claim to the heritage of all Israel. The Book of Deuteronomy is addressed simply to "Israel," ostensibly to Israel in the Mosaic period but actually to the community that survived the Assyrian invasions. In 2 Chr. 30, Hezekiah summoned both Israel and Judah to celebrate the Passover in Jerusalem, thereby restoring the unity of Israel.[4]

It is of course true that Hezekiah invites the survivors of Israel to celebrate the Passover in 2 Chronicles.[5] But this does not imply that the *Yehudim* thereby identified themselves as the whole of Israel – the very attempt to unify a greater Israel through the incorporation of northerners suggests exactly the opposite. And while the context of Deuteronomy's actual readers is indeed different from that of its implied audience, we must be careful not to make the mistake of imagining that the Israel of Deuteronomy is a representation of the world of the writers or readers.[6] Deuteronomy is addressed to "Israel," but that Israel is set in the *past*

Samaritans: Studies on Bible, History and Linguistics, ed. József Zsengellér, SJ 66 (Berlin: de Gruyter, 2011), 39–67 (50–51, 57).

[4] Collins, "Construction," 25.

[5] On the rise of pan-Israelite sentiment – or the attempt to rebuild an "Israel" under its own leadership – in Judah of the late eighth century BCE, see Finkelstein and Silberman, "Temple and Dynasty"; Nadav Na'aman, "The Israelite-Judahite Struggle for the Patrimony of Ancient Israel," *Bib* 91.1 (2010): 1–23; Koog P. Hong, "Once Again: The Emergence of 'Biblical Israel,'" *ZAW* 125.2 (2013): 278–88; Fleming, *Legacy of Israel*, 47–57. On the efforts of Hezekiah and Josiah to reunify the northern remnant under their own sovereignty, see Jonathan Rosenbaum, "Hezekiah's Reform and the Deuteronomistic Tradition," *HTR* 72.1–2 (1979): 23–44; Nadav Na'aman, "The Kingdom of Judah under Josiah," *TA* 18.1 (1991): 3–71; Williamson, *Israel*, 119–26; Christopher B. Hays, *The Origins of Isaiah 24–27: Josiah's Festival Scroll for the Fall of Assyria* (Cambridge: Cambridge University Press, 2019).

[6] For recent work on the origins of the Torah and Deuteronomy, cf. Gary N. Knoppers and Bernard M. Levinson, eds., *The Pentateuch as Torah: New Models for Understanding Its Promulgation and Acceptance* (Winona Lake: Eisenbrauns, 2007); Schorch, "Samaritan Version of Deuteronomy."

of both the actual and implied audience, which, it should be noted, is not explicitly identified as Israel.[7] Interpreters have been too quick to assume that the (actual) Jewish audience of these texts is the same as the Israel to which the texts are rhetorically addressed. But we must not overlook the curious fact that *the Hebrew Bible is scripture collected and edited by Jews, for Jews, about Israel.* Daniel Fleming explains:

> Here, we confront an underappreciated oddity. Historically, the Bible is Judah's book, the collected lore of Judah's survivors after defeat by Babylon in the early sixth century. ... Nevertheless, the story of origins and early life, including the founding of monarchy, is the story of Israel, the other kingdom. ... To explain its past, the people of Judah tell the story of Israel, only making sure that we know Judah was one part of a larger group.[8]

Biblical material is so familiar to interpreters that this oddity has gone largely unnoticed; the perspective of the texts tends to be assumed as the most obvious, natural outcome. But once one is attuned to notice it, one of the most striking things about the Hebrew Bible is how these texts, which are universally edited from the perspective of southern Judahites rather than northern Israelites, grapple with and construct not *Jewish* identity but *Israelite* identity, consistently constructing a biblical Israel larger than the Jews alone. "Why," James Linville wonders, "did the dialogue that this new elite in the Persian province of Judah engage in centre on an 'Israelite' heritage, in the first place, and not simply a 'Judaean' one?"[9] The biblical genealogical schemes and historical

---

[7] Linville, *Israel in the Book of Kings*, 34. Linville also rightly observes that there is "no evidence that Kings was intended to be an up-to-date history" and that the Deuteronomists may not have regarded the exile "as an event of bounded duration" to that point (70). See also Gary N. Knoppers, "History and Historiography: The Royal Reforms," in *The Chronicler as Historian*, eds. M. Patrick Graham, Kenneth G. Hoglund, and Steven L. McKenzie, JSOTSup 238 (Sheffield: Sheffield Academic, 1997), 178–203.

[8] Fleming, *Legacy of Israel*, xii. This fact raises many questions for those aiming to reconstruct the history of and relationship between ancient Israel and Judah, though that is not our concern in this study, which focuses instead on the reception of the biblical traditions long after any independent memory of the historical events had faded. See also Andrew Tobolowsky, "Israelite and Judahite History in Contemporary Theoretical Approaches," *CurBR* (2018): 33–58; Tobolowsky, *The Sons of Jacob*; Na'aman, "Patrimony"; Davies, *Origins*, 127–58; Alexander Rofé, "Ephraimite versus Deuteronomistic History," in *Reconsidering Israel and Judah: Recent Studies on the Deuteronomistic History*, eds. Gary N. Knoppers and J. Gordon McConville, SBTS 8 (Winona Lake: Eisenbrauns, 2000), 462–74; Harold Louis Ginsberg, *The Israelian Heritage of Judaism*, Texts and Studies of the Jewish Theological Society of America 24 (New York: Jewish Theological Seminary of America, 1982).

[9] Linville, *Israel in the Book of Kings*, 93.

frameworks, for example, consistently integrate northern Israelites and southern Judahites as subsets of a larger twelve-tribe body of Israel, with the Jews descended from common patriarchs and members of the same covenant with YHWH as their northern counterparts.[10] And as Fleming points out, the "Israel" terminology used throughout the biblical narratives puts distance between the exilic or post-exilic present and the past:

> Where the southern name [Judah] is contemporary or close to it in use by one of Judah's own, the northern name evokes antiquity in use that is in some sense foreign to the Judahite writers who selected it.[11]

Any accounting of the concept of Israel in the Second Temple Period must account for this curious fact. And in the process, we must not be too quick to identify the circumstances and people of the texts with their authors or audiences. While it is true that any recounting of the past serves to interpret and give meaning to the present – and is always tinted by the perspective of the present – this can be done through discontinuities as easily as similarities.[12] Moreover, because the past can be interpreted differently, later groups often come into conflict over how to interpret and apply a shared past – precisely what happened among those later groups claiming the legacy of biblical Israel. In any case, for the early Jewish groups that accepted biblical texts as authoritative (groups such as the Sadducees that held to a more limited set of authoritative texts must also not be forgotten), these narratives were read holistically as the story of Israel, as a single unified narrative of repeated violations of the terms of

---

[10] The historicity of the pre-exilic unity of Israel and Judah has been increasingly challenged, but what matters for the purpose of this study is that the Judahite biblical narratives construct such a picture. On the relationship of history to literary creation with respect to Israel and Judah, see Fleming, *Legacy of Israel* and Tobolowsky, *The Sons of Jacob*. For recent discussions and proposals on how northern traditions came to be incorporated in Judah's literature, see Ernst Axel Knauf, "Bethel: The Israelite Impact on Judean Language and Literature," in *Judah and the Judeans in the Persian Period* (Winona Lake: Eisenbrauns, 2006), 291–349; Nadav Na'aman, "Saul, Benjamin and the Emergence of 'Biblical Israel' (Part 1)," *ZAW* 121.2 (2009): 211–24; Israel Finkelstein, "Saul, Benjamin and the Emergence of 'Biblical Israel': An Alternative View," *ZAW* 123.3 (2011): 348–67; Hong, "Once Again"; Koog P. Hong, "The Deceptive Pen of Scribes: Judean Reworking of the Bethel Tradition as a Program for Assuming Israelite Identity," *Bib* 92.3 (2011): 427–41.

[11] Fleming, *Legacy of Israel*, 291.

[12] Cf. Berger, *Sacred Canopy*, 48; Mullen, *Narrative History*, 37–47; Bernard Lewis, *History: Remembered, Recovered, Invented* (Princeton: Princeton University Press, 1975).

the covenant culminating in the punishments for covenant disobedience and their own present situation.[13]

It is critically important to recognize that the implied circumstances occupied by the implied reader looks nothing like those of biblical Israel occupying the land of promise – though the biblical past and prophecies provide the substance for the aspirations of the present community.[14] Rather, Robert Carroll explains:

> In the narratives between Genesis and Chronicles, there may be discerned a metanarrative of a "homeland" occupied by the people, but the grand narrative of the Hebrew Bible (especially as constituted by Genesis–2 Kings) seems to reflect and to testify to a subtext of deported existence.[15]

Put another way, the biblical narratives consistently place the reader in the implied context of exile, in a place of alienation awaiting reconciliation. This perspective begins as early as the Eden story, which typologically establishes the themes of restoration eschatology,[16] and is carried forward throughout the other stories of Genesis, which dovetail nicely with the eschatological expectations attested in the prophetic corpus.[17]

Yet it is rarely noticed that far from appropriating the full heritage of Israel or constructing a post-exilic Israel comprised of the remnant from Judah, the biblical stories construct, emphasize, and idealize a unified

[13] See David Noel Freedman, *The Nine Commandments: Uncovering the Hidden Pattern of Crime and Punishment in the Hebrew Bible*, ABRL (New York: Doubleday, 2002), 179–80.

[14] According to Katherine M. Stott, "A Comparative Study of the Exilic Gap in Ancient Israelite, Messenian and Zionist Collective Memory," in *Community Identity in Judean Historiography: Biblical and Comparative Perspectives*, eds. Gary N. Knoppers and Kenneth A. Ristau (Winona Lake: Eisenbrauns, 2009), 41–58 (54–55), the biblical past is "represented as a golden age to which the present community aspires and in relation to which it imagines its future." But there is an inherent discontinuity between the present and both the biblical past and the imagined future, as the prophecies of Israel's restoration have not yet been fulfilled.

[15] Robert P. Carroll, "Deportation and Diasporic Discourses in the Prophetic Literature," in *Exile: Old Testament, Jewish, and Christian Conceptions*, ed. James M. Scott, JSJSup 56 (Leiden: Brill, 1997), 63–88 (64); cf. Shemaryahu Talmon, "'Exile' and 'Restoration' in the Conceptual World of Ancient Judaism," in *Restoration: Old Testament, Jewish and Christian Perspectives*, ed. James M. Scott, JSJSup 72 (Leiden: Brill, 2001), 107–46 (118–19).

[16] Jacob Neusner, *Judaism When Christianity Began: A Survey of Belief and Practice* (Louisville: Westminster John Knox, 2002), 55; cf. Genesis Rabbah 19:9.1–2. See also Gary A. Anderson, *The Genesis of Perfection: Adam and Eve in Jewish and Christian Imagination* (Louisville: Westminster John Knox, 2001), 207–08.

[17] As persuasively demonstrated by Jonathan Luke Huddleston, *Eschatology in Genesis*, FAT 57 (Tübingen: Mohr Siebeck, 2012).

twelve-tribe Israel and lament its broken present state, regularly depicting Judah as incomplete without its northern counterpart.[18] It is surely no accident that a quarter of Genesis, which provides Israel's primary origin myth, focuses on the primary *northern* patriarch Joseph rather than the southern fathers Judah or Benjamin (Gen 37–50). These chapters even culminate in an explanation of the preeminence of Ephraim (Gen 48). Judah, by contrast, is a minor player in Genesis, with the only chapter devoted to him (Gen 38) involving a ribald story of familial irregularity involving Judah and his daughter-in-law Tamar. The wanderings of Abraham and Jacob are likewise more typically situated in northern sites like Shechem (e.g. Gen 12:6; 33:18–19; 34), which eventually became the chief city not of the Jews but of the Samaritans.

In a post-exilic context, however, a narrative in which Joseph is seemingly lost or dead in an exilic situation resulting from his brothers selling him into slavery is especially relevant for a Jewish audience, given the context of the Syro-Ephraimite conflict and deportations of northern Israel.[19] Ultimately, although he had been reckoned permanently lost, Joseph's reunion with his brothers leads to the salvation of all Israel in the culmination of a greater divine plan.[20] As will be shown below, there is evidence that at least some Jews in the Second Temple period read the Joseph story in precisely this typological manner, paralleling Joseph's enslavement in Egypt with the present fate of the northern tribes scattered among the nations.[21] In much the same way Israel/Jacob thought Joseph had died in the patriarchal story, the northern tribes appear to be "dead," but they will be revealed and restored at the salvation and reconstitution of all Israel. In any case, the prominence of Joseph in the last quarter of Genesis provides an early hint of significant continuing concern about the northern house of Israel throughout the remainder of the biblical corpus and among the post-exilic Jewish community.[22]

---

[18] On the incorporation of a "tribal-genealogical" layer together with other narrative elements to create a pan-Israelite perspective after the exile, see Tobolowsky, *The Sons of Jacob*.

[19] The biblical Joseph narrative is not strictly limited to Genesis; also important is the recapitulation of Psalm 105:17–22, which says Joseph underwent physical "affliction" and was bound with iron while imprisoned in Egypt.

[20] As observed by Graham I. Davies, "Apocalyptic and Historiography," *JSOT* 5 (1978): 15–28 (24), "Such a pattern provided the perfect model for those who wished to maintain that after the long period of post-exilic history, in which Yahweh's activity on behalf of his people might appear even to have been suspended, a divine deliverance was yet to be expected."

[21] See the discussions on 4Q372 1 and the Testaments of the Twelve Patriarchs below.

[22] "For the Elohist, the Joseph story tells the history of the loss of Israel, the Northern Kingdom" (Jacqueline R. Isaac, "Here Comes this Dreamer," in *From Babel to Babylon: Essays on Biblical History and Literature in Honor of Brian Peckham*, eds. Joyce Rilett

Exodus carries this concern for all twelve tribes forward, as now all of Israel is enslaved and separated from the promised land, only to have YHWH miraculously free the nation from slavery in Egypt and lead them into the land by the hand of Moses. Along the way, YHWH renews his covenant with his people and – in the face of Israelite disobedience and unfaithfulness – postpones the restoration to the land, causing Israel to wander in the wilderness until the unfaithful generation has died out. Although on first glance this narrative serves as merely another foundation myth, the exodus was understood even in other biblical literature as typologically foreshadowing a future restoration from exile (e.g., Jer 16:14–15 MT; 23:7–8 MT; Isa 40–55) that would be a second exodus even greater than the first,[23] a sentiment that by no means disappeared in the Second Temple period.[24]

The covenant renewal and wilderness wanderings are not irrelevant, either, as many Jews (as will become evident below) regarded the initial

---

Wood, John E. Harvey, and Mark Leuchter, LHBOTS 455 [London: T&T Clark, 2006], 237–49 [247]). For a discussion of the Joseph novella as setting up Ephraimite and Judahite leadership in Israel, see T. Desmond Alexander, "The Regal Dimension of the תולדות־יעקב: Recovering the Literary Context of Genesis 37–50," in *Reading the Law: Studies in Honor of Gordon J. Wenham*, eds. J. Gordon McConville and Karl Möller, LHBOTS (New York: T&T Clark, 2007), 196–212.

[23] See Hans M. Barstad, *A Way in the Wilderness: The "Second Exodus" in the Message of Second Isaiah*, Journal of Semitic Studies Monograph Series (Manchester: University of Manchester Press, 1989); Anthony R. Ceresko, "The Rhetorical Strategy of the Fourth Servant Song (Isaiah 52:13–53:12): Poetry and the Exodus-New Exodus," *CBQ* 56.1 (1994): 42–55; Gregory M. Stevenson, "Communal Imagery and the Individual Lament: Exodus Typology in Psalm 77," *RestQ* 39 (1997): 215–30; Rikki E. Watts, "Consolation or Confrontation? Isaiah 40–55 and the Delay of the New Exodus," *TynBul* 41 (1990): 31–59; Sara Japhet, "Periodization between History and Ideology II," in *From the Rivers of Babylon to the Highlands of Judah: Collected Studies on the Restoration Period* (Winona Lake: Eisenbrauns, 2007), 416–31 (426).

[24] Holger Zellentin, "The End of Jewish Egypt: Artapanus and the Second Exodus," in *Antiquity in Antiquity: Jewish and Christian Pasts in the Graeco–Roman World*, eds. Gregg Gardner and Kevin Lee Osterloh, TSAJ 123 (Tübingen: Mohr Siebeck, 2008), 27–73; Rikki E. Watts, *Isaiah's New Exodus and Mark* (Tübingen: Mohr Siebeck, 1997); David W. Pao, *Acts and the Isaianic New Exodus*, WUNT 130 (Tübingen: Mohr Siebeck, 2000); Pitre, *Jesus*, 60–62, 90–91, 381–508; James M. Scott, "Exile and the Self-Understanding of Diaspora Jews in the Greco-Roman Period," in *Exile: Old Testament, Jewish, and Christian Conceptions*, ed. James M. Scott, JSJSup 56 (Leiden: Brill, 1997), 173–218; Jonathan A. Goldstein, "The Judaism of the Synagogues (Focusing on the Synagogue of Dura-Europos)," in *Judaism in Late Antiquity, Part 2: Historical Syntheses*, ed. Jacob Neusner, HdO 17 (Leiden: Brill, 1995), 109–57; N. T. Wright, "The Lord's Prayer as a Paradigm of Christian Prayer," in *Into God's Presence: Prayer in the New Testament*, ed. Richard N. Longenecker, McMaster New Testament Studies (Grand Rapids: Eerdmans, 2001), 132–54 esp. 138–47.

return from exile as disappointing and incomplete, looking to the wilderness wanderings as typologically prototypical of the current situation in which Israel remains wandering in the "wilderness of the peoples."[25] It goes without saying that the Torah contains these patriarchal and early Israelite narratives not out of an antiquarian interest but because of their rhetorical and typological application to the post-exilic situation.[26] These historical narratives provided the framework through which later readers would interpret the unfulfilled promises of the Israelite prophets, these stories provided the record of the covenant between YHWH and Israel, culminating in Israel's unfaithfulness and exile and YHWH's promises to renew his covenant with Israel in spite of their past rebellion. And whereas ancient Israelite theology seems to have centered on the concept of a present covenant between Israel and YHWH, the biblical narratives center on the prophetic promises of a future restored, regathered, and reunified Israel, re-chosen for special covenant with the God of Israel, having been called out from the midst of the nations among which Israel had been scattered. In Carroll's words, "The Bible is the great metanarrative of deportation, exile, and potential return."[27]

Early Judaism therefore developed in continuity with ancient Israelite ethno-religion but was also an outgrowth of multiple deportations and the experience of exile, different from its ancestor due to its changed sociopolitical situation and foundation upon a forward-looking (as opposed to present-focused) theology of restoration eschatology based on the prophets' promises.[28] This is a critically important point: through the collection and redaction of the prophetic literature and authoritative historical narratives of Israel that ultimately comprised the Hebrew Bible, exilic and post-exilic Jews established a continual reminder of the broken circumstances of the present, constructing an Israel *not* realized in the present. These early Jews thereby consistently situated themselves in a liminal space between the memory of a past "biblical" Israel and the hope for a future restored Israel.[29] Put another way, *at the root of exilic and*

[25] 1QM 1:1–3. See Chapter 10.
[26] Cf. Erich S. Gruen, *Diaspora: Jews amidst Greeks and Romans* (Cambridge: Harvard University Press, 2004), 1.
[27] Carroll, "Deportation," 64.
[28] See Nickelsburg and Kraft, "Early Judaism," 14.
[29] Cf. Bustenay Oded, "Exile – The Biblical Perspectives," in *Homelands and Diasporas: Greeks, Jews and Their Migrations*, ed. Minna Rozen, International Library of Migration Studies 2 (New York: Tauris, 2008), 85–92; Michael A. Knibb, "The Exile in the Literature of the Intertestamental Period," *HeyJ* 17.3 (1976): 253–72.

post-exilic Judaism we find not a redefinition of Israel limited to Jews/ Judahites but restoration eschatology – a theology looking backward to biblical Israel and forward to a divinely orchestrated future restoration of Israel far exceeding the small return of *Yehudim* in the Persian period.[30] This "in-between" perspective of restoration eschatology is foundational to the very earliest Jewish literature, which helped form, preserve, and give shape to the Jewish communities that survived and grew out of the context of Babylonian domination and exile.[31]

ISRAELITE RESTORATION ESCHATOLOGY

Before continuing, a brief note on terminology is in order. In the interest of clarity, I will follow E. P. Sanders in using the term "restoration eschatology" when discussing the future hopes of Israel's restoration held by many (though not all) early Jews,[32] reserving the term "apocalyptic" for references to revelatory material and motifs, "Apocalypticism" for the related philosophical worldview(s) on divine revelation and future expectation, and "apocalypse" for a genre of revelatory literature.[33] As such, it should be noted that "eschatology" in this context does not necessarily imply the end of the *world* but rather the end of the present *age* and the dawn of a new one. Thus throughout this study, "Israelite restoration eschatology" will refer specifically to the *theological conviction that Israel has fallen under the curses of YHWH's covenant and awaits a time of glorious redemption and restoration.*[34] This may or may not be

---

[30] E. P. Sanders, *Jesus and Judaism* (Minneapolis: Augsburg Fortress, 1985), 97: "In general terms it may be said that 'Jewish eschatology' and 'the restoration of Israel' are synonymous."

[31] Carroll, "Deportation," 64: "Deportation and diaspora are constitutive of the Jewish identity as it begins to emerge and evolve in the biblical narratives."

[32] Sanders, *Jesus and Judaism*, 90; E. P. Sanders, *Judaism: Practice and Belief 63* BC–66 CE (London: SCM, 1992), 289–98.

[33] For a discussion of the characteristics of the genre of apocalypse, see John J. Collins, *The Apocalyptic Imagination: An Introduction to Jewish Apocalyptic Literature* (Grand Rapids: Eerdmans, 1998), 1–42.

[34] Sanders, *Judaism*, 289–98, discusses four main themes of restoration eschatology: the restoration of the twelve tribes, the subjugation or conversion of the nations, the purification of the temple and Jerusalem, and the transformation of Israel into a pure and righteous people. As Sanders notes, these themes were also often accompanied by the messianic expectations. See also David E. Aune and Eric Clark Stewart, "From the Idealized Past to the Imaginary Future: Eschatological Restoration in Jewish Apocalyptic Literature," in *Restoration: Old Testament, Jewish and Christian Perspectives*, ed. James M. Scott, JSJSup 72 (Leiden: Brill, 2001), 147–77, which

envisioned in cosmic or otherworldly terms, but the basic expectation of Israel's restoration is the essential focus.

I want to emphasize that I am not positing the existence of a homogen-ous or monolithic Judaism or that all Jews in the Second Temple period believed the same things. Rather, what we now somewhat anachronistic-ally call "Judaism" was internally diversified, often featuring harsh polemical tensions between competing factions.[35] Nevertheless, Seth Schwartz rightly points out that such diversity should not be taken as an indication that no foundational common ground existed among ancient Jews, since "as far as we can tell most ancient Jews regarded themselves as a members of a single group and furthermore were so regarded by their neighbors, rulers, and others."[36] Schwartz emphasizes that disagreements and discussions often illustrate "not the absence of a normative center ... but *precisely* the typical functioning ... *within* a normative religious system."[37] That is, the diversity of Judaism involves a *shared discourse* tracing back to and limited by an authoritative body of scriptures regularly read in the synagogue, the Torah in particular.[38]

For example, John Collins notes that wisdom traditions and apocalyp-ticism "reflect different understandings of Judaism, each distinct from the traditional covenantal pattern" as defined by an emphasis on the history of the people, responsibility to keep the Torah, and ties to the land.[39] But

discusses the same four basic themes along with the additional apocalyptic themes of the restoration of the creation and paradise regained.

[35] Laurence H. Kant, "Jewish Inscriptions in Greek and Latin," *ANRW* 20.2: 671–713 (686). Cf. also Kraabel, "Roman Diaspora," 457.

[36] Schwartz, "Yannai and Pella," 219. Cf. Jeff S. Anderson, "From Communities of Texts to Religious Communities: Problems and Pitfalls," in *Enoch and Qumran Origins: New Light on a Forgotten Connection*, ed. Gabriele Boccaccini (Grand Rapids: Eerdmans, 2005), 351–55 (351); Cohen, *Beginnings of Jewishness*; Jacob Neusner, "Judaism and Christianity in the Beginning: Time for a Category-Reformation?," *BBR* 8 (1998): 229–38; Jacob Neusner, "What Is 'a Judaism'? Seeing the Dead Sea Library as the Statement of a Coherent Judaic Religious System," in *Theory of Israel*, eds. Alan J. Avery-Peck, Jacob Neusner, and Bruce D. Chilton, HOS 56 (Leiden: Brill, 2001), 3–21. For examples of variation in how Jewish identity was defined, see Barclay, *Jews in the Mediterranean Diaspora*, 402–18.

[37] Schwartz, "Yannai and Pella," 221.

[38] Cf. Michael L. Satlow, "Defining Judaism: Accounting for 'Religions' in the Study of Religion," *JAAR* 74.4 (2006): 837–60 (845); Schwartz, "Social Change," 232; Scott, "Self-Understanding," 181–82.

[39] Collins, *Between Athens and Jerusalem*, 23, (cf. George E. Mendenhall, *Law and Covenant in Israel and the Ancient Near East* (Pittsburgh: Presbyterian Board of Colportage, 1954); Klaus Baltzer, *The Covenant Formulary in Old Testament, Jewish and Early Christian Writings* (Philadelphia: Fortress, 1971); Delbert R. Hillers,

Collins nevertheless acknowledges that even those forms of Judaism that do not focus on the central role of the covenant law still remain tied in some way to Torah and covenant, despite the different perspectives they offer. In this sense, Sanders' observation about the foundational quality of the covenantal framework even when covenant is not overtly in view seems to hold.[40] It is not that Judaism was uniform but rather that there was a central grammar of discourse – covenant and restoration eschatology – that is shared across the various forms of Judaism in this period. Wisdom and apocalyptic literature need not focus on the basics of the covenant precisely because they can assume a shared covenantal outlook among their communities. Despite the tremendous diversity in early Judaism both in theology and practice, there remains no known Judaism in this period – apocalyptic, wisdom, or any other form – outside a covenantal framework.

Even Neusner, who coined the term "Judaisms" to sidestep "the problem of how to define a single 'Judaism' out of all the diverse data,"[41] ultimately argues that the various "Judaisms" are all tied together by a "formative Judaism" centered on the generative myth (and self-fulfilling prophecy) of exile and return.[42] Neusner argues that formative Judaism developed through the Babylonian Exile and return to the land and made that experience normative for all subsequent "Judaisms," which have shared the "conception that the Jews are in exile but have the hope of coming home"[43] as Jews have flourished in a perpetual diaspora.[44] This is, Neusner, argues, a narrative that each Judaism "retells in its own way and with its distinctive emphases."[45] Granted the correction that this motif of exile and restoration cuts deeper than the Babylonian Exile and

---

Covenant: The History of a Biblical Idea (Baltimore: Johns Hopkins University Press, 1969). See also John J. Collins, "Cosmos and Salvation: Jewish Wisdom and Apocalyptic in the Hellenistic Age," *HR* 17.2 (1977): 121–42.

[40] Sanders, *Paul and Palestinian Judaism*, 420–21.

[41] Neusner, "What Is 'a Judaism'?," 6.

[42] Cf. Jacob Neusner, *The Way of Torah: An Introduction to Judaism*, 5th ed. (Belmont: Wadsworth, 1993), 9–15; Jacob Neusner, "Exile and Return as the History of Judaism," in *Exile: Old Testament, Jewish, and Christian Conceptions*, ed. James M. Scott, JSJSup 56 (Leiden: Brill, 1997), 221–37; and especially the explanation in Neusner, "What Is 'a Judaism'?," 6.

[43] Neusner, *Way of Torah*, 14.

[44] Jacob Neusner, *Self-Fulfilling Prophecy: Exile and Return in the History of Judaism* (Boston: Beacon, 1987). For the diaspora as formative and central to Jewish identity, see Boyarin and Boyarin, "Diaspora."

[45] Neusner, *Way of Torah*, 15.

includes the Assyrian deportations of Israel as well, Neusner's "generative narrative" is essentially what I am calling restoration eschatology.[46]

DEUTERONOMY AND RESTORATION ESCHATOLOGY

The emphasis on the present incompleteness of Israel and promises of future restoration are especially apparent in Deuteronomy as read from a late Second Temple period perspective.[47] Although Deuteronomy may indeed have originated as part of an effort to reconstruct a unified Israel after the Assyrian campaigns,[48] the Israel established in the text looks nothing like the post-Assyrian kingdom of Judah or the weak Yehud in the Persian period, particularly since it "included the defunct nation of Israel."[49] The book is a constitution of sorts, but it is not presented as a constitution of the *present* people of Judah but instead rhetorically situated as the constitution of a *past* people – the unified twelve-tribe entity of Israel – from which the reader (whether in post-Assyrian Judah or the late

---

[46] For the concept of exile and return – that is restoration eschatology – as fundamental to the construction of all forms of Judaism, see Neusner, "Exile and Return" and Neusner, *Judaism When Christianity Began*, 55–66.

[47] Cf. David Lincicum, *Paul and the Early Jewish Encounter with Deuteronomy*, WUNT 284 (Tübingen: Mohr Siebeck, 2010); Matthew Thiessen, "The Form and Function of the Song of Moses (Deuteronomy 32:1–43)," *JBL* 123.3 (2004): 401–24; Matthew Thiessen, "4Q372 1 and the Continuation of Joseph's Exile," *DSD* 15 (2008): 380–95 (391–92); J. Gordon McConville, "Restoration in Deuteronomy and the Deuteronomic Literature," in *Restoration: Old Testament, Jewish and Christian Perspectives*, ed. James M. Scott, JSJSup 72 (Leiden: Brill, 2001), 11–40 (39–40). See also the analysis of the definition of Israel in Deuteronomy in Mullen, *Narrative History*, 55–86. On the importance of Deuteronomy in the Second Temple period, see Sidnie A. White Crawford, "Reading Deuteronomy in the Second Temple period," in *Reading the Present in the Qumran Library: The Perception of the Contemporary by Means of Scriptural Interpretation*, eds. Kristin De Troyer et al., SymS 30 (Leiden: Brill, 2005), 127–40.

[48] That an early form of what became Deuteronomy was composed in the seventh century BCE has been the prevailing scholarly opinion since W. M. L. De Wette, "Dissertatio critica qua Deuteronomium a prioribus Pentateuchi libris diversum alius cuiusdam auctoris opus esse monstratur" (PhD diss., Jena, 1805); cf. Duane L. Christensen, *Deuteronomy 1:1–21:9*, WBC 6A (Waco: Word, 2001), lxviii. It should be noted that if Deuteronomy was originally composed to appropriate Israel's heritage for those from Judah, it was a failure, as even the Samaritans – who traced their descent back to the North – claimed Deuteronomy as their own, a critical datum for any inquiry into the relationship between the Samaritans and Jews and when exactly the schism between the two groups happened, as discussed in Schorch, "Samaritan Version of Deuteronomy"; Nodet, *A Search for the Origins of Judaism*; Frank Moore Cross, "Aspects of Samaritan and Jewish History in Late Persian and Hellenistic Times," *HTR* 59.3 (1966): 201–11.

[49] Mullen, *Narrative History*, 83.

Second Temple period or even today) can work only by analogy.[50] Observing that the "Israel" of Deuteronomy no longer exists in the reader's present, Theodore Mullen explains:

> The "Israel" addressed by Moses is ideal, one that will exist in real terms only at a later time. This "Israel," too, will find itself outside the land as a result of exile. It has only the hope of [YHWH's] forgiveness and acceptance of its repentance to cling to in the attempt to regain this ideal time that had now been lost. ... The symbolic nature of the designation "Israel," [is] applied now to a nonexistent entity with the intention of *recreating* that very object.[51]

Put another way, as it stands in its final form, Deuteronomy does not construct a present Israelite polity but rather establishes a system of covenantal nomism and restoration eschatology that has dominated Jewish theology for millennia since.[52] Deuteronomy's pattern of obedience and blessing, disobedience and chastening, return and mercy, exile and restoration – together with an overarching theology of YHWH's grace – sows the seeds of restoration eschatology that come into full flower within the theological retellings of Israel's history, particularly in the Former Prophets, where Israel is shown to have repeatedly strayed from YHWH, received chastening, repented, and then experienced divine favor. Far from establishing a new Israel limited to the *Yehudim*, Deuteronomy emphasizes the essential unity of all twelve tribes of Israel and – as with the Prophets – climaxes with the prediction that Israel will rebel, break covenant, and be scattered in exile as punishment.[53]

---

[50] Thomas Römer, "Deuteronomy in Search of Origins," in *Reconsidering Israel and Judah: Recent Studies on the Deuteronomistic History*, eds. Gary N. Knoppers and J. Gordon McConville, SBTS 8 (Winona Lake: Eisenbrauns, 2000), 112–38; McConville, "Restoration in Deuteronomy," 11. For more on Deuteronomy as a constitution, see S. Dean McBride, "Polity of the Covenant People: The Book of Deuteronomy," *Int* 41.3 (1987): 229–44. Mullen, *Narrative History*, 87, argues that Deuteronomy is "a ritual manifesto of ethnic boundary formation for Israelite identity," rightly noting that "the 'today' of Deuteronomy could be ritually recovered at any time" through proper performance of the ritual activities distinguishing Israel (84). Nevertheless, Mullen fails to note that Deuteronomy's emphasis on the twelvefold structure of Israel limits the extent to which Israel can be ritually recovered until the restoration of which the end of the book speaks.

[51] Mullen, *Narrative History*, 57–58.

[52] On covenantal nomism as foundational to Judaism, see E. P. Sanders, "Patterns of Religion in Paul and Rabbinic Judaism," *HTR* 66 (1973): 455–78; Sanders, *Paul and Palestinian Judaism*; and Sanders, *Judaism*. On Deuteronomy as eschatological, see McConville, "Restoration in Deuteronomy," 39–40.

[53] Deuteronomy's pessimism about the inevitability of impending exile matches Linville's reading of the Josianic reforms in 2 Kings, which he sees as preparing the people for the inescapably imminent exile by accepting responsibility for the sins that will soon result in Judah joining the rest of Israel in exile (*Israel in the Book of Kings*, 226–53). Linville

Then they will say, "Because they forsook the covenant of YHWH ... YHWH uprooted them from their land in anger, fury and great wrath, and cast them into another land (as it is this day)." (Deut 29:25, 28)[54]

Moreover, YHWH will scatter you among all peoples, from one end of the earth to the other end of the earth; and there you will serve other gods, wood and stone, which you or your fathers have not known. (Deut 28:64)

Nevertheless, Deuteronomy does not conclude with failure and abandonment but rather promises that YHWH would not allow the covenant to remain broken. Instead, YHWH will ultimately regather his people, yet again showing them mercy and ending the cycle of disobedience and return once and for all:

Thus when all of these things have come upon you, the blessing and the curse which I have set before you, and you remember them in all nations where YHWH your God has banished you, and you return to YHWH your God and obey Him with all your heart and soul according to all that I command you and your children today, then YHWH your God will restore you from captivity. ...

Moreover, YHWH your God will circumcise your heart and the heart of your descendants, to love YHWH your God with all your heart and with all your soul, so that you may live. YHWH your God will inflict all these curses on your enemies and on those who hate you, those who persecuted you. And you shall again obey YHWH and observe all his commands that I command you today. (Deut 30:1–3a, 6–8)

In these passages, Deuteronomy promises the restoration and return of an Israel significantly larger in scope than that of the Jewish refugees from Babylon. Thus, in sharp contrast to Collins' assertion that Deuteronomy reflects Judaean appropriation of the heritage of Israel, Deuteronomy looks forward to a more comprehensive restoration. In the context of the late Judahite kingdom, this suggests a hope for the return of the (mostly northern) Israelites scattered by Assyria and their reconciliation and reunion with Judah – an expectation that would later broaden to include the exiles from Judah after their deportation to Babylon. The narrative framing of the book – with Israel in Moab on the cusp of entering the promised land – rhetorically situates the reader in a liminal

---

points out that the captivity paradoxically results in the reunification of Israel inasmuch as each of the rival monarchies has been shattered. On exile and restoration and the ending of Deuteronomy, cf. Thiessen, "Song of Moses."

[54] The "as it is this day" appears to be an aside referencing the fulfillment of this passage from the perspective of the present state of the editor/reader. The LXX strengthens this connection by translating this portion ὡσεὶ νῦν, "as now." According to m. Sanh. 10:3 and b. Sanh. 110b, R. Aqiba interpreted "as it is this day" here to mean the ten tribes would never return to the land. Cf. Scott, "Self-Understanding," 186–87.

space "in dispersion, outside the land, awaiting the realization of the promise."[55]

Readers of Deuteronomy are therefore rhetorically encouraged to locate themselves near the end of the "slavery/promise" stage, awaiting the great theophany ("promised presence") and subsequent "freedom/ fulfillment," this time not from Egypt but from "the ends of the earth" (Deut 30:4).[56] This understanding of Deuteronomy was prevalent throughout the Second Temple period, with the Song of Moses in Deut 32 and, to a lesser extent, Moses' blessing of Israel in Deut 33, taking special importance, being read as prophecies of Israel's present subjection to the nations and subsequent restoration and exaltation.[57]

Thus Deuteronomy and the Song of Moses in particular – the "end of the Torah," as it were – was understood as concluding with promises of restoration that remain unfulfilled throughout the Second Temple period, wrapping up the Pentateuch by establishing a permanent paradigm of restoration eschatology at the very core of Judaism.[58] The influence of Deuteronomy and particularly the Song of Moses are so strong that one scholar has remarked, "Deuteronomy 32 was a major source, the 'bible' so to speak, of the prophetic movement ... [it] has extremely close ties with especially the 7th–6th century prophecy. Virtually all the major themes of those prophets (including even the 'remnant') have their

---

[55] Watson, *Hermeneutics of Faith*, 471; cf. also McConville, "Restoration in Deuteronomy," 37; Linville, *Israel in the Book of Kings*, 226–53; Thiessen, "Song of Moses."

[56] For an analysis of this tripartite pattern in the biblical tradition, see Edward G. Newing, "A Rhetorical and Theological Analysis of the Hexateuch," *South East Asia Journal of Theology* 22.2 (1981): 1–15. Cf. also Christensen, *Deuteronomy 1:1–21:9*, lxxxviii.

[57] Richard J. Bauckham, "Tobit as a Parable for the Exiles of Northern Israel," in *Studies in the Book of Tobit: A Multidisciplinary Approach*, ed. Mark R. J. Bredin, LSTS 55 (London: T&T Clark, 2006), 140–64 (142). For a thorough look at the Song of Moses as it is used and interpreted in later Jewish and Christian tradition, see Richard H. Bell, "Deuteronomy 32 and the Origin of the Jealousy Motif in Romans 9–11," in *Provoked to Jealousy: The Origin and Purpose of the Jealousy Motif in Romans 9–11*, WUNT 63 (Tübingen: Mohr, 1994), 200–85 (209–85). Cf. also J. Ross Wagner, *Heralds of the Good News: Isaiah and Paul in Concert in the Letter to the Romans* (Leiden: Brill, 2003), 191–201; Thiessen, "Song of Moses"; Steven Weitzman, *Song and Story in Biblical Narrative: The History of a Literary Convention in Ancient Israel* (Bloomington: Indiana University Press, 1997), 69–70; Steven Weitzman, "Allusion, Artifice, and Exile in the Hymn of Tobit," *JBL* (1996): 49–61; Umberto Cassuto, "The Song of Moses (Deuteronomy Chapter xxxii 1–43)," in *Biblical and Oriental Studies: Bible* (Jerusalem: Magnes, 1973), 41–46.

[58] McConville, "Restoration in Deuteronomy," 39–40.

antecedents in Deuteronomy 32."[59] The influence may of course have gone the other direction, but that influence was certainly established by the time the Torah began to be authoritative and remained such throughout our period of inquiry. This restoration-eschatological paradigm – and the implied location of Israel as in exile and on the cusp of restoration established in Deuteronomy – remained prevalent in early Judaism as will be attested throughout the remainder of this study.

FORMER PROPHETS: LOSS OF ISRAELITE IDENTITY

Both the Former Prophets and Chronicles carry the restoration-eschatological theology of Deuteronomy forward, embedded in historical narratives that ostensibly explain the present (exilic) state of affairs.[60] Significantly, neither gives any support to the idea that the name "Israel" was appropriated by the southern "Judaeans" as is so often assumed. As for the Former Prophets, despite the narrator's condemnation of the northern kingdom's idolatry and its ultimate fate, the north retains the title of "Israel" throughout Kings. On this point, Knoppers observes:

Nevertheless, the authors of Kings do not speak of Judah, the southern kingdom, as Israel. In Kings Israel may refer to a multi-tribal entity, the united kingdom, the northern region of the nation, the northern kingdom, or exiled northerners (2 Kgs 17:6; 18:11), but the term Israel is never used to refer to either the southern kingdom or the Judahite exiles. The writers of Kings, as well as the writers of the other books in the Deuteronomistic History (or the Former Prophets), embrace a comprehensive understanding of the Israelite people.[61]

[59] George E. Mendenhall, "Samuel's 'Broken Rîb': Deuteronomy 32," in *A Song of Power and the Power of Song: Essays on the Book of Deuteronomy*, ed. Duane L. Christensen (Winona Lake: Eisenbrauns, 1993), 169–80.

[60] For a representative sample of recent approaches to the so-called Deuteronomistic History, see Thomas Römer, ed., *The Future of the Deuteronomistic History*, Bibliotheca Ephemeridum Theologicarum Lovaniensum 147 (Leuven: Leuven University Press, 2000) and the summary of several important recent works found in William M. Schniedewind, "The Problem with Kings: Recent Study of the Deuteronomistic History," *RelSRev* 22.1 (1996): 22–27. Cf. also Gary N. Knoppers, "Theories of the Redaction(s) of Kings," in *Books of Kings*, eds. André Lemaire and Baruch Halpern (Leiden: Brill, 2010), 69–88; Jeffrey C. Geoghegan, "'Until This Day' and the Preexilic Redaction of the Deuteronomistic History," *JBL* 122.2 (2003): 201–27. Since late Second Temple readers read the Deuteronomistic History as a unity, the various source and form critical concerns typical of modern scholarship are not a concern in this study.

[61] Knoppers, "Did Jacob Become Judah," 45.

Moreover, YHWH is the "God of Israel" and never "the God of Judah" in the Deuteronomistic History,[62] highlighting the broader corporate entity of which Judah is only a part – and this even after the fall of the northern kingdom.[63] It is striking that by the end of Kings – that is, where the reader's present meets the past – Israel is no longer in the picture, with Judah alone in view but still under the thumb of powerful foreign rule. And yet the name "Israel" is still never transferred to Judah. This tragic ending – of which the audience could be expected be aware in much the same way a modern film audience is not surprised when the *Titanic* sinks – is presented as the natural outcome of what is arguably the central theme of the Former Prophets: namely, Israel's rebellion against YHWH's covenant and consequent forfeiture of status and (ultimately) land. This theme is accentuated by the constant tension between the image of an ideal Israel and *actual* Israel.[64]

On the one hand, the Deuteronomic covenant constructs Israel in ideal terms as a twelve-tribe unity fully obedient to YHWH's covenant and enjoying the blessing of YHWH's favor. On the other hand, the Israel of the Former Prophets only comes close to matching this description in the book of Joshua, which is nevertheless punctuated by several proleptic warnings like the Achan incident (Jos 7) along the way.[65] Notably, the term "all Israel," denoting the union of all twelve tribes, appears seventeen times in Joshua, underscoring this theme of unity.[66] But after Joshua, Israel never comes close to matching the ideal. Indeed, the rest of the Former Prophets tells the story of Israel's decline and destruction, as the narrator regularly points out how Israel consistently falls short of its covenantal obligations. Barry Webb, for example, argues that in Judges the non-fulfillment of YHWH's promise of land is "the fundamental issue which the book as a whole addresses,"[67] highlighting the dramatic

---

[62] Zeitlin, "Hebrew, Jew and Israel," 367. Linville, *Israel in the Book of Kings*, 28, notes the peculiarity of this fact: "If the origins of the literature now contained in the Hebrew Bible lie within Judah-ism, then why is there absolutely no reference in this literature to Yahweh as the 'God of Judah'?"

[63] See Hjelm, *Jerusalem's Rise*, 30–92, 117–18.

[64] For more on the tragic character of the Former Prophets, see Flemming A. J. Nielsen, *The Tragedy in History: Herodotus and the Deuteronomistic History*, JSOTSup 251 (Sheffield: Sheffield Academic, 1997), esp. 154–60.

[65] Mullen, *Narrative History*, 56–57, observes that the deuteronomistic presentation of "Israel" relies on the paradox of Israel's election and obligations, the various resolutions of which construct "Israel" throughout.

[66] Cf. Grosby, *Biblical Ideas of Nationality*, 16.

[67] Barry G. Webb, *The Book of Judges: An Integrated Reading*, JSOTSup 46 (Sheffield: JSOT Press, 1987), 208.

tension between Israel's election and weakness depicted throughout the narrative. This contrast between the ideal Israel and the Israel of the narrative leads to a persistent sense of foreboding and entropy throughout the narrative of the Former Prophets, which the reader naturally expects to end in exile.[68]

In the face of Israel's chronic disobedience, YHWH decides "at the end of the Judges era not to *give* them the whole land originally promised."[69] By the end of Judges, Israel remains in the land, but its covenantal right to the land is tenuous at best due to repeated unfaithfulness. Inevitable judgment looms, since "in those days, there was no king in Israel, and everyone did what was right in his own eyes" (Judg 17:6; 19:1; 21:25).[70]

Samuel and Kings (1–4 Kingdoms)

Unfortunately, the rise of the monarchy does not rectify the problem of disobedience but itself represents a further rejection of YHWH (1 Sam 8:7), ultimately leading to even greater wickedness, just as Samuel warns.[71] Moreover, the account of Gideon and Abimelech (Judg 6–9) has already established a pessimistic perspective on kingship that serves proleptically to reinforce the ambivalence (at best) of 1 Samuel towards the institution of the monarchy.[72] It should be noted that although modern scholarship tends to distinguish pro- and anti-monarchical redactors of the Former Prophets, ancient readers did not draw such distinctions but rather grappled with the ambiguous picture presented in the final form of the narrative.[73]

In the final form, the rise of the monarchy is both a temporary respite with respect to Israel's political weakness and a continuation of the pattern of unfaithfulness extending from the exodus (cf. 1 Sam

---

[68] Linville, *Israel in the Book of Kings*, 91.

[69] Webb, *Judges*, 210. Cf. also Lambert, *How Repentance Became Biblical*, 105–06.

[70] On this phrase in Judges, see Shemaryahu Talmon, "'In Those Days There Was No King in Israel,'" *Imm* 5 (1974): 27–36.

[71] Ralph W. Klein, *1 Samuel*, WBC 10 (Waco: Word, 1983), 75.

[72] See David Jobling, *The Sense of Biblical Narrative: Structural Analyses in the Hebrew Bible*, 2 vols. JSOTSup 39 (Sheffield: Sheffield Academic, 1986), 1.86; cf. also Robert Polzin, review of *The Sense of Biblical Narrative: Structural Analyses in the Hebrew Bible II*, by David Jobling, *Bib* 69.1 (1988): 122.

[73] On anti-monarchical traditions among (particularly northern) Israelites and the decentralized nature of the northern kingdom reflected in the final biblical documents, see Fleming, *Legacy of Israel*, esp. 295–98. On the paradoxes inherent in the final form and their impact on the reader, see Linville, *Israel in the Book of Kings*, 85.

10:18–19) up to "this day" – that is, the reader's position in implied exile.[74] As such, much of the narrative of the monarchy makes use of the ironic disconnect between Israel's chronic disobedience and its political fate.[75] That is, despite unfaithfulness and the stated covenantal penalties for disobedience, Israel's political fortunes continue to improve until the division of the kingdoms marks the beginning of the inevitable decline. But even then, the (more) wicked north actually enjoys greater power and prosperity until its destruction by Assyria, at which point the consequences of Israel's disobedience come to full fruition, only to be followed by Judah's inevitable destruction a little over a century later. As might be expected given this trajectory, the story of Saul's rise and kingship is highly ironic, even tragic in character, "the story of a man not fitted for a job that should not have been opened."[76] But the dire warnings about the nature of monarchy in 1 Sam 8:7–18 are certainly not limited to the disaster of Saul's kingship. On the contrary, even David's model kingship is marred right at its high point by adultery, murder, and a military coup by his eldest son in 2 Sam 9–20, only reinforcing the sense of Israel's instability.[77]

Solomon's kingship marks the center of Israel's history as recounted in Kings, the high point of the monarchy, and a political golden age.[78] But, as Linville observes, "Even Solomon's reign in Kings seems undermined at an early stage."[79] Solomon brings the kingdom to its zenith but is also, in the words of Antti Laato, the "destroyer of the Israelite empire."[80] It is Solomon who breaks the Deuteronomic prohibitions for the king (Deut

---

[74] Klein, *1 Samuel*, 75–76.

[75] McConville, "Narrative and Meaning," 32–33; Robert Polzin, *Moses and the Deuteronomist: A Literary Study of the Deuteronomic History. I: Deuteronomy, Joshua, Judges* (Bloomington: Indiana University Press, 1980).

[76] Edwin M. Good, *Irony in the Old Testament*, 2nd ed., BLS 3 (Sheffield: Almond Press, 1981), 58; cf. Nielsen, *The Tragedy in History*, 124–35; Robert P. Gordon, *1 & 2 Samuel* (London: Continuum, 1984), 30–35.

[77] Cf. Linville, *Israel in the Book of Kings*, 90; McConville, "Narrative and Meaning," 33–34.

[78] Kings, however, hints that this "golden age" was in fact quite limited, as illustrated by the fact that Solomon had to receive part of his own land as a marriage bounty from the king of Egypt (1 Kgs 9:16). Cf. McConville, "Narrative and Meaning," 36–37.

[79] Linville, *Israel in the Book of Kings*, 90. See also Eric A. Seibert, *Subversive Scribes and the Solomonic Narrative a Rereading of 1 Kings 1–11*, LHBOTS 436 (New York: T&T Clark, 2006).

[80] Antti Laato, *A Star Is Rising: The Historical Development of the Old Testament Royal Ideology and the Rise of the Jewish Messianic Expectations*, USFISFJC 5 (Atlanta: Scholars Press, 1997), 78.

17:16–17) by acquiring numerous horses for himself, sending to Egypt for horses, and marrying many foreign wives.[81] The narrator makes these violations quite clear by recounting these deeds together (ironically at the end of a summary of Solomon's glorious tenure) in the same order as the prohibitions in Deuteronomy and immediately following with the declaration of Deuteronomic punishment (1 Kgs 10:26–11:13). Solomon also introduces new administrative districts, circumventing the traditional tribal-territorial boundaries established by YHWH (1 Kgs 4:7–19).[82] Moreover, of all the kings of Israel, Solomon's high taxes and conscription of labor best fulfill Samuel's warnings about the nature of monarchy in 1 Sam 8, warnings that conclude with Samuel's solemn declaration that YHWH will not listen to Israel's cries when this happens.[83] Even the Solomonic temple is itself ambiguous in character.[84] Nathan's prophecy shows its insignificance to YHWH (2 Sam 7:5–7), its location is connected with judgment (2 Sam 24:15–25), and Solomon's grand dedicatory prayer concedes both its insufficiency as a house for YHWH (1 Kgs 8:27) and its inability to restrain Israel's sin, which will inevitably result in exile (1 Kgs 8:46–48).

The apparent high point of the unified Israelite monarchy under Solomon is short-lived, as Israel's decline begins with the secession of the northern tribes from the monarchy governed by David's heirs behind a competing king, the Ephraimite Jeroboam I. Solomon's reign thus ironically marks both the political high point of Israel and a new low in

---

[81] Laato, *A Star Is Rising*, 79–80.

[82] Mordechai Cogan, *1 Kings: A New Translation with Introduction and Commentary*, AB 10 (New Haven: Yale University Press, 2008), 205; Laato, *A Star Is Rising*, 78; Baruch Halpern, "Sectionalism and the Schism," *JBL* 93.4 (1974): 519–32 (528–32); Tryggve N. D. Mettinger, *Solomonic State Officials: A Study of the Civil Government Officials of the Israelite Monarchy*, ConBOT 5 (Lund: Gleerup, 1971), esp. 111–23. But see the caution on this point of Simon J. de Vries, *1 Kings* (Grand Rapids: Zondervan, 2003), 71. It is also unclear whether this tradition, which may well be quite old, actually predates the twelve-tribe traditions, but from a narrative standpoint Solomon's redistricting divides traditional tribal territories already established at this point. See also G. Ernest Wright, "The Provinces of Solomon," *ErIsr* 8 (1967): 58–68; Yohanan Aharoni, "The Solomonic Districts," *TA* 3.1 (1976): 5–15.

[83] For more detail on the ambivalent portrayal of Solomon's reign, see McConville, "Narrative and Meaning," 35–38.

[84] Lyle M. Eslinger, *Into the Hands of the Living God*, JSOTSup 24 (Sheffield: Sheffield Academic, 1989), 145–47, highlights other flaws of Solomon within the narrative, arguing that the temple-building narratives suggest a Solomonic attempt to coerce unconditional sanction from YHWH, which the repetitions of the conditions in 1 Kgs 6:11–13 and 1 Kgs 9:3–9 demonstrate to be a failure.

the Former Prophets' narrative of Israel's continued decline, the result of Solomon's spiritual unfaithfulness and heavy-handed government.

Solomon's forfeiture of ten tribes and retention of one is obviously central to the evaluation of his reign, and to the message of Kings (1 Kgs 11,13, cf. 11,36; 15,4; 2 Kgs 8,19). It heightens the tension between the promise, which has no explicit conditions attached in 2 Sam 7, and its vulnerability because of Israel's unfaithfulness.[85]

This division into two kingdoms – and Israel's accompanying adoption of golden calves at Dan and Bethel to compete with the Jerusalem cult, itself an echo of the golden calf episode in Exod 32 – marks the end of Israel's political ascent and the beginning of the decline culminating in exile.[86] Both Kings and Chronicles emphasize this point and lament the continuation of this situation into the present, "Thus Israel has been in rebellion against the house of David *to this day*" (1 Kgs 12:19 // 2 Chr 10:19, my emphasis). With the significant words "to this day," the story constructs a present Israel that cannot solely be identified with the descendants of the southern kingdom. Rather, Israel remains divided and broken, with the bulk of Israel continuing in rebellion in the present moment as constructed in the narrative.[87]

To the confusion of many an unfortunate undergraduate, from this point forward "Israel" refers not only to the twelve tribes descended from the eponymous patriarch but also to the northern kingdom, the "house of Israel" (בית ישראל) in contrast to southern "the house of Judah" (בית יהודה).[88] Read in an

---

[85] McConville, "Narrative and Meaning," 37.

[86] On the golden calf episode from Exodus as archetypal for Israel's history, see Scott W. Hahn, *The Kingdom of God as Liturgical Empire: A Theological Commentary on 1–2 Chronicles* (Grand Rapids: Baker Academic, 2012), 167–69, 178–80, and the sources cited there.

[87] The "to this day" statements in the Deuteronomistic History have been an important part of the discussion of the date(s) of authorship/redaction, as discussed in Geoghegan, "Until This Day" and Jeffrey C. Geoghegan, *The Time, Place, and Purpose of the Deuteronomistic History: The Evidence of "Until This Day,"* BJS 347 (Providence: Brown Judaic Studies, 2006). What matters for this study, however, is that from the perspective of the *reader* (both real and implied), such statements in an anonymous, undated, and authoritative text featuring an omniscient narrator imply the continuation of such circumstances into the present not only of the author but *of the reader*. For more on "to this day" statements and their rhetorical role in constituting the audience in light of the stories being told (though focusing on their use in Genesis), see also Huddleston, *Eschatology in Genesis*, 35–40, 64–73.

[88] E.g. 1 Kgs 12:21; Jer 3:18; 11:17. These separate groups are never portrayed as completely unified even in the accounts of the monarchy (e.g. 2 Sam 2:4–11; 2 Sam 5:5), and the tenuous connection forged between them under David finally broke after

exilic or post-exilic context, it is striking that Kings focuses not on Judah but on the northern house of Israel until its destruction by Assyria, with sixteen chapters from 1 Kings 17–2 Kings 10, including the iconic ministries of Elijah and Elisha, focusing almost exclusively on the dominant, corrupt (according to the narrator), and doomed northern kingdom.[89] This shift highlights the ambiguity of the term "Israel" throughout the Hebrew Bible, an ambiguity that in fact renders the term all the more powerful as a transformative symbol.[90] McConville rightly observes the irony inherent in the apostate northern kingdom retaining the title "Israel," yet another illustration of the larger theme of Israel's loss of status:

> Kings is arguably *all about* a loss of identity, of which loss of land is finally a function. The division of the kingdom is a first manifestation of this. It is no mere "casting off" of the north. On the contrary, the king of the northern kingdom is regularly styled "the King of Israel," even though it is here that the most profound apostasy, even though he is not Davidic, and even though succession is largely by main force. Rather, separation is part of the problematic of being Israel. The question Who is Israel? hangs over these books.[91]

The tension between Israel's disobedience and its identity as YHWH's elect people is thus all the more prominent after the division of the kingdoms. After a period of sustained idolatry in the north, conflict between the two kingdoms ultimately leads to the Syro-Ephraimite conflict (2 Kgs 16; 2 Chr 28; Isa 7–12), in which Judah calls upon Assyria for assistance against Israel, Syria/Aram, and their allies.[92] The north is subsequently destroyed by the Assyrians in several major campaigns, most notably under Tiglath-Pileser III (2 Kgs 15:29, 16:9) and Shalmaneser (2 Kgs 17:3–6). Each campaign ends with significant deportations, with Israelites scattered across the Assyrian empire and new

---

Solomon's death. Cf. Yigal Levin, "Joseph, Judah and the Benjamin Conundrum," *ZAW* 116.2 (2006): 223–41 (esp. 225–226). As shown in Chapter 1, this division between the kingdoms is the source of Josephus' continued distinction between the terms "Israel" and "the Jews."

[89] Knoppers both highlights this fact and seeks to explain it in *Two Nations under God: The Deuteronomic History of Solomon and the Dual Monarchies*, 2 vols., HSM 52 and 53 (Leiden: Brill, 1993, 1994) (n.b. the discussion at I, 9). In spite of their presence in the north, both Elijah and Elisha are subversive figures who subtly protest the division between the kingdoms and the illegitimacy of Omride rule in the north (e.g. 1 Kgs 18:31–32; 2 Kgs 3:14), again highlighting this concern of the narrator.

[90] Mullen, *Narrative History*, 57.

[91] McConville, "Narrative and Meaning," 34. Cf. Webb, *Judges*.

[92] See Vann D. Rolfson, "The Syro-Ephraimite War: Context, Conflict, and Consequences," *Studia Antiqua* 2.1 (2002): 87–100.

inhabitants brought from outside the land to resettle Samaria – Kings' polemical explanation of the origins of those later identified with the Samaritans.[93] The narrator – typically scarce in his evaluation and terse in his judgments – at this point finally breaks into an extended and unusually emotional soliloquy explaining the situation and its causes in one of the most glaring examples of "retrospective or last-minute clarification" in the biblical narrative:[94]

The king of Assyria captured Samaria and carried Israel away into exile. . . . This happened because the children of Israel had sinned against YHWH their God. . . . They served idols, concerning which YHWH had said to them, "You must not do this thing." . . . They spurned his statutes and his covenant, the one he made with their ancestors, and his testimonies, which he testified against them. And they walked after the Nothing (הַהֶבֶל) and they became nothing (וַיֶּהְבָּלוּ); they walked after the nations that surrounded them, concerning whom YHWH had commanded them not to behave as they did.[95] And they abandoned all the commands of YHWH their God. So YHWH was very angry with Israel and removed them from his face; none was left except the tribe of Judah. . . . So Israel was carried away into exile from their own land to Assyria until this day. (2 Kgs 17:6–7a,12, 15–16a, 18, 23b)

Yet again, the exile of Israel – specifically that of the northern house – is depicted as continuing "to this day." By adopting the practices of the surrounding nations, Israel "became nothing," undifferentiated from the nations.[96] For Jewish readers in the Second Temple period, this continued

---

[93] For more detailed analysis of these deportations and their historical impact, see Knoppers, "Post-Exilic Israel," 153–60; Finkelstein, *Forgotten Kingdom*, 153–55; Finkelstein and Silberman, "Temple and Dynasty"; Davies, *In Search of "Ancient Israel,"* 69–70; Na'aman, "When and How"; Barmash, "Nexus"; Peter Dubovský, "Tiglath-pileser III's Campaigns in 734–732 BC: Historical Background of Isa 7; 2 Kgs 15–16 and 2 Chr 27–28," *Bib* 87.2 (2006): 153–70. For a more specific look at the fall(s) of Samaria, see also K. Lawson Younger, "The Fall of Samaria in Light of Recent Research," *CBQ* 61.3 (1999): 461–82; Gershon Galil, "The Last Years of the Kingdom of Israel and the Fall of Samaria," *CBQ* 57.1 (1995): 52–64; John H. Hayes and Jeffrey K. Kuan, "The Final Years of Samaria (730–720 BC)," *Bib* 72.2 (1991): 153–81.

[94] Sternberg, *Poetics*, 54–55, observes that the biblical narrator is typically laconic and scarce with evaluation but preserves "foolproof judgment" through "retrospective or last-minute judgment," by which "the narrative will often enlighten the naive or superficial toward the end." Mullen, *Narrative History*, 43, similarly notes the unusual display of emotion in this passage.

[95] After the prior equation of "walked after the Nothing . . . became nothing," this parallel clause implies that by walking after the surrounding nations, they became the surrounding nations.

[96] Cf. Mullen, *Narrative History*, 78. This notion of becoming nothing may allude to neo-Assyrian policies of deportation designed to produce ethnically mixed populations, thereby effectively eliminating rebellious peoples, as also reflected by the importation of

to stand in distinction to the return of Jews from Babylon since Jewish sources give no indication of Israelites who were resettled among the various regions of the Assyrian Empire ever returning to their homeland in any significant numbers.[97] Later biblical authors and, as will be seen below, many Jews around the turn of the era were conscious of this difference, with Israel's absence still keenly felt (despite or even exacerbated by the presence of the Samaritans).

Not to be outdone, Judah is similarly condemned for adopting the idolatrous "statutes which Israel had introduced" (2 Kgs 17:19), leading to its own series of deportations and destruction just over a century later. Thus, "YHWH rejected all the seed of Israel and afflicted them and gave them into the hand of plunderers until he had cast them from before his face" (2 Kgs 17:20). That the narrator declares this judgment upon the south even before it happens in the story casts the gloom of inevitable judgment over the later reform efforts of Hezekiah and Josiah, which are undertaken in the shadow of impending destruction.[98] Far from laying claim to the full heritage of Israel after the north's Assyrian destruction as suggested by Collins, Hezekiah's reforms are a dismal failure, all the more in that Hezekiah's just reign is followed by Manasseh's exceedingly wicked rule.[99] Josiah's reform – undertaken with the knowledge that future destruction was assured (2 Kgs 22:13–20) – does not stem the tide of judgment but rather prepares Judah for its transformation into an exilic people.[100] That is, Josiah sets the example for the narrator and reader to emulate as YHWH's people in exile.

The narrative therefore establishes a clear continuity between the implied audience and biblical Israel but rhetorically situates the reader in the liminal space between the Israels of the past and future – between punishment and restoration – at a time when both the ideal and the polity of Israel remain unrealized. That is, the present community of the reader

---

those from other nations to the region of Samaria. On neo-Assyrian policies of deportation and its application to the Israelite deportations, see Oded, *Mass Deportations*; Oded, "Assyrian Rule"; Na'aman, "Population Changes"; Younger, "Deportations"; Na'aman and Zadok, "Assyrian Deportations"; Galil, "Israelite Exiles in Media."

[97] Cf. the discussion on the Samaritans in Chapter 2.

[98] Cf. McConville, "Narrative and Meaning," 42–46; Mullen, *Narrative History*, 281; Hans-Detlef Hoffmann, *Reform und Reformen: Untersuchungen zu einem Grundthema der deuteronomistischen Geschichtsschreibung*, ATANT 66 (Zurich: TVZ, 1980), 154–55.

[99] McConville, "Narrative and Meaning," 42, 44. Cf. Collins, "Construction," 25.

[100] Linville, *Israel in the Book of Kings*, 226–53.

is rhetorically placed in continuity with biblical Israel and the restored Israel of the future but synonymous with neither. In Mullen's words, "the deuteronomistic history constitutes a two-way vision: it looks to the past to understand the present and to the future to restore the ideals that have been described as part of that past."[101] Put another way, the Former Prophets construct an Israel that remains in the second stage of the recurring cycle of apostasy, judgment, repentance, and salvation.[102] Or, as Linville puts it:

The readers in the post-monarchic world are transported into a narrative realm in which they are in a spiritually liminal, and so potentially transformative state. Somewhere betwixt and between the two ideals of retribution and salvation, they might reaffirm the covenant yet again and so have communion with the ancient god of Israel. ... There seems to me to be a deliberate paradox.[103]

By concluding on the threshold of restoration with Jehoiachin's release from prison, Kings further reinforces this paradox, as the reader remains in exile, looking back to Israel's destruction and forward towards its imminent restoration.[104] This story thus serves not as literature of appropriation and legitimation but as a permanent reminder of the incompleteness of Israel in the present and standardizes and sacralizes Jewish expectations of a fully restored Israel in the future, constructing an Israel that once was, now is not, and is to come.

CHRONICLES: ON THE THRESHOLD OF RESTORATION

Despite its relatively late authorship,[105] Chronicles exhibits a similar paradox, conspicuously summarizing the seventy years of Babylonian captivity in one

---

[101] Mullen, *Narrative History*, 284.

[102] Hans Walter Wolff, "Das Kerygma des deuteronomischen Geschichtswerks," *ZAW* 73 (1961): 171–86 (173–74).

[103] Linville, *Israel in the Book of Kings*, 251.

[104] Linville, *Israel in the Book of Kings*, 37. On the ending of 2 Kings as ambivalent, at least with respect to the Davidic kingship, see Donald F. Murray, "Of All the Years the Hopes – Or Fears? Jehoiachin in Babylon (2 Kings 25:27–30)," *JBL* 120.2 (2001): 245–65.

[105] That Chronicles was written later than and knew the Former Prophets as a source is a long-standing consensus. A wide range of dates for Chronicles have been proposed, from the late sixth century to the Maccabean era (ca. 160 BCE), but a date sometime in the fourth century, around the end of the Persian period and beginning of the Hellenistic period, holds the majority at present. Cf. Ralph W. Klein, *1 Chronicles: A Commentary on 1 Chronicles*, ed. Thomas Krüger, Hermeneia 13 (Minneapolis: Fortress, 2006), 13–16; Kai Peltonen, "A Jigsaw without a Model? The Date of Chronicles," in *Did Moses Speak Attic? Jewish History and Historiography in the Hellenistic Period*, ed.

sentence (2 Chr 36:20–21) and omitting any return from Babylon, instead concluding with Cyrus' decree that all of YHWH's people should return.[106] Thus, like Kings, Chronicles situates the reader in the space between retribution and salvation and on the cusp of restoration, looking back to Israel's heritage and destruction but with hope for Israel's future deliverance.[107]

In contrast to the Former Prophets, which trace Israel's decline back to an ideal established in Moses' time, Chronicles' sets up the Davidic/Solomonic kingdom as the standard, the time when a united Israel was at its political high point, and focuses specifically on the fate of the Davidic (Judahite) monarchy, an emphasis signaled by the careful language at the end of the genealogy, "Thus *all Israel* was enrolled by genealogies, and these are written in the book of the kings *of Israel*. And *Judah* was taken into exile *in Babylon* because of their unfaithfulness" (1 Chr 9:1). Yet again, "all Israel" is distinguished from the subset Judah, the only group of Israelites deported to Babylon. Recognizing the importance of the distinction between "all Israel" and "Judah" here, Sara Japhet goes so far as to argue that the Chronicler thus believes that "all Israel" had never in fact left the land.[108] The passage itself, however, does not suggest that "all Israel" was never exiled or that only Judah was exiled but that only Judah was exiled *to Babylon*. The other Israelites, as the reader of Chronicles is already aware, were taken into exile *but not to Babylon*.[109] This verse therefore accounts for the book's focus upon Judah as the frame begins to narrow. Nevertheless, for the purpose of understanding the distinction between the terms "Israel" and "the Jews" in later periods, such passages with their distinct language remain instructive.[110]

Lester L. Grabbe, JSOTSup 37 (Sheffield: Sheffield Academic, 2001), 225–73; Isaac Kalimi, "Die Abfassungszeit der Chronik – Forschungsstand und Perspektiven," *ZAW* 105.2 (1993): 223–33. For summaries of recent scholarship on Chronicles see Rodney K. Duke, "Recent Research in Chronicles," *CurBR* 8.1 (2009): 10–50 and John W. Kleinig, "Recent Research in Chronicles," *CurBS* 2 (1994): 43–76.

[106] Sara Japhet, "Exile and Restoration in the Book of Chronicles," in *The Crisis of Israelite Religion: Transformation of Religious Tradition in Exilic and Post-Exilic Times*, eds. Bob Becking and Marjo C. A. Korpel, OtSt 42 (Leiden: Brill, 1999), 33–44 (36).

[107] Japhet, "Exile and Restoration," 43. Japhet argues that by situating the restoration of Israel's destiny in the future rather than the past, the Chronicler opposes the perspective of Ezra-Nehemiah. The next chapter, however, will demonstrate that Ezra-Nehemiah similarly takes the position that Israel's restoration has not yet taken place.

[108] Japhet, "Exile and Restoration," 42.

[109] Japhet also points to the presence of Israelites in the land in 2 Chr 30:5, but the Chronicler places that event *before* the final Assyrian deportation, not after (see below).

[110] Knoppers, "Did Jacob Become Judah," 42, observes, "Indeed, the work plays on the different nuances of the name Israel – the patriarch Israel, the united kingdom of Saul,

Chronicles' nearly exclusive focus on the southern kingdom of Judah might at first glance seem to suggest either an anti-northern bias or that the Chronicler inclusively regards his own contemporary community as the heir to the heritage of all Israel.[111] Recent research, however, has demonstrated that Chronicles – along with its rejection of the idea that the restoration had already occurred – retains an open perspective towards the north and shows special concern for their plight, continuing to uphold the ideal of a restored (re)united twelve-tribe Israel.[112] For example, despite a general focus on Judah, the Chronicler goes out of his way to declare, "although Judah prevailed over his brothers and the leader came from him, the birthright belonged to Joseph" (1 Chr 5:2). The Chronicler also does not ignore the conquest and deportation of northern Israel, mentioning it four separate times (1 Chr 5:6, 22, 26; 2 Chr 30:9).[113] The genealogy, for example, declares that the Transjordan tribes of Reuben, Gad, and half of Manasseh (conspicuously referenced by their

---

David, and Solomon, the northern kingdom, the southern kingdom, the people of God, the future community of God's people, and so forth."

[111] The view that Chronicles is written with a sharp anti-northern bias was once standard, as can be seen in such works as Gerhard von Rad, *Das Geschichtsbild des chronistischen Werkes*, BWANT 3/4 (Stuttgart: Kohlhammer, 1930), 31; Otto Eissfeldt, *The Old Testament: An Introduction* (New York: Harper & Row, 1965), 531; Otto Plöger, *Theocracy and Eschatology*, trans. Stanley Rudman (Oxford: Blackwell, 1968), 38–41; and the summaries in Jacob M. Myers, *1 Chronicles: A New Translation with Introduction and Commentary*, AB 12 (Garden City: Doubleday, 1965), xxxii–xxxiv. For more details on the idea that only the descendants of the kingdom of Judah would make up "Israel" in the future envisioned by the Chronicler, see the discussion in Williamson, *Israel*, 97–98.

[112] Hugh G. M. Williamson, "Eschatology in Chronicles," *TynBul* 28 (1977): 115–54; Williamson, *Israel*, 69, 87–140; Sara Japhet, *The Ideology of the Book of Chronicles and Its Place in Biblical Thought*, BEATAJ 9 (Frankfurt: Lang, 1989), 308–24; Roddy L. Braun, "A Reconsideration of the Chronicler's Attitude toward the North," *JBL* 96.1 (1977): 59–62; Gary N. Knoppers, "'Battling against Yahweh': Israel's War against Judah in 2 Chr 13:2–20," *RB* 100.4 (1993): 511–32; Gary N. Knoppers, "Reform and Regression: The Chronicler's Presentation of Jehoshaphat," *Bib* 72.4 (1991): 500–24 (500–01, 523–24); Gary N. Knoppers, "Rehoboam in Chronicles: Villain or Victim?," *JBL* 109.3 (1990): 423–40; Gary N. Knoppers, "A Reunited Kingdom in Chronicles?," *Proceedings of the Great Lakes and Midwest Bible Societies* 9 (1989): 74–88; Gary N. Knoppers, "'YHWH Is Not with Israel': Alliances as a Topos in Chronicles," *CBQ* 58.4 (1996): 601–26 (622–26); Steven J. Schweitzer, *Reading Utopia in Chronicles*, JSOTSup 442 (London: T&T Clark, 2007), 9–11.

[113] Japhet rightly notes that Hezekiah's decree "does not speak of 'exile' or 'expulsion' but of 'captivity'" ("Exile and Restoration," 39–40). Together with the fact that this letter was sent in the first year of Hezekiah while Samaria's destruction took place in his sixth year (see below), this is best understood as not referring to the final deportation of Samaria.

tribal names rather than geography, as in 2 Kgs 15:29) were deported by Assyria and remain in exile "to this day" (1 Chr 5:26). The Chronicler does claim that although though the northern tribes as a whole remained in exile, a few from Ephraim and Manasseh returned and lived in Jerusalem, suggesting that at least some northerners returned with Judah (9:3). But as Knoppers explains, the reference to Ephraim and Manasseh in 9:3 "should not be pressed too far. The succeeding verses, which deal only with Judah, Benjamin, and Levi, neglect Ephraim and Manasseh entirely."[114]

Unlike Kings, Chronicles spends extra time blaming the rebellious northern tribes and Jeroboam I rather than Solomon's heavy hand for the division of the kingdom and loss of unity.[115] Nevertheless, the north remains an essential part of Israel and is not to be marginalized, as demonstrated by the inclusion of the northern tribes in the genealogy of chapters 2–8. Thus, although the Chronicler focuses on Judah, Levi, and Benjamin, these three tribes are presented in the context of a framework that necessarily includes the other tribes of Israel.[116] Along the same lines, Chronicles' report of Hezekiah's invitation for northerners to participate in the Passover celebration in Jerusalem suggests an attempt to reintegrate the remnant of the north under the Davidic dynasty in the wake of Assyrian invasions.[117] This is part of a larger pattern; the kings of Judah most highly evaluated in Chronicles – Asa, Jehoshaphat, Hezekiah, and Josiah – are all lauded for their efforts to unify with the "remnant" from the north (e.g. 2 Chr 34:9).[118] But the Chronicler makes it clear that Hezekiah's efforts failed, with his envoys unsuccessful in their attempts to gain northern allegiance, instead being "scorned and mocked" (2 Chr 30:10) by those to whom they were sent with the exception of "some from Asher, Manasseh, and Zebulun" (30:11). It is also surely no accident that in the Chronicler's time scheme Hezekiah's invitation *precedes* the final destruction of Samaria and consequent deportation by five years, implying that had the northerners only returned to the Davidic kingdom, they might have managed to avoid such a

---

[114] Gary N. Knoppers, *I Chronicles 1–9: A New Translation with Introduction and Commentary*, AB 12A (New York: Doubleday, 2003), 501.

[115] See Roddy L. Braun, "Solomonic Apologetic in Chronicles," *JBL* 92.4 (1973): 503–16.

[116] Klein, *1 Chronicles*, 46. Cf. also Knoppers, "Rehoboam in Chronicles."

[117] Collins, "Construction," 25.

[118] See Williamson, *Israel*, 119–31, who notes the distinctiveness of the Chronicler's application of the concept of "remnant" to those from the north (126, 131).

devastating fate.[119] This is an important point, as this passage is regularly cited as evidence that "Chronicles depicts a sizable Israelite remnant remaining in the land following the Assyrian invasions and deportations."[120]

Instead, Assyria did destroy the northern kingdom and returned a short time later under Sennacherib, devastating Judah and isolating Jerusalem, exiling and scattering many Judahites and Israelite refugees who had fled from the north during the prior Assyrian campaigns.[121] The efforts of the other kings of Judah meet with similar failures, and the northerners who reject their overtures similarly receive due recompense for their continued rebellion.[122] The Chronicler therefore does not – as Collins suggests based on the Hezekiah Passover narrative – declare surviving Judah to be the whole of Israel but instead highlights the continued incompleteness of Israel, a circumstance Hezekiah hopes to amend through his reforms. The Septuagint further emphasizes this negative present state with an addition at the end of Hezekiah's statement to the priests and Levites, "And your sons and your daughters and wives are captives in a land that is not theirs – *as it is even now* (ὁ καὶ νῦν ἐστιν)" (2 Chr 29:9).[123] Nevertheless, despite these past failures, the Chronicler continues to look forward to a future far better than that known in his

---

[119] Japhet, "Exile and Restoration," 40 n. 19, observes that 2 Kgs 18:10 places the fall of Samaria in the sixth year of Hezekiah while Chronicles puts Hezekiah's invitation to celebrate the Passover in his first year (2 Chr 29:37; 30:2), commenting, "One wonders whether this blurring of the historical sequence was not done on purpose." Despite her observation, Japhet still assumes that Chronicles regards the destruction of Samaria as "already a matter of the past" at this point in the story, but there is nothing in Chronicles to suggest that. Williamson's analysis of the Chronicler's portrayal of Hezekiah overlooks this fact, treating 30:6 as occurring after the fall of Samaria and therefore concluding that the Chronicler portrays Hezekiah as having been successful in reunifying north and south (*Israel*, 125–27).

[120] Knoppers, "Nehemiah and Sanballat," 321, citing 2 Chr 30:6–9.

[121] 2 Chr 32 // 2 Kgs 18–19 (esp. 18:13–25). Chronicles does not narrate the final sack of Samaria and deemphasizes Sennacherib's destructive work in Judah, focusing instead on Jerusalem's survival, but even in Chronicles it is clear Israel is still not united and that Judah itself did not fare especially well. An Assyrian source records that Sennacherib took 200,150 captives from the Southern Kingdom, a number that was surely inflated but still reflects significant destruction. See Barmash, "Nexus," 220–25; Marco de Odorico, *The Use of Numbers and Quantifications in the Assyrian Royal Inscriptions*, SAAS (Helsinki: Neo-Assyrian Text Corpus Project, 1995), esp. 171–87; J. B. Pritchard, ed., *Ancient Near Eastern Texts*, 3rd ed. (Princeton: Princeton University Press, 1969), 287–89. Inasmuch as northerners had fled south during earlier Assyrian campaigns, many were likely caught in the Assyrian net a second time.

[122] Braun, "Reconsideration," 60–62.

[123] See Scott, "Self-Understanding," 187. Cf. also 1 Chr 5:26.

present community, to a restoration of the unity and majesty of all Israel as in the time of David and Solomon.[124]

This hope for restoration fits closely together with Chronicles' replacement of the Deuteronomic History's model of accumulated sin or merit and inevitable decline with a more immediate system of reward and punishment, repentance and restoration, a model consistent with the concept of individual (rather than intergenerational) responsibility advocated in Ezekiel 18 (cf. also Jer 31:29–30 MT).[125] This shift has led some to see Chronicles as promoting a mechanistic principle of absolute divine justice.[126] Others, however, have observed that although Chronicles clearly emphasizes the connection between conduct and recompense, the prominent theme of repentance and consequent mercy serves to emphasize YHWH's benevolence and covenantal mercy over and against deserved retribution.[127] Those who repent (that is, turn from their disobedience) are restored straightaway, as changed behavior is swiftly followed by divine mercy that overcomes even the severest of divine punishments.[128]

---

[124] See Klein, *1 Chronicles*, 46–48; Japhet, "Exile and Restoration," 44; Manfred Oeming, *Das wahre Israel: Die "genealogische Vorhalle" 1 Chronik 1–9*, Beiträge zur Wissenschaft vom Alten und Neuen Testament (Stuttgart: Kohlhammer, 1990); Williamson, "Eschatology"; Rad, *Das Geschichtsbild*, 123–27. But cf. Donald F. Murray, "Dynasty, People, and the Future: The Message of Chronicles," *JSOT* 58 (1993): 71–92.

[125] See Japhet, *Ideology*, 161–76; Klein, *1 Chronicles*, 46. Chronicles consequently lacks Kings' persistent sense of entropy and some of the tension between Israel's history and the ideal of Israel is transferred to a tension between (ideal) past and present, as the ideal is always in reach but never achieved after Solomon.

[126] See the discussion in Japhet, *Ideology*, 150–65.

[127] This is the basic argument of Brian E. Kelly, *Retribution and Eschatology in Chronicles*, JSOTSup 211 (London: T&T Clark, 1996).

[128] David Lambert has recently challenged the idea that "repentance" is a biblical concept at all, suggesting that it postdates the Second Temple period, largely on the grounds that for earlier periods the world was understood as determined by divine fiat rather than human choice. See David A. Lambert, "Did Israel Believe that Redemption Awaited Its Repentance? The Case of Jubilees 1," *CBQ* 68.4 (2006): 631–50 and now especially *How Repentance Became Biblical*. The difference here mostly is a semantic one, however, as Lambert understands repentance as roughly equivalent to contrition or an inward sense of regret, sorrow, or remorse akin to what Stendahl calls the "introspective conscience" (*How Repentance Became Biblical*, 1, 9, 154–55; cf. Krister Stendahl, "The Apostle Paul and the Introspective Conscience of the West," *HTR* 56.3 (1963): 199–215). Lambert rightly objects to the importation of such introspective contrition to the biblical texts, but a concept of repentance understood as a change of behavior (sometimes including a rite of self-affliction, which again need not indicate inner contrition, as explained in *How Repentance Became Biblical*, 13–31) is a theme that

This principle is perhaps best illustrated by the dramatic difference between the portrayal of Manasseh in Kings and Chronicles. In Chronicles, while in the midst of his own personal exile – a punishment for his severe rebellion against YHWH – Manasseh repents and is astonishingly restored to his throne over Judah. Likewise, the Chronicler's own generation, who themselves continue to suffer the consequences of Israel's rebellion, will be restored if only they "humble themselves and pray and seek [YHWH's] face and turn from their wicked ways" (2 Chr 7:14).[129] Thus, although the north is clearly depicted as "in rebellion against the house of David to this day" (2 Chr 10:19 // 1 Kgs 12:19), those from the north are still but one act of repentance away from a full restoration. Even better, if those *in the land* "return to YHWH" wholeheartedly, even those who have been scattered in exile will be restored to the land (2 Chr 30:6–9).[130]

This close connection between repentance and restoration established throughout Chronicles puts additional emphasis on the way the book ends – with a call to all YHWH's people to return, spurring the merciful YHWH to restore Israel as promised. The Chronicler thus contemporizes the promises and original traditions of his *Vorlage* not by applying them to his own "restored" community but by transforming them into "a challenge that is presented afresh to each generation."[131] Thus Solomon

---

appears throughout biblical literature, as Lambert himself acknowledges, though he distinguishes this from the term "repentance" (71–90), which is precisely the term I am using for such change of behavior. That is, when I use the term "repentance" or "repent," I mean exactly what Lambert suggests for the term שוב (often translated "return"): "a dramatic change in direction, motion that is opposite in some fashion, a turning away/aside/around/back/off" (73), independent of a psychological state of sorrow or contrition. In addition, the use of "repentance" language need not presume that human agency precedes divine transformation, which (as Lambert notes) restoration passages often characterize as a prerequisite to repentance leading to restoration. Rather than regarding repentance as inherently based in human agency, it is possible to speak of divinely initiated repentance, which seems to most closely approximate the perspective of many biblical passages. The point is that Israel changes behavior (repents) through a divinely granted transformation/repentance, leading to Israel's restoration.

[129] On 2 Chr 7 as the utopian era of foundations both anticipating the future decline and desolation and providing the key to its revival, see Donald F. Murray, "Retribution and Revival: Theological Theory, Religious Praxis, and the Future in Chronicles," *JSOT* 88 (2000): 77–99 (92–96).

[130] Klein, *1 Chronicles*, 48.

[131] Kelly, *Retribution and Eschatology*, 181; cf. Sara Japhet, *I & II Chronicles: A Commentary*, OTL (Louisville: Westminster John Knox, 1993), 491; Hahn, *The Kingdom of God as Liturgical Empire*, 33.

prays that YHWH would "bring [the exiles] back again to the land which you gave *to them* and to their fathers" (2 Chr 6:25, my emphasis), a reminder to contemporary readers "that they too had been 'given' the land," if only they would return in faithfulness to YHWH.[132] The restoration has not yet happened, but it is ever within reach. In this manner, "the Chronicler indicates how Israel may continue to possess its inheritance ... and he holds out the possibility of a more extensive fulfilment."[133] This is all the more true in light of the fact that the allotted time of punishment (the seventy years predicted by Jeremiah) has long passed (2 Chr 36:20–21), though the promised restoration has not yet been fulfilled. In his concluding statement, the Chronicler thus enjoins the reader to emulate model penitents such as David, thereby participating in Israel's restoration and return to YHWH.[134] This conclusion would gain even more rhetorical punch for later readers for whom a proto-canon ended with 2 Chronicles (cf. Mt. 23:35), as the very last word of the Hebrew Bible is then the final word of the Chronicler: "let him go up" (ויעל).[135]

CONCLUSION: BETWEEN BIBLICAL ISRAEL AND RESTORATION

The narratives of the Torah, Former Prophets, and Chronicles thus position their readers, their communities, in a liminal position awaiting Israel's restoration. Each displays a relative negativity or ambivalence toward the present conditions of the implied audience and looks hopefully towards the future. As such, the Former Prophets and Chronicles are, in Steven Schweitzer's words, "*revolutionary texts* designed to challenge the *status quo* and question the way things presently are being done."[136] In much the same manner as utopias, these stories "seek to

---

[132] Kelly, *Retribution and Eschatology*, 181.

[133] Kelly, *Retribution and Eschatology*, 182; cf. Sara Japhet, "Post-exilic Historiography," in *Deuteronomistic Historiography in Recent Research (306)*, eds. Albert de Pury, Thomas Römer, and Jean-Daniel Machi (Sheffield: Sheffield Academic, 2000), 144–73 (166, 172).

[134] On David as a model penitent in Chronicles – and the observation that the location of the temple itself is based upon an act of penitence – see Gary N. Knoppers, *I Chronicles 10–29: A New Translation with Introduction and Commentary*, AB 12B (New York: Doubleday, 2004), 763–64.

[135] Tucker S. Ferda, "John the Baptist, Isaiah 40, and the Ingathering of the Exiles," *JSHJ* 10.2 (2012): 154–88 (158–59); Talmon, "'Exile' and 'Restoration,'" 118.

[136] Schweitzer, *Reading Utopia in Chronicles*, 18, emphasis his. Schweitzer applies utopian literary theory to Chronicles, arguing that Chronicles reframes Israelite history to

re-describe 'what is' in a way that disrupts the present order,"[137] critique
the present situation, and imagine alternative futures for the community,
providing a powerful system of meaning that can serve to bind the
community together moving forward.[138] Rather than doing this "from
nowhere" (ou-topos), however, these authors instead reframed and retold
the past to imagine a "better alternative reality" for the present
community.[139]

For these books, the present community, though in continuity with
Israel, does not even *approximate* Israel. Instead, the present situation and
community is situated in the liminal space between punishment and
restoration, between the curses of the covenant and the reconciliation of
Israel and YHWH.[140] The "better alternative reality" envisioned
throughout this literature consistently involves a restored Israel including
all twelve tribes and featuring perfect covenantal obedience and cultic
practice. There seems to have been less certainty or agreement about the

---

critique the present situation and imagine better alternatives for the future. In similar
fashion, David Janzen has argued that Chronicles is a fourth-century BCE argument for
the restoration of Davidic leadership as a client monarchy under within the Persian
Empire (*Chronicles and the Politics of Davidic Restoration: A Quiet Revolution*
[London: Bloomsbury, 2017]).

[137] Grassie, "Entangled Narratives," 152.

[138] These are the second and third stages of Paul Ricoeur's three-stage model for the
functions of utopia *vis-à-vis* ideological legitimation. See Paul Ricoeur, *Lectures on
Ideology and Utopia*, ed. George H. Taylor (New York: Columbia University Press,
1986), xxi–xxiii, 16–17, 179–80. For more on utopian or idealistic literature and
utopian literary theory in general, see in addition Steven J. Schweitzer, "Utopia and
Utopian Literary Theory: Some Preliminary Observations," in *Utopia and Dystopia in
Prophetic Literature*, ed. Ehud Ben Zvi, PFES (Göttingen: Vandenhoeck & Ruprecht,
2006), 13–26; Lyman Tower Sargent, "The Three Faces of Utopianism," *Minnesota
Review* 7.3 (1967): 222–30; Lyman Tower Sargent, "The Three Faces of Utopianism
Revisited," *Utopian Studies* 5.1 (1994): 1–37; and especially Steven J. Schweitzer,
"Reading Utopia in Chronicles" (PhD diss., University of Notre Dame, 2005), 31–35
and the many sources cited there. For more specific applications of utopian literary
theory to biblical criticism, see Schweitzer, *Reading Utopia in Chronicles*; Ehud Ben Zvi,
ed., *Utopia and Dystopia in Prophetic Literature*, PFES (Göttingen: Vandenhoeck &
Ruprecht, 2006); Roland Boer, *Novel Histories: The Fiction of Biblical Criticism*, PT
(Sheffield: Sheffield Academic, 1997); John J. Collins, "Models of Utopia in the Biblical
Tradition," in *A Wise and Discerning Mind: Essays in Honor of Burke O. Long*, eds.
Burke O. Long, Saul M. Olyan, and Robert C. Culley (2000), 51–67; Thomas P. Wahl,
"Chronicles: The Rewriting of History," *TBT* 26 (1988): 197–202; Mary Ann Beavis,
"The Kingdom of God, 'Utopia' and Theocracy," *JSHJ* 2.1 (2004): 91–106.

[139] Cf. Schweitzer, *Reading Utopia in Chronicles*, 175.

[140] Cf. Jonathan G. Campbell, "Essene-Qumran Origins in the Exile: A Scriptural Basis?,"
JJS 46.1–2 (1995): 143–56 (148).

restoration of the Davidic kingship, but a restoration of a unified monarchy under covenantally obedient Davidic rulers seems to be a part of the ideal future more often than not.[141]

The implication is that the only proper recourse for the reader of these texts, stuck between retribution and reconciliation, is to return to YHWH, in whose hands Israel's future rests.[142] In the implied present reflected in these narratives, Israel – having been destroyed and scattered but not yet restored – no longer exists in its fullness but is instead still awaiting redemption. The expectations of redemption reflected in these narratives are, of course, drawn from the classical Hebrew prophets, whose glorious prophecies of restoration undergirded the construction of Judaism itself. Indeed, these works – particularly the Deuteronomic History as the "former" part of the prophetic corpus – provide the framework for later interpretations of the prophets, reinforcing and reframing the Latter Prophets' predictions of punishment followed by miraculous restoration.

Finally, given that these works are all from the perspective of the southern kingdom, the incorporation of northern Israelite traditions and the emphasis on the unity of all Israel (both northern and southern tribes) also rhetorically establishes the dominant position of the *Yehudim/ Ioudaioi* relative to other claimants to the heritage of Israel. Indeed, these stories recognize Ephraim's primacy and importance while simultaneously arguing that Ephraim's failures led to Judah being designated the leading tribe of Israel and thereby diminishing any rival claims to authority within the people of Israel.[143] Indeed, "Israel remains in rebellion against the house of David to this day" (1 Kgs 12:19; 2 Chr 10:19). From the perspective of these southern editors, Israel's full restoration will not only feature the reunification and restoration of all twelve tribes but the proper submission of the rest of Israel to the *Yehudim* and Jerusalem's claim on YHWH's name.

---

[141] As suggested by 1 Chr 13:4–8; 2 Kgs 25:27–30, etc. For a strong argument that Chronicles still expects a restoration of the Davidic line, cf. Williamson, "Eschatology," 133–54. On the uncertain details of this imagined future, cf. Roland Boer's observations in his response to Schweitzer in Mark J. Boda et al., "In Conversation with Steven Schweitzer, *Reading Utopia in Chronicles* (LHBOTS, 442; London: T&T Clark International, 2007)," *JHebS* 9 (2009): 1–19 (13).

[142] Cf. Schweitzer's conclusion in Boda et al., "Conversation," 18.

[143] For a nuanced argument of this point, see T. Desmond Alexander, "Royal Expectations in Genesis to Kings," *TynBul* 49.2 (1998): 191–212; Alexander, "Royal Expectations."

4

Between Disaster and Restoration

The Prophets, Exile, and Restoration Eschatology

But what does "Israel" mean when a large part of the nation has been taken away into exile in Assyria? . . . The story of the prophetic books involves re-thinking who "Israel" is.

J. Gordon McConville[1]

The biblical narratives provide the frame for the proclamations of the Latter Prophets, themselves edited and collected in the shadow of exile.[2] Although the various prophets each have their own distinctive emphases, most of the prophetic books follow a common paradigm in which the prophet warns of the consequences of covenantal disobedience (especially exile), declares the covenant broken, and nevertheless promises a glorious future restoration. What is most surprising, however, given that these books were collected and codified by southern *Yehudim*, is the amount of attention the prophetic corpus pays to the northern Israelites.[3] Some books (like Hosea and Amos) are nearly exclusively focused on northern Israel, and even those with a more southern orientation continue to keep the north in view.[4] Modern scholarship has tended to interpret this continued attention to Israel as evidence that the *Yehudim* were narrowing the legacy of larger Israel to include only themselves, but a closer look at the prophetic corpus shows otherwise.

---

[1] J. Gordon McConville, *Exploring the Old Testament, Volume 4: A Guide to the Prophets* (Downers Grove: InterVarsity Press, 2002), xxiv.

[2] See especially Peter R. Ackroyd, *Exile and Restoration: A Study of Hebrew Thought of the Sixth Century BC (Louisville: Westminster John Knox, 1968).*

[3] See Coggins, *Samaritans and Jews*, 28–37.

[4] See Stephen D. Ricks, "The Prophetic Literality of Tribal Reconstruction," in *Israel's Apostasy and Restoration: Essays in Honor of Roland K. Harrison*, ed. Avraham Gileadi (Grand Rapids: Baker Books, 1988), 273–81.

ISAIAH: DESTRUCTION, RETURN, REUNION

Not only is the book of Isaiah of chief importance in the tradition, it has long been viewed as a prime witness to the transformation of the name Israel "both in the history of Israel and in the literary history" of the Bible itself.[5] That is, the concept of Israel has long been understood to narrow as one moves forward in the book, from a broader vision in First Isaiah to much more restrictive definitions in Second and especially Third Isaiah.[6] According to this view, Knoppers explains,

When the writers of Deutero-Isaiah speak of Israel, the remnant of Israel, or of Israel's return from exile, the assumption is that Israel designates Judah, the Babylonian Judean exiles, or some subset thereof. With respect to Trito-Isaiah, a further set of distinctions comes into view. If the title Israel is applied to the Babylonian exiles in Deutero-Isaiah, it can be further restricted in Trito-Isaiah "to a faithful individual or group within the community."[7]

Knoppers, however, has rightly questioned this old consensus as "problematic on a number of different counts,"[8] complaining that there is no evidence outside Isaiah itself for such shifts of meaning, as evidenced by the fact that various scholarly reconstructions have suggested dates for such transformations that differ by hundreds of years.[9] More importantly, it is unclear how a premodern reader operating under the assumption of unified authorship of Isaiah would read these passages as anything but indications of broader Israelite identity. After all, Isaiah of Jerusalem lived and prophesied during the Assyrian onslaught (cf. 2 Kgs 19–20 // 2 Chr 32), which Judah was the only kingdom among its neighbors to survive. As a result, although Isaiah was a southern prophet, more than half of the book (that is, First Isaiah) is concerned with the Assyrian threat, the destruction of the northern kingdom, and the future

---

[5] Reinhard G. Kratz, "Israel in the Book of Isaiah," *JSOT* 31.1 (2006): 103–28 (103).

[6] On the tripartite division of Isaiah (chaps. 1–39; 40–55; 56–66), see Christopher R. Seitz, *Zion's Final Destiny: The Development of the Book of Isaiah: A Reassessment of Isaiah 36–39* (Minneapolis: Fortress, 1991).

[7] Knoppers, "Did Jacob Become Judah," 48. The quote is from Hugh G. M. Williamson, "The Concept of Israel in Transition," in *The World of Ancient Israel: Sociological, Anthropological and Political Perspectives*, ed. Ronald E. Clements (Cambridge: Cambridge University Press, 1989), 141–61 (147), who further argues, "the author of Isaiah 40–55 ... was far less of a visionary than Ezekiel [!], addressing himself directly to the situation of his own community, whom he calls Jacob/Israel. Their lack of response, however, led to a shift in his aspirations and he seems to have experienced the need to narrow the meaning of Israel quite sharply."

[8] Knoppers, "Did Jacob Become Judah," 51.

[9] Knoppers, "Did Jacob Become Judah," 49.

restoration of the remnant of the north along with the salvation of Judah.[10] As Knoppers points out, it is "quite important" that the opening lines of the book use the term Israel to denote a broad concept not limited to those from Judah.[11] The operational definition of Israel in the first chapters of Isaiah, setting the tone for the rest of the work, therefore includes and even focuses on the northern kingdom of Israel rather than Judah.

Isaiah 7–12 in particular address the Syro-Ephraimite conflict and its consequences, the Assyrian invasion and deportation of both Aram (Damascus) and Ephraim (Samaria). But the prophet by no means suggests that Israel will be entirely extirpated, nor does the book hint at a forthcoming terminological transition. Rather, in the midst of proclaiming the destruction of the disobedient north, the prophet declares that a remnant will remain and return, adding that the rivalry between Israel and Judah will be what passes away:

Then on that day, root of Jesse will stand as a signal to the peoples, nations will seek him (OG/LXX: καὶ ὁ ἀνιστάμενος ἄρχειν ἐθνῶν), and his dwelling place will be glorious. And on that day YHWH will with his hand a second time recover the remaining remnant of his people – from Assyria, Egypt, Pathros, Cush, Elam, Shinar, Hamath, and from the islands of the sea.

> And he will lift a standard for the nations
> > and assemble the banished (OG/LXX:
> ἀπολομένους) ones of Israel.
> And he will gather the dispersed of Judah
> > from the four corners of the earth.
> Then the jealousy of Ephraim will depart,
> > and the hostility of Judah will be cut off.
> Ephraim will not be jealous of Judah,
> > and Judah will not be hostile towards Ephraim.
> And there will be a highway from Assyria
> > for the remnant of his people who will be left,
> Just as there was for Israel
> > in the day that they came out of Egypt.
> > > (11:10–13, 16)

---

[10] Kratz, "Israel," 127–28: "The texts surrounding the *Denkschrift* in Isaiah 5 and Isaiah 9 express this point more clearly and unite both kingdoms, the 'two houses of Israel', into 'Israel' as the one people of God, consisting of Ephraim (Samaria) and Judah (Jerusalem)."

[11] Knoppers, "Did Jacob Become Judah," 50. Cf. Hugh G. M. Williamson, *The Book Called Isaiah: Deutero-Isaiah's Role in Composition and Redaction* (Oxford: Clarendon, 1994), 153–54; Hugh G. M. Williamson, *Isaiah 1–5*, ICC (London: T&T Clark, 2006), 9–11.

The Old Greek version revises the prophecy of return in verse 16, placing the focus on those remaining in Egypt (where the translation originated), with the highway (διοδος) made not for the remnant in Assyria but for "my people left in Egypt" – that is the community of the translators.[12] The reference to the root of Jesse is further strengthened in the Greek, with the one who arises "ruling over the nations," which surely would have reinforced the restoration expectations among the Egyptian diaspora.[13] The translators did not, however, eliminate the earlier references to Assyria in vv. 11–13, focusing the attention on their own community's part in the restoration only in v. 16. This focus on the whole of Israel remains constant throughout First Isaiah, as Isa 17:4–11 and chapter 28 likewise focus on the impending destruction of Israel/Ephraim by Assyria, much of chapters 14–23 deals with the fate of the surrounding nations in the face of Assyrian (and Babylonian) power, and chapters 36–37 deal with the final Assyrian threat to Jerusalem after the destruction of Samaria.

The focus on "Israel" is by no means diminished after the transition to a new context in Deutero-Isaiah, which most interpreters have found problematic in light of the events of the previous centuries. Gordon McConville, for example, muses:

In Isa. 41:8 the prophet addresses "Israel." Historically, however, Israel no longer existed, since the largest part of it was destroyed for ever in 722 BC[E], and the Jewish exiles in Babylon had come from Judah. Why then does the prophet use this term (and its parallel, Jacob)?[14]

Williamson expresses similar puzzlement, asking, "What now *is* Israel?"[15] Given the presumption that Judah was all that remained of Israel by this time, the usual conclusion has been that the book here witnesses to a transition in Israel's meaning. No longer does Israel mean Israel; rather, when Deutero-Isaiah says Israel, he must now mean specific

---

[12] For more on Old Greek Isaiah, see Mirjam Van der Vorm-Croughs, *The Old Greek of Isaiah: An Analysis of Its Pluses and Minuses* (Atlanta: Society of Biblical Literature, 2014); J. Ross Wagner, *Reading the Sealed Book: Old Greek Isaiah and the Problem of Septuagint Hermeneutics* (Waco: Baylor University Press, 2013); Abi T. Ngunga, *Messianism in the Old Greek of Isaiah: An Intertextual Analysis*, FRLANT 245 (Göttingen: Vandenhoeck & Ruprecht, 2012); Isac Leo Seeligmann, *The Septuagint Version of Isaiah and Cognate Studies*, ed. Robert Hanhart and Hermann Spieckermann, FAT 40 (Tübingen: Mohr Siebeck, 2004).
[13] Scott, "Self-Understanding," 193; cf. also LXX Isa 27:12–13 and Zech 10:9–10.
[14] McConville, *Prophets*, 24.
[15] Williamson, "Concept of Israel," 142.

people from Judah, demonstrating a narrowing of scope in salvation history.[16] But the Jacob-became-Judah theory presumes what it must prove, as there is no clear indication in the text that Israel has come to mean Judah (or a specific group within Judah), nor would an ancient reader be predisposed to such a transition after having read the first thirty-nine chapters.[17] That is, although it is true that Deutero-Isaiah is centrally concerned with Zion/Jerusalem/Judah, that does not mean that the term Israel in these sections must *only* refer to these more limited reference points. Instead, as Knoppers points out, the very choice of the broader term "points to the people as a whole, rather than some part thereof."[18]

Limiting Deutero-Isaiah's scope to Judah has the helpful effect of limiting the prophet's scope to what actually happened historically with the return of some Jews from Babylon, thus protecting the prophet against overstatement. But ignoring the distinctive use of the broader term in this context and treating it as though the prophet actually means the narrower group misses the force of Deutero-Isaiah's proclamation that not only Judah but the whole people of Israel will be miraculously restored by the divine action of YHWH. The very point of these passages is that Judah's present restoration is only the beginning, that YHWH will in fact redeem and restore his whole people as promised in the past. This is certainly how ancient readers seem to have understood Isaiah, as evident from the interpretive alterations to Isa 40:1–4 in the Isaiah Targum, which adds that Jerusalem "is about to be filled with people of her exiles" along with several other alterations clearly placing the fulfillment of the passage in the future.[19]

---

[16] Thus John D. W. Watts, *Isaiah 1–33*, WBC 24 (Grand Rapids: Zondervan, 2005), 508, simply declares "Israel" to be "the exiles from Babylon" or "the Babylonian diaspora" (511), seemingly without any thought about the implications of such a terminological shift. Instead, Watts simply declares without argument, "While Israel was understood first to have a political role as the northern kingdom (1:2–7; chaps. 5, 10), in chaps. 40–48 the role has evolved so she here becomes simply YHWH's servant people in exile" (505), again ignoring the problem of the north's fate entirely. Remarkably, Baltzer entirely ignores the problem in his discussions of Second Isaiah, e.g. Klaus Baltzer, *Deutero-Isaiah: A Commentary on Isaiah 40–55*, Hermeneia 23C (Minneapolis: Fortress, 2000), 82–83, 95–102.

[17] Knoppers, "Did Jacob Become Judah," 52.

[18] Knoppers, "Did Jacob Become Judah," 54.

[19] For a comparison of Targum Isa 40:1–4 with the Hebrew text and analysis of the changes, see Ferda, "Ingathering of the Exiles," 182–83. The translation from the Targum here is Ferda's.

Far from being satisfied with and glorying in the present state of affairs, the prophet vividly proclaims the expectations of a more expansive restoration through the direct intervention of YHWH himself, hoping for more than merely a return of *Yehudim* from Babylon. Rather than limiting the scope to Judah's restoration from Babylon, the prophet proclaims the regathering of Israel from all four directions of the compass (Isa 43:5–7). Another example is even more telling:

> Listen to me, house of Jacob,
>> All the remnant of the house of Israel,[20]
> Those who have been carried since birth,
>> To those borne since leaving the womb.
> To old age, I am he,
>> To declining years I will carry.
> I have acted and I will bear,
>> I will carry and I will bring to safety.
>
> (Isa 46:3–4)

It is difficult to explain why, if the "remnant of the house of Israel" is in fact code for a small group of Judahite returnees from Babylon, the prophet uses such remarkably expansive language.[21] Indeed the larger frame of Deutero-Isaiah clearly includes – indeed focuses on – the whole of Israel, highlighting Israel's status as "my [=YHWH's] servant" (41:8; 44:21; 49:3; etc.). The salvation envisioned is expressly comprehensive:

> And now, says YHWH,
>> the one who formed me from the womb to be his servant,
> To restore Jacob to himself,
>> so that Israel might be gathered to him.
> He said to me,
> "It is too small for you to be my servant,
>> To establish the tribes of Jacob,
>> and to restore the survivors of Israel.
> I will make you a light of the nations,
>> to be my salvation to the ends of the earth."
>
> (Isa 49:5–6)

This passage makes that all-encompassing scope all the more explicit with its reference to "the tribes of Jacob," a phrase that "by definition includes more than the Judeans or the Judean exiles. If the writer had a very limited perspective, it would be odd to leap from that highly restrictive charge to

---

[20] MT: כל־שארית בית ישראל; OG/LXX: πᾶν τὸ κατάλοιπον τοῦ Ἰσραήλ.

[21] Knoppers, "Did Jacob Become Judah," 58.

an international mandate."[22] That international mandate to be a "light to the nations" (42:6) is especially striking, as it "closely aligns the restoration of the scattered tribes of Israel with the redemption of the nations."[23] Thus the fulfillment of the promise to Abraham that all nations would be blessed (Gen 22:18; 26:4) here coincides with the regathering of all Israel, with the servant fulfilling the mission for which Israel was chosen (cf. Exod 19:5–6).[24] The famous passage in Isa 52 likewise rather strikingly references oppression not by the Babylonians but the Assyrians, comparing the present situation to Israel's oppression in Egypt before the exodus:

Thus says YHWH: "You were sold without money and you will be redeemed without money." For thus says the Lord YHWH: "My people went down at first into Egypt to reside there. Then the Assyrian oppressed them without cause. Now then," declares YHWH, "What do I have here, since my people have been taken away without cause?" YHWH declares, "Those who rule over them howl, and my name is continually blasphemed all day long. My people will therefore know my name; thus in that day I am the one who is speaking, 'Here I am.'" How lovely on the mountains are the feet of him who brings good news! (Isa 52:3–7a)[25]

An ancient reader of Isaiah, who would of course read this prophetic book as a unity, would thus be continually reminded of both the Babylonian Exile but also of Assyria's destruction of Israel and the promise of a restoration of the Israelites scattered in the first half of the book, a miraculous event that still lay in the future. In addition, not only will Israel be regathered and restored (56:8, etc.), this restoration will have global implications. The poet's vision is therefore by no means limited to those from Judah, nor should it be assumed that "Israel" transitions to mean something narrower as the book goes on. If anything, rather than moving toward an increasingly limited definition of Israel, we find the very opposite. By the end of the book, the emphasis is that "[YHWH's] salvific intentions have the potential to include an

---

[22] Knoppers, "Did Jacob Become Judah," 59.

[23] Rafael Rodríguez, *If You Call Yourself a Jew: Reappraising Paul's Letter to the Romans* (Eugene: Cascade, 2014), 5.

[24] Cf. Abraham J. Heschel, *The Prophets*, Perennial Classics (San Francisco: HarperCollins, 2001), 17, 197–99, 269–71.

[25] Baltzer, *Deutero-Isaiah*, 371–75, suggests that this section is consciously connected with the account of Sennacherib's campaign in Isa 36–37 while also reminding of the Assyrian destruction of Israel. Watts, *Isaiah 1–33*, 775, observes that "two earlier exiles [Egypt and Assyria] are cited," but presumes that the Babylonian captivity is actually the topic here (apparently because the Assyrian captivity had ended?), despite the absence of Babylon from the passage.

international body of persons while excluding members of the intra-national community that fails to observe certain requisite behaviors."[26] Indeed, by the end of the book, YHWH declares, "they will declare my glory among the nations ... and I will also take some of them as priests and as Levites" (Isa 66:19c, 21). With such utopian language anticipating the end of exile and the reversal of the covenantal curses even to the point that the nations will have access to the holy, the final chapters implicitly extend the conditions of exile into the present.[27]

BOOK OF THE TWELVE: FROM NOT MY PEOPLE TO MY PEOPLE

Similar concern not only for Judah but also for the northern kingdom of Israel and its fate in the wake of its dissolution at the hands of Assyria is not only present but is strikingly prominent throughout the Book of the Twelve (Minor Prophets).[28] Hosea, the first of the Twelve, was himself a northern prophet who declared that YHWH had divorced Israel (that is, the northern kingdom) due to its idolatry – they are now "not my people" (לא עמי/οὐ λαός μου; Hos 1:9–2:1 [ET 1:10]), a phrase alluding to and

[26] Jill A. Middlemas, "Trito-Isaiah's Intra- and Internationalization: Identity Markers in the Second Temple period," in *Judah and the Judeans in the Achaemenid Period: Negotiating Identity in an International Context*, eds. Oded Lipschits, Gary N. Knoppers, and Manfred Oeming (Winona Lake: Eisenbrauns, 2011), 105–25 (122). Cf. also Christophe Nihan, "Ethnicity and Identity in Isaiah 56–66," in *Judah and the Judeans in the Achaemenid Period: Negotiating Identity in an International Context*, eds. Oded Lipschits, Gary N. Knoppers, and Manfred Oeming (Winona Lake: Eisenbrauns, 2011), 67–104 (95); Joseph Blenkinsopp, "Second Isaiah – Prophet of Universalism," *JSOT* 41 (1988): 83–103.
[27] Cf. Martien Halvorson-Taylor, *Enduring Exile: The Metaphorization of Exile in the Hebrew Bible*, VTSup 141 (Leiden: Brill, 2010), 107–49. There is no need, however, to argue that this amounts to "understanding the exile theologically rather than just historically" (as Bradley C. Gregory, "The Post-exilic Exile in Third Isaiah: Isaiah 61:1–3 in Light of Second Temple Hermeneutics," *JBL* 126.3 [2007]: 475–96 [488]), since a return of some from Judah does not end the exile of Israel as a whole.
[28] I here treat the Twelve as a collective volume, following James Nogalski, *Literary Precursors to the Book of the Twelve*, BZAW 217 (Berlin: de Gruyter, 1993); James Nogalski, *Redactional Processes in the Book of the Twelve*, BZAW 218 (Berlin: de Gruyter, 1993); James W. Watts and Paul R. House, eds., *Forming Prophetic Literature: Essays on Isaiah and the Twelve in Honor of John DW Watts*, JSOTSup 235 (Sheffield: Sheffield Academic, 1996). See also Paul L. Redditt, "Recent Research on the Book of the Twelve as One Book," *CurBS* 9 (2001): 47–80; Rainer Albertz, James Nogalski, and Jakob Wöhrle, eds., *Perspectives on the Formation of the Book of the Twelve: Methodological Foundations, Redactional Processes, Historical Insights* (Berlin: de Gruyter, 2012).

negating the covenantal language of "I will be your God and you will be my people" (Lev 26:12; cf. also 2 Sam 7:14).[29] Hosea further declares,

> Ephraim was mixed[30] with the peoples;
> Ephraim became an unturned cake. . . .
> Israel is swallowed up.
> They are now among the nations like a worthless vessel.
>
> (Hos 7:8, 8:8)

The covenant has been broken; Israel (= the north) is no longer YHWH's covenantal people and will be removed from YHWH's land and intermingled with the other nations, no longer a separate and distinct people, holy to YHWH.[31] Nevertheless, Hosea proclaims that the impending judgments will one day be reversed, when YHWH will again have mercy and call out to not-my-people, making them his people once again (Hos 2:1–3 [ET 1:10–2:1]; 2:23).[32] Some modern commentators have argued that such hopeful prophecies of restoration reflect later redaction of Hosea, but such redactional activity would only underscore the oddity of southern *Jewish* editors inserting prophecies of *northern Israel's* restoration. In any case, ancient readers read the book as a whole, looking forward to the fulfillment of these restoration promises. Hosea is

---

[29] Alternately, this may be rendered "my non-people" (alluding to Deut 32:21 or its prototype), still asserting ownership but declaring Israel to be no better than or indistinct from the outside nations. See Francis I. Andersen and David Noel Freedman, *Hosea: A New Translation with Introduction and Commentary*, AB 24 (Garden City: Doubleday, 1980), 198. Here and elsewhere in this chapter, biblical translations are from the Masoretic Text except where noted.

[30] Heb. בלל, a word denoting dispersion, separation, and confusion. In the LXX, the word is συναναμίγνυμι, a word both carrying a sexual connotation (cf. Hdt. *Hist.* 2.64; Homer, *Il.* 21.143; *Od.* 1.73) and meaning, "become included among" LSJ, s.v. μείγνυμι, 1092; LSJ, s.v. ἀμείγνυμι, 112; LSJ, s.v. συνανα-μείγνῡμι, 1695b. The idea is that Ephraim has become ethnically mixed with non-Israelites through the exile. In contrast, the *Ioudaioi* remain "unmingled" (ἄμικτον), which becomes a point of contention and accusation by their enemies (cf. *Ant.* 11.212).

[31] "Hosea is more radical still in his judgment, because he was convinced that Israel had ceased to be [YHWH's] people" (Baltzer, *Deutero-Isaiah*, 179). Andersen and Freedman suggest that both kingdoms are renounced here as "the title 'my people' applies to Israel as a whole, the twelve tribes," but it does not appear that Hosea was read this way in antiquity, as Jeremiah (alluding to Hosea) regards only the north as previously having been given her certificate of divorce (Jer 3:8), declaring that Judah will (in his own day) receive a similar fate (Andersen and Freedman, *Hosea*, 198).

[32] "Hosea, as a prophet to the Northern Kingdom, stands out in his vision of future divine reconciliation with Ephraim. The prophets generally anticipate the ultimate salvation of Israel in a unified nation led by a Davidic monarch, i.e., one descended from Judah" (Shani L. Berrin, *The Pesher Nahum Scroll from Qumran: An Exegetical Study of 4Q169* [Leiden: Brill, 2004], 110). Cf. also Andersen and Freedman, *Hosea*, 200, 202.

especially important since Jeremiah, Ezekiel, and Second Isaiah knew and were influenced by his preaching – the material of the first two chapters in particular.[33]

Like Hosea, Amos warns of impending judgment upon Israel for their abandonment of the covenant and breaches of social justice (Amos 1:1; 7:10–17). Amos hints of a similar future fate for Judah (2:4–5), but this does not detract from Amos' focus on the north. Israel will be destroyed, and the people will be taken "beyond Damascus" (5:27). Amos also startlingly asserts that Israel has no special status as God's holy covenantal people (anymore?), proclaiming, "Are you not like the sons of Ethiopia to me, children of Israel?" (Amos 9:7). But like Hosea, the book of Amos concludes with the promise of future restoration and reconciliation, as YHWH promises to consume the sinners from among his people but ultimately to restore the "fallen booth of David" and "restore the fortunes of my people Israel" (9:8–15).[34] Far from remaining abandoned in exile and apart from YHWH's favor, YHWH will in fact restore (northern) Israel after it has been punished.[35]

The full ironic force of Jonah depends on understanding Jonah's connection to the northern kingdom, with the reader, knowing that the Assyrians will later destroy Israel, expected to identify with Jonah's attitude.[36] Nahum, which immediately follows Jonah in the LXX, rejoices

---

[33] Cf. William L. Holladay, *Jeremiah I: A Commentary on the Book of the Prophet Jeremiah, Chapters 1–25*, Hermeneia 24A (Philadelphia: Fortress, 1986), 112 (cf. also 45–46); Walther Zimmerli, *Ezekiel I: A Commentary on the Book of the Prophet Ezekiel, Chapters 1–24*, ed. Frank Moore Cross and Klaus Baltzer, trans. Ronald E. Clements, Hermeneia (Philadelphia: Fortress, 1979), 43; Baltzer, *Deutero-Isaiah*, 104.

[34] See the discussions in Shalom M. Paul, *Amos: A Commentary on the Book of Amos*, Hermeneia (Minneapolis: Fortress, 1991), 344–56; Douglas K. Stuart, *Hosea-Jonah*, WBC 31 (Grand Rapids: Zondervan, 1988), 393–402; Francis I. Andersen and David Noel Freedman, *Amos: A New Translation with Introduction and Commentary*, AB 24A (New York: Doubleday, 1989), 870–93.

[35] "The restoration [envisioned in the epilogue of Amos] requires a united Israel under the rule of its long-standing dynasty (that of David). The returned people is called Israel, and the land includes not only the traditional territory of Israel but areas that belonged to Israel in the days of the united monarchy (the remnant of Edom and all of the other nations)." Andersen and Freedman, *Amos*, 893.

[36] As explained by Jonathan Magonet, "Jonah, Book of," *The Anchor Yale Bible Dictionary* 3:936–42 (941), "Given the role of Nineveh in Israelite history (the capital of the Assyrian Empire that destroyed the N Kingdom), the reader may well sympathize with an Israelite prophet who refused to go there to preach." For more discussion of the irony of Jonah, see David Marcus, *From Balaam to Jonah: Anti-prophetic Satire in the Hebrew Bible*, BJS 301 (Atlanta: Scholars Press, 1995), 93–159; Good, *Irony*, 39–55; Carolyn J. Sharp, *Irony and Meaning in the Hebrew Bible* (Bloomington: Indiana

in the destruction of Assyria, proclaiming the restoration not only of Judah (2:1 [ET 1:15]) but also of Jacob/Israel (2:3 [ET 2:2]).[37] Micah, a southern prophet roughly contemporary with Hosea, Amos, and Isaiah of Jerusalem around the fall of the northern kingdom to Assyria, similarly prophesies "concerning Samaria and Jerusalem" (Mic 1:1), castigating their breaches of covenant and social justice and declaring YHWH's judgment. Yet in the midst of declaring ruin for the northern kingdom, Micah agrees with the restoration promises found in Hosea and Amos, declaring, "I will surely assemble all of you, Jacob; I will surely gather the remnant of Israel and put them together like sheep in the fold, like a flock in the midst of its pasture" (Mic 2:12).

Likewise, significant passages in the post-exilic prophet Zechariah concern not only the restoration of Judah and Jerusalem but of Ephraim (Zech 9:13), the house of Israel (Zech 8:13).[38] Zechariah promises,

> I will strengthen the house of Judah,
> and I will save the house of Joseph,
> and will bring them back because I have compassion on them.

University Press, 2008), 176–86; and Mona West, "Irony in the Book of Jonah: Audience Identification with the Hero," *PRSt* 11 (1984): 232–42.

[37] Commentators have predictably identified the latter reference as referring to Judah with the title for the whole of Israel: "[T]he words *Jacob* and *Israel* here are both honorific titles for Judah as the whole of Israel. ... It would make little sense to say that Judah would be restored 'as' the pride of Israel if one were referring to the northern kingdom of Israel in the middle of the seventh century BCE. The former kingdom of Israel was no longer in existence" (Duane L. Christensen, *Nahum: A New Translation with Introduction and Commentary*, AB 24F [New Haven: Yale University Press, 2009], 264). If, however, the questionable assumption that the northern kingdom was out of view by this point is dropped, the passage serves as a promise of the restoration of both houses of Israel, as argued by Adam S. van der Woude, *Jona, Nahum*, POuT (Nijkerk: Callenbach, 1978), 118–19; Bob Becking, "Is het boek Nahum een literaire eenheid?," *NedTT* 32 (1978): 111–14.

[38] The mention of the "house of Israel" in 8:13 is striking enough to have given some interpreters pause, with some have suggesting that this verse is a gloss. E.g., Willem A. M. Beuken, *Haggai-Sacharja 1–8*, Studien zur Überlieferungsgeschichte der frühnachexilischen Prophetie (Assen: Van Gorcum, 1967), 168. Douglas R. Jones, "A Fresh Interpretation of Zechariah IX–XI," *VT* 12.3 (1962): 241–59 (109), rightly objects, "This is no interpolation. The restoration of the scattered northern people is an integral part of Zechariah's hope of salvation." Cf. also Ackroyd, *Exile and Restoration*, 215 n. 144. In any case, a Second Temple period reader certainly would understand this as promising the restoration of the north and its reunion with Judah. For more on Zech 1–8 as emphasizing the estrangement of the people from YHWH and looking forward to reconciliation, see Halvorson-Taylor, *Enduring Exile*, 151–98. For more on Zech 9–14 and its reception, see Kelly D. Liebengood, "Zechariah 9–14 as the Substructure of 1 Peter's Eschatological Program" (PhD diss., University of St. Andrews, 2011), 22–73.

They will be as though I had not rejected them [cf. Hosea/Amos],
      for I am YHWH their God and I will answer them.
Ephraim will be like a mighty man. . . .
I will whistle for them to gather them together,
      for I have redeemed them,
      and they will be as numerous as they were before,
        when I sowed them among the peoples.[39] . . .
I will bring them back from the land of Egypt
      and gather them from Assyria
and will bring them into the land of Gilead and Lebanon. (Zech 10:6–10)[40]

Similarly, the enigmatic prophecy of Zech 11 features the prophet cutting his second shepherd's staff, called "Union," symbolizing the broken brotherhood between Israel and Judah (Zech 11:14), yet another reminder of the prophet's concern with the totality of Israel, not just the southern kingdom.[41] Finally, the superscription in Malachi, the final book of the Twelve, says that the prophecy is "the word of YHWH to Israel through Malachi" (1:1), which, as Smith notes, reflects an "emphasis in Malachi on the New Israel, *made up of all the tribes.*"[42]

JEREMIAH: A NEW COVENANT WITH ISRAEL AND JUDAH

By the time of Jeremiah, the Assyrian destruction of the kingdom of Israel was over a century in the past. Jeremiah is fully conversant with the message of prior prophets (cf. the allusion to Hosea in Jer 3:8) that Israel had been "divorced" and was scattered, intermingled, and "not

---

[39] It is unclear whether ואזרעם here refers to a future sowing or the past; I have translated it as referring to a past (but still incomplete) action, though a future reading is entirely plausible given the imperfect form. Cf. Ralph Lee Smith, *Micah–Malachi*, WBC 32 (Nashville: Nelson, 1984), 263, which renders it as future. Either way, as Smith comments, "the results are the same. The emphasis is on the return" (266).

[40] For a fuller look at this passage and its restoration implications, see Smith, *Micah–Malachi*, 265–66.

[41] This difficult passage has led to differing interpretations, including the idea that the breaking of the staff is envisioned as a *future* event, though it is unclear what this would entail. See Smith, *Micah–Malachi*, 268–72.

[42] Smith, *Micah–Malachi*, 303 (my emphasis); cf. also Dumbrell, "Malachi." Ben Sira 48:10 also apparently conflates the Elijah prophecy of Mal 3:23–24 with Isa 49:6, adding that Elijah will "prepare the tribes of Israel" for restoration (see p. 322). Cf. David M. Miller, "The Messenger, the Lord, and the Coming Judgement in the Reception History of Malachi 3," *NTS* 53.1 (2007): 1–16 (7–8).

my people" any longer.[43] Jeremiah uses the fate of the north as an object lesson for Judah,[44] who has followed in its sibling's footsteps (Jer 3:6–10).[45] Yet Jeremiah continues to put a remarkably strong emphasis on the restoration not only of Judah but also of Israel – indeed, Judah's rebellion and punishment is in fact the guarantee of Israel's subsequent restoration, since Judah has made Israel look good by comparison:

And YHWH said to me, "Unfaithful Israel has proved herself more righteous than treacherous Judah. Go and proclaim these words toward the north and say, "Return, unfaithful Israel," declares YHWH.

> "I will not look upon you in anger.
> For I am gracious," declares YHWH.
> "I will not be angry forever."
> (Jer 3:11–12)[46]

This theme is so strong that some have even proposed that Jeremiah's early ministry was preoccupied with the reunification of northerners with the Josianic kingdom and the Jerusalem cultus, which provided the background for Jeremiah's concern with the north.[47] For later readers (and

---

[43] E.g. Jer 26:18; allusions to and reappropriations of the themes of Hosea are especially prominent in Jeremiah. Cf. William L. Holladay, *Jeremiah II: A Commentary on the Book of the Prophet Jeremiah, Chapters 26–52*, Hermeneia 24B (Philadelphia: Fortress, 1989), 45–47; Georg Fischer, *Das Trostbüchlein: Text, Komposition und Theologie von Jer 30–31* (Stuttgart: Katholisches Bibelwerk, 1993), 186–204.

[44] On the impact of Amos and especially Hosea on Jeremiah, see Jeremiah Unterman, *From Repentance to Redemption: Jeremiah's Thought in Transition*, JSOTSup 54 (London: Continuum, 1987), 151–66.

[45] The LXX of Jeremiah is markedly different from the MT. Although the LXX was in primary use among the diaspora and early Christian communities, unmarked references are to the MT for the sake of simplicity. For more on the difference between MT and LXX Jeremiah, see, e.g., Robert P. Carroll, *Jeremiah* (London: T&T Clark, 2004), 21–30; Gleason L. Archer, "The Relationship Between the Septuagint Translation and the Massoretic Text in Jeremiah," *TJ* 12.2 (1991): 139–50; Sven Soderlund, *The Greek Text of Jeremiah: A Revised Hypothesis* (Sheffield, England: JSOT Press, 1985); Bob Becking, "Jeremiah's Book of Consolation: A Textual Comparison Notes on the Masoretic Text and the Old Greek Version of Jeremiah XXX–XXXI," *VT* 44.2 (1994): 145–69; Jack R. Lundbom, "Haplography in the Hebrew Vorlage of LXX Jeremiah," *HS* 46.1 (2005): 301–20.

[46] See the discussions of this passage in Peter C. Craigie, Page H. Kelley, and Joel F. Drinkard, *Jeremiah 1–25*, WBC 26 (Grand Rapids: Zondervan, 1991), 53–58; Holladay, *Jeremiah I*, 118–20; Jack R. Lundbom, *Jeremiah 1–20: A New Translation with Introduction and Commentary*, Accordance electronic ed., AB (New Haven: Yale University Press, 1974), 305–12. Cf. also the similar themes in Ezek 16.

[47] See especially Holladay, *Jeremiah I*, 130–31 and the similar argument of Marvin A. Sweeney, "Jeremiah 30–31 and King Josiah's Program of National Restoration and

perhaps for Jeremiah himself and his editors after Jerusalem's fall), however, these calls to the north would have taken an entirely different and more eschatological character. In any case, like (Second) Isaiah, Jeremiah depicts this return in glorious language recalling the exodus from Egypt, proclaiming that Israel's return would be more miraculous than the deliverance from Egypt, a theme that carries throughout the rest of the book:

> "Therefore days are coming," declares YHWH, "when it will no longer be said, 'As YHWH lives, who brought the children of Israel out of the land of Egypt,' but, 'As YHWH lives, who brought the children of Israel from the land of the north and from all the countries where He had banished them.' For I will restore them to their own land which I gave to their fathers."[48] (Jer 16:14–15)

Most notably, at the climax of Jeremiah, the so-called "Book of Consolation" (Jer 30–33 MT), YHWH repeatedly promises not only to restore Judah but to "restore my people *Israel and Judah* from captivity" (30:3; cf. 31:27, 31; 33:14 MT).[49] The famous new covenant passage actually concludes an extended prophecy of *Ephraim's* return:

> Is Ephraim my dear son? ...
> I will surely have mercy on him, declares YHWH.
> (31:20)

> "See, days are coming," declares YHWH, "when I will make a new covenant with the house of Israel and the house of Judah. ... This is the covenant which I will make with the house of Israel after those days: I will put my law within them and will write it on their hearts, and I will be their God and they will be my people."[50]
> (Jer 31:31, 33)

Religious Reform," *ZAW* 108.4 (1996): 569–83. Cf. also Hays, *The Origins of Isaiah 24–27: Josiah's Festival Scroll for the Fall of Assyria*, 127–75, 235–36.

[48] The next verse proclaims that YHWH will send for many fishermen who will fish for "them" (ם; αὐτούς). This reference to "fishers" seems to be a proclamation of judgment rather than a continuation of the restoration promises in the preceding verse, but some nevertheless appear to have read it as part of the restoration promise (i.e. the fishers retrieve those returning), since it likely underlies the "fishers of humans" invitation in Mark 1:17 (=Matt 4:19). On Jer 16:16–18 as a message of judgment rather than restoration, see Holladay, *Jeremiah I*, 477–79.

[49] For more on the Book of Consolation, including significant bibliography, see Gerald L. Keown, Pamela L. Scalise, and Thomas G. Smothers, *Jeremiah 26–52*, WBC 27 (Nashville: Thomas Nelson, 1995), 148–202. See also Halvorson-Taylor, *Enduring Exile*, 43–106.

[50] Note the two-sided covenant formula "their God ... my people," which also appears in Hos 2:23; Lev 26:12; Jer 7:23; 11:4; 24:7; 30:22; 31:1; 32:38; Ezek 11:20; 14:11; 36:28; 37:23, 27; Zech 8:8.

YHWH will thus reunite both houses of Israel, restoring his covenant with them and making them again "my people" (Jer 31:31–34; cf. Hos 1:9–2:1, 2:23). But the promised new covenant requires Ephraim's return; the complete restoration of the descendants of the south will not precede the return of those from the northern kingdom but is inextricably linked with YHWH's restoration of Ephraim. Restoration from Babylon is insufficient; Ephraim must also be restored from the destruction wrought by Assyria. Even if that restoration is limited to "one from a city and two from a family" (3:14), Israel must be – will be – complete and reunified once again. Until then, the new covenant promise has not been and cannot be fulfilled.

On a terminological note, the later chapters of LXX Jeremiah also use *Ioudaios* language on six occasions, each of which specifically refers to the citizens of Judah at or around the time of Jerusalem's fall.[51] In contrast, Israel appears approximately eighty-eight times, always either paired with "Judah" (thus referring to northern Israel) or referring to the larger totality (e.g., 38:35–37 [31:35–37 MT]). It is also worth noting that when Jeremiah contrasts those already living in exile with those remaining in the land, he says those in exile are in fact the "good figs" (Jer 24:5–7), the remnant God will preserve, while those remaining in the land are the "bad figs, which are rotten and inedible" (24:8–10) and will be swept away. Jeremiah advises those in exile to settle down and prosper in the land of captivity (36:5–6 [MT 29:5–6]) and to "seek the welfare of the city where I have sent you into exile ... for in its welfare you will find your welfare" (36:7; [29:7 MT]). The community of exiles is also enjoined to heed the word of YHWH unlike those remaining in the land (29:16–20 MT).[52] Jeremiah thus provides the beginnings of an ethic for living and serving YHWH as a minority group outside the land, with those outside the land understood as in no way inferior to those in the land.[53]

EZEKIEL: CAN THESE BONES LIVE?

Like Jeremiah, the book of Ezekiel begins by calling attention to the twofold exile of Israel and Judah, with Ezekiel lying on his left side

---

[51] LXX Jer 33:2 (26:2 MT); 39:12 (32:12); 45:19 (38:19); 47:11 (40:11); 48:3 (40:3); and 51:1 (44:1).

[52] Dalit Rom-Shiloni, "Ezekiel as the Voice of the Exiles and Constructor of Exilic Ideology," *HUCA* (2005): 1–45 (16–17 n. 55).

[53] Note also the importance of the Sabbath in Jer 17:19–27, a distinguishing practice that became especially important in the diaspora.

390 days to represent Israel's "years of iniquity" (Ezek 4:4–5) and his right forty days for Judah's iniquity (4:6).[54] Many commentators have found the fact that Israel and Judah are addressed separately jarring. Walther Zimmerli, for example, argues that "house of Israel" does not denote the northern house but rather means "all Israel," while the reference to Judah is a later alteration such that in the final form of the text, "'Israel' has taken on a quite different and unexpected meaning."[55] Ancient readers, of course, did not read the reference to Judah as an interpolation, and the parable of Oholah (northern kingdom) and Oholibah (Judah) in Ezek 23 further demonstrates the maintenance of the distinction in the final form of the book. Nevertheless, Zimmerli is correct that "Israel" in Ezekiel tends to refer to the whole people, though that should not be understood as limiting the scope of Israel to those from Judah.

As with Jeremiah, Ezekiel's prophecies of Jerusalem's impending destruction are mixed with promises that YHWH would reunite both Israel and Judah (Ezek 34–36).[56] In that day, proclaims the prophet, Israel will be cleansed and restored, in proper covenantal relationship to YHWH once again (Ezek 36:24–28). Also like Jeremiah, Ezekiel argues against those remaining in Jerusalem who claimed that the wicked had already been removed from the land, leaving them as the "meat in the pot" (11:3), the true inheritors of the land (11:5). Ezekiel responds by

---

[54] The numbers are those of the MT. As William H. Brownlee, *Ezekiel 1–19*, WBC 28 (Waco: Word, 1986), 66, notes, these numbers suggest "a tradition close to that of the Deuteronomic History was being followed. ... In the light of the specific accusation of defiling [YHWH's] sanctuary in 5:11 (cf. chap. 8; 43:7–9; 44:6–8), the number is best understood as a general reference to the existence of the first temple. Alternatively, it may relate to the period of disunity of the covenant nation." Cf. also Zimmerli, *Ezekiel I*, 163–68. The differing numbers reflected in the LXX reflect a continuing interpretation of "Israel" and "Judah" in this case as specifically denoting the northern and southern kingdoms respectively and an effort to harmonize the text with the known dates of each respective exile. The LXX translator(s) may also have understood "right" and "left" in the passage as references to south and north, again reflecting this continuing concern. Cf. Brownlee, *Ezekiel 1–19*, 68; Zimmerli, *Ezekiel I*, 167–68 Kelvin G. Friebel, *Jeremiah's and Ezekiel's Sign-Acts: Rhetorical Nonverbal Communication*, JSOTSup 283 (Sheffield: Sheffield Academic, 1999), 535.

[55] Zimmerli, *Ezekiel I*, 163; cf. also Walther Zimmerli, "Israel im Buche Ezechiel," *VT* 8.1 (1958): 75–90.

[56] Ezekiel's concerns with the house of Israel are so emphatic that some earlier interpreters thought Ezekiel must have been a northerner. E.g., Moses Gaster, *The Samaritans: Their History, Doctrines and Literature*, SchwLect (London: Oxford University Press, 1925), 11–15, 138–40; James Smith, *The Book of the Prophet Ezekiel: A New Interpretation* (London: SPCK, 1931), 55–71.

declaring exactly the opposite, namely that those in exile – though neither obedient nor virtuous – are in fact the preserved remnant (11:16–20), even going so far as to depict the presence of YHWH leaving the temple and Jerusalem and heading east, as though YHWH was joining his people in exile (11:22–24), where YHWH will himself be "a little sanctuary" (מקדש מעט/ἁγίασμα μικρὸν; 11:16) for the exiles.[57] Although reduced in comparison to the presence in the temple, YHWH remains present among the exiles. On this point, Dalit Rom-Shiloni observes, "exile does not [for Ezekiel] bring separation from God."[58] Instead, "The exilic arena is in fact an advantageous context for future restoration of the covenant" (Ezek 20:1–38).[59] That is not to say, however, that exile is preferable to the alternative. The advantage is that, much like the Israelites in Egyptian captivity, those in exile are positioned to see the deliverance of YHWH, while those in the land remain in the space of judgment.[60]

The famous Valley of Dry Bones Vision (Ezek 37) addresses the restoration with vivid imagery – but Ezekiel is not proclaiming only the restoration of Judah, which had experienced a relatively short period of exile to that point. Rather, the vision addresses the fate of the *"whole house of Israel"* – including the northern kingdom, which the prophet equates with dry bones, on which there was no longer any hint of life.[61]

---

[57] See the discussion in Rom-Shiloni, "Voice of the Exiles," 17–18. Cf. also Zimmerli, *Ezekiel I*, 126; George A. Cooke, *The Book of Ezekiel*, ICC (Edinburgh: T&T Clark, 1985), 125; Paul M. Joyce, "Dislocation and Adaptation in the Exilic Age and After," in *After the Exile: Essays in Honour of Rex Mason*, eds. John Barton and David James Reimer (Macon: Mercer University Press, 1996), 45–58 (54). Note also the broadening of the scope from "your brothers" to "the whole house of Israel" among those rejected by Jerusalem in 11:15. In light of the temple of YHWH built at Elephantine, it is also worth asking whether Ezekiel here envisions a literal sanctuary of YHWH among the exiles in Babylon, though the imagery of YHWH himself being the sanctuary probably suggests otherwise.

[58] Rom-Shiloni, "Voice of the Exiles," 17.

[59] Rom-Shiloni, "Voice of the Exiles," 43–44; cf. also Joyce, "Dislocation and Adaptation."

[60] Rom-Shiloni, "Voice of the Exiles," 44. Rom-Shiloni rightly points out that this perspective of the exiles as the righteous remnant paves the way for the antipathy for the "people of the land" found in Ezra-Nehemiah. For further development of the latter point, see Rom-Shiloni, "From Ezekiel to Ezra-Nehemiah." Recall also the metaphor of good and bad figs in Jer 24:8–10, which expresses a similar sentiment.

[61] Walther Zimmerli, *Ezekiel II: A Commentary on the Book of the Prophet Ezekiel, Chapters 25–48*, Hermeneia 26B (Philadelphia: Fortress, 1979), 264, rightly observes that this vision "expresses the event of the restoration and regathering of the politically defeated all-Israel" and is not limited solely to the northern tribes. Neither, it should be added, is it limited to the southern tribes. A tradition ascribed to Rab in b. San. 92b associates the bones of Ezek 37 with Ephraimites.

The question, "Son of man, can these dry bones live?" (37:3) confronts skepticism over whether the seemingly long-dead house of Israel could ever be restored again. That is, is it beyond YHWH to be able to restore not only Judah but northern Israel also?

> Then he said to me, "Son of man, these bones are the whole house of Israel. They say, 'Our bones are dried up and our hope is lost. We are completely cut off.' Therefore prophesy and say to them, 'Thus says Lord YHWH, "Look! I will open your graves and bring you up from your graves, my people [cf. Hos 1:9–2:1], and I will bring you into the land of Israel. . . . I will put my spirit in you, and you will come to life, and I will place you on your own land, then you will know that I, YHWH have spoken and done it."' (Ezek 37:11–12, 14)

As if to ensure no ambiguity on this point, the next image highlights the division between the two houses of Israel and promises their reunion:

> "And you, son of man, take one stick and write on it, 'For Judah and for the sons of Israel associated with it.' Then take another stick and write on it, 'For Joseph (the stick of Ephraim) and all the house of Israel associated with him.' Then join them together into one stick so that they become one in your hand." (Ezek 37:16–17)

Notably, the two sticks are not divided into "Israel" and "Judah" but rather include both Joseph and Judah within Israel.[62] Ezekiel's vision depicts this miraculous reunification and salvation in dramatic fashion, as YHWH effectively raises Israel from the dead – this appears to be the first reference to resurrection in Israelite literature – to fulfill his promises. YHWH's power extends even beyond the grave, and he will indeed restore the house of Israel as promised. Much like Jeremiah, Ezekiel's restoration depends on an internal, spiritual change – in each case, those restored are given a new heart and a new spirit by which they can and will remain faithful to YHWH. Ezekiel closes with a vision of a magnificent new temple and a restored Israel comprised of all twelve tribes reunited with expanded territorial borders (40–48). Remarkably, in a passage reminiscent of Second Isaiah's expansive vision, Israel is here instructed to divide the land also "among the aliens who stay among you, who bring forth children in your midst. And they will be to you as the native-born among the children of Israel and will be allotted an inheritance with you among the tribes of Israel" (47:22).[63]

---

[62] See Zimmerli, *Ezekiel II*, 279–80 and Brownlee, *Ezekiel 1–19*, 192–97.

[63] This ruling involves a transformation of Num 34:13–15; see Leslie C. Allen, *Ezekiel 20–48*, WBC 29 (Grand Rapids: Zondervan, 1990), 281. Zimmerli notes that this ruling addresses a problem in the monarchy in which *gerim* were not permitted to own land,

THE PERPETUAL HOPE OF ESCHATOLOGICAL ISRAEL

Through its grounding in historical Israel and Judah and focus on the future, the prophetic corpus puts the reader in the liminal space between the tragedy of divine wrath and reconciliation through divine mercy, reinforcing hopes for the restoration and reunification of all twelve tribes scattered by Assyria and Babylon.[64] As summarized by Knoppers,

> Such oracles in Jeremiah, Ezekiel, Zechariah, and other books hardly speak with one voice, but they assume the survival of Israelites and Judahites in a variety of territories and prophesy their reconfiguration in some new political form within their ancestral land. But such prophetic passages are wishfully directed to the future; they do not refer in a past historical sense to something that has already occurred. According to the prophets, the deported northern groups never returned to the land of Israel.[65]

Moreover, the prophets (particularly Jeremiah and Ezekiel) frequently emphasize that Israel's return requires the correction of the *cause* of Israel's plight – that is, Israel must be ethically transformed in order to return and receive the blessings of the renewed covenant.[66] The fact that the twelve tribes have not returned in unity is evidence that Israel's infidelity has not yet been corrected and vice versa. But the prophets look forward to a new era of YHWH's favor and Israel's obedience, a time marked by the return and reunification of all Israel. The hope of the prophets is unparalleled, their visions of the future idyllic.

The theological perspective constructed during and after the exile thus involves both a continuity with the past covenantal relationship with

---

opening them to oppression. In the restored Israel, however, the *ger* "is to receive a share in the land allocation in the tribal area where he wishes to settle, and this surely means also that he is to be incorporated into that tribe" (*Ezekiel II*, 532).

[64] To borrow from David Lambert's three-stage model for the relationship between God and Israel, the prophetic corpus consistently portrays Israel (and the reader) in stage two, in which "effective communication between the people and their God ceases. ... God is now at war with his own people" (*How Repentance Became Biblical*, 97). The first stage is that of an active, unbroken covenant, what Lambert calls "a reasonably functional relationship." Stage three involves "anticipated return to a normal relationship." Lambert similarly concludes, "Much of prophetic literature, I would suggest, is framed within this dysfunctional stage [stage two] of the relationship" (97).

[65] Knoppers, *Jews and Samaritans*, 6.

[66] Konrad Schmid and Odil Hannes Steck, "Restoration Expectations in the Prophetic Tradition of the Old Testament," in *Restoration: Old Testament, Jewish and Christian Perspectives*, ed. James M. Scott, JSJSup 72 (Leiden: Brill, 2001), 41–81 (78): "[S]everal passages in Jeremiah and Ezekiel treat an *anthropological renewal* of God's people in the framework of the future salvific condition as an essential element of restoration" (emphasis original).

Israel's God and a hopeful expectation of the ultimate restoration of Israel to the benefits of that covenantal status as promised by the Hebrew prophets. Those who looked to the prophets and the biblical narratives as their own authoritative history were therein consistently confronted with constant reminders of the present incompleteness of Israel and instilled with future hopes of a full restoration.[67] The Judaism(s) established through these foundational texts is thus founded on God of Israel's promises to restore Israel, regathering, reunifying, and re-choosing his people for special relationship, calling them out from the midst of the nations among which they had been scattered, or in Neusner's words: "that story of exile and return, alienation and remission ... the paradigmatic statement in which every Judaism, from then to now, found its structure and deep syntax of social existence, the grammar of its intelligible message."[68]

Indeed, the Jewish scriptures, redacted during and after the exile, are held together by the restoration eschatology derived from these prophetic promises in the wake of destruction. This permanent outlook of hope for the future established in the prophets helps account for the enduring power of Judaism and its children. But this power is rooted in yet another paradox: perpetual hope in the face of present disappointment.[69] The situation in the Second Temple period fell far short of the triumphant declarations of Israel's future found throughout the prophets, as the promised restoration of all twelve tribes under a renewed covenant, free from the oppression of outside nations or empires, remained unfulfilled. Indeed, David Greenwood has called the numerous predictions regarding a restored northern kingdom, "perhaps the most conspicuous example in the Tanak of patently false prophecy."[70]

---

[67] Cf. the continued preeminence of restoration eschatology in the Targumim, for example. See Bruce D. Chilton, "Messianic Redemption: Soteriology in the Targum Jonathan to the Former and Latter Prophets," in *This World and the World to Come: Soteriology in Early Judaism*, ed. Daniel M. Gurtner, LSTS 74 (London: T&T Clark, 2011), 265–84.

[68] Neusner, *Judaism When Christianity Began*, 61.

[69] Neusner observes that the paradigm of exile and return "retained its power of self-evidence because that system in its basic structure addressed *but also created* a continuing and chronic social fact. ... It represents a self-sustaining system, which solves the very problem that to begin with it precipitates: a self-fulfilling prophecy" (*Judaism When Christianity Began*, 63–64). That is, by highlighting present alienation and promising future blessing if only the community should behave in a particular way, this paradigm easily adapts to the new circumstances of each generation.

[70] David C. Greenwood, "On the Jewish Hope for a Restored Northern Kingdom," *ZAW* 88.3 (1976): 376–85 (384).

Nevertheless, as is often the case with unfulfilled prophecy, the long delay did not quench the hope of fulfillment.[71] Indeed, as Jonathan Goldstein has observed, it was not *fulfilled* prophetic proclamations but the *unfulfilled* prophecies of restoration that were most formative in the Second Temple period, as circumstances continually fell far short of prophetic expectations.[72] The returnees from Babylon and many continuing to live in the diaspora continued to look to the prophets for direction, still expecting the eventual fulfillment of their pronouncements. Some, as we will see in the next chapter, went even farther, making significant efforts to bring about the fulfillment of the prophets' proclamations of Israel's restoration and the end of the age of wrath.

---

[71] Cf. Leon Festinger, Henry W. Riecken, and Stanley Schachter, *When Prophecy Fails: A Social and Psychological Study of a Modern Group That Predicted the Destruction of the World* (Minneapolis: University of Minnesota Press, 1956); Leon Festinger, *A Theory of Cognitive Dissonance* (Palo Alto: Stanford University Press, 1962); Robert P. Carroll, "Ancient Israelite Prophecy and Dissonance Theory," *Numen* 24.2 (1977): 135–51; J. Gordon Melton, "Spiritualization and Reaffirmation: What Really Happens When Prophecy Fails," *American Studies* 26.2 (1985): 17–29; Lorne L. Dawson, "When Prophecy Fails and Faith Persists: A Theoretical Overview," *Nova Religio: The Journal of Alternative and Emergent Religions* 3.1 (1999): 60–82; Chris Bader, "When Prophecy Passes Unnoticed: New Perspectives on Failed Prophecy," *JSSR* 38.1 (1999): 119–31; Simon Dein, "What Really Happens When Prophecy Fails: The Case of Lubavitch," *Sociology of Religion* 62.3 (2001): 383–401; Mathew N. Schmalz, "When Festinger Fails: Prophecy and the Watch Tower," *Religion* 24.4 (2011): 293–308.

[72] Goldstein, "Messianic Promises," 69–70. For a contrasting view, see Michael H. Floyd, "Was Prophetic Hope Born of Disappointment? The Case of Zechariah," in *Utopia and Dystopia in Prophetic Literature*, ed. Ehud Ben Zvi, PFES (Göttingen: Vandenhoeck & Ruprecht, 2006), 268–96, which argues that such a view too closely resembles the early Christian *adversos Judaeos* interpretations of the prophets. Floyd's warning is important, but the current study suggests that the interpretation that the restoration prophecies remained unfulfilled is not a Christian innovation but was rather (as Goldstein suggests) the dominant Jewish interpretation before the Common Era.

5

The Restoration of Israel in the Persian and Hellenistic Periods

Incomplete, Delayed, Failed

The first centuries of the post-exilic period could only have been puzzling for faithful believers: The glorious prophecies of restoration uttered by the true prophets were not being fulfilled. ... [D]espite the return of many exiles to the Promised Land, despite the completion of the Second Temple, it was clear to believing Israelites that they were still living in the "Age of Wrath."

Jonathan A. Goldstein[1]

While it is hardly controversial to observe that the biblical narratives of Israel are characterized by restoration eschatology and conclude with Israel in exile awaiting restoration, most modern scholars have treated the events narrated in Ezra-Nehemiah as the conclusion of the period of exile and the time thereafter as the post-restoration period. This is not, however, how Ezra-Nehemiah was read in the Second Temple period, nor is there any indication that Jews from the later Second Temple period regarded Israel's restoration as having taken place in those events.[2] Instead, although the protagonists of Ezra-Nehemiah identify their actions as critical to the promised restoration, their efforts end in disappointment.[3] In this respect, the events of Ezra-Nehemiah are part of a

---

[1] Goldstein, "Messianic Promises," 70.
[2] In Davies' words, "the 'restoration' of Judah under the Persians is really a scholarly rather than a biblical concept." Philip R. Davies, "'Old' and 'New' Israel in the Bible and the Qumran Scrolls: Identity and Difference," in *Defining Identities: We, You, and the Other in the Dead Sea Scrolls*, eds. Florentino García-Martínez and Mladen Popović (Leiden: Brill, 2007), 33–42 (35).
[3] "[Ezra,] Sheshbazzar, Zerubbabel, Haggai, Zechariah, and perhaps also Nehemiah – these all attempt to pick up prophetic predictions and to bring them to an initial fulfillment" (Koch, "Ezra," 196).

larger pattern throughout the Second Temple period, as various attempts were made to bring the promised restoration to its fulfillment – and similarly resulted in disappointment. Indeed, although Ezra-Nehemiah and other early Jewish texts such as 1 and 2 Maccabees record various attempts to restore Israel or appropriate the full legacy of that title, these very accounts confirmed for later readers that Israel had *not* been restored as promised but was instead incomplete, delayed, or failed, thereby cementing restoration eschatology as foundational to normative Judaism throughout the Second Temple period.

EZRA-NEHEMIAH: A "LITTLE REVIVING" AND HOPE FOR THE FUTURE

As for Ezra-Nehemiah and the transitional events of the Persian period, John Collins summarizes the current consensus as follows:

> The Babylonian exile effected a rather drastic reduction of empirical Israel. Nonetheless, the books of Ezra and Nehemiah speak of the returned exilic community as "Israel," whereas "the people of the land" are categorized as "foreigners" with whom the returned exiles are forbidden to intermarry. ... But the books of Ezra and Nehemiah are important for our present inquiry because they establish a precedent for viewing "Israel" as an intentional community that was not identical with "the people of the land."[4]

For most modern scholarship, Ezra-Nehemiah therefore is treated both as the fulfillment of the promises of return and as the transition point after which "Israel" has been narrowed to the remnant of the *Yehudim*, the southern tribes of Judah, Levi, and Benjamin.[5] This perspective is deeply flawed, however, both in its reading of Ezra-Nehemiah and in its straightforward application of that reading to the historical situation.

The first problem is that this view uncritically adopts the polemical perspective of Ezra-Nehemiah in ruling out rival claimants to Israelite heritage, effectively invalidating and erasing those not included among Israel by Ezra-Nehemiah and its protagonists. As we have already

---

[4] Collins, "Construction," 25–26.

[5] Cf. J. Gordon McConville, "Ezra-Nehemiah and the Fulfillment of Prophecy," *VT* 36.2 (1986): 205–24 (205). For examples of this line of thinking, see Wilhelm Rudolph, *Esra und Nehemiah samt 3*, HAT (Tübingen: Mohr, 1949), xxiii–xxiv; J. D. Newsome, "Toward a New Understanding of the Chronicler and His Purposes," *JBL* 94 (1975): 201–17 (214): "no breath of royalist or messianic hope stirs in Ezra-Nehemiah"; Sara Japhet, "Sheshbazzar and Zerubbabel against the Background of the Historical and Religious Tendencies of Ezra-Nehemiah," *ZAW* 94 (1982): 66–98 (72).

observed, Israelite status remained a matter of debate for centuries after the time of Ezra and Nehemiah. It is also not the case that Israel was identical with "the people of the land" prior to Ezra-Nehemiah; Canaanites, foreign sojourners (*gerim*), Judahites,[6] and non-Israelite Hebrews/*Ḥabiru* are present in the land throughout the narratives of pre-exilic Israel and various Torah legislation.[7] Indeed, the notion of Israelite status based solely on being an inhabitant of the land presumes something akin to modern birthright citizenship, an anachronistic concept in antiquity.[8] Ancient citizenship tended to involve class and lineage rather than birthplace or dwelling place. For example, most born in Ancient Rome (or Roman territories) were not Roman citizens, as such citizenship was passed down from the father through a legally recognized wife. Imperial Rome later changed the criteria for citizenship, but most free inhabitants of the Empire still remained non-citizens until citizenship was expanded in 212 CE. Likewise, citizenship in ancient Athens and Sparta was restrictive and not simply based on residence in the land or city.[9]

---

[6] It is increasingly recognized that Judahites did not conceive of themselves as Israelites until (at least) the fall of the northern kingdom in the late eighth century BCE. See, for example, Hong, "Once Again"; Na'aman, "Patrimony"; Fleming, *Legacy of Israel*, 11–16, 47–57.

[7] That "Hebrew" and "Israelite" were not synonymous in ancient Israel has long been established. See pp. 71–80 and Niels Peter Lemche, "The 'Hebrew Slave': Comments on the Slave Law Ex. XXI 2–11," *VT* 25.2 (1975): 129–44; H. L. Ellison, "The Hebrew Slave: A Study in Early Israelite Society," *EvQ* 45 (1973): 30–35; Rad, "Israel, Judah, and Hebrews in the Old Testament," *TDNT* 3: 357–59; Gray, "Habiru-Hebrew Problem."

[8] For more on the phenomenon of citizenship and the differences between various ancient and modern conceptions, see Derek Benjamin Heater, *A Brief History of Citizenship* (New York: New York University Press, 2004); J. G. A. Pocock, "The Ideal of Citizenship Since Classical Times," *Queen's Quarterly* 99.1 (1992): 35–55; Peter Riesenberg, *Citizenship in the Western Tradition: Plato to Rousseau* (Chapel Hill: University of North Carolina Press, 1994).

[9] Ancient Greek city-states offer intriguing parallels to biblical Israel, especially the twelve-tribe Amphictyonic League and the tribal structure of Athens, which Cleisthenes reconfigured from the traditional four birth-based tribes into ten regional tribes. For more on Roman citizenship, see A. N. Sherwin-White, *The Roman Citizenship* (Oxford: Oxford University Press, 1980). For more on citizenship in ancient Greece, see Heater, *Brief History*, 6–29; Brook Manville, *The Origins of Citizenship in Ancient Athens* (Princeton: Princeton University Press, 1997). For more on Cleisthenes' reconfiguration of Athens' tribal structure, see Aristotle, *Athenian Constitution* 20–22; Manville, *Origins*, 157–209. Martin Noth and others have proposed the ancient Israelite tribal structure to be analogous to the amphictyonic systems known among the Greeks, Old Latins, and Etruscans; cf. Martin Noth, *Das System der zwölf Stämme Israels* (Stuttgart: Kohlhammer, 1930); A. D. H. Mayes, "Israel in the Pre-Monarchy Period," *VT* 23.2 (1973): 151–70. But Noth's theory is no longer widely held, thanks in large part to Norman K. Gottwald, *Tribes of Yahweh: A Sociology of the Religion of Liberated*

The notion of a constructed people of Israel as a "status community" distinct from other inhabitants in the land thus probably predates Ezra and Nehemiah by centuries, while the notion of Israelite status based solely on being an inhabitant of the land is almost certainly anachronistic.[10] Instead, the reforms of Ezra and Nehemiah attempted to restore and uphold social and class distinctions derived from before the exile, albeit with important accommodations to the new context.[11] After all, the people deported by the Babylonians were from the royal house, temple service, and upper classes, while those who remained in the land were from poorer classes. That the returning elites were also emissaries of Persian authority only strengthened those distinctions.[12] The combination of exile and prophetically-fostered hopes of repatriation had also led to an emphasis on the maintenance of traditions and practices that would prevent assimilation, such as strict endogamy.[13]

Both Ezra and Nehemiah argued that these rules also excluded those who had remained in the land,[14] presumably at least partly on the basis of the proclamations of Jeremiah and Ezekiel that those who went into exile (in particular those from the deportation of 598 BCE) were in fact the

---

    Israel, 1250–1050 BCE (Sheffield: Sheffield Academic, 1979), 345–57. For a more recent approach arguing that the concept of a unified tribal confederacy was a late Persian-period development aimed at constructing a shared ethnic past, see Tobolowsky, *The Sons of Jacob*.

[10] For more on pre-exilic Israelite status, see Tobolowsky, *The Sons of Jacob*, 1–42; Fleming, *Legacy of Israel*, 276–322; Grosby, *Biblical Ideas of Nationality*, 13–68; Grosby, "Religion and Nationality in Antiquity: The Worship of Yahweh and Ancient Israel," *European Journal of Sociology* 32.2 (2009): 229–65; Niels Peter Lemche, *The Canaanites and Their Land: The Tradition of the Canaanites* (Sheffield: Sheffield Academic, 1999); Aloo Osotsi Mojola, "The 'Tribes' of Israel? A Bible Translator's Dilemma," *JSOT* 81 (1998): 15–29; Christiana van Houten, *The Alien in Israelite Law* (Sheffield: JSOT Press, 1991).

[11] Bob Becking, *Ezra, Nehemiah, and the Construction of Early Jewish Identity*, FAT 80 (Tübingen: Mohr Siebeck, 2011), 107. The sweeping condemnation of exogamy in Ezra-Nehemiah appears to be one of these innovations, as discussed in Ophir and Rosen-Zvi, *Goy*, 58–74.

[12] For a comparison of the citizenship reforms in fifth-century Athens and fifth–fourth-century Judah, including the important point that "the only citizens of the Achaemenid Empire were the Persian officials and members of the Persian elites" and that these were the ones who put the intermarriage rules into effect, see Lisbeth S. Fried, "No King in Judah? Mass Divorce in Judah and in Athens," in *Political Memory in and after the Persian Empire*, eds. Jason M. Silverman and Caroline Waerzeggers, Ancient Near East Monographs (SBL Press, 2015), 381–401 (398).

[13] Talmon, "Emergence of Jewish Sectarianism," 586–87.

[14] Cf. Saul M. Olyan, "Purity Ideology in Ezra-Nehemiah as a Tool to Reconstitute the Community," *JSJ* 35.1 (2004): 1–16; Ophir and Rosen-Zvi, *Goy*, 58–74.

righteous remnant, while those who remained behind had been rejected.[15] Ezra-Nehemiah therefore is not the origin of the idea of Israel as an intentional community not identical with the "people of the land," as Israel had always been a "status community." Instead, Ezra-Nehemiah witnesses to – and takes a distinct position in – an early stage of the debates over who properly holds Israelite status in the changed circumstances after the exile. Modern scholarly equation of "Israel" with the Jews after the period of Ezra-Nehemiah therefore represents an uncritical acceptance of the book's argument and application of that perspective to the historical situation.[16]

The second problem is that treating the events of Ezra-Nehemiah as the restoration or end of the period of exile runs counter both to the message of the book itself and how Ezra-Nehemiah was interpreted throughout the Second Temple period. This anti-eschatological reading of Ezra-Nehemiah has been the default since at least Wellhausen, for whom Ezra was the de facto founder of "Judaism," understood as a routinization of previously lively ancient Israelite religion.[17] That is, Ezra took the prophetic, living Israelite cultus and subjected it to rote legalism and exclusivism, establishing a "Jewish religion" no longer tied to ethnic or political (*völkisch*) unity but rather centering on individual acceptance and observance of the written Torah.[18] By limiting the fulfillment of the prophetic promises to the return of a few *Yehudim*, Ezra-Nehemiah represents the end of those eschatological hopes and the beginning of the new post-exilic Judaism based on legalism and creedal exclusivism. This exclusivity and anti-eschatological perspective are now regularly cited as evidence for the separate authorship of Ezra-Nehemiah and Chronicles, the latter of which as we have seen takes an inclusive view

---

[15] E.g., Jer 24, Ezek 11. See the sections on Jeremiah and Ezekiel in Chapter 4.

[16] For a critique of modern scholars' willingness to "accept the judgment of the text," see Lester L. Grabbe, "Triumph of the Pious or Failure of the Xenophobes? The Ezra-Nehemiah Reforms and Their Nachgeschichte," in *Jewish Local Patriotism and Self-Identification in the Graeco-Roman Period*, eds. Siân Jones and Sarah Pearce, LSTS (Sheffield: Sheffield Academic, 1998), 50–65.

[17] For the concept of routinization of charisma, see Max Weber, *From Max Weber: Essays in Sociology* (London: Routledge, 2009), 245–52; Max Weber, *On Charisma and Institution Building* (Chicago: University of Chicago Press, 1968). Wellhausen of course predated Weber, but the idea of *Spätjudentum* as an empty husk of ritual built around once living prophetic tradition anticipates Weber's concept without Weber's terminology. See Wellhausen, *Prolegomena to the History of Israel*, 404–10.

[18] E.g., Max Weber, *Ancient Judaism*, trans. Hans H. Gerth and Don Martindale (New York: Free Press, 1952), 336–82; see also the discussion and assessment of Weber's model in Talmon, "Emergence of Jewish Sectarianism."

of northern Israel and continues to hold eschatological hopes for a full Israelite restoration.[19] But while it is true that Ezra-Nehemiah rejects the claims of the "people of the land" and circumscribes Israelite status in the land to the returned exiles, a closer look shows that the book does not argue that the Judahite exiles now comprise all of Israel, nor does it take an anti-eschatological perspective.[20] Indeed, although Ezra-Nehemiah narrates multiple attempts to restore, renew, and redefine Israel in the wake of the exiles,[21] it is rarely noticed that according to the narrative of Ezra-Nehemiah, each of these efforts to restore Israel *failed*, with Israel's restoration remaining a future hope.

---

[19] E.g., Knoppers, "Did Jacob Become Judah," 40–43; Williamson, *Israel*, 69. The idea that Ezra-Nehemiah was edited by the same author(s) as Chronicles goes back at least to b. B. Bat. 15a and was long the critical consensus after L. Zunz, "Dibre-Hayamim oder die Bücher der Chronik," in *Die Gottesdienstlichen Vorträge der Juden, historisch Entwickelt* (Berlin: Asher, 1832), 13–36 and Franz Carl Movers, *Kritische Untersuchungen über die biblische Chronik* (Bonn: Habicht, 1834). See, e.g., the summary in Charles Cutler Torrey, *The Composition and Historical Value of Ezra-Nehemiah*, BZAW 2 (Giessen: Ricker, 1896), 1. The consensus has now shifted to an assumption of distinct authorship for the two works on the basis of differences in language, style, and thematic emphases as argued by Sara Japhet, "The Supposed Common Authorship of Chronicles and Ezra-Nehemia Investigated Anew," VT 18.3 (1968): 330–71 and Williamson, *Israel*; Hugh G. M. Williamson, *Ezra-Nehemiah*, WBC 16 (Louisville: Nelson, 1985). For more discussion, see Klein, *1 Chronicles*, 6–10; Knoppers, *1 Chronicles 1–9*, 73–89; Gary N. Knoppers, "Sources, Revisions, and Editions: The Lists of Jerusalem's Residents in MT and LXX Nehemiah 11 and 1 Chronicles 9," *Text* 20 (2000): 141–68; Tamara Cohn Eskenazi, *In an Age of Prose: A Literary Approach to Ezra-Nehemiah*, SBLMS 36 (Atlanta: Scholars Press, 1988), 14–34; Tamara Cohn Eskenazi, "The Structure of Ezra-Nehemiah and the Integrity of the Book," *JBL* 107.4 (1988): 641–56.

[20] McConville, "Ezra-Nehemiah," 205–24; on the continued eschatological hopes of Ezra-Nehemiah, see also Laato, *A Star Is Rising*, 221–30; on the parallels between Ezra-Nehemiah and the Exodus story, see Japhet, "Periodization between History and Ideology II," 426–28.

[21] Ezra-Nehemiah narrates not one but *three* returns to the land and restorations of Jerusalem occurring over about a century, those of Zerubbabel/Jeshua, Ezra, and Nehemiah, all of which share some overlapping features. See Lester L. Grabbe, "'Mind the Gaps': Ezra, Nehemiah, and the Judaean Restoration," in *Restoration: Old Testament, Jewish and Christian Perspectives*, ed. James M. Scott, JSJSup 72 (Leiden: Brill, 2001), 83–104, esp. 84–85; Lester L. Grabbe, "'They Shall Come Rejoicing to Zion' – or Did They? The Settlement of Yehud in the Early Persian Period," in *Exile and Restoration Revisited: Essays on the Babylonian and Persian Period in Memory of Peter R. Ackroyd*, eds. Gary N. Knoppers, Lester L. Grabbe, and Dierdre N. Fulton, LSTS 73 (London: T&T Clark, 2009), 116–27.

Shouts of Joy Mixed with Weeping

Cyrus' decree permitting the return to Judah (Persian Yehud) and rebuild Jerusalem and the temple doubtless stirred up hopes that the glorious restoration of Israel promised by the prophets had begun. That is, the temple would soon be rebuilt in splendor, Israel and Judah would be reunited in perfect obedience to YHWH, and the nations would flock to Jerusalem to pay homage to YHWH and his people Israel. The reality, however, did not match the expectations. Although the decree is presented in terms that clearly echo the prophets' promises of return,[22] the fact that only some from "Judah and Benjamin and the priests and Levites" arose and returned (Ezra 1:5) is the first indication that these events will fall short of those promises.[23] It is also worth noting that the book's polemic against potential rival Yahwists begins even in the decree itself, which goes out of its way to specify that "YHWH, the God of Israel, is the God who is in Jerusalem" (1:3). Most modern readers gloss over this detail because they already share the Judahite biases of the book and assume that YHWH's house properly belongs in Jerusalem, but those accustomed to a sanctuary of YHWH at Shechem or Bethel or Elephantine surely had other ideas.[24]

Despite their fear of the "peoples of the lands" (3:3), the initial returnees quickly set about rebuilding the Jerusalem temple, and the account of the people's response to the laying of the foundation of the temple is a fitting summary of the combination of optimism and disappointment found throughout Ezra-Nehemiah:

But many of the priests and Levites and heads of fathers' households and elders who had seen the first house wept with a loud voice when the foundation of this house was laid before their eyes, while many shouted aloud for joy, so that the

---

[22] See Williamson, *Ezra-Nehemiah*, 9–10.

[23] Ezra-Nehemiah may be overstating its case in this respect, as illustrated by a comparison of the genealogies with those of 1 Chronicles (e.g., Ezra 2:29 // 1 Chr 5:26). See Barmash, "Nexus," 230–31; but cf. the differing conclusions of Z. Kallai, "Nov, Noveh," in *Enziklopediya Mikra'it*, 5 (Jerusalem: Bialik, 1968), 684. In any case, even if some northerners did return and many had remained in the land, the biblical editors consider their return insufficient to regard their tribes as having returned. Regardless of "what really happened," the account in Ezra-Nehemiah – which shaped the Jewish imagination thereafter – was one in which the full restoration of the northern tribes has not yet taken place.

[24] For a corrective of the Jerusalem-centered assumptions of modern scholarship in light of evidence from Elephantine and Al Yahudu, see Gard Granerød, "Canon and Archive: Yahwism in Elephantine and Āl-Yāḫūdu as a Challenge to the Canonical History of Judean Religion in the Persian Period," *JBL* 138.2 (2019): 345.

people could not distinguish the sound of the shout of joy from the sound of the weeping of the people. (Ezra3:12–13a; cf. Hag2:3; Zech4:10)

This passage makes it clear that, although the return to the land and the rebuilding of the city and the temple are indeed important events guided by YHWH, the present state of affairs also leaves much to be desired, falling short of the new golden age promised by the prophets.[25] This conclusion is further reinforced by the events that immediately follow, in which the "enemies of Judah and Benjamin" (note: not "enemies of Israel"), who are later identified as chiefly from Samaria (4:10),[26] initially offer to aid the returnees in their building efforts (4:1–2). The leaders of the returnees rebuff these offers and dismiss any connection with these other worshipers of YHWH (4:3). Naturally, the people of the land do not take kindly to this rejection and take steps to prevent the construction (4:4–16).

This episode deserves a closer look, as it sets the precedent for the limitation of Israel to the "children of the exile" (בני הגולה) as opposed to the "people of the land" within the book and reveals much of what is at stake throughout Ezra-Nehemiah. First, the returnees seem to recognize that accepting this assistance amounts to an acceptance of cultic and political unity. Acceptance of such an offer would therefore effectively place Jerusalem in an inferior relationship with the much stronger city of Samaria (among others) and make the Jerusalem temple one among multiple shrines to YHWH, as these people have been continuously "sacrificing to [YHWH] since the days of Esarhaddon, who brought us up here" (4:2). Secondly, these "people of the land" are – of their own admission (!) – not Israelites but rather those who were brought by the Assyrians to resettle the land (cf. 2 Kgs 17). Regardless of whether these "people of the land" were in fact descended from Israel or those resettled by the Assyrians, the narrative presents them as non-Israelites; as such, their continued presence in the land is a symptom and consequence of exile, and restoration requires that they be replaced by legitimate Israelites. Although this passage is frequently read as a declaration that Israel has now been narrowed to the *Yehudim* alone, that is one thing this passage does not say. Instead, only a portion of Judah, Benjamin, and Levi have returned from exile, and most of the "children of the exile" – including the other tribes of Israel – remain abroad.

---

[25] McConville, "Ezra-Nehemiah," 210.
[26] Thus also Josephus, *Ant.* 11.84–115.

The returnees' rejection of this offer reflects three related convictions of the returnees: (1) the "people of the land" are not in fact legitimate Israelites, (2) the Jerusalem temple is the only legitimate shrine to YHWH, while those sacrificing elsewhere are idolaters and rebels by definition, and (3) fulfillment of Israel's promised restoration ultimately requires the reestablishment of Jerusalem and its temple under the proper leadership. The Jews' rejection of their offer would naturally be alarming to the "people of the land," who concluded that the Jews must be intending to rebel and reestablish Jerusalem's hegemony in the region – thus their warning to the Persian king, "The Jews who came from you to us have gone to Jerusalem; they are building that wicked and rebellious city" (4:12).

These concerns may have been warranted, as the initial returnees appear to have expected the revival of the Davidic monarchy (cf. Hag 2:6–9, 20–23), including the subjection of the nations (Hag 2:22) and presumably the reunification of Israel and Judah under Jerusalem's authority. It is probably no coincidence that Haggai's prophecies, including the declaration that YHWH is about to "shake the nations" (2:7) and "overthrow the throne of kingdoms and destroy the strength of the kingdoms of the nations" (2:22) came in the second year of Darius I (1:1; 2:10, 20), when news of the numerous significant revolts in the east – including Babylon, Elam, Persia, Media, Assyria, and Scythia – would have reached the Levant, and when Egypt began its own rebellion against the Persians. Several of the leaders of these revolts claimed descent from the last local leader of that region, something Zerubbabel could also claim.[27] But these hopes were not fulfilled, as the editor of the book was aware, and the book tells us nothing about Zerubbabel's fate.

---

[27] See Sabine Müller, "Darius I and the Problems of [Re-]Conquest: Resistance, False Identities and the Impact of the Past," in *Greece, Macedon and Persia*, eds. Timothy Howe, E. Edward Garvin, and Graham Wrightson (Oxford: Oxbow Books, 2015), 5–10. It took Darius over a year to put down these eastern uprisings, after which he engaged a successful campaign in Egypt in 519 or 518. The official Persian account of these revolts is found on the Bisitun inscription, on which see Amélie Kuhrt, *The Persian Empire: A Corpus of Sources from the Achaemenid Period* (London: Routledge, 2007), 135–57. On the eastern revolts, see Yigal Bloch, "The Contribution of Babylonian Tablets in the Collection of David Sofer to the Chronology of the Revolts against Darius I," *AoF* 42.1 (2015): 1–14; Willem J. Vogelsang, "Medes, Scythians and Persians: The Rise of Darius in a North–South Perspective," *IrAnt* 33 (1998): 195–224; Stefan Zawadzki, "Bardiya, Darius and Babylonian Usurpers in the Light of the Bisitun Inscription and Babylonian Sources," *Archäologische Mitteilungen aus Iran* 27 (1994): 127–45; M. A. Dandamaev, *A Political History of the Achaemenid Empire*, trans. Willem J. Vogelsang (Leiden: Brill, 1989), 114–31. On the Egyptian revolt, see Uzume Z. Wijnsma, "The Worst Revolt of the

Ezra's account of the completion and dedication of the temple similarly draws attention to the inferiority of the Second Temple when compared to the first.[28] Whereas Solomon's Temple was dedicated with a massive sacrificial feast of 22,000 oxen and 120,000 sheep (2 Chr 7:4) and glorious speech, the Second Temple is dedicated with comparatively few sacrifices – 100 bulls, 200 rams, 400 lambs (Ezra 6:17).[29] The concluding statement that "the elders of the Jews" (6:14) also offered "a sin offering of twelve male goats, corresponding to the number of the tribes of Israel" (Ezra 6:17), sounds an especially somber note in contrast to Solomon's dedication, which did not feature sin offerings. The juxtaposition between the "elders of the Jews" and the sin offering on behalf of the twelve tribes of Israel further underscores both the incompleteness of Israel and the continued hopes of a fuller (twelve-tribe) restoration.[30] The returnees from Babylon thereby serve as the vanguard on behalf of the rest of Israel, whose restoration appears to depend on this atoning work. The dedication of the Second Temple, however, lacks the tangible presence of God that characterized Solomon's dedication with fire from heaven and a cloud of glory. The absence of the signs of divine approval and presence that had distinguished the one built by Solomon once again draws attention to the incomplete state of the restoration. The rebuilding of the temple is a necessary and important step toward the fulfillment of the prophecies of restoration, but it is only a step.[31]

This theme is further reinforced by the fact that the narrative seamlessly passes into an account of the Passover celebration immediately following the dedication of the temple, as the Passover both celebrates the exodus from Egypt and looks forward to the future restoration (cf. Jer

---

Bisitun Crisis: A Chronological Reconstruction of the Egyptian Revolt under Petubastis IV," *JNES* 77.2 (2018): 157–73; Olaf E. Kaper, "Petubastis IV in the Dakhla Oasis: New Evidence about an Early Rebellion against Persian Rule and Its Suppression in Political Memory," in *Political Memory in and after the Persian Empire*, eds. Jason M. Silverman and Caroline Waerzeggers, Ancient Near East Monographs 13 (Atlanta: SBL Press, 2015), 125–50.

[28] McConville, "Ezra-Nehemiah," 210–11. On Ezra's echoes of Chronicles' account of Solomon's building efforts, see Williamson, *Ezra-Nehemiah*, 48; Nodet, "Israelites, Samaritans, Temples, Jews," 125.

[29] Joseph Blenkinsopp, *Ezra-Nehemiah: A Commentary* (Louisville: Westminster John Knox, 1988), 130.

[30] *Pace* Blenkinsopp, *Ezra-Nehemiah*, 130–31.

[31] Wayne O. McCready, "The 'Day of Small Things' vs. the Latter Days," in *Israel's Apostasy and Restoration: Essays in Honor of Roland K. Harrison*, ed. Avraham Gileadi (Grand Rapids: Baker Books, 1988), 223–36 (230).

6:14–21).[32] Likewise, the fact that the people are still called "exiles" (Ezra 6:16, 19, 20) throughout this passage – and indeed throughout the book itself – makes plain this negative view of the present state of affairs and the hope for further restoration.[33] But in case the reader misses all of these indicators, the narrator accentuates this sentiment with a remarkable anachronism, referring to the Persian ruler as "the king of Assyria" (Ezra 6:22) – surely no accident given the correct reference to the "king of Persia" only a few verses above (6:14). The implication is clear: regardless of who is now ruling the empire, Israel has not yet been freed from the oppression that began under Assyria, a freedom toward which the exiles look with hope as they observe the Passover.[34]

The positioning of the Ezra procession immediately after the Passover celebration at the rebuilt temple further accentuates the implications of this event and the hopes that it would inaugurate Israel's restoration. Although the events are separated by half a century, the narrative identifies them more closely than the chronology would suggest – the beginning of Ezra's procession is even concurrent with the Passover celebration (cf. Ezra 7:9). Moreover, as is evident by the prominence of the number twelve (cf. 8:1–14, 24), the hopes reflected in Ezra's procession are also for much more than just a restoration of the three southern tribes.[35] It is therefore unlikely to be coincidental that the terminology for the people shifts in the Ezra narratives. In contrast to the frequent references to "Jews" in the rest of Ezra-Nehemiah (nineteen times), that term is completely absent in the five chapters of the Ezra narratives, and "Judah"

---

[32] See Barry Douglas Smith, *Jesus' Last Passover Meal* (Lewiston: Mellen, 1993), 40–50. Cf. also Federico M. Colautti, *Passover in the Works of Josephus*, JSJSup 75 (Leiden: Brill, 2002); Pitre, *Jesus*, 447, "it should go without saying that to a first-century Jew there would have been no more evocative image of return from Exile than that of the Passover."

[33] בני־גלותא, בני־הגולה; cf. also Ezra 4:1; 8:35; 9:4; etc.

[34] Nodet, "Israelites, Samaritans, Temples, Jews," 125, misses the inference that the exile was still ongoing but correctly points out that "'Assyria' should not be viewed as a sloppy mistake, but as a coded message that now the Jerusalem temple is the only one for all of Israel, including any ancient returnees. In other words, the new temple is akin to Solomon's."

[35] Koch goes so far as to suggest that Ezra planned to reconstitute a twelve-tribe people by (among other things) unifying the Samarians and Judahites: "One might assume that he knew that a great portion of the tribes of former times had disappeared. He would attempt to establish new tribes out of the contemporary clans" ("Ezra," 194). Whether or not Koch's Samarian hypothesis is correct, he is surely right that Ezra's return is portrayed in a manner consistent with the expectation of a twelve-tribe restoration of Israel, whether by a miraculous return of northern Israelites or unification with Samarians. See also Dumbrell, "Malachi," 45–52.

appears only four times (excluding the personal name in 10:23) in the Ezra narratives but thirty-nine times in the rest of the book. Instead, "Israel" terminology comes to the forefront in the Ezra material, most notably in the edict of Artaxerxes, which empowers Ezra to take "any of the people of Israel" (7:13) – not just Judah, Benjamin, and Levi – who wish to go with him and establishes him as governor not over Judah but over the entire "Beyond the River province" – that is, over both Judah and Samaria (7:25).[36]

In this context, the account of Ezra's procession to the land suggests a self-conscious attempt at the fulfillment of restoration prophecies, echoing numerous prophetic passages, most notably Jeremiah 31 (MT; 38 LXX) and sections of Second Isaiah.[37] Many of these echoes account for what Grabbe calls "fairy tale features" of the story,[38] such as Ezra's rejection of an armed escort despite purportedly transporting more than twenty-five tons of gold (100 talents) and silver (750 talents) from Babylon to Jerusalem, a detail that connects with prophecies of YHWH's divine provision of a "straight path" (דרך ישרה; i.e., safe journey) upon Israel's restoration (cf. Jer 31:9; Isa 40:3), for which Ezra prays in Ezra 8:21.[39] It therefore appears to have been Ezra's aim, motivated by the messages of the exilic prophets, to rebuild a twelve-tribe Israel centered on the temple in Jerusalem, with his journey to Jerusalem – not accidentally beginning on Passover – an attempt to fulfill the promised second exodus (cf. Jer 16:14, Isa 52:7–12).[40]

Despite the initial optimism surrounding Ezra's return, the narrative does not portray that return as the successful fulfillment of the prophetic promises; instead, Ezra's efforts fail to achieve what he had hoped.[41] This is why even after his return to the land, Ezra rejoices not that the promises have been fulfilled but rather that God "has given us a little reviving in

---

[36] Cf. Dumbrell, "Malachi," 45.

[37] McConville has persuasively demonstrated numerous verbal and thematic parallels to Jer 31 (McConville, "Ezra-Nehemiah," 214–18; see esp. the parallel list on 215) and echoes of Isaiah (218–22). See also Williamson, *Ezra-Nehemiah*, 93.

[38] Grabbe, "Mind the Gaps," 92.

[39] "Indeed, the use of [דרך ישרה] in Ezra viii 21, in the sense of a safe journey, gives a meaning to [ישׁר] which is unique and which is probably explicable only in terms of the desire in Ezra to relate the return to the prophecy. Ezra's prayer is not simply that the returned exiles should have a safe journey, but that their return should in fact be that 'making straight a highway' of which the prophet speaks" (McConville, "Ezra-Nehemiah," 219).

[40] Cf. Koch, "Ezra," 184–89; Dumbrell, "Malachi," 46–47; Williamson, *Book Called Isaiah*, 93.

[41] Koch, "Ezra," 189.

our bondage, for we are slaves, yet God has not forsaken us in our bondage" (Ezra 9:8–9).[42] In spite of all the hope and optimism both at the beginning of the book and in his own procession to the land, Ezra acknowledges that the people are still "slaves," and the fear that characterizes the returnees in the narrative (e.g., Ezra 3:3; 4:4; Neh 2:2; 4:14) stands in sharp contrast to the promise that "Jacob will return and be quiet and at ease, and nothing will cause him to fear" (Jer 30:10). As put forward in the narrative, Ezra's actions are therefore "in no way exhaustive and conclusive, but are only a pre-eschatological step towards a future eschatological fulfillment."[43]

Nehemiah similarly reminds the reader that even those who had returned to the land remained in captivity, referring to the distress of "the remnant in the province who remain from the captivity" (1:3),[44] a phrase that calls attention to the fact that those in the land remained under foreign domination (hence מדינה) and were not truly free from the captivity (השבי, αἰχμαλωσία). They were instead the part from the captivity who were presently in the province – the captivity had not yet come to its end. Nehemiah's initial prayer (1:5–11) alludes to Solomon's temple dedication prayer (1 Kgs 8:22–53) and Deuteronomy 30:1–10 and petitions YHWH for the restoration promised in the latter.[45] Moreover, by the time the reader reaches the Nehemiah materials, especially the first-person narratives often called the Nehemiah memoir, the hopeful focus on Israel so evident in the early chapters of Ezra has been pared back to a focus on the Jews and the land of Judah.[46]

---

[42] This statement is reminiscent of Ezekiel's declaration that YHWH was "a little sanctuary" for the exiles (Ezek 11:16). See Harm van Grol, "'Indeed, Servants We Are': Ezra 9, Nehemiah 9, and 2 Chronicles 12 Compared," in *The Crisis of Israelite Religion: Transformation of Religious Tradition in Exilic and Post-exilic Times*, eds. Bob Becking and Marjo Christina Annette Korpel (Leiden: Brill, 1999), 209–27, for further analysis of this prayer and its implications. Williamson also notes the parallels to Deuteronomic language of exile in 9:7 and the emphatic "as we are today" as strong indicators that Ezra regards the exile as ongoing (*Ezra-Nehemiah*, 134–35). Cf. also Halvorson-Taylor, *Enduring Exile*, 6–7.

[43] Koch, "Ezra," 196.

[44] MT: הנשארים אשר־נשארו מן־השבי שם במדינה. LXX: οἱ καταλειπόμενοι οἱ καταλειφθέντες ἀπὸ τῆς αἰχμαλωσίας ἐκεῖ ἐν τῇ χώρᾳ.

[45] Cf. Knoppers, "Nehemiah and Sanballat," 310.

[46] See, for example, Neh 11–12, which lists where the returnees settled and only discusses the "sons of Judah" (Neh 11:25–30), "sons of Benjamin" (11:31–36), and the priests and Levites (12:1–26). "The focus upon the territory of Judah, as opposed to a larger territory of Israel, is telling" (Knoppers, "Did Jacob Become Judah," 41). On the Nehemiah memoir, see the discussion in Williamson, *Ezra-Nehemiah*, xxviii–xxxii and the arguments against the memoir as a separate source in Lester L. Grabbe, *Ezra-*

Even more significantly, Nehemiah's very mission to rebuild the walls of Jerusalem signals that the prophetic promises have not yet come to pass, as Zechariah (whose prophetic activity is mentioned in Ezra 5:1 and 6:14) had declared: "Jerusalem will be inhabited without walls ... because I will be for her a wall of fire around her and the glory in her midst," (Zech 2:8–9 [ET 2:4–5]).[47] Walls were very much needed in the time of Nehemiah, however, and any reader familiar with Zechariah's prophecy and Ezek 38:11 would notice the obvious gap between promise and current reality. This disconnect would obviously push any sense of fulfillment for Zechariah's prophecy into the future and away from the return depicted in Ezra-Nehemiah. Nehemiah's victories – rebuilding the walls of Jerusalem, resettling Jerusalem via lottery, and fighting to keep the priesthood pure – are indeed important for the preservation of Judah and therefore Israel. But they also serve as reminders that the prophets' promises remain unfulfilled. Indeed, though some have returned to the land, the whole people – including those in the land – remain in captivity, as the extended prayer in Nehemiah explains:

> See, we are slaves today,
> And as for the land which you gave to our fathers ...
> Indeed, we are slaves in it.
> Its rich yield goes to the kings
> Whom God has set over us because of our sins
> They rule over our bodies
> And over our cattle however they please,
> So we are in great distress.
>
> (Neh 9:36–37)[48]

In its final form, Ezra-Nehemiah thus starts on a hopeful note suggestive of the promised Israelite restoration but spirals steadily downward as it tells of the actual situation of the returnees to the land, ending both the Ezra and Nehemiah narratives with the disappointment and distress raised by the problem of intermarriage and (in Nehemiah) broken

---

Nehemiah (London: Routledge, 1998), 133–53. Cf. also Jacob L. Wright, *Rebuilding Identity*, BZAW 348 (Walter de Gruyter, 2004).

[47] This prophecy may have been a response to the cessation of the work on the walls (Ezra 4:12) forced by the "people of the land" under orders from Artaxerxes (4:23).

[48] Grol notes that the situation reflected in Neh 9 alters the traditional "sin → punishment → mercy = restoration" paradigm to a "sin → punishment → mercy = a little relief + a continuing servitude" paradigm (Grol, "Indeed, Servants We Are," 218–19). Nevertheless, Davies, "Old and New Israel," 35, observes, "there is implied hope that the slavery will one day be averted when the sins are finally forgiven." Cf. also Klein, *1 Chronicles*, 47.

Sabbaths, the latter of which "adds to the wrath on Israel" (Neh 13:18), implying that Israel is (still) already under wrath.[49] As such, the narratives of Ezra-Nehemiah, although including moments of victory, ultimately serve as a sad contrast to promises of the prophets,[50] and the sinful situations in Yehud further indicate that the days of prophetic fulfillment have not been reached.[51]

The Problem of Exogamy: Holiness as the Key to Israel's Restoration

These repeated failures provide the larger narrative context in which the book and its protagonists limit the term "Israel" to the "exiles"[52] over and against the "people of the land." More specifically, "Israel" is restricted to those from the exile who can prove their genealogical bona fides (Ezra 4:3; 9:2). This is not the same, however, as limiting "Israel" to the returnees from Judah, Benjamin, and Levi – it is not the case that "Israel is just Judah and Benjamin" in Ezra-Nehemiah as it is often understood.[53] The Jewish returnees are the sole legitimate representatives of Israel *in the land*. The rest of Israel (including many Jews who have not yet returned) remains in exile – those from other tribes who could prove their descent would also be included – while the "people of the land" are

---

[49] "Many scholars have found it improbable that the joyful ceremony of Neh. viii should lead so abruptly into the sombre act of confession in Neh. ix, x. Partly for this reason, therefore, critical reconstructions have tended to place Neh. viii directly after Ezra viii, and the confession and renewal in Neh. ix, x directly after Ezra's measures regarding marriage-abuse, i.e. following immediately upon the book of Ezra. ... This re-ordering of the material, however, also assumes a view on the part of the compiler that abuses could be purged, and a satisfactory *status quo* re-established through reforms. Such a reconstruction suffers from the difficulty that the books still end with Neh. xi–xiii, and therefore a jarring note. On my hypothesis, furthermore, namely that the books of Ezra-Nehemiah are characterized by celebration yet with reservations, a rationale exists for the transition from the joy of Neh. viii to the deliberately postponed (Neh. viii 9) lamentation of chs ix–x" (McConville, "Ezra-Nehemiah," 212 n. 22).

[50] *Pace* Japhet, "Exile and Restoration," 43; Japhet, "Post-exilic Historiography," 151.

[51] Grabbe, "Mind the Gaps," 97.

[52] That is, בני הגולה, "the children of the exile" (Ezra 4:1; 6:19–20; 8:35; 10:7, 16; בני גלותא in Ezra 6:16); העלים משבי הגולה, "those who came up from the exile" (Ezra 2:1 // Neh 7:6); העלות הגולה, "the exiles who went up" (Ezra 1:11); קהל הגולה, "the assembly of the exile" (Ezra 10:8, 12–16). The use of מעל הגולה, "the unfaithfulness of the exile" (Ezra 9:4; 10:6), is especially interesting, as it refers to the exile in the abstract rather than to the people specifically (see p. 158). Cf. also קהל האלהים, "assembly of God" (Neh 13:1).

[53] Rad, *Das Geschichtsbild*, 24. Similarly, Williamson, *Israel*, 69; Knoppers, "Did Jacob Become Judah," 40–42.

illegitimate squatters on Israel's land.[54] It is also worth noting that even the "people of the land" of Judah who could thereby justifiably be called *Yehudim* are not only not Israelites but are not *Yehudim* either.

In this view, the returned Jews are the vanguard of Israel's restoration, and their efforts are directly tied to the reconstitution of the whole people; that is, they are "engaged in the task of re-establishing the broader historical and theological reality of 'Israel.'"[55] They have separated themselves not only from the nations but also from other Yahwists in the land, all apparently in the hopes that the remainder of Israel would be restored under Jerusalem's authority. Interestingly, Ezra-Nehemiah here seems to represent an inversion of Kuhn's insider-outsider paradigm, as "Israel" denotes the in-group but "Jew" represents the holy *inner*-group that stands at the center of the larger in-group and is in fact the means of salvation for the larger group.[56] As such, Ezra-Nehemiah has no hesitation in also calling them the "children of Israel" (בני ישראל; Ezra 3:1; 6:16; 6:21; 7:7; Neh 2:10; 7:73; 9:1), or suggesting that what is good for the Jews is what is good for Israel (Neh 2:10).[57] But these references are also contextually limited by the book's frequent reminders that these "children of Israel" are not in fact the whole of the people (e.g., Ezra 1:5; 4:1, 10:9; Neh 11:4), which is still twelve tribes rather than three (e.g. Ezra 6:17; 8:35).[58]

---

[54] Grabbe, "Failure of the Xenophobes," 57. This accords with how the phrases "the peoples" (העמים) or "the peoples of the land" (עמי הארץ)are typically used to denote non-Israelites in Chronicles (e.g., 1 Chr 5:25; 16:8, 24, 26; 2 Chr 6:33; 7:20; 13:9; 32:13, 19). Cf. Knoppers, "Did Jacob Become Judah," 42. The Nehemiah memoir avoids this expression, instead referring to "the nations around us" (הגוים אשר סביבתינו; Neh 5:17; 6:6, 16; cf. Ezra 6:21). See Knoppers, "Nehemiah and Sanballat," 312.

[55] Blumhofer, *Future of Israel*, 17.

[56] Cf. Talmon, "Emergence of Jewish Sectarianism," 599.

[57] This comment involves a pun on Tobiah's name, suggesting that Nehemiah is bringing the "good" (תובה) to Israel that Tobiah (טוביה) not only cannot provide but, as (according to Nehemiah) an Ammonite, cannot participate in (Deut 23:4–7; cf. Neh 13:1). See Knoppers, "Nehemiah and Sanballat," 313; Joseph Blenkinsopp, *Ezra-Nehemiah: A Commentary*, OTL (Philadelphia: Westminster, 1988), 219.

[58] The same patterns hold in 1 Esdras as well, which is mostly identical to Ezra-Nehemiah with respect to Israel/Judah language. The following are the relevant verses in 1 Esd with variants from the parallels in Ezra-Nehemiah: 1 Esd 5:41 ("whole of Israel" // Ezra 2:64, Neh 7:66, "the whole assembly"); 1 Esd 7:10 ("children of Israel that were of the captivity" // Ezra 6:19, "the exiles"); 1 Esd 8:7 ("taught all Israel the just things and judgments" // Ezra 7:11 "commands of YHWH and his statutes to Israel"); 1 Esd 8:89 ("Jechoniah ... one of the children of Israel, called out" // Ezra 10:2 "Shecaniah ... yet now there is hope for Israel"). None of these is significant enough to warrant a separate treatment, as the argument about Ezra-Nehemiah here ultimately applies equally well to 1 Esdras.

In this context, the sharp critiques of exogamy found in the Ezra and Nehemiah narratives depend on three convictions: (1) the exile has not ended but is instead ongoing, and life in the land is not different from life abroad in this respect, (2) the "people of the land" who identify themselves as Yahwists and Israelites are not in fact Israelites but rather those God has rejected (cf. Jer 24, Ezek 11), while the rest of Israel remains abroad, and (3) the full and final restoration of Israel depends on "returning to YHWH" (Neh 1:9) in obedience and holiness (separation) from the non-Israelite nations. Intermarriage is so disastrous in the view of the book and its protagonists precisely because it represents a lack of obedience and separation and thereby threatens the final restoration, ensuring that wrath remains on Israel (cf. Ezra 9:13–14; Neh 13:18, 23–29).[59] This explains why Ezra 9:4 and 10:6 lament not the "unfaithfulness of the exiles" (that is, the people) as typically rendered into English but rather "the unfaithfulness of the exile" – the problem is that the exile had not resulted in faithfulness as it was supposed to.[60]

Many returnees, however, seem to have disagreed with this perspective, as the book itself (the Nehemiah memoir in particular) bears witness. Indeed, those who chose to marry outside the group of Jewish returnees seem to have accepted the Israelite status of the other Yahwists in the land and may no longer have held hopes of further restoration. In such a "realized eschatology," since the new age has already begun, maintaining the strict endogamy of the exile is no longer necessary for those in the land.[61] Nehemiah's enemies Tobiah and Sanballat, for example, are both Yahwists and self-identified Israelites, likely claiming to be from northern stock.[62] This claim seems to have been accepted by many, if not most, of the Jerusalem elites – including, as Nehemiah strikingly admits, the prophets (6:14) and even the high priest himself.[63] Knoppers' judgment

---

[59] Cf. McConville, "Ezra-Nehemiah," 216–17, 222–24. Either way, Ezra and Nehemiah are among those insisting that a more significant future restoration contingent upon adequate repentance and purity awaits.

[60] Heb: מעל הגולה; LXX: ἀσυνθεσίᾳ τῆς ἀποικίας. It is noteworthy that the Greek translator did not gloss the phrase as do many English translators.

[61] Cf. the similar judgment of R. Joshua to admit an "Ammonite" into the assembly (via marriage) in m. Yad 4:4. R. Joshua's rationale is that because none of the nations (including Israel and Judah!) have returned but instead, "Sennacherib, the king of Assyria, came and mingled all the nations," so prohibitions against intermarriage with Ammonites or Moabites are no longer coherent or applicable to the current situation.

[62] For more on the origins and Israelite self-identification of Tobiah and Sanballat, see Knoppers, "Nehemiah and Sanballat," 317–30 and the many references provided there.

[63] "It is entirely conceivable that a good many of Nehemiah's own supporters balked at including self-professed Israelites in the register of peoples whom Judeans could not marry" (Knoppers, "Nehemiah and Sanballat," 320). On the prophetic opposition to

that "like earlier prophets ... these prophets may have held to and promoted a comprehensive understanding of Israel" is most likely correct,[64] but we have already established that Ezra-Nehemiah similarly holds to a comprehensive understanding of Israel. The difference does not concern whether Israel is in fact larger than the community of returnees from the three southern tribes but rather concerns the status of the non-Jews in the land. For Nehemiah, regardless of their self-identification, these Yahwists who are opposed to Jerusalem's hegemony – and, at least in the case of Sanballat, sacrifice to YHWH elsewhere – are false Israelites (thus the significance of labeling Tobiah an "Ammonite" and Sanballat a "Horonite"), and their opposition to the rebuilding of Jerusalem's walls is in fact opposition to Israel, which will be unified under Jerusalem's sovereignty at the restoration.[65] Similarly, those Jews who have established kinship ties with these non-Israelites and their inadequate (non-Jerusalem-centered) worship of YHWH are endangering the welfare of Israel.

In this respect, the book and its protagonists want to have their cake and eat it too, circumscribing Israel in the land to the returnees from Judah, Benjamin, and Levi and those committed to Jerusalem's hegemony while simultaneously arguing that Israel in fact extends far beyond this community, which must maintain its purity and separation in order to facilitate the ultimate welfare of the whole people. Nevertheless, each episode of Ezra-Nehemiah begins in hope and ends in failure and disappointment,[66] with each failure prompting more rigorous efforts to purify the "holy seed," establish proper cultic observances, and separate from

---

Nehemiah, see Knoppers, "Nehemiah and Sanballat," 322–23; David Shepherd, "Prophetaphobia: Fear and False Prophecy in Nehemiah VI," *VT* 55 (2005): 232–50. That the protagonists of the book of Tobit are named Tobit and Tobias (= Tobiah) is an interesting bit of intertext here, especially given the prominence of the Tobiads after the period of Nehemiah (cf. 2 Macc 3:1–12; Jos. *Ant.* 12.4; Grabbe, "Failure of the Xenophobes," 58–60).

[64] Knoppers, "Nehemiah and Sanballat," 323.

[65] In this respect, Knoppers is correct in arguing "that what was going on in Nehemiah's Judah was not simply a debate about Judean identity but also a debate about Israelite identity. The two were distinct but very much related projects" ("Nehemiah and Sanballat," 320). It is worth noting that based on Zech 2:8–9 (ET 2:4–5), Nehemiah's opponents may have regarded the absence of walls as YHWH's will for restored Jerusalem (see p. 155).

[66] "Nehemiah's reforms were temporary, lasting only as long as he could maintain them by force. In the following century ... [we find] a community that took a rather different view from that of Nehemiah" (Grabbe, "Failure of the Xenophobes," 64).

the nations.[67] Indeed, the final chapter of Nehemiah sequentially epitomizes the failure of all three reform movements reflected in the book (each episode ending with Nehemiah's plea that God nevertheless remember him for his efforts), as the Jerusalem temple is misused and forsaken (13:4–14), the people are violating the Sabbath and thus Ezra's instruction (13:15–22), and exogamy continues to be practiced (13:22–31). For Ezra-Nehemiah, Israel is not as it should be, and those from Judah, Benjamin, and Levi must further repent, purify, and separate themselves for things to be set right. As such, Ezra-Nehemiah represents the beginning of the restorationist Jewish sectarianism that characterizes the later Second Temple period, with competing groups attempting to establish the correct halakha and thereby initiate Israel's restoration and the end of the age of wrath.[68]

Although there are indeed differences in perspective between the two works, it is mistaken to label Ezra-Nehemiah's eschatology "realized" and see it as at odds with the more hopeful perspective of Chronicles. For all the hopes of Israel's restoration reflected in the Ezra material and the reality that some Israelites indeed returned to the land of Judah, the returnees have continued in the behavior of their predecessors that led to the exile in the first place, and the ethical transformation that must accompany the restoration remains absent in the community of returnees. In the end, despite "a little reviving" (Ezra 9:8) including the rebuilding of the temple and the return of many Israelites, primarily from the southern tribes, Israel remains under Assyria (cf. Ezra 6:22, Neh 9:32), and the promised restoration therefore still lies in the future, contingent on proper obedience to YHWH's law.[69] As will be seen through the remainder of this study, unlike many modern interpreters, most early Jewish readers seem to have understood Ezra-Nehemiah in this manner, regarding the

---

[67] As noted by McConville, "Ezra-Nehemiah," 211–12, "[There is a] possibility that the compiler of Ezra-Nehemiah intended to end his work with the rather depressing re-emergence of problems which had beset the community, marital abuse in the centre. It is evident that Neh. xiii represents a low note. ... The clear implication is that, were the story of post-exilic community to be protracted, it would continue to follow the same chequered course that it has throughout our books. More important than the question of order, however, is the fact that mixed marriage is closely associated with the idea of slavery. ... It follows from this association of the mixed-marriage phenomenon with bondage to Persia that the problem which Ezra and Nehemiah face is actually complex, and will cease to exist only when bondage to Persia is a thing of the past." See also Grabbe, "Mind the Gaps," 84, 97, 100–01.

[68] Later groups would include the Maccabean Hasidim, the Pharisees, the Dead Sea Scroll sect, and the sects led by John the Baptist and Jesus. For Ezra and Nehemiah as the origin of Jewish sectarianism, see Talmon, "Emergence of Jewish Sectarianism," 593–601.

[69] Cf. Gregory, "Post-exilic Exile," 491.

Persian-period return(s) as by no means the fulfillment of Israel's restoration but rather still anticipating it.

DANIEL: ISRAEL'S RESTORATION DELAYED SEVENFOLD

As is evident from Ezra-Nehemiah, the optimism of the initial return from Babylon ultimately faded into disappointment as it became clear that the return had fallen far short of the prophetic promises, but as is often the case with failed predictions, those promises were not forgotten or abandoned but instead pushed into the future. The book of Daniel, with its apocalyptic periodizations of history and explanations of the present state of affairs dominated by imperial powers, provides an excellent example of how that dissonance between expectations and reality did just that, pushing the expectations of Israelite restoration into the future. Daniel also became exceedingly important in the first centuries BCE and CE, as by that point, "Daniel spread his light over all the prophets ... all the prophets were interpreted along the lines set out in Daniel."[70] Amid the court stories and apocalyptic visions, a central portion of Daniel answers the question of why, despite Jeremiah's prophecy of a seventy-year exile, the promised restoration of Israel had not yet happened:

> In the first year of [Darius'] reign, I, Daniel, understood in the books the number of years that, according to the word of YHWH to Jeremiah the prophet, must be fulfilled for the devastation of Jerusalem: seventy years. Then I turned to YHWH God to seek an answer [why this had not happened] by prayer and supplication with fasting and sackcloth and ashes. (Dan 9:2–3)

In response to the lack of fulfillment of Jeremiah's promise, Daniel attempts to intercede on behalf of the people,[71] offering a prayer of

---

[70] Klaus Koch, "Is Daniel Also among the Prophets?," *Int* 39.2 (1985): 117–30 (126). On Daniel's influence in the first centuries BCE and CE, see also Steve Mason, "Josephus, Daniel, and the Flavian House," in *Josephus and the History of the Greco-Roman Period*, eds. Morton Smith, Fausto Parente, and Joseph Sievers (Leiden: Brill, 1994), 161–91 (165–67); John J. Collins, *Daniel: A Commentary*, Hermeneia 27 (Minneapolis: Fortress, 1993), 90–112 (section by Adela Yarbro Collins).

[71] Gerald H. Wilson, "The Prayer of Daniel 9: Reflection on Jeremiah 29," *JSOT* 48 (1990): 91–99; John S. Bergsma, "The Persian Period as Penitential Era: The 'Exegetical Logic' of Daniel 9:1–27," in *Exile and Restoration Revisited: Essays on the Babylonian and Persian Period in Memory of Peter R. Ackroyd*, eds. Gary N. Knoppers, Lester L. Grabbe, and Dierdre N. Fulton, LSTS 73 (London: T&T Clark, 2009), 50–64 (57); Odil Hannes Steck, *Israel und das gewaltsame Geschick der Propheten: Untersuchung zur Überlieferung des deuteronomistischen Geschichtsbildes im Alten Testament*,

confession prominently featuring the schema of sin, exile, repentance, and restoration (9:4–19).[72] Significantly, Daniel specifies those remaining in need of restoration, mentioning "Judah [and] the inhabitants of Jerusalem" *plus* "all Israel, those who are nearby and those who are far away, in all the lands to which you have driven them" (Dan 9:7; cf. 2 Chr 6:36; Jer 16:16; 23:3–8; Isa 33:13; 57:19).[73] Judah is again distinguished as but a part of the totality of Israel, which includes exiles near and far from both Judah and the non-Judahite portions of Israel. As such, Goodblatt's proposal that Daniel serves as "the major exception to the preference for 'Israel'" observed in books composed in Hebrew because it reflects "non-Jewish usage" due to Persian/Aramaic influence is not only implausible but unnecessary.[74] Instead, as has been the case elsewhere throughout the biblical material, Daniel treats these terms as having a partitive relationship and, inasmuch as the book is set in the Babylonian Exile, its narratives depict those from Judah rather than from Israel. But when the focus expands to the whole people, the term "Israel" predictably reappears. In any case, in response to his prayer, Daniel receives an explanation from a heavenly messenger, Gabriel:

Spätjudentum und Urchristentum, WMANT 23 (Neukirchen-Vluyn: Neukirchener Verlag, 1967), 110–36.

[72] "The theology of the prayer is strongly Deuteronomic" (Collins, *Daniel*, 359). Collins, however, argues that the vision of vv. 24–27 does not reflect the Deuteronomic worldview reflected in the prayer and that the book of Daniel instead blames the gentile "beasts" (empires) and divine decree rather than Israel's sin for Israel's downtrodden situation (*The Apocalyptic Vision of the Book of Daniel*, HSM 16 [Missoula: Scholars Press, 1977], 95–96; Collins, *Daniel*, 360). This interpretation, however, is at odds with the fact that the decree amounts to a sevenfold multiplication of the *original* punishment, which assumes a Deuteronomic scheme of sin and punishment. The apocalyptic and Deuteronomic perspectives reflected in the chapter are therefore not at odds, upholding "apocalyptic determinism" (e.g. Bruce William Jones, "The Prayer in Daniel IX," *VT* 18.4 [1968]: 488–93 [493]) over and against Deuteronomic theology, but rather in concert, with the divine decree a response to Israel's violation of covenant. The gentile "beasts" have been given power only until Israel is restored, with Deuteronomic theology providing a necessary underpinning for the larger apocalyptic framework. Unfortunately, space does not permit a fuller exposition on this point, but it should suffice to say that the book of Daniel reflects continued concern with the incomplete restoration of Israel in the Hellenistic period. Some, such as Louis Francis Hartman and Alexander A. Di Lella, *The Book of Daniel*, AB 23 (Garden City: Doubleday, 1978), 245–46, have argued the prayer is a later addition to the apocalyptic portion of the chapter, but this is irrelevant when considering how it might have been understood by a first-century Jew or Christian.

[73] Pitre, *Jesus*, 59: "i.e., not just in Babylon. Here Daniel is using a distinct Hebrew phrase from the book of Jeremiah for describing *both* the Assyrian and Judean exiles" (his emphasis).

[74] Goodblatt, "Israelites Who Reside in Judah," 76–77.

Seventy sevens have been decreed for your people and your holy city, to complete the transgression, end sin, atone for iniquity, bring in everlasting righteousness, seal up vision and prophecy, and anoint the most holy. (Dan 9:24)

That is, since the people have not met the conditions of repentance stated in Jer 29:12–14, Israel's punishment had been multiplied seven-fold.[75] The desolation was now to last not seventy years but "seventy sevens" (Dan 9:24; that is, seventy *sabbatical* years), applying Leviticus 26:18, "If you do not obey me even after all these things, I will punish you seven times more for your sins" to Jeremiah's prophecy.[76] Despite the delay, Jerusalem would itself be rebuilt long before the restoration, "[your holy city] will be rebuilt, with streets and moat and in times of oppression" (9:25), an obvious allusion to the rebuilding of Jerusalem's walls under Nehemiah.[77] The passage thus makes it clear that the events of Ezra-Nehemiah were not the promised restoration; rather, another sixty-three "sevens" stood between those events and the promised redemption, the grand-jubilee announced by Gabriel.[78] That restoration – including atonement for Israel's sin – would come at the end of this extended period, at which point an "anointed one, the prince" (Dan 9:25–26) would be "cut off" (cf. Isa 53:8),[79] setting in motion the final restoration and the end of the age of wrath.[80] After this, Jerusalem and the sanctuary were to be "ruined" (שחת; LXX: [δια]φθείρω) yet again, an event both Josephus and early Christians connected with the Roman destruction of Jerusalem.[81]

---

[75] Bergsma, "Persian Period as Penitential Era," 55.

[76] See also Lev 26:21, 24, 28; 2 Chron 36:21. Cf. Bergsma, "Persian Period as Penitential Era," 55–58; Michael Fishbane, *Biblical Interpretation in Ancient Israel* (Oxford: Clarendon, 1985), 487–89; Anathea E. Portier-Young, *Apocalypse against Empire: Theologies of Resistance in Early Judaism* (Grand Rapids: Eerdmans, 2011), 271; Hartman and Di Lella, *Daniel*, 249–53; and Collins, *Daniel*, 352 and the sources cited there.

[77] Cf. Hartman and Di Lella, *Daniel*, 250–51.

[78] Cf. John S. Bergsma, *The Jubilee from Leviticus to Qumran: A History of Interpretation*, VTSup 115 (Leiden: Brill, 2007), 225–27, countering John E. Goldingay, *Daniel*, WBC 30 (Waco: Word, 1989), 267.

[79] For the links between the Suffering Servant of Isaiah 52:13–53:12 and this anointed one that is "cut off," see William H. Brownlee, "The Servant of the Lord in the Qumran Scrolls I," *BASOR* 132 (1953): 8–15 (12–15); cf. also Harold Louis Ginsberg, "The Oldest Interpretation of the Suffering Servant," *VT* 3.4 (1953): 400–4; Goldingay, *Daniel*, 300; and Portier-Young, *Apocalypse against Empire*, 272–76. The oft-repeated dictum that there is no evidence for the concept of a suffering and dying "anointed one" or of a messianic interpretation of the Suffering Servant in pre-Christian Judaism is therefore mistaken.

[80] Cf. Hartman and Di Lella, *Daniel*, 251–53.

[81] Cf. Josephus, *Ant.* 10.276. Most modern scholars, of course, interpret these verses as *ex eventu* references to Antiochus IV Epiphanes' desolation of Jerusalem "by corruption of

Daniel thus provides the earliest extant overt interpretation of the events of Ezra-Nehemiah and does not interpret the events of that book – important though they were – as fulfilling the promises of Israel's restoration. Rather, Daniel demonstrates that the expectation for a fuller restoration than that of Ezra-Nehemiah remained fervent well into the Hellenistic period, a period that featured its own attempts to fulfill the prophecies of restoration.[82] Michael Knibb aptly summarizes Daniel's position:

> The exile was now, and only now, to have its proper end, and in the author's view everything that has happened between the carrying away into captivity of [Israel and Judah] and the time of Antiochus was of little importance. Rather, this period is seen as a unity whose characteristic is sin. We are in a situation where the exile is understood as a state that is to be ended only by the intervention of God and the inauguration of the eschatological era.[83]

Moreover, as Pitre explains, "the messianic tribulation described by Gabriel, when read in context, is nothing less than the answer to Daniel's prayer for God to restore his scattered people from exile – including the Assyrian exiles."[84] Given its importance in the first century as the interpretive key to the other prophets and prophecies of the Bible, Daniel's treatment of the return from Babylon as an intermediate stage at best and emphatic expectations for a future restoration including both Israel and Judah is especially important for an understanding of early Jewish understandings of Israel and attitudes about the present. Like Deuteronomy and the biblical tradition preceding it, the book of Daniel places the reader in a liminal space, a time in which Israel remains scattered and indistinct but on the cusp of restoration.

I ENOCH: STILL AWAITING THE TRUE RESTORATION

A similar perspective is found in I Enoch,[85] which although set in the antediluvian past features apocalyptic visions that address the reader's future, with such eschatological proclamations coming as early as the first

---

the cult" (Collins, *Daniel*, 357; cf. Hartman and Di Lella, *Daniel*, 252–54). That Josephus would take these verses as referring to the Roman destruction is somewhat puzzling, as it is hard to imagine that he (like early Christians) would have understood the earlier, messianic parts of the prophecy as having been fulfilled prior to the Roman destruction of Jerusalem.

[82] Bergsma, "Persian Period as Penitential Era," 60–62.
[83] Knibb, "The Exile in the Literature of the Intertestamental Period," 255.
[84] Pitre, *Jesus*, 60.
[85] I Enoch is a compilation of five originally independent works composed in Hebrew and/ or Aramaic and attributed to the figure of Enoch from Genesis 5:21–24. For introductory

chapter.[86] Like Daniel, the Animal Apocalypse of 1 Enoch portrays the return from Babylon as limited and fundamentally flawed, as only three of the sheep returned to build the temple,[87] and the sacrifices offered in it were "polluted and not pure" (1 En. 89:73). James VanderKam explains:

Both [Daniel and the writer of the Animal Apocalypse] were aware that the historical movement in 538, however momentous to some, did not mark an ultimately significant or meaningful point in the history of God's dealings with his people. The time of Babylonian exile was merely the first part (the first 12 times) of a larger and longer-lasting phenomenon – the cruel reign of the seventy shepherds which would continue to the imminent end. The word exile never surfaces in the symbolic narrative of the Animal Apocalypse, but the language of dispersion is used and continues to be employed even after the end of the historical exile (see, e.g., 89:75). For the author, exile was an ongoing condition that would soon end with the final judgment.[88]

Furthermore, "all that had been destroyed and dispersed" (1 En. 90:33) do not return until after the eschatological throne is established, when the "Lord of the sheep" sits in judgment. In addition, the Animal Apocalypse connects the return of the sheep with their finally becoming obedient to their Lord (90:33–34).[89] An especially striking element of the Animal Apocalypse is its depiction of the fate of the gentiles at this future time.[90] Remarkably, the dispersed sheep return together with the various

---

matters on 1 Enoch, see E. Isaac, "1 (Ethiopic Apocalypse of) Enoch," in *OTP* 1, 5–89; George W. E. Nickelsburg, *1 Enoch: A Commentary on the Book of 1 Enoch*, Hermeneia (Minneapolis: Fortress, 2001); Matthew Black and James C. VanderKam, eds., *The Book of Enoch, or, 1 Enoch: A New English Edition: With Commentary and Textual Notes* (Leiden: Brill, 1985). The chronological elements of the Book of Dreams, more specifically in the Animal Apocalypse (chs. 85–90), are most relevant to this section, but that general eschatological perspective persists throughout the rest of the corpus. Translations of 1 Enoch are from Nickelsburg, *1 Enoch* unless otherwise noted.

[86] 1 En. 1:9 is of course known for its use in Jude 14–15, but more noteworthy in this context is 1 En. 1:6, which Ferda, "Ingathering of the Exiles," 180–81 n. 60, suggests is an allusion to Isa 40 to "signal eschatological restoration and the reversal of Israel's misfortunes."

[87] Patrick A. Tiller, *A Commentary on the Animal Apocalypse of 1 Enoch*, EJL 4 (Atlanta: Scholars Press, 1993), 38 n. 41, argues that *two* is the original reading of the passage.

[88] James C. VanderKam, "Exile in Jewish Apocalyptic Literature," in *Exile: Old Testament, Jewish, and Christian Conceptions*, ed. James M. Scott, JSJSup 56 (Leiden: Brill, 1997), 89–109 (100).

[89] A similar theme is present but lacks the emphasis on the return to the land in Jubilees, in which "restoration of a lost purity, not exile and return to the land, is the signature of the imminent eschaton." Betsy Halpern-Amaru, "Exile and Return in Jubilees," in *Exile: Old Testament, Jewish, and Christian Conceptions*, ed. James M. Scott, JSJSup 56 (Leiden: Brill, 1997), 127–44 (144).

[90] See Daniel C. Olson, *A New Reading of the Animal Apocalypse of 1 Enoch: "All Nations Shall be Blessed,"* SVTP 24 (Leiden: Brill, 2013); Matthew Thiessen, *Contesting Conversion: Genealogy, Circumcision, and Identity in Ancient Judaism and*

beasts (=gentiles), which also enter the house of the Lord, apparently having been made "good" like the sheep (90:33–34), thus providing an example of what has been called "flexible election."[91] The terms "Israel" and "Jew" do not appear in 1 Enoch, as they would be anachronistic in an antediluvian setting, but the eschatological perspective and view of the exile/diaspora reflected in 1 Enoch provides further evidence of later Jews not regarding the Persian-period returns narrated in Ezra-Nehemiah as having ended Israel's exile.

1 MACCABEES: AN EXCEPTION PROVING THE RULE

About three centuries after Ezra and Nehemiah, another effort was made to initiate Israel's restoration, this time through the military campaigns of the Maccabean Revolt and the establishment of the Hasmonean Dynasty. The accounts of these events are especially important to this study, as 1 Maccabees provides the primary basis (along with later rabbinic literature) for the insider/outsider paradigm. Kuhn explains:

The usage of Palestinian Jews is best seen in 1 Macc. In the true historical presentation of this book, where the author himself speaks, there is a consistent use of Ἰσραήλ. But there is also a consistent and exclusive use of Ἰουδαῖοι . . .

(1) when non-Jews are speaking. . . .
(2) In diplomatic correspondence, letters and treaties with non-Jewish states and rulers. . . .
(3) Ἰουδαῖοι, not Ἰσραήλ is also used by the Jews themselves in diplomatic communications with non-Jewish states. . . .
(4) Not merely in external affairs, but also in official domestic documents Ἰουδαῖοι is always used for the people, not Israel.[92]

In addition, although 1 Maccabees is only preserved in Greek, nearly all commentators have concluded it is based on a Hebrew original, so Goodblatt's linguistic version of the insider/outsider model likewise depends heavily on 1 Maccabees.[93] Unlike the other texts we have

---

Christianity (New York: Oxford University Press, 2011), 89–94; Nickelsburg, *1 Enoch*, 403.

[91] Ophir and Rosen-Zvi, *Goy*, 94–96.
[92] Kuhn, "Ἰουδαῖος κτλ," *TDNT* 3:360–61.
[93] Goodblatt, "Israelites Who Reside in Judah." On 1 Maccabees as deriving from an original Hebrew document, see Uriel Rappaport, *The First Book of Maccabees – Introduction, Hebrew Translation and Commentary* (Jerusalem: Yad Izhak Ben-Zvi, 2004), 9–10 and the sources cited there.

examined so far, 1 Maccabees uses "Israel" and "Israelites" (apparently) interchangeably with "Judaea" and *Ioudaioi*, with Israel and cognates appearing sixty-three times (3.12 per 1000 words) versus thirty-seven uses of *Ioudaios* (1.83/1000) and twenty-seven of Judah/Judaea (1.34/ 100), combining for sixty-four uses (3.17/1000). On the surface, this seems to run counter to the usual partitive relationship between these terms observed elsewhere in biblical literature and to favor Kuhn's reading of the data,[94] but sometimes the exceptions to a trend further illustrate the logic underlying the trend, and in the case of the link between restoration eschatology and Israel/*Ioudaioi* terminology, the Maccabean literature does just that.

First, it should be noted that although Kuhn is correct that the narrator's voice tends to use "Israel" in 1 Maccabees, the narrator by no means avoids *Ioudaios* when speaking in his own voice (cf. 1 Macc 1:29; 2:22:23; 4:2; 11:47; 11:49; 14:33, 34, 37, 40, 47, 51). Instead, the narrator actually prefers *Ioudaios* when speaking of the specific political entity and people of Judaea, tending toward "Israel(ites)" only when speaking on a grander, more cosmic, "biblical" scale. Consider the differences in the following narrative statements:

Very great wrath came upon Israel. (1 Macc 1:64)

When he had finished speaking these words, a *Ioudaios* came forward in the sight of all to offer sacrifice on the altar in Modein, according to the king's command. (1 Macc 2:23)

All his brothers and all those who had joined his father helped him; they gladly fought for Israel. (1 Macc 3:2)

This division moved out by night to fall upon the camp of the *Ioudaioi* and attack them suddenly. (1 Macc 4:1b–2)

Thus Israel had a great deliverance that day. (1 Macc 4:25)

They gained control of the land of Judah and did great damage in Israel. (1 Macc 7:22)

And he placed garrisons in [those cities] to harass Israel. (1 Macc 9:51)

So the king called the *Ioudaioi* to his aid, and they all rallied around him and then spread out through the city; and they killed on that day about one hundred thousand. (1 Macc 11:47)

And the sword rested from Israel. Jonathan dwelt in Michmash and began to judge the people, and he destroyed the impious out of Israel. (1 Macc 9:73)

---

[94] Thus as recently as Goodblatt, "Israelites Who Reside in Judah," 74–79.

And they threw down their arms and made peace. So the *Ioudaioi* gained glory in the sight of the king and of all the people in his kingdom, and they returned to Jerusalem with a large amount of spoil. (1 Macc 11:51)

He established peace in the land, and Israel rejoiced with great joy. (1 Macc 14:11)

An insider/outsider distinction between the terms cannot account for the variation shown in these narrative statements; that paradigm is insufficient even in the source upon which it is primarily built. A better explanation is provided by understanding the propagandistic aim of 1 Maccabees in light of Jewish expectations of restoration. In Jonathan Goldstein's words, "1 Maccabees is a history written to demonstrate the right of the Hasmonean dynasty ... to be hereditary high priests and princes ruling the Jews."[95] As already observed in Daniel, some Jews saw the events surrounding the Maccabean Revolt as "the end of days," the final period of tribulation before the "age of wrath" ended, ushering in the restoration of Israel. But the events following the mostly-victorious resistance against the Seleucids were not ultimately accompanied by a miraculous restoration of Israel and a messianic rule.[96] In this environment, 1 Maccabees constructs its narrative in such a way as to argue that the newly independent state of Judah/Judaea under Hasmonean rule is in fact at least the beginning of the fulfillment of the promises of Israel's restoration. Goldstein explains:

The predictions of how God after the end of the Babylonian exile would bring about a great restored Israel in a perfected world can be divided into two classes: those that could conceivably be fulfilled by Jewish mortals (e.g., conquest of Moab, Ammon, and Philistia; military security for Judaea), and those that could be fulfilled only by a supernatural power (e.g., creation of new heavens and a new earth, resurrection of the dead, streaming of the gentiles of their own free will to Jerusalem to learn the ways of the God of Jacob). The Hasmonaean propagandist does not touch the predictions that could be fulfilled only by a supernatural

---

[95] Goldstein, "Messianic Promises," 73. Following Goldstein, I will refer to the author of 1 Maccabees as the "Hasmonean propagandist." Cf. also Daniel R. Schwartz, "The Other in 1 and 2 Maccabees," in *Tolerance and Intolerance in Early Judaism and Christianity*, eds. Graham N. Stanton and Guy G. Stroumsa (Cambridge: Cambridge University Press, 1998), 30–37 (31–32).

[96] Goldstein, "Messianic Promises," 78: "More than one generation had elapsed by the time he wrote. It was therefore obvious to the Hasmonaean propagandist that the troubles had not been the prophesied prelude to the Last Days." Goldstein elsewhere observes that the author of 1 Macc repeatedly "took delight in exposing what he saw as the falsity of Daniel 7–12" (*I Maccabees*, AB 41 [Garden City: Doubleday, 1976], 560, cf. also 42–54), whereas Jason of Cyrene, the author of the work abridged in 2 Maccabees, preferred Daniel over 1 Macc (48–49).

power, but he exploits some of his opportunities to suggest that Hasmonaeans fulfilled those possible for mortals, as we shall see, and one could go on to trace the efforts of Hasmonaeans to fulfill them after the times narrated in 1 Maccabees.[97]

The military successes of the Hasmoneans against gentile oppressors "proved that the Age of Wrath was at last approaching its end,"[98] and 1 Maccabees goes out of its way to show how the Hasmoneans were in fact fulfilling the promises to Israel. The propagandist's use of "Israel" language is therefore a result of his attempt to connect the acts of the Hasmoneans to Israel's restoration. He applies the term Israel precisely because he is making a case about Israelite restoration. His characters, on the other hand, do not tend to use this terminology, as readers would know that this was not the language typically used by Judahites, most of whom were still using the default term *Ioudaios*, since the eschatological restoration of Israel had not yet taken place. The few times Israel is heard on the lips of a character within the story are always in theological or covenantal contexts like prayer (4:11, 30–31; 13:4), in which the term would be expected not because of an "insider/outsider" distinction but because it is the proper covenantal term – YHWH is the God of Israel, the full people of the covenant, not just the God of Judah. Again, recall that the Hasmonean state was called "Judah" and its people "Jews," as Kuhn himself acknowledges:

Hasmonean coins bear out this conclusion. Here היהודים [the Jews] is consistently used, since the reference is to official titles. It is of interest to compare the shekel which was probably minted during the great revolt of 66–70 AD. This bears the inscription שקל ישראל [Shekel of Israel], Cf. also the coins minted under Bar Cochba in 132–135 AD, which carry the inscriptions לגולת ישראל [for the redemption of Israel] and לחרות ישראל [for the freedom of Israel]. יהודים [Jews] on Hasmonean coins is the correct official inscription; the ישראל [Israel] of the rebellions proclaims a religio-political programme, namely, that we, the people of God, now throw off the yoke of the Gentiles, that the Messianic age is dawning, and that it brings with it the redemption (גאלה!) and freedom (הרות!), the dominion and glory, of the people of God.[99]

Goodblatt has further confirmed this conclusion, finding it "somewhat surprising,"[100] since it seems at odds with Kuhn's insider/outsider paradigm, which "would lead us to expect the use of the term 'Israel' as the

---

[97] Goldstein, "Messianic Promises," 75–76.
[98] Goldstein, "Messianic Promises," 76.
[99] Kuhn, "Ἰουδαῖος κτλ," *TDNT* 3: 361.
[100] Goodblatt, "Judeans to Israel," 10.

preferred self-designation."[101] Tomson is likewise at a loss at how to deal with this "witness to the striking phenomenon of 'outside speech,' in Hebrew, by Jewish officials,"[102] coming to the implausible conclusion that by using *Yehudim*, "the Hasmonean leaders portray themselves in a non-Jewish perspective."[103] Goodblatt sees this as an indicator of "the conflicted identity of the Hasmoneans" but confesses in the next breath that "a convincing explanation of Hasmonean usage still eludes me."[104] No such interpretive gymnastics or confusion is necessary once one recognizes that such usage as witnessed in 1 Maccabees is not "outside speech" at all but an application of the usual and proper ethnonym for the group in question. As we have repeatedly observed, *Yehudi/Ioudaios* was simply the standard way Jews of the period referred to themselves and their state, particularly in light of the "Israel" located in the region around Samaria.[105] Consequently, a reader in the Hasmonean period would be accustomed to *Ioudaios* or *Yehudi* in common speech for the people and nation.

In other words, instead of asking why 1 Maccabees (and the Hasmoneans) would use Jew/Judaean/Judah terminology and regarding that as anomalous, the better question is why 1 Maccabees so frequently and anomalously uses "Israel" language. The answer to that question is more straightforward. By using heightened biblical terminology, the Hasmonean propagandist associates the Hasmonean kingdom with the more historically and rhetorically powerful covenantal term "Israel." The author is at pains to convince the reader, for whom "Judah" terminology was normative, that Hasmonean Judah/Judaea should be understood as fulfilling God's promises about the restoration of Israel. As can be seen from the evidence presented above, the Hasmonean propagandist does not in fact treat "Israel(ites)" and Judah/*Ioudaios* as synonymous but instead restricts each term to its appropriate sphere. "Judah" language

---

[101] Goodblatt, "Judeans to Israel," 16. "Kuhn felt obliged to explain the use of "Israel" by the rebels. However, based on the evidence he himself adduced, the latter term is what we would have expected in any event. It is not so much the shift to "Israel" that requires explanation, but rather the use of 'Judeans" by the Hasmonean state" (Goodblatt, "Judeans to Israel," 35). Goodblatt further puzzles over this "anomaly" in Goodblatt, "Israelites Who Reside in Judah."

[102] Tomson, "Names," 129.

[103] Tomson, "Names," 132.

[104] Goodblatt, "Israelites Who Reside in Judah," 86.

[105] As noted by Boyarin, "The IOUDAIOI in John," 227: "Now the natural name for the citizens of this tiny Temple-State would be 'children of Judah' (בני יהודה) or 'Yahudim' (יהודים; Ἰουδαῖοι)."

continues as the default when speaking in a more mundane register – even Simon's response to Antiochus only claims "the legal rights of the Judeans over Judea's territory"[106] rather than the full territory of biblical Israel (1 Macc 15:28–36). In contrast, "Israel" language is preferred when rhetorically connecting the actions of Judah the Maccabee and the Hasmoneans with the eschatological promises to Israel.

The propagandist is thoroughgoing in his efforts to connect the Judah/ Judaea of the Hasmoneans with a restored Israel, also applying biblical language to "Israel's" enemies, speaking of such foes and locations as the "children of Esau" (5:3) and "the land of the Philistines" (3:41). Not only do these anachronisms provide continuity with historical Israel, they connect the deeds of the Hasmoneans with the promised conquests of these entities at the restoration of Israel (cf. Isa 11:14).[107] The repeated echoes of the language of heroic stories from the Former Prophets also serve to parallel the Hasmonean rulers with Israelite heroes of the past,[108] leaving the reader to infer what these parallels suggest about the Hasmoneans' role in fulfilling God's promises:

> The Hasmonaean propagandist did not wish to give up completely the possibility of leading his readers to believe that Mattathias' sons fulfilled the words of the prophets. Without echoing the words of the prophecies, he could tell of the deeds of his heroes that looked as if they were fulfillments and he could then leave it to Jewish Bible-readers to infer the point. He seems to have done so repeatedly.[109]

The anachronistic and biblical nature of these terms for "Israel's" enemies only reinforces the equally anachronistic and biblical nature of the author's use of Israel. In the same way that the Hasmoneans were not in fact fighting against Philistia or Moab, the Jewish state of the second century BCE was also not the same as Israel, either the historical entity or

---

[106] Katell Berthelot, "Reclaiming the Land (1 Maccabees 15:28–36): Hasmonean Discourse between Biblical Tradition and Seleucid Rhetoric," *JBL* 133.3 (2014): 539–59 (559).

[107] The Hasomonean annexation of Samaria (1 Macc 11:28–34) and campaigns of forced conversion (such as with the Idumaeans) also make additional sense in the context of an effort to restore Israel, though in this case the restoration would not be happening through the miraculous regathering of Israelites from the nations but through the conversion of those in the land and their subjection to Judah. On the conversions under the Hasmoneans, see Cohen, *Beginnings of Jewishness*, 16–24, 109–39; Shaye J. D. Cohen, "Religion, Ethnicity, and Hellenism in the Emergence of Jewish Identity in Maccabean Palestine," in *Religion and Religious Practice in the Seleucid Kingdom*, eds. Per Bilde et al. (Aarhus: Aarhus University Press, 1990), 204–23.

[108] E.g. the examples mentioned in Goldstein, *I Maccabees*, 6–8 and Goldstein, "Messianic Promises," 76–81.

[109] Goldstein, "Messianic Promises," 80.

the promised future entity. Nevertheless, the propagandist's use of these terms is rhetorically powerful, identifying the Hasmonean house as the rightful rulers of Israel-being-restored, suggesting through the very use of this language that the age of wrath was coming to an end through the Hasmoneans' reconquest of the land.[110] Thus, even in a book that uses it as frequently as 1 Maccabees, the title "Israel" is not used lightly but denotes a strong rhetorical claim about the present work of God to restore his people.

The same insight also makes sense of the choice of the revolutionaries in the revolts of 66–73 and 132–135 in adopting the term "Israel" – unlike the Hasmoneans, the rebels are thereby overtly laying claim to the promises of Israel's restoration.[111] Again, it is not the Hasmoneans who were anomalous in this regard but the rebels, who saw themselves as ushering in the final kingdom.[112] Such calculated rhetorical use of the term Israel shows that some early Jewish groups and factions did indeed constructively appropriate "Israel" terminology as a means of intentional community formation in continuity with historical Israel. But this is not the same as the straightforward appropriation of that title as though the *Ioudaioi* were now the sole heirs of the heritage of Israel,[113] nor does 1 Maccabees "equate Israelite with Judean."[114] Instead, these appropriations of the term "Israel" serve as rhetorical claims that the promised restoration of Israel was underway.

In this way, although just looking at the number of uses of the respective terms may give the impression that 1 Maccabees conflated these terms and in fact preferred Israel when referring to the present people, a fuller investigation shows the same basic principles we have observed so far. The difference is not (as has been suggested) between groups insistent on

---

[110] The age of wrath has not fully come to an end even for the propagandist, since only the actions of human beings associated with the end – and not yet the promised actions of God himself – have transpired. Nevertheless, "For the Hasmoneans and their propagandist, these facts proved that the Age of Wrath was at last approaching its full end" (Goldstein, "Messianic Promises," 76).

[111] On these rebel governments, see Goodblatt, *Elements*, 124–34; Goodblatt, "Judeans to Israel," 23–36.

[112] This is one conclusion Kuhn got right, as this "Israel" language marks the rebellions as messianic religious-political programs. Cf. Kuhn, "Ἰουδαῖος κτλ," *TDNT* 3:361.

[113] Collins, "Construction," 25.

[114] *Pace* John S. Bergsma, "Qumran Self-Identity: 'Israel' or 'Judah'?," *DSD* 15 (2008): 172–89 (172), who uses 1–2 Maccabees and Josephus as foils for the Dead Sea Scrolls' preservation of the distinction between these terms. But Josephus and 1–2 Maccabees do continue to distinguish between the terms, so the distinction is mistaken.

"living in the biblical world" who use these terms with the precision of the older biblical texts, and those groups who more liberally collapsed the difference between the terms.[115] Rather, the difference concerns the present position in the eschatological timetable. For the hopeful returnees in Ezra's day and the Hasmonean propagandist, the age of wrath was coming to an end, and God had begun the process of restoring Israel. Thus we see a revival of Israel language in each case. But even these authors do not use "Israel" as if it were synonymous with "the *Ioudaioi*"; rather, even those who appropriated the term did so under the heavy influence of restoration eschatology and made use of the rhetorical weight of the term "Israel." The principle is clear: *When Jews adopted "Israelite" language in this period, they were identifying with the historical covenant with Israel and the eschatological promises of Israelite restoration.*

2 MACCABEES: STILL AWAITING ISRAEL

The relationship between Israel terminology and restoration eschatology – and the rhetorical punch of 1 Maccabees' use of "Israel" – is further demonstrated by the lack of such language within 2 Maccabees, which is far less optimistic about the Hasmonean period.[116] In noting the difference between these books, Kuhn regarded 2 Maccabees as the signal example of supposed outsider accommodation, "If 1 Macc. is the best example of Palestinian Judaism, 2 Macc. is the best example of Hellenistic."[117] Written long after 1 Maccabees, 2 Maccabees is a composite work, with two letters purportedly written to the *Ioudaioi* of Egypt about the commemoration of the purification of the Second Temple preceding an anonymous abridgment of Jason of Cyrene's history of the wars of Judah the Maccabee and his brothers, which is no longer

---

[115] Bergsma, "Qumran Self-Identity," 187–89; cf. Shemaryahu Talmon, "The Community of the Renewed Covenant: Between Judaism and Christianity," in *The Community of the Renewed Covenant: The Notre Dame Symposium on the Dead Sea Scrolls*, eds. Eugene Ulrich and James C. VanderKam, CJAS 10 (Notre Dame: University of Notre Dame Press, 1994), 3–24 (12); Collins, "Construction," 25–26.

[116] On 2 Macc as less optimistic about the Hasmoneans, see Goldstein, "Messianic Promises," 74, 85–88, esp. 87. On differences between 1 and 2 Maccabees, see Daniel R. Schwartz, "On Something Biblical about 2 Maccabees," in *Biblical Perspectives: Early Use and Interpretation of the Bible in Light of the Dead Sea Scrolls*, eds. Michael E. Stone and Esther G. Chazon, STDJ 28 (Leiden: Brill, 1998), 223–32.

[117] Kuhn, "Ἰουδαῖος κτλ," *TDNT* 3:363.

Table 2 *Israel and Judah language in 1 & 2 Maccabees*

	Israel+	Per 1,000	Ioudaios	Per 1,000	Judaea	Per 1,000	Ioudaismos /Ioudaikos
1 Maccabees	63	3.44	37	2.02	30	1.64	0
2 Maccabees	5	0.42	59	4.95	11	0.92	5

extant.[118] In contrast to the pro-Hasmonean propaganda of 1 Maccabees:

> One purpose of the Abridged History is to oppose the dynastic claims of the Hasmonaeans. Another is to demonstrate that although the Second Temple is not yet the exclusive location for sacrificial worship demanded by Deuteronomy 12:5–14, there are important senses in which it is now God's Chosen Place.[119]

This antipathy towards Hasmonean claims manifests itself in the way 2 Maccabees handles Israel and *Ioudaios* terminology. In contrast to 1 Maccabees, 2 Maccabees avoids narrative use of Israel language entirely. The contrast between the two books is stark, as can be seen in Table 2. While 1 Maccabees uses "Israel" and cognates sixty-three times, 2 Maccabees uses the term only five times, restricted to prayer (1:25, 26), third-person reports of prayer (10:38; 11:6; 11:06), a reference to "the God of Israel" (9:5), and a reference (in a vision) to Jeremiah the prophet's love for "the family of Israel" (15:14) – in Kuhn's words, "always in strongly religious contexts."[120] Proportionally, 1 Maccabees uses Israel language over eight times more often than 2 Maccabees, which avoids it in the narrator's voice. On the flip side, because of its avoidance of Israel terminology, 2 Maccabees uses *Ioudaios* nearly two-and-a-half times as often as 1 Maccabees.

Although 1 and 2 Maccabees do not have a literary relationship comparable to that of the Synoptic Gospels, this sort of consistent differ-

---

[118] For more on the authorship and composite nature of 2 Maccabees, see Jonathan A. Goldstein, *II Maccabees*, AB 41A (Garden City: Doubleday, 1983), 1–54.

[119] Goldstein, "Messianic Promises," 85. See also Goldstein, *II Maccabees*, 17: "Where First Maccabees was written to prove the legitimacy of the Hasmonean dynasty of high priests and princes descended from the zealous priest Mattathias, our writer does not deign to mention Mattathias and pointedly makes every effort to show that Judas' brothers were at best ineffective and at worst tainted by treason and sin."

[120] Kuhn, "Ἰουδαῖος κτλ," *TDNT* 3:363.

ence in language suggests the epitomist of 2 Maccabees disagreed with the restoration associations implied by 1 Maccabees' application of "Israel" terminology to Hasmonean Judah.[121] In fact, 2 Maccabees makes it clear from the very start that Israel's restoration remains incomplete, with Jonathan's prayer in 1:24–29 asking God to "gather together our dispersed (*diasporan*) people, set free those enslaved among the Gentiles … Plant your people in your holy place, as Moses promised" (2 Macc 1:27–29). In Goldstein's words:

> Obviously, the author believed that Age [of Wrath] had not yet completely ended. … This prayer, in alluding to still unfulfilled promises and to continuing aspects of the Age of Wrath, does echo words of the Writing Prophets. Though the great prophetic forecasts for the post-exilic era had predicted a prompt ingathering of the exiled Jews [*sic*] and a prompt punishment of their oppressors, the author of Epistle 2 concedes the obvious truth, that those promises were still unfulfilled in 164 and even in 103 BCE. … Nevertheless, the author of Epistle 2 ends with the hope that the last remnants of the Age of Wrath will *speedily* pass away, with the renewed fulfilment of Exodus 15:17, i.e., a new Exodus by which the exiles will return to be planted again in God's Holy Place.[122]

In contrast to Goldstein's summary, however, Jonathan prays not for "the ingathering of the exiled Jews" but rather for the restoration of *Israel* (1:26). Indeed, this prayer contains two of 2 Maccabees' five uses of "Israel" but does not use *Ioudaios*. Significantly, the epitome following the letters tells of the struggle for *Judah's* (that is, the *Ioudaioi's*) independence under Hasmonean leadership, which the epitomist – in contrast to 1 Maccabees – is careful not to equate with *Israel's* restoration and independence. The second letter does, however, defend the Second Temple against suggestions that it was invalid because it lacked the glorious presence of the Lord manifested through the heavenly fire that accompanied God's election of Moses' tabernacle (Lev 9:24) and Solomon's temple (2 Chr 7:1–3). In response, the second letter suggests that the fire of the Second Temple was in fact the fire of the First Temple, miraculously preserved during the exile (2 Macc 1:19–36). The letter also grapples with the absence of the ark of the covenant and other temple implements by fabricating a tradition about Jeremiah hiding the ark in the

---

[121] "Unlike the Hasmonaean propagandist, our writer defined the conditions of the Present Age as falling far short of the predicted period of Israel's unending bliss" (Goldstein, "Messianic Promises," 85).

[122] Goldstein, "Messianic Promises," 74, 84.

wake of the Babylonian Exile, sealing it in a cave on the mountain from which Moses had looked upon the promised land, and declaring,

The place shall remain unknown until God gathers his people again and shows his mercy. Then the Lord will disclose these things, and the glory of the Lord and the cloud will appear, as they were shown in the case of Moses, and as Solomon asked that the place should be specially consecrated. (2 Macc 2:7–8)[123]

2 Maccabees therefore begins by asserting that the absence of the ark of the covenant and the glory of the Lord are evidence that Israel had not yet been restored as promised.[124] At the restoration of Israel, YHWH's presence would again be known as it had been in prior days. The present temple, although valid as a place of atonement and prayer, bears witness to Israel's continued exile through the absence of the ark and the cloud of glory. Similarly, the second letter expresses hopes for the return of those who have been scattered "from everywhere under heaven" (2:18) and for a restoration of "the kingship and the priesthood and the consecration" (2:17),[125] further illustrating the present lack and hopes for a full restoration. Goldstein rightly sums up the situation:

The bulk of the [second] letter (1:18–2:18) serves to prove that important aspects of the Age of Wrath have ended forever, especially some which had cast doubt on God's election of the second temple. The letter concludes with a vigorous expression (2:17–18) of confidence in the present situation of the Chosen People and of hope that God will speedily fulfill his promises and put an end to all aspects of the Age of Wrath. It also contains a prayer for the end of the Age of Wrath (1:24–29). Obviously, the author believed that Age had not yet completely ended.[126]

The Abridged History continues along the same trajectory, avoiding any identification of Hasmonean Judaea with "Israel," in fact seeking "to discredit the Hasmonaean dynasty, which by his time had "usurped" the high priesthood and the kingship."[127] Rather, the epitomist hopes for a true restoration of all of Israel in the future – seemingly accompanied by the resurrection of Dan 12:2 (cf. 2 Macc 7:9, 14). It should be noted,

---

[123] This tradition is in opposition to Jer 3:16, which declares that at the restoration, Israel will no longer remember or miss the ark of the covenant.

[124] Doubts about the presence of God in the Second Temple are evident as late as *Pesiq. R.* 160a.

[125] Following the textual emendation of Goldstein, *II Maccabees*, 187; Goldstein, "Messianic Promises," 83.

[126] Goldstein, "Messianic Promises," 74.

[127] Goldstein, "Messianic Promises," 87, continuing: "Our writer admired Judas Maccabeus and strove to discredit all other Hasmonaeans."

however, that 2 Maccabees does not suggest that the contemporary faithful are thereby precluded from sharing in YHWH's compassion in the midst of the age of wrath (7:6) and receiving the blessings of the covenant after enduring the suffering of this age (7:36). But it is a mistake to conclude from these verses, as does Guy Prentiss Waters, that "2 Maccabees 7 suggests that some Jews were explicitly not regarded as existing under either Deuteronomic curse or Deuteronomic exile."[128] A look at the immediate context – in which the seven brothers are being brutally slaughtered – is sufficient to demonstrate that the age of wrath is in full effect. Indeed, the brothers drink from the "ever-flowing life under God's covenant" only "after enduring a brief suffering" (7:36), which further accentuates the nature of the present age.

CONCLUSION: THE ENDURING ROOTS OF RESTORATION ESCHATOLOGY

The contrast between 1 and 2 Maccabees thus further illuminates the link between Israel terminology and restoration eschatology in Jewish literature. For 2 Maccabees, although *Ioudaioi* are indeed "Israelites," the larger body of Israel remains scattered in exile, and the *Ioudaioi* and the kingdom of Judah/Judaea are not synonymous with Israel, which will be restored in full sometime in the future. That 2 Maccabees also seems to have held some respect for the Samaritan temple at Mount Gerizim may also connect to this larger point, as a way of recognizing Samaritan claims to Israelite heritage even if they are not at present united with (or under) Judah as the Jewish author believes they should be.[129] On the other hand, in contrast to the other early Jewish literature examined so far, 1 Maccabees readily uses Israel language of the present people, a fact that helped provide the basis for Kuhn's insider/outsider paradigm. But a closer look at 1 Maccabees, especially once placed alongside 2 Maccabees, shows that Israel language is yet again closely tied to restoration hopes, rhetorically identifying the exploits of the Hasmoneans with Israel's restoration and the end of the age of wrath. As with the returnees in Ezra/Nehemiah, the Hasmonean propagandist thus constructively

---

[128] Guy Prentiss Waters, *The End of Deuteronomy in the Epistles of Paul*, WUNT 221 (Tübingen: Mohr Siebeck, 2006), 42 n. 78.

[129] See Goldstein, *II Maccabees*, 13.

appropriates "Israel" in the belief that the promised restoration is already taking place, although not complete.

Similarly, although Ezra-Nehemiah is evidence of early Jewish appropriation of the title of Israel, with some Jews circumscribing Israel to those who had been exiled, the book nowhere suggests that the restoration of Israel has been completed. Within the land, the only significant portion of Israel to have returned is from Judah, Benjamin, and Levi, and the rest of Israel (including most of the three tribes represented in the land) remains outside the land awaiting return, restoration, and reconciliation. This appropriation of Israelite heritage therefore does not limit Israel to the Jews but rather rhetorically positions the Jews as the authoritative center of larger Israel. This conclusion accords with the basic concept of Israel established throughout the foundational biblical literature of early Judaism, which largely amounts to a record and explanation of the events leading to the two exiles along with promises of Israel's subsequent return and large-scale restoration. But these prophecies were not fulfilled during the Persian, Hasmonean, or any other period. The twelve tribes were not reunited, Israel had not been restored as promised, the wealth of the nations had not poured into Jerusalem, and the nations had not yet submitted to Israel's God.[130]

This perspective also rhetorically establishes the dominant position of the *Yehudim/Ioudaioi* relative to other claimants to the heritage of Israel, such as those who had remained in the land during the Babylonian deportations. For those groups, such as the Samaritans, to participate in Israel's future, they must do so by submitting to the primacy of those from Judah. Only by giving up their rebellion against Jerusalem and the leadership of Judah can Ephraim and the rest of Israel participate in the promised restoration. It is therefore true that Ezra-Nehemiah, the Maccabean literature, and many other early Jewish works position the Jews at the theological and political center of Israel, which they argue should always be under Jewish leadership. Nevertheless, the very preservation of the distinction between the *Ioudaioi/Yehudim* and Israel in the biblical texts serves as a continued witness of the incompleteness of Israel in the present and keeps restoration eschatology at the very center of the consciousness of the Jews awaiting the fulfillment of the Hebrew prophets' promises. Those Jews who regarded the Prophets and the Writings as authoritative would regularly read of "Israel," painfully

---

[130] Sanders, *Jesus and Judaism*, 80.

aware that the polity of Israel so frequently mentioned in the scriptures no longer existed but also hopefully expecting that Israel would one day be restored as promised.[131]

In this light, we must therefore be alerted to the rhetorical power of "Israel" language in early Judaism and the claims inherent in its use. If the construction of Israel in biblical texts shaped the understanding of early Jewish groups, we should expect that, for the majority of Jews in our period, "Israel" is the covenantal term for the people of YHWH as a whole, but is also an entity in an incomplete and liminal state at present, still awaiting the time when YHWH will not only restore the Jews but restore and reunify all of the covenantal people, including the northern Israelites still believed to be scattered among the nations or awaiting restoration in some far-off place. Put another way, identification with "Israel" was always a theological claim in the Second Temple period, tying the individual or group in question to the biblical people in covenantal relationship with YHWH. And inasmuch as the narrative framework established in the biblical texts supplied a descriptive lexicon and grammar for the discourses and debates concerning Israelite identity for those coming afterwards, when we do hear the use of "Israel" in Jewish literature of the Second Temple period, our ears should therefore always be primed for eschatological, messianic, or theological-political claims.[132]

---

[131] In contrast, Sadducees and Samaritans, neither of whom accepted the prophetic material as authoritative, likely would not have shared this vision of Israel's restoration, though Samaritan eschatology does include a transition from the age of *fanuta* (divine displeasure) that has persisted since the time of Eli to an ideal future age. For more on Samaritan eschatology, see Ferdinand Dexinger, "Eschatology," in *A Companion to Samaritan Studies*, eds. Alan D. Crown, Reinhard Pummer, and Abraham Tal (Tübingen: Mohr Siebeck, 1993), 86–90; Ferdinand Dexinger, "Samaritan Eschatology," in *The Samaritans*, ed. Alan D. Crown (Tübingen: Mohr Siebeck, 1989), 266–92; Ferdinand Dexinger, *Der Taheb, ein "Messianischer" Heilsbringer der Samaritaner*, Kairos Religionswissenschaftliche Studien 3 (Salzburg: Müller, 1986); Alan D. Crown, "Dexinger's Der Taheb," *JQR* 80.1/2 (1989): 139–41.

[132] As also recognized by Bloch, "Israélite, juif, hébreu," 17, who otherwise follows Kuhn (without citation).

PART III

ISRAEL AND RESTORATION ESCHATOLOGY IN THE DIASPORA

6

Exile and Diaspora Theology

The logical point of departure for most Jews addressing the phenomenon of their dispersion would naturally have been the Bible.

Isaiah Gafni[1]

The first chapter showed that Josephus reserves Israel terminology for the pre-exilic period, when it could refer to the larger people group or the northern kingdom, and transitions to *Ioudaios* language when discussing contemporary Jews after the Babylonian Exile, explaining his shift in terminology by calling attention to the difference between the scope of the pre-exilic and post-exilic peoples. Josephus' explanation corresponds remarkably well with the biblical paradigm, in which Israel tends to refer either to the biblical entity or to an eschatological restoration of that people including but not limited to the Jews, that portion of Israel derived from the southern kingdom of Judah. As such, Josephus serves as a prime witness for the continued distinction between these terms and the groups they represent into the late first century. He also suggestively claims that "the ten tribes are beyond Euphrates until now" (*Ant.* 11.133). Of course, given the centrality of restoration eschatology in biblical literature, it should hardly be surprising if Josephus continues to hold out hope for a future restoration of all twelve tribes of Israel. It would therefore seem a natural next step to reexamine Josephus for other indications of this paradigm.

---

[1] Isaiah Gafni, *Land, Center and Diaspora: Jewish Constructs in Late Antiquity*, JSPSup 21 (Sheffield: Sheffield Academic, 1997), 21.

Curiously, Louis Feldman begins his study on Josephus' perspective on exile with exactly the opposite assertion, "One would expect that Josephus would have a positive attitude toward the concept of exile."[2] This seems an odd thing to expect from an upper-class priest who had fought against Rome – which Feldman concedes is evidence that Josephus had once held restorationist hopes – before witnessing the fall of his beloved city and Temple,[3] but Feldman presumes "three decades of ... living in luxurious exile in Rome" had been powerful enough to overcome such prior ideological commitments and experiences.[4] Feldman is not alone in this judgment; a surprising number of interpreters have concluded that Josephus not only did not take a negative view of exile but rather was positive about, even proud of, the diaspora.[5] This scholarly trajectory mostly derives from the later work of Abraham Schalit, who in the 1930s had characterized Josephus as a "reptile" but dramatically shifted his views after, and as Daniel Schwartz points out, likely in reaction to, the Holocaust.[6]

Beginning with the introduction to his Hebrew translation of the *Antiquities*, Schalit "cast Josephus as the first Jew to make a political program out of existence in the Diaspora, because he realized that in this way only would the future of the Jewish people be assured. This, according to the new Schalit, is the point of much of Josephus' politics, and is a praiseworthy one."[7] In any case, Schalit's shift toward a diaspora-positive and conciliatory Josephus was deeply influenced by his own political concerns and stand, as Schwartz notes, as yet another

---

[2] Feldman, "Exile in Josephus," 148.

[3] Cf. Feldman, "Exile in Josephus," 169: "It would seem likely that Josephus shared one of the major and distinctive tenets of the Pharisees, namely their apocalyptic hopes."

[4] Louis H. Feldman, "Restoration in Josephus," in *Restoration: Old Testament, Jewish and Christian Perspectives*, ed. James M. Scott, JSJSup 72 (Leiden: Brill, 2001), 223–61 (229).

[5] E.g., Betsy Halpern-Amaru, "Land Theology in Josephus' 'Jewish Antiquities,'" *New Series* 71.4 (1981): 201–29 (227–28); Feldman, "Exile in Josephus," 148–61; Daniel R. Schwartz, "From Punishment to Program, From Program to Punishment: Josephus and the Rabbis on Exile," in *For Uriel. Studies in the History of Israel in Antiquity Presented to Professor Uriel Rappaport* (Jerusalem: Zalman Shazar Center for Jewish History, 2005), 205–26; Adolf von Schlatter, *Die Theologie des Judentums nach dem Bericht des Josefus*, Beiträge zur Förderung schriftlicher Theologie (Gütersloh: Bertelsmann, 1932), 87.

[6] Daniel R. Schwartz, "On Abraham Schalit, Herod, Josephus, the Holocaust, Horst R. Moehring, and the Study of Ancient Jewish history," *Jewish History* 2.2 (1987): 9–28 (10).

[7] Schwartz, "On Abraham Schalit," 11; alluding to Abraham Schalit, ed., *Josephus, Jewish Antiquities [in Hebrew]*, 3 vols. (Jerusalem: Bialik, 1944), lxxxi.

reminder of how contemporary events so often have an impact on the historiography of antiquity – and Josephus and other ancients were no less vulnerable to this tendency than are we moderns. To his credit, Schwartz recognizes the disconnect between Josephus' earlier revolutionary actions and the idea that he took a positive view of the exile, observing that this positive perspective "is not to be found in Josephus' earlier work, the *Jewish War*, which he wrote a few years after he got off the boat from Judaea."[8] Instead, Schwartz observes,

Josephus' view of exile in the *Jewish War* is the plain and simple negative view expressed in the Bible. . . . So Josephus, in his *Jewish War*, although in Rome, was as far as exile is concerned right at home in Palestinian historiography. Which is only to be expected; what else should a priest from Jerusalem think about exile?[9]

Remarkably, Schwartz nevertheless concludes that Josephus *eventually* came to the positive view of exile:

Twenty years later, in contrast, he seems to have become reconciled with exile, viewing it as a "positive political program."[10]
We have seen that the early Josephus, who was a Judaean, considered exile like Judaeans did, and that the later Josephus, who had become a diasporan Jew, preferred to view exile positively. . . . Apart from some philological niceties, all we have done is show that Josephus exemplifies a familiar aspect of human nature, namely, that people come to posit situations they cannot change. Psychologists call it dissonance reduction, plain folks call it "if you can't beat'm, join'm."[11]

In this picture, Josephus represents the Roman diaspora Jew par excellence, having eventually adjusted to his diaspora circumstances and exchanged any eschatological or restorationist hopes for a positive view of the dispersion. More than that, he serves as an individual illustration of the transition from a traditional biblical view of exile to the more satisfied (enlightened?) perspective supposedly characteristic of diaspora Jews.[12]

---

[8] Schwartz, "Punishment to Program," 207.

[9] Schwartz, "Punishment to Program," 208–09.

[10] Schwartz, "Punishment to Program," 209.

[11] Schwartz, "Punishment to Program," 213. Dissonance reduction or not, it is difficult to believe Josephus so thoroughly abandoned his prior theological perspective. Given the usual mechanisms of cognitive dissonance, it is far more likely that he revised rather than wholly abandoned his cosmology in the wake of Rome's victory. Cf. Harold W. Attridge, *The Interpretation of Biblical History in the Antiquitates Judaicae of Flavius Josephus,* HDR (Missoula: Scholars Press, 1976), 183, cf. 149, 169.

[12] It is difficult to escape the sense through much of this literature that Josephus' positive views of the exile reflect more mature, enlightened sensibilities – that is, his views look more like those of his modern interpreters – than the crude eschatological hopes of his predecessors.

Indeed, it is now widely assumed that most Jews in the diaspora had abandoned the restoration eschatology of the Bible, having given up on any hope or expectation of restoration.[13] This sentiment is perhaps most poignantly expressed by A. T. Kraabel, who explains, "The Diaspora was not Exile; in some sense it became a Holy Land, too."[14]

This distinction between diaspora and exile was popularized by Karl Schmidt's 1935 *TWNT* article on *diaspora*,[15] which argues that as the passage of time "healed the severe wounds of the various deportations" and voluntary emigration and proselytism extended the diaspora, the prophetic understanding of exile as a curse had been replaced by a feeling of pride (*Hochgefühl*) in Jewish expansion across the world.[16] As proof, Schmidt cites Rolf Rendtorff's assessment that, whereas the Hebrew terms related to exile (e.g., *golah* and *galut*) are wholly negative,[17] the Septuagint translators coined the milder Greek term *diaspora* ("sown" or "scattered"), which could be neutral or even positive, to soften or conceal the negative prophetic assessment of exile:

> The Jewish diaspora appears in light of the prophetic judgment (Isa 35:8, Jer 23:24, Ezek 22:15) as an effect of divine criminal courts, and therefore as a curse, and only in Hellenistic optimism does D. judge otherwise. ... The Septuagint also ... has masked the terrible gravity of all those Hebrew expressions that mercilessly reveal the divine judgment of scattering over Israel with the veil of the word διασπορά.[18]

---

[13] This fact is perhaps most evident in several recent reference materials on diaspora Judaism. See, for example, Erich S. Gruen, "Judaism in the Diaspora," *EDEJ* 77–97, which consistently asserts that diaspora Jews no longer held hopes for restoration.

[14] A. Thomas Kraabel, "Unity and Diversity among Diaspora Synagogues," in *Diaspora Jews and Judaism: Essays in Honor of, and in Dialogue with, A. Thomas Kraabel*, eds. J. Andrew. Overman and Robert S. MacLennan, SFSHJ 41 (Atlanta: Scholars Press, 1992), 49–60 (58).

[15] Karl Ludwig Schmidt, "διασπορά," *TDNT* 2: 98–104; ET of Karl Ludwig Schmidt, "διασπορά," *TWNT* 2: 98–104. See also the same basic argument in Rudolf Schnackenburg, "Gottes Volk in der Zerstreuung. Diaspora im Zeugnis der Bibel," in *Schriften zum Neuen Testament. Exegese in Fortschritt und Wandel*, ed. Rudolf Schnackenburg (Munich: Kosel, 1971), 321–37. This paradigm is cited with approval by W. D. Davies, *The Territorial Dimension of Judaism*, 23 (Berkeley: University of California Press, 1982), 116–17, though he also calls attention to the need for more research on the question.

[16] Schmidt, "διασπορά," 2: 100.

[17] The term *galut* occurs three times in the Torah (Lev 18:6, 17, 18, 19), each meaning "uncover" in a sexual sense, and the LXX uses *apocalypsis* in these cases. Cf. Kiefer, *Exil und Diaspora*, 144–47, 484–95.

[18] F. M. Rendtorff, "Diaspora II. Evangelische," in *Die Religion in Geschichte und Gegenwart (RGG2)*, eds. Hermann Gunkel and Leopold Zscharnack, 1 (Tübingen:

This argument is oft-repeated and continues to be an especially popular notion in the field of diaspora studies.[19] Sociologist Robin Cohen, for example, has even repeatedly asserted that *diaspora* was used prior to the LXX to describe Greek colonization in the Mediterranean, despite the fact that not one occurrence of *diaspora* in the *TLG* refers to colonization.[20] Cohen may have been misled on this point by conflating *diaspora* with the term that most often renders *golah* in the LXX: *apoikia* (or *apoikesia*; 30× and 8×, respectively), a term meaning "away from home" and often applied to various Greek emigrations in the classical period.[21] That the LXX prefers the term also used for these classical Greek emigrations has been understood as further evidence that "the Alexandrian translators refused to face [the] reality" of the differences between the glorious history of Greek colonization and their own history of captivity and

Mohr, 1927), 1916–20 (1918): "Die jüdische Diaspora erscheint im Lichte des prophetischen Urteils (Jes. 35:8; Jer. 23:24; Ezech. 22:15) als Auswirkung göttlicher Strafgerichte und darum als Fluch, und erst hellenistischer Optimismus beurteilt die D. anders ... So hat auch die Septuaginta ... den furchtbaren Ernst aller jener hebräischen Ausdrücke, die das göttliche Zerstreuungsgericht über Israel schonungslos aufdecken, mit dem Schleier des Wortes διασπορά verhüllt."

[19] E.g., Minna Rozen, "People of the Book, People of the Sea: Mirror Images of the Soul," in *Homelands and Diasporas: Greeks, Jews and Their Migrations*, ed. Minna Rozen, International Library of Migration Studies 2 (New York: Tauris, 2008), 35–81 (43–44); Namsoon Kang, *Diasporic Feminist Theology: Asia and Theopolitical Imagination.* (Minneapolis: Fortress, 2014), 5–6; Caryn Aviv and David Shneer, *New Jews: The End of the Jewish Diaspora* (New York: New York University Press, 2005), 3.

[20] E.g., Robin Cohen, "Rethinking Babylon: Iconoclastic Conceptions of the Diasporic Experience," *Journal of Ethnic and Migration Studies* 21.1 (1995): 5–18 (6); Robin Cohen, "Diasporas and the Nation-State: From Victims to Challengers," *International Affairs* 72.3 (1996): 507–20 (507); Robin Cohen, "Diaspora: Changing Meanings and Limits of the Concept," in *Les diasporas dans le monde contemporain*, eds. W. Berthomière and C. Chivallon (Paris: Karthala-MSHA, 2006), 39–48 (40). Cf. also the inventive claim of Balasubramanyam Chandramohan, "Diasporic (Exilic; Migrant) Writings," *Encyclopedia of Postcolonial Studies* 144–50 (145): "The original use of the term by the Greeks connotes a triumphalist migration/colonization (*speiro* = to sow; and *dia* = over) from the point of view of the colonizer/occupier. Notions of civilizational/ masculine superiority underpinned such a use of the term." On this point, see the scathing criticisms of Stéphane Dufoix, "Des usages antiques de diaspora aux enjeux conceptuels contemporains," *Pallas Revue d'études antiques* 89 (2012): 17–33.

[21] Cf. Joseph Mélèze Modrzejewski, "How to Be a Jew in Hellenistic Egypt," in *Diasporas in Antiquity*, eds. Shaye J. D. Cohen and Ernst S. Frerichs, BJS 288 (Atlanta: Scholars Press, 1993), 65–91 (67–70). Modrzejewski rightly notes that "colony" or "Colonization" are problematic terms in these contexts because of their loaded modern connotations. Nevertheless, most Greek *apoikia* were of the voluntary variety and involved leaving one's home city to establish a foothold in a new territory. On Greek colonization, see David William Robertson Ridgway, "Colonization, Greek," *The Oxford Classical Dictionary*, 362–63.

deportation, instead apologetically and "retrospectively align[ing] the Jewish past with the Greek past."[22]

For all its present popularity, this argument therefore rests upon two basic pillars: (1) evidence that the Septuagint weakens the negative prophetic verdict on the exile in favor of a new "Hellenistic optimism" and (2) the idea that the passage of time and changing circumstances eventually changed the perspectives of those who voluntarily remained outside the land, such that most Jews felt at home in the diaspora and no longer looked forward to a return,[23] an argument more recently augmented by appeal to material evidence from the diaspora. Since this argument directly impacts the foundational assumptions with which many scholars now approach Jewish literature from the diaspora, we must address it before we are able to return to Josephus or evaluate any diaspora literature from the Hellenistic period and beyond.

EXILE, DIASPORA, AND EMIGRATION IN THE LXX

Diaspora in the LXX

Before Schmidt popularized the idea that the LXX softened the Hebrew Bible's negativity about exile, James Hardy Ropes had already shown through a brief but incisive analysis of *diaspeirō*, *diaspora*, and a comparison with other synonyms (chiefly *diaskoprizō*, *aichmalosia*, and *apoikia*) in the LXX that *diaspora*, "always standing in contrast with the idea of a visible unity of the nation, calls attention, usually with a certain pathos, to the absence of that unity."[24] Ropes' observations were buried in the middle of a commentary on the Epistle of James, however, and did not receive significant attention, easily overshadowed by the greater influence of the *TWNT* a few years later. The *TWNT* still did not go entirely unchallenged, however, as Isac Leo Seeligmann, after previously having offhandedly approved Schmidt's and Rendtorff's arguments,[25] called their conclusions into question as early as 1948:

---

[22] E.g., Modrzejewski, "How to Be a Jew," 70. As will be shown below, Philo's frequent use of the word (and Josephus' few examples) have been seen as particular evidence of an attempt to domesticate the exile and put a positive spin on the diaspora.

[23] For a discussion of this idea, see Gafni, *Land, Center, and Diaspora*, 27–30.

[24] James Hardy Ropes, *A Critical and Exegetical Commentary on the Epistle of St. James*, ICC (Edinburgh: T&T Clark, 1978), 122.

[25] Isac Leo Seeligmann, "Problemen en perspectieven in het moderne Septuagintaonderzoek," *JEOL* 7 (1940): 359–90 (75).

[LXX] Texts ... do express a complaint about the afflictions caused by exile, making us doubt the truth in the saying according to which the Alexandrian Jewry of the Septuagint [exchanged the traditional negative view for a more positive perspective]. Such a formulation of the situation does not do enough justice to the factor that translators use the term diaspora, amidst and as a synonym to many expressions denoting horror, abuse, and shame.[26]

The Schmidt/Rendtorff hypothesis nevertheless remained the default until a posthumously published study by Willem C. van Unnik persuasively demonstrated that neither the Septuagint nor later Hellenistic Jewish literature weakens the dire prophetic verdict but instead consistently present the diaspora as a continuing condition of judgment based on the curses of the Torah.[27] Van Unnik's thorough philological study first demonstrates that *diaspora* was not a technical term for emigration, colonization, or the dispersion of a people prior to its use in the LXX, instead serving as a term signifying a destructive scattering of something that was once a unified entity.[28] He then argues that this previous negative connotation was precisely the reason the Septuagint translators chose the term, as it matched the negative tone of these passages,[29] a conclusion that has since been further strengthened by David Reiner's observation that in the Hebrew Bible, the language of "scattering" (e.g., נדח, פוש, זרה) is considerably *more* negative than that of "exile" (*golah*).[30]

From there, van Unnik demonstrates that in the overwhelming majority of biblical passages in the Septuagint, both the noun *diaspora* and the verb *diaspeirein* carry a distinctly – often harshly – negative tone.[31] He further reinforces this point by observing that the use of the term in later Jewish literature from the Second Temple period corresponds with this negative view, consistently presenting the diaspora as a misfortune and

---

[26] Seeligmann, *Septuagint Version of Isaiah*, 100.

[27] Willem Cornelis van Unnik, *Das Selbstverständnis der jüdischen Diaspora in der hellenistisch-römischen Zeit*, ed. Pieter Willem van der Horst, AGJU 17 (Leiden: Brill, 1993).

[28] Unnik, *Das Selbstverständnis*, 74–76. Cf. Plutarch's citation of Epicurus in *Non posse* 27 (*Moralia* 1105A) and the use of *diaspora* in *Adv. Col.* 6, 1109F.

[29] Unnik, *Das Selbstverständnis*, 84–88. Cf. Modrzejewski, "How to Be a Jew," 66–69 for more on the apparent disconnect between the Hebrew terms and their translations. Van Unnik's observations about the negative charge of *diaspora* help account for the seeming lack of synonymity.

[30] David J. Reimer, "Exile, Diaspora, and Old Testament Theology," *SBET* 28.1 (2010): 3–17 (10–13): "[B]ehind the fear of 'exile' – bad enough in any case – is the yet more deep-seated anxiety concerning scattering" (13).

[31] Unnik, *Das Selbstverständnis*, 89–107.

punishment for Israel's sins.[32] That Philo and Josephus tend to avoid the term *diaspora* further confirms the negative connotation of the term, as their apologetic context is unsuited for outright negative judgments on the diaspora – though van Unnik also observes (as we will see more fully below) that neither abandons the prophetic picture of punishment and ultimate restoration.[33] In his discussion of the Babel episode, Philo actually goes a step further, explicitly stating that *diaspora* is a term of destruction:

Therefore Moses also says, "The Lord dispersed (*diespeiren*) them from that place," which is equivalent to "he scattered (ἐσκέδασεν) them," "he put them to flight (ἐφυγάδευσεν)," "he made them invisible (ἀφανεῖς ἐποίησε)."[34] For to sow (*speirein*) is for good purpose, but to disperse (*diaspeirein*) is the cause of bad things (κακῶν),[35] because the former happens for the sake of growth, increase, and generation of other things but the latter for destruction (ἀπωλείας) and decay (φθορᾶς). But God, the gardener, wishes to sow (*speirein*) excellence in everyone but to disperse (*diaspeirein*) and drive accursed impiety from the citizenship of the world so that the good-hating customs may at some time stop building the evil city and godless tower. (*Conf.* 196)

Philo helpfully puts *diaspeirein* in parallel with three other verbs – all negative – to clarify its meaning.[36] Nevertheless, he emphasizes that God uses the negative punishment of diaspora to destroy evil and thereby make room for productive outcomes.[37] In any case, in light of this passage and in the wake of van Unnik's philological tour de force, it is no longer tenable to argue that the Greek translators' choice of *diaspora* lessens the

---

[32] Unnik, *Das Selbstverständnis*, 108–47.

[33] Unnik, *Das Selbstverständnis*, 127–45. These authors and their perspectives on exile/diaspora/restoration will be addressed more thoroughly below.

[34] Philo's equation of these various terms serves as strong counterevidence to Feldman's claim (see below) that *fugē* is the standard and proper term for exile (Feldman, "Exile in Josephus," 145–46). In contrast, in addition to the terms used here, Philo also uses *elasis* as a synonym, paralleling it with *fugas* in *Flacc.* 184.

[35] Yonge's translation here misses the impact of the δέ and thus the distinction Philo makes between the two verbal forms. Charles Duke Yonge, *The Works of Philo: Complete and Unabridged* (Peabody: Hendrickson, 1993).

[36] Surprisingly, neither Kiefer nor van Unnik addresses this passage, where Philo defines the verbal form and emphasizes its negative sense, though van Unnik does reference the following paragraph's promise of restoration (Unnik, *Das Selbstverständnis*, 132).

[37] See Chapter 8 for more detailed discussion of Philo's idea that God uses the negative punishment of dispersion to produce a positive outcome. Cf. Phillip Michael Sherman, *Babel's Tower Translated: Genesis 11 and Ancient Jewish Interpretation* (Leiden: Brill, 2013), 273.

negative prophetic judgment in favor of a more optimistic perspective.[38] Instead, it appears that the translators chose *diaspora* in part because of its negative connotation (as van Unnik suggests), and in part to echo several key prophetic passages that speak of the people being "sown" in punishment, with a harvest to be reaped at the restoration (Hos 2:23; Jer 31:27 [38:27 LXX]). Thus the choice of *diaspora* serves as a way to actualize those prophecies – the people have not only been "scattered" nearly to dissolution, they are being "sown" in the expectation of a future harvest.[39] Thus this translation brings out both the punishment aspect of the curse of exile and the hope of restoration and harvest from among the nations.

Fugē, Apoikia, and Colonization

Although he addresses the term *diaspora*, van Unnik does not substantively discuss the use of *apoikia* and cognates, and now that the *diaspora* argument is unsuitable for this purpose, many point to the Septuagint's use of these terms as evidence of a positive perspective on exile.[40] Feldman, for example, argues that although classical Greek has a "standard word, namely φυγή [*fugē*]" for the concept of exile, "when the Septuagint deals with exile (גולה), it uses the language of emigration or colonization,"[41] continuing:

The picture one gets [in the LXX] is of the founding of a colony, since this, or the verb ἀποικίζω derived from the same stem, is the word used by Herodotus in referring to the colonies established by the Athenians in Iona (1.146) and by the Therans in Cyrene (4.155) and the colony which Aristagoras the Milesian is thinking of founding (5.124). The word ἀποικία is likewise used by Hecataeus of Abdera (*ap.* Diodorus, *Bibliotheca Historica* 40.3.3) is [*sic*] referring to the "colony" in Jerusalem and other cities established by Moses and his followers when they are allegedly driven by the Egyptians during a pestilence.[42]

---

[38] That is not to say that van Unnik is correct in regarding *diaspora* as *worse* than exile. It should instead be regarded as roughly equivalent in charge to the words it translates. Cf. Scott, "Self-Understanding," 180–85.

[39] This interpretation is found as late as the Rabbinic period, as evidenced in b. Pes. 87b. See Gafni, *Land, Center, and Diaspora*, 36 for further discussion.

[40] The LXX regularly translates *golah* ("exile") with *apoikia*, with that term occurring nine times in Ezra-Nehemiah, once in 3 Maccabees, seventeen times in Jeremiah, and twice in Baruch. The related word *apoikesia* ("going away from home") is likewise used in LXX 4 Kgs 24:15 (=2 Kgs 24:15). Cf. Kiefer, *Exil und Diaspora*, 217–18.

[41] Feldman, "Exile in Josephus," 145.

[42] Feldman, "Exile in Josephus," 145–46.

To further his point, Feldman highlights Philo's awareness of "the term φυγή as referring to exile" when speaking of the expulsion of Adam from the garden, the expulsion of Hagar by Abraham, the banishment of Cain, and banishment for homicide.[43] Feldman observes that although Philo is aware of this term, neither he nor the LXX, New Testament, or Josephus use this term to refer to the exile of the Israelites or the diaspora, instead preferring *apoikia* and cognates, which, he argues, "connotes those who have emigrated, who have settled in a far land, and who have been sent to colonize it, and has not the connotation of having been punished."[44] Thus the Hellenistic authors and translators who employed *apoikia* rather than *fugē* obviously did not believe themselves to be in exile but rather styled themselves "colonists," a positive perspective lacking the connotation of divine punishment.

But this argument assumes its conclusion, namely that *fugē* would have been the term of choice if the authors or translators had wished to communicate divine judgment. Feldman also seems not to have noticed how odd it would be for the Septuagint to employ a positive term to translate *golah* or *galut* given its use of the negatively charged *diaspora* in other cases.[45] In any case, none of these authors seem to have regarded *fugē* as an appropriate translation, and Feldman's examples from Philo may actually shed light on the reason: each of these examples was not just an exile but a permanent banishment with no hope of return. A closer look at the data shows that *fugē/feugōn* also carried this connotation of permanence in earlier Greek literature. In his discussion of the concept of *fugē* in Classical Greek literature, Timothy Perry explains:

> The third stock element of the exile [*fugē*] motif is the idea of permanence – the exiles of the Iliad and the Odyssey, whether they go into exile as the result of an act of homicide or as the result of a dispute, are all sundered permanently from their original communities. In other words, the exile loses his νόστος [*nostos*] ("homecoming" or "return home"), and even his desire for νόστος.[46]

True to form, every example of the nominal form of *fugē* in Philo, Josephus, or the New Testament involves either fleeing from danger (the

---

[43] Feldman, "Exile in Josephus," 146.
[44] Feldman, "Exile in Josephus," 146. Cf. also Modrzejewski, "How to Be a Jew," 69.
[45] Scott, "Philo and the Restoration of Israel," 563.
[46] Timothy Peter John Perry, "Exile in Homeric Epic" (PhD diss., University of Toronto, 2010), 18. For more on the concept of *nostos* and its relation to colonization, see Irad Malkin, *Returns of Odysseus: Colonization and Ethnicity* (Berkeley: University of California Press, 1998).

more common meaning of the word) or the sense of an individual banishment for a crime. The ambiguity between these two aspects of *fugē* is also noteworthy in understanding why the LXX translators chose not to use it, as the connotation of "flight" does not disappear even when the word refers to banishment.[47] Rather, the term came to denote banishment – which often followed rather than preceded the flight – precisely because those receiving this sentence were thereby compelled to flee (φεύγειν) the country to avoid being killed.[48] "Thus there was," Sara Forsdyke explains, "an equivalency between sentences of death and sentences of exile."[49] Contrary to Feldman's assertion that *fugē* is "clearly the standard word" for exile, *fugē* was not a technical term for the exile of a people. Instead, there was considerable slippage in the language of ancient authors, who lacked a technical vocabulary for these concepts and thus frequently lumped concepts like exile and emigration together:

Ancient authors often do not distinguish between exile and other forms of displacement: ancient consolatory treatises on exile, for example, often mix mythical and historical exiles with characters that today would be called fugitives (such as Patroclus) or voluntary exiles (such as Metellus Numidicus), and Seneca compares

---

[47] E.g., Demosthenes, *Against Aristocrates* 23.72: "What does the law order? That the one convicted of involuntary homicide must leave (ἀπελθεῖν) the country on certain appointed days by a prescribed route and flee (φεύγειν) until he is forgiven by one of the relatives of the deceased." The term clearly denotes an exile of sorts in this case but also clearly echoes the concept of flight from blood vengeance – the "flight" must continue until reconciliation with the family of the deceased. On the ambiguity between these two senses of "flight" and "banishment," see e.g., Jakob Seibert, *Die politischen Flüchtlinge und Verbannten in der griechischen Geschichte: von d. Anfängen bis zur Unterwerfung durch d. Römer* (Darmstadt: Wissenschaftliche Buchgesellschaft Abt. Verlag, 1979), 2–3; Hans-Joachim Gehrke, *Stasis: Untersuchungen zu den inneren Kriegen in den griechischen Staaten des 5. und 4. Jahrhunderts v. Chr.* (Munich: Beck, 1985), 216–17. For a more general discussion of Greek banishment for homicide, see Joseph Mélèze Modrzejewski, "La sanction de l'homicide en droit grec et hellénistique," in *Symposion* (Pacific Grove: 1990), 3–16.

[48] E.g., the archaic judgment of ἀτιμία, which denoted a formal "loss of honor," meaning a person (sometimes the person's family as well) receiving this sentence was rendered an "outlaw" and could be killed with impunity and without pollution by any member of the community. By the later fifth century, ἀτιμία had come to denote the loss of some or all citizenship rights but was no longer necessarily equivalent to the death penalty. See Adele C. Scafuro, "Atimia," *The Encyclopedia of Ancient History*, 923; Sara Forsdyke, *Exile, Ostracism, and Democracy: The Politics of Expulsion in Ancient Greece* (Princeton: Princeton University Press, 2005), 10–11; Serge Vleminck, "La valeur de ἀτιμία dans le droit grec ancien," *Les études classiques* 49 (1981): 251–65; A. R. W. Harrison, *The Law of Athens: Procedure, Volume* 2, 2nd ed. (London: Duckworth, 1998), 169–76; Douglas M. MacDowell, *Spartan Law*, ScotCS (Edinburgh: Scottish Academic, 1986), 73–75.

[49] Forsdyke, *Exile, Ostracism, and Democracy*, 11.

the loss of his *patria* in exile to the condition of the many immigrants in the Rome of his day (*Helv.* 6.2–3).[50]

It should therefore be no surprise that the LXX uses a different term, avoiding the connotations of "flight" and permanence that could be associated with *fugē* and preferring a term for displacement from one's homeland while leaving room for the hope of return.[51] The Septuagint's chosen term, *apoikia*, serves this purpose quite well,[52] as it is itself not a technical term for colonization or emigration but rather denotes being "away from home" in a neutral sense, taking on the charge of its surrounding context.[53] Thus it can have a negative sense, as in Bar 3:8, Josephus' reference to the expulsion of Abraham's sons by Hagar and Keturah (*Ant.* 1:216, 239, 255), or indeed the Septuagint, as well as a more positive meaning, such as when referring to Greek colonization.[54] As will be noted in our discussion of Philo, this flexibility had apologetic benefits while not eliminating the sense of prophetic judgment in these texts. Rather than attempting to spin the Jewish diaspora as a positive along the lines of Greek colonization, the Septuagint translators were more likely applying these passages to their own context, directly

---

[50] Jan Felix Gaertner, "The Discourse of Displacement in Greco-Roman Antiquity," in *Writing Exile: The Discourse of Displacement in Greco-Roman Antiquity and Beyond*, ed. Jan Felix Gaertner, MnemosyneSup 283 (Leiden: Brill, 2007), 1–20 (3).

[51] See, for example, Philo's acknowledgment that those abroad continue to long for a return home in *Conf.* 78. Cf. Scott, "Philo and the Restoration of Israel," 563, but note the objections of Sarah J. K. Pearce, "Jerusalem as 'Mother-City' in the Writings of Philo of Alexandria," in *Negotiating Diaspora: Jewish Strategies in the Roman Empire*, ed. John M. G. Barclay (London: T&T Clark, 2004), 19–37 (25–27). See the section on Philo below for more discussion of this passage. Cf. also Modrzejewski, "How to Be a Jew," 70, on the influence of restoration hopes on the LXX's choice of vocabulary.

[52] Kiefer, *Exil und Diaspora*, 217–18.

[53] Kiefer, *Exil und Diaspora*, 218. See also Talmon, "'Exile' and 'Restoration,'" 107; Modrzejewski, "How to Be a Jew," 67. Michel Casewitz, *Le vocabulaire de la colonisation en grec ancien. Etude lexicologique: les familles de κτίζω et de οἰκέω-οἰκίζω* (Paris: Klincksieck, 1985), also attempts to provide an overview of Greek terminology for colonization or emigration, but it is an untrustworthy resource – indeed, "deplorably inaccurate," in the words of A. J. Graham, review of *Le vocabulaire de la colonisation en grec ancien. Etude lexicologique: les familles de κτίζω et de οἰκέω-οἰκίζω*, by Michel Casewitz, *Classical Review* 37.2 (1987): 237–40.

[54] *Pace* Erich S. Gruen, "Diaspora and Homeland," in *Diasporas and Exiles: Varieties of Jewish Identity*, ed. Howard Wettstein (Berkeley: University of California Press, 2002), 18–46 (26–27), who argues the implications of the term when used by Jewish writers were "decidedly positive" (26), though the examples he cites are mixed at best rather than universally positive.

connecting their own experience of forced colonization under the Ptolemies as continuous with the biblical exiles.[55]

This tendency to actualize the biblical text and apply it to their own community is visible in key alterations to prophetic passages, such as Isa 11:15–16, where the highway from Assyria in the Hebrew version is altered to a highway for those remaining in Egypt – that is, for the community of the Greek translators.[56] Most of the LXX occurrences of *apoikia* can be found in Jeremiah, where there is no attempt to obscure the exilic undertones of these passages.[57] Instead, a number of these passages are translated in such a way as to apply more easily to a reader in Egypt. For example, Jer 29:4–7 (36:4–7 LXX) talks of an exile "to Babylon," but the Greek version leaves that qualifier out, giving an Alexandrian reader more of an opportunity to read the text as speaking to his own situation (cf. also Jer 35:4 [28:4 LXX]). Where Hebrew Jeremiah encourages those "in Babylon" to settle down and seek the good of the city where they are exiled, the Greek passage is easily applicable not only to the community in Babylon but anywhere.[58] Nevertheless, despite this admonition to make the best of the circumstances and settle down in the *apoikia*, this passage neither presents those circumstances as a positive nor repudiates the hope of return – quite the opposite. That *apoikia* and *aichmalosia* stand in parallel in LXX Jer 37:18 (30:18 MT) is further evidence that the translator at least in this instance did not envision *apoikia* as something distinct from exile as is often suggested. Scott's conclusion is therefore most likely correct:

By their choice of the term ἀποικία for גולה, the Ptolemaic Jews affirm the history of their people and, more importantly, their own place within that history as a continuation of exile "to this day." Moreover, the term occurs in many passages which speak of the return of the "colony" from exile, even as a future hope.[59]

Although he correctly argues that the LXX takes a largely negative view of the diaspora, Seeligmann nevertheless agrees with Schmidt that the Greek translators no longer embrace the Hebrew Bible's prophetic idea of exile as divine judgment for sin. Instead, Seeligmann contends that

---

[55] Scott, "Self-Understanding," 190.
[56] See p. 123. Seeligmann, *Septuagint Version of Isaiah*, 99, goes so far as to argue that Greek Isaiah transforms the king of Assyria into "the disguised, but not quite masked, figure of Antiochus Epiphanes."
[57] Scott, "Self-Understanding," 191.
[58] Scott, "Self-Understanding," 191.
[59] Scott, "Self-Understanding," 191–92.

the translators replaced this concept with the more pessimistic and negative idea of injustice (ἀδικία) inflicted by the nations upon Israel,[60] a shift often associated with a transition from prophetic to apocalyptic literature:[61]

[T]he *adikia* concept [was introduced] into the Greek translation, in particular of Isaiah where we find this concept in many instances without any support in the Hebrew text. ... One can hardly escape the impression that the actual content of the historical consciousness is fashioned by the novel notion of the injustice committed by the foreign nations, whereas the ancient biblical orientation – that of the rightful punishment meted out by God – has now become an esteemed tradition, no longer deeply felt or experienced.[62]

That the Septuagint amplifies the concept of the injustice of the nations toward Israel and Judah cannot be denied, but Seeligmann's contention that this is a novel concept first introduced in the Greek versions is mistaken. The (Hebrew) book of Habakkuk, for example, prominently features this theme of injustice, complaining to YHWH that the nations he has used as instruments of his justice toward Israel are more wicked than those against whom they are being used (cf. Hab 1:13, 17).[63] Zechariah echoes a similar sentiment, putting together the two notions Seeligmann finds so incompatible: "I [YHWH] am very angry with the carefree nations, for while I was only a little angry [at Jerusalem/Zion], they multiplied the disaster" (Zech 1:15). That is, although YHWH intended to use the nations in judgment against his people, the nations' treatment far exceeded justice and therefore demands its own retribution.[64] The LXX does not soften or eliminate the prophetic passages that declare exile to be a divine punishment; rather, like Zechariah, the Greek version holds these two things together as complementary rather than incompatible. In any case, the amplification of the theme of unjust oppression at the hand of the nations is hardly what one would expect if the Greek Bible embraced a positive "diaspora theology" as is so often assumed.

---

[60] Seeligmann, *Septuagint Version of Isaiah*, 99.

[61] For more on the relationship between prophetic and apocalyptic literature, see Lester L. Grabbe and Robert D. Haak, eds., *Knowing the End From the Beginning: The Prophetic, Apocalyptic, and Their Relationship*, JSPSup 46 (London: Continuum, 2003); Job Y. Jindo, "On Myth and History in Prophetic and Apocalyptic Eschatology," *VT* 55 (2005): 412–15; Lorenzo DiTommaso, "History and Apocalyptic Eschatology: Reply to J. Y. Jindo," *VT* 56.3 (2006): 413–18.

[62] Seeligmann, *Septuagint Version of Isaiah*, 100.

[63] Smith, *Micah–Malachi*, 103–04.

[64] Smith, *Micah–Malachi*, 188; cf. Ackroyd, *Exile and Restoration*, 176.

With respect to the terminology for exile in the LXX, Ropes' overview remains generally correct:

Of the words here considered, αἰχμαλωσία is obviously the most limited in application, referring to the captivity proper; ἀποικία and μετοικία are applicable to any portion, as well as to the whole, of the body of Jews residing in foreign parts; διασπορά can only be used with reference to the general scattering of Jews [sic]. Thus the αἰχμαλωσία was (e.g.) in Babylon; the Jews in any one place could be called ἀποικία (Jer 21:1, etc.); while ἡ διασπορά means the scattered state, or the scattered section, of the Jewish [sic] nation.[65]

That is, the Septuagint neither substantially softens nor hardens the prophetic perspective on the exile/diaspora. On the contrary, the LXX reinforces the restoration eschatology of its *Vorlage*, updating and expanding that perspective for a new context and serving as a constant reminder of the inadequacies of the present and of the prophetic promises of restoration to the communities for which it served as authoritative literature.

RESTORATION ESCHATOLOGY IN THE DIASPORA: A COMPLEX REALITY

That the Septuagint preserves and indeed sometimes amplifies traditional exilic theology (that is, restoration eschatology) does not, however, in itself disprove Schmidt's larger argument that Jewish attitudes toward exile became more positive as time passed and circumstances changed. The assumption underlying this larger case is that since, unlike the forced captivity under Babylon, most diaspora Jews could at least theoretically return to the land if they chose, the traditional negative view of exile or diaspora was unsustainable.[66] The dissonance between freely choosing to

---

[65] Ropes, *James*, 121–22.

[66] Scholarly opinion is divided on the accounts of voluntary Jewish emigrations; cf. Victor Tcherikover, *Hellenistic Civilization and the Jews*, trans. Shimon Applebaum (Peabody: Hendrickson, 1999), 56–57. See also the summary in Aryeh Kasher and Avigdor Shinan, "Jewish Emigration and Settlement in the Diaspora in the Hellenistic-Roman Period," in *Emigration and Settlement in Jewish and General History* (Jerusalem: Zalman Shazar Center, 1982), 65–91. For the idea that most Jews in the diaspora remained so voluntarily, see Collins, *Between Athens and Jerusalem*, 3–5; Menahem Stern, "The Jewish Diaspora," in *The Jewish People in the First Century: Historical Geography, Political History, Social, Cultural, and Religious Life and Institutions*, eds. Shmuel Safrai and Menahem Stern, CRINT 1 (Philadelphia: Fortress, 1974), 117–83 (170–80); Joseph Mélèze Modrzejewski, *The Jews of Egypt: From Ramses II to Emperor Hadrian*

live outside the land and the prophetic perspective of exile as a curse must have been reconciled by altering the negative judgment to a more positive one. Erich Gruen puts it this way:

> It is not easy to imagine that millions of ancient Jews dwelled in foreign parts for generations mired in misery and obsessed with a longing for Jerusalem that had little chance of fulfillment. . . . To imagine that they repeatedly lamented their fate and pinned their hopes on the recovery of the homeland is quite preposterous. . . . It seems only logical that Jews sought out means whereby to legitimize a diaspora existence that most of them had inherited from their parents and would bequeath to their descendants.[67]

This perspective is typically set against the "grim sense of diaspora and a correspondingly gloomy attitude . . . conventionally ascribed to Jews of the Second Temple,"[68] and much recent scholarship has shifted the attention from the center to the periphery, observing that diaspora Jews did not in fact live a miserable, anxious, insular existence but were often active and prosperous participants in the non-Jewish societies among which they lived. More Jews lived outside the land than inside, and numerous large and stable Jewish communities thrived throughout the Mediterranean, complete with "opportunities for economic advancement, social status, and even political responsibilities."[69] Kraabel, for example, argues that these material conditions demonstrate that diaspora Jews did not take a gloomy view of their circumstances but in fact felt completely at home in their non-Jewish settings, having rendered a geo-

(Princeton: Princeton University Press, 1995), 123–33. See also the discussion in Gafni, *Land, Center, and Diaspora*, 27–29.

[67] Gruen, "Diaspora and Homeland," 20; see also Daniel R. Schwartz, "Temple or City: What Did Hellenistic Jews See in Jerusalem," in *The Centrality of Jerusalem: Historical Perspectives*, eds. Marcel Poorthuis and C. Safrai (Kampen: Kok Pharos, 1996), 114–27 (118).

[68] Gruen, "Diaspora and Homeland," 21. For an example, see Marcel Simon, Verus Israel: A Study of the Relations between Christians and Jews in the Roman Empire AD 135–425, trans. H. McKeating (London: The Littman Library of Jewish Civilization, 1986), 132.

[69] Gruen, "Diaspora and Homeland," 20. Cf. Paul R. Trebilco, *Jewish Communities in Asia Minor*, SNTSMS 69 (Cambridge: Cambridge University Press, 2006); Leonard Victor Rutgers, *The Hidden Heritage of Diaspora Judaism*, Contributions to Biblical Exegesis and Theology (Leuven: Peeters, 1998), 20–21; Collins, *Between Athens and Jerusalem*, 3–5; Kasher and Shinan, "Jewish Emigration and Settlement"; Martin D. Goodman, ed., *Jews in a Graeco-Roman World* (New York: Oxford University Press, 1998); Stern, "The Jewish Diaspora," 117–83; Barclay, *Jews in the Mediterranean Diaspora*, 19–81; Irina Levinskaya, *The Book of Acts in Its Diaspora Setting* (Grand Rapids: Eerdmans, 1996), 127–93.

graphical center for Judaism unnecessary.[70] The influence of cosmopolitan Hellenism supposedly reinforced this shift, aiding in the "development of a Judaism which undercut the security of establishments of place and pedigree,"[71] with those Jews choosing to dwell outside the land developing a "diaspora theology" that deemphasized the centrality of the land and minimized the idea of scattering or exile as divine punishment.[72] Some, such as Haim Hillel Ben-Sasson, have even suggested that the concept of exile does not apply to the Second Temple period so long as the temple stood and Jews possessed the land (albeit under the control of an empire).[73]

Although he agrees with Kraabel that Jews generally had "a singular pride in the accomplishments of the diaspora," Gruen cautions against the idea that such positive attitudes were at odds with a devotion to Jerusalem and the temple, the "symbolic heart of Judaism."[74] Nevertheless, pride in the extent of the diaspora and allegiance to their new fatherlands had "eradicate[d] any idea of the 'doctrine of return.'"[75] That is, although the two drachma (half-shekel) payment (often mislabeled a "tithe") served as a repeated display of affection and allegiance from the diaspora, it also "signaled that the return was unnecessary," since YHWH and his Temple could thus be served satisfactorily without living in the land.[76] Thus Gruen argues that diaspora Jews did not view themselves as cut off from the center or somehow disconnected from their kinsfolk living in the land as one might expect of an "exilic" mentality;

---

[70] See especially Kraabel, "Unity and Diversity" and Kraabel, "Roman Diaspora," 458–59. Cf. also Ronald Charles, *Paul and the Politics of Diaspora* (Minneapolis: Fortress, 2014), 6–7.

[71] Schwartz, "Punishment to Program," 215.

[72] For the concept of "diaspora theology," see Kraabel, "Unity and Diversity," 29–31, though Kraabel puts the full flowering of this development after the destruction of the second Temple. Cf. also Schnackenburg, "Gottes Volk."

[73] Haim Hillel Ben-Sasson, "Galut," *EncJud* 7: 275–94 (275). Cf. also Oded, "Exile," 85; Daniel L. Smith, *The Religion of the Landless: The Social Context of the Babylonian Exile* (Bloomington: Meyer-Stone, 1989), 50–65.

[74] Gruen, "Diaspora and Homeland," 36.

[75] Gruen, "Diaspora and Homeland," 28.

[76] Gruen, "Diaspora and Homeland," 30–31; Schwartz, "Temple or City," 125–26, notes that this payment was not so much in support of the temple as it seems to have been a tax *to Jerusalem* for those who considered themselves citizens of that city. Shmuel Safrai, "Relations between the Diaspora and the Land of Israel," in *The Jewish People in the First Century: Historical Geography, Political History, Social, Cultural and Religious Life and Institutions*, eds. Menahem Stern and Shmuel Safrai, CRINT 1 (Philadelphia: Fortress, 1974), 184–215 (188–92), discusses the half-shekel tax at some length, also connecting it with the perceived bond between Jews and their capital city.

rather, they were fellow compatriots who had simply spilled over the borders of the territory but retained their fundamental identity and allegiance to Jerusalem.[77] This again he regards as evidence that Jews in the diaspora had no expectation of restoration, no longer regarding their current state as inferior to what might be expected in the future.[78] Gruen thereby concludes that those in the diaspora did not regard themselves as in exile.[79]

Thriving in Exile

That Jews not only thrived in the diaspora but often participated in non-Jewish society is indisputably evident in the archaeological and epigraphical record. But this does not mean that most Jews had replaced traditional restoration-eschatological theology with a positive, universalist, diaspora theology.[80] Evidence of prosperity is insufficient to come to such a sweeping conclusion; to suggest otherwise reflects a startlingly consumerist perspective.[81] There are indeed good reasons to reject old portrayals of diaspora Jewish life in overly negative terms, but we must be careful lest the pendulum swing so far as to suggest that diaspora Jews had dispensed with the restoration eschatology central to their own foundational narratives.[82] As John Barclay has shown, it is important to distinguish between assimilation, acculturation, and accommodation; it is therefore important to differentiate between the material circumstances, acculturation, and everyday psychology of group members on the

---

[77] Gruen, "Diaspora and Homeland," 33. Charles, *Paul and the Politics of Diaspora*, 9–10, however, observes that these dual loyalties sometimes put Jews in awkward positions with their non-Jewish neighbors, who were "upset that economic resources urgently needed for local festivals and the repair of public buildings were sent away to the 'homeland' of the Judeans."

[78] Gruen, "Diaspora and Homeland," 30–31.

[79] Gruen, *Diaspora*, 1–11; Gruen, "Diaspora and Homeland," 33–34; cf. Charles, *Paul and the Politics of Diaspora*, 6–7.

[80] Cf. Gruen, "Diaspora and Homeland," 20, 36–37.

[81] Rutgers, *Hidden Heritage*, 21–22, points out that a similar attention to material evidence among modern German Jews might be taken to suggest that they feel at home, but the survey data show otherwise. In contrast to Kraabel's conclusions, Rutgers observes that the impressive architecture and centralized locations of diaspora synagogues may not always have been the *result* of acquired status but rather an *attempt* to acquire status.

[82] See especially Rutgers, *Hidden Heritage*, 21–24. Cf. also Gruen, "Diaspora and Homeland," 20.

one hand and participation in a traditional group narrative theology on the other.[83]

For an instructive example, many Evangelical Christians in the United States hold to an apocalyptic eschatology that characterizes the present world as evil while simultaneously being prosperous, politically active citizens otherwise integrated into secular society. These comfortable suburban residents frequently signal their belief in a particular eschatological narrative through their staunch political and financial support of Israel, behavior remarkably analogous to those diaspora Jews who continued to send money to the Jerusalem Temple.[84] In each case, the donors have no intention of giving up their present comfortable position to relocate to Israel, but they continue to await the time of God's eschatological intervention, which will radically alter the status quo and make their present situation moot. Notably, in the case of modern Dispensationalist Christian supporters of Israel, much of that support of Israel is overtly for the purpose of accelerating the eschatological timetable – even if that should require another world war.[85]

To imagine that diaspora Jews holding traditional exilic/eschatological theology would necessarily experience everyday life in a nervous, unhappy manner, longing for return to the land, is as absurd as the suggestion that modern Christian believers in the Parousia live a miserable daily existence, unable to integrate with larger society as they await the eschaton. It is equally misguided to suggest that social integration necessarily indicates abandonment of traditional eschatological hopes. Such tension between integration and restoration/eschatological hopes goes back at least to Jeremiah's counsel to the exiles to "seek the welfare of the city where I have sent you into exile, and pray to YHWH on its behalf, for in its welfare you will find your welfare" (Jer 29:7 MT). But those exiles were no less exhorted to look forward to the time of restoration when YHWH would restore Israel and subjugate the nations to his chastened, chosen people. That future hope is, in fact, the very explanation Jeremiah provides for his counsel (Jer 29:10–14 MT): they must not

---

[83] See Barclay, *Jews in the Mediterranean Diaspora*, 82–98. As Barclay demonstrates, high levels of acculturation (e.g., scholarly expertise in Greek traditions) or assimilation (e.g., participation in local civic government) do not necessarily indicate accommodation or abandonment of traditional Jewish theology.

[84] Thanks to Sonya Cronin for reminding me of this point.

[85] See Yaakov Ariel, "An Unexpected Alliance: Christian Zionism and Its Historical Significance," *Modern Judaism* 26.1 (2006): 74–100; Hal Lindsey, *The Late Great Planet Earth* (Grand Rapids: Zondervan, 1970).

seek to rebel or return of their own accord before the appointed time when YHWH would restore them. Those who refused to accept this judgment and tried to rebel and initiate the return on their own would be destroyed (Jer 29:15–20 MT).

Jeremiah's counsel is relevant to the lack of any significant movement of return to Jerusalem in the diaspora until after the destruction of 70 CE, which is sometimes cited as evidence for the absence of traditional exilic theology or restoration eschatology in the diaspora.[86] But the prophets did not enjoin the people to attempt to return on their own. Instead, we find what Goldstein labels "the requirement of the full Age of Wrath, that Jews be loyal even to oppressors"[87] and promises of a restoration that would happen through divine action. In the meantime, the people are encouraged to make the best of their circumstances while hoping for better things from the future and are assured that even YHWH's punishments are for their ultimate benefit, that they remain under his ultimate protection even in exile (cf. Ezek 11:16).[88] There is therefore little reason to expect diaspora Jews to have clamored for return unless they believed that divine action had begun.[89] We do have evidence, however, of such movements after the destruction of Jerusalem in 70 CE, most notably in the Diaspora Revolt of 116–117 CE.[90] That revolts and messianic movements did eventually manifest suggests that previous inaction was not due to a lack of restoration theology (which surely did not suddenly arise *ex nihilo*) but rather to a conviction that the time of restoration had not yet come.

---

[86] E.g., Charles, *Paul and the Politics of Diaspora*, 9.

[87] Goldstein, "Messianic Promises," 83.

[88] Erich S. Gruen, "Judaism in the Diaspora," *EDEJ* 77–97 (91), observes that diaspora "authors who speak with reverence [about the land] do not demand the 'Return.' Commitment to one's local or regional community was entirely compatible with devotion to Jerusalem. The two concepts in no way represented mutually exclusive alternatives." Gruen implies that this is somehow different from the traditional prophetic perspective, but the prophets likewise do not demand a return. Instead, they promise that YHWH will intervene and ultimately bring about a return.

[89] Davies, *Territorial Dimension*, 120: "If the return were an act of divine intervention, it could not be engineered or forced by political or any other human means: to do so would be impious. That coming was best served by waiting in obedience for it: *men of violence would not avail to bring it in.*" Cf. also Boyarin and Boyarin, "Diaspora," 721–23.

[90] On the Diaspora Revolt, see Miriam Pucci Ben Zeev, *Diaspora Judaism in Turmoil, 116/ 117 CE: Ancient Sources and Modern Insights*, Interdisciplinary Studies in Ancient Culture and Religion (Leuven: Peeters, 2005); Miriam Pucci Ben Zeev, "The Uprisings in the Jewish Diaspora (116–117 CE)," in *The Cambridge History of Judaism, Vol 4: The Late Roman-Rabbinic Period*, ed. Stephen T. Katz (Cambridge: Cambridge University Press, 2006), 93–104.

The generally positive relations between Jews and their non-Jewish neighbors and governments in the diaspora have also been cited as further reason for a positive view of exile or diaspora for those in the dispersion. Robin Cohen, for example, states, "Despite occasional outbursts of hostility, philo-Semitism was the normal experience of the many Jewish communities scattered around the Greco-Roman world."[91] But this overstates the case, as those "occasional outbursts" served as stark reminders of the insecurity of diaspora existence, which had both ups and downs as Jewish experience varied across time and region.[92] Regardless of the prosperity of a given Jewish community at a specific point in time, that Israel remained under foreign domination remains an inescapable truth, and as long as they remained under foreign domination, Jews remained subject to the capriciousness of their gentile rulers and neighbors, a theme that persists in the Jewish literature of the period.[93]

Secure and prosperous circumstances thus do not by their mere existence negate the narrative of Jewish identity established in and reinforced through the sacred Jewish texts, which assert that the present circumstances, regardless of how good they may be, still fall short of the promises to Israel.[94] Even today, one can still defensibly assert, "Traditional Jewish texts always figured (and continue to figure) a mythic Zion as the eternal Jewish home, the place to which the Messiah would return Jews."[95] That concept has mostly transitioned into a more distant, otherworldly concept, but the hope of restoration has not entirely disappeared even in modern times. Irrespective of the positivity of daily circumstances, the foundational narrative of exile and restoration was ever present for Jews of the Second Temple period, promising a future time of restoration in which they would rule the nations rather than being subject

---

[91] Robin Cohen, *Global Diasporas: An Introduction*, 2nd ed. (London: Routledge, 2008), 24.

[92] Cf. Unnik, *Das Selbstverständnis*, 143.

[93] Tessa Rajak, *Translation and Survival: The Greek Bible of the Ancient Jewish Diaspora* (Oxford: Oxford University Press, 2009), 194.

[94] Philo, for example, says that after the restoration, "the good fortune of their fathers and ancestors will be considered as a small thing because of the bountiful abundance which they will have" (*Praem.* 168). Aristeas 249 also asserts that life abroad is a "reproach" even to the wealthy, a reminder that material prosperity does not prima facie eliminate hopes for restoration and return.

[95] Aviv and Shneer, *New Jews*, 4.

to the various governments and nations among which they dwelt.[96] Gruen is therefore right to say:

We can therefore abandon simplistic dichotomies. Diaspora Jews did not huddle in enclaves, isolated and oppressed, clinging to a heritage under threat. Nor did they assimilate to the broader cultural and political world, compromising their past, ignoring the homeland, and reckoning the Book (in Greek) as surrogate for the Temple. The stark alternatives obscure understanding. A complex set of circumstances, diverse and dependent on local conditions, produced a mixed, ambiguous, and varied picture.[97]

But to this we may add that although it was surely interpreted and actualized in various ways, restoration eschatology nevertheless remained near the center of Jewish theological expression throughout this period, whether in the diaspora or (however defined) in the homeland. Neither the Septuagint nor the often pleasant and prosperous circumstances of Jewish life in the diaspora gives evidence that diaspora Jews had dropped traditional restoration eschatology in favor of a more positive perspective on the dispersion.

That Day Has Not Yet Come

Remarkably, although Gruen concedes that Hellenistic Jewish texts regularly characterize diaspora as exile, he promptly dismisses the importance of that theme for the period in which the texts were written:

A caveat has to be issued from the start. The majority of these grim pronouncements [about exile] refer to the biblical misfortunes of the Israelites, expulsion by the Assyrians, the destruction of the Temple, and the Babylonian Captivity. Were they all metaphors for the Hellenistic diaspora? The inference would be hasty, and it begs the question.[98]

Instead, he argues, that perspective and those concerns are irrelevant by the Hellenistic period, since "redemption came, the promise of a new Temple was kept. The lamentations do not apply to current conditions."[99] Here we encounter the problematic root of the positive diaspora

---

[96] Carroll, "Deportation," 84, notes, "for many generations it must have represented no more than a conventional trope," but the point is that it nevertheless remained, waiting on just the right moment for the flame to be rekindled.

[97] Gruen, *Diaspora*, 6.

[98] Gruen, "Diaspora and Homeland," 20–21.

[99] Gruen, "Diaspora and Homeland," 24; cf. Charles, *Paul and the Politics of Diaspora*, 6–7.

theology argument: the presumption that most Jews regarded the promised return and restoration as already having come to pass at the beginning of the Persian period, such that the historical misfortunes of exile
could only apply to the "Hellenistic diaspora" metaphorically. Once the
return had already taken place, those who remained in the diaspora
necessarily legitimized their own situations, understanding themselves as
living in a post-restoration era no less than those living in the land.

Dismissing these texts and passages as inapplicable to the periods in
which they were written is what truly begs the question, however, as does
the assumption that those dwelling in the land could not be part of the
diaspora or exile. We have already observed that Ezra-Nehemiah, Daniel,
and the Maccabean literature undermine the idea that the restoration was
a past event, and the conditions of life in the land continued to fall far
short of prophetic promises in the succeeding centuries. Ezra-Nehemiah
even explicitly calls the returnees to the land "exiles" on multiple occasions (e.g., Ezra 4:1 6:16, 19, 20; 8:35; 10:6–8, 16). The similarities
between diaspora Jews and those living in the land therefore cut both
ways, since, as Tessa Rajak points out, "The Jews were in fact always a
minority in much of Palestine, subject to the same circumstances and the
same rulers as Jews further afield."[100] Indeed, *there is little evidence or
indication that even those living in the land believed the promised restoration had already taken place.*[101] As such, continued attention to the
biblical misfortunes, particularly the expulsion by the Assyrians, should
be no surprise in later literature, as those misfortunes marked the beginning of the present period of wrath, a period that would continue until the
promises of the prophets would be fulfilled. These texts served as a
continued reminder of the theological history underlying the present

---

[100] Rajak, *Translation and Survival*, 95. For more on the problems involved in
distinguishing "Diaspora" from "Palestinian" Judaism, see Barclay, *Jews in the
Mediterranean Diaspora*, 6–9, 82–102; cf. also Sean Freyne, "Studying the Jewish
Diaspora in Antiquity," in *Jews in the Hellenistic and Roman Cities*, ed. John
R. Bartlett (London: Routledge, 2002), 1–5 (4), who wonders whether living in Galilee
was "a form of Diaspora existence for a Jew."

[101] For example, though living in the land, the sect behind the Dead Sea Scrolls presents
itself as righteous people living in exile. See Noah Hacham, "Exile and Self-Identity in
the Qumran Sect and in Hellenistic Judaism," in *New Perspectives on Old Texts:
Proceedings of the Tenth International Symposium of the Orion Center for the Dead
Sea Scrolls and Associated Literature, January 2005*, eds. Esther G. Chazon, Betsy
Halpern-Amaru, and Ruth A. Clements, STDJ 88 (Leiden: Brill, 2010), 3–21 and
Chapter 9.

circumstances – no matter how good or bad – continuing to set the narrative framework for the people.

Moreover, it should not be presumed that diaspora Jews holding to a biblical/prophetic perspective of exile would regard themselves or their situation as inferior to those living in the land. Kraabel, for example, claims:

> [F]or biblical thought before the Common Era there was no positive theological symbol for life outside Palestine. The only two kinds of biblical "space" were Promised (or Holy) Land and Exile. Diaspora could only be Exile; and no one who read the Hebrew Scriptures carefully could come to any other conclusion than that Exile was punishment. On this point Christians and Jews saw the Old Testament in the same way; on a "biblical" basis, each group could view Jewish life in the western Diaspora only as flawed, and inferior to life in the Holy Land.[102]

On the contrary, Jeremiah and Ezekiel depict the exiles as better positioned for redemption than those who remained in the land.[103] Exile is indeed consistently presented throughout the Bible as punishment for the disobedience of the people, but it is not presented as a specific punishment of the *individuals* living in exile. Again, Jeremiah advises those going into exile to settle down, marry, and prosper, awaiting YHWH's restoration (Jer 29:4–7), since they are the "good figs" (24:5) in contrast to the rotten, split-open figs remaining in the land and awaiting destruction (29:17; 24:8–10). There is therefore no indication in the prophets that those living outside the land should regard themselves as inferior to those living in the land – if anything, we find the opposite. As will be shown below, this turns out to be especially important for understanding the Dead Sea sect.

Until Israel has been reconstituted and YHWH's manifest presence renewed among his people, life in the land is not qualitatively different than diaspora existence,[104] not because the diaspora is no longer to be regarded as a negative thing but because the ultimate positive of eschatological restoration has not yet taken place.[105] In this context, Gruen is correct to observe that "Jews seem to have felt no need to fashion a theory of Diaspora," but this is because there was nothing new to explain.

---

[102] Kraabel, "Roman Diaspora," 462; cf. also Simon, *Verus Israel*, 132.
[103] Cf. Jer 24; Ezek 11. See the sections on Jeremiah and Ezekiel above for more discussion on this point.
[104] E.g., Ezra 6:22; Neh 9:32.
[105] Erich S. Gruen, "Judaism in the Diaspora," *EDEJ* 77–97 (79); cf. Gruen, "Diaspora and Homeland," 28.

Location outside the land is not inferior to life within – but it is because both still await the time after Israel's restoration that will be superior to the inferior existence of all those living prior to the fulfillment of the prophets' promises.[106] All are on equal footing not because everything is right with the world but because it is not.

Good from Evil: Planting and Harvest

What then should be made of the positive statements about the spread of the Jews across the world in Philo, Josephus, and even in texts such as the Sibylline Oracles or later Rabbinic literature? If, as Daniel Schwartz explains, the diaspora "itself is an expression of divine grace,"[107] how could this not be understood as a positive perspective on exile in sharp contrast to traditional restoration eschatology that sees the exile/diaspora as a negative to be overcome? We will of necessity address these specific statements as we examine these texts in more depth, but the short answer is found in the distinction between something being a positive in itself versus yielding positive results. In Genesis, for example, Joseph declares to his brothers that God took what was meant for evil and brought good from it (Gen 50:20). Similarly, the prophets often declare that YHWH's chastisements of Israel will culminate in Israel's ultimate redemption.[108] Israel had been appointed as a kingdom of priests through which all nations would be blessed (Gen 22:18, 26:4; Exod 19:5–6) but instead exceeded the other nations in wickedness, thus becoming a curse (e.g., Ezek 5:5–9; Zech 8:13). YHWH has therefore sown Israel (Hos 2:23) among the nations (cf. 7:8), where the prophet promises in the wake of exile that Israel will become a "light to the nations" (Isa 49:6, 9). Those "not my people" scattered among the nations will multiply into an immeasurable number to be harvested at the time of redemption and vindication (Hos 2:1–2 [ET 1:10–11]). The means of punishment thus provides the avenue for even greater redemption.[109] Whereas at the

---

[106] Gafni, *Land, Center, and Diaspora*, 58–78, notes that increased calls for loyalty to the land only emerged after active messianism was rendered taboo in the wake of the Bar Kokhba disaster, observing that this contrasts with modern assumptions that the two would have necessarily gone together. Prior to the middle of the second century CE, location in the land was not the priority – restoration of the people was more central.

[107] Schwartz, "Punishment to Program," 213.

[108] Cf. Heschel, *The Prophets*, 183, 277.

[109] Cf. b. Pesachim 87b; Origen, *Contra Celsum* 1.55.

exodus YHWH displayed his power in Egypt, this time, thanks to the dispersion, YHWH's wisdom will be displayed among all the nations (Jer 16:14–15). Thus for these later interpreters, the fact that the Jews have spread so widely only further attests to continued divine protection even in the midst of diaspora. It is not the diaspora that is the source of pride but the continued relationship with YHWH.[110]

The idea that the diaspora would ultimately turn out for the best is therefore neither a new development nor should it be understood as contradicting the disciplinary nature of exile. Rather, both elements regularly appear together in the tradition: the exile is indeed punishment, but YHWH nevertheless will bring about redemptive results for his people.[111] Thus YHWH in his faithfulness always brings good from evil. Philo makes the same basic point in *Conf.* 171, explaining, "Even punishment is not entirely disadvantageous (ἐπιζήμιον), since it is a hindrance of doing wrong and a correction/restoration (ἐπανόρθωσις)." Even more relevant is Philo's assertion that "many have been trained (ἐσωφρονίσθησαν) by going abroad (ἀποδημίαις)," since they have been separated from "the idols (εἴδωλα) of pleasure" and the things that had previously inflamed their passions (*Praem.* 19).[112] Thus exile and diaspora simultaneously serve as punishment for sin and the means for redemption, the greater good brought out of redemptive chastisement. In YHWH's wisdom, the exile/diaspora sets the stage for all of his promises to be accomplished at once, as YHWH continues in his faithfulness to bring good out of disobedience and redemption from evil circumstances, even using evil itself to produce redemption for Israel. As will be further demonstrated below, the pride shown in the spread of the Jews across the world should not be confused with the idea that the diaspora is good in itself, nor does such pride negate hopes for future redemption.

---

[110] This point will be more thoroughly discussed below, as many of the passages that are seen as rejoicing in the diaspora itself are better understood as rejoicing in something *else* that the diaspora has brought into relief.

[111] It should be noted, however, that such optimism, although typical, is not universal in the Hebrew Bible, as illustrated by the uncertainty of Lamentations, the discourses of Job, etc. Nevertheless, the idea that the scattering of exile (or diaspora) is an unmitigated positive does not appear anywhere in the biblical tradition.

[112] See also Philo's appeal to the metaphor of surgery in *Praem.* 33–34. The same basic understanding of divine punishment as corrective and redemptive can be seen in Heb 12:5–11 and Rev 3:19, each of which connects unpleasant discipline (*paideia*) with divine love and concern and the need for repentance.

CONCLUSION: RESTORATION ESCHATOLOGY IN THE DIASPORA

We can therefore conclude that there is no evidence that diaspora Jews transitioned away from traditional exile theology and adopted a positive "diaspora theology" in its place. Instead, as will be shown more clearly in the following chapters, the traditional perspective of restoration eschatology mediated through the Jewish scriptures remained influential, though everyday diaspora life was often prosperous and pleasant.[113] This conclusion runs counter to those who have attributed the idea of diaspora as divine punishment to Christian anti-Judaism.[114] Harry Attridge is therefore correct to conclude:

It was not Christians, but Jews of the Hellenistic period themselves who viewed the fact of the diaspora in negative terms. They did so not because of the social and economic facts of life in the diaspora, but because scripture itself indicated that dispersion was an act of God designed to punish transgression of the covenant and to call the people of Israel to repentance.[115]

And, we may add: to lead to subsequent redemption and exaltation above the nations, who also would ultimately benefit from Israel's chastisement. To be sure, later Christian apologists appropriated this theological perspective on the diaspora; their primary innovation, however, was to suggest that the diaspora following the destruction of the Second Temple (which they claimed was the result of Jesus' crucifixion) would be perpetual, thus stripping away any eschatological hopes of return not tied to Jesus. Those arguing that such negativity about the diaspora must have arisen from Christians have not fully appreciated the persistence of traditional exilic theology – and its accompanying hopeful future-oriented restoration eschatology – in the generative myth of exile and return embedded in early Jewish theology. Moreover, as the succeeding chapters will demonstrate, Jewish literature of the Second Temple period continued to maintain the restoration-eschatological sense of the term "Israel" with remarkable consistency.

---

[113] Grabbe, "Israel's Historical Reality," 22–23.

[114] E.g., Kraabel, "Unity and Diversity," 30; Cohen, *Global Diasporas*, 24–25; Jules Isaac, *The Teaching of Contempt: Christian Roots of Anti-Semitism*, trans. Helen Weaver (New York: Holt, Rinehart, & Winston, 1964).

[115] Harold W. Attridge, review of *Das Selbstverständnis der jüdischen Diaspora in der hellenistisch-römischen Zeit*, by Willem Cornelis Van Unnik, *JAOS* 115.2 (1995): 323–24 (324).

7

Israel, Jews, and Restoration Eschatology in Josephus

Josephus had a bigger fish to fry – he expected the "return" to encompass the whole world. It would not come about as the result of another military confrontation between Rome and the Jews; rather it will transpire peacefully and naturally. Until that happens (and in order for it [to] happen) the Jews must be faithful to the Law. . . . They should leave politics to God, who in His own time will bring this all about.

Michael Tuval[1]

If, as the previous chapter has demonstrated, there is little evidence of an exile-positive "diaspora theology" that had replaced the traditional restoration-eschatological framework among most Jews in the diaspora, there is little reason to expect Josephus to have abandoned his own restorationist perspective after coming under Roman patronage. Moreover, as has already been demonstrated, Josephus' employment of Israel terminology and statements about the fate of the northern Israelites corresponds closely with the same patterns in distinctly restorationist works, suggesting that this paradigm remained influential for Josephus. Reconstructing Josephus' view of exile and potential restoration eschatology is complicated not only by the passage of time between *War* and his other works but also his Roman patronage and apologetic purposes. Feldman, for example, is far too credulous in regarding Josephus' effusive praise for his patrons' beneficence toward him – and the "striking" absence of any expression of "pain at being exiled" in Josephus' *Life* –

---

[1] Michael Tuval, *From Jerusalem Priest to Roman Jew: On Josephus and the Paradigms of Ancient Judaism*, WUNT 357 (Tübingen: Mohr Siebeck, 2013), 283.

as an indication that he took a positive view of the concept of exile.[2] Nor should the absence of a direct expression of a hope or prayer to return to Jerusalem be understood as evidence that Josephus took a positive view of the present circumstances or had abandoned restoration hopes.[3] On the contrary, open declaration of restoration hopes or dissatisfaction with his situation while under the patronage of the Flavian emperors would have been imprudent, so we should expect that if Josephus gives any evidence of such hopes, it will be muted and indirect.[4]

Indeed, in a recent monograph, Michael Tuval demonstrates many differences between the priestly, Temple-focused "Judaean" perspective reflected in Josephus' *Jewish War* and the more diaspora-oriented and Torah-focused perspective of the *Antiquities*,[5] concluding that Josephus "began his career as a Temple Judean, but in the course of time became a Diaspora Jew."[6] In the process, Tuval notes that the view of eschatology reflected in the two works does exhibit a significant shift, but in exactly the opposite direction to that suggested by Feldman, Daniel Schwartz, and others.[7] Tuval argues that whereas *War* had been characterized by a certain "dead-endedness,"[8] the later *Antiquities* contains a much more robust and coherent eschatology, including the end of Roman domination and the ultimate triumph of Israel.[9] As a Jewish apologist under Roman patronage, Josephus simultaneously defends the misfortunes of his people and upholds the legitimacy of Roman rule by presenting the latter through the lens of the providence of God and the former through the lens of God's justice in response to disobedience.[10] In so doing, he is able to argue that the Jews are neither weak nor are they a hateful people who should be feared by the Romans, while simultaneously arguing that Jews should not resist Roman rule. Instead, the Romans rule providentially, and the disasters that have befallen the Jews are the result of their

---

[2] Feldman, "Exile in Josephus," 148–49.

[3] Feldman, "Exile in Josephus," 149.

[4] Cf. James C. Scott, *Domination and the Arts of Resistance: Hidden Transcripts* (New Haven: Yale University Press, 1990); John M. G. Barclay, *Pauline Churches and Diaspora Jews*, WUNT 275 (Tübingen: Mohr Siebeck, 2011), 301–16, 331–44.

[5] Tuval, *From Jerusalem Priest to Roman Jew*.

[6] Tuval, *From Jerusalem Priest to Roman Jew*, 276.

[7] Tuval, *From Jerusalem Priest to Roman Jew*, 188–90, 282–83.

[8] Tuval, *From Jerusalem Priest to Roman Jew*, 188.

[9] Tuval, *From Jerusalem Priest to Roman Jew*, 189, 282–83.

[10] Martin Braun, "The Prophet Who Became a Historian," *The Listener* 56 (1956): 53–57; Paul Spilsbury, "Flavius Josephus on the Rise and Fall of the Roman Empire," *JTS* 54.1 (2003): 1–24.

disobedience to the divine dictates, with Rome as the latest tool of divine punishment.[11] In this sense, Schwartz is correct in observing that for Josephus, "the Diaspora is not something which will hopefully soon be overcome by divine grace; it itself is an expression of divine grace,"[12] but the idea that every expression of grace is positive in itself is mistaken. Rather, in *Antiquities*, Josephus presents *everything*, positive or negative, as an expression of providence (e.g., *Ant.* 10.277–80), including the calamities brought in response to disobedience, which are providentially provided to train and discipline Israel for its ultimate dominion.

Josephus' solution does not depart from traditional restoration eschatology but rather embraces it, advocating that the Jews quietly serve their Roman masters while subtly encouraging his Jewish readers to wait "patiently for the 'rod of empire' to move away from the Romans ... [and] devote themselves to re-establishing themselves as God's favored clients by scrupulous observance of the laws of Moses."[13] Josephus is thereby able to pacify his Roman patrons and defend the justice of God while simultaneously preserving an undercurrent of hope for the future restoration and dominion of Israel – which, as we have already observed, is not synonymous with the *Ioudaioi* in Josephus.

JOSEPHUS' VIEW OF EXILE

Nevertheless, in addition to assuming that diaspora Jews had generally abandoned restoration eschatology, many interpreters cite passages in which Josephus allegedly expresses his pride in the diaspora as proof that he took a positive view of exile rather than retaining restoration hopes.[14] For example, Betsy Halpern-Amaru claims, "The dispersion of the Jews in his own day is favorably commented upon by Josephus both in the *War* (II, 399 [sic, 2.398]) and in *Against Apion* (II, 282)."[15] A closer look at these passages, however, shows that although each passage references the

---

[11] Cf. Helgo Lindner, *Die Geschichtsauffassung des Flavius Josephus in Bellum Judaicum: Gleichzeitig ein Beitrag zur Quellenfrage*, AGJU 12 (Leiden: Brill, 1972), 30.

[12] Schwartz, "Punishment to Program," 213.

[13] Spilsbury, "Rise and Fall," 21. For Josephus' view of Roman power as grim and pragmatic rather than positive, see Arthur M. Eckstein, "Josephus and Polybius: A Reconsideration," *ClAnt* (1990): 175–208.

[14] E.g., Schlatter, *Theologie des Judentums*, 87; Nils A. Dahl, *Das Volk Gottes: eine Untersuchung zum Kirchenbewusstsein des Urchristentums*, 2 (Oslo: Dybwad, 1941), 93; Gerhard Delling, *Die Bewältigung der Diasporasituation durch das hellenistische Judentum* (Göttingen: Vandenhoeck & Ruprecht, 1987), 64–65.

[15] Halpern-Amaru, "Land Theology," 226 n. 52.

wide geographical spread of the Jewish people, neither actually presents the dispersion in favorable terms. The former occurs in the midst of Agrippa's warning about rebelling against Rome, observing that such actions would not only imperil the rebels but that:

[I]ndeed the danger concerns not only those Jews who dwell here but also those who dwell in other cities, for there is no people upon the habitable world among which there is not some portion of you, whom your enemies will strike down ... on account of the ill-advised actions of a few men. (*War* 2.398–399a)

This is by no means a statement of pride in the dispersion of the people but rather describes a delicate and dangerous situation. Similarly, the second passage exhibits pride not in the conditions of diaspora but in the recognition of the superior nature of the Jews' customs across the world:[16]

Not only that but also the multitude have long had a great zeal to follow our piety, for there is no city of the Greeks, nor any barbarians or nation whatsoever where our custom of rest on the seventh day has not yet come or where our fasts and lighting of lamps and many of our food prohibitions are not observed. They also try to imitate our harmony with one another, our distribution of substance, our diligence in our trades, and our endurance in our calamities [ἀνάγκαις] on account of our laws. For most amazingly, our law prevails by its own strength, lacking the bait of pleasure for attraction, and just as God pervades the whole world, our Law has passed through the whole world also. (*Ag. Ap.* 2.282–84)

Far from taking pride in the diaspora, Josephus takes pride in the superiority of his people's laws and customs that have given them such fortitude in spite of their calamities – the difficult conditions themselves are not worthy of pride but rather require fortitude and endurance (καρτερικός).[17] These examples are not anomalous, either. For example, in addition to the above, Feldman cites *War* 6.442 and 7.43 as evidence of "the pride with which Josephus refers to the spread of the Jews throughout the inhabited world," such that "that he did not regard the exile in pejorative terms."[18] The first of these occurs in perhaps the most negative context possible for Josephus: right at the end of his account of the fall of Jerusalem, where he does not glorify the spread of the Jews but rather laments,

---

[16] Unnik, *Das Selbstverständnis*, 142.
[17] Unnik, *Das Selbstverständnis*, 143.
[18] Feldman, "Exile in Josephus," 149. Feldman also cites *Ant.* 14.114, which also lacks the supposed pride in the spread of the Jews Josephus allegedly exhibits.

Neither [Jerusalem's] great antiquity, nor its vast riches, nor the wandering [διαπεφοιτηκὸς] of its nation throughout the whole civilized world, nor the greatness of the veneration paid to it on a religious account, have been sufficient to preserve it from being destroyed. And thus the siege of Jerusalem ended. (*War* 6.442)

The mention of the Jews' spread in *War* 7.43 occurs at the beginning of Josephus' explanation of why a pogrom against the Jews in Syrian Antioch occurred, with Josephus explaining that "as much as the Jewish *genos* is scattered [παρέσπαρται] across the civilized world, it is all the more intermingled with Syria." He then proceeds to explain that "about this time ... all men had taken up a great hatred against the Jews" (7.46–47). It goes without saying that these statements do not reflect the pride about the diaspora Feldman's summary would suggest. Along the same lines, although Feldman is surely correct that Josephus spends so much time on his account of Esther to "show what Jews can do in an alien environment and how God will rescue them,"[19] this is quite different from suggesting that environment is a good in itself. Rather, Josephus uses these stories to demonstrate God's faithfulness *in spite of* the context of captivity – and highlight the certainty of ultimate rescue for those who continue to serve God. It is difficult to escape the sense that many of Josephus' modern interpreters desperately want him to be positive about the diaspora and latch onto any possible indication of such a view, ignoring all evidence to the contrary.

Diaspora in Josephus

Feldman's tortured analysis of *diaspeirō* in Josephus offers a signal example of preconceptions interfering with interpretation. Although Josephus never uses the noun *diaspora*,[20] he does use verbal forms of *diaspeirō* in decidedly negative contexts, such as in the mouth of Haman, the archenemy of the Jews (*Ant.* 11.212), which Feldman somehow regards as evidence that Josephus "did not view the exile negatively," continuing:

The fact that he (*Ant.* 11.212) closely follows the Septuagint's version (Esther 3:8) that the Jews are "a nation scattered (διεσπαρμένον) among the nations in all your

---

[19] Feldman, "Restoration in Josephus," 226

[20] Josephus' avoidance of this term is seen as evidence of his pride in the spread of the Jews in Schlatter, *Theologie des Judentums*, 87.

kingdom" indicates that for him the verb διασπείρω from which Diaspora is derived is not to be viewed negatively, inasmuch as this word is put into the mouth of the Jews' arch-enemy Haman, and especially since he has Haman add immediately thereafter, in phrases that have no counterpart in the Hebrew original or in the Septuagint, that the Jews are unsociable (ἄμικτον, "unmingled," – a term used of Centaurs and Cyclopes) and incompatible (ἀσύμφυλον, "unsuitable," "not akin"). Since these are stock charges similar to those used by the Alexandrian Jew-baiters whom Josephus answers in his essay *Against Apion*, we may assume that Josephus did not view the scattering of the Jews in a negative sense.[21]

This conclusion is puzzling to say the least. That Josephus places *additional* insults on the lips of Haman does not diminish the negative sense of what comes immediately before, as the continued insults only clarify that Haman was not flattering the Jews by referencing their scattered state. Instead, Feldman assumes that the LXX takes a positive view of the diaspora (despite the strong evidence to the contrary discussed above) and that Josephus' use of LXX source material necessarily means that he is taking a similarly positive perspective. But even if these premises were true, are we really to imagine they should supersede the Josephan context in which the great enemy of the Jews uses this term as part of a statement reviling the Jews? Such a conclusion is obviously untenable.

Feldman also points to Josephus' pride that Jewish priests manage to keep strict account of their marriages even in the dispersion (διεσπαρμένοι; *Ag. Ap.* 1.33) as yet further evidence the term is "certainly not [used] in a negative sense" here.[22] But as before, Josephus' pride is not in the conditions of diaspora but in the priests' steadfast commitment to faithfulness *even in the far more difficult and suboptimal conditions of dispersion.* That Josephus also uses this term to describe the punishment of Israel for following the impious ways of Jeroboam (*Ant.* 8.271) further reinforces the negative connotations of this term and its underlying concept in Josephus.[23] Far from portraying it as a positive, Josephus consistently associates the word *diaspeirō* with "disgrace and slavery."[24]

---

[21] Feldman, "Exile in Josephus," 160; cf. also Feldman, "Restoration in Josephus," 224–26.

[22] Feldman, "Exile in Josephus," 160–61.

[23] Even Feldman, "Restoration in Josephus," 225, acknowledges that the term is here used in a negative sense and associated with punishment and acknowledges that it tends to have such a negative sense in other writers, but he nevertheless claims this is the only such negative use in Josephus.

[24] Unnik, *Das Selbstverständnis*, 142.

COVENANT THEOLOGY, EXILE, AND RESTORATION
IN JOSEPHUS

In stark contrast to his allegedly positive view of the exile or diaspora, Josephus states his traditional covenantal perspective right at the beginning of the *Antiquities*:

> One may especially learn from this history that those who follow after the purpose of God and do not dare to transgress [his] well-legislated laws are established in all things beyond belief [πέρα πίστεως][25] and that happiness [εὐδαιμονία] is set before them as honor from God. But inasmuch as they apostatize from the precise observance of these laws, the practicable things become impracticable, and whatever seemingly good thing they labor over is turned into incurable misfortunes.
>
> (*Ant.* 1.14)

It is difficult to imagine a more characteristically Deuteronomic statement than that God rewards those who obey his laws, while calamity awaits those who do not obey. Josephus steadfastly applies this principle throughout his account, blaming the many sufferings of his people on disobedience against the good legislation given by Moses, calling attention to the deportations of Israel and Judah as the prime examples of this perspective.[26] Josephus repeatedly emphasizes the punitive nature of these deportations, appealing to the connection between retention of the land and obedience to God to explain the history of the *Ioudaioi*.[27] It should be noted that Josephus' stated interest is not the history of *Israel* but of the *Ioudaioi*, the contemporary people of which he is a part.

Josephus goes out of his way to portray the circumstances of his own day as divine punishment for disobedience not only in the *War* (as Schwartz recognizes) but also in the *Antiquities*.[28] For example, Josephus expands on Deuteronomy to have Moses specifically warn the people of dispersion and slavery throughout the world, better connecting that passage to the present (post-70 CE) conditions:

> since having been elevated [by your wealth] into disdain and belittling of virtue, you will also lose the goodwill of God. And when you have made him your enemy,

---

[25] The phrase πέρα πίστεως is interesting here, as it could just as easily be rendered "beyond faithfulness" – that is, God is overfaithful to those who keep his laws.

[26] See Attridge, *The Interpretation of Biblical History*, 67–107; Lincicum, *Paul and the Early Jewish Encounter*, 180–81; Spilsbury, "Rise and Fall."

[27] Halpern-Amaru, "Land Theology," 219.

[28] Cf. Attridge, *The Interpretation of Biblical History*, 67–107; Lindner, *Die Geschichtsauffassung des Flavius Josephus*, 30 (focusing on *War*); Braun, "The Prophet Who Became a Historian."

the land you will acquire will be seized back again from you, beaten in arms with the greatest of disgraces, and having been scattered [σκεδασθέντες] throughout the whole world, you will fill land and sea with your slavery. After you experience these trials, your repentance and remembrance of the laws you did not keep will be useless. (*Ant.* 4.190–191a)

This passage closely matches Josephus' descriptions of the aftermath of the revolt against Rome (e.g., *Ant.* 20.166), conflating the events of 587/ 86 BCE and 70 CE and viewing both through the lens of divine punishment.[29] The connection between 4.190–191 and 20.166 makes it clear that Schwartz's attempt to distinguish the "divine punishment pure and simple" found in the *War* from the more positive "divine corrective" found in the *Antiquities* on the basis of the wording of 20.166 is misguided.[30] For Josephus, as with his biblical source material (e.g., Jer 30:11), God's punishment of Israel is never solely punitive but is always corrective, at least on the level of the people as a whole. In any case, Josephus' final summary of Moses' giving of the Torah again straightforwardly presents a classic Deuteronomic perspective on the exile:

Moses foretold, as God had declared to him, that after disobeying his worship they would suffer the following evils: Their land would be filled with weapons of their enemies and their cities razed and their temple burned to ashes, and having been sold for slavery to men who would never have pity on their afflictions, but suffering these things they would repent to no benefit. Nevertheless, the God who created you will return to your citizens both your city and your temple. But the loss of these will happen not once, but often. (*Ant.* 4.312–14)

By adding that this was to happen "not once, but often," Josephus suggests that the present (post-70 CE) circumstances are part of this continued pattern of punishment for disobedience and hints that the present captivity is not final but will be followed by the return promised in the previous clause.[31] Josephus does not limit his attention on these themes to the Pentateuch, either, expanding on several passages in his account of the monarchy to explain the exile or extend the consequences to the destruction of the Second Temple.[32] For example, in his account of

---

[29] Halpern-Amaru, "Land Theology," 220. See also Unnik, *Das Selbstverständnis*, 141–42.
[30] Schwartz, "Punishment to Program," 210.
[31] Halpern-Amaru, "Land Theology," 221. Kylie Crabbe has observed that by framing Jerusalem's destruction as divine punishment, Josephus subtly "disempowers Rome," as Israel's God remains in charge, with Rome only an instrument of destruction ("Being Found Fighting against God: Luke's Gamaliel and Josephus on Human Responses to Divine Providence," *ZNW* 106.1 [2015]: 21–39 [26]).
[32] Halpern-Amaru, "Land Theology," 222.

Solomon's revelatory dream after the dedication of the first Temple, Josephus retains the biblical warning that Israel would be "cast out of the land which [God] had given their fathers," to which he appends, "and settle them as foreigners in other lands," applying hindsight to connect the prophetic warning with the events of history. Josephus also substantially alters the meeting between the prophet Azariah and King Asa in 2 Chr 15:2–6 to include a prophecy that if the people turned away from proper worship and obedience, "your cities will be laid waste and the nation sowed (σπαρήσεται) all over the earth to lead the life of aliens and wanderers"[33] (*Ant.* 8.296–97).

Josephus' version of Ahijah's prophecy against Jeroboam from 1 Kgs 14:15–16 is especially significant for this study, as Josephus here specifically blames the sin of Jeroboam for the dispersion of Israel:

> The multitude will also share in the same punishment: they will be driven from the good land and dispersed (διασπαρέν) to places beyond the Euphrates because they followed the impious ways of their king [Jeroboam] and worshiped the gods he made. (*Ant.* 8.271)

Not only is this entire passage strangely absent from our Greek versions (and probably Josephus' own), the statement about Israel following Jeroboam's impieties does not appear in the Hebrew Bible. Yet again, Josephus has added material to emphasize the connection between disobedience and dispersion.[34] Even more significantly, like the biblical narratives, Josephus specifically blames Jeroboam and his introduction of idolatry in the northern kingdom for Israel's exile. He further emphasizes this point in *Ant.* 9.280–82, blaming the "sedition which they raised against Rehoboam" and Jeroboam's "bad example" for the calamities that ultimately befell the northern kingdom. Josephus thus retains and even augments the first half of the traditional prophetic restoration-eschatological perspective, and (as shown in the first chapter) connects this theme to the dispersion of Israel and the deportation of Judah later in the work (e.g., *Ant.* 9.278–80; 10.183–85; 11.8), emphasizing that the present dispersed state of Israel (still "beyond the Euphrates," *Ant.* 11.132–33) is the result of Israel's disobedience.[35]

---

[33] Cf. Azriel Shochet, "Josephus' Outlook on the Future of Israel and Its Land," in *Yerushalayim*, eds. Michael Ish-Shalom et al., 1 (Jerusalem: Mosad Ha-Rav Kook, 1953), 43–50 (47).

[34] Cf. Unnik, *Das Selbstverständnis*, 139–40.

[35] *Pace* Feldman, "Exile in Josephus," 153–54, Josephus does not limit the punishment to the demolition of the Israelite government. Feldman here glosses over the second half of

The Land and the World

In this light, Josephus' decision to diminish the importance of the land covenant only serves to emphasize the connection between obedience and land/dominion by making a distinction between the *eternal* covenant with the people and the *conditional* promise of land (and Temple),[36] thus alleviating some of the tensions present in the biblical stories that tie these elements together. In the process, Josephus reworks prophetic passages to emphasize that Israel would become so numerous that they would fill the whole world.[37] This has led some, such as Halpern-Amaru, to conclude that Josephus had abandoned traditional hopes of restoration, instead seeing the diaspora as permanent and positive:

Josephus replaces the classical messianic eschatology with his own vision of future blessings: a glorious people whose eternal existence is assured by divine blessing and promise; a people who have a motherland, but whose population is so great that they overflow into every island and continent. It is not a portrait true to the classical Biblical end of days; rather it is a reflection of the Hellenistic world – a motherland (as a point of reference) with an extensive eternal diaspora which might even be seen as colonial in character.[38]

But Josephus does not in fact eliminate the promise of land, nor does he ever characterize the present dispersion as having fulfilled the patriarchal promises. Instead, he plays up the conditional nature of Israel's dominion and possession of the land and takes advantage of the ambiguity of the Greek word *gē* by expanding the promises of Israel's possession of the land (*gē*) to apply to the whole earth (*gē*).[39] For example, whereas the

---

Josephus' account of these events (9: 280–82), which clearly portrays the deportation of the north as part of that punishment.

[36] Cf. Halpern-Amaru, "Land Theology," 229.

[37] *Ant.* 1.282; 4.115–16. These blessings may allude to a curse in *Sib. Or.* 3.271, "The whole earth will be filled with you and every sea," only Josephus converts this curse into a blessing planned by God from the beginning. That does not mean, however, that the actual means of filling the earth and sea is positive, as will be discussed below. Cf. Halpern-Amaru, "Land Theology," 227.

[38] Halpern-Amaru, "Land Theology," 228; see also Feldman, "Exile in Josephus," 153; see also Schalit, *Josephus, Jewish Antiquities* [in Hebrew], lxxxi.

[39] On the ambiguity of this term (shared also by the Hebrew *aretz*), see Daniel R. Schwartz, "The End of the ΓΗ (Acts 1:8): Beginning or End of the Christian Vision?," *JBL* 105.4 (1986): 669–76. This ambiguity and the development toward a more totalizing interpretation provides a helpful explanation for the trend toward what W. D. Davies, "Reflections on Territory in Judaism," in *"Sha'arei Talmon": Studies in Bible, Qumran, and the Ancient Near East Presented to Shemaryahu Talmon*, eds. M. Fishbane, Emanuel Tov, and W. W. Fields (Winona Lake: Eisenbrauns, 1992), 339–44 (342–43), calls the "transcendentalizing and spiritualizing of the Land" in later Judaism and Christianity.

biblical promise to Jacob promises that his seed would be given "the land on which you lie" (Gen 28:13), Josephus expands this promise to give "the dominion of the land [*gēs*]" to Jacob's descendants, "who will fill earth [*gē*] and sea, as far as the sun beholds them" (*Ant.* 1.282).⁴⁰ Given Josephus' circumstances as a client of the Roman emperors, the breadth Josephus assigns to this promise is striking.

Balaam's Oracles

Josephus' summary of Balaam's first three oracles similarly promises that the people would become so numerous that they would fill not only the land of Canaan but the whole world (*pasa hē gē*) and that "the civilized world [οἰκουμένην] is set before them to be their eternal dwelling" (*Ant.* 4.115–16).⁴¹ Once again, the emphasis Josephus places on this point has been understood as indicating that Josephus saw the exile/diaspora as not only "very positive" but eternal,⁴² but exile or diaspora is not mentioned here, nor does Josephus suggest that Balaam's prophecies have been fulfilled.⁴³ In fact, the details Josephus includes suggest that the ultimate fulfillment of Balaam's blessings lie beyond Josephus' own day, as Balaam claims this widespread people will be invincible in war and have dominion, neither of which resembles the diaspora circumstances of which Josephus was allegedly so fond.⁴⁴ Josephus explicitly says the final

---

See also the discussions of similarly expanded expectations in Philo (p. 236 below) and the pesharim (p. 276 below).

⁴⁰ Tuval, *From Jerusalem Priest to Roman Jew*, 189: "It seems that his view of this triumph was not perceived only in the narrow terms of the restoration of the Judeans to their land – rather it was to be universal."

⁴¹ *Pace* Per Bilde, "Josephus and Jewish Apocalypticism," in *Understanding Josephus: Seven Perspectives*, ed. Steve Mason, JSOTSup 32 (Sheffield: Sheffield Academic, 1998), 35–63 (52), who sees this passage as expanding and elaborating Balaam's first blessing, Josephus' summary is a pastiche of Balaam's first *three* oracles, sequentially summarizing the various promises, including distinction from the nations (first oracle, Num 23:9; *Ant.* 4.114), innumerable offspring (first oracle, Num 23:10; *Ant.* 4.115–16), divine presence and blessing (second oracle, Num 23:21–23; *Ant.* 4.116), wide geographical spread (third oracle, Num 24:5–7; *Ant.* 4.116), and ultimate military victory (third oracle, Num 24:8–9; *Ant.* 4.116–17). Josephus stops short of summarizing the fourth oracle (24:15–24), surely due to its messianic content.

⁴² Feldman, "Exile in Josephus," 153; Halpern-Amaru, "Land Theology," 226–28.

⁴³ Unnik, *Das Selbstverständnis*, 142.

⁴⁴ Per Bilde, *Flavius Josephus between Jerusalem and Rome: His Life, His Works, and Their Importance* (Sheffield: Sheffield Academic, 1988), 188.

fulfillment of Balaam's words remains in the future in his allusive summary of Balaam's fourth oracle a few paragraphs later:

Balaam fell on his face and foretold what sufferings would befall kings and what would befall the most distinguished cities (some of which had not yet begun to be inhabited), events that have happened by land and sea both to the people born in previous times and also in my own memory, from all of the things which have come to the end he predicted, one might judge what will also happen in the future. (*Ant.* 4.125)

As Per Bilde points out, "the concluding clause can only be taken to refer to the coming messianic salvation and restoration of Israel."[45] The fourth oracle of Balaam to which he alludes here of course contains the famous prediction that "a star will come from Jacob and a scepter will rise from Israel" (Num 24:17) and was foundational to the messianic hopes of the Dead Sea Scroll community (e.g., 4QTest) and the Bar Kokhba revolt of 132–135 CE, with Bar Kokhba himself deriving his title ("son of a star") from the passage.[46] The passage goes on to promise that Israel will finally crush the Moabites, the Edomites, and the Amalekites, and that the Kittim will come to destruction after their ships first afflict Asshur and Eber. The Kittim were identified with the Romans in Josephus' time (cf. Old Greek Dan 11:30; 1QpHab 3:4, 9–11; etc.), and Edom was also identified with Rome in later rabbinic traditions,[47] so through his coy citation of this prophecy (which, as Feldman acknowledges,[48] he had no reason to mention otherwise) Josephus subtly reminds his readers that Rome would ultimately experience the same fate as the other eminent cities of the past, while Israel would receive the eternal dominion promised in the remainder of Balaam's oracle, the content of which he surely could not reproduce here.

Song of Moses

Were this the only place Josephus makes such a move, one might overlook it as unreflective of Josephus' own views and an indication that he

---

[45] Bilde, "Josephus and Jewish Apocalypticism," 52.

[46] Cf. See Davies, "Apocalyptic and Historiography," 17–18; Spilsbury, "Rise and Fall," 18.

[47] For the rabbinic evidence, see Louis Ginzberg, *The Legends of the Jews*, trans. S. H. Glick, 7 vols. (Philadelphia: Jewish Publication Society of America, 1968), 3.380 and the passages cited in Vol. 6 (1928) 133 n. 782. Cf. Feldman, "Exile in Josephus," 166.

[48] Feldman, "Exile in Josephus," 166.

"wished somehow to satisfy his Jewish readers, who might well have recognized an allusion to Rome here,"[49] but this is only the first of three passages in the *Antiquities* in which Josephus calls attention to unfulfilled biblical prophecies while remaining vague as to their contents. The second is the Song of Moses (Deut 32), which Josephus says, "contained a prediction of what was to happen afterward, in accordance with which everything has happened and is happening, since he in no way deviated from the truth" (*Ant.* 4.303).[50] Josephus is again vague about the latter contents of this song for good reason, as verses 34–42 tell of the eventual vindication and redemption of Israel after they had been scattered (διασπερῶ αὐτούς, 32:26 LXX) as punishment for disobedience. Josephus' subtle treatment of the Song – particularly his assessment that the predictions not only have happened but are still happening – suggests that he believes this vindication still lies in the future.[51]

Daniel's Visions

But the most striking indication of Josephus' restoration hopes is found in his delicate handling of Daniel's visionary material.[52] Josephus presents Daniel as "one of the greatest of the prophets" (*Ant.* 10.266), distinguished from others by prophesying not only future events "but also the time of their accomplishment" (10.266) and also because he prophesied good things rather than misfortunes (10.267).[53] But Josephus then

---

[49] Feldman, "Exile in Josephus," 166.

[50] See Lincicum, *Paul and the Early Jewish Encounter*, 177–80. Cf. Philo, Mos. 2.288, "Some of these [prophecies] have already come to pass, while others are still looked for, since confidence in the future is assured by fulfillment in the past."

[51] Davies, "Apocalyptic and Historiography," 18.

[52] On the importance of Daniel for Josephus, see Christopher T. Begg, "Daniel and Josephus: Tracing Connections," in *The Book of Daniel in the Light of New Findings*, ed. Adam S. van der Woude, BETL 106 (Leuven: Peeters, 1993), 539–45; Mason, "Josephus, Daniel, and the Flavian House," 190–91; Goldstein, *I Maccabees*, 558–68; Louis H. Feldman, *Josephus's Interpretation of the Bible*, HCS (Berkeley: University of California Press, 1998), 629–57; Géza Vermes, "Josephus' Treatment of the Book of Daniel," *JJS* 42.2 (1991): 149–66.

[53] Josephus' claim that Daniel predicted the time of fulfillment surely refers to Daniel's seventy sevens (Dan 9:24–27). N. T. Wright, "Israel's Scriptures in Paul's Narrative Theology," *Th* 115.5 (2012): 323–29 (324), connects this reference to Daniel's prophetic timetable to *J.W.* 6.312, where Josephus says the revolt owed to an oracle which said a ruler would arise from Judea *at that time*. Cf. also Roger T. Beckwith, "Daniel 9 and the Date of Messiah's Coming in Essene, Hellenistic, Pharisaic, Zealot and Early Christian Computation," *RevQ* 10.4 (1981): 521–42.

nowhere openly presents those good things or the time frame of their accomplishment.[54] He does, however, recount Nebuchadnezzar's dream in which the stone destroys the fourth kingdom of iron (Dan 2:44–45; *Ant.* 10.205–9). But he declines to provide the meaning of the dream, commenting,

> And Daniel also revealed to the king the meaning of the stone, but I have not thought it proper to relate this, since I am expected to write about the past and not the future. If, however, anyone has so keen a desire for exact information that he will not stop short of inquiring more closely but wishes to learn about the hidden things that are to come, let him take the trouble to read the Book of Daniel, which he will find among the sacred writings. (*Ant.* 10.210)

This is an especially flimsy pretense in light of Josephus' theological agenda throughout the *Antiquities*, which began with an appeal that the reader learn from the past (*Ant.* 1.14–15).[55] Neither Josephus nor any other extant ancient historian ever expresses such a sentiment elsewhere,[56] and as with Balaam's oracle, if Josephus were truly concerned only with the past, he had little reason to mention this vision at all – except as a subtle reminder to knowledgeable (Jewish) readers that Daniel promises the future downfall of Rome.[57] Roman readers, on the other hand, were highly unlikely to take the trouble. Josephus very clearly identifies this fourth kingdom as Rome,[58] explaining after a summary of Daniel's vision of the goat and the ram (Dan 8; *Ant.* 10.269–75) that Daniel had predicted the desolation of the temple by Antiochus Epiphanes and "also wrote about Roman empire and that it would be desolated by them" (10:276; cf. Dan 9:24–27). Josephus is deliciously ambiguous here, as Jewish and Roman readers would read this concluding statement very differently, with Roman viewers understanding "it" as the temple and "them" as the Romans, while readers familiar with Dan 9:26 and connecting it also with the stone of Nebuchadnezzar's dream already

---

[54] Attridge, *The Interpretation of Biblical History*, 105.

[55] For Josephus as consistently using history in the service of theology, see Halpern-Amaru, "Land Theology," 221; Attridge, *The Interpretation of Biblical History*, 109–44.

[56] On the contrary, Thucydides (1.22.4) says history is valuable in part precisely because it provides a guide to the future. Cf. Feldman, "Exile in Josephus," 167.

[57] Feldman, "Exile in Josephus," 167–69. Cf. Tuval, *From Jerusalem Priest to Roman Jew*, 282–83.

[58] So Barclay, *Pauline Churches*, 314; Spilsbury, "Rise and Fall," 12–13; Bilde, "Josephus and Jewish Apocalypticism," 188; Mason, "Josephus, Daniel, and the Flavian House," 171; Davies, "Apocalyptic and Historiography," 18; Feldman, "Exile in Josephus," 167–71. Cf. also *Exod Rab.* 35:5.

discussed would understand Josephus as referring to the destruction of the Roman Empire by "our nation."[59]

It is surely no accident that Josephus is so vague and allusive in precisely these passages – or that he chooses to call attention to these specific passages about the future. He pays remarkably little attention to the classical prophets,[60] instead looking to Balaam and Daniel for his eschatological perspective.[61] That choice is telling, since Balaam and Daniel were also central to the messianic eschatology for the Dead Sea Scrolls sect and in the Bar Kokhba revolt, and these very prophetic passages likely served together as the "ambiguous oracle" that Josephus

---

[59] My translation follows the text of the *editio maior*, in which "it" and "them" are ambiguous. An alternate reading, "that Jerusalem would be taken by them and the temple desolated" (αἱρεθήσεται τὰ Ἱεροσόλυμα καὶ ὁ ναὸς ἐρημωθήσεται), is found in John Chrysostom's *Adv. Jud.* 5.8. That reading, followed by Marcus in the LCL, eliminates the ambiguity and is therefore probably secondary, the result of Chrysostom's attempt to clarify Josephus' meaning. On the ambiguity of Josephus' statement and its function in the passage, see Jay Braverman, *Jerome's Commentary on Daniel: A Study of Comparative Jewish and Christian Interpretations of the Hebrew Bible*, CBQMS 7 (Washington, DC: Catholic Biblical Association of America, 1978), 109–11. Some, such as Robert Eisler, *The Messiah Jesus and John the Baptist according to Flavius Josephus' Recently Rediscovered "Capture of Jerusalem" and Other Jewish and Christian Sources*, trans. Alexander H. Krappe (New York: MacVeagh, Dial, 1931), have suspected an interpolation here, a claim first rebutted by Marcus in *Jewish Antiquities, Volume VI*, 310–11 n. c and then in Feldman, "Exile in Josephus," 170 n. 48. Feldman notes that either way, Josephus' omission of any direct discussion of Dan 9:24–27 despite his significant attention to Daniel suggests reluctance to broach the subject of Rome's downfall with a Roman audience. He was apparently not so reluctant as to avoid signaling that end to his more informed Jewish readers, however.

[60] Cf. Halpern-Amaru, "Land Theology," 224; Joseph Blenkinsopp, "Prophecy and Priesthood in Josephus," *JJS* 25 (1974): 239–62. Feldman, "Bibliography of Josephus," 411, explains this paucity of attention to the prophets by remarking, "it is precisely because Josephus is writing a history rather than a work of theology that he does so. Moreover, his rationalistic pagan readers might have found the concept of prophecy difficult to accept." But this explanation is implausible. First of all, it takes Josephus' coy explanation for why he chooses not to provide the interpretation of Daniel's prophecy at face value, as though Josephus took a modern view of the role of the historian vs. the role of theologian or reporter of miracles, something Feldman himself acknowledges elsewhere that Josephus does not do ("Exile in Josephus," 167–69). Secondly, the idea that Josephus' Roman pagan readers would have had difficulty accepting the concept of prophecy is entirely unfounded, especially since Josephus makes such a fuss in *Ant.* 10.277–80 about Daniel's prophecies serving as proof that divine providence truly governs the affairs of human beings.

[61] Halpern-Amaru, "Land Theology," 224. Although Halpern-Amaru expresses surprise on this point, the use of Balaam's prophecy in particular makes sense since it is found in the Torah, which had more universally agreed authority than the classical prophets. That is, Balaam's prophecies, inasmuch as they were contained in the Torah, seem to have been regarded as having Mosaic authority.

credits as having undergirded the first revolt.[62] Graham Davies' judgment is therefore correct:

His excuse that such things are not the business of a historian like him will deceive few. It was better, in Rome, to keep quiet about such hopes. That Josephus shared in them is clear enough, and his disagreement with the Zealots will not therefore have been over the hope of a glorious future for the Jews as such, but over the time, and also the manner, of its coming.[63]

Each prophetic passage predicts Israel's ultimate dominion and an end to gentile domination after a period of affliction,[64] and throughout Josephus' summaries, the reader in the know can fill in the blanks, assured (as Josephus makes explicit) that Rome's dominion had been given by God and (as Josephus leaves implicit) that God will destroy Rome and exalt Israel in the future.

In this context, Josephus' prophecy that Vespasian would become the ruler of the whole world (*J. W.* 6:313) should not be understood as though Josephus saw Vespasian as the messiah and therefore Roman rule as permanent. Instead, given Josephus' handling of the prophecies of Balaam and Daniel, it seems more likely that he understood Vespasian as the leader of the Kittim who would afflict Asshur and Eber (Num 24:24) and the ruler who would destroy the city and the sanctuary (Dan 9:26) before his kingdom was itself destroyed at Israel's ultimate ascendance (Dan 9:27).[65] This would make Vespasian analogous to Nebuchadnezzar and Josephus analogous to Jeremiah (with whom Josephus explicitly identifies himself),[66] who declared that Nebuchadnezzar had been divinely appointed to rule over all the nations

---

[62] See e.g., Valentin Nikiprowetzky, "Josephus and the Revolutionary Parties," in *Josephus, the Bible, and History*, eds. Louis H. Feldman and Gohei Hata (Detroit: Wayne State University Press, 1989), 216–36 (228). Craig A. Evans, "The Star of Balaam and the Prophecy of Josephus Concerning Vespasian," in *Scribal Practice, Text and Canon in the Dead Sea Scrolls*, eds. Peter W. Flint, John J. Collins, and Ananda Geyser-Fouch (Brill, 2019), 297–333, argues that the Balaam oracle alone is the "ambiguous oracle," but it is unlikely that passage was read in isolation, especially given the centrality of Daniel in this period.

[63] Davies, "Apocalyptic and Historiography," 19. Davies was perhaps overoptimistic in his assessment, however, as some scholars have surprisingly taken Josephus at face value here, e.g., Mason, "Josephus, Daniel, and the Flavian House," 173; Feldman, "Bibliography of Josephus," 411.

[64] Cf. Davies, "Apocalyptic and Historiography," 17–19.

[65] Cf. Nikiprowetzky, "Josephus and the Revolutionary Parties," 228–29.

[66] On Josephus' identification with Jeremiah, see Mason, "Josephus, Daniel, and the Flavian House," 176–77; Shaye J. D. Cohen, "Josephus, Jeremiah, and Polybius," *HistTh* (1982): 366–81.

(Jer 28:14) and punish Judah for its unfaithfulness, though the Babylonian kingdom would ultimately be punished and Israel restored.

Other Indications of Restoration Eschatology

Indications of Josephus' eschatological hopes are not limited to these passages, either, but can be found across the full Josephan corpus, with these hopes at the very root of Josephus' overall perspective. For example, Josephus hints at his eschatological hopes in his speech to his countrymen (*J.W.* 5.367), where he states that God and the dominion, after having gone around various nations, were *now* (νῦν) in Italy – implying that Rome's dominance was only temporary.[67] This idea of the rotation of empire from one nation to another again appears to derive from Daniel, and Josephus again hints at the Romans' eventual downfall.[68] His disagreement with rebels here is therefore not with respect to the final outcome of that prophecy but rather the manner and timing of its fulfillment.[69] Whereas they saw the present military action as the means of Rome's final overthrow, Josephus read Daniel 9:24–27 as predicting another desolation of the temple to precede that overthrow and expected Israel's final victory and exaltation through divine intervention rather than human military action. Feldman expresses skepticism on this point, suggesting "It seems very unlikely that Josephus, having been commissioned by the Romans to urge the Jews to surrender, would have ventured to suggest such an anticipation in clear defiance of his Roman hosts."[70] On the contrary, such subtle rhetoric is *precisely* what should be expected from Josephus, as can be seen in the analogous example of Jeremiah, who urged his countrymen to serve Babylon while assuring them that the deportation and Babylon's supremacy would be of limited duration (Jer 27:17; 29:10).[71]

---

[67] Cf. Marinus de Jonge, "Josephus und die Zukunftserwartungen seines Volkes," in *Josephus-Studien: Untersuchungen zu Josephus, dem antiken Judentum und dem Neuen Testament, Otto Michel zum 70. Geburtstag gewidmet*, eds. Otto Betz, Klaus Haacker, and Martin Hengel (Göttingen: Vandenhoeck & Ruprecht, 1974), 205–19 (211–12); Halpern-Amaru, "Land Theology," 225.

[68] Mason, "Josephus, Daniel, and the Flavian House," 190–91.

[69] See Jonge, "Josephus," 215.

[70] Feldman, "Exile in Josephus," 170.

[71] See Tucker S. Ferda, "Jeremiah 7 and Flavius Josephus on the First Jewish War," *JSJ* 44.2 (2013): 158–73.

Josephus makes the same move in *Against Apion*, referring to the Romans as those "who are *now* lords of the civilized world," again hinting at the limited nature of said lordship. He further reinforces this point later in the treatise by observing that changes have brought the great imperial powers of the past into subjection to others, quietly implying a similar eventuality for Rome, though in the most general possible terms (*Ag. Ap.* 2.127).[72] A few paragraphs later, Josephus references other strong and pious peoples who had been subjected and the numerous great temples that had been burned, making the bold statement that "no one reproached those sufferers but those who did these things" (*Ag. Ap.* 2.129–31), implying that the Romans would eventually be reproached for their violent subjugation of the Jews – but again in a general, indirect manner.[73]

Such hopes also provide a plausible explanation for the lack of attention paid to Ezra and Nehemiah in *Antiquities*,[74] which Feldman sees as evidence that, "the concept of return from exile was not for Josephus a matter of major importance."[75] To the contrary, Josephus did not view these figures as especially important because (unlike Feldman) he did not see them as marking the promised end to Israel's exile, which in Josephus' view was ongoing.[76] As we have already seen, the biblical accounts portray Ezra's efforts at restoration as having failed, and Nehemiah's heroic efforts were needed precisely because the promised restoration remained a future hope rather than a present (or past) reality. As is also true across much Second Temple literature, Josephus' treatment of these figures is in keeping with the biblical portrayal, though he also emphasizes their loyalty to their imperial patrons and the quality of their leadership.

JOSEPHUS' APOCALYPTIC QUIETISM

Josephus was no Roman shill who had gone native after years of luxurious living under Flavian patronage to the point that as "the supporter and

---

[72] So Barclay, *Pauline Churches*, 314. Cf. Blenkinsopp, "Prophecy and Priesthood in Josephus," 262.

[73] Cf. Barclay, *Pauline Churches*, 314–16.

[74] See Louis H. Feldman, "Josephus' Portrait of Ezra," *VT* 43 (1993): 190–214; Feldman, "Restoration in Josephus," 231–49.

[75] Feldman, "Exile in Josephus," 160.

[76] Feldman, "Restoration in Josephus" focuses on "the restoration period" – that is, the period of Ezra, Nehemiah, Cyrus, and Zerubbabel – while dismissing any idea that Josephus held hopes for any other sort of restoration, especially "the establishment of an independent nation, so abhorrent to him" (Feldman, "Restoration in Josephus," 253).

admirer of the Romans,"[77] he found "the establishment of an independent nation . . . abhorrent."[78] On the contrary, although he stays vague due to political prudence,[79] he repeatedly implies in subtle tones that Roman rule will be temporary, to be followed by the righteous rule of Israel.[80] Even Josephus' conciliatory perspective toward the Romans depends on the idea that Roman rule will be temporary, meaning Jeremiah's counsel to the Babylonian exiles remains the best course of action for those under Roman rule.[81] Essentially, Josephus counsels his Jewish readers to "wait it out" – any attempt to speed the process in advance of God's own intervention is both foolish and impious.[82]

Josephus is indeed ever at pains to distance himself and other Jews of his day from the militant nationalism that spawned the revolt and to explain that despite those recent events, most Jews were peaceable and no threat to rebel. But it was not the idea of Israel's restoration or dominion that was so abhorrent to Josephus but rather the foolish and impious means by which the radical insurrectionists had attempted to bring it about. Instead, Josephus advocates a quietistic and conciliatory approach, characterizing this as the only appropriate Jewish response to Roman authority and thereby marginalizing those who rebelled. But again, this is merely a difference in approach, not an abandonment of eschatological hopes.[83] Josephus argues along these lines in his speech to his countrymen, just after hinting at the temporary (but inexorable) nature of Roman rule:

> In short, there is no instance where our ancestors triumphed by arms or lacked success without them when they had committed their cause to God. If they sat still, they conquered, as purposed by their judge, but when they fought, they always fell. (*J.W.* 5.390)

Josephus therefore counsels his Jewish interlocutors (and readers) to wait patiently for the "rod of empire" to move away from the Romans while scrupulously devoting themselves to obeying God's laws, thereby

---

[77] Feldman, "Restoration in Josephus," 251

[78] Feldman, "Restoration in Josephus," 253.

[79] Davies, "Apocalyptic and Historiography," 18. Cf. Halpern-Amaru, "Land Theology," 225; F. F. Bruce, "Josephus and Daniel," *ASTI* 4 (1965): 148–62 (160).

[80] Jonge, "Josephus," 212: "It is clear that Josephus expects a glorious future for an Israel that is obedient to God. The Roman Empire is not the final one."

[81] As demonstrated by Spilsbury, "Rise and Fall." Cf. Jonge, "Josephus," 210.

[82] Nikiprowetzky, "Josephus and the Revolutionary Parties," 228–29. Cf. Bilde, *Flavius Josephus*, 188;

[83] Bilde, *Flavius Josephus*, 188.

positioning themselves for the redemption and dominion promised to Israel when the time comes for God's intervention.[84] This is a similar position to that advocated by Jesus, Paul, and numerous other early Jewish apocalyptic thinkers, who argued against violent action on the basis that redemption will only come through God's sovereign action – and will only benefit those who have not stained themselves with unrighteous violence.

ISRAEL'S RESTORATION IN JOSEPHUS

Thus, despite his vague and allusive treatments of eschatological matters, Josephus does provide enough hints that a coherent eschatological picture emerges. After allusively recounting Balaam's oracles, Josephus narrates Balaam's advice to Balak about how a temporary victory over the people may be won:

Complete destruction will not befall the race of the Hebrews, neither by war nor by pestilence and scarcity of the fruit of the ground, nor will any other unexpected cause destroy it [cf. Num 23:23], for God's providence is theirs to save them from all evil and to permit no such suffering to come upon them under which all of them would be destroyed. But a few sufferings may befall them and for a short time, under which they will appear to be humiliated. Then they will blossom to the fear of those having brought the harm upon them. (*Ant.* 4.127–28)

This is a strikingly subversive statement in light of the sufferings that had befallen the Jews in Josephus' day, under which they certainly appeared to be humiliated.[85] Josephus has the Midianite prophet declare not only that those humble circumstances are only an appearance (δοκοῦντες) and ephemeral, he promises that those who brought the harm upon them will ultimately fear "the race of the Hebrews." As Spilsbury argues, this uncharacteristically bold statement also confirms the identity of the stone in Nebuchadnezzar's dream which Josephus summarizes but does not explain.[86] Balaam's declaration that the people would fill the whole world (*pasa hē gē*) and that "the civilized world [οἰκουμένην] is set before them to be their eternal dwelling" (*Ant.* 4.115–16) also parallels a key detail of the dream-stone: "but the stone increased to such a degree that the whole earth seemed to be filled with it" (*Ant.* 10.207),

---

[84] Spilsbury, "Rise and Fall," 21.
[85] Spilsbury, "Rise and Fall," 19, calls this "a somewhat uncharacteristic flourish" given Josephus' restraint throughout his treatments of Daniel and Balaam.
[86] Spilsbury, "Rise and Fall," 19.

further indicating that Josephus read Daniel and Balaam's prophecies together.[87]

We have therefore come full circle, finding that Josephus' restoration hopes also inform his understanding of the present worldwide spread of the people. The diaspora is not a positive thing but a punishment, a chastening of the people. But it also has the effect of laying the groundwork for the future dominion of the people, so God (or providence, in Josephus' terminology) uses a negative to produce the ultimate positive result for his people, who will inherit not only the land but dominion of the whole world.[88] But one more detail yet remains to be clarified: whereas Spilsbury says Josephus interpreted the stone as "the Jewish [*sic*] nation dispersed abroad,"[89] these passages connect to yet another allusive reminder that Josephus' people would not always be subject to Roman dominion. As we have already noted, when Josephus explains why he has begun to use the term *Ioudaioi*, he looks back to the time of Ezra:

When these *Ioudaioi* learned of the king's piety towards God, and his kindness towards Ezra, they loved [him] most dearly, and many took up their possessions and went to Babylon, desiring to go down to Jerusalem. But the whole people of Israel [ὁ πᾶς λαὸς τῶν Ἰσραηλιτῶν] remained in that land; so it came about that only two tribes [δύο φυλὰς] came to Asia and Europe and are subject to the Romans. But the ten tribes are beyond Euphrates until now and are a boundless multitude, not to be estimated by numbers. (*Ant.* 11.132–33)

Although Rome has subjugated the *Ioudaioi*, the rest of Israel is not only beyond Roman dominion but innumerable. Here Josephus ever so subtly suggests that even Roman power will be insufficient to withstand the eventual dominion of this boundless multitude.[90] The dispersion not only includes the *Ioudaioi* currently subject to the Romans but also the rest of Israel – and when the whole people is considered, the extent of Nebuchadnezzar's dream-stone is already mighty indeed.[91]

---

[87] Spilsbury, "Rise and Fall," 20. Cf. Tuval, *From Jerusalem Priest to Roman Jew*, 282–83.

[88] Thus, although Josephus does not cite the prophecies of Second Isaiah in connection with the return from Babylon (as noted in Feldman, "Restoration in Josephus," 252), his eschatological picture actually looks remarkably similar to the expansive vision in the later chapters of Isaiah in which Israel is not only restored but rules the entire world and receives the nations as an inheritance (e.g. Isa 49:19–20).

[89] Spilsbury, "Rise and Fall," 20.

[90] Cf. the concerns of Petronius about the number of the Jews in Philo, *Legat.* 214.

[91] Barmash, "Nexus," 233, "In either case, Josephus assumes that the population of Jews [*sic*] 'beyond the Euphrates' consists of the descendents [*sic*] of the northerners."

Thus, upon close examination, Josephus' eschatological hopes are more comprehensive than just expecting an independent state of *Ioudaioi*,[92] though he carefully conceals his hopes with hidden-tran-script-style passages.[93] Such subtlety was not beyond Josephus, as he elsewhere contrasts Moses' open revelation with the need of the "wisest among the Greeks" to hide their true sentiments from all but a few (*Ag. Ap.* 2.168–69). How much more must Josephus have felt the need to veil his own restoration eschatology from his Roman patrons while still leaving room for fellow insiders to discern the truth! Although at pains to avoid offending his Roman patrons, who would not have appreciated the view that Israel was only temporarily scattered and subservient as punishment for disobedience (but cf. *Ant.* 1.14), Josephus does not imagine that the Israelites will always remain beyond the Euphrates,[94] nor that "the two tribes ... subject to the Romans" will remain so forever.[95] Of course, until God intervenes and reunites the two tribes with "the entire people of Israel," any effort by the two tribes alone to speed the eschatological timetable will necessarily result in failure. This last element suggests that, at least for Josephus, the continued distinction between these terms depends in large measure upon restoration eschat-ology – the continued hope of the full restoration of the whole twelve-tribe entity of Israel. So we see that Josephus' distinction between

---

[92] Cf. Bilde, *Flavius Josephus*, 188, 226.

[93] Davies, "Apocalyptic and Historiography," 18: "Naturally he expresses himself cautiously, to avoid offending his Roman readers, but there can be little doubt about his meaning." Feldman observes that if Josephus' eschatology was indeed similar to contemporary apocalypticists, "Josephus certainly was careful to conceal his eschatological beliefs or to wrap them in ambiguity" (Feldman, "Exile in Josephus," 171 n. 49). On hidden transcripts, see Scott, *Domination and the Arts of Resistance*; Barclay, *Pauline Churches*, 301–16, 331–44; Richard A. Horsley, *Hidden Transcripts and the Arts of Resistance: Applying the Work of James C. Scott to Jesus and Paul*, SemeiaSt 48 (Leiden: Brill, 2004).

[94] *Pace* Feldman, "Restoration in Josephus," 225, who flatly claims, "Josephus presents no prophecies or hope of the return of the ten tribes."

[95] Feldman, "Exile in Josephus," 172, shortly after acknowledging that Josephus shared the apocalyptic hopes of the Pharisees, reverses course and concludes that Josephus, whose luxurious Roman life Feldman regularly emphasizes, only took such a position when "talking to his fellow-countrymen ... but his deepest felt sentiments, as seen in his *Life* are to view the Diaspora positively. ... Josephus clearly regarded the exile as everlasting and never foresees an end to it." On the contrary, it is far more likely that Josephus took pains to appeal to his Roman patrons by concealing his deepest sentiments (nowhere more than in *Life*, where he is establishing his own credibility to this Roman audience) than that he occasionally injected subtle eschatological hopes into his work merely to appeal to his Jewish readers.

Ioudaioi and Israel is not haphazard but is connected with his traditional understanding of the exilic status of Israel and his eschatological hopes – hopes that also inform his quietistic and conciliatory stance toward Roman dominion.[96] Of course, none of this should be surprising, as "in this respect Josephus agreed not only with the Bible but also with Palestinian literature of the Second Temple period, Josephus' more immediate predecessors."[97]

---

[96] Tuval, *From Jerusalem Priest to Roman Jew*, 283.
[97] Schwartz, "Punishment to Program," 208.

8

Israel and Restoration in Philo of Alexandria

Philo's separate uses of these terms are indeed puzzling to the modern reader, who may expect "Israel" and "Jews" – or, in the case of the Biblical nation in Moses's time, "Israel" and "Hebrews" – to be synonymous. For Philo, however, "Israel" may represent something else ... Philo may regard "Israel" and "Jews" – or "Hebrews" – as overlapping in meaning but not necessarily synonymous.

Ellen Birnbaum[1]

The massive literary corpus of Philo of Alexandria provides another important test case from the first century CE.[2] Due to the highly allegorical and philosophical nature of most of the Philonic corpus, the relationship between restoration eschatology and Israel terminology is more difficult to assess for Philo than for Josephus, and there has been significant debate

---

[1] Ellen Birnbaum, *The Place of Judaism in Philo's Thought: Israel, Jews, and Proselytes*, BJS 290 (Atlanta: Scholars Press, 1996), 28.

[2] The bibliography on Philo is extensive and growing rapidly. The first port of call for Philo research is the now three-volume annotated bibliography: Roberto Radice and David T. Runia, *Philo of Alexandria: An Annotated Bibliography 1937–1986*, VCSup 8 (Leiden: Brill, 1988); David T. Runia and Helena Maria Keizer, *Philo of Alexandria: An Annotated Bibliography 1987–1996, with Addenda for 1937–1986*, VCSup 57 (Leiden: Brill, 2000); David T. Runia, *Philo of Alexandria: An Annotated Bibliography 1997–2006, with Addenda for 1987–1996*, VCSup 109 (Leiden: Brill, 2011). The *Studia Philonica Annual* serves as another primary avenue. The primary textual basis used here is the PHILO-T module included in *Accordance Bible Software 13*, which is derived from the Norwegian Philo Bibliography Project also represented in Peder Borgen, Kåre Fuglseth, and Roald Skarsten, *The Philo Index: A Complete Greek Word Index to the Writings of Philo of Alexandria*, 2nd ed. (Leiden: Brill, 2000). For an excellent short introduction to Philo and the Philonic corpus, see Peder Borgen, "Philo of Alexandria," in *Jewish Writings of the Second Temple period*, ed. Michael E. Stone, CRINT 2 (Philadelphia: Fortress, 1984), 233–82.

about both Philo's understanding of Israel and his eschatological perspective, though these two questions are generally considered independently. We will consider the latter question first before taking a closer look at the related matter of Philo's use of the term "Israel."

APOIKIA, DISPERSION, AND EXILE IN PHILO

The discussion about Philo's perspective on the diaspora and potential eschatological hopes largely follows the same contours we have observed in the larger discussion about diaspora Judaism to this point; as Collins notes, "The majority of scholars have tended to discount his interest in practical nationalism."[3] Like other Jewish authors writing in Greek, Philo follows the LXX in preferring the term *apoikia* for the exile/diaspora, which, together with his high level of acculturation, some have regarded as evidence that Philo did not hold to traditional restoration-eschatological hopes but rather took a positive view of the present circumstances.[4] Philo does make ample use of the ambiguity of the term, sometimes characterizing the diaspora as the "colonization" of the world,[5] most notably in the apologetic work *Against Flaccus* 45–46:

For no one land can contain the Jews because of their populousness, for which reason they inhabit many of the most prosperous and fertile countries of Europe and Asia ... regarding the holy city, in which is established the holy temple of the Most High God, as their metropolis, but regarding as their fatherlands those regions in which their fathers, grandfathers, and even more remote ancestors dwelt, in which they were born and raised, and to some of which they even came at their very foundation, sent to establish a colony (*apoikia*) as a favor to the founders.[6]

---

[3] Collins, *Between Athens and Jerusalem*, 133.

[4] E.g., Gruen, "Diaspora and Homeland," 27–28; Feldman, "Exile in Josephus," 146; Andrea Lieber, "Between Motherland and Fatherland: Diaspora, Pilgrimage and the Spiritualization of Sacrifice in Philo of Alexandria," in *Heavenly Tablets: Interpretation, Identity and Tradition in Ancient Judaism (1)*, eds. Lynn Lidonnici and Andrea Lieber, JSJSup 119 (Leiden: Brill, 2007), 193–210 (195–98). These arguments presume that *apoikia* is a positive term in the LXX and elsewhere, which we have already seen is not the case (see pp. 188–97). By contrast, Scott, "Philo and the Restoration of Israel," 563, rightly notes that even if Philo could not read Hebrew, he was "aware of the prevalent usage of ἀποικία with reference to the exiles."

[5] Kiefer, *Exil und Diaspora*, 400–02.

[6] Harry A. Wolfson, *Philo: Foundations of Religious Philosophy in Judaism, Christianity, and Islam*, 2 vols. (Cambridge: Harvard University Press, 1947), 402–03, argues that Philo saw the diaspora "as natural growth ... analogous to that of the Roman Empire" but simultaneously and paradoxically understood the dispersion in scriptural terms as "captivity, as divine punishment." See also Scott, "Philo and the Restoration of Israel," 556–62; Unnik, *Das Selbstverständnis*, 127–37; Kiefer, *Exil und Diaspora*, 399–402.

Philo here says nothing of the punitive nature of exile, instead high-lighting the Jews' vast population, which could not be contained in one country,[7] a fact he ties to the Abrahamic promise.[8] He also calls attention to Jews' patriotism toward their new homelands, though acknowledging that they continue to regard Jerusalem as their capital city, likely deriving this image from LXX Isa 1:26 and also echoing Greek colonial imagery and the concept of a capital city.[9] Philo has Agrippa I express similar sentiments in his letter to Gaius (*Legat.* 281–83), indicating that Jerusalem is the *metropolis* of the Jews, who live in "every region of the civilized world" (καθ' ἕκαστον κλίμα τῆς οἰκουμένης; *Legat.* 283).[10] But Philo's role as an apologist should not be forgotten; it is surely no coincidence that such statements occur in explicitly apologetic contexts.[11]

In particular, Philo's statements to this end should be considered in light of Egyptian colonial rhetoric, including the claim that Egypt sent out numerous colonies on account of its excessive population, including the nation of the Jews.[12] Philo counters these claims by asserting that his people were in fact the most populous nation (*Congr.* 3; *Virt.* 64) – more populous than the Egyptians (*Mos.* 1.8, 149) – and are colonizing the world, including Egypt itself.[13] Remarkably, he also refers to the exodus itself in colonial terms as a "migration from here" (τῆς ἐνθένδε ἀποικίας;

---

[7] Cf. also *Mos.* 2.232.

[8] *Congr.* 3; *Spec.* 1.7. Cf. also *Somn.* 1.175. See Scott, "Philo and the Restoration of Israel," 559–62.

[9] See the discussions of this image in Pearce, "Jerusalem"; Aryeh Kasher, "Jerusalem as a Metropolis in Philo's National Consciousness," *Cathedra* 11 (1979): 45–56; Aryeh Kasher, *The Jews in Hellenistic and Roman Egypt: The Struggle for Equal Rights*, TSAJ 7 (Tübingen: Mohr Siebeck, 1985); Yehoshua Amir, *Die hellenistische Gestalt des Judentums bei Philon von Alexandrien*, Forschungen zum jüdisch-christlichen Dialog 5 (Neukirchen-Vluyn: Neukirchener Verlag, 1983); Isaak Heinemann, "The Relationship between the Jewish People and Their Land in Hellenistic Jewish Literature," *Zion* 13 (1948): 1–9. Cf. also *Conf.* 77–78. See Scott, "Philo and the Restoration of Israel," 559.

[10] In this passage Philo also indirectly explains that *Ioudaios* is not merely a geographical term, since the *Ioudaioi* are not geographically tied but are scattered everywhere. See Maren R. Niehoff, *Philo on Jewish Identity and Culture*, TSAJ 86 (Tübingen: Mohr Siebeck, 2001), 33. On the authorship of Agrippa's letter, see Daniel R. Schwartz, *Agrippa I: The Last King of Judaea*, TSAJ 23 (Tübingen: Mohr Siebeck, 1990), 179, 200–02; Solomon Zeitlin, "Did Agrippa Write a Letter to Gaius Caligula?," *New Series* 56.1 (1965): 22–31.

[11] Cf. Unnik, *Das Selbstverständnis*, 136.

[12] Cf. Diod. Sic. 1.28.1–29.6. Note also the testimony of Hecataeus of Abdera cited in Diod. Sic. 40.3.1–8, in which the claim is that the Jews were cast out of Egypt because of a pestilence related to their presence in the land. Interestingly, the word *apoikia* is still used in this (negative) context of expulsion.

[13] See Scott, "Philo and the Restoration of Israel," 557–62.

Mos. 1.71, cf. 1.170), appropriating and reframing Egyptian propaganda about the Jews' origins.[14] Philo also makes the implications of such great populousness clear through Petronius, the governor of Syria, who regards the task of fighting all the Jews as too perilous to undertake (*Legat.* 214–15), confirmed by the multitude that appears in Phoenicia a few paragraphs later (*Legat.* 226–27).[15]

Like Josephus, Philo interprets the patriarchal promises expansively, with Israel's promised domain not limited to the land but "to extend up to the very ends of the universe (ἄχρι τῶν περάτων τοῦ παντὸς εὐρύνεται) . . . inheriting all the parts of the world" (τῶν τοῦ κόσμου κληρονόμον μερῶν; *Somn.* 1.175).[16] Gruen argues that these sentiments together indicate that Philo "eradicates any idea of the 'doctrine of return,'"[17] but as we have already observed with Josephus, such statements are not at odds with traditional restoration eschatology. Similarly, despite his apologetic flourishes about the extent of Jewish population and expansion, Philo nowhere indicates that these patriarchal promises have been fulfilled or that the various Jewish *apoikiai* enjoy the sovereignty one would expect of a colony. Rather, Philo is fully aware that, whereas the Greek colonialists ruled the colonies they founded, in the words of David Winston, "the position of the Jewish emigrants was generally one of a tolerated

---

[14] Philo uses the same terminology as Hecataeus but reframes it to speak positively about the Hebrews' migration from Egypt. Niehoff, *Philo on Jewish Identity*, 35, reads these passages as critiquing overattachment to the land and making specific claims about Jewish identity in the diaspora: "Moses, when approaching the land of Israel, was moreover shocked by the Jewish [*sic*] population which had remained there. Although Moses naturally treated them as kinsfolk (συγγενεῖς), he quickly discovered that they had abandoned all their ancestral customs and sense of belonging (*Mos.* 1.239). Philo stresses in this context that the group of inauthentic Jews "had been attached to the soil" (ἐφιλοχώρησεν), while the virtuous ones had gone abroad." Niehoff is mistaken and misreads Philo's reference to Edom (*Mos.* 1.240) as referring to "inauthentic Jews," applying terminology Philo himself never uses in this tractate. Philo also does not suggest that "Jews" had gone abroad as a result of their virtue or that being attached to the land had been a bad thing. The negative aspect in the passage was that Edom had forgotten its ties to Israel, while the Israelites had remembered their kinship and retained their ancestral customs despite being abroad. This portrayal is indeed informative of Philo's notion of diaspora life, but it does not suggest that Philo sees "attachment to the soil" of the holy land as a negative.

[15] Recall Josephus' subtlety when discussing the "innumerable" descendants of the ten tribes not under Roman rule in *Ant.* 11.133. For more on Philo's recasting of diaspora existence as a marker of strength rather than weakness, see Lieber, "Between Motherland and Fatherland."

[16] See Scott, "Philo and the Restoration of Israel," 559–62. See also the discussions of the parallel expectations in Josephus (pp. 219–20 above) and the pesharim (p. 276 below).

[17] Gruen, "Diaspora and Homeland," 28.

community, and nowhere that of masters."[18] In keeping with that understanding, Philo elsewhere characterizes the diaspora in traditional terms, connecting the concept with the classic schema of sin and punishment,[19] while also acknowledging that those abroad continue to yearn for a return to their native homeland (cf. *Conf.* 78).[20]

These seemingly incompatible perspectives (e.g., is the diaspora the result of overpopulation or divine punishment?) have proven difficult to reconcile. Van Unnik, for example, argues that Philo was psychologically conflicted, attempting to suppress the negative implications of diaspora for the concrete situation in which he lived but unable entirely to forget the negative theology so deeply rooted in scripture and the restoration hopes of his countrymen.[21] Others have ignored or denied the presence of any negativity toward exile or argued that Philo's eschatology changed later in his life due to the difficult events of Gaius' reign.[22] A more

---

[18] David Winston, review of *Das Selbstverständnis der jüdischen Diaspora in der hellenistisch-römischen Zeit*, by Willem Cornelis Van Unnik, *AJSR* 20.2 (1995): 399–402 (401); cf. Yehoshua Amir, "Philo's Version of the Pilgrimage to Jerusalem," in *Jerusalem in the Second Temple period*, eds. Aharon Oppenheimer, Uriel Rappaport, and Menaham Stern (Jerusalem: Yad Izhak Ben-Zvi, 1980), 154–65 (156).

[19] See, for example, *Conf.* 118–21, where Philo clearly depicts being geographically dispersed (*diaspeirō*) as "punishments ... inflicted by God" (119). The same sentiment can be seen in *Spec.* 2.169–70, where Philo discusses the expulsion of the Canaanites and the near disappearance of their race – and then says these events were to teach those who replaced them (i.e., Israel) that the "same fate" befalls all who practice evil deeds, alluding to Israel's exile in the same terms as Lev 18:24–30 and hinting that a similar situation exists at present in the land. Philo also refers to those dwelling in the ends of the earth as "in slavery" in *Praem.* 164. For more on Philo's negative characterization of the exile, see Scott, "Philo and the Restoration of Israel," 562–66.

[20] Philo's meaning in this passage and its application to those in the diaspora is disputed. Scott, "Philo and the Restoration of Israel," 563, cites this passage as illustrating Philo's own desires for return, but Pearce, "Jerusalem," 25–27, argues that Philo here distinguishes between sojourners and colonists, arguing that the latter do *not* in fact wish for a return to the mother city. The point of dispute is the function of the final μεν ... δὲ clause, which could either distinguish "colonists" from "sojourners" (as Pearce) or the two conflicted attitudes of colonists/sojourners (as Scott). Nevertheless, as will be seen below, even if Pearce is correct in her construal of this passage, *Praem.* 117 is problematic for the argument that Philo draws a hard distinction between those in *apoikia* and those who hope for restoration. Note also the ambivalence of Flaccus toward his exile in *Flacc.* 159. The view of Niehoff, *Philo on Jewish Identity*, 35–36, that Philo both recognizes the tendency of colonists to gradually regard their new land as the homeland while also regarding allegiance to the mother city of Jerusalem as of prime importance seems most likely correct here (though see the criticisms of Pearce, "Jerusalem," 27–31).

[21] Unnik, *Das Selbstverständnis*, 137.

[22] For an example of the former, see Gruen, "Diaspora and Homeland," 27–37. For the latter, see Berndt Schaller, "Philon von Alexandreia und das 'Heilige Land,'" in *Das Land Israel in biblischer Zeit*, ed. Georg Strecker, GTA 25 (Göttingen: Vandenhoeck &

plausible explanation, however, is that Philo's positive eschatological hopes provide the common thread that ties all these elements together.[23] That is, in much the same way we already saw with Josephus, although the diaspora is the result of divine judgment for sin, it simultaneously sets the stage for Israel's future rule, chastening and training the people (cf. *Praem.* 19, 115) as they multiply and gain strength. The positive aspects of the diaspora thus derive from the restoration and victory Philo envisions in the future.

As already discussed in Chapter 6, Philo's discussion of the Babel episode is manifestly clear that diaspora is a term of destruction, "for to sow (*speirein*) is for good purpose, but to disperse (*diaspeirein*) is the cause of bad things (κακῶν)" (*Conf.* 196). But Philo does not end the discussion there, as he explains God uses the destructive punishment of diaspora for redemptive purposes, wishing "to sow (*speirein*) excellence in everyone but to disperse (*diaspeirein*) and drive accursed impiety from the citizenship of the world" (196). As he has already established in the same tractate, "Even punishment is not harmful (ἐπιζήμιον), since it is a hindrance of doing wrong and a correction (ἐπανόρθωσις)" (171; cf. *Praem.* 33–34). Philo therefore argues that a divinely ordered diaspora ultimately clears away evil so that the righteous may return to greater prosperity.[24] But he again does not stop there; instead, he emphasizes that once diaspora has done its negative work, it will be followed by restoration:

For when these are scattered (σκεδασθέντων), those who long ago fled (πεφευγότες) the tyranny of folly may, at one proclamation (κηρύγματι), find the path of return [cf. Isa 40:3], with God having both written and confirmed the proclamation, as the oracles make clear, in which he expressly states, "Even if your diaspora is from one end of heaven to the other end of heaven, he will gather you together from there" [Deut 30:4]. (*Conf.* 196–197)[25]

Lest the reader object that this promise of return applies only metaphorically or spiritually,[26] Philo has already clarified only a few

Ruprecht, 1983), 172–87 (180–81). See also the discussion in Scott, "Philo and the Restoration of Israel," 573–75.

[23] See Scott, "Philo and the Restoration of Israel," 573–75; Thomas H. Tobin, "Philo and the Sibyl: Interpreting Philo's Eschatology," *SPhiloA* 9 (1997): 84–103 (102–03).

[24] Sherman, *Babel's Tower Translated*, 273.

[25] Cf. *Somn.* 2.277–290.

[26] E.g., Betsy Halpern-Amaru, "Land Theology in Philo and Josephus," in *The Land of Israel: Jewish Perspectives*, ed. Lawrence A. Hoffmann (Notre Dame: University of Notre Dame Press, 1986), 65–93 (85); Gruen, "Diaspora and Homeland," n. 50. Both Halpern-

paragraphs earlier (*Conf.* 190) that those who interpret these passages literally should not be criticized, as that interpretation is "equally" (ἴσως) true, though those who stop at that point are missing the deeper truths conveyed in the scriptures.[27] In the words of E. P. Sanders, "Philo, despite his allegorizing, maintained the traditional hope for the restoration of Israel."[28] Indeed, although it rarely surfaces, this undercurrent runs deeply throughout the Philonic corpus.

RESTORATION IN PHILO

Philo's restoration hopes are nowhere more evident than in his aptly named treatise *On Rewards and Punishments*, an exposition of Leviticus 26 and Deuteronomy 28–30 that serves as a capstone for his Exposition on the Torah (*Praem.* 1–4).[29] The treatise is divided into two primary sections, of which the latter is especially important for our investigation. The first section (7–78) establishes the ethical paradigm of the treatise by examining the rewards and punishments of biblical persons, whose examples demonstrate the connections between ethics and outcomes.[30] Philo's comments about Enoch are noteworthy for his understanding of diaspora and exile, as he cites Enoch as an example of the ethical "contests that concern repentance" (15), showing that the rewards for turning away from wickedness and toward virtue are *apoikia* and solitude (μόνωσις), respectively (16). "Many have been trained (ἐσωφρονίσθησαν) through going abroad (ἀποδημίαις)," he explains, since departures from home leave behind "the images (εἴδωλα) of pleasure"

Amaru and Gruen ignore this passage entirely, arguing that there are no appreciable indications of restoration eschatology in the Philonic corpus outside *On Rewards and Punishments*, which they argue is entirely allegorical.

[27] This is consistent with Philo's statements elsewhere about the allegorical vs. literal sense of the scriptures, e.g., *Migr.* 89–93; cf. Peder Borgen, "Philo of Alexandria. A Critical and Synthetical Survey of Research since World War II," *ANRW* 21.1:98–154 (126–28).

[28] Sanders, *Jesus and Judaism*, 86.

[29] Peder Borgen, "'There Shall Come Forth a Man': Reflections on Messianic Ideas in Philo," in *The Messiah: Developments in Earliest Judaism and Christianity*, ed. James H. Charlesworth, PSJCO (Minneapolis: Fortress, 1992), 341–61 (343). On the outline and structure of the *Exposition of the Torah* and *On the Life of Moses* I and II, see Borgen, "Philo of Alexandria," 233–41; Erwin Ramsdell Goodenough, "Philo's Exposition of the Law and His *De vita Mosis*," *HTR* 26.2 (1933): 109–25.

[30] Cf. Tobin, "Philo and the Sibyl," 96. Cécile Dogniez and Marguerite Harl, *Le Deutéronomie* (Paris: Cerf, 1992), 284, argue that the first portion of *Praem.* has Deut 28:1–14 in view throughout.

through which the passions could be inflamed (19). Nevertheless, he warns:

> There are also snares in a foreign land similar to those at home into which the unwary who rejoice in the society of the multitude must become entangled. ... For just as the bodies of those just beginning to recover from a long illness are easily affected since they have not yet built their strength, so also the soul which is now healing. Its intellectual vigor is flaccid and trembling so as to fear, lest that passion get excited again, which gets stirred up by living together with purposeless people.
>
> (*Praem.* 20–21)

The allusions to Israel's idolatry and reeducation through departure from the land are difficult to miss, and Philo warns the reader against falling prey to the same temptations while living among foreign nations, since rewards await those adequately trained through their migrations. The lesson seems to be that those in *apoikia* will, by their pursuit of virtue, gain solitude, avoiding entanglement with the practices of the foreign "purposeless people" among whom they live. In so doing, the "healing" brought by the *apoikia* can take full effect.

That Philo then presents Cain's banishment as the prime example of individual punishment is also significant, especially given his explanation that banishment is worse than death since, while "human beings see death as the end of all punishments, in the view of the divine tribunal it is scarcely the beginning of them" (70).[31] Philo's later discussion of the horrors of exile and slavery, which he calls the "most intolerable evil, which wise men are willing to die to avoid" (137) further develops his discussion of Cain's punishment, though in this case it is applied to the people more generally (137–140). As he retells these stories of the past, Philo also reminds the reader that the rewards of the Torah are not only for individual human beings but are offered to whole houses and families – specifically the twelve tribes (57), which enjoyed prosperity in keeping with their virtue (66).

Then, after a lacuna of uncertain length,[32] the second section (79–172) focuses on the blessings and curses of the Torah decreed for the future.[33]

---

[31] Cf. also *Abr.* 54; *Conf.* 120–21, 196.

[32] Tobin, "Philo and the Sibyl," 96 notes that this lacuna must have at least described the punishments of Korah and his supporters and provided a transition from the first section to the second. Cf. also Leopold Cohn and Paul Wendland, eds., *Philonis Alexandrini Opera Quae Supersunt*, 6 vols. plus indices by Leisegang (Berlin: de Gruyter), 5.xxviii–xxix; F. H. Colson, *Philo, Volume VIII: On the Special Laws, Book 4. On the Virtues. On Rewards and Punishments*, 10 vols., LCL 341 (Cambridge: Harvard University Press, 1939), 455.

[33] Cf. Borgen, "There Shall Come Forth a Man," 348.

This section follows the basic outline of Leviticus 26, with support from Deuteronomy 28 and 30, interpreting these passages eschatologically rather than as general principles for observance or nonobservance of Torah.[34] Thomas Tobin has summarized the basic structure is as follows:

(1) Lev 26:3–13 Blessings for keeping the commandments (*Praem.* 79–126);

(2) Lev 26:14–39 Punishments for not keeping the commandments (*Praem.* 127–162);

(3) Lev 26:40–45 Restoration after repentance (*Praem.* 163–72).[35]

Although Leviticus 26 provides the backbone for the passage, Philo actually cites and alludes directly to Deuteronomy more often throughout the section, with Deut 28 corresponding to the first two components and Deut 30:1–10 functioning as the equivalent of Lev 26:40–45.[36] Philo blends the literal and allegorical senses throughout this section, portraying Israel as the "seeing part" (*Praem.* 44) of the world, superior to all other peoples (43), analogous to the human soul with respect to the body.[37] The exile and restoration of Israel thus serves as the image of the soul's disobedience and return to virtue, and Philo also associates Israel's restoration with a worldwide ethical transformation to virtue (89–97). As a result, although in some passages he uses the language of the soul while in others he more plainly paraphrases the scriptural passages he interprets, he is speaking of both aspects throughout (cf. *Praem.* 61, 65, 158). In Tobin's words, "As one reads this section, one is not really in doubt that Philo is writing about the future fate of the Jewish [*sic*] people, although who constitutes this people is complex."[38] The eschatological picture Philo paints is remarkably detailed and has been delineated by Ferdinand Dexinger and summarized by Birger Pearson as follows:

---

[34] Tobin, "Philo and the Sibyl," 96–97.

[35] Tobin, "Philo and the Sibyl," 97.

[36] Tobin, "Philo and the Sibyl," 97.

[37] Philo's treatment of Israel is reminiscent of how the city and individual are related in Plato's *Republic* or the way the macrocosmos is also a representation of human nature in the *Timaeus*. Similar concepts and imagery abound in early Christian teaching as well, with Israel depicted as "the salt of the earth" and the "light of the world" (Matt 5:13–14). For similar approaches in later Jewish authors, see Ithamar Gruenwald, "Major Issues in the Study and Understanding of Jewish Mysticism," in *Judaism in Late Antiquity, Part 2: Historical Syntheses*, ed. Jacob Neusner, HdO 17 (Leiden: Brill, 1995), 1–49 (esp. 45–46).

[38] Tobin, "Philo and the Sibyl," 97. Cf. also Collins, *Between Athens and Jerusalem*, 136.

Starting point

(a) Enmity between man and beast (*Praem.* 85, 87)

(b) Assault of enemies (*Praem.* 94; cf. Psalm 2)

Messianic occurrences

(a) Exemplary Status of Israel (*Praem.* 114)

(b) Leadership of a "man" (*Praem.* 95, 97; cf. Num 24:7 [LXX])

(c) Gathering of Israel (*Praem.* 165)

(d) Passage out of the wilderness (*Praem.* 165; cf. Isa 40)

(e) Divine manifestations (*Praem.* 165)

(f) Arrival at cities in ruins (*Praem.* 168)

Results

(g) Peace in nature (*Praem.* 89; cf. Isa 11:6)

(h) Peace among nations (*Praem.* 95, 97)

(i) Rebuilding of cities (*Praem.* 168)[39]

Early in this second section, Philo calls attention to the negative present situation, which is characterized in particular by the assault and victory of the enemies of the "class of human beings not far from God" (84). He proclaims that if the nation is pious, their enemies will not even attack them due to their virtue, which will have even the wild animals at peace with them (91–93). If, however, some enemies insist upon indulging their uncontrollable lust for war, Philo explains that the blessed will easily vanquish them with the help of a messianic figure, "'For a man will come forth,'" says the oracle [Num 24:7 LXX], leading an army and waging war, and he will subdue great and populous nations, with God sending the assistance suitable for holy men" (*Praem.* 95).[40] Philo's citation of the plainly messianic Septuagintal version of Balaam's prophecy is striking here – all the more in that he nowhere diminishes the literal sense of the

---

[39] Birger A. Pearson, "Christians and Jews in First-Century Alexandria," *HTR* 79.1/3 (1986): 206–16 (208–09), summarizing Ferdinand Dexinger, "Ein 'messianisches Szenarium' als Gemeingut des Judentums in nachherodianischer Zeit," *Kairós* 17 (1975): 249–78 (254–55).

[40] Halpern-Amaru, "Land Theology," 82, notes with some surprise that Philo (like Josephus) turns not to the classical prophets but to Balaam when addressing a messianic theme. As previously noted, this should not be surprising, since Balaam's prophecy occurs in the Torah proper and thereby carries not only the weight of the Midianite prophet but of Moses, giving it a greater authority in this period than even the declarations of the classical prophets, especially at the end of a commentary on the Torah itself.

passage or follows it up with an allegorical interpretation.[41] Remarkably, even the victory through this messianic figure and the irresistible and eternal dominion he attains will be "bloodless" (ἀναιμωτί), emphasizing the importance of virtue and minimizing the role played by violence in the restoration (97).[42]

Throughout the second section, Philo consistently contrasts "what you now endure" (ὃ νῦν ὑπομένεις; *Praem.* 106) with the blessings of the eschatological future, such as superabundant life and perfect health (*Praem.* 110). Notably, Philo specifically identifies the present circumstance as *diaspora*, arguing on the basis of the Torah's promises that the most important thing for those in that state is to obey Moses:

> If a nation does so, it will sit upon all the nations just as the head upon the body, having favor visible from all around. ... I say this concerning those wishing to imitate the excellent and marvelous things of beauty so that they will not despair of a transformation (μεταβολὴν) for the better, nor of a return (ἐπάνοδον), as it were, from a *diaspora* of the soul which evil has cultivated from to virtue and wisdom. (*Praem.* 114–115)

Philo encourages his reader not to despair of the long-awaited transformation and restoration from diaspora (!) but to commit to obeying the Torah fully, for once the nation fully obeys the commands, it will be exalted above all the nations. Philo's language here shifts between the level of the nation and that of the individual soul, thereby echoing the parallel emphases found in the prophets of moral transformation and the return from diaspora to better things.[43] For Philo, these two aspects (microcosm: soul // macrocosm: Israel) are inseparable, as he emphasizes in *Praem.* 93–97 that the promised eschatological blessings are contingent upon the people's obedience to the commands and their embodiment of the virtues found in the Torah.[44] Israel cannot obtain or retain its inheritance unless it is obedient, so it must be transformed into an obedient nation for the promised restoration to occur. Philo therefore counsels the reader to repent (116), as this draws the favor of God, whose favor (ἵλεως) makes such transformation and return easy. After all, Philo explains,

---

[41] For a more thorough evaluation of this passage and the messianism reflected in it, see Borgen, "There Shall Come Forth a Man."

[42] Cf. Tobin, "Philo and the Sibyl," 100–01.

[43] As noted by Kyle B. Wells, *Grace and Agency in Paul and Second Temple Judaism: Interpreting the Transformation of the Heart* (Leiden: Brill, 2014), 189, Philo's individual application follows the lead of Deut 29:17–18.

[44] Cf. Borgen, "There Shall Come Forth a Man," 357.

Just as God could easily collect the exiles (ἀπῳκισμένους) in the utmost parts [of the earth] with one command, bringing them from the end [of the earth] to whatever place he should choose, so also the merciful savior can easily lead back the soul after its long wandering … from a pathless place to a road [cf. Isa 40:3], once it has determined to flee without looking back, by no means a disgraceful flight but rather a salvation which would not be wrong to call better than any return from exile (καθόδου). (*Praem.* 117)[45]

This passage is pregnant with the language of exile and return, and Philo again lumps the transformation of the soul to virtue together with a literal return – in fact using the certain expectation of the latter as evidence that the soul can be transformed, which he explains is an even greater salvation than just a return to one's homeland. Remarkably, Feldman cites this passage as evidence that "Philo does not regard the Jews who, in his day, were living in the Diaspora as 'exiles' … The word which he here uses for exiles connotes those who have emigrated, who have settled in a far land, and who have been sent to colonize it, and has not the connotation of having been punished thus."[46] This is simply incorrect, as Feldman ignores the substance of the statement in favor of overinterpreting (and wrongly at that) a term borrowed from the LXX. The very fact that Philo here connects these exiles with a future return at a single divine command overturns Feldman's basic premise. This reference to a regathering of "exiles" or those "away from home" (ἀπῳκισμένους) is also problematic to the strong distinction Pearce makes between "colonists" and "those abroad" in *Conf.* 77–78.[47] Philo further develops the parallel of the transformation of the soul and a literal return from exile in the succeeding paragraphs, this time working in the opposite direction:

The God of all things peculiarly calls himself the God of this mind, and this [mind] his chosen people, not the portion of any particular rulers (ἀρχόντων) but of the one and true ruler, the holy of holies.[48] This is the mind which was a little while before yoked under many pleasures and desires and myriad necessities from evil things and desires, but God crushed the evil things of its slavery (τούτου τὰ κακὰ τῆς δουλείας; cf. Lev 26:13), delivering it [the mind] to freedom. (*Praem.* 123–24)

---

[45] The Greek κάθοδος is often used of the return of an exile to his country (e.g., Herodotus 1.60, 61; Thucydides 3.85, 5.16). Philo's language in this passage is pregnant with the concepts of exile and restoration.

[46] Feldman, "Exile in Josephus," 146.

[47] Pearce, "Jerusalem," 25–27.

[48] An allusion to Deut 32:8–9, where the nations are distinguished and Israel is marked out as the special possession of YHWH. Philo directly quotes this passage in *Plant.* 59, again in the context of a discussion of diaspora and return.

Again, Philo portrays the present time as under the yoke of slavery awaiting God's deliverance to freedom, both with respect to the metaphorical application to the mind/soul and the empirical application to the people. As his focus shifts to punishments, Philo's language shifts rather dramatically away from the allegorical or metaphorical register; in Burton Mack's words, "something is triggered in Philo that allows for the language of apocalyptic to surface."[49]

From this point on, he speaks of desolated families and emptied cities (133; cf. Lev 26:31),[50] cannibalism (134; cf. Lev 26:26–29; Deut 28:53–57), and the most intolerable evil of all – the enslavement of the people by their enemies both by force and through voluntary submission (138–140; cf. Lev 26:17, 33; Deut 28:29–44). Although the people was once prosperous thanks to the blessings of obedience, he says, "Those seeing their cities razed to their foundations will not believe that they were ever inhabited, and they will make their appearance a proverb for all the sudden disasters from brilliant prosperity" (150; cf. Deut 29:22–28). Those who refused to heed the commandments did violence even to the land by not observing the prescribed Sabbatical years and will receive the punishment for their conduct, while the land enjoys its rest and recovers from its abuse like an athlete recovers from exertions (150–157; cf. Lev 26:34–35). Philo's language is so plain in this section that Mack, for example, confesses, "The reader accustomed to the allegories of wisdom and the soul is stunned. .... The topic of punishment has simply become the occasion for a kind of apocalyptic projection."[51]

Philo's straightforward language is not limited to the discussion of punishments, however, but also extends to the restoration to follow these desolations after the land has had its rest. Philo concludes his treatise with a detailed exposition of a robust restoration eschatology in passages corresponding to Lev 26:40–45 and Deut 30:1–10. He begins with an exhortation, observing that the curses are not intended to destroy but should rather be received as a warning and instruction; if only those who had gone astray would reproach themselves and confess their sins, they would find favor with God (*Praem* 162–163; cf. Deut 30:1–3). In a

---

[49] Burton L. Mack, "Wisdom and Apocalyptic in Philo," *SPhiloA* 3 (1991): 21–39 (31).

[50] In keeping with his previous statements about the nature of exile/diaspora, Philo explains the desolated cities serve "for the warning of those able to be instructed" (*Praem.* 133; cf. Deut 29:22–28).

[51] Mack, "Wisdom and Apocalyptic in Philo," 32. Cf also Ulrich Fischer, *Eschatologie und Jenseitserwartung im hellenistischen Diasporajudentum*, BZNW 44 (Berlin: de Gruyter, 1978), 210; Tobin, "Philo and the Sibyl," 94.

passage worth quoting more fully, Philo then triumphantly expresses his expectation that after obtaining God's favor through repentance, the nation will be restored all at once through divine intervention:

For even though they may be at the utmost parts of the earth (cf. Deut 30:4), serving as slaves to those enemies who led them away into captivity, they will all be set free in one day (cf. *Praem.* 117), as though by a single watchword, with their universal change to virtue causing terror among their masters, for they will set them free, ashamed to govern those better than themselves. (*Praem.* 164)

But when they have obtained this unexpected freedom, those who a short time before were scattered (οἱ σποράδες) in Greece and barbarian lands, among the islands, and across the continents, will rise up with one zeal to hasten from every direction and locale to one place pointed out to them, guided by a certain vision more divine than human in nature, unseen by others but visible only to those being restored (ἀνασῳζομένοις), employing three helpers (παρακλήτοις) for their reconciliation with the Father. The first is the forebearance and kindness (χρηστότητι) of the one being invoked,[52] who always prefers pardon to punishment. Second is the piety of the founders of the nation, because they, with souls freed from their bodies exhibit sincere and naked service to the ruler are not accustomed to making ineffectual requests on behalf of their sons and daughters, since their reward granted by the father is that their prayers be heard. (165–66)

Third and most of all is because of that quality by which the goodwill of those mentioned above is overtaken, and that is the improvement of those brought to treaties and agreements [cf. Isa 33:7] who have scarcely been able to come from a pathless place to a road [cf. Isa 40:3; Jer 38:9 LXX],[53] the end of which is none other than pleasing God as sons please a father. (167)

And when they return, cities which were ruins shortly before will be rebuilt, and the desert will be inhabited, and the barren will be changed into fertility, and the good fortunes of their fathers and ancestors will be considered a small portion because of the bountiful abundance which they will have in their possession. (168)

As Tobin observes, "it is difficult not to register initial surprise at the corporate, this-worldly aspects of [this treatise's] eschatology."[54] Not only does Philo put forward unvarnished restoration theology in keeping with traditional, this-worldly interpretations of the Torah passages he is paraphrasing, he specifies that these promises apply to those scattered "in

---

[52] The word for "kindness" (χρηστότητι) would have been pronounced very similarly to χρίστος, since η and ι were pronounced so similarly in this period, making for an evocative pun in this context of restoration, particularly given the messianic references to the messianic figure of Balaam's prophecy in *Praem.* 94–97. Similarly, Paul twice appears to make similar plays on this word in a messianic context (Rom 2:4; 11:22).
[53] Cf. Ferda, "Ingathering of the Exiles," 180.
[54] Tobin, "Philo and the Sibyl," 94.

Greece and barbarian lands," language that connects with his statements elsewhere about the geographic dispersion of his people. Far from allegorizing or distancing this language from the real world, Philo reads both together, such that:

... the allegorical interpretation of the soul transformed by suffering is embedded within that larger story. Thus, when the time comes for Israel to be restored, it will take place by means of the moral transformation accomplished by God through the sufferings of exile and their effects in the souls of the individual exiles.[55]

Numerous biblical echoes abound throughout these passages, but space only allows for calling attention to a few. Peder Borgen is almost certainly correct in connecting the divine vision (τινος θειοτέρας ὄψεως) here with the divine vision (θεία τις ὄψις) in the cloud that Philo says guarded and guided the Hebrews during the exodus (*Mos.* 2.252), linking this eschatological scenario with the idea of a new exodus (cf. Jer 16:14–15). This literal restoration is also contingent upon a divinely orchestrated "universal change to virtue" (*Praem.* 164), echoing the connection between repentance and restoration in Deuteronomy, Jeremiah, and Ezekiel in particular. As with his source material, Philo portrays the agency of this change ambiguously or synergistically, with *Praem.* 163 apparently upholding human agency while *Praem.* 164 hints at a determined divine decree.[56] Philo further explores this ambiguity in *Praem.* 165–167, explaining that the restoration will be the result of God's mercy and the merits of the patriarchs together with the "improvement" of the nation that essentially activates first two factors.[57]

At any rate, Philo emphasizes that the true restoration will involve not only a reunification of the people and return to the land but first and foremost a transformation to obedience while in exile. The restoration of the people – complete with the rule of the entire world, which will be

---

[55] David I. Starling, *Not My People: Gentiles as Exiles in Pauline Hermeneutics*, BZNW 184 (Berlin: de Gruyter, 2011), 33.

[56] On the question of divine and human agency in Deuteronomy, Jeremiah, and Ezekiel, see Wells, *Grace and Agency*, 25–64. On divine vs. human agency in Philo, see Wells, *Grace and Agency*, 188–208; John M. G. Barclay, "By the Grace of God I Am What I Am: Grace and Agency in Philo and Paul," in *Divine and Human Agency in Paul and His Cultural Environment*, eds. John M. G. Barclay and Simon Gathercole, Library of Biblical Studies 335 (London: T&T Clark, 2006), 140–57; John M. G. Barclay, "Grace within and beyond Reason: Philo and Paul in Dialogue," in *Paul, Grace and Freedom: Essays in Honour of J. K. Riches*, eds. Paul Middleton, Angus Paddison, and Karen Wenell (London: T&T Clark, 2009), 9–21.

[57] On the restoration as the result of God's mercy, cf. Ezek 20:44, 36:22. On the "merits of the fathers," cf. Deut 4:37; M. Avot 2:2; b. Sot. 10b.

subject to the universal principles of the Torah – will immediately accompany the turn to virtue (*Praem.* 164). This emphasis on the connection between a return to virtue and Israel's restoration is markedly similar to the views reflected in Josephus (as seen above) and the Dead Sea Scrolls (see below), as well as Paul's concern with spirit-provided virtue in his communities.

When this happens, not only will the nation itself be exalted, the very order of the world will be reversed. Philo declares that the enemies of the nation (τοῦ ἔθνους), who had previously rejoiced in their misfortunes and mocked them by "turning their lamentations into ridicule and celebrating their unlucky days as public festivals" (171), will themselves fall under the curses that had previously come upon the nation only for "a warning and admonition" (170). As Borgen has shown, this description of the nation's enemies is by no means haphazard but corresponds with the descriptions of the Jews' enemies in *To Flaccus* and *Embassy to Gaius*, serving notice that Philo does indeed look forward to the ultimate overthrow of Rome and indicating that the eschatological motifs of this treatise were more central to Philo's thought than has generally been appreciated.[58] As a result, this passage is obviously problematic for those committed to the image of Philo as a universalizing diaspora Jew with a positive view of the present and thus no significant hopes of restoration, as Gruen's attempts to dismiss it illustrate:

Philo, in a puzzling passage, does make reference to Jews [*sic*] in Greek and barbarian islands and continents, enslaved to those who had taken them captive, and ultimately to strive for the one appointed land; *Praem. et Poen.* 164–65. . . . But the language must be metaphorical and the sense is allegorical, with messianic overtones, as the Jews [*sic*] will be conducted by a divine and superhuman vision.[59]

On the contrary, the passage is only "puzzling" if one comes to it with preconceptions about Philo's view of diaspora and restoration, convinced

---

[58] Borgen, "There Shall Come Forth a Man," 359, lists the following parallels: "1) enemies rejoiced in the misfortunes of the nation (*Praem.* 169 and *Gaium* 122, 137, 353–54, 359, 361, 368; *Flacc.* 34)[,] 2) enemies showed cruelty (*Praem.* 171 and *Flacc.* 59–66)[,] 3) enemies rejoiced in their lamentations (*Praem.* 171 and *Gaium* 197, 225)[,] 4) enemies proclaimed public holidays on the days of their misfortunes and feasted on their mourning (*Praem.* 171 and *Flacc.* 116–18)." Borgen also notes (359–60) that the principle of reversal emphasized here in *Praem.* is also central in *Flacc.* 167–70.

[59] Gruen, "Diaspora and Homeland," n. 50. See also Halpern-Amaru, "Land Theology," 85, who also claims these sections should be understood as merely metaphorical.

that he could not hold to the views he puts forward here.[60] It is unclear why "the language must be metaphorical," and the idea that the returnees will be divinely guided has no bearing on whether the sense is allegorical, since Philo was not a post-Enlightenment materialist.[61] Rather, Philo explains only a few lines earlier that the prophetic utterance "*also* speaks allegorically of the soul" (*Praem.* 158), implying that it does not *solely* have an allegorical meaning.[62] This dual commitment to both the literal sense and the allegorical or symbolic understanding of the scriptures is by no means unusual in Philo, either, as he elsewhere complains about those who wrongly believe that the allegorical understanding is all that matters (*Migr.* 89–92) and reminds the reader on at least two other occasions in this tractate that both the literal and metaphorical meanings are in play (*Praem.* 61, 65).[63] Indeed,

[60] As stated by Tobin, "Philo and the Sibyl," 94, "One needs, of course, to be careful about one's surprise. While his thought has a universalizing character to it, Philo is also deeply concerned about Jewish identity as a community and the role the Jewish people should play in his more universalizing ways of thinking." Cf. also Birnbaum, *Place of Judaism*; Ellen Birnbaum, "The Place of Judaism in Philo's Thought: Israel, Jews, and Proselytes," in *Society of Biblical Literature 1993 Seminar Papers(290)*, ed. Eugene H. Lovering (Atlanta: Scholars Press, 1996), 54–69.

[61] Pearson, "Christians and Jews," 209, rightly notes that even if Philo himself preferred not to interpret these themes in a literal sense, "the importance of this 'messianic scenario' in Philo's treatise is that it represents contemporary Alexandrian tradition." Given the richness of Philo's allusive treatments of scripture throughout the treatise, a reader unfamiliar with the Jewish Scriptures could scarcely have followed Philo's arguments in this treatise. Cf. Ferda, "Ingathering of the Exiles," 180–81.

[62] Tobin, "Philo and the Sibyl," 99.

[63] The idea that Philo is a thoroughly committed allegorist – despite his clear statements to the contrary – often underlies the arguments of those who claim he did not hold traditional restoration hopes. For example, most of the objections to a Philonic eschatology put forward by Mack, "Wisdom and Apocalyptic in Philo," depend on a view of "Wisdom" and "Apocalyptic" as distinct and competing modes of thought with no possibility for carryover. Thus Mack critiques Borgen for "shift[ing] worldviews when interpreting these passages" (34), from Philo's wisdom paradigm to an apocalyptic paradigm Mack finds unimaginable for Philo. As Mack concludes, "Philo was a child of wisdom and the diaspora synagogue. He was hardly a strong candidate for an apocalyptic persuasion. Because he was not, the turn he took with its language in *De praemiis et poenis* is singularly unconvincing. Wisdom in Philo? Yes. Apocalyptic? No" (39). More recent scholarship has, however, shown that the boundary between Wisdom and Apocalyptic traditions is more porous than previously appreciated. The publication of 4QInstruction in 1999 was especially important, as it provides an example of a wisdom text with a clearly apocalyptic worldview. That Philo should exhibit characteristics of both wisdom and apocalyptic traditions should therefore be no surprise, as the two traditions are not inherently at odds with one another. Rather, as Matthew J. Goff, "Wisdom and Apocalypticism," in *The Oxford Handbook of Apocalyptic Literature*, ed. John J. Collins (Oxford: Oxford University Press, 2014), 52–68 (53), explains, "There is, however, no inherent aspect of either genre that prevents one of these traditions from

in the capstone for his commentary on the Torah, Philo brings both the metaphorical/allegorical sense (that is, the lessons pertaining to right living) and the literal sense (Israel's return) into vision, for as Borgen reminds us, these two aspects are intertwined for Philo:

> Since the foundation of the Hebrew nation and its native land is the cosmic and national laws of Moses, their divine virtues and wisdom, it follows that the return to these laws, virtues, and wisdom is the basis of the national and geographical return to Palestine. Thus the literal and allegorical interpretations are interwoven, and the concrete national and "messianic" eschatology and the general, cosmic principles belong together.[64]

Although often claimed otherwise, the eschatological perspective Philo displays here is not limited to *On Rewards and Punishments*, either.[65] On the contrary, these overtly eschatological passages provide a clearer lens through which Philo's more subtle handling of these matters elsewhere can be understood.[66] All too often interpreters have worked the opposite direction, not recognizing eschatological themes in Philo's more difficult philosophical material and then, on the basis of the supposed absence of those themes elsewhere, denying the significance or even the presence of

influencing the other. Moreover, in the late Second Temple period both wisdom and apocalypticism are shaped by the same broad intellectual currents of the Hellenistic age." The reminder of George W. E. Nickelsburg, "The Search for Tobit's Mixed Ancestry. A Historical and Hermeneutical Odyssey," *RevQ* 17 (1996): 339–49 (340), is especially applicable in this case: "modern scholarly categories that we use to interpret ancient texts (such as wisdom, apocalyptic, eschatology, and folklore) are our own inventions; and while they are helpful for heuristic purposes, they should not be conceived of as hermeneutically sealed and mutually exclusive entities in the ancient cultures that we wish to understand and explicate." The primary basis for Mack's argument – that Philo could not simultaneously be so thoroughly philosophical and allegorical while holding to such vulgar apocalyptic or eschatological hopes – thus falls flat. It should also be noted that Philo's noteworthy mysticism could just as easily be connected with a revelatory/ apocalyptic framework. Cf. David Winston, *Logos and Mystical Theology in Philo of Alexandria* (Cincinnati: Hebrew Union College Press, 1985); Maren R. Niehoff, "What Is in a Name? Philo's Mystical Philosophy of Language," *Jewish Studies Quarterly* 2.3 (1995): 220–52; Scott D. Mackie, "Seeing God in Philo of Alexandria: Means, Methods, and Mysticism," *JSJ* 43.2 (2012): 147–79.

[64] Borgen, "There Shall Come Forth a Man," 360.

[65] *Pace* Halpern-Amaru, "Land Theology," 85; Mack, "Wisdom and Apocalyptic in Philo"; Gruen, "Diaspora and Homeland," n. 50.

[66] For example, Goodenough's conviction that Philo held traditional restoration hopes was based on his reading of *On Dreams*, which he understood as a veiled attack on Roman rule (Erwin Ramsdell Goodenough and H. L. Goodhart, *The Politics of Philo Judaeus: Practice and Theory with a General Bibliography of Philo* [New Haven: Yale University Press, 1938]), an interpretation also followed (although in more measured terms) by Collins, *Between Athens and Jerusalem*, 133–34.

those themes here. But once those eschatological themes are discerned here, their impact can be detected throughout the Philonic corpus. For all his apparent emphasis on the universal, Philo consistently argues for a particular (Jewish) perspective as the superior embodiment of the universal and cosmic principles.[67] At bottom, Philo is an apologist, not a universalist philosopher.[68] Where he highlights non-Jewish peoples and philosophical principles as worthy of praise, he does so because they serve as examples for principles he finds in the Torah, which is the ultimate embodiment of the cosmic/universal *Logos*.[69] Philo not only advocates for the special supremacy and wisdom of the Torah but fully expects all other nations ultimately to abandon their own ancestral customs and honor the Torah alone after observing the renewal of the people to whom it was given (*Mos.* 2.43–44).[70]

This should, of course, be no surprise given the high degree of eschatological fervor in works popular among Philo's contemporaries like 3 Maccabees or the Sibylline Oracles.[71] Tobin has, for example, shown numerous points of connection between Philo's eschatological statements and the militantly nationalist eschatology of the *Sib. Or.* 3 and 5, demonstrating that Philo does not abandon restoration eschatology as reflected in the Sibylline Oracles but rather thoroughly revises that eschatology away towards an emphasis on Torah-observance and the practice of virtue as the means to restoration and away from anything that could serve as the basis for any sort of uprising against Roman or other authority.[72] As Collins explains, "Where Philo's eschatology differs from that of many apocalyptic writers and from that of most of the sibylline books is not so much in the actual concepts as in the degree of urgency,"[73] and "the fact that Philo still finds some place for national eschatology indicates that messianic beliefs must have been widespread in his time, even in Egyptian Judaism."[74] For all Philo's emphasis on the allegorical and ethical value of the Torah, it is difficult to disagree with Scott's conclusion that "Philo looks forward to the

---

[67] Cf. Alan Mendelson, *Philo's Jewish Identity*, BJS 161 (Atlanta: Scholars Press, 1988), 113; Borgen, "There Shall Come Forth a Man," 342–43, 360–61; Peder Borgen, *Philo of Alexandria: An Exegete for His Time*, NovTSup 86 (Leiden: Brill, 1997), 206;

[68] See especially Collins, *Between Athens and Jerusalem*, 132.

[69] On the *Logos* in Philo, see Winston, *Logos and Mystical Theology*.

[70] As Borgen, "There Shall Come Forth a Man," 347, observes, Philo's expectation that the world will ultimately submit to Torah is fully in keeping with his restoration hopes.

[71] For a closer look at 3 Maccabees, see Chapter 8.

[72] Tobin, "Philo and the Sibyl," 97–98.

[73] Collins, *Between Athens and Jerusalem*, 136.

[74] Collins, *Between Athens and Jerusalem*, 137.

ingathering of the exiles, the defeat of the nation's enemies, the reign of the Messiah and the Jewish [*sic*] nation over the world, and universal peace based on harmony with the law of God."[75]

ALL ISRAEL AND THE JEWS IN PHILO

In contrast to Scott's summary, however, Philo clearly identifies the people who will be awakened and restored from their exilic state of servitude not as "the Jewish nation" but as "Israel" (*Praem.* 44) – that is, he explains, the people "originally divided into twelve tribes" (*Praem.* 57). Indeed, the term *Ioudaios* never appears in this tractate, despite being the significantly more common term in the Exposition as a whole.[76] In fact, although he uses the term Israel (79) or Israelite (1) a combined eighty times in the extant Greek works,[77] *Philo never uses Israelite as synonymous with Ioudaios*, nor does he ever refer to the contemporary people as Israel or Israelites.[78] The degree of separation between the terms across the Philonic corpus is striking: *Ioudaios* appears frequently in the Exposition (twenty times) and non-exegetical treatises (eighty-one times) but never in the Allegory,[79] while only three of the eighty instances of Israel occur outside the Allegory (*Abr.* 57, *Praem.* 44, and *Legat.* 4).[80]

Remarkably, with the exception of *Embassy to Gaius*, Philo never even uses Israel and *Ioudaios* (or *Ioudaikos*) in the same treatise,[81] and even in

---

[75] Scott, "Philo and the Restoration of Israel," 573.

[76] See Birnbaum, *Place of Judaism*, 45. The Philonic corpus is typically divided into three categories: (1) the Exposition, in which Philo paraphrases and interprets the Torah, (2) the Allegory, which consists of allegorical expositions of stories mostly from the Torah, and (3) the thematic or non-exegetical works, which are individual treatises dealing with specific political, philosophical, or apologetic topics. For more on these three divisions and which treatises are included within each category, see Borgen, "Philo of Alexandria," 233–52.

[77] This count includes the Greek fragment of *QE* 2.47. Because there is at present no extant Greek text of *QGE*, the four other references to Israel (*QG* 3.49; 4.233; *QE* 2.30, 37) and the numerous periphrastic substitutions for Israel found in the translations of those works will not be addressed here.

[78] David M. Hay, "Philo of Alexandria," in *Justification and Variegated Nomism*, eds. D. A. Carson, P. T. O'Brien, and M. A. Seifrid, 1 (Grand Rapids: Baker Academic, 2001), 357–79 (369), states it plainly, "Philo does not use 'Israel' and 'the Jews' as identical terms." Cf. also Birnbaum, *Place of Judaism*, 55.

[79] The term *Ioudaikos* also appears three times in *Flacc.* and eight times in *Legat.*

[80] Cf. Birnbaum, *Place of Judaism*, 47–48, 61–62, 122–26.

[81] Birnbaum, *Place of Judaism*, 26–27. Cf. also Dahl, *Das Volk Gottes*, 107–08; Ophir and Rosen-Zvi, *Goy*, 136.

Table 3 *Israel and the Jews in Philo*

	Israel+	Per 1,000	*Ioudaios*	Per 1,000
Allegory	77	0.34	0	0.00
Exposition	2	0.01	20	0.13
Flacc.	0	0.00	28	3.14
Legat.	1	0.06	44	2.51
Other	0	0.00	9	0.32

that case, the terms are separated by 113 paragraphs, as Philo begins the treatise by highlighting the historical relationship between God and the nation of Israel, emphasizing the term's allegorical meaning, "the seeing nation" (*Legat.* 4).[82] It is not until *Legat.* 117 that Philo first uses the term *Ioudaios*, which he uses forty-three times (plus eight uses of *Ioudaikos*) thereafter to refer to the contemporary people. Although he clearly implies a link between the terms, Philo does not use the two terms synonymously even in this treatise.[83] Elsewhere, only eleven of the eighty instances of Israel occur outside discussions directly tied to the biblical nation or patriarch (of which forty-five occur in direct quotations of scripture).[84] Instead, like Josephus, Philo employs *Ioudaios* as the "usual way of referring to contemporary Jews in their socio-political situation,"[85] while Israel appears only in other contexts.[86]

---

[82] Harvey, *True Israel*, 222: "This introductory usage establishes a philosophical point about vision, rather than a political or social one about the people."

[83] *Pace* Birnbaum, *Place of Judaism*, 105–07, although Philo clearly intends the reader to *associate* Israel and the Jews (as *Place of Judaism*, 191), he does not *identify* them as the same entity. That is, the Jews seem to be presented as related to (i.e., descended from) Israel, but Philo nowhere explicitly identifies the two terms. Given the distinction he holds between the terms everywhere else, it is probably best to recognize the subtle handling of them here as well. It is a subtle difference, and I otherwise agree with the analysis of the rhetorical function of the use of "Israel" presented in *Place of Judaism*, 189–91.

[84] Birnbaum places these references in four categories: references interpreting "Israel" using the etymological meaning of "seeing" (49); uninterpreted references, usually in biblical quotations (15); interpretations not related to the etymology (17); and references where the interpretation is unclear but the metaphor of "seeing" is used (2). Birnbaum's total (83) differs slightly from mine because she includes the four uses from the English *QEG* but not the fragment of *QE* 2.47. See Birnbaum, *Place of Judaism*, 61–67, 101–27.

[85] Runia, "Philonic Nomenclature," 15; cf. also 18.

[86] Birnbaum, *Place of Judaism*, 28. *Contra* the many interpreters who simply assume these terms are synonymous, e.g., Peder Borgen, *Bread from Heaven: An Exegetical Study of the Concept of Manna in the Gospel of John and the Writings of Philo*, NovTSup 10 (Leiden: Brill, 1965), 115–18; Peder Borgen, "Philo of Alexandria. A Critical and

The differing quotations of Balaam's oracles in the Allegory and Exposition are especially instructive. Whereas Philo retains the names "Jacob" and "Israel" (as in the LXX) in the Allegory, he substitutes "Hebrews" for both names each time he quotes this passage in the Exposition, thus avoiding the word "Israel" (*Conf.* 72; *Mos.* 1.278, 284, 289). As Birnbaum notes, "Because Balaam's oracles appear as direct quotations both in the Bible and in Philo's rendition, the consistent change from the original "Jacob" and "Israel" to "Hebrews" is especially salient."[87] Philo similarly avoids "Israel" in the two treatises on Moses even when paraphrasing quotations from scripture in which "Israel" appears.[88] Philo even tends to use different words to describe Israel and the *Ioudaioi* as collectives, preferring *genos* for Israel but *ethnos* and sometimes *laos* for *Ioudaioi*, clearly marking out the latter as a nation but framing the former in more ambiguous terms.[89]

Even more significantly, "*Philo portrays the relationship between God and 'Israel' and between God and the Jews in different ways,*"[90] and he characterizes the membership of each group differently, further suggesting that the two terms are not to be understood as identical.[91] There is, moreover, no indication that any sort of insider/outsider distinction is in play.[92] Rather, the appearance of Israel in *Praem.* 44, at the very end of

---

Synthetical Survey of Research since World War II," *ANRW* 21.1:98–154 (113–15); Gerhard Delling, "The 'One Who Sees God' in Philo," in *Nourished with Peace: Studies in Hellenistic Judaism in Memory of Samuel Sandmel*, eds. Frederick E. Greenspahn, Earle Hilgert, and Burton L. Mack (Chico: Scholars Press, 1984), 27–41; and Annie Jaubert, *La notion d'Alliance dans le judaïsme aux abords de l'ère chrétienne*, PS (Paris: Seuil, 1963), 407–14.

[87] Birnbaum, *Place of Judaism*, 49.

[88] Birnbaum, *Place of Judaism*, 27

[89] Cf. Birnbaum, *Place of Judaism*, 222–23. Observing that Philo avoids "Israel" and prefers "Hebrews" for the biblical people in the Exposition and noting that his use of "Israel" in the Allegory is nearly always accompanied by the etymology, Birnbaum argues that Philo does not use "Israel" to describe the "real nation" (*Place of Judaism*, 43). But the presence of the etymological explanation does not negate the fact that he does frequently use "Israel" of the biblical people throughout the *Allegory*, though not in the *Exposition*.

[90] Birnbaum, *Place of Judaism*, 223 (emphasis hers).

[91] "Because the distinguishing mark of 'Israel' is its ability to see God, it would seem that anyone who qualifies – whether Jew or non-Jew – may be considered part of 'Israel'" (Birnbaum, *Place of Judaism*, 224). "In contrast to 'Israel,' who sees God, the Jews constitute the community of people – past and present – who believe in and worship God by observing specific laws and customs" (223).

[92] *Pace* Birnbaum, *Place of Judaism*, 12–13, 28–29, 55–56, 117, 120–21, 159, who does not offer evidence for an insider/outsider distinction but proposes different audiences for Philo's works as a *possible* explanation for the different terminology across the various

the Exposition, where Philo otherwise avoids the term, hints at a more plausible solution: as with Josephus, for Philo, "Israel" is an aspirational identity deeply tied to eschatology. That is, Philo's philosophical interpretations of Israel are intertwined with and complementary to his eschatological outlook.[93] Throughout his corpus, Philo constructs "Israel" as a class of virtuous people who embody the principles of the Torah and have come to "see God,"[94] even explaining that the word itself means "the sight of God."[95] This meaning of "Israel" is set opposite the word "Pharaoh," which he interprets as "dispersion" (σκεδασμός; *Somn.* 2.211). Philo thereby presents "Israel" as overcoming "dispersion," a theme that can hardly be accidental. As long as "dispersion" reigns, "Israel" does not. This theme corresponds with his eschatological vision,

works, e.g., "Both passages are found in works that are probably intended at least in part for 'outsiders'" (121). I find implausible the idea that the Exposition was targeted at "'outsiders,' i.e., people who are not familiar with Judaism and who may be put off by its claims to an exclusive relationship with God or by the seeming burden of its laws" (159), especially given the level of familiarity with the text Philo appears to assume at different points through the Exposition. Given the exhortation at the end of *Praem.*, it seems more plausible to identify the Exposition as targeted at those on the margins of what Philo regarded as proper Jewish practice, that is, those liable to be swayed into not adequately keeping the Torah, on the verge of what he would regard as apostasy, or those tending toward a more militant nationalism.

[93] As argued by Jaubert, *La notion d'Alliance*, the various levels on which this term is used all work together: "Because Israel is a spiritual people, it is the collection of pious souls; what applies to all counts also for each one" (407). For the related point that Philo's exegetical and historical writings illuminate each other, see Borgen, *Philo of Alexandria*; Peder Borgen, "Application of and Commitment to the Laws of Moses. Observations on Philo's Treatise On the Embassy to Gaius," in *In the Spirit of Faith: Studies in Philo and Early Christianity in Honor of David Hay*, eds. David T. Runia and G. E. Sterling, BJS 332 (Atlanta: Scholars Press, 2001), 86–101.

[94] *Pace* Isaak Heinemann, *Philons griechische und jüdische Bildung: Kulturgleichende Untersuchungen zu Philons Darstellung der jüdischen Gesetze* (Hildesheim: Olms, 1973), 483, although Philo says little about the covenant with Israel in his extant work (but cf. *Mut.* 53), he is clearly aware of and upholds Israel's special covenantal status, as is evident in his eschatology. His consistent emphasis on the importance of fulfilling the principles of the Torah and his connection of that obedience with restoration is fully in keeping with a framework of a form of "covenantal nomism," though not in "soteriological" terms as put forth by E. P. Sanders, "The Covenant as a Soteriological Category and the Nature of Salvation in Palestinian and Hellenistic Judaism," in *Jews, Greeks and Christians: Religious Cultures in Late Antiquity*, ed. Robert G. Hamerton-Kelly (Leiden: Brill, 1976), 11–44 (41). Cf. Hay, "Philo of Alexandria," 370. As Birnbaum, *Place of Judaism*, 36 n. 21 observes, some of the confusion in this regard owes to interpreters conflating Philo's "Israel" with "the Jews," which is not in fact identical with the former. Rather, "Israel" is the covenantal people who fulfill the Torah and "see God."

[95] E.g., *Ebr.* 82; cf. *Leg.* 2.34; *Post.* 63, 92; *Deus.* 144.

wherein those who are obedient to Torah and have thereby come to see God are restored and exalted above all other nations.[96] In both the philosophical and eschatological material, "Israel" is therefore an aspirational category related to but not the same as "the Jewish nation," which has descended from the Israel of the past but is not identical to Israel.[97]

Intriguingly, Philo's "Israel" does not include all Jews, some of whom have been cut off due to disobedience (*Det.* 107–108; *Virt.* 156–157; *Praem.* 152, 172),[98] leaving only the roots of the tree (*Praem.* 172),[99] while proselytes who imitate Abraham's example can be incorporated (152, 172).[100] Branches may be cut away from the tree due to their unfaithfulness, but the tree itself will always be preserved, with new shoots regenerating it to life (*Praem.* 172).[101] Fuller is therefore correct to conclude that, "even while Philo holds on to the restoration of 'Israel' (per his definition), he does not envision that event as being the exclusive heritage of the Jews."[102] Taken together, Philo's eschatological picture and explanation of Israel are striking. For Philo, not all who have been descended from Israel are in fact Israel (that is, "the seeing ones"); instead, that status is something to be attained through the practice of virtue, as defined by the Torah. Philo further explains that Israel, though not a visible, identifiable people or nation at present,[103] will be raised up again in the future when the nation has learned from its migrations and obeys the Torah fully. In that day, the "seeing nation" will itself be visible,

---

[96] This is one treatise where Philo refers to "Israel" as an ἔθνος.

[97] Cf. Donald A. Hagner, "The Vision of God in Philo and John: A Comparative Study," *JETS* 14 (1971): 81–93; Scott D. Mackie, "Seeing God in Philo of Alexandria: The Logos, the Powers, or the Existent One?," *SPhiloA* 21 (2009): 25–48; Mackie, "Seeing God in Philo."

[98] Hay, "Philo of Alexandria," 369, "'Israel' seems regularly to denote the community of all who 'see God,' and Philo does not claim that all Jews are inside that circle or that all Gentiles are outside." Cf. also Birnbaum, *Place of Judaism*, 225–26.

[99] The parallels to the olive tree allegory in Rom 11:17–24 here are inescapable.

[100] See Per Jarle Bekken, *The Word Is Near You: A Study of Deuteronomy 30:12–14 in Paul's Letter to the Romans in a Jewish Context*, BZNW 144 (Berlin: de Gruyter, 2007), 213–17.

[101] Borgen, "There Shall Come Forth a Man," 348: "If the Jewish [sic] nation in this way is for a while rejected, proselytes take over the role of the native citizens. Then, finally, restoration and return will take place and the curses will be turned upon the persecutors of the nation (*Praem.* 152–72)." Cf. also Halpern-Amaru, "Land Theology," 83.

[102] Michael E. Fuller, *The Restoration of Israel: Israel's Re-Gathering and the Fate of the Nations in Early Jewish Literature and Luke-Acts*, BZNW 138 (Berlin: de Gruyter, 2006), 92 (his emphasis).

[103] Birnbaum, *Place of Judaism*, 43: "Israel" seems to describe an entity which cannot be easily identified with a particular social group."

and the eschatological promises to Israel will be accomplished. Perhaps even more remarkably, Philo explains that although the restoration is but a hope at present, this "hope is joy before joy ... because reaching what is coming also proclaims the gospel of the perfect good" (*Praem.* 161).[104]

Philo's metaphorical/ethical interpretation is therefore thoroughly linked to his eschatological understanding of Israel, since the ethical dimension is the necessary precursor to the eschatological aspect.[105] Perhaps the most startling sentiment in this eschatological scenario is that, in the face of Jewish disobedience, Philo argues that proselytes can actually take the role of native citizens.[106] Those descended from Israel who rightly practice the principles of the Torah are incorporated in the renewed people at the restoration while those who do not are cut off.[107] This draws remarkably close to Paul's argument about gentile incorporation, though Paul goes a step further in not regarding circumcision and full observance of the food laws as necessary for full proselytism.[108] Nevertheless, the basic principles of Philo's eschatology and understanding of Israel appear to be closer to Paul's than generally appreciated.[109]

Overall, Philo's conception and construction of Israel also appears to match closely with that of Josephus, as each of them discourages violent rebellion while emphasizing the need to keep the Torah to facilitate Israel's future restoration. For both Philo and Josephus, "Israel" remains an aspirational identity tied to the past and hoped for in the eschatological future, and when he speaks of the historic people of God and of

---

[104] Gk. φθάνουσα τὸ μέλλον καὶ πλῆρες ἀγαθὸν εὐαγγελίζεται. I have overtranslated εὐαγγελίζεται here to draw out the parallel to New Testament language; both Philo and the New Testament authors obviously derive this language from the LXX's use of the term in restoration contexts. Note also the use of φθάνω, a word that Paul also uses in the context of restoration in Rom 9:31.

[105] Cf. Starling, *Not My People*, 33.

[106] Cf. also the discussion of repentance (μετάνοια) and proselytism in *Virt.* 175–86, the treatise immediately preceding *Praem.*

[107] Cf. Collins, *Between Athens and Jerusalem*, 136.

[108] Philo himself is aware of radical allegorists in his own community who do not regard keeping the literal laws as necessary so long as one understands their noetic symbolism (*Migr.* 89–90). Cf. Gregory E. Sterling, "Thus Are Israel: Jewish Self-Definition in Alexandria," *SPhiloA* 7.8 (1995): 12 (15–16); David M. Hay, "Philo's References to Other Allegorists," *SPhilo* 6 (1979–80): 41–75. Paul seems not to have gone so far, however, as his resistance to gentile circumcision as the proper means of entering the covenant seems to be based on something other than allegorical interpretation.

[109] This lacuna in scholarship has only recently begun to be addressed, most notably in Bekken, *The Word Is Near You*, 115–230 and Wells, *Grace and Agency*, 188–208. Cf. also Barclay, "Grace within and beyond Reason."

the future people restored from exile, he uses "Israel" or "Hebrews." But like Josephus, Philo does not use that term to refer to his contemporary *ethnos* or *genos*. Rather, for Philo, *Ioudaios* is the proper term for the contemporary people, while "Israel" is used in past, allegorical, philosophical, spiritual, or eschatological contexts.

9

Exile and Israel's Restoration in the Dead Sea Scrolls

The *Yaḥad* is actively anticipating the *eschatological, pan-Israelite restoration of the twelve tribes*. They are the vanguard, the spearhead of the incoming of the lost tribes in the eschatological era. . . . The point is, the *Yaḥad* does not see the post-exilic state of Judah as the sole heir of biblical Israel.

John Bergsma[1]

That the sect behind the Dead Sea Scrolls looked forward to the restoration of Israel is widely recognized.[2] The sect's self-identification vis-à-vis Israel and other related terms, however, is less well understood, as is the scrolls' depiction of exile.[3] What follows will demonstrate that the

---

[1] Bergsma, "Qumran Self-Identity," 188.

[2] E.g., Frank Moore Cross, *The Ancient Library of Qumran* (London: Duckworth, 1958); Paul Garnet, *Salvation and Atonement in the Qumran Scrolls*, WUNT 3 (Tübingen: Mohr Siebeck, 1977); Philip R. Davies, "Eschatology at Qumran," *JBL* 104.1 (1985): 39–55; Shemaryahu Talmon, "Waiting for the Messiah: The Spiritual Universe of the Qumran Covenanters," in *Judaisms and their Messiahs at the Turn of the Christian Era*, eds. Jacob Neusner, William Scott Green, and Ernest S. Frerichs (Cambridge: Cambridge University Press, 1987), 111–37; Talmon, "Emergence of Jewish Sectarianism"; John C. Poirier, "The Endtime Return of Elijah and Moses at Qumran," *DSD* 10.2 (2003): 221–42; Thiessen, "4Q372."

[3] The sect behind the scrolls has long been called the "Qumran community," as in Knibb's classic introduction, Michael A. Knibb, *The Qumran Community*, Cambridge Commentaries on Writings of the Jewish and Christian World 200 BC to AD 200 (Cambridge: Cambridge University Press, 1987). See also, for example, the first line of James H. Charlesworth, "Community Organization in the Rule of the Community," *EDSS* 1:133–36 (133). The "Qumran community" is often seen as a monastic/ascetic group either connected with or split off from the larger body of Essenes; cf. Géza Vermes, *The Complete Dead Sea Scrolls in English* (London: Penguin Books, 2004), 26; James C. VanderKam, *The Dead Sea Scrolls Today* (Grand Rapids: Eerdmans, 1994), 6. But as

sectarian scrolls attest to a group that did not believe Israel's restoration had taken place even for those living in the land. Indeed, the Yaḥad presents itself as having rejoined wider Israel in exile to await the final and authentic restoration of all Israel. As with the other literature so far examined, the sect's theology of exile and restoration had a significant impact on its preferred nomenclature, with the sect retaining essentially biblical distinctions between these important terms.[4]

Until fairly recently, a scholarly consensus held that the sect identified itself as "Judah," building primarily on the language of 1QpHab 8:1-3:

Its interpretation concerns all observing the Torah in the House of Judah, whom God will free from the house of judgment on account of their toil and their loyalty to the Teacher of Righteousness.[5]

This reference has often been read as identifying the sect with the "House of Judah," seen as loyal to the Teacher of Righteousness.[6] John Bergsma, however, has pointed out that this passage does not unambiguously identify the sect as Judah but rather uses partitive language to identify a group of righteous people not *as* Judah but *in* Judah.[7] The same document later confirms this point in the statement, "'Lebanon' refers to the

<hr>

observed by John J. Collins, "The Yahad and the 'Qumran Community,'" in *Biblical Traditions in Transmission: Essays in Honor of Michael A. Knibb*, eds. Charlotte Hempel and Judith M. Lieu, JSJSup 111 (Leiden: Brill, 2006), 81–96 (82), "there is no evidence that any of the Scrolls were written specifically for a community that lived by the Dead Sea." See also John J. Collins, *Beyond the Qumran Community: The Sectarian Movement of the Dead Sea Scrolls* (Grand Rapids: Eerdmans, 2010); see also Sarianna Metso, "Whom Does the Term Yahad Identify?," in *Biblical Traditions in Transmission: Essays in Honour of Michael A. Knibb*, eds. Charlotte Hempel and Judith M. Lieu, JSJSup 111 (2008), 215–35. In what follows, I will assume that the scrolls were the product of a sect that probably included members at the settlement of Qumran, but I do not claim that the sect was exclusively based at Qumran nor that all the scrolls kept by the sect were of sectarian origin. On the archaeology of Qumran and the identification of that site with the sectarians behind the scrolls, I follow Jodi Magness, *The Archaeology of Qumran and the Dead Sea Scrolls* (Grand Rapids: Eerdmans, 2003).

[4] Cf. Talmon, "Community," 12; Bergsma, "Qumran Self-Identity," 187.

[5] The notion of suffering and faithfulness to the Teacher of Righteousness being rewarded by rescue from judgment found here is remarkably analogous to Paul's notion of fidelity and suffering together with Christ, rewarded by salvation from sin and death (e.g., Rom 8:17).

[6] Cf. David Flusser, "Pharisäer, Sadduzäer und Essener im Pescher Nahum," in *Qumran*, eds. Karl Erich Grözinger et al. (Darmstadt: Wissenschaftliche Buchgesellschaft, 1981), 121–66 (140–41); Joseph D. Amusin, "Éphraïm et Manassé dans le Péshèr de Nahum (4 Q p Nahum)," *RevQ* 4 (1963): 389–96 (394); André Dupont-Sommer, "Le Commentaire de Nahum découvert près de la Mer Morte (4QpNah): Traduction et Notes," *Sem* 13 (1963): 55–88 (78); Knibb, *Qumran Community*, 216; Berrin, *Pesher Nahum*, 110–11; Bergsma, "Qumran Self-Identity," 179–86, 205–208.

[7] Bergsma, "Qumran Self-Identity," 185.

Council of the Yaḥad [עצת היחד], and 'animals' are the naïve of Judah who obey the Torah" (1QpHab 12:3–5a). This passage clearly differentiates between the Yaḥad and those "of Judah who obey the Torah" – conclusive proof that this work does not identify the sect as "Judah." Nevertheless, CD 7:9–15 has also been interpreted as a passage in which the sect identifies itself as Judah:

> When God visits the land to return the deeds of the wicked upon them, when the word of the prophet Isaiah son of Amoz comes to pass, which says [Isa 7:17], "Days are coming upon you and upon your people and upon your father's house that have never come before, since the departure of Ephraim from Judah," when the two houses of Israel separated, Ephraim detaching from Judah. All who rebelled were handed over to the sword, but all who held strong escaped to the land of the north, as it says [Amos 5:27], "I will exile the Sikkut of your king and the Kiyyune of your images from my tent [to] Damascus."

This passage has frequently been interpreted as referring to the sect's ("Judah's") separation from the group's opponents ("Ephraim"), using Isaiah 7:17 as [an allegory] signifying contemporary rivals."[8] But both the verse in Isaiah and its recollection here refer to Ephraim departing from Judah, not vice versa, and since CD presents the group as having "left the land of Judah" (6:5), an allegorical reading would more closely identify the group with *Ephraim* in this passage rather than Judah.[9] Likewise, Amos 5:27 refers to the exile of the *northern kingdom* (that is, Ephraim), not Judah, naturally pairing with the prior verse about Ephraim's rebellion. It does not appear, however, that the sect identifies itself specifically with either party in this case.[10] Instead, CD merely cites a prophecy of a time of strife (the present day of CD) so great as to recall the original split between the northern and southern kingdoms, which came with severe cost. That CD so prominently recalls the division between the kingdoms and the subsequent Assyrian exile is important and will be revisited below.

---

[8] Berrin, *Pesher Nahum*, 111. Cf. Collins, "Construction," 30; Flusser, "Pharisäer, Sadduzäer und Essener."

[9] This specific identification is equally unlikely, however, given the use of "Ephraim" in the pesharim (see below).

[10] The passage depicts those who went into exile "to the land of the north" as the righteous, while the wicked perished by the sword, paralleling the sect's own example of the righteous going into exile to await restoration, while the wicked remain behind. This notion of the righteous going into exile with the wicked left behind likely borrows from the "good figs" of Jer 24 and the "meat in the pot" of Ezek 11 (see discussions of each in Chapter 4). See also the discussion of attitudes toward the diaspora in Chapter 6 and the discussion of the implications of the sect's voluntary exile in Hacham, "Exile and Self-Identity," 14–15.

In any case, the sectarian scrolls do not straightforwardly label the group *Yehudim*, though they do acknowledge their origins in the southern kingdom of Judah and regard neither "Judah" nor *Yehudi* as negative or "outsider" terms.[11] Rather, Judah includes both righteous and wicked, and examination of the approximately thirty-two incidences of "Judah" in the scrolls suggests that the sect is exceedingly careful in how it uses the term, typically employing subset language as reflected in the quotes from 1QpHab above or "all who did evil in Judah" (CD 20:26–27) to denote parts of a larger whole called "Judah." Interestingly, the "land of Judah" is typically cast in a negative light, as can be seen by passages such as CD 6:5, where the sect is portrayed as having left the land, though the "House of Judah" includes both the righteous and the wicked, with its charge thus depending on what qualifier is paired with it.[12] In addition to the fact that the group's enemies were no less associated with Judah than the group itself, Bergsma argues that the group's strong priestly/Levite leadership may be another reason the group avoided identifying itself as "Judah" or *Yehudim*:

This is a society governed by priests who are proud of their Levitical, Aaronic, and Zadokite lineages. The tribe that consistently is given primacy in the documents is Levi, *followed by* Judah. Since the Levitical/ Zadokite leadership of the *Yahad* probably wrote many of the documents themselves, they strongly resist suppressing their own tribal heritage under that of Judah.[13]

Indeed, Levi and other priestly nomenclature is prominently featured throughout the core sectarian scrolls (CD, *Community Rule*, 1QSa, *War*), where Levi is regularly presented in an overwhelmingly positive manner and nearly always mentioned in a leadership context.

When referring to itself as a whole, the sect tends to prefer cognates of "Israel" rather than "Judah," which some have interpreted as a consequence of the supposed insider/outsider distinction between the terms.[14] And at first glance, the scrolls' marked preference for "Israel" might indeed suggest that their use of these terms differed from their more Hellenized counterparts. But yet again, a closer examination shows that the cause for the difference lies

---

[11] Harvey, *True Israel*, 41: "'Judah' is applied to both 'good' and 'bad' in Qumran Literature ... It is applied to both the producers of Qumran Literature and their opponents in other groups." Oddly, on the same page, Harvey refers to "a distinctive use of the phrase 'House of Judah' as a name for the Community."

[12] For example, "the cruel Israelites in the House of Judah" (4Q171 1–2 ii 13) or the aforementioned quote in 1QpHab 8:1–3. See Bergsma, "Qumran Self-Identity," 186.

[13] Bergsma, "Qumran Self-Identity," 187.

[14] E.g. Tomson, "Names," 136; Goodblatt, "Israelites Who Reside in Judah," 78–80; Goodblatt, "Varieties of Identity," 16–17.

elsewhere – specifically in the sect's beliefs about their location on the eschatological timetable. The first thing to note is that although the term Israel appears
frequently, the sect "generally refrained from simply calling [itself] 'Israel.'"[15]
Rather, the sectarians consistently identify themselves as a faithful *subset* within
Israel,[16] only one part of the larger whole remaining in exile, the firstfruits of the
eschatological harvest. On this basis, Sanders concludes:

> The members seem to have been conscious of their status as sectarians, chosen
> from out of Israel, and as being a *forerunner of [eschatological] Israel*, which God
> would establish to fight the decisive war.[17]

The sect does not, therefore, present itself as "the true Israel" as is often
claimed; instead, the sect's self-understanding as eschatological forerunners
shapes its nomenclature. Once again, the use of the term "Israel" is pregnant
with eschatological and apocalyptic meaning. But unlike most of the other
material covered in this study, the Yaḥad does not restrict the word Israel to the
past or eschatological future; instead, the Yaḥad portrays itself as already
participating in the eschatological future. Whereas Philo, for example, expects
a *future* wide-scale transformation to virtue immediately preceding Israel's
return to the land, the foundational scrolls assert that its members have *already*
experienced this awakening to virtue by following the Teacher of
Righteousness. Although the full restoration has not yet occurred, the sect is
the breakthrough, the leading edge of the divine movement. In their exiled,
wilderness community, the sect is ritually fulfilling the Deuteronomic requirements for Israel's full restoration.[18] All that remains for the eschatological
promise to be fulfilled is for the rest of Israel to experience the same transformation and then restoration to the land.

Indeed, "Yaḥad," the term most clearly associated with the sect in 1QS
and elsewhere, has strong restoration underpinnings, recalling Deut 33:5

---

[15] Sanders, *Paul and Palestinian Judaism*, 247. See also Collins, "Construction," 25–42
(esp. 28–29). Contra Robert Hayward, "The New Jerusalem in the Wisdom of Jesus Ben
Sira," *SJOT* 6.1 (1992): 123–38 (136).

[16] E.g., CD 1:4–5; 4:2; 6:5). Harvey, *True Israel*, 189–218, convincingly demonstrates that
the Qumran sect did not regard itself as the "true Israel," listing numerous instances in
which Israel is envisioned as much larger than the sect, even including the wicked

[17] Sanders, *Paul and Palestinian Judaism*, 245. Bergsma, "Qumran Self-Identity" has
convincingly demonstrated this with respect to the so-called "foundational documents"
(CD, Community Rule, 1QSa, 1QpHab, 1QM, 4QMMT, War, the Temple Scroll,
and 1QH).

[18] Lambert, *How Repentance Became Biblical*, 141. Note that this is not the same as
suggesting that the sect is a penitential movement "motivated, at least in part, by a
desire to induce Israel to repent" (122). Cf. also Lambert, "Did Israel Believe," 646.

and Ps 133:1.[19] The former celebrates the kingship of God when the tribes of Israel were unified (*yaḥad*) in the days of Moses.[20] The latter is a prayer specifically for the reunification of Israel and Judah, represented in the poetic form of the Psalm by the dew of Mt. Hermon (in the north) coming down upon the mountains of Zion (in the south).[21] The first line celebrates the unity (*yaḥad*) of these brothers dwelling together,[22] and the psalm closes with the assertion that such unity in Zion is the fulfillment of YHWH's promise of "life always."[23] 11QPs[a] makes the restoration context even more explicit with a closing line not elsewhere attested, "Peace upon Israel" (11Q5 xxiii 11).[24] The sect evidently regards itself as participating in this pan-Israelite restoration, but as will be seen below, although that restoration is understood as presently underway, it is not yet complete.

THE YAḤAD AS ESCHATOLOGICAL FORERUNNER: THE FOUNDATIONAL SCROLLS

Damascus Document

The Damascus Document portrays the group as the "repentant/returnees/ captives of Israel,"[25] who were exiled into the land of "Damascus" where

---

[19] "Yaḥad" appears more than fifty times in 1QS and appears in many other core sectarian texts.

[20] Collins, "The Yaḥad," 84.

[21] As Lauren Chomyn explains, Ps 133 highlights "a sense of continuity between Israel's perceived golden age and its utopian future" ("Dwelling Brothers, Oozing Oil, and Descending Dew: Reading Psalm 133 Through the Lens of Yehudite Social Memory," *SJOT* 26.2 [2012]: 220–34 [220]). See also Adele Berlin, "On the Interpretation of Psalm 133," in *Directions in Biblical Hebrew Poetry*, ed. E. R. Follis, JSOTSup 40 (Sheffield: Sheffield Academic, 1987), 141–47 (142).

[22] Othmar Keel has persuasively argued for a Zion-centered cultic interpretation in which the "brothers" are worshiping together in Jerusalem in "Kultische Brüderlichkeit – Ps 133," *FZPhTh* 23 (1976): 68–80.

[23] See also Mic 2:12; Ezra 4:3. "Brothers" (אחים) and "life" (חיים) represent a framing wordplay in the first and last lines – further confirming Keel's cultic reading of the Psalm – as shown in Mitchell Dahood, *Psalms*, AB (Garden City: Doubleday, 1970), 253. Cf. Leslie C. Allen, *Psalms 101–150*, WBC 21 (Waco: Word, 1983), 279.

[24] 11QPs[a] does not include "life," which does appear in 11QPs[b] (11Q6 7 5).

[25] That is, שבי ישראל (CD 4:2; 6:5; 8:16). The phrase is ambiguous and can mean any of the three listed options; Jonathan G. Campbell, *The Use of Scripture in the Damascus Document 1–8, 19–20*, BZAW 228 (Berlin: de Gruyter, 1995), 153, observes, "this ambiguity is remarkably similar to what is found in Isa 59 or Ps 106, on both of which it cannot be doubted our writer has drawn." Cf. also Martin G. Abegg, "Exile and the Dead Sea Scrolls," in *Exile: Old Testament, Jewish, and Christian Conceptions*, ed. James M. Scott, JSJSup 56 (Leiden: Brill, 1997), 111–25 (112–13); Talmon, "Community," 244. Lambert objects to the oft-used translation "penitents of Israel," observing that the

they became participants in the "new covenant," through which Israel would be restored.[26] Significantly, this takes place 390 years into the "age of wrath,"[27] an allusion to the years of the iniquity of the house of Israel in Ezekiel 4:5 and a strong indication that the sect did not understand the return of the *Yehudim* from Babylon as Israel's reconciliation or the conclusion of Israel's exile, though they may have regarded *Judah's* exile as having been completed after the forty years mentioned in Ezek 4:6.[28]

---

group is not continuously engaged in penitence or repentance ("Did Israel Believe," 648; *How Repentance Became Biblical*, 133–142 [esp. 140–42]). Lambert is correct that the group is not continuously engaged in penitence, and where this terminology appears, it denotes that the group *has* turned aside from prior error or sin to live the correct way. Lambert therefore suggests the translation "those who *have* turned" (*How Repentance Became Biblical*, 134, 141; cf. "Did Israel Believe," 649).

[26] CD 6:19; 8:21; 19:33; 20:12; 1QpHab 2:3. Whether CD's use of "Damascus" is literal or symbolic is secondary to the point that the sect regarded itself (and the larger body of Israel) as still in exile, still awaiting the promised restoration. What is significant is that the sect ties the events in "Damascus" to Amos 5:27 (a passage about the exile of the north) and the split between the two houses of Israel (CD 7:9b–16). For more on CD and historical reconstructions based on it, see Ben Zion Wacholder, *The New Damascus Document: The Midrash on the Eschatological Torah of the Dead Sea Scrolls: Reconstruction, Translation and Commentary*, 56 (Leiden: Brill, 2007); Maxine L. Grossman, *Reading for History in the Damascus Document: A Methodological Method*, STDJ 45 (Leiden: Brill, 2002); Philip R. Davies, *The Damascus Covenant: An Interpretation of the "Damascus Document,"* LHBOTS 25 (London: Continuum, 1983); Louis Ginzberg, *An Unknown Jewish Sect* (New York: Jewish Theological Seminary of America, 1976).

[27] בקץ חרון (CD 1:5). Some have attempted to connect the 390 years with specific dates in the effort to pin down the origins of the sect, but most argue that the number should not be taken overly literally, due to its symbolic and allusive nature. On the 390 years pinpointing the emergence of the "new covenant" community around 180 BCE, see Shemaryahu Talmon, "The New Covenanters of Qumran," *Scientific American* 225.5 (1971): 72–83; Talmon, "Emergence of Jewish Sectarianism," 606; for other discussions, see Michael A. Knibb, "Exile in the Damascus Document," *JSOT* 25 (1983): 99–117 (113); Campbell, *Use of Scripture*, 153–54; Gert Jeremias, *Der Lehrer der Gerechtigkeit*, SUNT 2 (Göttingen: Vandenhoeck & Ruprecht, 1963), 151–52; Isaac Rabinowitz, "A Reconsideration of 'Damascus' and '390 Years' in the 'Damascus' ('Zadokite') Fragments," *JBL* 73.1 (1954): 11–35.

[28] Lawrence H. Schiffman, "The Concept of Restoration in the Dead Sea Scrolls," in *Restoration: Old Testament, Jewish and Christian Perspectives*, ed. James M. Scott, JSJSup 72 (Leiden: Brill, 2001), 203–22 (220); see also Collins, "Construction," 28; Campbell, *Use of Scripture*, 148, "Indeed, CD does not mention the sixth century BCE return directly, because the writer considered the exile to have ceased only with the foundation of his own community. This should not lead us to accept that the jump from Nebuchadnezzar's deportation to the sect's foundation is historically accurate. Rather, it signifies only that, for the writer, nothing worthy of note took place in between these two episodes, with no implications as to the duration of the intervening period."

Israel, however, has remained in the period of wrath long after the events recounted in Ezra-Nehemiah, and the birth of the community, "the covenant and faithfulness they established in Damascus – that is, the new covenant" (CD 20:12), is what marks the beginning of the end of that age.[29] The appositional structure in this statement ensures that the reader understands that this is not just any covenant but is "the new covenant" (Jer 31:31 MT), the one specifically associated with Israel's restoration and the end of the age of wrath.[30] The community therefore presents its own origin as the true beginning of Israel's restoration – as of yet but a root (CD 1:7; cf. 1QpHab 14:18), the forerunner of fully restored Israel.

In this context, it is no coincidence that CD 7:12–13 recalls the separation between the two houses of Israel (Isa 7:17) and the Assyrian invasion (Amos 5:27), continuing to emphasize the sect's comprehensive vision of exile and restoration.[31] Remarkably, this detail is routinely missed by modern interpreters. Davies, for example, suggests that the sect "regards itself as . . . continuing to suffer the divine punishment of Israel initiated at the time of the exile under Nebuchadnezzar,"[32] overlooking the fact that the exile referenced in CD was initiated over a century earlier by the Assyrians. Similarly, Martin Abegg suggests that Amos 5:27 is here "'updated' in their understanding to have relevance for the sixth-century exile," but provides no warrant for such a reading.[33] Instead, the group does not mention the return of the sixth century because that event is ultimately irrelevant to the end of Israel's exile, and although the group itself is beginning to experience the firstfruits of that age of salvation, the sect still considers itself – and the rest of Israel – in exile.[34]

Community Rule

The same concept is prominent in the Community Rule, where the group is identified with those who "prepare the way of YHWH in the wilderness" (1QS 8:12b–14; 9:18–20), a reference to Isaiah's prophecy of

---

[29] Cf. Pitre, *Jesus*, 450.
[30] On the new covenant in the Damascus Document and the community of the Scrolls, see Stephen J. Hultgren, *From the Damascus Covenant to the Covenant of the Community: Literary, Historical, and Theological Studies in the Dead Sea Scrolls*, STDJ 66 (Leiden: Brill, 2007), 77–140.
[31] Cf. the demonstrations of interconnected Bible usage throughout CD, particularly noting the prominence of passages dealing with the Assyrian exile in Campbell, *Use of Scripture*.
[32] Davies, "Eschatology at Qumran," 52.
[33] Abegg, "Exile and the Dead Sea Scrolls," 118.
[34] Cf. Campbell, *Use of Scripture*, 148, 149; Abegg, "Exile and the Dead Sea Scrolls," 120.

Israelite restoration (Isa 40:3; cf. Mark 1:3; John 1:23). The centrality of the "covenant of mercy" (1:8; cf. 1:16, 18, 20, etc.) and the document's emphasis on the role of the holy spirit in the community (1QS 9:3–4) suggest the influence of new covenant theology, an idea further strengthened by the reference to circumcision of "the lower nature," which "establishes a foundation of truth for Israel, that is, for the Yaḥad of the eternal covenant" (1QS 5:5–6). The same theme appears also in 4Q177 9 6–8, which discusses those of the house of Judah "who have circumcised themselves spiritually in the last generation." Remarkably, even native-born Israelites must be initiated into the covenant of the Yaḥad to participate in the eschatological restoration; the group apparently regards the rest of Israel as remaining under the curses of the broken covenant, requiring a new entry into the covenant.[35] The recitations at initiation (1QS 1:24–2:18) prominently feature Deuteronomic theology and look a good deal like the appeal for restoration in Dan 9, while "the dominion of Belial" (1:23–24; 2:19; et al.) seems to refer to the exilic age of wrath, Israel's "time of tribulation."

As discussed above, Deuteronomy promises that Israel will turn back to YHWH and experience a circumcision of the heart in exile at the time of the restoration (Deut 30:6), a theme further developed by Jeremiah and Ezekiel and underlying the prayer of appeal tradition in the Second Temple period.[36] The Yaḥad seems to have regarded itself as the necessary and sufficient episode of repentance to initiate the restoration of Israel, seeing itself as the acceptable atonement for Israel's sin:

When such men exist in Israel, then the counsel of the Yaḥad will truly be established, an "eternal planting" [Jub 16:26], a temple for Israel, a secret holy of Holies for Aaron, true witnesses to justice, chosen by grace to atone for the land and to repay the wicked their due [Dan 9:24].[37] ...

---

[35] 1QS 2:25b–3:9a; 5:10b–15a. This also seems to have been the case in John the Baptist's movement and early Christianity, as baptism in the Jordan seems to have represented a new exodus, a new return to the land of promise, joining the new covenant through repentance. Cf. Colin Brown, "What Was John the Baptist Doing?," *BBR* 7 (1997): 37–50; Ferda, "Ingathering of the Exiles."

[36] The prayers of Daniel 9 and Baruch are obvious examples. See pp. 161 and 332.

[37] This "mystery" language is prominent in the scrolls and often seems tied to Israel's restoration, the details of which have been shrouded in mystery until the revelation to the group. Such a use of "mystery" language is remarkably similar to that found in the Pauline literature (e.g. Rom 11:25; 16:25; 1 Cor 2:7; 4:1). Cf. T. J. Lang, *Mystery and the Making of a Christian Historical Consciousness: From Paul to the Second Century*, BZNW 219 (Berlin: de Gruyter, 2015); Samuel I. Thomas, *The "Mysteries" of Qumran: Mystery, Secrecy, and Esotericism in the Dead Sea Scrolls*, EJL 25 (Leiden:

They will be a blameless and true house in Israel, upholding the covenant of eternal statutes. They will be an acceptable sacrifice, atoning for the land and ringing in the verdict against evil, so that perversity ceases to exist.

(1QS 8:4b–7a; 8:9–10)

"Israel" is therefore conceived of as larger than the Yaḥad, which is an atonement for Israel, possessing special revelation from the "Interpreter" (דורש) not revealed to the rest of Israel. Rather, the Yaḥad is set apart to "prepare the way of YHWH in the wilderness," serving as the atoning sacrifice that will spur the restoration. The combination of divine foreordination and human action in this formulation is noteworthy, as God has specifically set apart the Yaḥad to perform the actions necessary to instigate the restoration:[38]

They will atone for the guilt of transgression and the rebellion of sin, becoming an acceptable sacrifice for the land through the flesh of burnt offerings, the fat of sacrificial portions, and prayer – becoming, in effect, justice itself, a sweet savor of righteousness and blameless behavior, a pleasing freewill offering. (1QS 9:4–5)[39]

As in CD, the group thus serves as the forerunner, with its obedience making way for the coming of the "prophet and the messiah(s) of Aaron and Israel" (1QS 9:10–11), and the group "preparing the way in the wilderness" (1QS 9:19–20), preceding and preparing for their coming – and the restoration of Israel associated with their arrival. Similar conceptions of Israel needing to attain a sufficient degree of righteousness prior

---

Brill, 2009); Matthew J. Goff, "The Mystery of Creation in 4QInstruction," *DSD* 10 (2003): 163–85; Markus N. Bockmuehl, *Revelation and Mystery in Ancient Judaism and Pauline Christianity* (Tübingen: Mohr, 1990).

[38] Lambert objects to the idea that the sect "believed Israel's redemption depended on its repentance," instead emphasizing divine agency, arguing that they saw themselves as simply part of the divinely ordained plan for redemption ("Did Israel Believe," 649–50). However, as observed by Wells, *Grace and Agency*, 150–53, these ideas are not necessarily mutually exclusive, since participation in the divinely foreordained plan may be understood as voluntary, while voluntary participation also depends on divine grace: "It is possible that under the direct determination and foreordination of God, creatures possess the capacity as effective agents to perform acts which influence God" (153). Thus it is likely that the sectarians believed their repentance is the *divinely foreordained* precursor to Israel's restoration. In any case, the group's view of its practices as the fulfillment of the Deuteronomic promises associated with Israel's restoration is significant for the purposes of this study regardless of how they envisioned the interaction between divine and human agency. See also the discussions of divine and human agency at n. 129 in Chapter 3 and n. 65 in Chapter 10. Cf. also Heschel, *The Prophets*, 253, 310, 333–34, 367.

[39] The parallels to Paul's language of presenting oneself as a "living and holy sacrifice" (Rom 12:1) and becoming the "righteousness of God" (2 Cor 5:21) here are striking.

to the restoration were likely foundational to John the Baptist's ministry and the earliest Jesus movement and are also reflected in R. Eliezer's views against R. Joshua in b. Sanh. 97b–98a.[40]

4QMMT

A similarly distinct restoration-eschatological theology is also elucidated in 4QMMT,[41] in which the writers of the letter explain that they have "separated from the multitude of the people" (4Q397 14–21 7) not due to "disloyalty or deceit or evil" (4Q397 14–21 8–9) but rather because of the biblical promises of exile and restoration, which tell of a time in which Israel will stray and rebel (4QMMT[c] 7–23; cf. Deut 31:29).[42] The key is

---

[40] John's ministry is of course framed in "forerunner" language within the Gospels, and John and Jesus preached repentance in advance of the impending "kingdom of God," which is best understood as denoting the promised restoration. Cf. Ferda, "Ingathering of the Exiles"; Brown, "John the Baptist"; Joan E. Taylor, *The Immerser: John the Baptist within Second Temple Judaism* (Grand Rapids: Eerdmans, 1997); Sanders, *Jesus and Judaism*; Pitre, *Jesus*. On Rabbinic discussions on this point, cf. Neusner, *In the Aftermath of Catastrophe*, 87–95, 140–66; Hyam Maccoby, "Naḥmanides and Messianism: A Reply," *JQR* 77.1 (1986): 55–57.

[41] There has been an explosion of scholarship on the Halakhic Letter in recent years. For introductory matters, see Lawrence H. Schiffman, "Miqtsat Má asei Ha-Torah," *EDSS* 1: 558–60; Hanne von Weissenberg, *4QMMT: Reevaluating the Text, the Function, and the Meaning of the Epilogue* (Leiden: Brill, 2009); Elisha Qimron et al., "Some Works of the Torah," in *The Dead Sea Scrolls: Hebrew, Aramaic, and Greek Texts with English Translations: Damascus Document II, Some Works of the Torah, and Related Documents*, eds. James H. Charlesworth and Henry W. M. Rietz, PTSDSSP (Tübingen: Mohr Siebeck, 2006), 187–251; Albert L. A. Hogeterp, "4QMMT and Paradigms of Second Temple Jewish Nomism," *DSD* 15.3 (2008): 359–79. On the limitations of the composite reconstruction of the text, see Elisha Qimran, "The Nature of the Reconstructed Composite Text of 4QMMT," *SBLSym* Reading 4QMMT: New Perspectives on Qumran Law and History (1996): 9–14.

[42] The authors and audience of the document are unclear. Some have treated it as a polemical letter or treatise written from the sect or even the Teacher of Righteousness himself to a royal figure aiming to persuade the latter of the group's halakhic positions after the group's schism from the temple. See, e.g., Elisha Qimron and John Strugnell, *Qumran Cave 4: V: Miqsat Ma'ase Ha-Torah*, DJD 10 (Oxford: Clarendon, 1994), 114–16, 120–21; John Strugnell, "MMT: Second Thoughts on a Forthcoming Edition," eds. Eugene Ulrich and James C. VanderKam, CJAS 10 (Notre Dame: University of Notre Dame Press), 57–73. This hypothesis relies on importing a variety of assumptions into the reading of the text and has thus been called into question. See Charlotte Hempel, "The Context of 4QMMT and Comfortable Theories," in *The Dead Sea Scrolls*, ed. Charlotte Hempel, STDJ 90 (Leiden: Brill, 2010), 275–92; Gareth Wearne, "4QMMT: A Letter to (Not from) the Yaḥad," in *Law, Literature, and Society in Legal Texts from Qumran*, eds. Jutta Jokiranta and Molly Zahn, STDJ 128 (Leiden: Brill, 2019), 99–126. The proper position of 4Q397 frags. 14–21 in the epilogue

to understand "[the events of] the generations," that is, the overarching narrative and plan of history in "the book of Moses, the book[s of the pr]ophets and Davi[d]" (4Q397 14–21 10). The covenant had established blessings and curses for Israel; the blessings were fulfilled in the days of Solomon (4QMMT^c 18; cf. 1 Kings 8:56), while the curses "came in the days of [Jer]oboam son of Nebat and up to the ex[i]le of Jerusalem and Zedekiah, king of Judah" (4Q398 11–13 18b–20).[43] The division between the kingdoms is again surprisingly central, this time as the beginning point of the curses promised in the covenant, which resulted in the exiles of both Israel and Judah. There is, however, no indication that, as Waters argues, "4QMMT conceives of the epoch of the Deuteronomic curses to cease with the exile of Jerusalem."[44] Quite the contrary, the point is that the fullness of the curses had fallen on Israel and Judah by the time of the exile of Jerusalem, as the letter establishes that the covenantal curse remains in force and points to the promise of restoration "in the last days," citing Deut 4:30 and 30:1–2 (4QMMT^c 12b–14). The authors believe they are living in that time of restoration, as they explain, "it is now the last days, when those of Israel will return to the To[rah …] and will never turn back" (4QMMT^c 21–22),[45] redeemed from the covenantal curse and delivered from exile. In this light, the letter admonishes the recipient:

And we have also written to you some of the works of the Torah which we think are good for you and for your people, for we s[a]w that you have intellect and knowledge of Torah. Reflect on all these matters and seek from him that he may support your counsel and keep the evil scheming and counsel of Belial far from

is also uncertain, as discussed by Weissenberg, *4QMMT*, 102–04, 222, who suggests they should follow 4Q398 frags. 11–13 and should be understood as referring to halakhic disagreement. Nevertheless, it is clear from the number (6) and temporal range of the manuscripts that the document was important to the sect, as argued by Steven D. Fraade, "To Whom It May Concern: 4QMMT and Its Addressee(s)," *RevQ* 19.4 (2000): 507–26. What follows will therefore treat it as sectarian, though it should be noted that if MMT did originate outside the sect, it would only demonstrate the wider scope of these eschatological ideas.

[43] Translation from Florentino García Martínez and Eibert J. C. Tigchelaar, *The Dead Sea Scrolls Study Edition*, 2 vols. (Leiden: Brill, 1998), 803.

[44] Waters, *End of Deuteronomy*, 46.

[45] Cf. CD 4:4, 6:11; 1QSa 1:1; 1QpHab 7:7–12, 9:6. See Qimron et al., "Some Works," 193. Cf. Moshe J. Bernstein, "The Employment and Interpretation of Scripture in 4QMMT: Preliminary Observations," in *Reading 4QMMT: New Perspectives on Qumran Law and History*, eds. John Kampen and Moshe J. Bernstein, SymS 6 (Atlanta: Scholars Press, 1994), 29–51 (48–50); Lincicum, *Paul and the Early Jewish Encounter*, 76–79.

you, so that at the end time, you may rejoice in finding the essence of our words true. And it shall be reckoned to you as righteousness when you do what is upright and good before him, for your good and that of Israel.

(4Q398 14–17 ii 2–8; =4QMMT^c 26–32)

The letter suggests that observing its halakhic rulings is good not only for the recipient but for the whole of Israel, which is understood as a larger group including but not limited to the senders and the recipient of the letter.[46] This conclusion and its focus on the good of Israel as a whole corresponds well with the sect's self-representation in CD and 1QS as a forerunner in the larger restoration of Israel, the first to have fully repented/returned (שוב) as written in Deuteronomy and the prophets. More significantly, they do not typologize the exile but regard it as an empirical reality in their own day and experience. Their separation is not figuratively or allegorically related to the exile but is presented as actually rejoining the rest of Israel in the exile that began with the Assyrian deportations and has continued to their own day.[47] The community, with its proper halakha, is the vanguard of Israel's restoration, and their repentance/return is the preparation for and example by which the rest of Israel will soon be restored, complete with the restoration of the Davidic and Aaronic lines. Nevertheless, although all of Israel (that is, all twelve tribes) will be restored as promised, not every individual Israelite is guaranteed to participate in that restoration. If the reader of 4QMMT wishes to participate in Israel's restoration (s)he must follow the distinctive halakha represented therein.

TWELVE-TRIBE RESTORATION IN THE DEAD SEA SCROLLS

War Scroll

The War Scroll makes it clear just how comprehensive the sect expected this eschatological restoration to be, as the eschatological battle will be fought between:

the forces of the sons of darkness, the army of Belial: the troops of Edom, Moab, the sons of Ammon, the [Amalekites], Philistia, and the troops of the Kittim of Assyria, supported by those who have violated the covenant. The sons of Levi, the sons of Judah, and the sons of Benjamin, those exiled to the wilderness, will fight

---

[46] Collins, "Construction," 34.

[47] Based on 4Q398 11–13 18–20, one might even extend the time of wrath further back even to the division of the kingdoms.

against them with [. . .] against all their troops, at the return of the exiles (גולת) of the sons of light from "the wilderness of the peoples." (1QM 1:1–3)

The sect thus identifies itself as comprised of Levi, Judah, and Benjamin (the traditional southern tribes), with the tribe of Levi listed first and suggesting priestly leadership. These southern tribes will ultimately be joined by the "exiles of the sons of light from the wilderness of the peoples," an allusion to the "house of Israel," having already undergone the judgment "in the wilderness of the peoples" (Ezek 20:35) prior to its restoration to the land (cf. Ezek 20:39–44). Unfortunately, the significance of this reference to the northern Israelites uniting with the southern tribes in the battle has been widely missed. Abegg, for example, notes the citations of Ezek 20, suggesting that they "may be interpreted as [the sect's] exile from Jerusalem and the Temple."[48] It is true that "those exiled to the wilderness" from Levi, Judah, and Benjamin are to be identified with the sect; but those in "the wilderness of the peoples" are better understood as a *second group* in distinction from the sect itself, namely the "house of Israel" referenced in Ezek 20.

The eschatological battle will therefore be fought by all "twelve tribes of Israel" (1QM 3:14; 5:1–2), with the three southern tribes finally united with the eschatologically restored northern tribes. As such, Pitre rightly concludes:

The famous "sons of light" appear to be nothing less than the reunited twelve tribes of Israel. Note that this group seems to include both the "exiled" of Judah, Benjamin, and Levi (i.e., the Babylonian exiles of the southern kingdom), and those who returned "from the desert of the nations" (i.e., the Assyrian exiles of the northern tribes). Second, this group is an eschatological remnant of Israel: they are elsewhere described as "the remnant, the survivors of your covenant" who are redeemed and become "an eternal nation." (1QM13:8–10)[49]

Remarkably, the Romans (Kittim) are identified with the Assyrians, further illustrating that the current conditions are seen as continuous with the period of exile initiated by the Assyrian deportations of Israel. The impending war will finally bring that period to an end, with all twelve tribes of Israel reunited once again.

4Q372 1

The same three tribes, albeit with Judah first and Levi last, are listed in 4Q372 1, which is generally thought to be pre-sectarian but influential in

[48] Abegg, "Exile and the Dead Sea Scrolls," 124.
[49] Pitre, *Jesus*, 115.

the development of the sect. This fragmentary text depicts "Joseph" and his brothers as "cast into lands which he did not k[now], among unknown nations and scattered in all the world" (10–11). Meanwhile, "fools" (=Samaritans) living in Joseph's land (11–12) revile "the tent of Zion," likely alluding to Ezra 4:4–23 and perhaps to the passages in Nehemiah dealing with Sanballat (particularly Neh 4:2),[50] and provoke "Judah, Levi, and Benjamin" (14) to jealousy and anger. All the while, the true Joseph and his brothers remain "given into the hands of foreigners who were devouring his strength and breaking all his bones until the time of the end" (14–15).[51] But Joseph and his brothers will return and offer sacrifices and praise when God "will destroy [the foreigners] from the entire world" (4Q372 1 22).

Eileen Schuller's initial publication points out that fragment is strongly anti-Samaritan, with "Joseph" a cipher for the northern tribes over and against the Samaritans (="fools") who claim to be descended from Joseph.[52] Florentino García Martínez further argues that Joseph should be seen as a multivalent figure in 4Q372 1, being simultaneously the patriarch and also the northern tribes,[53] though Michael Knibb does not see any "real influence from the story of the patriarch Joseph" discernible in 4Q372.[54] It should be noted, however, that Joseph does not represent *all* the northern tribes but only speaks as their representative (cf. line 19, "my brothers"). In both the patriarchal narrative and the present situation, "Joseph" is imprisoned and afflicted in a foreign land

---

50 Cf. Eileen M. Schuller, "4Q372 1: A Text about Joseph," *RevQ* 14 (1991): 349–76 (371–76); Michael A. Knibb, "A Note on 4Q372 and 4Q390," in *The Scriptures and the Scrolls: Studies in Honor of A. S. van der Woude on the Occasion of his 65th Birthday,* eds. Florentino García Martínez, Anthony Hilhorst, and C. J. Labuschagne (Leiden: Brill, 1992), 164–70 (166–70); Florentino García Martínez, "Nuevos textos no biblicos procedentes de Qumrán," *EstBíb* 49 (1991): 116–23 (124–25). Note that the Samarians in Ezra 4 readily admit their foreign (non-Israelite) origins rather than claiming descent from Joseph, a sentiment with which the fragment would surely agree.

51 Cf. Eileen M. Schuller and Moshe J. Bernstein, "4QNarrative and Poetic Composition," in *Wadi Daliyeh II: The Samaria Papyri from Wadi Daliyeh and Qumran Cave 4, XXVIII: Miscellanea, Part 2,* eds. Douglas M. Gropp et al., DJD 28 (Oxford: Clarendon, 2001), 151–205; Abegg, "Exile and the Dead Sea Scrolls"; Thiessen, "4Q372."

52 Schuller and Bernstein, "4QNarrative and Poetic Composition," 170. Cf. also Schuller, "A Text about Joseph." Schuller argues that the fragment predates the sect, but there is nothing in the fragment at odds with distinctly sectarian literature.

53 García Martínez, "Nuevos textos," 124. Allegue arrives at the same conclusion in J. Vázquez Allegue, "Abba Padre! (4Q372 1, 16) Dios como Padre en Qumrán," *Estudios Trinitarios* 32 (1998): 167–86 (179).

54 Knibb, "A Note on 4Q372 and 4Q390," 170.

and must wait the appointed time of his release, which culminates in reunification with his brothers and their divine rescue (from famine in the biblical story, from exile and foreign rule in 4Q372 1). Knibb's protests notwithstanding, there can be little doubt of the allusion to Genesis, which serves as a prototype for the current situation of the northern tribes, suggesting that they will be restored as was their ancestor Joseph.

Remarkably, although the anti-Samaritan themes have been widely recognized, the text's concern with the fate of the actual northern tribes has frequently been downplayed, presumably because that concern is seen as implausible by this time. Abegg, for example, comments, "The focus of the text ... does not appear to be the fate of the Joseph tribes as much as the status of the peoples who dwelt in their place. ... [The Assyrian] exile itself is subordinate to the Samaritan problem."[55] But such anti-Samaritan rhetoric in no way reduces the fate of "the Joseph tribes" to a secondary concern but is grounded in the belief that the rightful occupants of Samaria remain in exile among the nations. As long as the Samaritans are fulfilling the role of the "foolish nation" (גוי נבל) of the Song of Moses (Deut 32:21; cf. 4Q372 1 11–14), they serve as a constant and stinging reminder that the curse of exile has not yet been reversed. As Matthew Thiessen points out, "through the interpretation of the foolish people [from Deut 32] as the Samaritans, the author has re-narrated himself and his readers into the exilic period of Deut 32's historical scheme."[56] Thus the Samaritan problem *is* the problem of the continuing Assyrian exile; the fate of the northern tribes is inextricably linked to the fate of the impostors now living in their land – and the fate of the southern tribes remains tied to that of their northern brothers, as each awaits restoration and reunification.[57]

In this context, the fact that this fragment is the first extant extrabiblical Jewish text in which YHWH is addressed as "father" is probably no coincidence,[58] since father language for YHWH in the Hebrew Bible is most commonly associated with the Exodus and, in the prophets, the restoration from Assyrian exile.[59] Thiessen therefore rightly concludes:

---

[55] Abegg, "Exile and the Dead Sea Scrolls," 117.
[56] Thiessen, "4Q372," 393.
[57] Thiessen, "4Q372," 395.
[58] See Allegue, "Abba Padre"; Mary Rose D'Angelo, "Theology in Mark and Q: Abba and 'Father' in Context," *HTR* 85.2 (1992): 149–74.
[59] See the discussion in Pitre, *Jesus*, 139.

The Samaritans function as a reminder to the southern tribes (Levi, Judah, and Benjamin) that, while they might be tempted to conclude that the exile is over, Israel (Joseph) still endures God's punishment. Restoration has not been achieved: Joseph is still in foreign lands. Whatever polemic might be found in this fragment is not directed against the Samaritans at Mount Gerizim, but against those in the south who espoused a theology, perhaps dependent upon Ps 78 where God is said to utterly reject Joseph, that claimed that the fate of the descendants of Joseph was unrelated to the fate of Levi, Judah, and Benjamin. 4Q372 1, with the help of Deut 32, demonstrates that Ps 78 cannot be read as God's utter rejection of the northern tribes. While they remain in exile, full restoration is yet to come, even for those currently in the land. Through such means, the author attempts to convince his readers that the southern tribes' fate remains bound to the fate of the northern tribes.[60]

For Israel to be complete, "Joseph and his brothers" will have to return to their rightful land, joining "Judah, Benjamin, and Levi" at the restoration, accompanied by judgment on the "fools" and other nations. 4Q372 1 thus demonstrates ongoing concern the Assyrian exile among those who continued to hope for the fulfillment of the prophets' promises. The incomplete restoration of Israel and expectations of a future restoration of the northern tribes were foundational to their theological reflection and identity.

THE PESHARIM: ISRAEL'S RESTORATION FROM THE WILDERNESS

The pesharim, line-by-line commentaries on prophetic texts, bear further witness to the sect's self-understanding, the status of Israel, and expectations of restoration. For example, the Isaiah pesher connects Isaiah's prophecy of the eschatological Jerusalem with Ezekiel's eschatological vision (Ezek 48:31), reading them both as representing a renewed twelve-tribe Israel.[61] More significantly, the pesherist connects Isaiah 10:24–27, which promises that Assyrian dominion would be temporary, with Ezekiel's promised return from "the wilderness of the peoples" (4Q161 5–6 15–20), the same passage used by 1QM 1:3 when referring to Israel's reunion with Levi, Judah, and Benjamin. Moreover, although

---

[60] Thiessen, "4Q372," 395.

[61] David Flusser, "The Isaiah Pesher and the Notion of Twelve Apostles in the Early Church," in *Qumran and Apocalypticism* (Grand Rapids: Eerdmans, 2007), 305–26 (300–11). Cf. also Yigael Yadin, "Some Notes On: The Newly Published 'Pesharim' of Isaiah," *IEJ* 9.1 (1959): 39–42.

the manuscript is too fragmentary to be certain, this return from the "wilderness of the peoples" appears to be incorporated again in the interpretation of Isa 21:14–15 in 4Q165 5 6,[62] further confirming the centrality of this imagery to the sect.[63]

Likewise, the Psalms pesher refers to the same restoration "[of] the ones who will return from the wilderness, who will live a thousand generations in virtue.[64] To them and their descendants belongs all the inheritance of Adam [or 'humanity'] forever" (4QpPs[a] iii 1–2). Thus at the restoration, Israel will inherit not only the land of Israel but in fact the whole world, an expansion of the promise likely due to the ambiguity inherent in *ha-aretz* (cf. Ps 37:9–11), which can refer either to "the land" (i.e., the promised land) or "the earth" in a more comprehensive sense, which is how the sect and eventually early Christians understood the promise.[65] At any rate, this pesher again characterizes Israel as still "in the wilderness," awaiting its fuller restoration and dominion – which the Genesis pesher claims will be accompanied by a Davidic messiah:

When Israel has the dominion, there [will not] be cut off someone who sits on the throne of David. For "the staff" [Gen 49:10] is the covenant of royalty [and the thou]sands of Israel are "the standards." [Blank] Until the messiah of righteousness comes, the branch of David – for to him and to his descendants has been given the covenant of the kingdom of his people for everlasting generations.

(4Q252 v 2–4)

The interpretation is clear: David's heir does not yet rule because Israel does not (yet) have the dominion, but when Israel is fully restored and receives dominion (cf. Dan 7:14), David's kingdom will be unending. 4QFlorilegium preserves a similar expectation, as "the shoot of David" will arise together with "the interpreter of the Torah," the former of whom will "deliver Israel" (4QFlor 1 i 11–13).

Some have argued that the "return from the wilderness" in the Psalms pesher refers specifically to the sect's return to Jerusalem, with the Yaḥad understanding itself as the true Israel,[66] but this interpretation is

---

[62] Cf. Abegg, "Exile and the Dead Sea Scrolls," 124.

[63] 4Q285 5 appears to connect this event with the advent and presence of a "shoot … from the stump of Jesse," a "bud from David," who may or may not be the same figure as "the Prince of the Congregation." Cf. Abegg, "Exile and the Dead Sea Scrolls," 124 n. 44.

[64] Note the parallels to Philo's expectations in *Praem.* again here.

[65] Pitre, *Jesus*, 333, notes that passages referring to eschatological destruction of the land/earth are similarly ambiguous. See also the discussions of the same expanded expectations of inheriting the entire world in the sections on Josephus (p. 219–20) and Philo (p. 236) above.

[66] E.g., Abegg, "Exile and the Dead Sea Scrolls," 124.

untenable as there is no evidence elsewhere that the sect regards itself as such.[67] Indeed, the Psalms pesher itself mentions "the cruel Israelites in the house of Judah" (4QpPs^a ii 14) and "wicked Israelites" (4QpPs^a iii 12), who oppose and "plot to destroy those who obey the Torah in the Council of the Yaḥad" (4QpPs^a ii 15). Similarly, Pesher Habakkuk mentions the "traitors of the new covenant," calling them "cruel Israelites who will not believe" what is coming in the last days (that is, judgment and restoration; 1QpHab 2:3–10). There are indeed Israelites outside the sect, including some who have abandoned the sect. These disobedient Israelites are under the curse and will ultimately perish, not participating in Israel's restoration, meaning that for the sect, Israel's redemption does not require the redemption of every Israelite. Likewise, that the Psalms pesher specifies that the "cruel Israelites" are "in the house of Judah" further confirms that the sect uses these terms very much in their biblical sense, with those of "the house of Judah" seen as a subset of the larger body of Israel. Judah also includes the righteous, however, as Pesher Habakkuk clarifies:

The interpretation of the word concerns the Wicked Priest, that he will be paid back for what he did to the poor, for "Lebanon" refers to the Council of the Yaḥad [עצת היחד], and "animals" are the naïve of Judah who obey the Torah.
(1QpHab 12:3–5a; see also 1QpHab 8:1–3 above)

In contrast, the sect is called the Yaḥad or "the poor" (cf. also 4QpPs^a ii 10) and is identical with neither "Israel" nor "Judah."[68] That both the enemies and allies of the sect are from "the house of Judah" should not be surprising, as we have already seen that the sect appears to regard the rest of Israel as still in exile. The house of Judah will experience its own time of persecution at the end, prior to Israel being permanently planted in its own place (4QFlor 1–3 ii 1–2; 4QFlor 4 6–7). The wicked of Israel,

---

[67] Harvey, *True Israel*, 189–218.
[68] That the sect understands "Lebanon" as a reference to its leadership is interesting in light of the later Rabbinic propensity to interpret "Lebanon" as referring to the temple. Since the sect appears to regard itself as somehow atoning for Israel, this interpretation of "Lebanon" suggests the sect understood itself as somehow functioning as a replacement temple – as potentially suggested by the reference to the "temple of humanity" in 4QFlor 1 i 6. But note the caution of David Flusser, "Two Notes on the Midrash on 2 Sam vii," *IEJ* 9 (1959): 99–109 (102 n. 11), who points out that the phrase could also be understood "sanctuary among mankind." For the community as a new sanctuary in this passage, see Géza Vermes, "The Symbolical Interpretation of Lebanon in the Targums: The Origin and Development of an Exegetical Tradition," *JTS* 9.1 (1958): 1–12.

however, will ultimately be wiped out along with "the cruel of the nations," while "the poor" will inherit the lofty mountain of Israel, the holy mountain (= Jerusalem; 4QpPs^a iii 7–13; 4QpPs^a iv 1–5; cf. 1QpHab 5:3). As in 1QM, the restoration from the wilderness pictured in the pesharim involves other Israelites joining with the sect in a much larger event. Even Gilead and the half-tribe of Manasseh from the Transjordan will ultimately be gathered (קבץ) at the restoration (4QpPs^a 13 5–6).

The details of this final restoration are further described in 11QMelchizedek (11Q13), the "oldest purely exegetical text from Qumran,"[69] a messianic text that interprets Lev 25, Isa 61, Isa 52, and Dan 9:26 together with a few Psalms to describe the last days, in which the "jubilee to the captives" will be proclaimed (11QMelch 2 4; cf. Isa 61:1).[70] The exile is portrayed as having been extended to ten jubilees,[71] when the "day of atonement" will be fulfilled, atoning "for all the sons of [light] and the people[e who are pre]destined to Mel[chi]zedek" (11QMelch 2 6–8; cf. 1QM 1:1–4). The fragment suggests this "year of Melchiz[edek]'s favor" (11QMelch 2 9; cf. Isa 62) and atonement for Israel will occur when "an anointed one will be cut off," citing Dan 9:26 (11QMelch 2 18). The clear messianic overtones – and overlaps with passages and interpretations later used by early Christians – of this text's vision of final restoration further round out the eschatological expectations found in the sectarian scrolls.

Ephraim and Manasseh: On Distinguishing Ephraim from "Ephraim"

The propensity of the pesharim to use coded language does give reason for further investigation, however, as the references to "Ephraim" and "Manasseh," particularly in Pesher Nahum, do seem to depart from the traditional biblical meanings of these tribal terms:

[Nah 3:1] Its interpretation: it is the city of Ephraim, the seekers of smooth things [דורשי הלקות], in the final days, since they walk in treachery and lie[s.] (4QpNah 3–4 ii 2)

[Nah 3:4] [Its] interpretation [con]cerns the deceived of Ephraim, who with their fraudulent teaching and lying tongue, who through their deceptive teaching and lying tongue and dishonest lip lead many astray. (4QpNah 3–4 ii 8)

---

[69] Annette Steudel, "Melchizedek," *EDSS* 282–84.
[70] Cf. 4QMMT^c 11–13 4; cf. CD 4:4, 6:11; 1QSa 1:1; 1QpHab 7:7–12, 9:6.
[71] Cf. Dan 9:20–27; 1 En 89; 4QPseudo-Moses^{a-e}; 4Q180–181.

[Nah 3:7b] Its interpretation concerns the seekers of smooth things, whose evil deeds will be exposed to all Israel in the final time; many will perceive their wrongdoing and will hate them and loathe them for their hubris. And when the glory of Judah is re[ve]aled, the naïve of Ephraim will flee from their assembly and desert the ones who misdirected them and will join the [man]y of [I]srael. (4QpNah 3–4 iii 3)

[Nah 3:9] Its interpretation: They are the wick[ed of Juda]h, the house of Peleg/ division, which joined to Manasseh. "She, too, w[ent] into exile [a captive,] with chains" [Nah 3:10]. Its interpretation concerns Manasseh, in the last time, in which his kingdom over Is[rael] will be brought low. (4QpNah 3–4 iv 3)

[Ps 37:14–15] Its interpretation concerns the wicked of Ephraim and Manasseh who will attempt to lay hands on the Priest and the members of his council in the period of trial that will come upon them. But God will save them from their power and afterwards will hand them over to the wicked nations for judgment.
(4QpPs[a] ii 18)

Both terms certainly refer to Judahite opponents of the sect. "Ephraim" has typically been identified with the Pharisees, since the phrase "seekers of smooth things" (דורשי חלקות), associated with the "city of Ephraim" in 4QpNah 3–4 ii 2, is a pun on "seekers/interpreters of halakha" (פרושי/דורשי הלכות) and thought to be a jab at the halakhic leniency of the Pharisees.[72] The mention of crucifixion in 1QpNah 3–4 i 7–8 also appears to reference events concerning the Pharisees recorded by Josephus in *Ant.* 13.379–83 and *J.W.* 1.96–98, which has been understood as confirming this identification.[73] As for "Manasseh," although there is less in the way of helpful material to aid identification, this term is typically associated with the Sadducees.[74] Obviously, as Shani Berrin points out, neither the Pharisees nor the Sadducees originated from northern stock:

Ephraim no longer refers to genealogical non-Judahites and to the geographical area inhabited by them. Instead … Ephraim is used consistently within Qumran literature as a technical term for … the Pharisees. The sect's self-designation as "Judah" leads to the labeling of their opponents as Ephraim.[75]

---

[72] Cf. Berrin, *Pesher Nahum*, 94–96; Joseph D. Amusin, "The Reflection of Historical Events of the First Century BC in Qumran Commentaries (4Q 161; 4Q 169; 4Q 166)," *HUCA* 48 (1977): 123–52 (142–46). The long consensus on this point has been rightly challenged by Gregory L. Doudna, *4Q Pesher Nahum: A Critical Edition* (Sheffield: Sheffield Academic, 2001), 577–99. On the "seekers of smooth things," see Matthew A. Collins, *The Use of Sobriquets in the Qumran Dead Sea Scrolls*, LSTS 67 (London: T&T Clark, 2009), 186–91.

[73] See the discussion in Berrin, *Pesher Nahum*, 224–31.

[74] Cf. Berrin, *Pesher Nahum*, 268–72.

[75] Berrin, *Pesher Nahum*, 110.

On the surface, this use of "Ephraim" and "Manasseh" in the pesharim therefore seems to violate the traditional distinction between *Yehudim* and the rest of Israel found in the other scrolls so far. We have already observed, however, that the sect does not in fact designate itself as "Judah" as Berrin assumes. A closer examination shows that the use of these terms in the pesharim does not undermine the traditional use of tribal language found elsewhere in the scrolls but in fact *presumes* the traditional senses of these terms, typologically and analogically applying these labels to opponents in much the same way a modern Christian calling someone a "Pharisee" presumes the hearer will make the connection with the Pharisees scolded by Jesus for their hypocrisy in the Synoptic Gospels. In a modern context, such labeling is especially common in Christian sermons on the Synoptics, where the "Pharisees" in the text are often interpreted as "types" of modern hypocrites. The pesharim are similar to much modern expository preaching in that sense – although constrained by the lemma, their interpretation typologizes the lemma to fit the present situation.

Such typologizing interpretation becomes necessary and prominent once the sacred text becomes fixed, requiring the *interpretation* rather than the *text* to be the flexible element, a phenomenon Armin Lange and Zlatko Pleše have labeled "transpositional hermeneutics."[76] Flexible as it may be, such recontextualization still depends on the historical sense of the text, all the more in groups especially concerned with their own connection to sacred history like that in the scrolls. Berrin observes that the pesherists operated with exactly this sort of appreciation for multivalence in the face of the need for recontextualization:

The author of pesher does not take the eschatological significance of biblical prophecy as its only intended meaning. Rather, the pesher application would have superseded, but not invalidated, the earlier historical significance that the original prophet himself believed to be the subject of his prophecy. The words of the prophet Nahum would have been perceived as applicable to Assyria, but as ultimately important because of their applicability to the end-time. ... In this view, pesher does in fact presuppose an originally meaningful base-text. ... It is possible that the modern supposition of the irrelevance of the original context of the base-text of pesher has its origins in a mistaken analogy with early Christian exegesis.[77]

---

[76] Armin Lange and Zlatko Pleše, "Transpositional Hermeneutics: A Hermeneutical Comparison of the Derveni Papyrus, Aristobulus of Alexandria, and the Qumran Pesherim," in *The Dead Sea Scrolls in Context: Integrating the Dead Sea Scrolls in the Study of Ancient Texts, Languages, and Cultures*, eds. Armin Lange et al., VTSup 2 (Leiden: Brill, 2011), 895–922.

[77] Berrin, *Pesher Nahum*, 15–16.

The pesharim thus presume a shared understanding of what these terms denote and how they might apply to contemporary *Yehudim*. Later Rabbinic works often make similar moves, with terms like Edom (= Rome) and Lebanon (= the temple) applied typologically to modern entities, though no one would suggest that the Rabbis were unaware of the initial sense of these terms in their historical or biblical context. Rather, that shared understanding of the biblical context – often in extraordinarily clever exegetical combinations – is precisely what informs the present typological sense and makes metareferential use of the language and motifs possible, especially given the polyvalent meanings of these terms in their biblical contexts.[78]

In the case of the pesharim, starting with the interpretation of "Manasseh" rather than "Ephraim" is instructive, as the sect looks forward to the day "Manasseh's" kingdom will be cast down (4QpNah 3–4 iv 3), and the wicked king handed over to the Gentiles for judgment (4QpPs[a] ii 18). Rather than referring to a party (e.g., the Sadducees), the term instead appears to refer to an individual king,[79] although his partisans are condemned with him (e.g., "the nobles of Manasseh," 4QpNah 3–4 iii 9). "Manasseh" therefore alludes less to the tribal name than to the notorious king of Judah who was blamed for the Babylonian Exile (cf. 2 Kgs 23:26). To call a Judahite king "Manasseh" would therefore be an especially severe insult, identifying him with the king the Former Prophets identify as the worst in the history of Judah. The most likely candidate for "Manasseh" is Aristobulus II – who, in a remarkably convenient parallel to the imprisonment of the biblical Manasseh in 2 Chr 33:11–13 and the apocryphal Prayer of Manasseh known in 4Q381, was imprisoned by the Romans before returning to the throne and eventually being deposed again.[80] Aristobulus' allegiance to the Sadducees also corresponds to the Sadducean characteristics associated with "Manasseh's" partisans elsewhere in the scrolls.[81] The term is therefore associated with the Sadducees but by association rather than direct reference.

78 Cf. Ida Fröhlich, "Qumran Names," in *The Provo International Conference on the Dead Sea Scrolls: Technological Innovations, New Texts, and Reformulated Issues*, STDJ 30 (Leiden: Brill, 1999), 294–305 (300).

79 As correctly observed by Doudna, *4Q Pesher Nahum*, 588.

80 Berrin, *Pesher Nahum*, 271–76; Doudna, *4Q Pesher Nahum*, 666.

81 Cf. Berrin, *Pesher Nahum*, 269. For more on Manasseh's Sadducean characteristics, see Amusin, "Éphraïm et Manassé"; André Dupont-Sommer, "Observations sur le Commentaire de Nahum découvert près de la mer Morte," *Comptes rendus de*

Ephraim, on the other hand, recalls the tribe most clearly associated with the northern kingdom, which was sometimes called "Ephraim" itself (cf. Ps 108:8; Isa 11:13; etc.) because its kings (most notably Jeroboam I) came from the tribe of Ephraim.[82] In the same way that for many modern Christians the epithet "Pharisee" carries the force of "hypocrite" due to familiarity with the Gospel narratives, the force of this epithet depends on Ephraim's association with those who rebelled against the house of David, split Israel in two, established the worship of golden calves in Dan and Bethel, and ultimately led to the exile of Israel. In this light, to label opponents "Ephraim" is to call them schismatics and idolaters who have broken from the truth just as Ephraim did under Jeroboam and to imply that they will receive similar punishment.[83] The "house of Peleg" (4QpNah 3–4 iv 3) seems to be another way of saying "schismatics," furthering this charge.[84]

Berrin and others have rightly recognized the implications of labeling one's opponents with terms traditionally denoting the northern kingdom, but because of the mistaken identification of the sect as "Judah," the full force of these epithets has been missed.[85] That the biblical "Ephraim" and "Manasseh" were brothers would also be convenient if Aristobulus' brother and rival Hyrcanus II benefited from Pharisaic support as some have argued.[86] In that case, the sect could thus insult each of the rival kings and their partisans with clever filial epithets that labeled each of their kingships wicked and illegitimate. At any rate, the force of the insults thus does not contradict but rather depends on the historical sense of the

l'Académie des Inscriptions et belles-lettres 4 (1963): 221–27; Eyal Regev, "How Did the Temple Mount Fall to Pompey?," *JJS* 48 (1997): 276–89.

[82] Doudna rightly points out that whereas Manasseh is treated as a singular in 4QpNah, Ephraim is treated as a collective people (*4Q Pesher Nahum*, 589). I am not persuaded, however, by his argument that Ephraim is distinct from the "seekers of smooth things."

[83] Berrin, *Pesher Nahum*, 105–11, notes that 4QpHos includes "Ephraim" in the lemma, which likely influenced the decision to employ this terminology, which then appears in other pesharim even when it does not occur in the lemma. Unfortunately, it is unclear how the term is interpreted and used in 4QpHos due to the poor preservation of the text; for this reason, 4QpHos will not be examined in detail here.

[84] Cf. Berrin, *Pesher Nahum*, 271–75.

[85] E.g. Berrin, *Pesher Nahum*, 110. To be fair, Berrin does observe that Judah does at times seem to refer to "the Jewish nation as a whole" rather than the sect alone, although she then follows the majority of commentators in understanding Judah as the sect itself (205–08).

[86] The construction of a Hyrcanus II/Pharisee alignment has come into question in recent years, however. See Berrin, *Pesher Nahum*, 222–33; (Doudna, *4Q Pesher Nahum*, 737–38); Anthony J. Saldarini, *Pharisees, Scribes, and Sadducees in Palestinian Society* (Wilmington: Glazier, 1988), 94.

terms in the context of the restoration eschatology prominent elsewhere in the sectarian literature. Pesher Habakkuk's reference to "the family of Absalom" is instructive on this point, as it reflects the same sort of typological labeling of the sect's enemies:

[Hab 1:13b] Its interpretation refers to the house of Absalom and the members of their council, who kept quiet when the Teacher of Righteousness was rebuked and did not help him against the Man of the Lie, *[Blank]* who had rejected the Torah in the presence of their entire council. (1QpHab 5:9–12)

Again, the pesher uses biblical language typologically, this time identifying those who rose up against the Teacher of Righteousness with Absalom, who staged an ultimately failed coup against his father David – akin to someone in the USA calling a traitor "Benedict Arnold." As with the prior sobriquets, this insult presumes intimate familiarity with the narratives of Israel. Again, the coded application to contemporary opponents does not negate the normal understanding of the term but rather depends upon it. In keeping with this conclusion, "Ephraim" appears to be used in its more generic traditional sense in the scrolls outside the pesharim (cf. 4QTest 1 27//4Q379 22 ii 113; CD 7:12–13, 14:1; 4Q460 9 i 9–11; 11Q19 24:13; 44:13).

In any case, because of the tendency of the pesharim to assume a shared insider framework as foundational for figurative language and creative epithets (much like apocalyptic literature), it is important not to lean too heavily on the terminology in these specific scrolls as a key for all uses elsewhere, as it is difficult for outsiders to discern reliably between Ephraim and "Ephraim," not to mention the possibility of deliberately ambiguous usage.[87] There is therefore no reason to suspect, as Boyarin suggests, that the use of Ephraim/Manasseh terminology in the pesharim indicates that groups of Jews not aligned with the Jerusalem power base would generally have been called Ephraim and Manasseh as opposed to *Yehudim*.[88] If that were the case, it would make no sense that the pesherists, who believed the temple to be impure and were themselves not aligned with the Jerusalem elites, would have regarded such labels as insulting. In the end, it should suffice to say that the pesharim provide no reason to doubt the centrality of Israelite restoration eschatology – and the related distinction between Judah and Israel – that we have found elsewhere in the scrolls. Instead, the metareferential uses of the pesharim

---

[87] Cf. the advice on polyvalent language in Hays, *Faith of Jesus Christ*, 161.
[88] Boyarin, "The IOUDAIOI in John," 230.

depend upon this larger framework to give these epithets their power in a new context. Taken together with the evidence from the foundational scrolls, the pesharim therefore provide additional support for the sect's identity as only a part of "Israel," the majority of which remains under the curse.

ISRAEL AND RESTORATION IN THE OTHER SCROLLS

Of the remaining evidence within the scrolls, 4QApocryphon of Jeremiah[c], after first recounting the destruction of Jerusalem and Israel's captivity, states, "[Speak to] the children of Israel and to the children of Judah and Benjamin [saying] 'Seek my statutes every day and ke[ep] my commands [and do not go] after the idols of the nations …'" (4Q385b 16 ii 6–9), more evidence of a continued distinction between "Israel" and the subset "Judah/Benjamin." 4Q434, one of the Barkhi Nafshi ("Bless YHWH, my soul") hymns with a salvation-history element, is especially significant. In Abegg's words, this manuscript "certainly praises God for the future deliverance of Israel,"[89] for example:

> He has favored the needy and has opened their eyes so that they see his paths, and their ear[s] so they hear his teaching. He has "circumcised the foreskin of their hearts" [Deut 10:16] and has saved them because of his grace and has set their feet firm on the path and has not abandoned them in their m[a]ny hardships. … He judged them with much mercy. The sorrowful judgments were to test them. And abundant in [his] mercy, he has hidden them among the nations (בגוים) [. . .] man he saved them. He did not judge them by a mass of nations, and he did not [abandon] them in the midst of the peoples and hid them in [. . .]. "He turned darkness into light before them and twisting paths into a plain" [Isa 42:16]. (4Q434 1 i 3b–9)

The scroll gets increasingly fragmentary but later cites Hosea's promises of restoration of (northern) Israel, again employing the motif of restoration "from the wilderness" (4Q434 3 ii 2–3). Similarly, 4QPseudo-Moses[a–e], another prophetic text schematized according to Sabbaths and jubilees,[90] tells of Solomon's kingdom (4Q385a 13 ii 1–3) and subsequent split of Israel (4Q387a 2 7) and declares that Israel's exile

---

[89] Abegg, "Exile and the Dead Sea Scrolls," 125.
[90] The manuscripts underlying this text are especially difficult; see Devorah Dimant, "New Light from Qumran on the Jewish Pseudepigrapha – 4Q390," in *Proceedings of the International Congress on the Dead Sea Scrolls – Madrid, 18–21 March 1991*, eds. J. Trebolle Barrera and L. Vegas Montaner (Leiden: Brill, 1992), 405–48.

and desolation would be extended, lasting ten jubilees,[91] with "Israel [kept] from [being] a people" during that period (4Q387 2 ii 1–iii 1; 4Q388a 1 ii 4). The text also melds the theme of Israel's exile (4Q387 2 ii 10–11) with the events of Antiochus IV and the Maccabean Revolt (4Q387 2 ii 7–9), which the author appears to view with disfavor. The return from Babylon is deemed insufficient, as the returnees continue to do evil, with the exception of the very first who returned to the land to rebuild the temple (4Q390 1 2–6). In consequence, the returnees will again be delivered into the hands of their enemies (4Q390 1 7b–9a), with Israel's restoration still a future hope presumably dealt with after the fragments of the composition cut off. At any rate, the fragments we do have make several things clear: Israel remains in exile at present, the result of rebellion dating back to the division of the kingdoms after Solomon, and the return of the *Yehudim* from Babylon was an inadequate restoration to fulfill the eschatological promises of the prophets.

In 4QPseudo-Ezekiel, the prophet asks when YHWH will fulfill promise to "rescue my people, giving them the covenant" (4Q385 2 1), only to be told that it will appear as though Israel's exile has extended well beyond the expected time (4Q385 3 2–5), though the days will soon be shortened and Israel will indeed return to its land in full. Pseudo-Ezekiel's interpretation of Ezekiel 37 is also significant in that it gives second century BCE evidence for a belief in the eschatological resurrection of the righteous associated with the restoration of Israel, suggesting a more ancient origin for this belief than previously thought.[92]

The Temple Scroll, whether of sectarian or non-sectarian provenance,[93] prominently features all twelve tribes of Israel (cf. 11Q19 23; 11Q20 6; 11Q19 39–41;) along with warnings that they "will be dispersed to many lands" (11Q19 59:2) and promises of Israel's subsequent redemption, including a remarkable passage combining the language of Hosea and Jeremiah:

---

[91] In this respect, it closely parallels the ten jubilees or seventy sevens of Daniel 9:20–27, the Animal Apocalypse of 1 En 89, the Melchizedek scroll (11Q13), and (probably) Ages of Creation (4Q180–181).

[92] Devorah Dimant, "Pseudo-Ezekiel," *EDSS* 1:282–84 (283–84).

[93] Cf. Florentino García Martínez, "Temple Scroll," *EDSS* 2:927–33; Yigael Yadin, "Is the Temple Scroll a Sectarian Document?" in *Humanising America's Iconic Book*, eds. G. Tucker and D. Knight (Chico: Scholars Press, 1982), 153–69; Elisha Qimron and Florentino García Martínez, *The Temple Scroll: A Critical Edition with Extensive Reconstructions* (Beer-Sheva: Ben-Gurion University of the Negev Press, 1996).

Afterwards, they will return to me with all their heart and all their soul, in agreement with all the words of this Torah, and I will save them from the hands of their enemies and redeem them from the hand of those who hate them and bring them into the land of their fathers. I will redeem them and multiply them and rejoice in them. And I will be their God and they will be my people.

(11Q19 59:9–13; cf. Hos1:9–2:1 [ET 1:9–10]; Jer31:31–34)

At this time, in "the day of creation," YHWH says, "I will create my temple, establishing it for myself for all days, according to the covenant which I made with Jacob at Bethel" (11Q19 29:9–10). The Temple Scroll thus expects a new temple – built by God himself – at the eschaton, when all Israel is restored as promised.[94]

Finally, "Words of the Heavenly Lights" (4Q504–506) offers perhaps the most extended and thoroughgoing example of the restoration eschatology observed throughout the scrolls, as this document from the second century BCE portrays Israel as remaining in the exilic age of wrath and prays for restoration:

You have raised us through the years of our generations [disciplining us] with terrible disease, famine, thirst, even plague and the sword – [every reproa]ch of your covenant. For you have chosen us as your own [as your people from all] the earth. That is why you have poured out your fury upon us [your ze]al, the full wrath of your anger. That is why you have caused [the scourge of your plagues] to cleave to us, that of which Moses and your servants the prophets wrote: You [wou]ld send evil ag[ain]st us in the Last Days [...] (4Q504 iii 7–14)

Nevertheless, you did not reject the seed of Jacob nor spew Israel out, making an end of them and voiding your covenant with them. ... You have not abandoned us among the nations; rather, you have shown covenant mercies to your people Israel in all [the] lands to which you have exiled them. You have again placed it on their hearts to return to you, to obey your voice [according] to all that you have commanded through your servant Moses.

[In]deed, you have poured out your holy spirit upon us [br]inging your blessings to us. You have caused us to seek you in our time of tribulation [that we might po]ur out a prayer when your chastening was upon us. We have entered into tribulation [cha]stisement and trials because of the wrath of the oppressor.

(4Q504 v 7–18)

Despite the fragmentary nature of this text, it would be difficult to produce a clearer statement of the restoration eschatology we have

---

[94] Sanders, *Jesus and Judaism*, 84–85. Again, the sect seems to have regarded itself as the eschatological "temple of humanity," "not made with hands," finally serving as an adequate atonement for Israel. Passages like this one in the Temple Scroll therefore may well have been interpreted in this manner.

already witnessed elsewhere in the scrolls. The speaker clearly depicts Israel as remaining in exile and sees himself as part of a larger group that has been awakened to obedience and return. New covenant language is again central, as the group has received the holy spirit and had the covenant "placed on their hearts to return to [God], to obey [his] voice," causing them to seek YHWH and await the restoration of Israel for which the speaker prays.

CONCLUSIONS: ISRAEL, JUDAH, AND RESTORATION ESCHATOLOGY IN THE DEAD SEA SCROLLS

Despite the sectarians' residence in the land, the literature found in the Dead Sea Scrolls consistently rejects the identification of the return from Babylon as Israel's restoration. Rather, this literature consistently represents the exile of Israel as ongoing, with Israel "expected to remain in exile until the time of God's judgment on the nations (1QM 1:2–3)."[95] In fact, the notion of a continuing exile was so foundational to the sect's thinking that, after some important but unknown event, they withdrew themselves to the wilderness – "the new Sinai – so as to prepare for the coming of God."[96] Indeed, when the sect refers to itself as "in exile" or the "repentant captives of Israel," this is not merely a rhetorical claim or typological application of scripture to its own separation from the Jerusalem establishment. Instead, the sect straightforwardly portrays itself as having withdrawn from the wicked in the land to rejoin the larger body of Israel that has remained in exile for centuries.[97] In so doing, the sectarians see themselves as having "repented/returned" to appropriate fulfillment of the Torah for those in exile, ritually fulfilling the Deuteronomic requirements associated with the divinely orchestrated restoration and return of all Israel.

The scrolls thereby portray Israel's restoration as first and foremost involving a return to virtue and obedience that ultimately culminates in an eschatological reunion of all twelve tribes, regathered to their land, with the nations subjugated to Israel. They regard their community as the vanguard of this return to virtue, which has already happened for them

---

[95] Abegg, "Exile and the Dead Sea Scrolls," 123.
[96] Abegg, "Exile and the Dead Sea Scrolls," 125.
[97] My conclusions in this respect are therefore similar to Talmon's ("The New Covenanters of Qumran"; "Emergence of Jewish Sectarianism," 605–07).

through the revelation of the Teacher of Righteousness, which was itself the indication that the restoration was imminent. They do not regard this turn of events as of their own initiative but regard themselves as the vanguard of renewed Israel, participating in the (re)new(ed) covenant promised by Jeremiah after the curses of the Torah had been carried out upon Israel, transformed by the divine presence in their midst. Their community, set aside for obedience by God, has thus become the necessary atonement in exile to bring about the final eschatological restoration of all Israel; their existence and obedience are the final necessary steps outlined for Israel's restoration in Deuteronomy.

As for nomenclature, the sect handles Israel and Jew/Judahite terminology with subtlety and clearly does not equate this term with Judah and its cognates, instead using the terms in their biblical senses, understanding Judah as a *subset* of Israel, the larger people of God. And although preferring the more comprehensive and eschatologically freighted terminology of "Israel," the sect is only a righteous subset within the larger people of Israel. More specifically, the Yaḥad presents itself as comprised of the southern tribes of Levi, Judah, and Benjamin. But as a priestly Levite-led group distancing itself from the Judaean state apparatus and effectively rejoining the rest of Israel in exile, looking towards the eschatological restoration, the sect does not identify itself as "Judah," although it is comprised solely of southerners. The sect is therefore neither "Israel" nor "Judah," though it is comprised of a part of each, with its members both *Yehudim* and children of Israel. Even the sect's preferred name "Yaḥad" likely alludes to the eschatological unity between both houses of Israel associated with the restoration. Although on the one hand the sect regards itself as having taken the first steps of repentance towards this restoration – in fact serving as an atonement for the rest of Israel – it is clearly aware of the absence of the other (northern) Israelite tribes who will join together with the sectarians (and other *Yehudim* joining them) at the eschatological restoration.

Although those who initially returned from Babylon to rebuild the temple were righteous, that return and restoration was an abortion, since Israel remained in exile and the Judahite returnees continued in their wickedness. Disillusioned by the present state of Judaea, the sect has rejoined the rest of Israel in exile, where the "good figs" (Jer 24:5) await the divinely initiated restoration. The sectarians thus regard themselves as exiles within the exile – exiles from rebellious Judah within the continuing exile of Israel. Their recognition of the present state of affairs and divinely initiated repentance (observance of correct halakha) have established the roots of the righteous community (Yaḥad); it is now only a matter of time before God acts to restore all Israel, with the sectarians at the forefront of God's sovereign plan.

Israel, Jews, and Restoration in Other Second Temple Narrative Literature

> Much of the literature of the Second Temple period recognizes a category of exile after the destruction of Jerusalem in 587/86, but it does not recognize any return in subsequent centuries. This literature ... represents Israel as being in exile for centuries; virtually in permanent exile.
>
> Robert P. Carroll[1]

The prevalence of eschatological hopes throughout the Jewish literature of the Second Temple period is widely recognized in scholarly literature – even by those like Gruen who dismiss the relevance of this fact to the period in which these texts were written.[2] Nevertheless, scant attention has been paid to the relationship between restoration eschatology and the use of Israel terminology in these texts.[3] Instead, most have followed Kuhn's suggestion that Israel terminology is preferred among texts that are "religious rather than historical or political."[4] That is:

---

[1] Robert P. Carroll, "Israel, History of (Post-Monarchic Period)," *The Anchor Yale Bible Dictionary* 3:567–76 (575).

[2] Cf. Gruen, "Diaspora and Homeland," 20–21; see p. 204. On the prevalence of restoration eschatology in these texts, see Pitre, *Jesus*, 1–130; Carroll, "Exile! What Exile?"; Knibb, "The Exile in the Literature of the Intertestamental Period"; Knibb, "Exile in the Damascus Document"; Knibb, "A Note on 4Q372 and 4Q390"; Scott, "Self-Understanding."

[3] This corpus includes what is often problematically called "intertestamental" (that is, between the Old and New Testaments) literature or categorized into the subgroups of pseudepigrapha or apocrypha.

[4] Kuhn, "Ἰουδαῖος κτλ," *TDNT* 3: 361

Ἰσραήλ is always used in such works and never Ἰουδαῖοι. ... Examples of this type of writing are Sir., Jdt., Tob., Bar., Pss. Sol, 4 Esr., Test. XII, 3 En. Ἰσραήλ is found on innumerable occasions in these works, but never Ἰουδαῖος.[5]

This distinction between "religious" and "historical" works, however, cannot adequately account for the fact that even among Kuhn's listed examples, Tobit and Judith present themselves as (quasi-) historical narratives. It is no coincidence, however, that the texts Kuhn designates as "religious" or "insider" works are either set in the biblical past or prominently express expectations for Israel's restoration (or both), while *Ioudaios*/Jew terminology appears nearly exclusively in post-exilic or contemporary narrative contexts, not in references to biblical Israel or the future restored people. This distinction – and its connection to restoration eschatology – becomes apparent upon a close examination of the narrative literature from the Second Temple period, a task to which we now turn.

SECOND TEMPLE TEXTS WITH A PRE-EXILIC OR NORTHERN ISRAELITE SETTING

A variety of Second Temple texts are set in the pre-exilic biblical past or refer specifically to northern Israelites as distinct from southern Judahites/Jews. In addition to works covered in previous chapters, this group most notably includes Tobit, Judith, Jubilees, the Testaments of the Twelve Patriarchs, and Joseph and Aseneth.[6] As shown in Table 4, texts in this category overwhelmingly favor Israel language to the near-complete exclusion of *Ioudaios*/*Yehudi* language. Much of this literature also includes references to a restored, eschatological Israel comprised of all twelve tribes.

---

[5] Kuhn, "Ἰουδαῖος κτλ," *TDNT* 3: 361–62.

[6] Joseph and Aseneth is a Greek novella about the patriarch Joseph likely written between the first century BCE and the second century CE, though a dating in the Ptolemaic period (before 30 BCE) seems most likely. See Randall D. Chesnutt, *From Death to Life: Conversion in Joseph and Aseneth*, JSPSup 16 (London: Black, 1995), 80–85. The book is especially notable for its perspective on conversion; for a discussion of conversion in this work, see Chesnutt, *From Death to Life* and Jill Hicks-Keeton, *Arguing with Aseneth: Gentile Access to Israel's Living God in Jewish Antiquity* (Oxford University Press, 2018). The focus on the figure of Joseph is also noteworthy given that patriarch's identification with the northern kingdom. For Jos. Asen. as an allegory of apostate Israel and its redemption, see John C. O'Neill, "What is Joseph and Aseneth About?," *Hen* 16 (1994): 189–98. Since Jos. Asen. only refers to Israel in a patriarchal context, it will not be addressed in detail here.

Table 4 *Israelites and Jews in Second Temple texts with a pre-exilic or Northern Israelite setting*[a]

	Israel	Per 1,000	*Ioudaios*	Per 1,000
Tobit (G[I])	17	2.35	1	0.14
Tobit (G[II])	4	0.73	0	0.00
Judith	50	5.45	0	0.00
Jubilees	112	2.19	0	0.00
Mart. Ascen. Isa.*	5	3.33	0	0.00
Jos. Asen.	7	0.85	0	0.00
Liv. Pro.[b]	7	2.60	2	0.74
T. Moses[L]	2	0.61	0	0.00
4 Baruch	4	0.96	0	0.00

[a] Since T. Mos. is not fully extant in Greek, the Latin version was used. Similarly, the entries marked with asterisks (Jubilees and Mart. Ascen. Isa.) use the English text of Robert Henry Charles, ed., *The Apocrypha and Pseudepigrapha of the Old Testament in English: With Introductions and Critical and Explanatory Notes to the Several Books*, 2 vols. (Oxford: Clarendon, 1913) as a proxy due to extremely fragmentary Hebrew and Greek texts. The tables in this chapter and the next do not include texts that use either term, authors only known through quotations by other later authors (e.g., Eupolemus, Artapanus, and Cleodemus Malchus), or overly fragmentary texts. In addition, the date and provenance of many of these texts are disputed, with some potentially written after the Second Temple period or of Christian provenance, but these have been included since there is at least some possibility that they fall within our period (all instances of Israel in Mart. Ascen. Isa. are in chs. 2–3, for example, a section likely of Jewish provenance). For more on Christian interpolations and problems of provenance in early Jewish literature in general, see James R. Davila, *The Provenance of the Pseudepigrapha: Jewish, Christian, or Other?* (Leiden: Brill, 2005).
[b] Both uses of *Ioudaioi* in Lives of the Prophets refer to those from the kingdom of Judah (1:4; 4:2).

Tobit

Perhaps the best example of the continued use of "Israel" in Second Temple literature to distinguish those descended from northern stock from their southern kinsmen appears in the book of Tobit.[7] Composed

[7] On the basis of fragments from one Hebrew and four Aramaic manuscripts found at Qumran, it is generally agreed that Tobit was originally composed in a Semitic language, though there is insufficient evidence to determine whether that language was Hebrew or Aramaic. The full narrative survives in both Greek and Latin manuscripts, with two primary Greek versions: a shorter version (G[I]) preserved in Codices Vaticanus and Alexandrinus and a longer form (G[II]) represented in Sinaiticus. A third text-form

sometime in the third or second century BCE, Tobit cannot be identified with any specific location or Jewish group, which makes it especially important for this study, as "it seems to represent some kind of 'popular Judaism.'"[8] The book tells the story of a pious Naphtalite taken into Assyrian captivity by Shalmaneser, where he and his family are ultimately preserved through two interconnected tragic circumstances with divine aid: Tobit is healed from blindness, while his future daughter-in-law, Sarah, is delivered from the demon Asmodeus, who had the nasty habit of killing Sarah's betrothed on the night of the wedding.

Strikingly, Tobit is nowhere described as a Jew;[9] instead, the book employs the term "Israel" and cognates seventeen times while avoiding

---

survives only in part (Tob 6:9–12:22) and is likely secondary to the others. As demonstrated in Joseph A. Fitzmyer, "The Aramaic and Hebrew Fragments of Tobit from Qumran Cave 4," *CBQ* 57.4 (1995): 655–75, the longer G[II] version features more frequent Semiticisms and tends to correspond more readily to the five Qumran manuscripts of Tobit and is on that basis generally regarded as an earlier version than G[I], which features a shorter, more tightly edited, and more idiomatically Greek text. Sinaiticus, however, contains numerous textual problems, making it difficult to restore a coherent longer recension in spots. Unless otherwise noted, the citations and references in this chapter will be to the G[II] text, though the differences between these recensions do not make an appreciable difference for my argument; what holds for G[II] also holds for G[I] in this regard, though the former includes more distinct references to "Israel." For more on the text of Tobit, see Stuart Weeks, "Restoring the Greek Tobit," *JSJ* 44.1 (2013): 1–15; Stuart Weeks, Simon Gathercole, and Loren Stuckenbruck, eds., *The Book of Tobit: Texts from the Principal Ancient and Medieval Traditions. With Synopsis, Concordances, and Annotated Texts in Aramaic, Hebrew, Greek, Latin, and Syriac* (Berlin: de Gruyter, 2004); Stuart Weeks, "Some Neglected Texts of Tobit: The Third Greek Version," in *Studies in the Book of Tobit: A Multidisciplinary Approach*, ed. Mark R. J. Bredin, LSTS 55 (London: T&T Clark, 2006), 12–42; Fitzmyer, "Fragments"; Joseph A. Fitzmyer, "4QpapTobit[a] ar, 4QTobit[b–d] ar, and 4QTobit[e]," in *Qumran Cave 4. XIV: Parabiblical Texts, Part 2*, ed. James C. VanderKam, DJD 19 (Oxford: Clarendon, 1995), 1–76 + plates i; Joseph A. Fitzmyer, "The Significance of the Hebrew and Aramaic Texts of Tobit from Qumran for the Study of Tobit," in *The Dead Sea Scrolls: Fifty Years after their Discovery (1947–1997)*, eds. Lawrence H. Schiffman et al. (Jerusalem: Israel Exploration Society, 2000), 418–25; Joseph A. Fitzmyer, *Tobit*, CEJL (Berlin: de Gruyter, 2003), 3–15; Armin Schmitt, "Die hebräischen Textfunde zum Buch Tobit aus Qumran 4QTob[e] (4Q200)," *ZAW* 113.4 (2001): 566–82; Robert Hanhart, *Septuaginta: Vetus Testamentum Graecum Auctoritate Academiae Scientiarum Gottingensis editum VIII.5: Tobit* (Göttingen: Vandenhoeck & Ruprecht, 1983), 31–55.

8 Ophir and Rosen-Zvi, *Goy*, 100. Cf. John J. Collins, "The Judaism of the Book of Tobit," in *The Book of Tobit: Text, Tradition, Theology*, eds. Géza G. Xeravits and József Zsengellér, JSJSup 98 (Leiden: Brill, 2004), 23–40 (39); Gruen, *Diaspora*, 148–58.

9 As observed by Beattie and Davies, "Hebrew," 82 n. 32. The choice to name the protagonists Tobit and Tobias is also especially interesting in light of Nehemiah's opposition to Tobiah, who appears to identify as from northern Israelite stock, and the

the term *Ioudaios*.[10] In keeping with this distinction, the book emphasizes the northern identity of its protagonists and their relationship to their southern kindred from the very start, explaining that the tribe of Naphtali had "deserted from the house of David and Jerusalem" (1:4).[11] Nevertheless, Tobit demonstrates his righteousness by refusing to sacrifice "to the calf that Jeroboam the king of Israel had erected in Dan" (1:5),[12] instead going alone to Jerusalem for the proper festivals (1:6). It is noteworthy that instead of calling Jeroboam "son of Nebat," as is typical in Kings, the narrator draws further attention to the distinction between northern Israelites and southern Judahites by introducing Jeroboam as "the king of Israel." Once in exile, Tobit and his family continue to observe proper ritual regulations such as burial of the dead and keeping the festivals (though obviously not in Jerusalem) and especially by maintaining the boundaries set between Israel and the nations.[13]

The very existence of a novella like Tobit is evidence for a continued concern for the northern tribes among early Jews. In case there was any doubt that the promised restoration of all Israel was still possible in light

---

prominence of the Tobiad family after that period (cf. Josephus, *Ant.*, 12.157–236). See pp. 156–61.

[10] The only exception is found in the Sinaiticus version of Tob 11:17, which says "all the *Ioudaioi* in Nineveh" (πᾶσιν τοῖς Ιουδαίοις τοῖς οὖσιν ἐν Νινευη) rejoice upon learning of Tobit's good fortune. The shorter recension (G¹) from Vaticanus/Alexandrinus, on the other hand, has only "all his kinsmen in Nineveh" (πᾶσι τοῖς ἐν Νινευη ἀδελφοῖς αὐτοῦ). Since G^II generally appears to be the earlier version and the *Ioudaios* reading introduces a potential anachronism, the G^II reading was more likely corrected by the later editor (or a scribe) to produce the G¹ reading, which preserves the distinction observed elsewhere in the book. In either case, the G^II reading involves an uncharacteristic slip either by the author or a later translator, editor, or scribe, though the group indicated by *Ioudaioi* is ambiguous and does not clearly refer to a northerner (like Tobit). As such, it could refer to Tobit's southern kinsmen taken into Assyrian exile. But *pace* Richard J. Bauckham, "Anna of the Tribe of Asher," in *Gospel Women: Studies of the Named Women in the Gospels*, GTA 25 (London: Bloomsbury, 2002), 77–107 (77), it is nevertheless a significant departure from the language found elsewhere in the book and does not suggest that the terms were understood as equivalent.

[11] Miller, "Group Labels," 108, "Since one of the book's main emphases is the unity of the twelve tribes of Israel and the necessity of their restoration, it is also possible that 'Israel' was used, at least in part, for its covenantal or eschatological significance."

[12] G¹ omits the reference to Jeroboam and instead talks of sacrifice to "Baal the heifer." *Pace* Fitzmyer, *Tobit*, 106, the reference to Jeroboam's apostasy is not "a peculiar anachronism" but a commonplace understanding in the Second Temple period with respect to Jeroboam's apostasy as beginning the period of the covenantal curses, a view derived from 2 Kgs 17:5–17. E.g., Josephus, *Ant.* 8.271; 9.280–82; CD 7:12–13; 14:1; 4QMMT^c 19.

[13] Bauckham, "Tobit as a Parable," 145.

of the apparent absence of northern Israelites, this romantic fairy tale provides assurance that some northerners have indeed retained their Israelite heritage and tribal distinctions in exile. Indeed, the fundamental plot conflict is between Tobit's family and the conditions of exile. The three misfortunes to be overcome – Tobit's loss of property, Tobit's blindness, and Sarah's lack of a husband – are personal manifestations of the descriptions of Israel's punishment in Deuteronomy and the prophets.[14] Above all, the protagonists must overcome (with divine help) the central challenge of exile: maintenance of their distinctive tribal ancestry, which chiefly depends on endogamy.[15] Inasmuch as the misfortunes of Tobias and Sarah serve as obstacles to their marriage and consequent production of heirs, they specifically highlight the difficulty of maintaining their tribal heritage in exile.[16] Even the basic geography of the exiled community is a major obstacle.[17] Although Tobias and Sarah are from the same family in Naphtali (Tob 1:1; 3:7; 6:11) and were set apart for one another from the creation of the world (6:18), they are unknown to one another because of the dispersion of the Israelites. The

---

[14] Bauckham, "Tobit as a Parable," 147–49, lists the following parallels: (1) The plundering of Tobit's goods mirrors the predictions of Deut 28:30–31, 33, 51; cf. 2 Kgs 21:14. (2) Blindness matches closely with Isa 59:9–10; Lam 3:1–2, 6; Mic 7:8–9. Bauckham does not mention it in this section but notes elsewhere (153) that Isa 9:1–2 is also noteworthy as it specifically mentions blindness in connection with the exile of Naphtali. (3) Sarah's desolation mirrors that of Jerusalem in Isa 62:4; Lam 1:1; etc. Bauckham also discusses other connections between Tobit and the prophecies of exile throughout, such as the connection between Anna spending her waking hours watching the road for Tobias as fulfilling the curse of Deut 28:32. See also Will Soll, "Misfortune and Exile in Tobit: The Juncture of a Fairy Tale Source and Deuteronomic Theology," *CBQ* 51.2 (1989): 209–31 (222).

[15] Cf. Amy-Jill Levine, "Diaspora as Metaphor: Bodies and Boundaries in the Book of Tobit," in *Diaspora Jews and Judaism: Essays in Honor of, and in Dialogue with, A. Thomas Kraabel*, eds. J. A. Overman and Robert S. MacLennan, SFSHJ 41 (Atlanta: Scholars Press, 1992), 105–18 (105); Jill Hicks-Keeton, "Already/Not Yet: Eschatological Tension in the Book of Tobit," *JBL* 132.1 (2013): 97–117 (115).

[16] Cf. Bauckham, "Tobit as a Parable," 141.

[17] Levine, "Diaspora as Metaphor," 106, observes that even the historical and geographical inaccuracies in the story function to call attention to the fact that "things are not as they should be" in exile, while endogamy provides the stability otherwise missing in this unstable world. For a list of the historical and geographical inaccuracies in the book of Tobit, see Carey A. Moore, *Tobit: A New Translation with Introduction and Commentary*, AB 40 (Garden City: Doubleday, 1996), 10; Hicks-Keeton, "Already/Not Yet," 112–13 n. 39 observes that these inaccuracies function to make Tobit ahistorical and potentially more accessible to the Hellenistic-era reader.

miraculous intervention of angel-in-disguise Raphael/Azariah is ultimately required if the exile-crossed lovers are to preserve their family line.[18]

A key point that is often overlooked, however, is that endogamy for
Tobit does not merely involve the avoidance of gentile intermarriage but
extends to the preservation of tribal, clan, and familial lines. The solution
is not merely a matter of, as Levine suggests, marrying "a nice Jewish girl"
to maintain Jewish identity in the diaspora.[19] On the contrary, *the narrative depends on the fact that the protagonists are not Jews at all* – they are
Naphtalites in danger of losing their distinctive tribal association due to
the diaspora.[20] If Sarah were to marry a Jewish man, that would be as
much a tragedy in this narrative as if she were to marry a gentile, for in
doing so she would lose her tribal distinction, and her father (who had no
other child) would be left without an inheritance in Israel at the restoration, a hope without which there was no reason to live (Tob 3:15).[21] The
concern for specific tribal membership is highlighted throughout the
book, from Tobit's precision about his geographical origins (Tob 1:2)
and his acts of charity primarily for people of his own tribe (1:3, 16), to
his marriage within his own tribe and clan (1:9) and expectations for his
son to do the same (4:12).[22] The importance of maintaining not only
Israelite identity but also specific tribal distinctions is especially accentuated when Tobit quizzes a young "Israelite" (in fact the angel Raphael)
about his tribal heritage to determine his trustworthiness as a traveling
companion for his son (Tob 5:5–12). The familial language that pervades

---

[18] Bauckham, "Tobit as a Parable," 148, observes that Raphael's name itself echoes the
theme of God's healing (רפא) in numerous restoration promises, as does the vocabulary of
healing throughout Tobit.

[19] Levine, "Diaspora as Metaphor," 117. Cf. Soll, "Misfortune and Exile in Tobit," 225;
Pekka Pitkänen, "Family Life and Ethnicity in Early Israel and in Tobit," in *Studies in the
Book of Tobit: A Multidisciplinary Approach*, ed. Mark R. J. Bredin, LSTS 55 (London:
T&T Clark, 2006), 104 (106).

[20] "One would expect that Tobit would limit his scope to fellow Israelites, but he seems to
go even further in focusing on fellow Naphtalites only, as far as marriage is concerned"
(Pitkänen, "Family Life," 113).

[21] A precedent established with the daughters of Zelophehad in Num 27, 36; Josh 17:3–6.
Cf. Will Soll, "The Family as Scriptural and Social Construct in Tobit," in *The Function
of Scripture in Early Jewish and Christian Tradition*, eds. Craig A. Evans and Jack
A. Sanders, JSNTSup 154 (Sheffield: Sheffield Academic, 1998), 166–75 (171).

[22] Bauckham, "Tobit as a Parable," 151–52. Cf. also Soll, "Family," 173–74; Levine,
"Diaspora as Metaphor," 107–08; Irene Nowell, "The Book of Tobit: An Ancestral
Story," in *Intertextual Studies in Ben Sira and Tobit: Essays in Honor of Alexander
A. Di Lella, O. E. M*, eds. Jeremy Corley and Vincent Skemp, CBQMS 38 (Washington,
DC: Catholic Biblical Association of America, 2005), 3–13 (12).

the narrative further highlights the importance of endogamy not only within Israel but specifically within tribe and clan.[23]

This emphasis on the maintenance of tribal and familial distinctions is explicitly tied to eschatological hopes throughout the book. Tobit, for example, enjoins his son to marry within his father's tribe specifically so that his posterity may inherit the land as promised to the patriarchs (4:12). Levine notes that for Tobit, "The telos of endogamy is thus the ingathering of the exiles. By identity-determining kinship ties the land is reobtained; the land is now the result, rather than the origin, of community self-definition."[24] Jill Hicks-Keeton adds,

The hope of Israel's restoration grounds Tobit's practical advice. Tobias should conduct himself – as Tobit has – in a way that will preserve Israelite identity so that they will be returned to the promised land. This relationship between the theological affirmation and the ethical exhortations therefore emerges: Israelites in the Diaspora should act in a way that both expects and engenders God's faithfulness in the ingathering.[25]

These eschatological expectations so central to the narrative are made especially explicit in the final two chapters, in which Tobit rejoices at the reversals of his misfortunes (ch. 13) and gives his final words and blessing before his death (ch. 14). Tobit's declaration of praise after his son's wedding – and the discovery that the reversals of misfortune were all due to divine intervention through the angel Raphael in response to his own and Sarah's prayers – treats his own story as paradigmatic for the people of Israel as a whole. That is, God's action on Tobit's behalf serves as evidence that God has not abandoned Israel in exile but will surely restore them as promised. The passage is rife with restoration-eschatological themes,[26] emphasizing both the mercy of God and the importance of repentance and righteousness in the punishment of diaspora to facilitate the restoration:

---

[23] On fraternal/familial language and relationships in Tobit, see Vincent T. M. Skemp, "ΑΔΕΛΦΟΣ and the Theme of Kinship in Tobit," *EThL* 75 (1999): 92–103; Hicks-Keeton, "Already/Not Yet," 115–16; Soll, "Family"; Paul Deselaers, *Das Buch Tobit: Studien zu seiner Entstehung, Komposition und Theologie*, OBO 43 (Göttingen: Vandenhoeck & Ruprecht, 1982), 309–15.

[24] Levine, "Diaspora as Metaphor," 108–09.

[25] Hicks-Keeton, "Already/Not Yet," 115–16.

[26] Weitzman, "Allusion, Artifice, and Exile," has convincingly demonstrated that the hymn of praise in Tobit 13 is modeled on and alludes to the Song of Moses in Deut 32 and that the allusive themes of this song have been "shaped by a larger allusive strategy that governs Tobit as a whole" (50).

Acknowledge him before the nations, O children of Israel;
       for he has scattered (*diespeiren*) you among them.
He has shown you his greatness even there . . .
In the land of my exile (αἰχμαλωσίας) I acknowledge him,
       and show his power and majesty to a nation of sinners . . .
"Turn back, you sinners, and do what is right before him;
       perhaps he may look with favor upon you and show you mercy." . . .
A bright light will shine to all the ends of the earth;
       many nations will come to you from far away,
   the inhabitants of the remotest parts of the earth to your holy name,
       bearing gifts in their hands for the King of heaven.
Generation after generation will give joyful praise in you;
       the name of the chosen city will endure forever.

(Tob 13:3–4a, 6e, 11 NRSV)[27]

Whereas Tob 3:2–6 presented a lament for the circumstances of exile, this prayer involves the reversal of those circumstances, with the wording of 13:5b closely paralleling 3:4b, thereby highlighting the reversal of the very scattering among the nations described in the early chapters.[28] Tobit goes on to declare that the "children of the righteous . . . will be gathered together" and that Jerusalem would be rebuilt with gold and precious stones to serve as the Lord's house once again (13:14–15) – an especially remarkable statement given that in the context of the narrative the first temple had not yet been destroyed (cf. 14:4). Tobit's hope is that a "remnant of my descendants should survive to see [Jerusalem's] glory" (13:16), again emphasizing the importance of the survival of his family line.

By maintaining their Naphtalite heritage and preserving their right to inheritance in the land, the protagonists of the book of Tobit demonstrate their continued faith in the coming restoration that will not only involve Judah and Jerusalem but even Naphtali, the first tribe to have been taken into exile.[29] The prophets, of course, promised the restoration of all Israel, including the specific mention of Naphtali in one especially widely cited prophecy:

---

[27] G^{II} has a lacuna from 13:6–10a, likely the result of parablepsis, but these verses are found in G^I and some of the material from the lacuna is found in Aramaic 4Q196, which suggests that Sinaiticus is indeed defective. See Fitzmyer, *Tobit*, 304.

[28] As observed by Bradley C. Gregory, "The Relationship between the Poor in Judea and Israel Under Foreign Rule: Sirach 35:14–26 among Second Temple Prayers and Hymns," *JSJ* 42.3 (2011): 311–27 (323).

[29] Cf. 2 Kgs 15:29.

Previously he brought the land of Zebulun and the land of Naphtali into contempt,[30] but finally he will make the way by the sea glorious, the land beyond the Jordan, Galilee of the nations.

> The people who walked in darkness
> have seen a great light.
> Those who lived in a land of darkness
> on them the light has shined.
> (Isa 9:1–2 [MT 8:23–9:1])

The preservation of specific tribal lineages in exile is instrumental to the promised restoration, for if, as Levine asserts, "Naphtali, like the rest of the Northern tribes, permanently lost both its connection to the land and its self-identity,"[31] how could the restoration promised by the prophets, one that includes Naphtali, come to pass? How could Naphtali be restored if there is no Naphtali left to restore? This is of course the very question underlying the book itself; the continuation of Tobit's Naphtalite line is critically important to the fulfillment of the prophets' promises and requires God's providential oversight in the midst of exile. The book of Tobit thus reassures its protagonists – and through them the reader – that a faithful remnant of Naphtali *must* be preserved somewhere, awaiting the final restoration. As Bauckham notes, "A narrative so embedded in such specific tribal loyalty can scarcely serve as the paradigm for a restoration of the nation in a sense that would exclude this tribe from it."[32] The story of Tobit and his family thus serves as a model for the survival of all the various tribes of Israel, without whom the restoration cannot be complete.[33]

From his vantage point at the beginning of Israel's exile, Tobit then addresses the remainder of that exile in his deathbed testament,[34] directing his son to flee with his family to Media where they would be "safer than in Assyria and Babylon" (Tob 14:4) because of the impending destruction of Nineveh prophesied by Nahum, thereby putting Tobit's faithful family in one of the traditional locations of the northern tribes (as

---

[30] LXX: "Do this quickly, O land of Zebulun, land of Naphtali."

[31] Levine, "Diaspora as Metaphor," 107; cf. the objections on this point in Bauckham, "Tobit as a Parable," 154–59.

[32] Bauckham, "Tobit as a Parable," 151–52.

[33] Bauckham, "Tobit as a Parable," 152.

[34] On the Deuteronomic themes of Tobit's testament in ch. 14, see Alexander A. Di Lella, "The Deuteronomic Background of the Farewell Discourse in Tob 14:3–11," *CBQ* 41.3 (1979): 380–89; Alexander A. Di Lella, "A Study of Tobit 14:10 and Its Intertextual Parallels," *CBQ* 71.3 (2009): 497–506.

already observed in Josephus above).[35] The exile itself will continue far longer, scattering "all of our kindred, inhabitants of the land of Israel," including the desolation of both Samaria and Jerusalem (14:4). Most notably, Tobit does not portray the return from Babylon and building of the Second Temple as the end of the exile. Instead, Tobit treats that return as only a partial mercy preceding the actual times of fulfillment:

> But God will again have mercy on them, and God will bring them back into the land of Israel; and they will rebuild the temple of God, but not like the first one until the period when the times of fulfillment shall come. After this they all will return from their exile and will rebuild Jerusalem in splendor; and in it the temple of God will be rebuilt, just as the prophets of Israel have said concerning it. Then the nations in the whole world will all be converted (ἐπιστρέψουσιν) and worship God in truth. They will all abandon their idols, which deceitfully have led them into their error; and in righteousness they will praise the eternal God. All the Israelites who are saved in those days and are truly mindful of God will be gathered together; they will go to Jerusalem and live in safety forever in the land of Abraham, and it will be given over to them. Those who sincerely love God will rejoice, but those who commit sin and injustice will vanish from all the earth.
>
> (Tob 14:5–7 NRSV)

This passage is critically important, as each statement contrasts the final fulfillment of the prophets' restoration promises with the return from Babylon, emphasizing the inadequacy of that return and of the Second Temple.[36] Thus, like so much of what we have already examined, Tobit considers the return from Babylon incomplete at best. Yes, the Jerusalem temple has been rebuilt, but it remains inferior to the first one (14:5), and the promised restoration only comes some time later, "when the proper time is fulfilled" (οὗ ἂν πληρωθῇ ὁ χρόνος τῶν καιρῶν; 14:5). At that time, in contrast to small return to Jerusalem from Babylon, *all* of the exiles (ἐπιστρέψουσιν ἐκ τῆς αἰχμαλωσίας αὐτῶν πάντες) will return and rebuild Jerusalem "in splendor" or "honorably" (ἐντίμως; 14:5) as opposed to the paltry rebuilding job after the return from Babylon. And in that glorious

---

[35] Levine, "Diaspora as Metaphor," 107 n. 9 points out that "Tobit is consistent with if not the origin of other notices that the so-called 'ten lost tribes' were living in Media and its environs," an explanation that reappears in other literature throughout the Second Temple period. Cf. also the discussion in Yehoshua M. Grintz, "Tobit, Book of," *EncJud* 15:1183–87 (1186).

[36] Knibb, "The Exile in the Literature of the Intertestamental Period," 268: "There could hardly be a more explicit statement of the view … that the return from the exile in the sixth century had only a provisional character, and that the post-exilic cultus was defective. The decisive change in Israel's condition of exile was only to come when the 'times of the age' were completed." See also Fuller, *The Restoration of Israel*, 30–31.

Jerusalem, the temple will be rebuilt just as the prophets of Israel have said concerning it – unlike the inadequate contemporary building that comes nowhere close to fulfilling the expansive promises of the prophets. Then all the nations of the world will abandon their idols and worship Israel's God, in sharp contrast to the gentile domination throughout the Second Temple period. Finally, the passage specifies that the "all" who will be saved among Israel are those who are "mindful of God in truth" (that is, those like Tobit and his family), while the unjust will disappear, having been eliminated through the exile. As Bauckham explains,

> Tobit's eschatological prospect is not simply the restoration of the exiles of Judah, but, more importantly for the message of the book, the return of the exiles of the northern tribes to the land of Israel and their reconciliation to Jerusalem as the national and cultic centre.[37]

We have already observed that the same eschatological expectations expressed in these final chapters also govern the central narrative, which shows how God has been actively engaged in preserving a remnant to restore when the time is right, and that preservation is itself the assurance of the final ingathering.[38] Tobit's story – and the divine assistance he receives – serves as a paradigm for God's continued oversight of all of

---

[37] Bauckham, "Tobit as a Parable," 141.

[38] See Hicks-Keeton, "Already/Not Yet"; Cf. Manfred Oeming, "Jewish Identity in the Eastern Diaspora in Light of the Book of Tobit," in *Judah and the Judeans in the Achaemenid Period: Negotiating Identity in an International Context*, eds. Oded Lipschits, Gary N. Knoppers, and Manfred Oeming (Winona Lake: Eisenbrauns, 2011), 545–62 (557). Some scholars (e.g., Frank Zimmermann, *The Book of Tobit*, Dropsie College ed., Jewish Apocryphal Literature (New York: Harper, 1958); Deselaers, *Das Buch Tobit*), however, have found the overt eschatological nature of these chapters to be so at odds with the rest of the book that they declared them to be later additions. This position has become increasingly untenable, first by the presence of these chapters among the fragments of Tobit found among the Dead Sea Scrolls, and second by better literary analysis demonstrating the integrity of Tobit as a whole and the thematic correspondence between these chapters and the narrative itself. For a fuller discussion of the integrity of Tobit and why "there is no serious reason to think that the Book of Tobit, as we have it today, is not integral," see Fitzmyer, *Tobit*, 42–45 (here 45) and Irene Nowell, "Tobit: Narrative Technique and Theology" (PhD diss., The Catholic University of America, 1983). For fuller discussions of the Deuteronomic themes of the final two chapters and their connection to the rest of the story, see Weitzman, "Allusion, Artifice, and Exile"; Di Lella, "Deuteronomic Background"; Stuart Weeks, "A Deuteronomic Heritage in Tobit?," in *Changes in Scripture: Rewriting and Interpreting Authoritative Traditions in the Second Temple period*, eds. Hanne von Weissberg, Juha Pakkala, and Marko Marttila (Berlin: de Gruyter, 2011), 389–404.

pious Israel in exile.[39] In so doing, the book of Tobit provides answers to natural questions about Israel's fate among those looking forward to Israel's restoration but questioning how all Israel could be restored if there were no northern Israelites remaining to be restored.[40] The answer is that God has continued to preserve a pious remnant of all of Israel – even the first small tribe to have been taken into exile. A remnant of northerners have indeed remained faithful in exile, keeping their lineages pure and awaiting the "times of fulfillment" when they will be restored together with the rest of Israel. The book of Tobit therefore demonstrates that the restoration of all Israel – explicitly understood to be more than the Jews alone – is assured sometime in the future when the proper time is fulfilled.[41]

Judith

The book of Judith tells the heroic story of a beautiful and pious widow who saves her city of Bethulia by seducing and then beheading the

---

[39] Hicks-Keeton, "Already/Not Yet," 110. Cf. also Bauckham, "Tobit as a Parable," 151–54; David McCracken, "Narration and Comedy in the Book of Tobit," *JBL* (1995): 401–18 (417–18).

[40] Bauckham's suggestion that the book was written for an audience of northern Israelites ("Tobit as a Parable," 154–63) is implausible. Firstly, the idea that "the Jews of northern Mesopotamia were predominantly descended from the northern Israelite exiles ... while those of Media were descended from those Israelites of the northern tribes who settled there in the eighth century, perhaps augmented later by others" (158) is fatally flawed by the fact that these "Jews" would by definition have lost their distinct northern identities – thus being called "Jews." That distinct tribal heritage is precisely what is at issue in Tobit, and although I see no reason to reject the idea that many Jews in this period were descended in part from northern stock, the mixture between different tribes and groups is a challenge to an eschatological expectation that "all Israel" will be restored, including a distinct remnant from each specific tribe. *Pace* Bauckham and others who situate the book in the eastern diaspora, I therefore agree with Fitzmyer, *Tobit*, 54 in finding the book more likely to have arisen in or around the Levant, where the absence of northern Israelites was evident and imagining various tribes awaiting restoration in the unknown East would be less far-fetched, since there would be no readily apparent empirical evidence to the counterpart. For a list of those taking an eastern diaspora view, see Moore, *Tobit*, 42–43.

[41] Fuller, *The Restoration of Israel*, 29 n. 62: "[T]he narrative as a whole emphasizes that the Diaspora community should live righteously in view of the restoration." Fuller is mistaken, however, in arguing that "the implicit appeal of the writing is for all Jews [*sic*] to return to the Land" (32), as the narrative presumes that such a return must be divinely administered – not to mention that the return must include Naphtalites and other Israelites in addition to Jews. The story thus advocates righteous living in the diaspora and expectation of restoration but not an attempt to return absent divine intervention.

Assyrian general Holofernes. Like Tobit, Judith is ostensibly set in the Assyrian period, so it should come as no surprise that Judith prefers "Israel" and cognates (which occur fifty times) and entirely eschews the term *Ioudaios*. Nevertheless, the text's numerous anachronisms and historical inaccuracies belie the text's ancient setting and signal the reader to see through the Assyrian-period veneer and understand the story as applicable to the contemporary (Hasmonean) period.[42] For example, the antagonists in the story are "Nebuchadnezzar, king of the Assyrians," depicted as ruling from Nineveh (1:1),[43] and his chief general Holofernes,[44] who loses his head while prosecuting the campaign against Judith's city of Bethulia, the name of which is a pun along the lines of "virginville"[45] – all symbolic names and settings indicating the story's fantastic and parabolic nature. As Philip Esler explains, "the text announces at the outset that it will draw on history, but will take extreme liberties in the manner it does so."[46]

The story itself has previously been labeled a novella, folktale, legend, or parabolic history,[47] but it seems to fit best into a category of "ludic"

---

[42] Ellen Juhl Christiansen observes that the contemporary readers would easily have gotten this message, comparing the fictional setting of Judith to Hans Christian Andersen's fairy tale, "The Ugly Duckling," "which for all Danish readers clearly is a story about Andersen himself, how he grew up in poverty and became famous, while readers from other countries would easily miss this point" ("Judith: Defender of Israel – Preserver of the Temple," in *A Pious Seductress: Studies in the Book of Judith*, ed. Géza G. Xeravits, DCLS 14 [Berlin: de Gruyter, 2012], 70–84 [71 n. 3]). On Judith as a Hasmonean-era composition, see Benedikt Otzen, *Tobit and Judith*, GAP 11 (London: Continuum, 2002), 132–35; Carey A. Moore, *Judith: A New Translation with Introduction and Commentary*, AB 40 (New York: Doubleday, 1985), 67–70; Philip F. Esler, "Ludic History in the Book of Judith: The Reinvention of Israelite Identity?," *BibInt* 10.2 (2002): 107–43 (107).

[43] Esler compares the story's introduction of Nebuchadnezzar as king of the Assyrians as "akin to beginning with, 'When Napoleon was the emperor of Russia'" ("Ludic History," 117).

[44] This is a Persian name and may be linked to the Holofernes who prosecuted a campaign against Egypt on behalf of Artaxerxes III Ochus in the mid fourth century BCE. Cf. Esler, "Ludic History," 119–20.

[45] Ophir and Rosen-Zvi, *Goy*, 109; Judith H. Newman, "Bethulia," *NIDB* 1:449.

[46] Esler, "Ludic History," 117.

[47] For Judith as a novella or folktale, see Moore, *Judith*, 71–78. This category is further parsed into "legend" by Monika Hellmann, *Judit – eine Frau im Spannungsfeld von Autonomie und göttlicher Führung. Studie über eine Frauengestalt des Alten Testament*, EHS (Frankfurt: Lang, 1992), 52–62 and Otzen, *Tobit and Judith*, 125–26. "Parabolic history" (parabolische Geschichts-erzählung) is suggested by Ernst Haag, *Studien zum Buche Judith: Seine theologische Deutung und literarische Eigenart*, TThSt (Trier: Paulinus, 1963), 63 and Hans J. Lundager Jensen, "Juditbogen," in *Tradition og nybrud. Jødedommen i hellenistik tid*, eds. Troels Engberg-Petersen and Nils Peter

alternate historical fantasy.[48] Such stories are superficially situated in the past but in fact take place in an imagined world clearly diverging from the actual (typically well-known) past, in some cases reversing the winners and losers of key conflicts or enacting virtual vengeance on past villains to the delight of the contemporary audience, akin to several recent films by Quentin Tarantino.[49] Whereas the historical Nebuchadnezzar of Babylon had destroyed Jerusalem and the temple centuries after the Assyrians had destroyed and scattered the kingdom of Israel, the book of Judith imagines a world in which these outcomes were drastically different, with Israel, Jerusalem, and the temple preserved by the heroic actions of a piously deceptive widow. This time, the story will have a happy ending.[50]

This alternate history only thinly veils its connection to the Hasmonean period, as the "Assyrians" (Ἀσσύριοι) serve as an easy representation of Seleucid Syria (Συρία). Judith, on the other hand, stands as the model for those sharing her name, "Jew/Jewess" (though she is from the tribe of Simeon), and also evokes the figure of Judah the Maccabee, the masculine counterpart of her name.[51] Lest a reader miss these signals, the book explains that the "Israelites who lived in Judaea" (Jdt 4:1) who heard of Holofernes' approach were terrified "for they had only recently returned from exile" and reconsecrated the altar and temple (4:3; cf. also 5:18–19),[52] further emphasizing the fanciful nature of the Assyrian setting. Placing the story in the Assyrian period does, however, symbolically represent Seleucid rule as but a continuation of the foreign domination stretching back to the Assyrians, with their defeat through Judith's actions

Lemche, FBE (Kopenhaven: Museum Tusculanum, 1990), 153–89 (158) but protested as ontologically prioritizing violence and war rather than peace by Christiansen, "Judith," 70–71 n. 1.

[48] Cf. Esler, "Ludic History," 117–21. On Judith as thereby creating a "counter-discourse" in the context of Hasmonean propaganda, see Benedikt Eckhardt, "Reclaiming Tradition: The Book of Judith and Hasmonean Politics," *JSP* 18.4 (2009): 243–63.

[49] E.g., "Inglourious Basterds" (2009) or "Django Unchained" (2012). The writing of "virtual" or "counterfactual" history is a recent phenomenon even in scholarly historiography, as seen in Niall Ferguson, ed., *Virtual History: Alternatives and Counterfactuals* (London: Picador, 1997) and J. Cheryl Exum, *Virtual History and the Bible* (Leiden: Brill, 2000).

[50] Esler, "Ludic History," 118.

[51] Cf. Tal Ilan, *Jewish Women in Greco-Roman Palestine: An Inquiry into Image and Status*, TSAJ 44 (Tübingen: Mohr Siebeck, 2006), 54 n. 28; Esler, "Ludic History," 136. Cf. also Nicolae Roddy, "The Way It Wasn't: The Book of Judith as Anti-Hasmonean Propaganda," *Studia Hebraica* 8 (2008): 269–77, which argues that Judith is highly critical of Hasmonean policies and thereby fancifully portrays how things *should* have been conducted.

[52] Note the exceedingly negative use of *diaspora* in 5:19.

marking the beginning of the end (or the end of the beginning) of that period. In the fantasy world of the story, Judith's actions entirely erase the consequences and memory not only of the Babylonian Exile but also of the initial Assyrian victory over Israel.

It is also worth noting that the "Israelites" throughout the story – in sharp contrast to the biblical stories – are consistently portrayed as faithful and righteous, which puts them in position to receive divine deliverance. In this sense, the message of the book of Judith is similar to that of 1 Maccabees in that the victories of the Hasmonean period are suggestively portrayed as the beginning of an age of righteousness and divine favor. That is, like the activity of Judah the Maccabee in 1 Maccabees, the righteousness represented by Judith herself is salvific for the larger body of Israel and is part of the divine plan for Israel's salvation, including not only Judaea but traditionally northern territory such as Samaria (1:9; 4:4) and the Jezreel Valley (3:9).[53] Such a reading provides an explanation for why, despite the territorial setting of Judaea throughout the work, Judith is the only figure associated with the corresponding ethnonym or tribal label for that territory (her name). That is, she represents *Jewish* righteousness and action ultimately leading to the salvation of all Israel. Remarkably, however, Judith herself is not in fact descended from Judah but rather Simeon (Jdt 8:1; 9:2),[54] and the geographic location of Bethulia, which is suggestive of Shechem (Jdt 4:6; 6:11),[55] further reinforces the larger Israelite vision of the book. That is, when Israel is unified under Jewish authority based in Jerusalem, all Israel enjoys God's favor.

Goodblatt has argued that Judith should be understood as a representative example of how the people of Hasmonean Judaea typically identified themselves, calling the state Judah/Judaea (cf. Jdt 1:12; 3:9; 4:1, 3, 7, 13, 8:21; 11:19) but the people by the alleged insider term "Israel," thus

---

[53] For a discussion of the oddity of Judith thereby being the only "Jew" in the story, see Esler, "Ludic History," 136–37.

[54] Beattie and Davies, "Hebrew," 82 n. 32, mistakenly conclude on the basis of the name of Judith's husband that she is from the tribe of Manasseh. Nevertheless, that her husband's name is connected with "forgetting" (Gen 51:51) may be yet another ludic wink from the author.

[55] Judith H. Newman, "Bethulia," *NIDB* 1:449. *Pace* Christiansen, "Judith," 71, who concludes that "Bethulia is without a doubt another name for Jerusalem." But Jerusalem appears eighteen times in the book and is consistently depicted as a separate place from Bethulia, which is located in the northern region. On the northern location of Bethulia in Judith, see also Otzen, *Tobit and Judith*, 94–97; Moore, *Judith*, 150–51.

confirming Kuhn's model.[56] But the historical-fantasy genre and symbolic nature of the story should caution against such a straightforward transference of its terminology to the contemporary Hasmonean world – unless, of course, one wishes to argue that they typically called Antiochus "Nebuchadnezzar," the Seleucids "Assyria," the Seleucid capital "Nineveh," and their neighbors "Canaanites." Instead, it is more suitable to understand Judith's use of "Israel" terminology as part of the Assyrian-period framing with the effect of connecting the contemporary (faithful) inhabitants of Judaea with their Israelite forebears. "Israel" is once again preferred because the subjects in question are not (at least ostensibly) contemporary Jews but rather "Israelites" of the imagined past.

Jubilees

The second-century BCE book of Jubilees is an extended retelling of the pre-Mosaic past to alleviate difficulties found in Genesis and Exodus and support specific halakhic interpretations,[57] such as in calendrical

---

[56] Goodblatt, "Israelites Who Reside in Judah," 80–82.

[57] Jubilees was originally written in Hebrew but survived in Ge'ez (Ethiopic), likely through an intermediate Greek translation. Hebrew fragments from fourteen different copies of the book were found among the Dead Sea Scrolls. These finds have confirmed the Ge'ez version as reasonably faithful to the wording of the Hebrew copies. For more on the text of Jubilees, see James C. VanderKam, "Recent Scholarship on the Book of Jubilees," *CurBR* 6.3 (2008): 405–31 (406–09) and James C. VanderKam, *The Book of Jubilees: A Critical Text*, 2 vols. CSCO (Leuven: Peeters, 1989) and the resources cited in each. The book was written sometime before 100 BCE, but there is some debate as to when in the second century BCE it falls. For more on the dating of Jubilees, see VanderKam, "Jubilees," 407–09; Jonathan A. Goldstein, "The Date of the Book of Jubilees," *Proceedings of the American Academy for Jewish Research* 50 (1983): 63–86; Michael Segal, *The Book of Jubilees: Rewritten Bible, Redaction, Ideology and Theology*, JSJSup 117 (Leiden: Brill, 2007), 35–41. For Jubilees as "rewritten Bible," see Sidnie A. White Crawford, "The Rewritten Bible at Qumran," in *The Hebrew Bible and Qumran*, ed. James H. Charlesworth (Bibal Press, 1998), 173–95 (183–84), but note the problems inherent to that terminology as discussed by Crawford (174–77) and Moshe J. Bernstein, "Rewritten Bible: A Generic Category Which has Outlived Its Usefulness?," *Text* 22 (2005): 169–96. For Jubilees as an apocalypse, see John J. Collins, "The Genre of the Book of Jubilees," in *A Teacher for All Generations: Essays in Honor of James C. VanderKam*, eds. Eric F. Mason et al., JSJSup 2 (Leiden: Brill, 2012), 737–55; Leslie Baynes, *The Heavenly Book Motif in Judeo-Christian Apocalypses, 200 BCE–200 CE*, JSJSup 152 (Leiden: Brill, 2012), 109–34; Martha Himmelfarb, "Torah, Testimony, and Heavenly Tablets: The Claim to Authority of the Book of Jubilees," in *A Multiform Heritage: Studies on Early Judaism and Christianity in Honor of Robert A. Kraft*, ed. Benjamin G. Wright (Atlanta: Scholars Press, 1999), 19–29 (21–25). Contra Todd

matters.[58] Given its pre-Mosaic context, it should be no surprise that Jubilees uses the term Israel and cognates 112 times but avoids *Yehudim* and cognates. The book features two eschatological pericopes: 1:5–29 and 23:8–31,[59] each of which draws heavily from Deuteronomy, particularly Deut 29–31,[60] with Jub 1:15 reading Deut 30:1–2 together with Jeremiah 29:13–14 to establish the restoration-eschatological model that governs the rest of the book.[61] Significantly, although Jubilees is obviously aware of the returns from Babylon narrated in Ezra-Nehemiah, the book does not understand those events as the promised eschatological restoration.[62] Instead, Israel's restoration cannot have taken place until the Torah is properly interpreted and faithfully obeyed – obedience and restoration are interconnected (Jub 23:24–31).[63] The

R. Hanneken, *The Subversion of the Apocalypses in the Book of Jubilees* (Atlanta: Society of Biblical Literature, 2012).

[58] For more on Jubilees and calendrical matters, see VanderKam, "Jubilees," 413–15, 421–23; Annie Jaubert, "Le calendrier des Jubilés et de la secte de Qumrân. Ses origines bibliques," *VT* 3.3 (1953): 250–64; Annie Jaubert, "Le calendrier des Jubilés et les jours liturgiques de la semaine," *VT* 7.1 (1957): 35–61; Leora Ravid, "The Book of Jubilees and Its Calendar – A Reexamination," *DSD* 10.3 (2003): 371–94; James C. VanderKam, "2 Maccabees 6,7a and Calendrical Change in Jerusalem," *JSJ* 12.1 (1981): 52–74; James C. VanderKam, "Studies in the Chronology of the Book of Jubilees," in *From Revelation to Canon: Studies in the Hebrew Bible and Second Temple Literature* (Leiden: Brill, 2002), 522–44.

[59] The originality of these chapters to Jubilees has been questioned by both Michel Testuz, *Les idées religieuses du Livre des Jubilés* (Paris: Droz, 1960) and Gene L. Davenport, *The Eschatology of the Book of the Jubilees*, StPB 20 (Leiden: Brill, 1971), but the presence of these chapters in the Qumran copies of Jubilees suggest that they were part of the work at a very early date, and more recent work has treated these passages as integral to the book. See, for example, James M. Scott, *On Earth As in Heaven: The Restoration of Sacred Time and Sacred Space in the Book of Jubilees*, JSJSup 91 (Leiden: Brill, 2005); Lambert, "Did Israel Believe"; Wells, *Grace and Agency*, 147–63; George J. Brooke, "Exegetical Strategies in Jubilees 1–2: New Light from 4QJubilees^a," in *Studies in the Book of Jubilees*, eds. Matthias Albani, Jörg Frey, and Armin Lange, TSAJ 65 (Tübingen: Mohr Siebeck, 1997), 39–57; Ben Zion Wacholder, "Jubilees as the Super Canon: Torah-Admonition versus Torah-Commandment," in *Legal Texts and Legal Issues: Proceedings of the Second Meeting of the International Organization for Qumran Studies, Cambridge, 1995, Published in Honour of Joseph M. Baumgarten*, eds. Moshe J. Bernstein, Florentino García Martínez, and John Kampen, STDJ 23 (Leiden: Brill, 1997), 195–211.

[60] Cf. Brooke, "Exegetical Strategies in Jubilees 1–2."

[61] Wells, *Grace and Agency*, 147–49.

[62] Halpern-Amaru, "Exile and Return," 140.

[63] Wells, *Grace and Agency*, 149–50. Lambert, "Did Israel Believe," 633, has argued that Jubilees emphasizes "a dramatic, *divinely* initiated transformation of human nature … rather than a *humanly* initiated repentance" (emphasis his), thereby providing a solution to the problems of human vs. divine agency reflected in Deuteronomy. Although Lambert is correct in highlighting Jubilees' emphasis on divine transformation, VanderKam notes

book's overriding focus on chronology is deeply rooted in these eschatological hopes; the point is that God's plan for Israel's restoration continues to operate according to the ordained timetable.[64] The *telos* of history for Jubilees is therefore the eschatological restoration of Israel to obedience, such that God's will is done on earth – specifically in the land of Israel – as it is in heaven.[65] Jubilees depicts this future period in terms that suggest "a mythic recovery of paradise lost,"[66] including thousand year lifespans and eschatological blessings, along with the judgment of the wicked. Despite the Persian-period returns from Babylon, that restoration obviously remains a future hope for the implied reader of Jubilees.

SECOND TEMPLE TEXTS SET AFTER THE BABYLONIAN EXILE

In contrast to works set in a pre-exilic or northern Israelite context, the term *Ioudaios* and cognates appears frequently in Second Temple

that the return precedes the divine transformation of Israel's nature in Jubilees just as it does in Deut 30:1–10, calling into question Lambert's hard distinction between human and divine agency in Jubilees ("Jubilees," 425). Wells, *Grace and Agency*, 152, also objects that Lambert's argument assumes "that if something is divinely foreordained, it is divinely initiated," countering that Jubilees presents Israel's transformation as foreordained but still resulting from their repentance brought on by the experience of exile. Wells concludes that for Jubilees, "Restoration is on offer and must begin with Israel's turning" (161). Nevertheless, even in Wells' picture, Israel's turning is the result of the divine action of exile, which spurs Israel's repentance. Lambert has also more recently moderated his emphasis here, observing that although Jubilees does emphasize divine transformation, it does not share modern interpreters' concerns about agency (*How Repentance Became Biblical*, 126). See also John C. Endres, "Eschatological Impulses in Jubilees," in *Enoch and the Mosaic Torah: The Evidence of Jubilees*, eds. Gabriele Boccaccini and Giovanni Ibba (Grand Rapids: Eerdmans, 2009), 323–37 (328, 335); Todd R. Hanneken, "The Status and Interpretation of Jubilees in 4Q390," in *A Teacher for All Generations: Essays in Honor of James C. VanderKam*, eds. Eric F. Mason et al., JSJSup 2 (Leiden: Brill, 2012), 407–28 (427 n. 42).

[64] On the distinctive calendar and chronology of Jubilees, see Jaubert, "Le calendrier des Jubilés et de la secte de Qumrân"; Julian Morgenstern, "The Calendar of the Book of Jubilees, Its Origin and Its Character," *VT* 5.1 (1955): 34–76; Jaubert, "Le calendrier des Jubilés et les jours liturgiques de la semaine"; VanderKam, "2 Maccabees 6,7a"; Joseph M. Baumgarten, "The Calendars of the Book of Jubilees and the Temple Scroll," *VT* (1987): 71–78; VanderKam, "Chronology."

[65] Scott, *On Earth as in Heaven*, 8. See also David A. Lambert, "How the 'Torah of Moses' became Revelation: An Early, Apocalyptic Theory of Pentateuchal Origins," *JSJ* 47.1 (2016): 22–54; Baynes, *Heavenly Book*, 109–34; Florentino García Martínez, "The Heavenly Tablets in the Book of Jubilees," in *Studies in the Book of Jubilees*, eds. Matthias Albani, Jörg Frey, and Armin Lange, TSAJ 65 (Tübingen: Mohr Siebeck, 1997), 243–60.

[66] Halpern-Amaru, "Exile and Return," 142.

Table 5 *Israelites and Jews in Second Temple texts set after the*
Babylonian Exile

	Israel	Per 1,000	*Ioudaios*	Per 1,000
1 Macc	63	3.44	37	2.02
2 Macc	5	0.42	59	4.95
3 Macc	7	1.37	29	5.67
4 Macc[a]	2	0.25	1	0.13
Aristeas	0	0.00	17	1.31
Add Esth	7	3.23	5	1.38
Susanna (OG)	5	6.31	1	1.26
Susanna (θ')	3	2.65	1	0.88
Bel (OG)	0	0.00	1	1.11
Bel (θ)	0	0.00	1	1.15

[a] Although 4 Maccabees uses Israel language twice (17:22 and 18:1, each in the
context of elevated rhetoric) and *Ioudaios* and *Ioudaismos* ("Judaism") once
apiece, no clear pattern can be established from these occurrences, so 4 Macc will
not be examined in depth. The term *Ioudaikos* ("Jewish") also appears five times
in Aristeas and once in 2 Maccabees (which also includes three uses of
Ioudaismos) but appears nowhere else in the corpus discussed in this chapter.

narrative texts with a setting in the period after the Babylonian Exile. In
these texts, *Ioudaios* is regularly used to denote the contemporary people
descended from the kingdom of Judah, while Israel terminology tends to
appear in other contexts, such as prayer. In addition to works covered in
earlier chapters, this category most notably includes 3 Maccabees and the
Letter of Aristeas, along with a few minor or fragmentary examples.[67]
Table 5 shows the frequency of the two ethnonyms in these works; a
comparison with Tables 4 and 6 is instructive with respect to the frequency of the respective terms in different contexts.

3 Maccabees

The book of 3 Maccabees, written in Greek between the late third century
BCE and 70 CE, tells of the persecution and deliverance of Alexandrian

[67] E.g., Bel and the Dragon, part of the Greek additions to Daniel, in which the Babylonians
complain, "the king has become a Jew" (28). Collins, *Daniel*, 415 notes that such a
reference is in keeping with the rise of conversion in the Hasmonean period. Other
examples, such as the citations of Pseudo-Hecataeus found in Josephus or Origen, are
too fragmentary and incomplete for consideration here.

Jews in the time of Ptolemy IV Philopator (221–204 BCE).[68] When referring to the contemporary people the book consistently uses the term *Ioudaios*, which appears twenty-eight times. In contrast, "Israel" occurs only in prayer (2:6, 10, 16; 6:4, 9; 7:23) or as part of a stock reference to God, "the eternal savior of Israel" (7:16). Several prayers specifically refer to biblical Israel, reminding God of his saving action in the exodus from Egypt (2:6; 6:4) or his election of Israel (2:16).

The distinction between the two terms is sharp in 3 Maccabees, as is the overarching theme of exile and exodus, with Ptolemy twice compared to the Pharaoh of the exodus period (2:6–7; 6:4) and the prayer of the pious elder Eleazar referencing the impieties committed in exile (ἀποικία; 6:10). Gruen, however, downplays the importance of the latter reference to exile, arguing, "the sins, not the location, provide the grounds for potential destruction."[69] Nevertheless, the exilic/diaspora context and the subservient status of the Jews (and indeed "Israel," as stated in the prayers) should not be ignored, as evident from the surrounding context of the prayer and indeed the story in general.[70] After all, only a few verses earlier, Eleazar describes his people as "perishing as foreigners in a foreign land" (6:3), comparing the circumstances to the time before the exodus, and a few verses later, he concludes his prayer with the plea that God fulfill his promise not to "neglect them in the land of their enemies" (6:15; cf. Lev 26:44). Eleazar recognizes that the (possible) sins of the people may be the immediate cause of the impending destruction, but that destruction (and perhaps even those sins) are only made possible by the conditions of exile. This larger context affords more probability to Scott's suggestion that the use of *paroikia* after the Jews' deliverance (6:36; 7:19) carries the connotation of a temporary "sojourn" like that of biblical Israel (cf. Gen 47:4; Num 20:15; Deut 26:5), eventually to be ended by a new exodus.[71]

---

[68] See Sara Raup Johnson, "Maccabees, Third Book of," *EDEJ* 907–8; H. Anderson, "3 Maccabees," in *OTP*, 509–29.

[69] Gruen, "Diaspora and Homeland," 27.

[70] Noah Hacham, "The Third Book of Maccabees: Literature, History and Ideology" (PhD diss., Hebrew University of Jerusalem, 2002), 147–73, argues that a strong undercurrent in 3 Macc depicts a serious problem in the relationship between the gentile regime and the Jews.

[71] Scott, "Self-Understanding," 192; cf. also Schwartz, "Temple or City," 115, "This passage bespeaks, in other words, a longing for the end of the exile." *Pace* Gruen, "Diaspora and Homeland," n. 83.

Letter of Aristeas

The term *Ioudaios* appears seventeen times in the Letter of Aristeas, a legendary account of the translation of the Torah into Greek during the reign of Ptolemy II Philadelphus (285–247 BCE), each in reference to the contemporary, post-exilic people. In contrast, "Israel" and cognates never occur, as Aristeas discusses neither biblical Israel nor the eschaton. One oddity in the story is worth special attention, however: the sending of "six elders from each tribe" (32, 39, 46, 47–50), which at least initially appears to presume a united twelve tribes in the post-exilic period. But when the men from each tribe are listed in 47–50, the names of the tribes are never mentioned; instead the tribes are listed by number (first, second, etc.). That the first elder mentioned for the first tribe is named "Joseph" and the first from the second tribe is "Judah" is surely no accident, however, again nodding in the direction of the biblical kingdoms and tribal structure. Although hardly noticed by modern scholars, this conceit of elders being sent from all twelve tribes at a time when the twelve tribes no longer existed as such lends a playful, fairy-tale air to the story, especially given the absence of "Israel" and the tribal names from the account, while also accentuating the special, miraculous authority of the Alexandrian Greek translation for all Yahwists.[72]

Although Aristeas does not directly discuss the eschaton, a few hints of a restoration-eschatological perspective do slip through the cracks. First, the narrative ostensibly occurs on the heels of the deportation of tens of thousands of Jews to Egypt, many of whom were reduced to slavery (12–14); their emancipation and Ptolemy's benefaction in sponsoring the Greek translation could only be a partial compensation for such "miserable bondage" (15). This context is further reinforced by the sentiment reflected in the elder's answer to the king's question of how one could be patriotic:

> "By keeping it in mind," he said, "that it is good to live and die in one's own land, but residence abroad (ξενία) brings both disgrace to the day-laborer and reproach to the wealthy, as though they had been banished (ἐκπεπτωκόσιν) for a crime." (249)

---

[72] Sandra Gambetti has recently made the intriguing argument that Aristeas reflects a conflict between Samaritans and Jews in Alexandria and that the original Alexandrian Greek translation was Samaritan in origin, a theory that gives more significance to the criticisms of the Alexandrian scrolls in Arist. 30. Gambetti, "Syrian Politics," 34–43. If Gambetti's theory is correct, the twelve-tribe theme in Aristeas might serve the rhetorical function of trying to unite Alexandrian Yahwists, though emphasizing Jewish leadership (cf. Arist. 30, which references the "law of the Jews," not "of Israel"). A context of Jewish/Samaritan conflict would also account for the complete avoidance of "Israel" language in the text.

In the context of the deportation mentioned earlier in the book, it is hard to escape the conclusion that Aristeas presents life outside the land as less than ideal even for those who have prospered in the diaspora. Gruen, however, dismisses this interpretation, arguing,

> In the context of the whole work, a disparagement of Egypt as a residence for Jews would be absurd. ... In this instance, the king asks how he might be a genuine lover of his country. The first part of the answer, which contrasts native land and foreign residence, seems curiously irrelevant. ... Like so many of the swift and brief retorts by Jewish sages at the banquet, this one is bland and unsatisfying, containing statements that barely pertain to the king's query. The passage, whatever its significance, can hardly serve as a touchstone for the thesis that diaspora Jews were consumed with a desire to forsake their surroundings.[73]

On the contrary, the apparent disconnect between the question and answer does not diminish its importance but does the opposite, suggesting that the sentiment was so significant as to warrant inclusion even with the barest pretense. Moreover, that Gruen finds the content "bland and unsatisfying" is a matter of aesthetics, not historical judgment – Gruen appears unwilling even to consider that the book could actually mean what it says here. It hardly seems absurd that a book that begins by establishing a setting of deportation and slavery would take a generally negative view of the circumstances of life in Egypt. This is, of course, not the same as saying that "diaspora Jews were consumed with a desire to forsake their surroundings," as Gruen suggests. Instead, it marks a recognition of the inferiority of the present diaspora conditions – not to a life in Judaea hardly less subservient to foreign dominance than the life experienced by those in Alexandria – but rather to a future divinely orchestrated restoration superior to all present conditions, regardless of geographical location. In any case, the Letter of Aristeas restricts itself to the *Ioudaios* terminology exactly as one would expect from a text focusing on contemporary post-exilic Jews rather than on the biblical or eschatological people of Israel.

Susanna and Additions to Esther

One Second Temple text that does use "Israelite" to refer to contemporary Jews is the story of Susanna, part of the Greek additions to Daniel and set in the Babylonian deportation of Judah. This unusual case is further

---

[73] Gruen, "Diaspora and Homeland," 26.

complicated by differences between the two Greek versions.[74] The Old Greek version uses Israel five times; four of these refer to the characters within the story as "children of Israel" (Sus 28, 48 [2x], 57), while the fifth is similar, marking Susanna's husband as "from the people of Israel" (7). The OG uses *Ioudaios* once, referring to Susanna as a "Jewess" in vs. 22. Theodotion, on the other hand, refers to "the Jews" who came to Susanna's husband because he was the "most honored of them" (Sus 4 θ') but lacks the references to Susanna's husband and the synagogue assembly as children of Israel (7 and 28), with that term used only in the climactic scene in which Daniel castigates the "sons of Israel" for having unjustly condemned a "daughter of Israel" (48) and rebukes the elders for having taken advantage of "daughters of Israel" (57). This last example, which occurs in both versions, is especially unusual in Second Temple literature, as "Israel" is negatively contrasted with "Judah":

[Daniel] said to him, "Why is your seed perverted, as of Sidon and not of Judah? Beauty deceived you, the polluted desire [deceived you]. Thus you did to the daughters of Israel, and they had intercourse with you because they were afraid, but a daughter of Judah surely did not endure your disease of lawlessness."

(Sus 56–57 OG)

[Daniel] said to him, "Seed of Canaan and not of Judah! Beauty deceived you, and desire turned your heart. Thus you did to the daughters of Israel, and they had intercourse with you because they were afraid, but a daughter of Judah would not endure your wickedness." (Sus 56–57 θ')

Remarkably, this passage distinguishes between Susanna as a "daughter of Judah" and "daughters of Israel" in general, though Susanna was also herself called a "daughter of Israel" in v. 48.[75] These designations are evidently not envisioned as mutually exclusive, with "daughters of Judah" apparently being a subset of the "daughters of Israel" possessing superior virtue when compared to the larger group. This understanding is further strengthened by OG Sus 22, where Susanna is called "the Jewess" at the very point she responds to the elders' threat. In any case, Susanna retains the concept of *Ioudaioi* as a subset of the larger body of Israel;

---

[74] Although they share a common outline, there are significant differences between the Old Greek and Theodotion. The OG is shorter and focuses more on the sin of the elders, while θ' is expanded and focuses more on Susanna. Most scholars hold that θ' presupposes the OG, as there is substantial agreement between the two. The original language of the book is another problem, as it is generally thought to have been composed in Hebrew, though the relationship between the two Greek redactions and (a) hypothetical Hebrew version(s) complicates matters. See Collins, *Daniel*, 426–28.

[75] Collins, *Daniel*, 434 notes that the comparison in v. 57 is "problematic" given v. 48.

what is unusual is the portrayal of *Ioudaioi* as the more righteous subset of Israel – the opposite of what one would expect from Philo, for example. As a result of this distinction, some have suggested that the story derives from a particular dispute in the time of the author, perhaps in the context of Jewish–Samaritan antagonism.[76]

Perhaps the most significant exception to the pattern observed throughout this literature can be found in the Greek additions to Esther, in which "Israel" – which does not appear in the Hebrew version of the book – occurs seven times.[77] Of these, four occur in stock phrases in the context of prayer (13:9, 13; 14:1), including one reference to historical Israel (14:5). But the remaining three occurrences are unusual in that they refer to Esther's contemporaries and the implied reader not as "Jews," as does Hebrew Esther, but in elevated fashion as "Israel" (10:9, 13; 13:18). On closer examination, however, these instances are less exceptional than they seem, as two appear in the context of Mordecai's apocalyptic dream and refer to God's cosmic-level salvation of his people who cried out to him (10:9) and the subsequent celebration of Purim "forever among his people Israel" (10:13). The third refers to "all Israel" crying out in prayer (13:18), connecting closely with 10:9 and also appearing in a cultic context.[78] As will be shown in the next chapter, apocalyptic/eschatological works universally prefer the term Israel, so the apocalyptic quality and cosmic scope of these sections – which unlike Hebrew Esther also directly and repeatedly mention God – seems the best explanation for their use of Israel terminology.

CONCLUSION: ISRAEL IN SECOND TEMPLE NARRATIVE LITERATURE

As has been the case with the other corpora examined so far, Israel terminology in the narrative literature of the Second Temple period is highly correlated with a setting in the biblical past, an eschatological/ restorationist context, or in ritual or prayer contexts that often imply one

---

[76] Collins, *Daniel*, 434; Carey A. Moore, *Daniel, Esther, and Jeremiah: The Additions*, AB 44 (Garden City: Doubleday, 1977), 112.

[77] Since Esther provides an inversion of his linguistic version of the insider/outsider model, Goodblatt, "Israelites Who Reside in Judah," 77, suggests Hebrew Esther was influenced by "outsider" Persian usage but does not address the Greek additions.

[78] 13:18 does not appear in the Lucianic recension, likely due to haplography.

or both of the biblical/eschatological contexts.[79] It is, therefore, no coincidence that the texts Kuhn designates "religious" or "insider" works are either set in the biblical past or express expectations for Israel's restoration as constructed in prophetic literature (or both). Conversely, *Ioudaios* terminology appears nearly exclusively in post-exilic or contemporary contexts but not in references to biblical Israel or the future restored people. Instead, Israel terminology is universally preferred when referring to the pre-exilic biblical people or in eschatological or cultic contexts even in texts that otherwise speak of "Jews." Moreover, although rarely recognized or acknowledged in modern scholarship, the maintenance of a distinction between Jews and northern Israelites persists with surprising regularity in these texts, some of which show continued concern for the restoration not only of Jews but also of northern Israelites, while others are suggestive of rivalry or conflict between Jews and those who eventually came to be called Samaritans. Those continued eschatological hopes and the rivalry between Jews and Samaritans provide further reasons for the continued maintenance of a distinction between these terms and the partitive relationship between them.

---

[79] *Pace* Esther G. Chazon, "'Gather the Dispersed of Judah:' Seeking a Return to the Land as a Factor in Jewish Identity of Late Antiquity," in *Heavenly Tablets: Interpretation, Identity and Tradition in Ancient Judaism*, eds. Lynn R. LiDonnici and Andrea Lieber, JSJSup 119 (Leiden: Brill, 2007), 157–75 (174), there is no evidence of a distinction in eschatological hopes between "Palestinian" and diaspora prayers.

Israel in Second Temple Eschatological
and Apocalyptic Literature

After Ezra, a marked preference will reveal itself for the name Israel, which, while recalling the glorious memories of the past, is strongly linked to theocratic, messianic, and eschatological hopes.[1]

Renée Bloch

So far, this study has shown that the term Israel is closely correlated with restoration eschatology throughout early Jewish literature, tending to appear in contexts involving the biblical past or eschatological future rather than in contemporary post-exilic contexts. It should therefore come as no surprise that apocalyptic and eschatological texts from the Second Temple period consistently prefer the term Israel, while the term *Ioudaios* is vanishingly rare in these works (see Table 6). A closer look at these texts will further demonstrate a strong correlation between restoration eschatology and Israel terminology. Moreover, these texts consistently agree that the Persian-period returns from Babylon did not mark the end of the exilic age of wrath, instead rhetorically situating the reader in the liminal space between exile and the final eschatological restoration in much the same fashion as prior biblical literature. That restoration is consistently linked with the regathering and restoration not only of the Jewish diaspora but of the northern tribes of Israel, further highlighting an understanding of Israel as the full twelve-tribe people including but not limited to the Jews.

---

[1] Bloch, "Israélite, juif, hébreu," 17 ["À partir d'Esdras, une préférence marquée se manifestera pour le nom Israël qui, tout en rappelant les souvenirs glorieux du passé, se trouve fortement lié à l'espérance théocratique, messianique et eschatologique"].

Table 6 *Israelites and Jews in wisdom, apocalyptic, and eschatological texts*[a]

	Israel	Per 1,000	*Ioudaios*	Per 1,000
Sirach	18	0.96	0	0.00
Pss. Sol.	32	6.49	0	0.00
Baruch	19	7.29	0	0.00
4 Ezra[L]	12	0.68	0	0.00
2 Baruch[S]	11	0.61	0	0.00
T. Reu.	3	2.11	0	0.00
T. Sim.	3	2.59	0	0.00
T. Levi	13 (4)	4.35	0	0.00
T. Jud.	7	2.17	0	0.00
T. Iss.	1	0.97	0	0.00
T. Zeb.	2	1.34	0	0.00
T. Dan	10 (3)	8.27	0	0.00
T. Naph.	5 (1)	3.41	0	0.00
T. Gad	2	1.73	0	0.00
T. Ash.	1 (1)	1.01	0	0.00
T. Jos.	5 (1)	1.87	0	0.00
T. Benj.	7 (5)	4.40	0	0.00
T. Sol. A	9	1.10	1 (1)	0.12 (0.12)
Sib. Or.	2 (2)	0.07	6	0.20

[a] Since 4 Ezra and 2 Baruch are not fully extant in Greek, the Latin and Syriac versions, respectively, were used for these texts. Numbers in parentheses denote appearances in obvious Christian interpolations. Each use of Israel in the Sibylline Oracles, for example, occurs in a clearly Christian passage (1.360, 366), while the six uses of *Ioudaios* are scattered enough (including one from a section as late as the seventh century; 14.340) and their meaning ambiguous enough as to undermine any attempt to establish consistent tendencies across the corpus. The Sibylline Oracles will therefore not be examined in detail here, though it is worth noting that 2.170–76 suggests that the return of the ten tribes corresponds to the reversal of gentile domination over Israel (see Bauckham, "Anna," 101). For more on Christian interpolations and problems of provenance in early Jewish literature in general, see Davila, *The Provenance of the Pseudepigrapha*.

THE WISDOM OF BEN SIRA

Although typically categorized as a wisdom text, the Wisdom of Ben Sira "blurs the boundaries" between wisdom and apocalyptic literature and demonstrates significant hopes for Israel's restoration.[2] These

---

[2] Benjamin G. Wright III, "Conflicted Boundaries: Ben Sira, Sage and Seer," in *Congress Volume Helsinki 2010*, ed. Martti Nissinen, VTSup 148 (BRILL: 2012), 229–53 (229). Cf. also James D. Martin, "Ben Sira's Hymn to the Fathers: A Messianic Perspective," *OtSt* 24

expectations are most evident in the prayer of Sir 36:1–17,[3] which entreats God to "hasten the appointed time and remember the oath" (36:7) and take action on behalf of his people:

> Gather all the tribes of Jacob
>> and give them their inheritance, as at the beginning.
> Have mercy, Lord, on the people called by your name,
>> on Israel, whom you have made like your firstborn. . . .
> Give witness to those you created in the beginning,
>> and awaken the prophecies spoken in your name.
> Reward those waiting for you
>> and let your prophets be found trustworthy.
>
> (Sir. 36:10–11, 14–15)

Such concern for the reconciliation and gathering of the exiles – which Ben Sira specifically grounds in the promises of the prophets – is especially striking coming from someone who might be expected to regard the exile as already having ended. Jerusalem and the temple had been rebuilt centuries earlier and improved in his own day (cf. Sir 50), and Ben Sira himself lived in the land, enjoying a relatively prosperous life as part of the retainer class in Judaea in the early second century BCE.[4] The eschatological

---

(1986): 107–23. Restoration eschatology is nevertheless omitted from the list of Sirach's concerns in Patrick W. Skehan and Alexander A. Di Lella, *The Wisdom of Ben Sira: A New Translation with Notes, Introduction and Commentary*, Abhandlungen zum christlich-jüdischen Dialog 39 (Garden City: Doubleday, 1987), 75–92. On the problems of the category of "wisdom literature," see Will Kynes, *An Obituary for" Wisdom Literature": The Birth, Death, and Intertextual Reintegration of a Biblical Corpus* (New York: Oxford University Press, 2018); Will Kynes, "The 'Wisdom Literature' Category: An Obituary," *The Journal of Theological Studies* 69.1 (2018): 1–24.

[3] The book itself was originally written by Jesus ben Sira in Hebrew in the early second century BCE (198–175 BCE) and translated into Greek by Ben Sira's grandson at the end of the second century BCE. The analysis in this section is based on the Greek text except where noted, though the basic argument works for either version. For the Hebrew text(s), see Yigael Yadin, *The Ben Sira Scroll from Masada* (Jerusalem: Israel Exploration Society, 1965); Alexander A. Di Lella, *The Hebrew Text of Sirach: A Text-Critical and Historical Study*, Studies in Classical Literature (The Hague: Mouton, 1966); Benjamin G. Wright III, *No Small Difference: Sirach's Relationship to its Hebrew Parent Text* (Atlanta: Scholars Press, 1989); Pancratius C. Beentjes, *The Book of Ben Sira in Hebrew: A Text Edition of All Extant Hebrew Manuscripts and a Synopsis of All Parallel Hebrew Ben Sira Texts*, VTSup 68 (Leiden: Brill, 1997). The versification of Sirach varies among modern editions and versions; this section follows the versification in Alfred Rahlfs, ed., *Septuaginta* (Stuttgart: Deutsche Bibelgesellschaft, 2006) unless otherwise noted.

[4] See Benjamin G. Wright III and Claudia V. Camp, "Who has Been Tested by Gold and Found Perfect?," in *Praise Israel for Wisdom and Instruction: Essays on Ben Sira and Wisdom, the Letter of Aristeas and the Septuagint*, JSJSup 131 (Leiden: Brill, 2008), 71–96; Richard A. Horsley, *Scribes, Visionaries, and the Politics of Second Temple*

sentiments of this chapter are therefore so striking that some scholars have challenged its authenticity. John Collins, for example, finds these statements "so alien to the thought world of Ben Sira that it must be regarded as a secondary addition," and sees no reason for such animosity toward foreign rulers in the time of Antiochus III, who had assisted in rebuilding Jerusalem and the temple, suggesting that the prayer fits better in the Maccabean period.[5] Such an argument, however, presumes that the benefaction of a foreign ruler would eliminate hopes for restoration among the people still under foreign rule, an unlikely proposition at best.

Moreover, the prayer is thoroughly integrated into and in keeping with the rest of the composition, particularly the material from the previous chapter – which itself already includes an appeal for God to vindicate his people and judge the nations.[6] Far from being a stark departure from Ben Sira's thought elsewhere, the prayer is instead consistent with the concerns with injustice and oppression addressed in the surrounding context and as observed by Bradley Gregory, "flows from prior understandings of the theological status of the poor and of the nature of Israel's election" with the transition from the individual to the national reflected in the prayer mirroring a widely attested phenomenon in early Jewish literature.[7] That similar eschatological sentiments can be found elsewhere in the book (see below) further confirms the authenticity of this prayer – which was, in any case, integral to the book by the first century – and the importance of Israel's restoration to the Ben Sira tradition.[8]

Judea (Louisville: Westminster John Knox, 2007), 123–45. Gregory, "Poor in Judea," 321 also notes Ben Sira's concern for the poor and how he connects the fate of the poor with that of Israel as similarly striking given his social location.

[5] John J. Collins, *Jewish Wisdom in the Hellenistic Age* (Edinburgh: T&T Clark, 1998), 23, 110–11. Cf. also Theophil L. Middendorp, *Die Stellung Jesu Ben Siras zwischen Judentum und Hellenismus* (Leiden: Brill, 1973), 125–32; Lutz Schrader, *Leiden und Gerechtigkeit: Studien zu Theologie und Textgeschichte des Sirachbuches*, BBET 27 (Frankfurt: Lang, 1994), 87–95; Burkard M. Zapff, *Jesus Sirach 25–51*, NEchtB (Würzburg: Echter, 2010), 236.

[6] See Greg Schmidt Goering, *Wisdom's Root Revealed: Ben Sira and the Election of Israel*, JSJSup 139 (Leiden: Brill, 2009), 204–13; Skehan and Di Lella, *The Wisdom of Ben Sira*, 420; Fuller, *The Restoration of Israel*, 36–37; Gregory, "Poor in Judea."

[7] Gregory, "Poor in Judea," 313. See also Marco Zappella, "L'immagine di Israele in Sir 33 (36), 1–19 secondo il ms. ebraico B e la tradizione manoscritta greca. Analisi letteraria e lessicale," *RivB* 42.4 (1994): 409–46; Maria Carmela Palmisano, *"Salvaci, Dio dell'Universo!": studio dell'eucologia di Sir 36H, 1–17*, AnBib 163 (Rome: Pontifical Biblical Institute, 2006).

[8] A similar prayer also occurs in MS B of Sirach 51, also known as the "Prayer of Jesus, son of Sirach," which is attested in both Greek and Hebrew MSS and thought to be authentic to Sirach, though the earliest MSS do not contain the portion between 51:12 and 13 that

Along these lines, Michael Fuller concludes, "The basic perspective of Sirach is that until Jews [*sic*] outside Palestine return, even those within Palestine remain in exile."[9] Fuller is correct about the restoration-eschatological perspective of Sirach but with one major flaw: Ben Sira never mentions the *Ioudaioi* but instead consistently speaks of "Israel." Goodblatt, of course, regards this as due to the "insider" nature of the text, which was composed in Hebrew,[10] but Miller rightly points out that other explanations may be preferable:

[Goodblatt's] reliance on the statistical correlation between the Hebrew language and 'Israel' sometimes masks alternative explanations. ... It is significant that Ben Sira never uses *Ioudaios*, but it is possible that "Israel" was chosen not because it was the standard label in Ben Sira's time, but because it suited the elevated nature of his discourse. Of the seventeen occurrences of "Israel" in the Greek text of Ben Sira (excluding the prologue),[11] eleven refer to the period between Moses and Jeroboam; three more refer to [Ben Sira's] own time, but in a liturgical context (50.13, 20, 23); 36.11 is a prayer, as is the Hebrew poem included between 51.12 and 13.[12]

Indeed, Ben Sira's use of "Israel" precisely matches the pattern we have observed elsewhere, either referring to (1) pre-exilic biblical Israel (2) the diachronic "people of God" in prayer or liturgy, or (3) restored eschatological Israel. The prayer in 36:10–11 is especially instructive, as "Israel" occurs in parallel with "the tribes of Jacob," an even more pregnant phrase specifically calling attention to the tribal structure of the nation. The consistent use of "Israel" elsewhere in Sirach thus accords with a concern not only for the return of "the Jews" but for the restoration of all twelve tribes to their ancestral inheritance. Remarkably, Fuller nevertheless dismisses Sirach's mention of the tribes, apparently assuming such hopes were implausible by Ben Sira's time:

---

mentions the dispersion and gathering of Israel. Skehan and Di Lella argue that this dispersion/gathering passage nevertheless dates to the mid first century BCE (perhaps composed at Qumran), supplying in any another witness to restoration eschatology within the Ben Sira tradition. See Skehan and Di Lella, *The Wisdom of Ben Sira,* 569.

[9] Fuller, *The Restoration of Israel,* 42.

[10] Cf. Goodblatt, "Israelites Who Reside in Judah," 76; Goodblatt, "Varieties of Identity," 16.

[11] There are twenty-one instances of "Israel" in the Hebrew version, thanks to the three instances in the psalm between 51:12 and 13.

[12] Miller, "Group Labels," 108–09. I disagree with Miller's conclusion that 50:23 clearly denotes the people of Ben Sira's own day, though it is clearly in a cultic context either way.

The author of Sirach does not envision Israel's restoration as a return to the tribal confederacy. It is more likely that he is simply drawing on the symbolic value of the tribes to the Land in his hope that all the people of Israel (i.e., the Diaspora) will return to the Land. In some writings, the actual tribes are mentioned, making it difficult to discern whether the writer is further emphasizing Israel's relationship to the Land or hoping for an actual restoration of the twelve tribes themselves upon their historic allotments of territories (e.g., T. 12 Patr.; 11QTcol. xxiv)[13]

On the contrary, the fact that Ben Sira specifically prays for the resumption of the traditional tribal allotments/inheritance (κατακληρονόμησον) upon the restoration of the tribes makes it clear that he does expect a return to an (idealized) tribal confederacy "as in days of old" (36:10).[14] It is odd that Fuller ignores this specific request, only to note that some other early Jewish texts actually appear to hold such hopes. Nor is it "difficult to discern" whether those texts that mention the specific tribal names hope for "an actual restoration of the twelve tribes" themselves as Fuller suggests; such comments are a signal example of willfully ignoring the continued hopes for the restoration of the northern tribes in early Jewish literature. If, as we have seen, "Throughout the Second Temple period, the assumption was that the northern tribes still existed,"[15] there is no reason to doubt that Ben Sira did in fact hope for a return to the tribal confederacy.

This conclusion is further strengthened by the fact that Ben Sira's hopes for the restoration of all Israel appear elsewhere in the book. Specifically, Ben Sira also emphasizes Israel's restoration in its account of Elijah (48:10).[16] But just how Ben Sira's discussion of Elijah fits in the context of the larger encomium of Israel's heroes (44:1–50:24) and Sirach's emphasis on northern Israel in this larger section have all too often been missed.[17] Immediately before the Elijah passage, Sirach recounts

---

[13] Fuller, *The Restoration of Israel*, 38 n. 94.

[14] "As in days of old" is the Hebrew reading, which echoes the new exodus passage in Isa 51:9 (cf. also Mic 7:20; Ps 44:2).

[15] Barmash, "Nexus," 232.

[16] For more on the portrayal of Elijah in Sirach, see Pancratius C. Beentjes, "De stammen van Israël herstellen: Het portret van Elia bij Jesus Sirach," *ACEBT* 5 (1984): 147–55.

[17] See, for example, Fuller, *The Restoration of Israel*, 41–42. On the encomium of Israel's heroes in Sirach 44:1–50:24, see Martin, "Ben Sira's Hymn to the Fathers"; Burton L. Mack, *Wisdom and the Hebrew Epic: Ben Sira's Hymn in Praise of the Fathers* (Chicago: University of Chicago Press, 1985); Pancratius C. Beentjes, "Ben Sira 44:19–23 – The Patriarchs: Text, Tradition, Theology," in *Studies in the Book of Ben Sira: Papers of the Third International Conference on the Deuterocanonical Books, Papa, Hungary, 18–20 May 2006(127)*, eds. Géza G. Xeravits and József Zsengellér, JSJSup 127 (Leiden: Brill, 2008), 209–28.

Solomon's sin, explaining that in consequence, "the rule was divided, and a rebel kingdom arose out of Ephraim. But the Lord ... gave a remnant to Jacob, and to David a root from his own family" (47:21–22). "Jacob" here seems to refer to the northern remnant as an antithetical parallel to the root from David's family (that is, Judah), shedding further light on the meaning of the "tribes of Jacob" in ch. 36. The following verses further clarify these events, focusing on how Jeroboam's influence led to Israel/Ephraim's exile:[18]

> And Jeroboam the son of Nebat, who caused Israel to sin
>   and gave to Ephraim their sinful path.
> And their sins multiplied greatly
>   until they were removed from their land.
> For they sought every kind of evil,
>   until just punishment came upon them.
>
>   (47:24–25)

It is at this point that Ben Sira introduces Elijah (and then Elisha) as heroic figures for having done great wonders in opposing the idolatry of the northern kingdom, which nevertheless did not repent but were "plundered from their land and scattered in all the earth," while "the people were left few in number but with a ruler from the house of David" (48:15). But Israel's scattering is not final, for Elijah was taken up (48:9) and:

> Ordained for reproofs at the appointed time,
>   to stop the wrath [of the Lord] before [it becomes] fury
> To turn the hearts of the parents to their children
>   and to restore the tribes of Jacob.
>
>   (48:10)

Ben Sira here quotes the promise of Malachi 3:24 [ET 4:6] that Elijah will "turn the hearts of their parents to their children" but adds an element most likely from Isa 49:6, "and to restore the tribes of Jacob" – that is, the northern tribes among whom Elijah ministered that had been "scattered over all the earth" (48:15).[19] This scattering is a different event

---

[18] Leo Garrett Perdue, "Ben Sira and the Prophets," in *Intertextual Studies in Ben Sira and Tobit: Essays in Honor of Alexander A. Di Lella, O. F. M*, eds. Jeremy Corley and Vincent Skemp, CBQMS 38 (Washington, DC: Catholic Biblical Association of America, 2005), 132–54 (147).

[19] Pancratius C. Beentjes, "Prophets and Prophecy in the Book of Ben Sira," in *Prophets, Prophecy, and Prophetic Texts in Second Temple Judaism (427)*, eds. Michael H. Floyd and Robert D. Haak, LHBOTS 427 (London: T&T Clark, 2006), 135–50 (141–42); Miller, "The Messenger," 7–8.

from what Ben Sira narrates later, when "the kings of Judah came to an end" (49:4) and the "chosen city of the sanctuary" was burned (49:5). Similarly, the description of Elisha immediately following that of Elijah "concentrates on the sins of the people of the northern kingdom."[20]

In keeping with his expectations of a more expansive restoration, Ben Sira's narration of the return from Babylon is limited and brief, and the absence of Ezra from the list is especially striking given Ben Sira's scribal heritage.[21] Fuller observes that this is due to Ben Sira's eschatological views:

> For a writer who esteems the Temple so highly, it is striking that those who were instrumental in its construction and the wider restoration of the 6th century receive such brief acclaim. But Sirach plays down their role ... That is, the author maintains that the return and restoration under Persia was *not* completed in the 6th century.[22]

In their place, Ben Sira effusively praises another figure through whose action he hopes the promised restoration will be swiftly fulfilled: his contemporary, the high priest Simon II, "the leader of his brothers and the pride of his people" (50:1).[23] In repairing and fortifying the temple and city,[24] Simon has "considered how to save his people from ruin" (50:4), and Ben Sira represents Simon as having completed the work begun by Nehemiah, preparing Jerusalem and the sanctuary for the final ingathering.[25] Ben Sira describes Simon's glory in performing his priestly duties (50:5–21) to the satisfaction of God and the admiration of the people, culminating in Simon's pronunciation of the priestly blessing

---

[20] Perdue, "Ben Sira and the Prophets," 149.

[21] That is not to say that he regards this event as unimportant, as Ben Sira clearly sees Nehemiah's work as fulfilling prophecy. But like many others, such as the author of Tobit, that work, although important, was not the fulfillment of the promised restoration but only an intermediate step.

[22] Fuller, *The Restoration of Israel*, 39–40.

[23] This phrase only appears in the Hebrew version and is left out of the Greek as the translation tends to downplay Simon's importance. For more on the portrayal of Simon in Sirach, see Otto Mulder, *Simon the High Priest in Sirach 50: An Exegetical Study of the Significance of Simon the High Priest as Climax to the Praise of the Fathers in Ben Sira's Concept of the History of Israel* (Leiden: Brill, 2003); Otto Mulder and Renate Egger-Wenzel, "Two Approaches: Simon the High Priest and YHWH God of Israel/God of All in Sirach 50," in *Ben Sira's God: Proceedings of the International Ben Sira Conference, Durham-Ushaw College 2001*, BZAW 321 (Berlin: de Gruyter, 2002), 221–34.

[24] The Hebrew of Ben Sira 50:1 says that the house was "visited" rather than "repaired," which may indicate that Ben Sira believed the divine presence had returned to the temple in Simon's day, while the Greek translation is less optimistic about Simon's work here.

[25] Cf. Fuller, *The Restoration of Israel*, 40.

"over the whole assembly of the children of Israel" (50:20),[26] but the absence of the tribes of Jacob and incompleteness of Israel is keenly felt throughout the section, which is immediately followed by a plea for mercy and deliverance so that Israel may experience peace "as in the days of old" (50:23).[27] Although Ben Sira views Simon II as having (perhaps) accomplished the necessary preparatory work for Israel's restoration, even Simon's efforts still fall short of the promise, as that final ingathering has yet to take place.

Moreover, the presence of the rival Shechemites, whom Ben Sira bitterly denounces as "not a nation" and "the foolish people" (50:25–26; cf. Deut 32:21), provides a persistent testimony to Israel's absence and the fact that the restoration remains but a future hope.[28] That hope seemed even more distant by the time Ben Sira's grandson translated the book into Greek, and the translation understandably downplays the significance of Simon's work and line, which were diminished by the events of the Maccabean period. The hope for Israel's restoration remains prominent in Greek Sirach but with less immediacy and vibrancy. Nevertheless, even in the diminished Greek version, the book of Sirach unmistakably portrays Israel's restoration as incomplete, with the bulk of Israel ("the tribes of Jacob") remaining in exile and the situation of those in the land limited until the rest of Israel is restored. Despite living in the land with a functioning Temple run by an admirable heir of the Zadokite priesthood, the author prays for restoration promised by the prophets, highlighting the solidarity of those in the land with those still in exile by the plea, "have mercy on *us*" (36:1) and "all those called by your name" (36:11).[29] Until all of Israel has been restored, even those in the land await the fulfillment of the promises. And in keeping

---

[26] Sir 50:13 and 50:20 both refer to Simon's activity before the "assembly of Israel," which some may read as problematic in that they appear to refer to the present-day people as "Israel." This is, however, a stock phrase in the context of priestly liturgy (cf. Deut 31:30; 1 Kgs 8:14, 22, 55; 2 Chr 6:3, 12, 13; Josh 8:35), as the priests specifically serve on behalf of and to bless the "assembly of Israel." It should be also noted that in this context, those gathered to the temple are properly the assembly "of Israel" in a partitive sense, even if much of Israel remains absent and unrestored, thereby being blessed in absentia by the priest, with Ben Sira's additional prayer for mercy and restoration especially applying to that absent group.

[27] My translation follows the Hebrew here; the Greek says, "as at the beginning" rather than "as in days of old."

[28] On the Samaritans as a reminder of the absence of the northern tribes, see pp. 272–75 and Thiessen, "4Q372."

[29] Cf. Fuller, *The Restoration of Israel*, 41 n. 102.

with this hope, for Ben Sira, "Israel" is not equivalent to "the Jews" but rather denotes the full twelve-tribe people scattered among the nations awaiting glorious restoration.

PSALMS OF SOLOMON

The Psalms of Solomon is a collection of eighteen psalms with a distinctive eschatological focus, holding firmly to the rightful authority of the Davidic house and looking forward to the advent of a Davidic messiah.[30] The Pss. Sol. consistently portray Israel as still in exile due to disobedience (e.g., 9:1–2), including prayers calling upon the Lord to "gather together the dispersed (*diasporan*) of Israel" (8:28, my translation; cf. 7:8; 9:1–2; 11:1–9) and expressing faith that the promises of Israel's restoration will be fulfilled.[31] That restoration will involve the advent of a Davidic messiah who will overthrow current usurpers and "reign as king in Jerusalem, ingather the diaspora tribes, and judge the peoples and nations of the earth with righteous wisdom."[32]

Ioudaios terminology does not appear in Pss. Sol. In contrast, the term "Israel" appears thirty-two times in Pss. Sol. but is never used in reference

---

[30] On the latter, see Kenneth R. Atkinson, "On the Herodian Origin of Militant Davidic Messianism at Qumran: New Light from Psalm of Solomon 17," *JBL* 118.3 (1999): 435–60 and Benedikt Eckhardt, "PsSal 17, die Hasmonäer und der Herodompeius," *Journal for the Study of Judaism* 40.4 (2009): 465–92. Pss. Sol. were composed sometime between the invasion of Pompey in 63 BCE and the early portion of the Common Era, and there is some debate as to whether they were originally written in Hebrew or Greek, though they survive only in a few medieval Greek and Syriac MSS. For a Greek critical edition, see Robert B. Wright, *The Psalms of Solomon: A Critical Edition of the Greek Text*, Jewish and Christian Texts Series (London: T&T Clark, 2007); the translations of Pss. Sol. cited here are from Robert B. Wright, "Psalms of Solomon," in *OTP*, 639–70 except where noted. On the date of Pss. Sol., see Kenneth R. Atkinson, "Herod the Great, Sosius, and the Siege of Jerusalem (37 BCE) in Psalm of Solomon 17," *NovT* 38.4 (1996): 313–22. On the language of Pss. Sol., see Jan Joosten, "Reflections on the Original Language of the Psalms of Solomon," in *The Psalms of Solomon: Language, History, Theology*, eds. Eberhard Bons and Patrick Pouchelle, EJL (Atlanta: SBL Press, 2015), 31–48. The various psalms were likely composed by several authors, with the final redactor affixing the first and eighteenth psalms as an introduction and conclusion to the collection. All are anti-Hasmonean except Pss. Sol. 17, which is most likely anti-Herodian. Cf. Atkinson, "Herod the Great"; Atkinson, "Herodian Origin."

[31] Note again the highly negative use of *diaspora* and view of the present circumstances. Ferda, "Ingathering of the Exiles," 179, sees "clear echoes of Isa 40" in Pss. Sol. 11:1–7, looking forward to "the returning exiles."

[32] Atkinson, "Herodian Origin," 448.

to the contemporary Jewish people.[33] Rather, the term always refers either to the diachronic people of God (e.g., "God of Israel,"[34] "Israel his servant forever"[35]) or to the historical/biblical or eschatological people.[36] Lest one should imagine that these texts merely prefer the "insider" term functionally equivalent to the outsider term "Jews," several passages clarify that the "Israel" of Pss. Sol. denotes the full tribal heritage of Israel, restored in the days of the Davidic messiah, who will rule with a rod of iron:[37]

> He will gather a holy people
>   whom he will lead in righteousness;
> and he will judge the tribes of the people
>   that have been made holy by the Lord their God.
> *And he will distribute them upon the land*
>   *according to their tribes;*
> the alien and the foreigner will no longer live near them.
> He will judge peoples and nations in the wisdom of his righteousness.
>   (Pss. Sol. 17:26, 28–29, my emphasis)

> This is the majesty of the king of Israel
>   which God knew,
> to raise him over the house of Israel
>   to discipline it. . . .
> Blessed are those born in those days
>   to see the good fortune of Israel
> *which God will bring to pass in the assembly of the tribes.*
> May God dispatch his mercy upon Israel.
>   (Pss. Sol. 17:42, 44–45a, my emphasis)

The eschatological restoration envisioned by Pss. Sol. is therefore not merely the "hope that all Jews [*sic*] will return to Jerusalem"[38] or "the

---

[33] Count based on the Greek text from Herbert E. Ryle and Montague R. James, *Psalms of the Pharisees, Commonly Called the Psalms of Solomon: The Text Newly Revised from All the MSS* (New York: Columbia University Press, 1891), 2–153. One additional occurrence of "Israel" is found in a variant of 2:24, where the reading is either "Jerusalem" or "Israel."

[34] Pss. Sol. 4:1; 9:8; 16:3.

[35] Pss. Sol. 12:6. Cf. also 5:18; 7:8; 8:26, 34; 11:7, 9; 14:5; 18:1, 3. Because most of these are also clearly in the context of discussing exile/diaspora and/or eschatological restoration, they could easily be placed in the biblical/eschatological category as well.

[36] Pss. Sol. 8:28; 9:1, 2, 11; 10:5, 6, 7, 8, 11:1, 6, 7, 8, 9; 12:6; 17:4, 21, 42, 44, 45; 18:5.

[37] Cf. Ps. 2:9; Isa 11:4. De Jonge notes that for the Pss. Sol., the power of this messiah is such that "military operations are not necessary. The King has only to speak and his enemies are defeated" (Marinus de Jonge, "The Expectation of the Future in the Psalms of Solomon," *Neot* 23.1 [1989]: 93–117 [102]). This is reminiscent of Philo's vision of a "bloodless" conquest under a messianic figure in *Praem.* 97.

[38] So Kenneth R. Atkinson, "Solomon, Psalms of," *EDEJ* 1238–41 (1239), referencing Pss. Sol. 11.

release and return of the dispersed Jews [*sic*] to Israel,"[39] as is frequently suggested, since Pss. Sol. nowhere mentions "Jews" (*Ioudaioi*). Rather, these psalms hope for restoration and return for *Israel* – including all of the non-Judahite tribes – from their dispersion among the "mixed nations (συμμίκτων ἐθνῶν)" (17:15; cf. 9:1–2).[40] Moreover, in contrast to the Hasmonean or Herodian kingdoms, which were ruled by non-Davidic stock and did not include the plenum of Israel, Pss. Sol. look forward to the day of the Davidic Messiah,[41] who will gather the tribes of Israel and rule in righteousness as promised. The bitter indictment of the "sinners" who set up a non-Davidic kingdom in 17:4–6 and the foreigner who took their place illustrates the first concern the passages quoted above illustrate the second – these two themes appear to work together in this corpus, most evidently in *Pss. Sol.* 17, and throughout Pss. Sol., "Israel" terminology is employed in contexts closely linked to restoration eschatology.

TESTAMENTS OF THE TWELVE PATRIARCHS

Although the received form of the Testaments of the Twelve Patriarchs is a Christian redaction, its conception of Israel and use of terminology reflected throughout is in continuity with the patterns observed elsewhere.[42] These texts purport to be a record of the deathbed words of

---

[39] Jonge, "Expectation of the Future," 101.

[40] The declaration of William Scott Green, "Messiah in Judaism: Rethinking the Question," in *Judaisms and their Messiahs at the Turn of the Christian Era*, eds. Jacob Neusner, William Scott Green, and Ernest S. Frerichs (Cambridge: Cambridge University Press, 1987), 1–13 (3), that Pss. Sol. 17 is "neither apocalyptic nor eschatological" is puzzling in light of these eschatological features. Similarly, Burton L. Mack, "Wisdom Makes a Difference: Alternatives to 'Messianic' Configurations," in *Judaisms and Their Messiahs at the Turn of the Christian Era*, eds. Jacob Neusner, W. S. Green, and Ernst Frerichs (Cambridge: Cambridge University Press, 1988), 15–48 (40), objects that the chapter contains no eschatological hopes, since "the poetry is exuberant, even celebrative. It does not express longing or expectation." That eschatological hopes could not be expressed with exuberant, celebrative poetry in anticipation of final vindication is nonsense, as Dan 7:9–14 and Rev 19 are but two of many examples of exactly that.

[41] Cf. Joseph L. Trafton, "What Would David Do? Messianic Expectation and Surprise in Pss. Sol. 17," in *The Psalms of Solomon: Language, History, Theology*, eds. Eberhard Bons and Patrick Pouchelle, EJL 40 (Atlanta: SBL Press, 2015), 155–74.

[42] A number of texts from the Dead Sea Scrolls feature material parallel to some of the Testaments and may contain earlier source material for these texts. What follows attempts to avoid obviously Christian passages and will therefore not address T. Levi 10, 14, 16–17, 18:9 or T. Benj. 11, all of which prominently feature distinctly Christian material. For more on the provenance of the Testaments of the Twelve Patriarchs, see Marinus de Jonge, *Pseudepigrapha of the Old Testament as Part of Christian Literature:*

the twelve sons of Israel/Jacob, including exhortations and prophecies of their descendants' future. Since these texts are set in the biblical past and deal with the eschatological future, it should be no surprise that "Israel" and cognates occur approximately fifty-nine times and "Judah" ('Ιούδας) thirty-seven times.[43] The Testaments emphasize the separation of the northern and southern houses of Israel, and Judah and the disappearance of "Joseph" look forward to the future reunification and restoration of all twelve tribes with surprising frequency.[44]

T. Joseph, for example, recounts a vision of beasts in ch. 19 that begins with twelve stags, nine of whom are "dispersed over all the earth," followed

The Case of the Testaments of the Twelve Patriarchs and the Greek Life of Adam and Eve, SVTP (Leiden: Brill, 2003); Marinus de Jonge, "Christian Influence in the Testaments of the Twelve Patriarchs," *NovT* 4.3 (1960): 182–235; Marinus de Jonge, "The Pre-Mosaic Servants of God in the Testaments of the Twelve Patriarchs and in the writings of Justin and Irenaeus," *VC* 39 (1985): 157–70; Marinus de Jonge, "The Transmission of the Testaments of the Twelve Patriarchs by Christians," *VC* 47.1 (1993): 1–28; Marc Philonenko, *Les interpolations chrétiennes des Testaments des douze patriarches et les manuscrits de Quomràn*, 35 (Paris: Presses universitaires de France, 1960).

[43] Most (17) of these are found in combination with Levi, as these two tribes and patriarchs are envisioned as ruling Israel. Another fourteen uses are specifically in reference to the patriarch. The remaining six refer to the tribe or kingdom of Judah in general.

[44] Cf. Marinus de Jonge, "The Future of Israel in the Testaments of the Twelve Patriarchs," *Journal for the Study of Judaism* 17.2 (1986): 196–211 (196). De Jonge distinguishes two types of eschatological passages, those following the Sin-Exile-Return (SER) template and those following a Levi-Judah (LJ) template. Cf. Jonge, "Future of Israel"; Marinus de Jonge, *Jewish Eschatology, Early Christian Christology, and the Testaments of the Twelve Patriarchs: Collected Essays of Marinus de Jonge*, NovTSup 63 (Leiden: Brill, 1991); Marinus de Jonge, *The Testaments of the Twelve Patriarchs: A Study of Their Text, Composition and Origin*, SVTP (Assen: van Gorcum, 1953). Each fits nicely in the category of restoration eschatology, and the LJ paradigm (also a prominent element in the Dead Sea Scrolls) emphasizes both the primacy of the southern kingdom and the twelve-tribe structure of Israel. Both of these appear to be from a pre-Christian form of the tradition, though the Christian redaction has added elements to each, such as Levi's sin including the mistreatment and rejection of Jesus by the priests. Doron Mendels, *The Land of Israel as a Political Concept in Hasmonean Literature: Recourse to History in Second Century BC Claims to the Holy Land*, TSAJ 15 (Tübingen: Mohr Siebeck, 1987), 102, sees the early Jewish layer of the work reflecting "the anxiety of the writer concerning the wholeness of the nation, and its continuity as one entity consisting of twelve tribes." For other material on Israel and eschatology in the Testaments, see Jacob Jervell, "Ein Interpolator interpretiert: Zu der christlichen Bearbeitung der Testamente der zwölf Patriarchen," in *Studien zu den Testamenten der zwölf Patriarchen*, eds. Christoph Burchard et al. (Berlin: Töpelmann, 1969), 30–61; Anders Hultgård, *L'eschatologie des Testaments des Douze patriarches: 1, Interprétation des Textes* (Uppsala: Almqvist & Wiksell, 1977); Anders Hultgård, *L'eschatologie des testaments des Douze Patriarches: 2, Composition de l'ouvrage textes et traductions* (Uppsala: Almqvist & Wiksell, 1982).

into dispersion afterwards by the other three (T. Jos. 19:2).[45] Even more significantly, T. Naphtali includes two apocalyptic visions about the scattering of Israel, with the first including Joseph catching hold of a winged bull and being swept away from his brothers. This vision is followed by another, in which the twelve sons of Jacob depart on "the Ship of Jacob" (T. Naph. 6:2), which is then broken up by an intense storm:

> And Joseph escaped in a light boat while we were scattered about on ten planks; Levi and Judah were on the same one. Thus we were all dispersed, even to the outer limits. (T. Naph. 6:6–7)[46]

Notably, while the brothers are scattered "to the outer limits," Levi and Judah remain together, representing the separation of the other Israelite tribes from the southern kingdom. Upon recounting his dream to Jacob, Naphtali receives the following explanation:

> "These things must be fulfilled at their appropriate time, once Israel has endured many things." Then my father said, "I believe that Joseph is alive, for I continually see that the Lord includes him in the number with you."[47] And he kept saying tearfully, "You live, Joseph, my son, and I do not see you, nor do you behold Jacob who begot you." He made me shed tears by these words of his. I was burning inwardly with compassion to tell him that Joseph had been sold, but I was afraid of my brothers.
>
> Behold, my children, I have shown you the last times, all things that will happen in Israel. "Command your children that they be in unity with Levi and Judah, for through Judah will salvation arise for Israel, and in him will Jacob be blessed."
>
> (T. Naph. 7:1–8:2)

T. Naphtali depicts Joseph as separated and apparently lost in exile, mirroring the fate of their forefather in Egypt.[48] But like the patriarch, he will one day be restored to his brothers in the last days. The scattering of Israel – even to the point of the tribes forgetting their Israelite heritage – is likewise prominent in T. Asher:

---

[45] As noted in Jonge, "Christian Influence," 215–17, T. Jos. 19 "is an extremely complicated chapter" (215), plagued by textual problems and significant Christian redaction, but there is little reason in my view to regard the opening two verses as owing to that Christian redaction, especially since the view of the exiles characterized here is common through the Testaments.

[46] Except where noted, translations in this section are from Howard Clark Kee, "Testaments of the Twelve Patriarchs," in *OTP*, 775–828.

[47] This seems to be a meta-aware reference to the fact that the Jewish scriptures continue to keep all twelve tribes of Israel in view, including them in restoration promises despite their apparent absence.

[48] As discussed further below, a similar typological interpretation of the Joseph story can be found in 4Q372 1. The combination of that theme and the Levi-Judah emphasis of this section are almost certainly pre-Christian.

You will be scattered to the four corners of the earth; in the dispersion (*en diaspora*) you will be regarded as worthless, like useless water, until such time as the Most High visits the earth. . . . For this reason, you will be scattered like Dan and Gad, my brothers, you shall not know your own lands, tribe, or language.

(T. Asher 7:3, 6)

This passage exhibits the same concern as the book of Tobit – loss of tribal heritage in exile – but unlike Tobit does not imagine that a righteous remnant managed to preserve their identity. Nevertheless, restoration is still promised, as one day, "he will gather you together in faith through his compassion" (T. Asher 7:7). T. Dan 6:4 envisions this restoration as contingent on Israel's return to faithfulness, proclaiming, "on the day in which Israel trusts, the enemy's kingdom will be brought to an end." Similarly, the Testament of Benjamin also looks forward to the time when the "twelve tribes will be gathered" together to the temple (9:2), connecting this restoration with the restoration of Joseph (10:1), the resurrection of the patriarchs (10:6; cf. T. Judah 24–25), and YHWH revealing "his salvation to all nations" (T. Benj. 10:5).[49]

Contrary to the suggestions of some previous interpreters focused on Christian redaction of the Testaments, these eschatological passages are not indicators of continued Christian concerns about the fate of "the Jews"[50] – indeed, the term *Ioudaios* never appears in the Testaments. Instead, the Testaments consistently highlight the continuing exile of Israel with particular emphasis on the fate of the north, expecting that all twelve tribes would one day be restored through divine intervention. And as with so many other sources examined so far in this study, "Israel" in the Testaments of the Twelve Patriarchs denotes a larger group than the Jews, remarkably including even those who may have forgotten their tribal and ethnic heritage as Israelites (T. Asher 7:6). These texts thus provide yet further evidence of the persistence of restoration eschatology and the concern for all twelve tribes of Israel even beyond the Second Temple period while also showing easily how these strands could be reshaped to serve Christian theological purposes.

---

[49] The Christian redactor of course continues with Jesus, who was not believed "when he appeared as God in the flesh" (10:8–9), presiding over the final judgment. Although the final form of this passage is obviously Christian (as with the Testaments as a whole), it seems more likely that the emphasis on Israel's restoration throughout owes to an earlier pre-Christian version or source.

[50] E.g., Jonge, "Future of Israel," 210–11.

BARUCH

The (Greek) book of Baruch presents itself as having been written in Babylon by Baruch, the scribe of Jeremiah (cf. Jer 32:12; 36; 43:3; 45:1–5), and sent back to those remaining in Jerusalem by those already in exile (Bar 1:5–13).[51] The book lacks any instances of *Ioudaios*, while "Israel" appears nineteen times in five short chapters. The very structure of the book corresponds to an exile-repentance-restoration model, as the book opens with a lengthy prayer of confession (1:1–3:8) followed by a wisdom poem in the middle (3:9–4:4) and concludes with a poem of prophetic consolation (4:5–5:9).[52] Baruch does, however, go out of its

---

[51] Watson, *Hermeneutics of Faith*, 455. The dating of the book is uncertain, with most placing it somewhere between 200–60 BCE but with little precision. David G. Burke, *The Poetry of Baruch: A Reconstruction and Analysis of the Original Hebrew Text of Baruch 3:9–5:9* (Chico: Scholars Press, 1982), 26–28 provides a range of opinions, as does Shannon Burkes, "Wisdom and Law: Choosing Life in Ben Sira and Baruch," *JSJ* 30.3 (1999): 253–76 (269 n. 42). Burke places it in the Maccabean Period (180–100 BCE), while George W. E. Nickelsburg, *Jewish Literature between the Bible and the Mishnah* (Philadelphia: Fortress, 1981), 113 suggests 164 BCE as the date. Walter Harrelson, "Wisdom Hidden and Revealed according to Baruch (Baruch 3.9–4.4)," in *Priests, Prophets, and Scribes: Essays on the Formation and Heritage of Second Temple Judaism in Honour of Joseph Blenkinsopp*, eds. Eugene C. Ulrich et al., JSOTSup 149 (Sheffield: Sheffield Academic, 1992), 158–71 (159), argues for a final form of the book sometime in the late second or early third century. Moore, *Daniel, Esther, and Jeremiah*, 260, suggests the early second century BCE but thinks the third section could be later. Watson, *Hermeneutics of Faith*, 456–58, however, has shown the book to be dependent in some spots on Theodotion's version of Daniel, which suggests the book was composed sometime in the first century BCE, a judgment also held on other grounds by James L. Crenshaw, *Old Testament Wisdom: An Introduction*, 3rd ed. (Louisville: Westminster John Knox, 2010), 195–96. The dependence on Theodotion also suggests the book was written in Greek, making Baruch a problematic case for Goodblatt's linguistic version of Kuhn's paradigm (cf. Goodblatt, "Israelites Who Reside in Judah"; Goodblatt, "Varieties of Identity"). For other views on the original language of Baruch, see Emanuel Tov, *The Septuagint Translation of Jeremiah and Baruch: A Discussion of an Early Revision of the LXX of Jeremiah 29–52 and Baruch 1:1–3:8*, 8 (Cambridge: Harvard University Press, 1976), 111–33, 165; Moore, *Daniel, Esther, and Jeremiah*, 257; Odil Hannes Steck, *Das Buch Baruch, Der Brief des Jeremia, Zusätze zu Ester und Daniel*, ATD (Göttingen: Vandenhoeck & Ruprecht, 1998).

[52] Burke, *Poetry of Baruch*, 6–7, 20–23; Burkes, "Wisdom and Law," 269. Nickelsburg, *Jewish Literature*, 109, identifies four independent sections, distinguishing 1:1–14 as a separate introduction. See also George W. E. Nickelsburg, "The Bible Rewritten and Expanded," in *Jewish Writings of the Second Temple period*, ed. Michael E. Stone, CRINT 2 (Philadelphia: Fortress, 1984), 89–156 (140–46). Odil Hannes Steck, *Das apokryphe Baruchbuch: Studien zu Rezeption und Konzentration "kanonischer" Überlieferung*, FRLANT 160 (Göttingen: Vandenhoeck & Ruprecht, 1993) and Marko Marttila, "The Deuteronomic Ideology and Phraseology in the Book of Baruch," in *Changes in Scripture: Rewriting and Interpreting Authoritative Traditions in the*

way to distinguish the kingdom and territory of Judah as a subset of Israel, using the term Ἰούδα on seven occasions for that purpose (1:3, 8 [2x], 15; 2:1, 23, 26).

The first, confessional portion of the book is mostly modeled on the prayer of Daniel 9,[53] confessing that the curses of Deuteronomy have fallen upon "the people of Israel and Judah" (2:1; cf. 2:26).[54] The prayer of confession concludes with an appeal to Moses' promise of restoration (2:27–35),[55] declaring that this confession itself is part of the divinely granted repentance to accompany and initiate restoration:

> For you have put the fear of you in our hearts so that we would call upon your name;[56] and we will praise you in our exile [*apoikia*], for we have put away from our hearts all the iniquity of our ancestors who sinned against you. See, we are today in our exile [*apoikia*] where you have scattered [*diespeiras*] us, to be reproached and cursed and punished for all the iniquities of our ancestors, who forsook the Lord our God. (Bar 3:7–8)[57]

This opening prayer is followed by a wisdom poem in which Baruch explains that because Israel has neglected wisdom (3:12–14), namely the revelation of the Torah (3:35–4:1),[58] Israel is growing old among its

---

Second Temple period, eds. Hanne von Weissberg, Juha Pakkala, and Marko Marttila, BZAW 419 (Berlin: de Gruyter, 2011), 321–46 (321–22) similarly find four divisions, but see the division between the first two in the middle of 1:15. Steck, *Das apokryphe Baruchbuch*, 265 (followed by Marttila, "Deuteronomic Ideology"), argues convincingly that these sections form an intentional unity. Watson, *Hermeneutics of Faith*, 455, agrees, "there is logic to this arrangement, which should not too quickly be subjected to source-critical disintegration into originally independent fragments." Watson further notes that "The three parts of the book have their respective backgrounds in the law, the wisdom literature, and the prophets – that is, in all three sections of the scriptural canon" (456).

[53] Burkes, "Wisdom and Law," 269. See also Marttila, "Deuteronomic Ideology," 324. For a critique of the terminology of "penitential prayer," see Lambert, *How Repentance Became Biblical*, 33–49; David A. Lambert, "Fasting as a Penitential Rite: A Biblical Phenomenon?," *HTR* 96.4 (2003): 477–512; see also the discussions at n. 129 in Chapter 3 and n. 65 in Chapter 10.

[54] Watson, *Hermeneutics of Faith*, 460: "[I]n *Baruch*, the disasters that have now taken place show that the curse of the law is the controlling factor of Israel's whole history, from the exodus to the present. Paul is not alone in claiming that the whole of Israel's existence is subject to the curse of the law." Cf. Marttila, "Deuteronomic Ideology."

[55] Cf. Pitre, *Jesus*, 450; Watson, *Hermeneutics of Faith*, 462

[56] Wells, *Grace and Agency*, 138, notes the echo of LXX Jer 39:40 (32:40 MT) here.

[57] Translations of Baruch in this section are from the NRSV unless otherwise noted. In light of Chapter 6, the exceedingly negative use of the terms *apoikia* and *diaspeirō* in this passage is striking.

[58] The poem echoes Deut 30:12–13 to demonstrate that wisdom cannot be attained through human means (3:29–30) but goes on to assert that the Lord himself has presented wisdom

enemies in a foreign land, "defiled with the dead" and "counted among those in Hades" (3:10–11).[59] The wisdom poem concludes with an exhortation that Israel fully turn and be restored (4:2–6), after which the book progresses into a prophecy of consolation heavily dependent on Second Isaiah,[60] declaring that Israel will be restored and Jerusalem's enemies ruined and destroyed. As Wells explains, "Dead in exile, incompetent Israel will be reconstituted by God as a competent moral agent. The gift of a new heart along with the gift of Torah allows Israel to respond to God and obey unto life."[61] In keeping with the pattern set forth in prior biblical literature, Baruch therefore rhetorically situates the reader in the liminal space between exile and restoration, poised to receive the promise but as yet unable to enter.[62]

4 EZRA

Similar themes emerge in the apocalypse of 4 Ezra,[63] which was written in the wake of the destruction of the Second Temple and goes even further in its vision of a future messianic restoration of Israel that supersedes the incomplete restoration of Judah from Babylon, placing special emphasis on the miraculous return of the northern tribes:

---

to Israel in the form of the Torah revealed to Moses. Cf. Wells, *Grace and Agency*, 140–43.

[59] Marttila, "Deuteronomic Ideology," 331–32, shows that the wisdom poem is closely connected to the preceding section, as both are strongly influenced by Deut 4 and 30.

[60] Burkes, "Wisdom and Law," 274–75; Marttila, "Deuteronomic Ideology," 334; Ferda, "Ingathering of the Exiles," 178–79.

[61] Wells, *Grace and Agency*, 146. Burkes, "Wisdom and Law," 271 n. 47 notes the similarity of this theme in Baruch with that of Ezekiel 37's valley of dry bones. Wells, *Grace and Agency*, 136–37 notes several other key points of contact with Ezekiel, particularly in the metaphor of Israel receiving a new heart as accompanying the end of the exile.

[62] Watson, *Hermeneutics of Faith*, 472. Cf. also Steck, *Das apokryphe Baruchbuch*, 267–68; Scott, "Paul's Use," 647–50.

[63] 4 Ezra was probably composed in Hebrew but is extant in Latin, Syriac, and a few Greek quotations from Christian church fathers. The analysis here is based on the Latin text of Robert Lubbock Bensly, ed., *The Fourth Book of Ezra: The Latin Version, Edited from the MSS*, TS 2 (Cambridge: Cambridge University Press, 1895), though a more recent critical edition of the work can be found in Albertus F. J. Klijn, *Der lateinische Text der Apokalypse des Esra*, TUGAL 131 (Berlin: Academie, 1983). For a full discussion of the text of 4 Ezra, including a listing of the few unambiguous Greek quotations from early church fathers, see Michael E. Stone, *Fourth Ezra: A Commentary on the Book of Fourth Ezra*, Hermeneia 41 (Minneapolis: Fortress, 1990), 1–9.

And as for your seeing him gather to himself another multitude that was peace-able, *these are the ten tribes which were led away from their own land into captivity in the days of King Hoshea, whom Shalmaneser the king of the Assyrians led captive*; he took them across the river, and they were taken into another land. But they formed this plan for themselves, that they would leave the multitude of the nations and go to a more distant region, where mankind race had never lived, that there at least they might keep their statutes which they had not kept in their own land. For at that time the Most High performed signs for them, and stopped the channels of the river until they had passed over. ... Then they dwelt there until the last times; and now, when they are about to come again, the Most High will stop the channels of the river again, so that they may be able to pass over. Therefore you saw the multitude gathered together in peace. *But those who are left of your people, who are found within my holy borders, shall be saved.*

(4 Ezra 13:40–49, my emphasis)[64]

For 4 Ezra, a restoration that does not include the ten tribes deported by Assyria is by definition incomplete.[65] The final eschatological restor-ation must include "another multitude" comprising the bulk of Israel, while "those who are left of your people" (that is, Baruch's people, those from Judah) will be saved as well.[66] But 4 Ezra does not envision the eschatological gathering of Israel *from among* the nations as is often stated in the biblical prophets. Rather, in what may be a development of the tradition reflected in Tobit, in which Tobias and his family migrate to preserve their tribal heritage, the apocalyptic writer explicitly states that the northern tribes have withdrawn themselves from "the multitude of the nations" by traveling to a distant region in which no one else had ever lived (4 Ezra 13:41–45).[67] 4 Ezra thereby assuages any concern that the lineage of the northerners may have been adulterated by living among the nations for so long while also apparently eliminating any room for the concomitant salvation of the nations themselves.[68] In any case, 4 Ezra

---

[64] Translation from Bruce M. Metzger, "The Fourth Book of Ezra," in *OTP*, 517–59.

[65] The manuscripts of 4 Ezra vary between nine and ten tribes. The problem owes to ambiguity in the biblical materials as to how Levi and the two half-tribes of Ephraim and Manasseh are counted. As a result, the northern tribes are sometimes considered ten tribes and other times nine or nine and a half in early Jewish literature. See Schuller, "A Text about Joseph," 361. Cf. Stone, *Fourth Ezra*, 404, who concludes that the less common "nine and a half" is probably original.

[66] Cf. in this context John 10:16, which refers to sheep from another sheepfold who must be incorporated to create "one flock."

[67] See Levine, "Diaspora as Metaphor," 109 n. 9. The name of this legendary land likely derives from Deut 29:28, as shown by William A. Wright, "Note on the 'Arzareth,'" *Journal of Philology* 3 (1871): 113–14. On the river crossing and its relationship to later legends about the Sabbath river, see Barmash, "Nexus."

[68] Cf. Pitre, *Jesus*, 347 n. 307.

never mentions "the Jews," instead preferring "Israel," which appears twelve times and consistently refers to the full twelve-tribe nation in this work, providing yet another example of Israel terminology occurring in the context of restoration eschatology, including a particular emphasis on the restoration of northern Israelites.

2 BARUCH

Similarly written in the wake of the destruction of the Second Temple, perhaps even as a rejoinder to 4 Ezra,[69] the Syriac Apocalypse of Baruch (2 Baruch) begins by explicitly calling attention to the fate of the northern tribes:

Have you seen all that this people are doing to me, the evil things which the two tribes which remained have done – more than the ten tribes which were carried away into captivity? For the former tribes were forced by their kings to sin, but these two have themselves forced and compelled their kings to sin.

(2 Bar 1:2–3; cf.Jer 3)[70]

Later in the book, the vision of the "black seventh waters," a part of the so-called "Apocalypse of the Clouds," tells of the idolatry of the "nine and a half tribes" who followed Jeroboam and Jezebel until "the time of their captivity," when they were deported by Shalmaneser the king of Assyria (2 Bar 62). The book then concludes with Baruch writing two letters, one carried by an eagle to the nine and a half tribes – presumably because a human messenger could not find them – and the other sent to those that were at Babylon by means of three men (77:19).[71] The nine and a half tribes are thus envisioned as still in exile somewhere across the

---

[69] On 2 Baruch as a rejoinder to 4 Ezra, see John J. Collins, "Apocalypse," *EDEJ* 341–46 (344). For an argument that the literary relationship goes the other direction, see Pierre-Maurice Bogaert, *L'Apocalypse Syriaque de Baruch. Introduction, Traduction du Syriaque et Commentaire* (Paris: Cerf, 1969), 113–14, 284–88. For a synopsis of the two works, see Klaus Berger, *Synopse des Vierten Buches Esra und der Syrischen Baruch-Apokalypse*, TANZ (Tübingen: Francke, 1992).

[70] Translations of 2 Baruch from Klijn, *Der lateinische Text* unless otherwise noted.

[71] There is some textual variation here as to the number of tribes, with most Latin MSS have "ten," a few minor MSS have "nine," and the Syriac, two Arabic, and two Ethiopic MSS have "nine and a half." Stone, *Fourth Ezra*, 404, has persuasively argued that the last of these is most likely original. See also Bogaert, *L'Apocalypse Syriaque de Baruch*, 339–52 and the related discussion of the "two tribes" (1:2–4) versus "two and a half tribes" (62:5; 63:3; 64:5) in Liv Ingeborg Lied, *The Other Lands of Israel: Imaginations of the Land in 2 Baruch*, JSJSup 129 (Leiden: Brill, 2008), 38–39 n. 40 and the sources referenced there.

Euphrates (77:22), separated from those from Judah who have been exiled to Babylon. Nevertheless, Baruch assures the northern tribes that they are not forgotten, since "Are we not all, the twelve tribes, bound by one captivity as we also descend from one father?" (2 Bar 78:4). He then admonishes those tribes to repent and await restoration, concluding that "he will not forever forget or forsake our offspring, but with much mercy assemble all those again who were dispersed" (2 Bar 78:7). After a lengthy discourse in which Baruch summarizes what has happened to Zion since the deportation of the northern tribes and declares the characteristics of the impending eschatological reversal, Baruch warns,

Remember that once Moses called heaven and earth to witness against you and said, "If you trespass the law, you shall be dispersed. And if you shall keep it, you shall be planted." And also other things he said to you when you were in the desert as twelve tribes together. (2 Bar 84:2–3)

Given these strong restoration-eschatological themes, it should be no surprise that 2 Baruch limits Israel language to the full twelve-tribe entity (ten times) or the northern kingdom (62:3) while avoiding Jew/Judahite language except for three references to kings of Judah, strong evidence that 2 Baruch understands "Jew" to denote someone specifically from Judah.

TESTAMENT OF MOSES

These same themes also appear in the Testament of Moses (also called the Assumption of Moses), which presents itself as the secret prophecies of Moses transmitted to Joshua before Moses' death. The central narrative of Test. Mos. portrays the "ten tribes" as having rebelled against "two holy tribes" in Jerusalem (2:4), establishing "kingdoms for themselves according to their own ordinances" (2:5).[72] Ultimately the sins of the ten tribes filter down to the other two, leading to the following exchange upon the deportation of the two tribes by the "king from the east" who burns the holy temple (3:1):

Then, considering themselves like a lioness in a dusty plain, hungry and parched, the two tribes will call upon the ten tribes, and shall declare loudly, "Just and holy is the Lord. For just as you sinned, likewise we, with our little ones, have now been

---

[72] For introductory material on Test. Mos., most likely a first-century BCE composition with Christian interpolations, see Johannes Tromp, *The Assumption of Moses. A Critical Edition with Commentary* (Leiden: Brill, 1992); Johannes Tromp, "Moses, Assumption of," *EDEJ* 970–72; Kenneth R. Atkinson, *I Cried to the Lord: A Study of the Psalms of Solomon's Historical Background and Social Setting*, JSJSup 84 (Leiden: Brill, 2004).

led out with you." Then, hearing the reproachful words of the two tribes, the ten tribes will lament and will say, "What shall we, with you, do, brothers? Has not this tribulation come upon the whole house of Israel?" (3:4–7)[73]

After a captivity lasting "seventy-seven years" (3:14),

Then some parts of the tribes will arise and come to their appointed place [Jerusalem], and they will strongly build its walls. Now, the two tribes will remain steadfast in their former faith, sorrowful and sighing because they will not be able to offer sacrifices to the Lord of their fathers. But the ten tribes will grow and spread out among the nations during the time of their captivity. (4:7–9)[74]

Yet again, Israel's restoration is portrayed as incomplete, with only "some parts of the tribes" having returned after Cyrus' decree and only "the two tribes" continuing to serve the Lord faithfully. Nevertheless, Test. Mos. assures the reader that God will eventually visit the earth, at which point Israel would be fully saved, crushing the nations and looking down upon them from the heights of heaven (10:7–10).[75] Like Josephus (*Ant.* 11.132–33) but in contrast to 4 Ezra, the Testament of Moses portrays the ten tribes as multiplying and increasing to huge numbers among the nations of their exile. Moreover, in keeping with its restorationist focus, Test. Mos. entirely avoids *Ioudaios* language in favor of "ten tribes"/"two tribes" terminology, with both uses of "Israel" referring to the twelve tribes as a whole.

CONCLUSION: ESCHATOLOGICAL ISRAEL IN THE SECOND TEMPLE PERIOD

Although Second Temple literature is by no means univocal, a thorough review has demonstrated a striking degree of consistency with respect to how ethnic terminology for Israel and the Jews is used across these texts. This is especially true in apocalyptic and eschatologically focused texts, which universally favor the term Israel as they focus on the biblical past and eschatological future. In the process, these texts show a surprising degree of concern about the fate of the northern tribes of Israel, and many express the expectations of a future Israelite restoration specifically

---

[73] Translation from John Priest, "Testament of Moses," in *OTP*, 919–34.
[74] Translation from Priest, "Testament of Moses."
[75] Ferda, "Ingathering of the Exiles," 180 n. 60, notes that Test. Mos. 10 twice echoes Isa 40 while describing the final ingathering, reading Isa 40 "as a description of the end-time when God comes to vindicate Israel and fulfill his promises to them."

including these tribes, though the means of that salvation is not uniform across the various texts. This correlation between Israel terminology, concern for the fate of the northern tribes, and restoration eschatology is unlikely to be accidental, particularly given its connection to earlier biblical uses of the same terminology. Put another way, it is evident that the terms "Israel" and *Ioudaioi/Yehudim* operate within their own semantic domains throughout Second Temple literature, and it appears those domains are ultimately governed by the narratives established in what eventually became the Jewish Scriptures, which ensured that Jewish communities continued to "remember" the difference between the extent of their present communities and the totality of Israel, the restoration of which still lay in the future.

I 2

Israel, Hebrews, Jews, and Restoration Eschatology

Some have proposed that remnant theology remained strong, and that all the parties and sects of Jesus' day saw themselves as the remnant, the "true Israel." But it is a striking fact that, in the surviving literature, no group applies either title to itself during its own historical existence.

E. P. Sanders[1]

After examining a wide variety of evidence from the Second Temple period in some detail, several conclusions can now be drawn. Remarkably, the one perspective not significantly represented in this body of evidence is the one usually assumed by modern scholars: namely, that Israel is equivalent to the Jews (*Ioudaioi/Yehudim*). Rather than being an accurate historical or sociological reconstruction of the data, that assumption is best characterized as a theological position based on later polemics. Moreover, there is also no ancient evidence that suggests "Jew" should be understood as an outsider term while "Israelite" and "Hebrew" function as insider terms. Instead, the evidence is overwhelming that the three terms and the concepts they represent are neither synonymous nor coextensive in the Second Temple period, with each having its own specific nuance, overlapping with but not identical to the meaning of the others.

Throughout the period covered by this book, one constant is that Israel is the name either for the tribes of the biblical northern kingdom or for the twelve-tribe covenantal people of YHWH; a totalizing adjective is sometimes used to clarify that the latter meaning is in view (e.g., "all Israel"). Since neither entity existed in anything resembling its pre-exilic form after

---

[1] Sanders, "Jesus and Judaism," 96.

the destructive events of the Neo-Assyrian and Neo-Babylonian periods, Israelite status thereafter became a matter of conflict and contestation throughout the Second Temple period, with a number of variously related communities claiming to be heirs of the legacy of the biblical children of Jacob.[2] Both Jews and Samaritans, for example, considered themselves Israelites, though many Jews disregarded Samaritan claims to Israelite status as illegitimate. Neither group, however, identified Samaritans as Jews, which means that throughout our period of inquiry there were communities of self-identified Israelites who were not Jews – indeed, when "Israel" appears in pre-Christian Graeco-Roman sources, it refers to Samaritans rather than Jews.[3] Samaritan claims to Israelite status are not the only evidence for a continued distinction between the terms, however, as Jewish literature from this period also consistently distinguishes between the Jews (*Ioudaioi/Yehudim*) and Israel.

The best explanation of this fact is that the *partitive* relationship between Israel and Judah established in biblical literature persisted within the tradition. That is, "Jew" continues to refer to the subset of Israel specifically derived from the kingdom of Judah either by descent, marriage, or (eventually) proselytism/conversion. Because Judah is only part of Israel, the Samaritans, who claimed to be derived from the northern tribes of Israel rather than Judah, could claim Israelite heritage without being considered Jews or, as some have mistakenly suggested, "half-Jews."[4] Moreover, since only a small portion of the descendants of exiles from the kingdom of Judah ever returned to the land, a wide range of early Jewish texts ranging from the Torah to works written well into the Common Era portray Israel's exile as incomplete at best, with Israel remaining under the covenantal curses for disobedience, awaiting the promised redemption. Many of these texts continue to show a surprising degree of concern with the fate of the northern tribes scattered by Assyria in the eighth century BCE.

The prevalence of this concern for the northern kingdom in so much early Jewish literature suggests that although there has been no lack of

---

[2] Knoppers, *Jews and Samaritans*, 12.

[3] Grabbe, "Israel's Historical Reality," 13. See p. 60.

[4] E.g., Albert S. Geyser, "Israel in the Fourth Gospel," *Neot* 20 (1986): 13–20 (15); Stanley E. Porter and Cynthia Long Westfall, "A Cord of Three Strands: Mission in Acts," in *Christian Mission: Old Testament Foundations and New Testament Developments*, McMaster New Testament Studies (Eugene: Wipf and Stock, 2010), 108–34 (116). By contrast, Idumaeans, who had been forcibly circumcised in the second century BCE, were sometimes labeled "half-Jews," as shown by Josephus, *Ant.* 14.403.

research on Jewish messianism and eschatology in the Second Temple period, most of these studies have neglected a (perhaps *the*) key element of restoration eschatology: Jews in this period did not anticipate merely a *Jewish* restoration but a full restoration of *all Israel*. In keeping with this expectation, Jewish literature in this period consistently distinguishes between Israel (the whole) and the Jews (one part of the whole). Consequently, early Jewish texts that deal either with pre-exilic history or the eschatological restoration consistently prefer the term Israel, while those texts that refer to the contemporary (post-exilic) *ethnos* avoid that term, consistently preferring *Ioudaios* except when referring to biblical or eschatological Israel or in contexts of prayer or ritual. Many of these prayers confess Israel's past transgression and request divine reconciliation, further reinforcing a connection between Israel terminology and restoration eschatology.[5] Thus Israel is the covenantal term for the full people of YHWH, but is also a scattered, fragmented, and incomplete entity at present. Only after YHWH fully restores and reunites his people will "all Israel" be complete again.

This difference in terminology is therefore not due to an insider/outsider distinction but instead owes to the long historical and theological background of the terms and the overarching impact of the biblically mediated social memory of a past twelve-tribe Israel of which Judah was only one part. This distinction explains why the Hasmonaean state called itself Judah rather than Israel, a fact that has caused significant confusion among interpreters holding to the insider/outsider paradigm.[6] But neither Persian Yehud nor Hasmonaean Judaea could claim to be Israel, especially given the Samaritan presence not far north of Jerusalem and how far short conditions fell of the promises of restoration, though the testimony of 1 Maccabees suggests that at least some hoped the Hasmonean

---

[5] In keeping with Lambert, *How Repentance Became Biblical*, 33–49, I prefer the terminology of "appeal" rather than "penitence," since the latter tends to imply an introspective contrition not necessarily implied by these prayers. Notable examples already observed above include Neh 1:5–11; Dan 9:4–19; 2 Macc 1:24–29; Tob 3:2–6; Bar 1:1–3:8. For more on the development of these prayer traditions in early Judaism, see Mark J. Boda, Daniel K. Falk, and Rodney Alan Werline, eds., *The Origins of Penitential Prayer in Second Temple Judaism* (Leiden: Brill, 2006); Mark J. Boda, Daniel K. Falk, and Rodney Alan Werline, eds., *The Development of Penitential Prayer in Second Temple Judaism* (Atlanta: Scholars Press, 2007); Mark J. Boda, Daniel K. Falk, and Rodney Alan Werline, eds., *The Impact of Penitential Prayer beyond Second Temple Judaism* (Atlanta: Scholars Press, 2008).

[6] E.g., Goodblatt, "Israelites Who Reside in Judah," 84, 86.

kingdom would result in the restored Israel promised by the biblical prophets.

Since the kingdom of Judah included other tribes, most notably Benjamin and Levi, *Ioudaios* does double duty as a tribal label and an umbrella term including other tribes, introducing further ambiguity since some Jews were more Jewish (that is, from the tribe of Judah) than others. Moreover, throughout the Second Temple period, "the patriarchs and their tribal lineages remained central to the Jewish conception of their own history,"[7] with tribal distinctions continuing to be observed far longer than is often appreciated.[8] Moreover, if *Ioudaios* is also understood as an umbrella label including other tribes, this helps account for its use in "outsider" contexts, as the term distinguishes the larger group (Judah, Levi, Benjamin) from outsiders not associated with the descendants of the kingdom of Judah, while fellow Jews distinguished themselves from one another by tribe and other markers, such as language or geography.[9] Once again, a diagram is helpful, illustrating how various markers can serve as subsets of a larger whole when identifying oneself within or among groups (see Figure 3).

The third term, "Hebrew" (*Hebraios*) is often used to refer to someone from ancient, biblical Israel, especially in the pre-monarchy period, and also serves as a less ambiguous way of referring to the whole people in the period of the divided monarchies. Applied to contemporaries, it seems to carry an ethno-linguistic nuance throughout the Second Temple period, referring to a speaker (or perhaps reader) of a Semitic tongue, more commonly Aramaic but also potentially including what we call Hebrew today. Thus a Jew who spoke only Greek or Latin is not a "Hebrew," but an Aramaic-speaking Jew or Samaritan would be. The Samaritan, however, although a Hebrew, would not be a "Jew." Thus a Hebrew is not

---

[7] Rajak, *Translation and Survival*, 107. On the continued importance of tribal descent in Jewish identity, see also Daniel R. Schwartz, *Studies in the Jewish Background of Christianity* (Tübingen: Mohr, 1992), 8–9. *Pace* Michael Satlow, who suggests that tribal identity was "long-defunct" by the first century CE (*How the Bible Became Holy* (New Haven: Yale University Press, 2014), 301 n. 7).

[8] In addition to Tobit and the numerous examples in the Dead Sea Scrolls, the humorous explanations for why Esther 2:5 calls Mordecai both יהודי איש ("man of Judah" or "Jew/Judahite") and איש ימיני ("Benjaminite") offered in b. Meg. 12b–13a further attest to the persistence of the tribal sense of the term. As Lowe, "Who Were the ΙΟΥΔΑΙΟΙ," 106, points out, the tribal meaning of יהודי is also preserved in m. Sotah 8:1 and m. Taanith 4:5.

[9] E.g., in the New Testament, Jews not from Judaea are frequently referred to by their place of origin: Mary Magdalene, Saul of Tarsus, Joseph of Arimathea, Jesus of Nazareth, etc. (Thanks to Jodi Magness for reminding me of this point.)

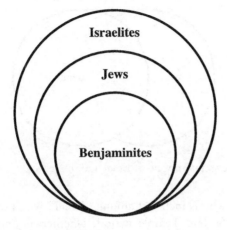

Figure 3 Umbrella terms and nested identities

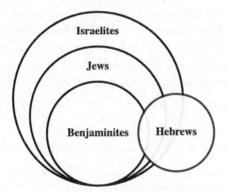

Figure 4 Israelites, Jews, Benjaminites, and Hebrews

necessarily an Israelite or a Jew, and a Jew or Israelite is not necessarily a Hebrew. Mapping "Hebrew" on the previous graphical illustration of terms results in something like Figure 4.

Similarly, although Jews are Israelites, not all Israelites are Jews, and some, such as Philo or the Dead Sea Scroll sectarians, even suggest that not all Jews are necessarily Israelites, adopting the biblical prophetic view that individuals can be cut off from Israel through disobedience and unfaithfulness to the covenant. That is, although Jews are a subset of Israel, Israelite status is something that can be lost, so being Jewish does not – at least for many of these authors – necessarily guarantee Israelite status (see Figure 5).

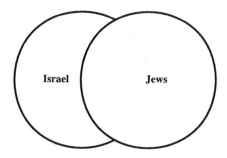

Figure 5 Prophetic/sectarian view of Israel and the Jews

Thus exactly who is included among "Israel" was a matter of dispute throughout the Second Temple period, whether among Jews debating with other Jews or among Jews and Samaritans. The Samaritans present a special problem as non-Jews with a claim to Israelite heritage, while Jewish assessments of Samaritans vary, with some Jews apparently accepting their claim to Israelite status and others rejecting it entirely.[10] But at least some of those rejecting Samaritan claims seem not to have regarded them as gentiles; they were instead a *tertium quid*, something between Israelite and gentile.[11] Samaritans, on the other hand, although

---

[10] The son of the high priest Eliashib who married the daughter of Sanballat would likely fall in the first group, while Nehemiah would certainly fall in the latter group (Neh 13:28).

[11] This seems to be the case in Matthew, Luke-Acts, and John in the New Testament, for example. Cf. Knoppers, *Jews and Samaritans*, 220–21; Vanmelitharayil John Samkutty, *The Samaritan Mission in Acts*, LNTS 328 (London: T&T Clark, 2006). Similarly, even after the Second Temple period, "most [Tannaitic] passages concerning the Samaritans mention non-Jews and *kutim* as separate categories" (Schiffman, "The Samaritans in Tannaitic Halakhah," 325–26); it is not until sometime between the mid-second and fourth centuries that the Samaritans are more clearly distinguished from Israelites and classed with foreigners or *goyim*. Cf. Ophir and Rosen-Zvi, *Goy*, 185–92; Shahar, "Imperial Religious Unification Policy"; Rocco Bernasconi, "Tannaitic 'Israel' and the Kutim," in *Entre lignes de partage et territoires de passage: les identités religieuses dans les mondes grec et romain. "Paganismes," "judaïsmes," "christianismes,"* eds. Nicole Belayche and Simon C. Mimouni, Collection de la Revue des Études Juives 47 (Leuven: Peeters, 2008), 365–92; Yitzhak Magen and N. Carmin, *The Samaritans and the Good Samaritan*, trans. Edward Levin, Judea and Samaria Publications (Jerusalem: Israel Antiquities Authority, 2008); Pieter W. van der Horst, "Anti-Samaritan Propaganda in Early Judaism," in *Persuasion and Dissuasion in Early Christianity, Ancient Judaism, and Hellenism* (Leuven: Peeters, 2003), 25–44; Yehudah Elitsur, "Samaritans in Tannaitic Texts," in *Israel and the Bible: Studies in Geography, History, and Biblical Thought*, eds. Amos Frisch and Yoel Elitsur (Ramat Gan: Bar Ilan University Press, 2000), 393–414; Reinhard Pummer, "Samaritanism in Caesarea Maritima," in

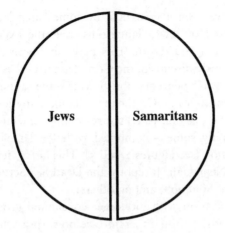

Figure 6 All Israel comprised of Jews and Samaritans

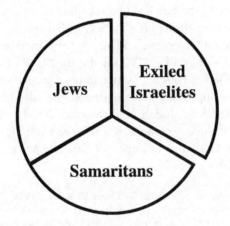

Figure 7 All Israel including Jews, Samaritans, and exiles

disputing the validity and centrality of the Jerusalem sanctuary, apparently did not deny their Jewish counterparts the right to consider themselves part of Israel (as in Figures 6 and 7).[12]

In Figure 6, Samaritans and Jews comprise the two parts of Israel,
corresponding to the ancient northern and southern kingdoms of Israel;

Religious Rivalries and the Struggle for Success in Caesarea Maritima, ed. Terence
L. Donaldson, SCJ (Waterloo: Wilfrid Laurier University Press, 2000), 181–202.
[12] Hjelm, "Changing Paradigms," 164.

this seems to have been a view held by some Samaritans. In Figure 7, Israel is comprised of Jews, Samaritans, and the exiles of Israel still awaiting restoration and return. This may have been the view of Ezra (though as previously discussed, the term "Samaritan" is anachronistic in that period) and was apparently the view of some rabbinic sages at least until the third century CE.[13] On the other hand, many Jews in this period regarded Samaritans as non-Israelites, restricting Israelite status to Jews – whether all or only some – combined with the Israelites still in exile awaiting restoration (see Figures 2 and 5). This latter view seems to have been shared by Nehemiah, Josephus, the Dead Sea Scroll sect, Ben Sira, and the Psalms of Solomon, among others.

Given its association with the larger covenantal group and eschato-logical expectations, it should therefore be no surprise that when Second Temple Jewish groups do use "Israel" self-referentially, the use of that term tends to reflect eschatological, messianic, or political claims – as is the case in Ezra-Nehemiah, 1 Maccabees, the Dead Sea Scrolls, the Jewish Revolt of 66–73 CE, the Bar Kokhba rebellion of 132–35 CE, and early Christianity.[14] Indeed, throughout the Second Temple period, the concept of Israel is always theological, and to identify with Israel is always a theological claim – after all, YHWH is not the "God of the Jews" alone but always the "God of Israel."[15] Often implied in such self-application is that although the opponents of such groups may also be "Jews" in that they are descended from Judah (and therefore Israel), the restorationist group may regard these opponents as excluded from "Israel" in its sense of the "people of God" due to improper halakhic practices.[16] Such a use

---

[13] As concluded by Shahar, "Imperial Religious Unification Policy," 118, "Up to the beginning of the third century, the Jews of Palestine tended to relate to their Samaritan neighbors as to distant relatives. In most areas of life, the Samaritan was seen as a kind of inferior Jew [sic] of unclear origins who did not take proper care to observe a number of religious laws." Similarly, Bernasconi, "Tannaitic 'Israel,'" 392; Ophir and Rosen-Zvi, *Goy*, 186–91.

[14] Davies, "Old and New Israel," 35, notes the "remarkable, detailed parallels" between the Dead Sea Scroll sect as presented in CD and the Ezra-Nehemiah stories in their presentation of Israel. Jennifer Eyl is therefore correct to argue that Paul's self-referential use of "Israelite" leverages the antiquity and authority associated with that term ("'I Myself Am an Israelite,'" 163), though it is not the case that "Israelite" amounts to "a really, *really* ancient Judean" (154–55), nor does Paul proclaim the "Judean deity" (150) but rather the God of Israel.

[15] Cf. Kaatz, *Die mündliche Lehre*, 43; Zeitlin, "Hebrew, Jew and Israel," 366–67; Kuhn, "Ἰουδαῖος κτλ," *TDNT* 3: 360. See n. 60 in Chapter 1.

[16] This also happens in later rabbinic literature, as pointed out by Bernasconi, "Tannaitic 'Israel'," 391–92: "Their [The Samaritans'] genealogical belonging to Israel is not

of the term marks the group as a part of the chosen remainder of Israel in position for (or already participating in) the promised restoration, whereas their opponents are not part of the group in line for eschatological salvation.[17] Moreover, as illustrated by Ezra-Nehemiah and the Dead Sea sect, some groups seem to have concluded that the final, complete restoration of all Israel depended on their keeping correct halakha.

In this context, rather than speaking merely of a variegated Judaism (or Judaisms) in the Second Temple period, it is more accurate to speak of multiple forms of *Israelism,* as various Yahwistic groups claimed the heritage and legacy of Israel in the new contexts brought about by the destruction and dissolution of the historical kingdoms of Israel and Judah and reshaped by the literature and traditions developed in exile. Judaism is only one of these forms of Israelism; the Samaritans comprise another. What ultimately became Christianity also arose in this formative context, as Jesus himself proclaimed the end of the Age of Wrath and the

negated, however, by classifying them among the classes of doubtful status, they are prevented from entering the congregation of Israel by way of marriage. ... the decisive element that prevents them from entering the congregation of Israel is not their genealogical status, but rather their understanding of impurity rules. Both cases clearly exhibit an arbitrary character and are the result of precise ideological choices, the effect of which is that there are Israelites and even Judeans (in the case of the Sadducees) that are excluded from 'Israel.'" The same phenomenon of Israelites and Jews being excluded from the "assembly" (*ekklesia*) due to ideological or halakhic differences is evident in earliest Christianity as well as the Dead Sea Scrolls.

[17] This also helps account for why, despite their widespread use in the Second Temple period, cognates of "Jew" rarely appear in Jewish sources after the second century CE and are "virtually nonexistent from the fifth and following centuries" (Baker, "A 'Jew' by Any Other Name," 166; cf. Kraemer, "Meaning of the Term Jew"). Along with the destruction of the temple and failures of the revolts of the late first and early second century, Christian claims to Israelite status (e.g., Justin Martyr, *Dial.* 11:5; Barn 4:6–7, 14:5) – and hostility toward the Jews – likely influenced the growing preference for Israel terminology in Jewish literature after the second century. (cf. Daniel Boyarin, "Justin Martyr Invents Judaism," *CH* 70.3 [2001]: 427–61). Like their Christian rivals, the rabbis regarded themselves as part of the congregation of Israel – albeit incomplete _ while those outside are not truly Israelites, and their choice of language reflects this theological claim. For Israel as still incomplete in rabbinic literature, see m. Sanh. 10:3; b. Sanh. 110b–111a; Gen. Rab. 98.2.4–5; 98.11.2. Cf. Jacob Neusner, *Genesis Rabbah: The Judaic Commentary to the Book of Genesis, A New American Translation*, 3 vols. (Atlanta: Scholars Press, 1985), 1.ix. On restoration eschatology in the *Amidah*, see Reuven Kimelman, "The Daily 'Amidah and the Rhetoric of Redemption," *JQR* 79.2/3 (1988): 165–97. It should also be noted that rabbinic literature also frequently inhabits an idealized space in which Israel is dwelling in the land with a functioning temple under proper Torah regulations, a context in which one would expect Israel terminology in the Second Temple period as well.

ingathering of all Israel – that is, the coming of the "kingdom of God" and the restoration of all twelve tribes of Israel (cf. Matt 19:28 // Luke 22:30). In this light, Paul's "all Israel" in Romans 11:26 also takes on more significance, as although certainly an ethnic term including Jews, "all Israel" is not the same as "all Jews" but is almost certainly a reference to the full twelve-tribe totality, which Paul, as an apocalyptic Jew, seems to have expected to be restored.[18] Thus although Christianity initially began as an apocalyptic/restorationist Jewish sect, it quickly – especially once gentiles began to be incorporated as equal members – became something else, yet another competing form of Israelism.

---

[18] See Staples, "All Israel."

Bibliography

Abegg, Martin G. "Exile and the Dead Sea Scrolls." Pages 111–25 in *Exile: Old Testament, Jewish, and Christian Conceptions*. Edited by James M. Scott. JSJSup 56. Leiden: Brill, 1997.

Abraham, Kathleen. "West Semitic and Judean Brides in Cuneiform Sources from the Sixth Century BCE: New Evidence from a Marriage Contract from Āl-Yahudu." *Archiv für Orientforschung* (2005): 198–219.

Accordance Bible Software 13. Altamonte Springs, FL: Oak Tree Software, Inc., 2019.

Ackroyd, Peter R. *Exile and Restoration: A Study of Hebrew Thought of the Sixth Century BC*. Louisville, KY: Westminster John Knox, 1968.

——. "An Inheritance Division among Judeans in Babylonia from the Early Persian Period." Pages 148–82 in *New Seals and Inscriptions: Hebrew, Idumean, and Cuneiform*. Edited by Meir Lubetski. HBM 7. Sheffield: Sheffield Phoenix, 2007.

Aharoni, Yohanan. "The Solomonic Districts." *TA* 3.1 (1976): 5–15.

Albertz, Rainer, James Nogalski, and Jakob Wöhrle, eds. *Perspectives on the Formation of the Book of the Twelve: Methodological Foundations, Redactional Processes, Historical Insights*. Berlin: de Gruyter, 2012.

Alexander, Philip S. "How Did the Rabbis Learn Hebrew?" Pages 71–89 in *Hebrew Study from Ezra to Ben-Yehuda*. Edited by William Horbury. Edinburgh: T&T Clark, 1999.

Alexander, T. Desmond. "Royal Expectations in Genesis to Kings." *TynBul* 49.2 (1998): 191–212.

——. "The Regal Dimension of the תולדות־יעקב: Recovering the Literary Context of Genesis 37–50." Pages 196–212 in *Reading the Law: Studies in Honor of Gordon J. Wenham*. Edited by J. Gordon McConville and Karl Möller. LHBOTS. New York, NY: T&T Clark, 2007.

Allegue, J. Vázquez. "Abba Padre! (4Q372 1, 16) Dios como Padre en Qumrán." *Estudios Trinitarios* 32 (1998): 167–86.

Allen, Graham. *Intertextuality*. 2nd ed. The New Critical Idiom. London: Routledge, 2011.

Allen, Leslie C. *Psalms 101–150*. Accordance/Thomas Nelson electronic ed. WBC 21. Waco, TX: Word, 1983.

Ezekiel 20–48. Accordance electronic ed. WBC 29. Grand Rapids, MI: Zondervan, 1990.

Amir, Yehoshua. "Philo's Version of the Pilgrimage to Jerusalem." Pages 154–65 in *Jerusalem in the Second Temple period*. Edited by Aharon Oppenheimer, Uriel Rappaport, and Menahem Stern. Jerusalem: Yad Izhak Ben-Zvi, 1980.

Die hellenistische Gestalt des Judentums bei Philon von Alexandrien. Forschungen zum jüdisch-christlichen Dialog 5. Neukirchen-Vluyn: Neukirchener Verlag, 1983.

Amusin, Joseph D. "Éphraïm et Manassé dans le Péshèr de Nahum (4 Q p Nahum)." *RevQ* 4 (1963): 389–96.

"The Reflection of Historical Events of the First Century BC in Qumran Commentaries (4Q 161; 4Q 169; 4Q 166)." *HUCA* 48 (1977): 123–52.

Andersen, Francis I., and David Noel Freedman. *Hosea: A New Translation with Introduction and Commentary*. AB 24. Garden City, NY: Doubleday, 1980.

Amos: A New Translation with Introduction and Commentary. Accordance electronic ed. AB 24A. New York, NY: Doubleday, 1989.

Anderson, Gary A. *The Genesis of Perfection: Adam and Eve in Jewish and Christian Imagination*. Louisville, KY: Westminster John Knox, 2001.

Anderson, H. "3 Maccabees." Pages 509–29 in OTP 2. Edited by James H. Charlesworth. Garden City, NY: Doubleday, 1985.

Anderson, Jeff S. "From Communities of Texts to Religious Communities: Problems and Pitfalls." Pages 351–55 in *Enoch and Qumran Origins: New Light on a Forgotten Connection*. Edited by Gabriele Boccaccini. Grand Rapids, MI: Eerdmans, 2005.

Anon. "Die Gedenkakrobatik Des Talmuds." Völkischer Beobachter (Berlin: 1939 Jan 21): 5.

Archer, Gleason L. "The Relationship between the Septuagint Translation and the Massoretic Text in Jeremiah." *TJ* 12.2 (1991): 139–50.

Ariel, Yaakov. "An Unexpected Alliance: Christian Zionism and Its Historical Significance." *Modern Judaism* 26.1 (2006): 74–100.

Ashton, John. "The Identity and Function of The Ἰουδαῖοι in the Fourth Gospel." *NovT* 27.1 (1985): 40–75.

Understanding the Fourth Gospel. Oxford: Oxford University Press, 1993.

Atkinson, Kenneth R. "Herod the Great, Sosius, and the Siege of Jerusalem (37 BCE) in Psalm of Solomon 17." *NovT* 38.4 (1996): 313–22.

"On the Herodian Origin of Militant Davidic Messianism at Qumran: New Light from Psalm of Solomon 17." *JBL* 118.3 (1999): 435–60.

I Cried to the Lord: A Study of the Psalms of Solomon's Historical Background and Social Setting. JSJSup 84. Leiden: Brill, 2004.

"Solomon, Psalms of." *EDEJ* 1238–41.

Attridge, Harold W. *The Interpretation of Biblical History in the Antiquitates Judaicae of Flavius Josephus*. HDR. Missoula, MT: Scholars Press, 1976.

Review of *Das Selbstverstdndnis der jüdischen Diaspora in der hellenistisch-römischen Zeit*, by Willem Cornelis van Unnik. *Journal of the American Oriental Society* 115.2 (1995): 323–24.

Atzmon, Gil et al. "Abraham's Children in the Genome Era: Major Jewish Diaspora Populations Comprise Distinct Genetic Clusters with Shared Middle Eastern Ancestry." *American Journal of Human Genetics* 86.6 (2010): 850–59.

Aune, David E., and Eric Clark Stewart. "From the Idealized Past to the Imaginary Future: Eschatological Restoration in Jewish Apocalyptic Literature." Pages 147–77 in *Restoration: Old Testament, Jewish and Christian Perspectives*. Edited by James M. Scott. JSJSup 72. Leiden: Brill, 2001.

Aviv, Caryn, and David Shneer. *New Jews: The End of the Jewish Diaspora*. New York, NY: New York University Press, 2005.

Bachmann, Michael. "Verus Israel: Ein Vorschlag zu einer 'mengentheoretischen' Neubeschreibung der betreffenden paulinischen Terminologie." *NTS* 48.4 (2002): 500–12.

Bader, Chris. "When Prophecy Passes Unnoticed: New Perspectives on Failed Prophecy." *JSSR* 38.1 (1999): 119–31.

Baker, Cynthia M. "A 'Jew' by Any Other Name." *JAJ* 2 (2011): 153–80.

———. *Jew*. New Brunswick, NJ: Rutgers University Press, 2017.

Baltzer, Klaus. *The Covenant Formulary in Old Testament, Jewish and Early Christian Writings*. Philadelphia, PA: Fortress, 1971.

———. *Deutero-Isaiah: A Commentary on Isaiah 40–55*. Accordance electronic ed. Hermeneia 23C. Minneapolis, MN: Fortress, 2000.

Barclay, John M. G. *Jews in the Mediterranean Diaspora: From Alexander to Trajan (323 BCE–117 CE)*. Berkeley, CA: University of California Press, 1996.

———. "By the Grace of God I Am What I Am: Grace and Agency in Philo and Paul." Pages 140–57 in *Divine and Human Agency in Paul and His Cultural Environment*. Edited by John M. G. Barclay and Simon Gathercole. Library of Biblical Studies 335. London: T&T Clark, 2006.

———. "Grace within and beyond Reason: Philo and Paul in Dialogue." Pages 9–21 in *Paul, Grace and Freedom: Essays in Honour of J. K. Riches*. Edited by Paul Middleton, Angus Paddison, and Karen Wenell. London: T&T Clark, 2009.

———. *Pauline Churches and Diaspora Jews*. WUNT 275. Tübingen: Mohr Siebeck, 2011.

Barmash, Pamela. "At the Nexus of History and Memory: The Ten Lost Tribes." *AJSR* 29.2 (2005): 207–36.

Barrett, C. K. *The Second Epistle to the Corinthians*. Black's New Testament Commentaries. London: Black, 1973.

Barstad, Hans M. *A Way in the Wilderness: The "Second Exodus" in the Message of Second Isaiah*. Journal of Semitic Studies Monograph Series. Manchester: University of Manchester Press, 1989.

———. *The Myth of the Empty Land: A Study in the History and Archaeology of Judah during the "Exilic" Period*. SO 28. Oslo: Scandinavian University Press, 1996.

———. "After the 'Myth of the Empty Land': Major Challenges in the Study of Neo-Babylonian Judah." Pages 3–20 in *Judah and the Judeans in the Neo-Babylonian Period*. Edited by Oded Lipschits and Joseph Blenkinsopp. Winona Lake, IN: Eisenbrauns, 2003.

Bauckham, Richard J. "Anna of the Tribe of Asher." Pages 77–107 in *Gospel Women: Studies of the Named Women in the Gospels*. GTA 25. London: Bloomsbury, 2002.

"Tobit as a Parable for the Exiles of Northern Israel." Pages 140–64 in *Studies in the Book of Tobit: A Multidisciplinary Approach*. Edited by Mark R. J. Bredin. LSTS 55. London: T&T Clark, 2006.

Baumgarten, Joseph M. "The Calendars of the Book of Jubilees and the Temple Scroll." *VT* (1987): 71–78.

Baynes, Leslie. *The Heavenly Book Motif in Judeo-Christian Apocalypses, 200 BCE–200 CE*. JSJSup 152. Leiden: Brill, 2012.

Beattie, D. R. G., and Philip R. Davies. "What Does Hebrew Mean?" *JSS* 56.1 (2011): 71–83.

Beavis, Mary Ann. "The Kingdom of God, 'Utopia' and Theocracy." *JSHJ* 2.1 (2004): 91–106.

Becking, Bob. "Is het boek Nahum een literaire eenheid?" *Nederlands theologisch tijdschrift* 32 (1978): 111–14.

———. "Jeremiah's Book of Consolation: A Textual Comparison Notes on the Masoretic Text and the Old Greek Version of Jeremiah XXX–XXXI." *VT* 44.2 (1994): 145–69.

———. "Do the Earliest Samaritan Inscriptions Already Indicate a Parting of the Ways?" Pages 213–22 in *Judah and the Judaeans in the Fourth Century BCE*. Edited by Oded Lipschits, Gary N. Knoppers, and Rainer Albertz. Winona Lake, IN: Eisenbrauns, 2007.

———. *Ezra, Nehemiah, and the Construction of Early Jewish Identity*. FAT 80. Tübingen: Mohr Siebeck, 2011.

———. "Yehudite Identity in Elephantine." Pages 403–19 in *Judah and the Judeans in the Achaemenid Period: Negotiating Identity in an International Context*. Edited by Oded Lipschits, Gary N. Knoppers, and Manfred Oeming. Winona Lake, IN: Eisenbrauns, 2011.

Beckwith, Roger T. "Daniel 9 and the Date of Messiah's Coming in Essene, Hellenistic, Pharisaic, Zealot and Early Christian Computation." *RevQ* 10.4 (1981): 521–42.

Beek, M. A. Review of *Achtzehngebet und Vaterunser und der Reim*, by Karl Georg Kuhn. *Vox Theologica* 21 (1950): 21–22.

Beentjes, Pancratius C. "De stammen van Israël herstellen: Het portret van Elia bij Jesus Sirach." *ACEBT* 5 (1984): 147–55.

———. *The Book of Ben Sira in Hebrew: A Text Edition of All Extant Hebrew Manuscripts and a Synopsis of All Parallel Hebrew Ben Sira Texts*. VTSup 68. Leiden: Brill, 1997.

———. "Prophets and Prophecy in the Book of Ben Sira." Pages 135–50 in *Prophets, Prophecy, and Prophetic Texts in Second Temple Judaism(427)*. Edited by Michael H. Floyd and Robert D. Haak. LHBOTS 427. London: T&T Clark, 2006.

———. "Ben Sira 44:19–23 – The Patriarchs: Text, Tradition, Theology." Pages 209–28 in *Studies in the Book of Ben Sira: Papers of the Third International Conference on the Deuterocanonical Books, Papa, Hungary, 18–20 May 2006(127)*. Edited by Géza G. Xeravits and József Zsengellér. JSJSup 127. Leiden: Brill, 2008.

Begg, Christopher T. "Daniel and Josephus: Tracing Connections." Pages 539–45 in *The Book of Daniel in the Light of New Findings*. Edited by Adam S. van der Woude. BETL 106. Leuven: Peeters, 1993.

Bekken, Per Jarle. *The Word Is Near You: A Study of Deuteronomy 30:12–14 in Paul's Letter to the Romans in a Jewish context*. BZNW 144. Berlin: de Gruyter, 2007.

Bell, Richard H. "Deuteronomy 32 and the Origin of the Jealousy Motif in Romans 9–11." Pages 200–85 in *Provoked to Jealousy: The Origin and Purpose of the Jealousy Motif in Romans 9–11*. WUNT 63. Tübingen: Mohr, 1994.

Ben Zvi, Ehud, ed. *Utopia and Dystopia in Prophetic Literature*. PFES. Göttingen: Vandenhoeck & Ruprecht, 2006.

Ben-Sasson, Haim Hillel. "Galut." *EncJud* 7:275–94.

Bennema, Cornelis. "The Identity and Composition of ΟΙ ΙΟΥΔΑΙΟΙ in the Gospel of John." *TynBul* 60.2 (2009): 239–63.

Bensly, Robert Lubbock, ed. *The Fourth Book of Ezra: The Latin Version, Edited from the MSS*. TS 2. Cambridge: Cambridge University Press, 1895.

Bentley, G. Carter. "Ethnicity and Practice." *Comparative Studies in Society and History* 29.1 (1987): 24–55.

Berger, Klaus. *Synopse des Vierten Buches Esra und der Syrischen Baruch-Apokalypse*. TANZ. Tübingen: Francke, 1992.

Berger, Peter L. *The Sacred Canopy: Elements of a Sociological Theory of Religion*. Garden City, NY: Doubleday, 1967.

Bergsma, John S. *The Jubilee from Leviticus to Qumran: A History of Interpretation*. VTSup 115. Leiden: Brill, 2007.

"Qumran Self-Identity: 'Israel' or 'Judah'?" *DSD* 15 (2008): 172–89.

"The Persian Period as Penitential Era: The 'Exegetical Logic' of Daniel 9:1–27." Pages 50–64 in *Exile and Restoration Revisited: Essays on the Babylonian and Persian Period in Memory of Peter R. Ackroyd*. Edited by Gary N. Knoppers, Lester L. Grabbe, and Dierdre N. Fulton. LSTS 73. London: T&T Clark, 2009.

Berlin, Adele. "On the Interpretation of Psalm 133." Pages 141–47 in *Directions in Biblical Hebrew Poetry*. Edited by E. R. Follis. JSOTSup 40. Sheffield: Sheffield Academic, 1987.

Bernard, John Henry. *A Critical and Exegetical Commentary on the Gospel according to St. John*. 2 vols. ICC. T&T Clark, 1928.

Bernasconi, Rocco. "Tannaitic 'Israel' and the Kutim." Pages 365–92 in *Entre lignes de partage et territoires de passage: les identités religieuses dans les mondes grec et romain. "Paganismes," "judaïsmes," "christianismes."* Edited by Nicole Belayche and Simon C. Mimouni. Collection de la Revue des Études Juives 47. Leuven: Peeters, 2008.

Bernstein, Moshe J. "The Employment and Interpretation of Scripture in 4QMMT: Preliminary Observations." Pages 29–51 in *Reading 4QMMT: New Perspectives on Qumran Law and History*. Edited by John Kampen and Moshe J. Bernstein. SymS 6. Atlanta, GA: Scholars Press, 1994.

"Rewritten Bible: A Generic Category Which has Outlived Its Usefulness?" *Text* 22 (2005): 169–96.

Berrin, Shani L. *The Pesher Nahum Scroll from Qumran: An Exegetical Study of 4Q169*. Leiden: Brill, 2004.

Berthelot, Katell. "Reclaiming the Land (1 Maccabees 15:28–36): Hasmonean Discourse between Biblical Tradition and Seleucid Rhetoric." *JBL* 133.3 (2014): 539–59.

Betz, Hans Dieter. "Wellhausen's Dictum 'Jesus Was Not a Christian, but a Jew' in Light of Present Scholarship." *Studium* 45.2 (1991): 83–110.

Beuken, Willem A. M. *Haggai-Sacharja 1–8*. Studien zur Überlieferungsgeschichte der frühnachexilischen Prophetie. Assen: Van Gorcum, 1967.

Bilde, Per. *Flavius Josephus between Jerusalem and Rome: His Life, His Works, and Their Importance*. Sheffield: Sheffield Academic, 1988.

"Josephus and Jewish Apocalypticism." Pages 35–63 in *Understanding Josephus: Seven Perspectives*. Edited by Steve Mason. JSOTSup 32. Sheffield: Sheffield Academic, 1998.

Birnbaum, Ellen. "The Place of Judaism in Philo's Thought: Israel, Jews, and Proselytes." Pages 54–69 in *Society of Biblical Literature 1993 Seminar Papers(290)*. Edited by Eugene H. Lovering. Atlanta, GA: Scholars Press, 1996.

The Place of Judaism in Philo's thought: Israel, Jews, and Proselytes. BJS 290. Atlanta, GA: Scholars Press, 1996.

Black, Matthew, and James C. VanderKam, eds. *The Book of Enoch, or, I Enoch: A New English Edition: With Commentary and Textual Notes*. Leiden: Brill, 1985.

Blenkinsopp, Joseph. "Prophecy and Priesthood in Josephus." *JJS* 25 (1974): 239–62.

Ezra-Nehemiah: A Commentary. Louisville, KY: Westminster John Knox, 1988.

"Second Isaiah – Prophet of Universalism." *JSOT* 41 (1988): 83–103.

Ezra-Nehemiah: A Commentary. OTL. Philadelphia, PA: Westminster, 1988.

"The Bible, Archaeology and Politics; Or the Empty Land Revisited." *JSOT* 27.2 (2002): 169–87.

Bloch, Renée. "Israélite, juif, hébreu." *Cahiers Sioniens* 5 (1951): 11–31.

Bloch, Yigal. "The Contribution of Babylonian Tablets in the Collection of David Sofer to the Chronology of the Revolts against Darius I." *Altorientalische Forschungen* 42.1 (2015): 1–14.

Blumhofer, Christopher Mark. *The Gospel of John and the Future of Israel*. Vol. *177*. SNTSMS. Cambridge: Cambridge University Press, 2020.

Bockmuehl, Markus N. *Revelation and Mystery in Ancient Judaism and Pauline Christianity*. Tübingen: Mohr, 1990.

Boda, Mark J., Daniel K. Falk, and Rodney Alan Werline, eds. *The Origins of Penitential Prayer in Second Temple Judaism*. Leiden: Brill, 2006.

Boda, Mark J., Daniel K. Falk, and Rodney Alan Werline, *The Development of Penitential Prayer in Second Temple Judaism*. Atlanta, GA: Scholars Press, 2007.

Boda, Mark J., Matthew Forrest Lowe, Roland Boer, and Steven J. Schweitzer. "In Conversation with Steven Schweitzer, Reading Utopia in Chronicles (LHBOTS, 442; London: T&T Clark International, 2007)." *JHebS* 9 (2009): 1–19.

Boer, Roland. *Novel Histories: The Fiction of Biblical Criticism*. PT. Sheffield: Sheffield Academic, 1997.

Bogaert, Pierre-Maurice. *L'Apocalypse Syriaque de Baruch. Introduction, Traduction du Syriaque et Commentaire*. Paris: Cerf, 1969.

Böhm, Martina. *Samarien und die Samaritai bei Lukas: eine Studie zum religion-shistorischen und traditionsgeschichtlichen Hintergrund der lukanischen Samarientexte und zu deren topographischer Verhaftung.* WUNT 111. Tübingen: Mohr Siebeck, 1999.

"Wer gehörte in hellenistisch-römischer Zeit zu 'Israel'? Historische Voraussetzungen für eine veränderte Perspektiv auf neutestamentliche Texte." Pages 181–202 in *Die Samaritaner und die Bibel: Historische und literarische Wechselwirkungen zwischen biblischen und samaritanischen Traditionen = The Samaritans and the Bible: Historical and Literary Interactions Between Biblical and Samaritan Traditions.* Edited by Jörg Frey, Ursula Schattner-Rieser, and Konrad Schmid. SJ 70. Berlin: de Gruyter, 2012.

Borgen, Peder. *Bread from Heaven: An Exegetical Study of the Concept of Manna in the Gospel of John and the Writings of Philo.* NovTSup 10. Leiden: Brill, 1965.

"Philo of Alexandria. A Critical and Synthetical Survey of Research since World War II." *ANRW* 21.1:98–154.

"Philo of Alexandria." Pages 233–82 in *Jewish Writings of the Second Temple period.* Edited by Michael E. Stone. CRINT 2. Philadelphia, PA: Fortress, 1984.

"'There Shall Come Forth a Man': Reflections on Messianic Ideas in Philo." Pages 341–61 in *The Messiah: Developments in Earliest Judaism and Christianity.* Edited by James H. Charlesworth. PSJCO. Minneapolis, MN: Fortress, 1992.

Philo of Alexandria: An Exegete for His Time. NovTSup 86. Leiden: Brill, 1997.

"Application of and Commitment to the Laws of Moses. Observations on Philo's Treatise On the Embassy to Gaius." Pages 86–101 in *In the Spirit of Faith: Studies in Philo and Early Christianity in Honor of David Hay.* Edited by David T. Runia and G. E. Sterling. BJS 332. Atlanta, GA: Scholars Press, 2001.

Borgen, Peder, Kåre Fuglseth, and Roald Skarsten. *The Philo Index: A Complete Greek Word Index to the Writings of Philo of Alexandria.* 2nd ed. Leiden: Brill, 2000.

Bornhäuser, Karl. *Das Johannesevangelium, eine Missionsschrift für Israel.* Gütersloh: 1928.

Bourdieu, Pierre. *Outline of a Theory of Practice.* Translated by Richard Nice. CSSCA. Cambridge: Cambridge University Press, 1977.

"Social Space and Symbolic Power." *Sociological Theory* 7.1 (1989): 14–25.

"Identity and Representation: Elements for a Critical Reflection on the Idea of Region." Pages 220–28 in *Language and Symbolic Power.* Cambridge, MA: Harvard University Press, 1991.

"The Practice of Reflexive Sociology (The Paris Workshop)." Pages 216–60 in *An Invitation to Reflexive Sociology.* Edited by Pierre Bourdieu and Loïc J. C. Wacquant, 1992.

Boyarin, Daniel. "Justin Martyr Invents Judaism." *Calwer Hefte* 70.3 (2001): 427–61.

"The IOUDAIOI in John and the Prehistory of Judaism." Pages 216–39 in *Pauline Conversations in Context: Essays in Honor of Calvin J. Roetzel*. Edited by Janice Capel Anderson, Philip Sellew, and Claudia Setzer. JSNTSup 221. London: Sheffield Academic, 2002.

Boyarin, Daniel, and Jonathan Boyarin. "Diaspora: Generation and the Ground of Jewish Identity." *Critical Inquiry* 19 (1993): 693–725.

Braun, Martin. "The Prophet Who Became a Historian." *The Listener* 56 (1956): 53–57.

Braun, Roddy L. "Solomonic Apologetic in Chronicles." *JBL* 92.4 (1973): 503–16.

——— "A Reconsideration of the Chronicler's Attitude toward the North." *JBL* 96.1 (1977): 59–62.

Braverman, Jay. *Jerome's Commentary on Daniel: A Study of Comparative Jewish and Christian Interpretations of the Hebrew Bible*. CBQMS 7. Washington, DC: Catholic Biblical Association of America, 1978.

Brettler, Marc Zvi. "Judaism in the Hebrew Bible? The Transition from Ancient Israelite Religion to Judaism." *Catholic Biblical Quarterly* 61.3 (1999): 429–47.

Brooke, George J. "Exegetical Strategies in Jubilees 1–2: New Light from 4QJubileesa." Pages 39–57 in *Studies in the Book of Jubilees*. Edited by Matthias Albani, Jörg Frey, and Armin Lange. TSAJ 65. Tübingen: Mohr Siebeck, 1997.

Broshi, Magen, and Israel Finkelstein. "The Population of Palestine in Iron Age II." *BASOR* (1992): 47–60.

Brown, Colin. "What Was John the Baptist Doing?" *BBR* 7 (1997): 37–50.

Brownlee, William H. "The Servant of the Lord in the Qumran Scrolls I." *BASOR* 132 (1953): 8–15.

——— *Ezekiel 1–19*. Accordance/Thomas Nelson electronic ed. WBC 28. Waco, TX: Word, 1986.

Brubaker, Rogers. "Ethnicity without Groups." *European Journal of Sociology* 43.2 (2002): 163–89.

——— *Ethnicity without Groups*. Cambridge, MA: Harvard University Press, 2004.

——— "Ethnicity, Race, and Nationalism." *Annual Review of Sociology* 35 (2009): 21–42.

Bruce, F. F. "Josephus and Daniel." *Annual of the Swedish Theological Institute* 4 (1965): 148–62.

Bruneau, Philippe. "Les Israélites de Délos et la juiverie délienne." *BCH* 106.1 (1982): 465–504.

Brunner, Jerome. "Life as Narrative." *Social Research* 54.1 (1987): 11–32.

Burke, David G. *The Poetry of Baruch: A Reconstruction and Analysis of the Original Hebrew text of Baruch 3:9–5:9*. Chico, CA: Scholars Press, 1982.

Burkes, Shannon. "Wisdom and Law: Choosing Life in Ben Sira and Baruch." *JSJ* 30.3 (1999): 253–76.

Byrne, Brendan. *Romans*. SP 6. Collegeville, MN: Liturgical Press, 1996.

Cadbury, Henry J. "The Hellenists." Pages 59–73 in *The Beginnings of Christianity(Part I)*. 5. Edited by F. J. Foakes Jackson and Kirsopp Lake. London: MacMillan, 1933.

Campbell, Jonathan G. "Essene-Qumran Origins in the Exile: A Scriptural Basis?" *JJS* 46.1–2 (1995): 143–56.

The Use of Scripture in the Damascus Document 1–8, 19–20. BZAW 228. Berlin: de Gruyter, 1995.

Carroll, Robert P. "Ancient Israelite Prophecy and Dissonance Theory." *Numen* 24.2 (1977): 135–51.

"The Myth of the Empty Land." Pages 79–93 in *Ideological Criticism of Biblical Texts*. Edited by David Jobling and Tina Pippin. Semeia 59. Atlanta, GA: Scholars Press, 1992.

"Israel, History of (Post-Monarchic Period)." *The Anchor Yale Bible Dictionary* 3:567–76.

"Deportation and Diasporic Discourses in the Prophetic Literature." Pages 63–88 in *Exile: Old Testament, Jewish, and Christian Conceptions*. 56. Edited by James M. Scott. JSJSup 56. Leiden: Brill, 1997.

"Exile! What Exile? Deportation and the Discourses of Diaspora." Pages 62–79 in *Leading Captivity Captive: "The Exile" as History and Ideology*. Edited by Lester Grabbe. Sheffield: Sheffield Academic, 1998.

Jeremiah. London: T&T Clark, 2004.

Casewitz, Michel. *Le vocabulaire de la colonisation en grec ancien. Etude lexicologique: les familles de κτίζω et de οἰκέω-οἰκίζω*. Paris: Klincksieck, 1985.

Casey, Maurice. "Some Anti-Semitic Assumptions in the 'Theological Dictionary of the New Testament.'" *NovT* 41.3 (1999): 280–91.

Cassuto, Umberto. "The Song of Moses (Deuteronomy Chapter xxxii 1–43)." Pages 41–46 in *Biblical and Oriental Studies: Bible*. Jerusalem: Magnes, 1973.

Ceresko, Anthony R. "The Rhetorical Strategy of the Fourth Servant Song (Isaiah 52:13–53:12): Poetry and the Exodus-New Exodus." *Catholic Biblical Quarterly* 56.1 (1994): 42–55.

Chancey, Mark A. *The Myth of a Gentile Galilee*. Cambridge: Cambridge University Press, 2002.

Chandramohan, Balasubramanyam. "Diasporic (Exilic; Migrant) Writings." *Encyclopedia of Postcolonial Studies* 144–50.

Charles, Robert Henry. *The Testaments of the Twelve Patriarchs*. London: Black, 1908.

Charles, Robert Henry, ed. *The Apocrypha and Pseudepigrapha of the Old Testament in English: With Introductions and Critical and Explanatory Notes to the Several Books*. 2 vols. Oxford: Clarendon, 1913.

Charles, Ronald. *Paul and the Politics of Diaspora*. Minneapolis, MN: Fortress, 2014.

Charlesworth, James H. "Community Organization in the Rule of the Community." *EDSS* 1:133–36.

Chazon, Esther G. "'Gather the Dispersed of Judah:' Seeking a Return to the Land as a Factor in Jewish Identity of Late Antiquity." Pages 157–75 in *Heavenly Tablets: Interpretation, Identity and Tradition in Ancient Judaism*. Edited by Lynn R. LiDonnici and Andrea Lieber. JSJSup 119. Leiden: Brill, 2007.

Chesnutt, Randall D. *From Death to Life: Conversion in Joseph and Aseneth*. JSPSup 16. London: Black, 1995.

Chilton, Bruce D. "Messianic Redemption: Soteriology in the Targum Jonathan to the Former and Latter Prophets." Pages 265–84 in *This World and the World to Come: Soteriology in Early Judaism*. Edited by Daniel M. Gurtner. LSTS 74. London: T&T Clark, 2011.

Chomyn, Lauren. "Dwelling Brothers, Oozing Oil, and Descending Dew: Reading Psalm 133 Through the Lens of Yehudite Social Memory." *SJOT* 26.2 (2012): 220–34.

Christensen, Duane L. *Deuteronomy 1:1–21:9*. Accordance/Thomas Nelson electronic ed. WBC 6A. Waco, TX: Word, 2001.

———. *Nahum: A New Translation with Introduction and Commentary*. Accordance electronic ed. AB 24F. New Haven, CT: Yale University Press, 2009.

Christiansen, Ellen Juhl. "Judith: Defender of Israel – Preserver of the Temple." Pages 70–84 in *A Pious Seductress: Studies in the Book of Judith*. Edited by Géza G. Xeravits. DCLS 14. Berlin: de Gruyter, 2012.

Cogan, Mordechai. *1 Kings: A New Translation with Introduction and Commentary*. Accordance electronic ed. AB 10. New Haven: Yale University Press, 2008.

Coggins, Richard J. *Samaritans and Jews: The Origins of Samaritanism Reconsidered*. WUNT 111. Atlanta, GA: John Knox, 1975.

———. "The Samaritans in Josephus." Pages 257–73 in *Josephus, Judaism and Christianity*. Edited by Louis H. Feldman and Gohei Hata. Leiden: Brill, 1987.

Cohen, Robin. "Rethinking Babylon: Iconoclastic Conceptions of the Diasporic Experience." *Journal of Ethnic and Migration Studies* 21.1 (1995): 5–18.

———. "Diasporas and the Nation-State: From Victims to Challengers." *International Affairs* 72.3 (1996): 507–20.

———. "Diaspora: Changing Meanings and Limits of the Concept." Pages 39–48 in *Les diasporas dans le monde contemporain*. Edited by W. Berthomière and C. Chivallon. Paris: Karthala-MSHA, 2006.

———. *Global Diasporas: An Introduction*. 2nd ed. London: Routledge, 2008.

Cohen, Ronald. "Ethnicity: Problem and Focus in Anthropology." *Annual Review of Anthropology* 7.1 (1978): 379–403.

Cohen, Shaye J. D. "Josephus, Jeremiah, and Polybius." *History and Theory* (1982): 366–81.

———. *From the Maccabees to the Mishnah*. Philadelphia, PA: Westminster, 1987.

———. "Religion, Ethnicity, and Hellenism in the Emergence of Jewish Identity in Maccabean Palestine." Pages 204–23 in *Religion and Religious Practice in the Seleucid Kingdom*. Edited by Per Bilde, Troels Engberg-Pedersen, Lise Hannestad, and Jan Zahle. Aarhus: Aarhus University Press, 1990.

———. "'Those Who Say They Are Jews and Are Not': How Do You Know a Jew in Antiquity When You See One." Pages 1–45 in *Diasporas in Antiquity*. Edited by Shaye J. D. Cohen and Ernst S. Frerichs, 1993.

———. "Ioudaios: 'Judaean' and 'Jew' in Susanna, First Maccabees, and Second Maccabees." Pages 211–20 in *Geschichte - Tradition - Reflexion: Festschrift für Martin Hengel zum 70. Geburtstag*. 1. Edited by H. Cancik, H. Lichtenberger, and P. Schäfer. 1. Tübingen: Mohr Siebeck, 1996.

———. *The Beginnings of Jewishness: Boundaries, Varieties, Uncertainties*. Berkeley, CA: University of California Press, 1999.

Cohn, Leopold, and Paul Wendland, eds. *Philonis Alexandrini Opera Quae Supersunt*. 6 vols. plus indices by Leisegang. Berlin: de Gruyter.

Colautti, Federico M. *Passover in the Works of Josephus*. JSJSup 75. Leiden: Brill, 2002.

Collins, John J. "Cosmos and Salvation: Jewish Wisdom and Apocalyptic in the Hellenistic Age." *HR* 17.2 (1977): 121–42.

The Apocalyptic Vision of the Book of Daniel. HSM 16. Missoula, MT: Scholars Press, 1977.

Daniel: A Commentary. Accordance electronic ed. Hermeneia 27. Minneapolis, MN: Fortress, 1993.

Jewish Wisdom in the Hellenistic Age. Edinburgh: T&T Clark, 1998.

The Apocalyptic Imagination: An Introduction to Jewish Apocalyptic Literature. Grand Rapids, MI: Eerdmans, 1998.

"Models of Utopia in the Biblical Tradition." Pages 51–67 in *A Wise and Discerning Mind: Essays in Honor of Burke O. Long*. Edited by Burke O. Long, Saul M. Olyan, and Robert C. Culley, 2000.

Between Athens and Jerusalem: Jewish Identity in the Hellenistic Diaspora. 2nd ed. Grand Rapids, MI: Eerdmans, 2000.

"The Construction of Israel in the Sectarian Rule Books." Pages 25–42 in *Judaism in Late Antiquity: Theory of Israel (Pt. 5 Vol. 1)*. Edited by Alan J. Avery-Peck, Jacob Neusner, and Bruce D. Chilton. Leiden: Brill, 2001.

"The Judaism of the Book of Tobit." Pages 23–40 in *The Book of Tobit: Text, Tradition, Theology*. Edited by Géza G. Xeravits and József Zsengellér. JSJSup 98. Leiden: Brill, 2004.

"The Yahad and the 'Qumran Community.'" Pages 81–96 in *Biblical Traditions in Transmission: Essays in Honor of Michael A. Knibb*. Edited by Charlotte Hempel and Judith M. Lieu. JSJSup 111. Leiden: Brill, 2006.

Beyond the Qumran Community: The Sectarian Movement of the Dead Sea Scrolls. Grand Rapids, MI: Eerdmans, 2010.

"Apocalypse." *EDEJ* 341–46.

"The Genre of the Book of Jubilees." Pages 737–55 in *A Teacher for All Generations: Essays in Honor of James C. VanderKam*. 2. Edited by Eric F. Mason, Samuel I. Thomas, Alison Schofield, and Eugene Ulrich. JSJSup 2. Leiden: Brill, 2012.

Collins, John J., and Gregory E. Sterling, eds. *Hellenism in the Land of Israel*. CJAS. Notre Dame, IN: University of Notre Dame Press, 2001.

Collins, Matthew A. *The Use of Sobriquets in the Qumran Dead Sea Scrolls*. LSTS 67. London: T&T Clark, 2009.

Colson, F. H. *Philo, Volume VIII: On the Special Laws, Book 4. On the Virtues. On Rewards and Punishments*. 10 vols. LCL 341. Cambridge, MA: Harvard University Press, 1939.

Cooke, George A. *The Book of Ezekiel*. ICC. Edinburgh: T&T Clark, 1985.

Cooperman, Alan, Gregory A. Smith, Conrad Hackett, and N. Kuriakose. "A Portrait of Jewish Americans: Findings from a Pew Research Center Survey of US Jews." Washington, DC: Pew Research Center, 2013.

Cowey, James M. S., and Klaus Maresch. *Urkunden des Politeuma der Juden von Herakleopolis (144/3–133/2 v. Chr.)(P. Polit. Iud.)*. Wiesbaden: Westdeutscher Verlag, 2001.

Crabbe, Kylie. "Being Found Fighting against God: Luke's Gamaliel and Josephus on Human Responses to Divine Providence." *ZNW* 106.1 (2015): 21–39.

Craigie, Peter C., Page H. Kelley, and Joel F. Drinkard. *Jeremiah 1–25.* Accordance electronic ed. WBC 26. Grand Rapids, MI: Zondervan, 1991.

Cranfield, Charles E. B. *A Critical and Exegetical Commentary on the Epistle to the Romans.* 2 vols. ICC. Edinburgh: T&T Clark, 1979.

Crenshaw, James L. *Old Testament Wisdom: An Introduction.* 3rd ed. Louisville, KY: Westminster John Knox, 2010.

Cronin, Sonya S. *Raymond Brown, "The Jews," and the Gospel of John: From Apologia to Apology.* LNTS 504. London: T&T Clark, 2015.

Cross, Frank Moore. *The Ancient Library of Qumran.* London: Duckworth, 1958.

——— "Aspects of Samaritan and Jewish History in Late Persian and Hellenistic Times." *HTR* 59.3 (1966): 201–11.

——— "Samaria and Jerusalem in the Era of Restoration." Pages 173–202 in *From Epic to Canon: History and Literature in Ancient Israel.* Baltimore, MD: Johns Hopkins University Press, 2000.

Crossley, James G. "What a Difference a Translation Makes! An Ideological Analysis of the *Ioudaios* Debate." *Marginalia Review of Books* (2014): http://marginalia.lareviewofbooks.org/difference-translation-makes-ideo logical-analysis-ioudaios-debate-james-crossley

Crown, Alan D., ed. *The Samaritans.* Tübingen: Mohr Siebeck, 1989.

Crown, Alan D., "Dexinger's Der Taheb." *JQR* 80.1/2 (1989): 139–41.

——— "Redating the Schism between the Judaeans and the Samaritans." *JQR* 82.1–2 (1991): 17–50.

——— "Another Look at Samaritan Origins." Pages 133–55 in *New Samaritan Studies of the Société d'Études Samaritaines III–IV: Essays in Honour of G. D. Sixdenier.* Edited by Alan D. Crown and Lucy Davey. Studies in Judaica 5. Sydney: Mandelbaum, 1995.

Crown, Alan D., and Reinhard Pummer. *A Bibliography of the Samaritans: Revised, Expanded and Annotated.* ATLA Bibliography. Lanham, MD: Scarecrow Press, 2005.

Crown, Alan D., Reinhard Pummer, and Abraham Tal, eds. *A Companion to Samaritan Studies.* Tübingen: Mohr Siebeck, 1993.

D'Angelo, Mary Rose. "Theology in Mark and Q: Abba and 'Father' in Context." *HTR* 85.2 (1992): 149–74.

Dahl, Nils A. *Das Volk Gottes: eine Untersuchung zum Kirchenbewusstsein des Urchristentums.* 2. Oslo: Dybwad, 1941.

Dahood, Mitchell. *Psalms.* AB. Garden City, NY: Doubleday, 1970.

Dandamaev, M. A. *A Political History of the Achaemenid Empire.* Translated by Willem J. Vogelsang. Leiden: Brill, 1989.

Daube, David. "Jesus and the Samaritan Woman: The Meaning of συγχράομαι." *JBL* 69.2 (1950): 137–47.

Davenport, Gene L. *The Eschatology of the Book of the Jubilees.* StPB 20. Leiden: Brill, 1971.

Davies, Graham I. "Apocalyptic and Historiography." *JSOT* 5 (1978): 15–28.

Davies, Philip R. *The Damascus Covenant: An Interpretation of the 'Damascus Document.'* LHBOTS 25. London: Continuum, 1983.

——— "Eschatology at Qumran." *JBL* 104.1 (1985): 39–55.

In Search of "Ancient Israel": A Study in Biblical Origins. 2nd ed. JSOTSup 148. Sheffield: Sheffield Academic, 1992.

"Exile? What Exile? Whose Exile?" Pages 128–38 in *Leading Captivity Captive: "The Exile" as History and Ideology.* Edited by Lester Grabbe. Sheffield: Sheffield Academic, 1998.

"'Old' and 'New' Israel in the Bible and the Qumran Scrolls: Identity and Difference." Pages 33–42 in *Defining Identities: We, You, and the Other in the Dead Sea Scrolls.* Edited by Florentino García-Martínez and Mladen Popović. Leiden: Brill, 2007.

The Origins of Biblical Israel. LHBOTS 485. London: T&T Clark, 2007.

Davies, W. D. *The Territorial Dimension of Judaism.* Vol. (23). 23. Berkeley, CA: University of California Press, 1982.

"Reflections on Territory in Judaism." Pages 339–44 in *"Sha'arei Talmon": Studies in Bible, Qumran, and the Ancient Near East Presented to Shemaryahu Talmon.* Edited by M. Fishbane, Emanuel Tov, and W. W. Fields. Winona Lake, IN: Eisenbrauns, 1992.

Davila, James R. *The Provenance of the Pseudepigrapha: Jewish, Christian, or Other?* Leiden: Brill, 2005.

Dawson, Lorne L. "When Prophecy Fails and Faith Persists: A Theoretical Overview." *Nova Religio: The Journal of Alternative and Emergent Religions* 3.1 (1999): 60–82.

DeConick, April D. "Jesus the Israelite?" *Forbidden Gospels Blog* (2007): http://aprildeconick.com/forbiddengospels/2007/09/jesus-israelite.html

Dein, Simon. "What Really Happens When Prophecy Fails: The Case of Lubavitch." *Sociology of Religion* 62.3 (2001): 383–401.

Delling, Gerhard. "The 'One Who Sees God' in Philo." Pages 27–41 in *Nourished with Peace: Studies in Hellenistic Judaism in Memory of Samuel Sandmel.* Edited by Frederick E. Greenspahn, Earle Hilgert, and Burton L. Mack. Chico, CA: Scholars Press, 1984.

Die Bewältigung der Diasporasituation durch das hellenistische Judentum. Göttingen: Vandenhoeck & Ruprecht, 1987.

Deselaers, Paul. *Das Buch Tobit: Studien zu seiner Entstehung, Komposition und Theologie.* OBO 43. Göttingen: Vandenhoeck & Ruprecht, 1982.

Dexinger, Ferdinand. "Ein 'messianisches Szenarium' als Gemeingut des Judentums in nachherodianischer Zeit." *Kairós* 17 (1975): 249–78.

"Limits of Tolerance in Judaism: The Samaritan Example." Pages 88–114 in *Judaism, Jewish and Christian Self-Definition, Vol. 2.* Edited by E. P. Sanders. London: SCM, 1981.

Der Taheb, ein "Messianischer" Heilsbringer der Samaritaner. Kairos Religionswissenschaftliche Studien 3. Salzburg: Müller, 1986.

"Samaritan Eschatology." Pages 266–92 in *The Samaritans.* Edited by Alan D. Crown. Tübingen: Mohr Siebeck, 1989.

"Der Ursprung der Samaritaner im Spiegel der frühen Quellen." Pages 67–140 in *Die Samaritaner.* Edited by Ferdinand Dexinger and Reinhard Pummer. WF 604. Darmstadt: Wissenschäftliche Buchgesellschaft, 1992.

"Eschatology." Pages 86–90 in *A Companion to Samaritan Studies.* Edited by Alan D. Crown, Reinhard Pummer, and Abraham Tal. Tübingen: Mohr Siebeck, 1993.

"Samaritan Origins and the Qumran Texts." *Annals of the New York Academy of Sciences* 722.1 (1994): 231–49.

Dexinger, Ferdinand, and Reinhard Pummer, eds. *Die Samaritaner*. WF 604. Darmstadt: Wissenschäftliche Buchgesellschaft, 1992.

Di Lella, Alexander A. *The Hebrew Text of Sirach: A Text-Critical and Historical Study*. Studies in Classical Literature. The Hague: Mouton, 1966.

———. "The Deuteronomic Background of the Farewell Discourse in Tob 14:3–11." *Catholic Biblical Quarterly* 41.3 (1979): 380–89.

———. "Wisdom of Ben Sira." *The Anchor Yale Bible Dictionary* 6:931–44.

———. "A Study of Tobit 14:10 and Its Intertextual Parallels." *Catholic Biblical Quarterly* 71.3 (2009): 497–506.

Dimant, Devorah. "New Light from Qumran on the Jewish Pseudepigrapha – 4Q390." Pages 405–48 in *Proceedings of the International Congress on the Dead Sea Scrolls—Madrid, 18–21 March 1991*. Edited by J. Trebolle Barrera and L. Vegas Montaner. Leiden: Brill, 1992.

———. "Pseudo-Ezekiel." *EDSS* 1: 282–84.

Ditommaso, Lorenzo. "History and Apocalyptic Eschatology: Reply to J. Y. Jindo." *VT* 56.3 (2006): 413–18.

Dodd, C. H. *According to the Scriptures: The Sub-Structure of New Testament Theology*. London: Collins, 1965.

Dogniez, Cécile, and Marguerite Harl. *Le Deutéronomie*. Paris: Cerf, 1992.

Doudna, Gregory L. *4Q Pesher Nahum: A Critical Edition*. Sheffield: Sheffield Academic, 2001.

Dubovský, Peter. "Tiglath-pileser III's Campaigns in 734–732 BC: Historical Background of Isa 7; 2 Kgs 15–16 and 2 Chr 27–28." *Bib* 87.2 (2006): 153–70.

Dufoix, Stéphane. "Des usages antiques de diaspora aux enjeux conceptuels contemporains." *Pallas Revue d'études antiques* 89 (2012): 17–33.

Duke, Rodney K. "Recent Research in Chronicles." *CurBR* 8.1 (2009): 10–50.

Dumbrell, William J. "Malachi and the Ezra-Nehemiah Reforms." *RTR* 35.2 (1976): 42–52.

Dunn, James D. G. *Romans 9–16*. Accordance/Thomas Nelson electronic ed. WBC 38B. Nashville, TN: Nelson, 1988.

———. "Who Did Paul Think He Was? A Study of Jewish–Christian Identity." *NTS* 45.2 (1999): 174–93.

Dupont-Sommer, André. "Observations sur le Commentaire de Nahum découvert près de la Mer Morte." *Comptes rendus de l'Académie des Inscriptions et belles-lettres* 4 (1963): 221–27.

———. "Le Commentaire de Nahum découvert près de la Mer Morte (4QpNah): traduction et notes." *Sem* 13 (1963): 55–88.

Dušek, Jan. *Aramaic and Hebrew Inscriptions from Mt. Gerizim and Samaria between Antiochus III and Antiochus IV Epiphanes*. CHANE. Leiden: Brill, 2012.

Eastman, Susan Grove. "Israel and the Mercy of God: A Re-reading of Galatians 6.16 and Romans 9–11." *NTS* 56.3 (2010): 367–95.

Eckhardt, Benedikt. "PsSal 17, die Hasmonäer und der Herodompeius." *JSJ* 40.4 (2009): 465–92.

"Reclaiming Tradition: The Book of Judith and Hasmonean Politics." *JSP* 18.4 (2009): 243–63.

Eckstein, Arthur M. "Josephus and Polybius: A Reconsideration." *Classical Antiquity* (1990): 175–208.

Egger, Rita. *Josephus Flavius und die Samaritaner: eine terminologische Untersuchung zur Identitätsklärung der Samaritäner.* NTOA 4. Göttingen: Presses Universitaires Fribourg, 1986.

Eisler, Robert. *The Messiah Jesus and John the Baptist according to Flavius Josephus' Recently Rediscovered "Capture of Jerusalem" and Other Jewish and Christian Sources.* Translated by Alexander H. Krappe. New York, NY: MacVeagh, Dial, 1931.

Eissfeldt, Otto. *The Old Testament: An Introduction.* New York, NY: Harper & Row, 1965.

Elitsur, Yehudah. "Samaritans in Tannaitic Texts." Pages 393–414 in *Israel and the Bible: Studies in Geography, History, and Biblical Thought.* Edited by Amos Frisch and Yoel Elitsur. Ramat Gan: Bar Ilan University Press, 2000.

Elliot, John H. "Jesus the Israelite Was Neither a 'Jew' Nor a 'Christian': On Correcting Misleading Nomenclature." *JSHJ* 5.2 (2007): 119–54.

Ellison, H. L. "The Hebrew Slave: A Study in Early Israelite Society." *EvQ* 45 (1973): 30–35.

Endres, John C. "Eschatological Impulses in Jubilees." Pages 323–37 in *Enoch and the Mosaic Torah: The Evidence of Jubilees.* Edited by Gabriele Boccaccini and Giovanni Ibba. Grand Rapids, MI: Eerdmans, 2009.

Eskenazi, Tamara Cohn. *In an Age of Prose: A Literary Approach to Ezra-Nehemiah.* SBLMS 36. Atlanta, GA: Scholars Press, 1988.

"The Structure of Ezra-Nehemiah and the Integrity of the Book." *JBL* 107.4 (1988): 641–56.

Esler, Philip F. "Ludic History in the Book of Judith: The Reinvention of Israelite Identity?" *Biblical Interpretation Series* 10.2 (2002): 107–43.

Conflict and Identity in Romans: The Social Setting of Paul's Letter. Minneapolis, MN: Fortress, 2003.

Eslinger, Lyle M. *Into the Hands of the Living God.* JSOTSup 24. Sheffield: Sheffield Academic, 1989.

Evans, Craig A. "The Star of Balaam and the Prophecy of Josephus Concerning Vespasian." Pages 297–333 in *Scribal Practice, Text and Canon in the Dead Sea Scrolls.* Edited by Peter W. Flint, John J. Collins, and Ananda Geyser-Fouch. Brill, 2019.

Exum, J. Cheryl. *Virtual History and the Bible.* Leiden: Brill, 2000.

Eyl, Jennifer. "'I Myself Am an Israelite': Paul, Authenticity and Authority." *JSNT* 40.2 (2017): 148–68.

Ezzy, Douglas. "Theorizing Narrative Identity." *Sociological Quarterly* 39.2 (1998): 239–52.

Feldman, Louis H. "Flavius Josephus Revisited: The Man, His Writings, and His Significance." *ANRW* 21.2:763–862.

"A Selective Critical Bibliography of Josephus." Pages 330–448 in *Josephus, the Bible, and History.* Edited by Louis H. Feldman and Gohei Hata. Detroit, MI: Wayne State University Press, 1989.

"Josephus' Attitude toward the Samaritans: A Study in Ambivalence." Pages 23–45 in *Jewish Sects, Religious Movements, and Political Parties: Proceedings of the Third Annual Symposium of the Philip M. and Ethel Klutznick Chair in Jewish Civilization Held on Sunday-Monday, October 14–15, 1990*. Edited by Menachem Mor. SJC. Omaha, NE: Creighton University Press, 1992.

"Josephus' Portrait of Ezra." *VT* 43 (1993): 190–214.

"The Concept of Exile in Josephus." Pages 145–72 in *Exile: Old Testament, Jewish, and Christian Conceptions*. Edited by James M. Scott. JSJSup 56. Leiden and New York, NY: Brill, 1997.

Josephus's Interpretation of the Bible. HCS. Berkeley, CA: University of California Press, 1998.

"Restoration in Josephus." Pages 223–61 in *Restoration: Old Testament, Jewish and Christian Perspectives*. Edited by James M. Scott. JSJSup 72. Leiden: Brill, 2001.

Ferda, Tucker S. "John the Baptist, Isaiah 40, and the Ingathering of the Exiles." *JSHJ* 10.2 (2012): 154–88.

"Jeremiah 7 and Flavius Josephus on the First Jewish War." *JSJ* 44.2 (2013): 158–73.

Ferguson, Niall, ed. *Virtual History: Alternatives and Counterfactuals*. London: Picador, 1997.

Festinger, Leon. *A Theory of Cognitive Dissonance*. Palo Alto, CA: Stanford University Press, 1962.

Festinger, Leon, Henry W. Riecken, and Stanley Schachter. *When Prophecy Fails: A Social and Psychological Study of a Modern Group That Predicted the Destruction of the World*. Minneapolis, MN: University of Minnesota Press, 1956.

Finkelstein, Israel. "The Archaeology of the Days of Manasseh." Pages 169–87 in *Scripture and Other Artifacts: Essays on the Bible and Archaeology in Honor of Philip J. King*. Edited by Michael D. Coogan, J. Cheryl Exum, and Lawrence E. Stager. Louisville, KY: Westminster John Knox, 1994.

"Saul, Benjamin and the Emergence of 'Biblical Israel': An Alternative View." *ZAW* 123.3 (2011): 348–67.

The Forgotten Kingdom: The Archaeology and History of Northern Israel. Ancient Near East Monographs. Atlanta, GA: Society of Biblical Literature, 2013.

Finkelstein, Israel, and Neil Asher Silberman. "Temple and Dynasty: Hezekiah, the Remaking of Judah and the Rise of the Pan-Israelite Ideology." *JSOT* 30.3 (2006): 259–85.

Fischer, Georg. *Das Trostbüchlein: Text, Komposition und Theologie von Jer 30–31*. Stuttgart: Katholisches Bibelwerk, 1993.

Fischer, Ulrich. *Eschatologie und Jenseitserwartung im hellenistischen Diasporajudentum*. BZNW 44. Berlin: de Gruyter, 1978.

Fishbane, Michael. *Biblical Interpretation in Ancient Israel*. Oxford: Clarendon, 1985.

Fitzmyer, Joseph A. "The Languages of Palestine in the First Century AD." *Catholic Biblical Quarterly* 32 (1970): 501–31.

A Wandering Aramean: Collected Aramaic Essays. SBLMS 25. Chico, CA: Scholars Press, 1979.

"The Aramaic and Hebrew Fragments of Tobit from Qumran Cave 4." *Catholic Biblical Quarterly* 57.4 (1995): 655–75.

"4QpapTobit[a] ar, 4QTobit[b-d] ar, and 4QTobit[e]." Pages 1–76 + plates i in *Qumran Cave 4. XIV: Parabiblical Texts, Part 2.* Edited by James C. VanderKam. DJD 19. Oxford: Clarendon, 1995.

"New Testament Kyrios and Maranatha and Their Aramaic Background." Pages 218–35 in *To Advance the Gospel: New Testament Studies.* Edited by Joseph A. Fitzmyer. Grand Rapids, MI: Eerdmans, 1998.

"The Significance of the Hebrew and Aramaic Texts of Tobit from Qumran for the Study of Tobit." Pages 418–25 in *The Dead Sea Scrolls: Fifty Years after Their Discovery (1947–1997).* Edited by Lawrence H. Schiffman, Emanuel Tov, James C. VanderKam, and Galen Marquis. Jerusalem: Israel Exploration Society, 2000.

Tobit. CEJL. Berlin: de Gruyter, 2003.

Fleming, Daniel E. *The Legacy of Israel in Judah's Bible: History, Politics, and the Reinscribing of Tradition.* Cambridge: Cambridge University Press, 2012.

Floyd, Michael H. "Was Prophetic Hope Born of Disappointment? The Case of Zechariah." Pages 268–96 in *Utopia and Dystopia in Prophetic Literature.* Edited by Ehud Ben Zvi. PFES. Göttingen: Vandenhoeck & Ruprecht, 2006.

Flusser, David. "Two Notes on the Midrash on 2 Sam vii." *IEJ* 9 (1959): 99–109.

"Pharisäer, Sadduzäer und Essener im Pescher Nahum." Pages 121–66 in *Qumran.* Edited by Karl Erich Grözinger, Norbert Ilg, Hermann Lichtenberger, and Gerhard-Wilhelm Pabst. Darmstadt: Wissenschaftliche Buchgessellschaft, 1981.

"The Isaiah Pesher and the Notion of Twelve Apostles in the Early Church." Pages 305–26 in *Qumran and Apocalypticism.* Grand Rapids, MI: Eerdmans, 2007.

Flynn, Kevin. *The Digital Frontier: Mapping the Other Universe.* Los Angeles, CA: Quotable Publishing, 1985.

Forsdyke, Sara. *Exile, Ostracism, and Democracy: The Politics of Expulsion in Ancient Greece.* Princeton, NJ: Princeton University Press, 2005.

Fraade, Steven D. "To Whom It May Concern: 4QMMT and Its Addressee(s)." *RevQ* 19.4 (2000): 507–26.

Fredriksen, Paula. "Compassion Is to Purity as Fish Is to Bicycle and Other Reflections on Constructions of 'Judaism' in Current Work on the Historical Jesus." Pages 55–67 in *Apocalypticism, Anti-Semitism and the Historical Jesus: Subtexts in Criticism.* Edited by John S. Kloppenborg and John W. Marshall. JSNTSup 275. London: T&T Clark, 2005.

Freedman, David Noel. *The Nine Commandments: Uncovering the Hidden Pattern of Crime and Punishment in the Hebrew Bible.* ABRL. New York, NY: Doubleday, 2002.

Frey, Jörg. "Qumran Research and Biblical Scholarship in Germany." Pages 529–64 in *The Dead Sea Scrolls in Scholarly Perspective: A History of Research.* Edited by Devorah Dimant. STDJ 99. Leiden: Brill, 2012.

Freyne, Sean. "Behind the Names: Samaritans, Ioudaioi, Galileans." Pages 389–401 in *Text and Artifact in the Religions of Mediterranean Antiquity: Essays in Honour of Peter Richardson (9)*. Edited by Stephen G. Wilson and Michel Desjardins. SCJ 9. Waterloo, ON: Wilfrid Laurier University Press, 2000.

———. "Studying the Jewish Diaspora in Antiquity." Pages 1–9 in *Jews in the Hellenistic and Roman Cities*. Edited by John R. Bartlett. London: Routledge, 2002.

Friebel, Kelvin G. *Jeremiah's and Ezekiel's Sign-Acts: Rhetorical Nonverbal Communication*. JSOTSup 283. Sheffield: Sheffield Academic, 1999.

Fried, Lisbeth S. "No King in Judah? Mass Divorce in Judah and in Athens." Pages 381–401 in *Political Memory in and after the Persian Empire*. Edited by Jason M. Silverman and Caroline Waerzeggers. Ancient Near East Monographs. Atlanta, GA: SBL Press, 2015.

Fröhlich, Ida. "Qumran Names." Pages 294–305 in *The Provo International Conference on the Dead Sea Scrolls: Technological Innovations, New Texts, and Reformulated Issues*. STDJ 30. Leiden: Brill, 1999.

Fuller, Michael E. *The Restoration of Israel: Israel's Re-Gathering and the Fate of the Nations in Early Jewish Literature and Luke-Acts*. BZNW 138. Berlin: de Gruyter, 2006.

Funk, Wolfgang. *The Literature of Reconstruction: Authentic Fiction in the New Millennium*. London: Bloomsbury, 2015.

Gadamer, Hans-Georg. *Truth and Method*. London: Continuum, 2004.

Gadenz, Pablo T. *Called from the Jews and from the Gentiles: Pauline Ecclesiology in Romans 9–11*. WUNT 267. Tübingen: Mohr Siebeck, 2009.

Gaertner, Jan Felix. "The Discourse of Displacement in Greco-Roman Antiquity." Pages 1–20 in *Writing Exile: The Discourse of Displacement in Greco-Roman Antiquity and Beyond*. Edited by Jan Felix Gaertner. MnemosyneSup 283. Leiden: Brill, 2007.

Gafni, Isaiah. *Land, Center and Diaspora: Jewish Constructs in Late Antiquity*. JSPSup 21. Sheffield: Sheffield Academic, 1997.

Galil, Gershon. "The Last Years of the Kingdom of Israel and the Fall of Samaria." *Catholic Biblical Quarterly* 57.1 (1995): 52–64.

———. "Israelite Exiles in Media: A New Look at ND 2443+." *VT* 59.1 (2009): 71–79.

Gambetti, Sandra. "When Syrian Politics Arrived in Egypt: 2nd Century BCE Egyptian Yahwism and the Vorlage of the LXX." Pages 1–43 in *Alexandria: Hub of the Hellenistic World*. Edited by Jörg Frey, Benjamin Schliesser, and Tobias Nicklas. WUNT. Tübingen: Mohr Siebeck, 2020.

García Martínez, Florentino. "Nuevos textos no biblicos procedentes de Qumrán." *EstBíb* 49 (1991): 116–23.

———. "The Heavenly Tablets in the Book of Jubilees." Pages 243–60 in *Studies in the Book of Jubilees*. Edited by Matthias Albani, Jörg Frey, and Armin Lange. TSAJ 65. Tübingen: Mohr Siebeck, 1997.

———. "Temple Scroll." *EDSS* 2:927–33.

García Martínez, Florentino, and Eibert J. C. Tigchelaar. *The Dead Sea Scrolls Study Edition*. 2 vols. Leiden: Brill, 1998.

Garnet, Paul. *Salvation and Atonement in the Qumran Scrolls*. WUNT 3. Tübingen: Mohr Siebeck, 1977.

Gaster, Moses. *The Samaritans: Their History, Doctrines and Literature*. SchwLect. London: Oxford University Press, 1925.

Gehrke, Hans-Joachim. *Stasis: Untersuchungen zu den inneren Kriegen in den griechischen Staaten des 5. und 4. Jahrhunderts v. Chr.* Munich: Beck, 1985.

Geoghegan, Jeffrey C. "'Until This Day' and the Preexilic Redaction of the Deuteronomistic History." *JBL* 122.2 (2003): 201–27.

The Time, Place, and Purpose of the Deuteronomistic History: The Evidence of "Until this Day." BJS 347. Providence, RI: BJS, 2006.

Gerdmar, Anders. *Roots of Theological Anti-Semitism: German Biblical Interpretation and the Jews, from Herder and Semler to Kittel and Bultmann*. Studies in Jewish History and Culture 20. Leiden: Brill, 2009.

Geyser, Albert S. "Israel in the Fourth Gospel." *Neot* 20 (1986): 13–20.

Ginsberg, Harold Louis. "The Oldest Interpretation of the Suffering Serv*Ant*." *VT* 3.4 (1953): 400–4.

The Israelian Heritage of Judaism. Texts and Studies of the Jewish Theological Society of America 24. New York, NY: Jewish Theological Seminary of America, 1982.

Ginzberg, Louis. *The Legends of the Jews*. Translated by S. H. Glick. 7 vols. Philadelphia, PA: Jewish Publication Society of America, 1968.

An Unknown Jewish Sect. New York, NY: Jewish Theological Seminary of America, 1976.

Gitelman, Zvi Y. *Religion or Ethnicity?: Jewish Identities in Evolution*. New Brunswick, NJ: Rutgers University Press, 2009.

Goering, Greg Schmidt. *Wisdom's Root Revealed: Ben Sira and the Election of Israel*. JSJSup 139. Leiden: Brill, 2009.

Goff, Matthew J. "The Mystery of Creation in 4QInstruction." *DSD* 10 (2003): 163–85.

"Wisdom and Apocalypticism." Pages 52–68 in *The Oxford Handbook of Apocalyptic Literature*. Edited by John J. Collins. Oxford: Oxford University Press, 2014.

Goldingay, John E. *Daniel*. Accordance/Thomas Nelson electronic ed. WBC 30. Waco, TX: Word, 1989.

Goldstein, Jonathan A. *I Maccabees*. Accordance electronic ed. AB 41. Garden City, NY: Doubleday, 1976.

II Maccabees. AB 41A. Garden City, NY: Doubleday, 1983.

"The Date of the Book of Jubilees." *Proceedings of the American Academy for Jewish Research* 50 (1983): 63–86.

"How the Authors of 1 and 2 Maccabees Treated the 'Messianic' Promises." Pages 69–96 in *Judaisms and Their Messiahs at the Turn of the Christian Era*. Edited by Jacob Neusner, William Scott Green, and Ernest S. Frerichs. Cambridge: Cambridge University Press, 1988.

"The Judaism of the Synagogues (Focusing on the Synagogue of Dura-Europos)." Pages 109–57 in *Judaism in Late Antiquity, Part 2: Historical Syntheses*. Edited by Jacob Neusner. HdO 17. Leiden: Brill, 1995.

Good, Edwin M. *Irony in the Old Testament.* 2nd ed. BLS 3. Sheffield: Almond Press, 1981.

Goodblatt, David. "From Judeans to Israel: Names of Jewish States in Antiquity." *JSJ* 29.1 (1998): 1–36.

Elements of Ancient Jewish Nationalism. Cambridge: Cambridge University Press, 2006.

"'The Israelites who Reside in Judah' (Judith 4:1): On the Conflicted Identities of the Hasmonean State." Pages 74–89 in *Jewish Identities in Antiquity: Studies in Memory of Menahem Stern.* Edited by Lee I. Levine and Daniel R. Schwartz. TSAJ 130. Tübingen: Mohr Siebeck, 2009.

"Varieties of Identity in Late Second Temple Judah (200 BCE–135 CE)." Pages 11–27 in *Jewish Identity and Politics between the Maccabees and Bar Kokhba: Groups, Normativity, and Rituals.* Edited by Benedikt Eckhardt. Leiden: Brill, 2011.

Goodenough, Erwin Ramsdell. "Philo's Exposition of the Law and His *De vita Mosis.*" *HTR* 26.2 (1933): 109–25.

Goodenough, Erwin Ramsdell, and H. L. Goodhart. *The Politics of Philo Judaeus: Practice and Theory with a General Bibliography of Philo.* New Haven, CT: Yale University Press, 1938.

Goodman, Martin D., ed. *Jews in a Graeco-Roman World.* New York, NY: Oxford University Press, 1998.

Goodspeed, Edgar J. *Problems of New Testament Translation.* Chicago, IL: University of Chicago Press, 1945.

Gordon, Robert P. *1 & 2 Samuel.* London: Continuum, 1984.

Gottwald, Norman K. *Tribes of Yahweh: A Sociology of the Religion of Liberated Israel, 1250–1050 BCE.* Sheffield: Sheffield Academic, 1979.

Grabbe, Lester L. *The Roman Period.* Minneapolis, MN: Fortress, 1992.

Ezra-Nehemiah. London: Routledge, 1998.

"Triumph of the Pious or Failure of the Xenophobes? The Ezra-Nehemiah Reforms and Their Nachgeschichte." Pages 50–65 in *Jewish Local Patriotism and Self-Identification in the Graeco-Roman Period.* Edited by Siân Jones and Sarah Pearce. LSTS. Sheffield: Sheffield Academic, 1998.

"Israel's Historical Reality after the Exile." Pages 9–32 in *The Crisis of Israelite Religion: Transformation of Religious Tradition in Exilic and Post-exilic Times.* Edited by Bob Becking and Marjo Christina Annette Korpel. Leiden: Brill, 1999.

"'Mind the Gaps': Ezra, Nehemiah, and the Judaean Restoration." Pages 83–104 in *Restoration: Old Testament, Jewish and Christian Perspectives.* Edited by James M. Scott. JSJSup 72. Leiden: Brill, 2001.

"'They Shall Come Rejoicing to Zion' – or Did They? The Settlement of Yehud in the Early Persian Period." Pages 116–27 in *Exile and Restoration Revisited: Essays on the Babylonian and Persian Period in Memory of Peter R. Ackroyd.* Edited by Gary N. Knoppers, Lester L. Grabbe, and Dierdre N. Fulton. LSTS 73. London: T&T Clark, 2009.

Grabbe, Lester L., and Robert D. Haak, eds. *Knowing the End From the Beginning: The Prophetic, Apocalyptic, and Their Relationship.* JSPSup 46. London: Continuum, 2003.

Graham, A. J. Review of *Le vocabulaire de la colonisation en grec ancien. Etude lexicologique: les familles de κτίζω et de οἰκέω-οἰκίζω*, by Michel Casewitz. *Classical Review* 37.2 (1987): 237–40.

Granerød, Gard. "Canon and Archive: Yahwism in Elephantine and Āl-Yāḫūdu as a Challenge to the Canonical History of Judean Religion in the Persian Period." *JBL* 138.2 (2019): 345.

Grassie, William J. "Entangled Narratives: Competing Visions of the Good Life." *Sri Lanka Journal of the Humanities* 34.1–2 (2008): 143–66.

Gray, Mary F. "The Habiru-Hebrew Problem in the Light of the Source Material Available at Present." *HUCA* 29 (1958): 135–97.

Green, William Scott. "Messiah in Judaism: Rethinking the Question." Pages 1–13 in *Judaisms and Their Messiahs at the Turn of the Christian Era*. Edited by Jacob Neusner, William Scott Green, and Ernest S. Frerichs. Cambridge: Cambridge University Press, 1987.

Greenwood, David C. "On the Jewish Hope for a Restored Northern Kingdom." *ZAW* 88.3 (1976): 376–85.

Gregory, Bradley C. "The Post-exilic Exile in Third Isaiah: Isaiah 61:1–3 in Light of Second Temple Hermeneutics." *JBL* 126.3 (2007): 475–96.

"The Relationship between the Poor in Judea and Israel under Foreign Rule: Sirach 35:14–26 among Second Temple Prayers and Hymns." *JSJ* 42.3 (2011): 311–27.

Grintz, Jehoshua M. "Hebrew as the Spoken and Written Language in the Last Days of the Second Temple." *JBL* 79.1 (1960): 32–47.

Grintz, Yehoshua M. "Tobit, Book of." *EncJud* 15:1183–87.

Grol, Harm van. "'Indeed, Servants We Are': Ezra 9, Nehemiah 9, and 2 Chronicles 12 Compared." Pages 209–27 in *The Crisis of Israelite Religion: Transformation of Religious Tradition in Exilic and Post-exilic Times*. Edited by Bob Becking and Marjo Christina Annette Korpel. Leiden: Brill, 1999.

Grosby, Steven Elliott. *Biblical Ideas of Nationality: Ancient and Modern*. Winona Lake, IN: Eisenbrauns, 2002.

"Religion and Nationality in Antiquity: The Worship of Yahweh and Ancient Israel." *European Journal of Sociology* 32.2 (2009): 229–65.

Grossman, Maxine L. *Reading for History in the Damascus Document: A Methodological Method*. STDJ 45. Leiden: Brill, 2002.

Gruen, Erich S. "Diaspora and Homeland." Pages 18–46 in *Diasporas and Exiles: Varieties of Jewish Identity*. Edited by Howard Wettstein. Berkeley, CA: University of California Press, 2002.

Diaspora: Jews amidst Greeks and Romans. Cambridge, MA: Harvard University Press, 2004.

"Judaism in the Diaspora." *EDEJ* 77–97.

Gruenwald, Ithamar. "Major Issues in the Study and Understanding of Jewish Mysticism." Pages 1–49 in *Judaism in Late Antiquity, Part 2: Historical Syntheses*. Edited by Jacob Neusner. HdO 17. Leiden: Brill, 1995.

Grundmann, Walter. *Die 28 Thesen der sächsischen Volkskirche erläutert*. Schriften der Deutschen Christen. Dresden: Deutsch-christlicher, 1934.

Jesus der Galiläer und das Judentum. Leipzig: Wigand, 1940.

Haag, Ernst. *Studien zum Buche Judith: Seine theologische Deutung und litera-rische Egenart*. TThSt. Trier: Paulinus, 1963.

Hacham, Noah. "The Third Book of Maccabees: Literature, History and Ideology." PhD diss., Hebrew University of Jerusalem, 2002.

——— "Exile and Self-Identity in the Qumran Sect and in Hellenistic Judaism." Pages 3–21 in *New Perspectives on Old Texts: Proceedings of the Tenth International Symposium of the Orion Center for the Dead Sea Scrolls and Associated Literature, January 2005*. Edited by Esther G. Chazon, Betsy Halpern-Amaru, and Ruth A. Clements. STDJ 88. Leiden: Brill, 2010.

Hagner, Donald A. "The Vision of God in Philo and John: A Comparative Study." *JETS* 14 (1971): 81–93.

Hahn, Scott W. *The Kingdom of God as Liturgical Empire: A Theological Commentary on 1–2 Chronicles*. Grand Rapids, MI: Baker Academic, 2012.

Hall, Jonathan M. *Ethnic Identity in Greek Antiquity*. Cambridge: Cambridge University Press, 1997.

——— "Ethnic Identity in Greek Antiquity." *Cambridge Archaeological Journal* 8.2 (1998): 265–83.

——— *Hellenicity: Between Ethnicity and Culture*. Chicago, IL: University of Chicago Press, 2002.

Halpern, Baruch. "Sectionalism and the Schism." *JBL* 93.4 (1974): 519–32.

Halpern-Amaru, Betsy. "Land Theology in Josephus' 'Jewish Antiquities.'" *New Series* 71.4 (1981): 201–29.

——— "Land Theology in Philo and Josephus." Pages 65–93 in *The Land of Israel: Jewish Perspectives*. Edited by Lawrence A. Hoffmann. Notre Dame, IN: University of Notre Dame Press, 1986.

——— "Exile and Return in Jubilees." Pages 127–44 in *Exile: Old Testament, Jewish, and Christian Conceptions*. Edited by James M. Scott. JSJSup 56. Leiden: Brill, 1997.

Halvorson-Taylor, Martien. *Enduring Exile: The Metaphorization of Exile in the Hebrew Bible*. VTSup 141. Leiden: Brill, 2010.

Hamilton, Mark W. "Who Was a Jew? Jewish Ethnicity during the Achaemenid Period." *Restoration Quarterly* 37.2 (1995): 102–17.

Hanhart, Robert. *Septuaginta: Vetus Testamentum Graecum Auctoritate Academiae Scientiarum Gottingensis editum VIII.5: Tobit*. Göttingen: Vandenhoeck & Ruprecht, 1983.

Hanneken, Todd R. "The Status and Interpretation of Jubilees in 4Q390." Pages 407–28 in *A Teacher for All Generations: Essays in Honor of James C. VanderKam*. 2. Edited by Eric F. Mason, Samuel I. Thomas, Alison Schofield, and Eugene Ulrich. JSJSup 2. Leiden: Brill, 2012.

——— *The Subversion of the Apocalypses in the Book of Jubilees*. Atlanta, GA: Society of Biblical Literature, 2012.

Harrelson, Walter. "Wisdom Hidden and Revealed according to Baruch (Baruch 3.9–4.4)." Pages 158–71 in *Priests, Prophets, and Scribes: Essays on the Formation and Heritage of Second Temple Judaism in Honour of Joseph Blenkinsopp*. Edited by Eugene C. Ulrich, John W. Wright, Robert P. Carroll, and Philip R. Davies. JSOTSup 149. Sheffield: Sheffield Academic, 1992.

Harrison, A. R. W. *The Law of Athens: Procedure, Volume 2.* 2nd ed. London: Duckworth, 1998.

Hartman, Louis Francis, and Alexander A. Di Lella. *The Book of Daniel.* Accordance electronic ed. AB 23. Garden City, NY: Doubleday, 1978.

Harvey, Graham. *The True Israel: Uses of the Names Jew, Hebrew, and Israel in Ancient Jewish and Early Christian Literature.* AGJU 35. Leiden: Brill, 1996.

Hawthorne, Gerald F., and Ralph P. Martin. *Philippians.* Accordance electronic ed. WBC 43. Waco, TX: Word, 2004.

Hay, David M. "Philo's References to Other Allegorists." *SPhilo* 6 (1979): 41–75.

"Philo of Alexandria." Pages 357–79 in *Justification and Variegated Nomism.* 1. Edited by D. A. Carson, P. T. O'Brien, and M. A. Seifrid. 1. Grand Rapids, MI: Baker Academic, 2001.

Hayes, Christine E. *Gentile Impurities and Jewish Identities.* New York, NY: Oxford University Press, 2002.

Hayes, John H., and Jeffrey K. Kuan. "The Final Years of Samaria (730–720 BC)." *Bib* 72.2 (1991): 153–81.

Hays, Christopher B. *The Origins of Isaiah 24–27: Josiah's Festival Scroll for the Fall of Assyria.* Cambridge: Cambridge University Press, 2019.

Hays, Richard B. *Echoes of Scripture in the Letters of Paul.* New Haven, CT: Yale University Press, 1989.

The Faith of Jesus Christ: The Narrative Substructure of Galatians 3:1–4:11. rev. ed. Grand Rapids, MI: Eerdmans, 2002.

Hayward, Robert. "The New Jerusalem in the Wisdom of Jesus Ben Sira." *SJOT* 6.1 (1992): 123–38.

Head, Peter M. "The Nazi Quest for an Aryan Jesus." *JSHJ* 2.1 (2004): 55–89.

Heater, Derek Benjamin. *A Brief History of Citizenship.* New York, NY: New York University Press, 2004.

Heiber, Helmut. *Walter Frank und sein Reichsinstitut für Geschichte des neuen Deutschlands.* Stuttgart: Deutsche Verlags-Anstalt, 1966.

Heinemann, Isaak. "The Relationship between the Jewish People and Their Land in Hellenistic Jewish Literature." *Zion* 13 (1948): 1–9.

Philons griechische und jüdische Bildung: Kulturgleichende Untersuchungen zu Philons Darstellung der jüdischen Gesetze. Hildesheim: Olms, 1973.

Hellmann, Monika. *Judit – eine Frau im Spannungsfeld von Autonomie und göttlicher Führung. Studie über eine Frauengestalt des Alten Testament.* EHS. Frankfurt: Lang, 1992.

Hellwald, Friedrich Von. "Zur Characteristik des jüdischen Volkes." *Das Ausland* 45.26 (1872): 901–6.

Hempel, Charlotte. "The Context of 4QMMT and Comfortable Theories." Pages 275–92 in *The Dead Sea Scrolls.* Edited by Charlotte Hempel. STDJ 90. Leiden: Brill, 2010.

Hengel, Martin. *Judaism and Hellenism: Studies in Their Encounter in Palestine during the Early Hellenistic Period.* Translated by John Bowden. London: SCM, 1974.

Heschel, Abraham J. *The Prophets.* Perennial Classics. San Francisco, CA: HarperCollins, 2001.

Heschel, Susannah. "Nazifying Christian Theology: Walter Grundmann and he Institute for the Study and Eradication of Jewish Influence on German Church Life." *Calwer Hefte* 63.4 (1994): 587–605.

The Aryan Jesus: Christian Theologians and the Bible in Nazi Germany. Princeton, NJ: Princeton University Press, 2008.

Hicks-Keeton, Jill. "Already/Not Yet: Eschatological Tension in the Book of Tobit." *JBL* 132.1 (2013): 97–117.

Arguing with Aseneth: Gentile Access to Israel's Living God in Jewish Antiquity. Oxford: Oxford University Press, 2018.

Hillers, Delbert R. *Covenant: The History of a Biblical Idea.* Baltimore, MD: Johns Hopkins University Press, 1969.

Himmelfarb, Martha. "Torah, Testimony, and Heavenly Tablets: The Claim to Authority of the Book of Jubilees." Pages 19–29 in *A Multiform Heritage: Studies on Early Judaism and Christianity in Honor of Robert A. Kraft.* Edited by Benjamin G. Wright. Atlanta, GA: Scholars Press, 1999.

Hjelm, Ingrid. *The Samaritans and Early Judaism: A Literary Analysis.* JSOTSup 303. Sheffield: Sheffield Academic, 2000.

"What Do Samaritans and Jews Have in Common? Recent Trends in Samaritan Studies." *CurBR* 3.1 (2004): 9–59.

Jerusalem's Rise to Sovereignty: Zion and Gerizim in Competition. JSOTSup 404. London: T&T Clark, 2004.

"Changing Paradigms: Judaean and Samarian Histories in Light of Recent Research." Pages 161–79 in *Historie og Konstruktion: Festskrift til Niels Peter Lemche i anledning af 60 års fødselsdagen den 6. September 2005.* Edited by Mogens Müller, Thomas L. Thompson, and Niels Peter Lemche. Copenhagen: Museum Tusculanum, 2005.

"The Samaritans in Josephus' Jewish 'History.'" Pages 27–39 in *Proceedings of the Fifth International Congress of the Société d'Études Samaritaines: Helsinki, August 1–4, 2000: Studies in Memory of Ferdinand Dexinger.* Edited by Haseeb Shehadeh, Habib Tawa, and Reinhard Pummer. Paris: Geuthner, 2006.

"Mt. Gerizim and Samaritans in Recent Research." Pages 25–41 in *Samaritans: Past and Present: Current Studies.* Edited by Menachem Mor and Fredrick V. Reiterer. SJ 53. Berlin: de Gruyter, 2010.

"Samaritans: History and Tradition in Relationship to Jews, Christians and Muslims: Problems in Writing a Monograph." Pages 173–84 in *Samaria, Samarians, Samaritans: Studies on Bible, History and Linguistics.* Edited by József Zsengellér. SJ 66. Berlin: de Gruyter, 2011.

Hoffmann, Hans-Detlef. *Reform und Reformen: Untersuchungen zu einem Grundthema der deuteronomistischen Geschichtsschreibung.* ATANT 66. Zürich: TVZ, 1980.

Hogeterp, Albert L. A. "4QMMT and Paradigms of Second Temple Jewish Nomism." *DSD* 15.3 (2008): 359–79.

Holladay, Carl R. "Paul and His Predecessors in the Diaspora: Some Reflections on Ethnic Identity in the Fragmentary Hellenistic Jewish Authors." Pages 429–60 in *Early Christianity and Classical Culture: Comparative Studies in*

Honor of Abraham J. Malherbe. 110. Edited by John T. Fitzgerald, Thomas H. Olbricht, and L. Michael White. NovTSup 110. Leiden: Brill, 2003.

Holladay, William L. *Jeremiah I: A Commentary on the Book of the Prophet Jeremiah, Chapters 1–25.* Accordance electronic ed. Hermeneia 24A. Philadelphia, PA: Fortress, 1986.

Jeremiah II: A Commentary on the Book of the Prophet Jeremiah, Chapters 26–52. Accordance electronic ed. Hermeneia 24B. Philadelphia, PA: Fortress, 1989.

Hong, Koog P. "The Deceptive Pen of Scribes: Judean Reworking of the Bethel Tradition as a Program for Assuming Israelite Identity." *Bib* 92.3 (2011): 427–41.

"Once Again: The Emergence of 'Biblical Israel.'" *ZAW* 125.2 (2013): 278–88.

Honigman, Sylvie. "'Politeumata' and Ethnicity in Ptolemaic and Roman Egypt." *Ancient Society* 33 (2003): 61–102.

Hooker, Morna D. *From Adam to Christ: Essays on Paul.* Eugene, OR: Wipf & Stock, 2008.

Horsley, Richard A. *Galilee: History, Politics, People.* Valley Forge, PA: Trinity Press International, 1995.

Hidden Transcripts and the Arts of Resistance: Applying the Work of James C. Scott to Jesus and Paul. SemeiaSt 48. Leiden: Brill, 2004.

Scribes, Visionaries, and the Politics of Second Temple Judea. Louisville, KY: Westminster John Knox, 2007.

Horst, Pieter W. van der. "Anti-Samaritan Propaganda in Early Judaism." Pages 25–44 in *Persuasion and Dissuasion in Early Christianity, Ancient Judaism, and Hellenism.* Leuven: Peeters, 2003.

Houten, Christiana van. *The Alien in Israelite Law.* Sheffield: JSOT Press, 1991.

Hübner, Hans. *Gottes Ich und Israel: Zum Schriftgebrauch des Paulus in Römer 9–11.* Göttingen: Vandenhoeck & Ruprecht, 1984.

Huddleston, Jonathan Luke. *Eschatology in Genesis.* FAT 57. Tübingen: Mohr Siebeck, 2012.

Hultgård, Anders. *L'eschatologie des Testaments des Douze patriarches: 1, Interprétation des Textes.* Uppsala: Almqvist & Wiksell, 1977.

L'eschatologie des testaments des Douze Patriarches: 2, Composition de l'ouvrage textes et traductions. Uppsala: Almqvist & Wiksell, 1982.

Hultgren, Stephen J. *From the Damascus Covenant to the Covenant of the Community: Literary, Historical, and Theological Studies in the Dead Sea Scrolls.* STDJ 66. Leiden: Brill, 2007.

Ilan, Tal. *Jewish Women in Greco-Roman Palestine: An Inquiry into Image and Status.* TSAJ 44. Tübingen: Mohr Siebeck, 2006.

Isaac, Benjamin. "Ethnic Groups in Judaea under Roman Rule." Pages 257–67 in *The Near East under Roman Rule.* Edited by Aryeh Kasher and Aharon Oppenheimer. Brill, 1998.

Isaac, E. "1 (Ethiopic Apocalypse of) Enoch." Pages 5–89 in *OTP* 1. Edited by James H. Charlesworth. 1. New York, NY: Doubleday, 1983.

Isaac, Jacqueline R. "Here Comes This Dreamer." Pages 237–49 in *From Babel to Babylon: Essays on Biblical History and Literature in Honor of Brian*

Peckham. Edited by Joyce Rilett Wood, John E. Harvey, and Mark Leuchter. LHBOTS 455. London: T&T Clark, 2006.

Isaac, Jules. *The Teaching of Contempt: Christian Roots of Anti-Semitism.* Translated by Helen Weaver. New York, NY: Holt, Rinehart, & Winston, 1964.

Jacobs, Andrew S. "A Jew's Jew: Paul and the Early Christian Problem of Jewish Origins." *JR* 86.2 (2006): 258–86.

Janzen, David. *Chronicles and the Politics of Davidic Restoration: A Quiet Revolution. Vol. 655.* London: Bloomsbury, 2017.

Japhet, Sara. "The Supposed Common Authorship of Chronicles and Ezra-Nehemia Investigated Anew." *VT* 18.3 (1968): 330–71.

"Sheshbazzar and Zerubbabel against the Background of the Historical and Religious Tendencies of Ezra-Nehemiah." *ZAW* 94 (1982): 66–98.

The Ideology of the Book of Chronicles and Its Place in Biblical Thought. BEATAJ 9. Frankfurt: Lang, 1989.

I & II Chronicles: A Commentary. OTL. Louisville, KY: Westminster John Knox, 1993.

"Exile and Restoration in the Book of Chronicles." Pages 33–44 in *The Crisis of Israelite Religion: Transformation of Religious Tradition in Exilic and Post-Exilic Times.* Edited by Bob Becking and Marjo C. A. Korpel. Oudtestamentlsche Studiën 42. Leiden: Brill, 1999.

"Post-exilic Historiography." Pages 144–73 in *Deuteronomistic Historiography in Recent Research (306).* Edited by Albert de Pury, Thomas Römer, and Jean-Daniel Machi. Sheffield: Sheffield Academic, 2000.

"Periodization between History and Ideology II." Pages 416–31 in *From the Rivers of Babylon to the Highlands of Judah: Collected Studies on the Restoration Period.* Winona Lake, IN: Eisenbrauns, 2007.

Jaubert, Annie. "Le calendrier des Jubilés et de la secte de Qumrân. Ses origines bibliques." *VT* 3.3 (1953): 250–64.

"Le calendrier des Jubilés et les jours liturgiques de la semaine." *VT* 7.1 (1957): 35–61.

La notion d'Alliance dans le judaïsme aux abords de l'ère chrétienne. PS. Paris: Seuil, 1963.

Jensen, Hans J. Lundager. "Juditbogen." Pages 153–89 in *Tradition og nybrud. Jødedommen i hellenistik tid.* Edited by Troels Engberg-Petersen and Nils Peter Lemche. FBE. Kopenhaven: Museum Tusculanum, 1990.

Jeremias, Gert. *Der Lehrer der Gerechtigkeit.* SUNT 2. Göttingen: Vandenhoeck & Ruprecht, 1963.

"Karl Georg Kuhn (1906–1976)." Pages 297–312 in *Neutestamentliche Wissenschaft nach 1945: Hauptvertreter der deutschsprachigen Exegese in der Darstellung ihrer Schüler.* Edited by Cilliers Breytenbach and Rudolf Hoppe. Neukirchen-Vluyn: Neukirchener Verlag, 2008.

Jervell, Jacob. "Ein Interpolator interpretiert: Zu der christlichen Bearbeitung der Testamente der zwölf Patriarchen." Pages 30–61 in *Studien zu den Testamenten der zwölf Patriarchen.* Edited by Christoph Burchard, Johannes Thomas, Jacob Jervell, and Walther Eltester. Berlin: Töpelmann, 1969.

Jewett, Robert. *Romans: A Commentary.* Accordance electronic ed. Hermeneia 66. Minneapolis, MN: Fortress, 2007.

Jindo, Job Y. "On Myth and History in Prophetic and Apocalyptic Eschatology." *VT* 55 (2005): 412–15.

Joannès, Francis, and André Lemaire. "Trois tablettes cunéiformes à onomastique ouest-sémitique (collection Sh. Moussaïeff) (Pls. I–II)." *Transeu* (1999): 17–34.

Jobling, David. *The Sense of Biblical Narrative: Structural Analyses in the Hebrew Bible.* 2 vols. JSOTSup 39. Sheffield: Sheffield Academic, 1986.

Johnson, Sara Raup. "Maccabees, Third Book of." *EDEJ* 907–8.

Jones, Bruce William. "The Prayer in Daniel IX." *VT* 18.4 (1968): 488–93.

Jones, Douglas R. "A Fresh Interpretation of Zechariah IX–XI." *VT* 12.3 (1962): 241–59.

Jonge, Marinus de. *The Testaments of the Twelve Patriarchs: A Study of Their Text, Composition and Origin.* SVTP. Assen: van Gorcum, 1953.

——— . "Christian Influence in the Testaments of the Twelve Patriarchs." *NovT* 4.3 (1960): 182–235.

——— . "Josephus und die Zukunftserwartungen seines Volkes." Pages 205–19 in *Josephus-Studien: Untersuchungen zu Josephus, dem antiken Judentum und dem Neuen Testament, Otto Michel zum 70. Geburtstag gewidmet.* Edited by Otto Betz, Klaus Haacker, and Martin Hengel. Göttingen: Vandenhoeck & Ruprecht, 1974.

——— . "The Pre-Mosaic Servants of God in the Testaments of the Twelve Patriarchs and in the writings of Justin and Irenaeus." *Vigiliae christianae* 39 (1985): 157–70.

——— . "The Future of Israel in the Testaments of the Twelve Patriarchs." *JSJ* 17.2 (1986): 196–211.

——— . "The Expectation of the Future in the Psalms of Solomon." *Neot* 23.1 (1989): 93–117.

——— . *Jewish Eschatology, Early Christian Christology, and the Testaments of the Twelve Patriarchs: Collected Essays of Marinus de Jonge.* NovTSup 63. Leiden: Brill, 1991.

——— . "The Transmission of the Testaments of the Twelve Patriarchs by Christians." *Vigiliae christianae* 47.1 (1993): 1–28.

——— . *Pseudepigrapha of the Old Testament as Part of Christian Literature: The Case of the Testaments of the Twelve Patriarchs and the Greek Life of Adam and Eve.* SVTP. Leiden: Brill, 2003.

Joosten, Jan. "Reflections on the Original Language of the Psalms of Solomon." Pages 31–48 in *The Psalms of Solomon: Language, History, Theology.* Edited by Eberhard Bons and Patrick Pouchelle. EJL. Atlanta, GA: SBL Press, 2015.

Josephus. *Jewish Antiquities, Volume VI.* Translated by Ralph Marcus. LCL 489. Cambridge, MA: Harvard University Press, 1937.

Joyce, Paul M. "Dislocation and Adaptation in the Exilic Age and After." Pages 45–58 in *After the Exile: Essays in Honour of Rex Mason.* Edited by John Barton and David James Reimer. Macon, GA: Mercer University Press, 1996.

Junginger, Horst. "Das Bild des Juden in der nationalsozialistischen Judenforschung." Pages 171–220 in *Die kulturelle Seite des Antisemitismus:*

Zwischen Aufklärung und Shoah. Edited by Andrea Hoffmann. Studien & Materialien des Ludwig-Uhland-Instituts der Universität Tübingen. Tübingen: Tübinger Vereinigung für Volkskunde, 2006.

Kaatz, Saul. *Die mündliche Lehre und ihr Dogma*. Leipzig: Kaufmann, 1923.

Kahneman, Daniel. *Thinking, Fast and Slow*. New York, NY: Farrar, Straus and Giroux, 2011.

Kalimi, Isaac. "Die Abfassungszeit der Chronik – Forschungsstand und Perspektiven." *ZAW* 105.2 (1993): 223–33.

Kallai, Z. "Nov, Noveh." Page 684 in *Enziklopediya Mikra'it*. 5. 5. Jerusalem: Bialik, 1968.

Kang, Namsoon. *Diasporic Feminist Theology: Asia and Theopolitical Imagination*. Minneapolis, MN: Fortress, 2014.

Kant, Laurence H. "Jewish Inscriptions in Greek and Latin." *ANRW* 20.2:671–713.

Kaper, Olaf E. "Petubastis IV in the Dakhla Oasis: New Evidence about an Early Rebellion against Persian Rule and Its Suppression in Political Memory." Pages 125–50 in *Political Memory in and after the Persian Empire*. Edited by Jason M. Silverman and Caroline Waerzeggers. Ancient Near East Monographs 13. Atlanta, GA: SBL Press, 2015.

Kartveit, Magnar. "Josephus on the Samaritans – His Tendenz and Purpose." Pages 109–20 in *Samaria, Samarians, Samaritans: Studies on Bible, History and Linguistics*. Edited by József Zsengellér. SJ 66. Berlin: de Gruyter, 2011.

Kasher, Aryeh. "Jerusalem as a Metropolis in Philo's National Consciousness." *Cathedra* 11 (1979): 45–56.

The Jews in Hellenistic and Roman Egypt: The Struggle for Equal Rights. TSAJ 7. Tübingen: Mohr Siebeck, 1985.

Kasher, Aryeh, and Avigdor Shinan. "Jewish Emigration and Settlement in the Diaspora in the Hellenistic-Roman Period." Pages 65–91 in *Emigration and Settlement in Jewish and General History*. Jerusalem: Zlaman Shazar Center, 1982.

Kee, Howard Clark. "Testaments of the Twelve Patriarchs." Pages 775–828 in *OTP* 1. Edited by James H Charlesworth. Doubleday, 1983.

Keel, Othmar. "Kultische Brüderlichkeit – Ps 133." *FZPhTh* 23 (1976): 68–80.

Keel, Othmar, and Christoph Uehlinger. *Gods, Goddesses, and Images*. Minneapolis: Fortress, 1998.

Kelly, Brian E. *Retribution and Eschatology in Chronicles*. JSOTSup 211. London: T&T Clark, 1996.

Keown, Gerald L., Pamela L. Scalise, and Thomas G. Smothers. *Jeremiah 26–52*. Accordance/Thomas Nelson electronic ed. WBC 27. Nashville, TN: Thomas Nelson, 1995.

Kiefer, Jörn. *Exil und Diaspora: Begrifflichkeit und Deutungen im antiken Judentum und in der hebräischen Bibel*. Arbeiten zur Bibel und ihrer Geschichte. Berlin: Evangelische Verlagsanstalt, 2005.

Kimelman, Reuven. "The Daily 'Amidah and the Rhetoric of Redemption." *JQR* 79.2/3 (1988): 165–97.

Kittel, Gerhard *Die Judenfrage*. Stuttgart: Kohlhammer, 1933.

Klawans, Jonathan. *Impurity and Sin in Ancient Judaism*. Oxford: Oxford University Press, 2004.

Klein, Ralph W. *1 Samuel*. Accordance/Thomas Nelson electronic ed. WBC 10. Waco, TX: Word, 1983.

1 Chronicles: A Commentary on 1 Chronicles. Edited by Thomas Krüger. Accordance electronic ed. Hermeneia 13. Minneapolis, MN: Fortress, 2006.

Kleinig, John W. "Recent Research in Chronicles." *Currents in Research: Biblical Studies* 2 (1994): 43–76.

Klijn, Albertus F. J. *Der lateinische Text der Apokalypse des Esra*. TUGAL 131. Berlin: Academie, 1983.

Knauf, Ernst Axel. "Bethel: The Israelite Impact on Judean Language and Literature." Pages 291–349 in *Judah and the Judeans in the Persian Period*. Winona Lake, IN: Eisenbrauns, 2006.

Knibb, Michael A. "The Exile in the Literature of the Intertestamental Period." *HeyJ* 17.3 (1976): 253–72.

"Exile in the Damascus Document." *JSOT* 25 (1983): 99–117.

The Qumran Community. Cambridge Commentaries on Writings of the Jewish and Christian World 200 BC to AD 200. Cambridge: Cambridge University Press, 1987.

"A Note on 4Q372 and 4Q390." Pages 164–70 in *The Scriptures and the Scrolls: Studies in Honor of A. S. van der Woude on the Occasion of His 65th Birthday*. Edited by Florentino García Martínez, Anthony Hilhorst, and C. J. Labuschagne. Leiden: Brill, 1992.

Knoppers, Gary N. "A Reunited Kingdom in Chronicles?" *Proceedings of the Great Lakes and Midwest Bible Societies* 9 (1989): 74–88.

"Rehoboam in Chronicles: Villain or Victim?" *JBL* 109.3 (1990): 423–40.

"Reform and Regression: The Chronicler's Presentation of Jehoshaphat." *Bib* 72.4 (1991): 500–24.

"'Battling against Yahweh': Israel's War Against Judah in 2 Chr 13:2–20." *RB* 100.4 (1993): 511–32.

Two Nations under God: The Deuteronomic History of Solomon and the Dual Monarchies. 2 vols., HSM 52 and 53 (Leiden: Brill, 1993, 1994).

"'YHWH Is Not with Israel': Alliances as a Topos in Chronicles." *Catholic Biblical Quarterly* 58.4 (1996): 601–26.

"History and Historiography: The Royal Reforms." Pages 178–203 in *The Chronicler as Historian*. Edited by M. Patrick Graham, Kenneth G. Hoglund, and Steven L. McKenzie. JSOTSup 238. Sheffield: Sheffield Academic, 1997.

"Sources, Revisions, and Editions: The Lists of Jerusalem's Residents in MT and LXX Nehemiah 11 and 1 Chronicles 9." *Text* 20 (2000): 141–68.

I Chronicles 1–9: A New Translation with Introduction and Commentary. AB 12A. New York, NY: Doubleday, 2003.

I Chronicles 10–29: A New Translation with Introduction and Commentary. AB 12B. New York, NY: Doubleday, 2004.

"In Search of Post-Exilic Israel: Samaria after the Fall of the Northern Kingdom." Pages 150–80 in *In Search of Pre-Exilic Israel*. Edited by John Day. JSOTSup 406. London: T&T Clark, 2004.

"What has Mt. Zion to Do with Mt. Gerizim?" *SR* 34 (2005): 307–36.

"Mt. Gerizim and Mt. Zion: A Study in the Early History of the Samaritans and Jews." *SR* 34.3–4 (2005): 309–37.

"Revisiting the Samarian Question in the Persian Period." Pages 265–90 in *Judah and the Judeans in the Persian Period*. Edited by Oded Lipschits and Manfred Oeming. Winona Lake, IN: Eisenbrauns, 2006.

"Nehemiah and Sanballat: The Enemy without or Within?" Pages 305–31 in *Judah and the Judeans in the Fourth Century BCE*. Edited by Oded Lipschits, Gary N. Knoppers, and Rainer Albertz. Winona Lake, IN: Eisenbrauns, 2007.

"Cutheans or Children of Jacob? The Issue of Samaritan Origins in 2 Kings 17." Pages 223–40 in *Reflection and Refraction: Studies in Biblical Historiography in Honour of A. Graeme Auld*. Edited by Robert Rezetko, Timothy Henry Lim, and W Brian Aucker. VTSup 113. Leiden: Brill, 2007.

"Theories of the Redaction(s) of Kings." Pages 69–88 in *Books of Kings*. Edited by André Lemaire and Baruch Halpern. Leiden: Brill, 2010.

"Did Jacob Become Judah? The Configuration of Israel's Restoration in Deutero-Isaiah." Pages 39–67 in *Samaria, Samarians, Samaritans: Studies on Bible, History and Linguistics*. Edited by József Zsengellér. SJ 66. Berlin: de Gruyter, 2011.

Jews and Samaritans: The Origins and History of Their Early Relations. New York, NY: Oxford University press, 2013.

Knoppers, Gary N., and Bernard M. Levinson, eds. *The Pentateuch as Torah: New Models for Understanding Its Promulgation and Acceptance*. Winona Lake, IN: Eisenbrauns, 2007.

Koch, Klaus. "Ezra and the Origins of Judaism." *JSS* 19 (1974): 173–97.

"Is Daniel Also among the Prophets?" *Int* 39.2 (1985): 117–30.

Koselleck, Reinhart. "Introduction and Prefaces to the Geschichtliche Grundbegriffe." *Contributions to the History of Concepts* 6.1 (2011): 1–37.

Kraabel, A. Thomas. "The Roman Diaspora: Six Questionable Assumptions." *JJS* 33.1–2 (1982): 445–64.

"New Evidence of the Samaritan Diaspora has Been Found on Delos." *BA* 47.1 (1984): 44–46.

"Unity and Diversity among Diaspora Synagogues." Pages 49–60 in *Diaspora Jews and Judaism: Essays in Honor of, and in Dialogue with, A. Thomas Kraabel*. Edited by J. Andrew. Overman and Robert S. MacLennan. SFSHJ 41. Atlanta, GA: Scholars Press, 1992.

Kraemer, Ross Shepard. "On the Meaning of the Term Jew in Greco-Roman Inscriptions." *HTR* 82.1 (1989): 35–53.

Kratz, Reinhard G. "Israel in the Book of Isaiah." *JSOT* 31.1 (2006): 103–28.

Kristeva, Julia. *Revolution in Poetic Language*. New York, NY: Columbia University Press, 1984.

Kuhn, Karl Georg. "Die inneren Voraussetzungen der jüdischen Ausbreitung." *Deutsche Theologie* 2 (1935): 9–17.

"Die Entstehung des talmudischen Denkens." *Forschungen zur Judenfrage* 1 (1937): 63–80.

"Weltjudentum in der Antike." *Forschungen zur Judenfrage* 2 (1937): 9–29, 64.

Review of Blut und Geld im Judentum, by Hermann Schroer. *Historische Zeitschrift* 156 (1937): 313–16.

"Ursprung und Wesen der talmudischen Einstellung zum Nichtjuden." *Forschungen zur Judenfrage* 3 (1938): 199–234.

Die Judenfrage als weltgeschichtliches Problem. Schriften des Reichsinstituts für Geschichte des neuen Deutschlands. Hamburg: Hanseatische Verlagsanstalt, 1939.

"Der Talmud, das Gesetzbuch der Juden: Einfuhrende Bemerkungen." Pages 226–33 in *Zur Geschichte und rechtlichen Stellung der Juden in Stadt und Universität Tübingen: Aus den Jahresbänden der wissenschaftlichen Akademie des NSD-Dozentenbundes/Wissenschaftliche Akademie Tübingen des NSD-Dozentenbundes 1 (1937–1939).* Edited by Thomas Miller. Tübingen: Mohr Siebeck, 1941.

"Die Schriftrollen vom Toten Meer: Zum heutigen Stand ihrer Veröffentlichung." *EvT* 11.1–6 (1951): 72–75.

Kuhrt, Amélie. *The Persian Empire: A Corpus of Sources from the Achaemenid Period.* London: Routledge, 2007.

Kynes, Will. *An Obituary for "Wisdom Literature": The Birth, Death, and Intertextual Reintegration of a Biblical Corpus.* New York, NY: Oxford University Press, 2018.

"The 'Wisdom Literature' Category: An Obituary." *JTS* 69.1 (2018): 1–24.

Laato, Antti. *A Star Is Rising: The Historical Development of the Old Testament Royal Ideology and the Rise of the Jewish Messianic Expectations.* USFISFJC 5. Atlanta, GA: Scholars Press, 1997.

Lambert, David A. "Fasting as a Penitential Rite: A Biblical Phenomenon?" *HTR* 96.4 (2003): 477–512.

"Did Israel Believe that Redemption Awaited Its Repentance? The Case of Jubilees 1." *Catholic Biblical Quarterly* 68.4 (2006): 631–50.

How Repentance Became Biblical: Judaism, Christianity, and the Interpretation of Scripture. New York, NY: Oxford University Press, 2016.

"How the 'Torah of Moses' Became Revelation: An Early, Apocalyptic Theory of Pentateuchal Origins." *JSJ* 47.1 (2016): 22–54.

Lang, T. J. *Mystery and the Making of a Christian Historical Consciousness: From Paul to the Second Century.* BZNW 219. Berlin: de Gruyter, 2015.

Lange, Armin, and Zlatko Pleše. "Transpositional Hermeneutics: A Hermeneutical Comparison of the Derveni Papyrus, Aristobulus of Alexandria, and the Qumran Pesherim." Pages 895–922 in *The Dead Sea Scrolls in Context: Integrating the Dead Sea Scrolls in the Study of Ancient Texts, Languages, and Cultures.* 2. Edited by Armin Lange, Emanuel Tov, Matthias Weigold, and Bennie H. Reynolds III. VTSup 2. Leiden: Brill, 2011.

Lemaire, André. "Judean Identity in Elephantine: Everyday Life according to the Ostraca." Pages 365–74 in *Judah and the Judeans in the Achaemenid Period: Negotiating Identity in an International Context.* Edited by Oded Lipschits, Gary N. Knoppers, and Manfred Oeming. Winona Lake, IN: Eisenbrauns, 2011.

Lemche, Niels Peter. "The 'Hebrew Slave': Comments on the Slave Law Ex. XXI 2–11." *VT* 25.2 (1975): 129–44.

"The Understanding of Community in the Old Testament and in the Dead Sea Scrolls." Pages 181–93 in *Qumran between the Old and New Testaments.* Edited by Frederick H. Cryer and Thomas L. Thompson. JSOTSup 290. Sheffield: Sheffield Academic, 1998.

The Israelites in History and Tradition. London: SPCK, 1998.

The Canaanites and Their Land: The Tradition of the Canaanites. Sheffield: Sheffield Academic, 1999.

Leon, Harry Joshua. *The Jews of Ancient Rome.* Peabody, MA: Hendrickson, 1995.

Leoni, Tommaso. "The Text of Josephus's Works: An Overview." *JSJ* 40.2 (2009): 149–84.

Levenson, Jon D. *Resurrection and the Restoration of Israel: The Ultimate Victory of the God of Life.* New Haven, CT: Yale University Press, 2006.

Levin, Yigal. "Joseph, Judah and the Benjamin Conundrum." *ZAW* 116.2 (2006): 223–41.

Levine, Amy-Jill. "Diaspora as Metaphor: Bodies and Boundaries in the Book of Tobit." Pages 105–18 in *Diaspora Jews and Judaism: Essays in Honor of, and in Dialogue with, A. Thomas Kraabel.* Edited by J. A. Overman and Robert S. MacLennan. SFSHJ 41. Atlanta, GA: Scholars Press, 1992.

The Misunderstood Jew: The Church and the Scandal of the Jewish Jesus. San Francisco, CA: HarperOne, 2006.

Levinskaya, Irina. *The Book of Acts in Its Diaspora Setting.* Grand Rapids, MI: Eerdmans, 1996.

Lewis, Bernard. *History: Remembered, Recovered, Invented.* Princeton, NJ: Princeton University Press, 1975.

Liebengood, Kelly D. "Zechariah 9–14 as the Substructure of 1 Peter's Eschatological Program." PhD diss., University of St. Andrews, 2011.

Lieber, Andrea. "Between Motherland and Fatherland: Diaspora, Pilgrimage and the Spiritualization of Sacrifice in Philo of Alexandria." Pages 193–210 in *Heavenly Tablets: Interpretation, Identity and Tradition in Ancient Judaism (1).* Edited by Lynn Lidonnici and Andrea Lieber. JSJSup 119. Leiden: Brill, 2007.

Lied, Liv Ingeborg. *The Other Lands of Israel: Imaginations of the Land in 2 Baruch.* JSJSup 129. Leiden: Brill, 2008.

Lifshitz, Baruch. "Papyrus grecs du désert du Juda." *Aeg* 42 (1962): 240–56.

Lightfoot, J. B. *Saint Paul's Epistle to the Philippians.* London: Macmillan, 1903.

Lincicum, David. *Paul and the Early Jewish Encounter with Deuteronomy.* WUNT 284. Tübingen: Mohr Siebeck, 2010.

Lindemann, Andreas. "Samaria und die Samaritaner im Neuen Testament." *WD* 22 (1993): 51–76.

Lindemann, Gerhard. "Theological Research about Judaism in Different Political Contexts: The Example of Karl Georg Kuhn." *Kirchliche Zeitgeschichte* (2004): 331–38.

Lindner, Helgo. *Die Geschichtsauffassung des Flavius Josephus in Bellum Judaicum: Gleichzeitig ein Beitrag zur Quellenfrage.* AGJU 12. Leiden: Brill, 1972.

Lindsey, Hal. *The Late Great Planet Earth.* Grand Rapids, MI: Zondervan, 1970.

Linville, James Richard. *Israel in the Book of Kings: The Past as a Project of Social Identity.* JSOTSup 272. Sheffield: Sheffield Academic, 1998.

Liverani, Mario. "The Ideology of the Assyrian Empire." Pages 297–317 in *Power and Propaganda: A Symposium on Ancient Empires.* Edited by Mogens Trolle Larsen. Copenhagen: Akademisk, 1979.

"The Growth of the Assyrian Empire in the Habur/Middle Euphrates Area: A New Paradigm." *SAAB* 2.2 (1988): 81–98.

Lowe, Malcolm. "Who Were the ΙΟΥΔΑΙΟΙ?" *NovT* 18.2 (1976): 101–30.

"ΙΟΥΔΑΙΟΙ of the Apocrypha: A Fresh Approach to the Gospels of James, Pseudo-Thomas, Peter, and Nicodemus." *NovT* 23.1 (1981): 56–90.

Lozachmeur, Hélène et al. *La collection Clermont-Ganneau: Ostraca, épigraphes sur jarre, étiquettes de bois.* 2 vols. Mémoires de l'Académie des inscriptions et belles-lettres. Paris: Boccard, 2006.

Lundbom, Jack R. *Jeremiah 1–20: A New Translation with Introduction and Commentary.* Accordance electronic ed. AB. New Haven, CT: Yale University Press, 1974.

"Haplography in the Hebrew Vorlage of LXX Jeremiah." *Hebrew Studies* 46.1 (2005): 301–20.

Macchi, Jean-Daniel. *Les Samaritains: Histoire d'une légende, Israël et la province de Samarie.* MdB 30. Geneva: Labor et Fides, 1994.

Israël et ses tribus selon Genèse 49. OBO 171. Freiburg: Universitätsverlag, 1999.

Maccoby, Hyam. "Naḥmanides and Messianism: A Reply." *JQR* 77.1 (1986): 55–57.

MacDowell, Douglas M. *Spartan Law.* ScotCS 107. Edinburgh: Scottish Academic, 1986.

MacIntyre, Alasdair. *After Virtue.* Notre Dame, IN: University of Notre Dame Press, 1981.

Mack, Burton L. *Wisdom and the Hebrew Epic: Ben Sira's Hymn in Praise of the Fathers.* Chicago, IL: University of Chicago Press, 1985.

"Wisdom Makes a Difference: Alternatives to 'Messianic' Configurations." Pages 15–48 in *Judaisms and Their Messiahs at the Turn of the Christian Era.* Edited by Jacob Neusner, W. S. Green, and Ernst Frerichs. Cambridge: Cambridge University Press, 1988.

"Wisdom and Apocalyptic in Philo." *SPhiloA* 3 (1991): 21–39.

Mackie, Scott D. "Seeing God in Philo of Alexandria: The Logos, the Powers, or the Existent One?" *SPhiloA* 21 (2009): 25–48.

"Seeing God in Philo of Alexandria: Means, Methods, and Mysticism." *JSJ* 43.2 (2012): 147–79.

Magen, Yitzhak. "Mt. Gerizim – A Temple City." *Qadmoniot* 33.2 (2000): 74–118.

"The Dating of the First Phase of the Samaritan Temple on Mount Gerizim in Light of the Archaeological Evidence." Pages 157–211 in *Judah and the Judeans in the Fourth Century BCE.* Edited by Oded Lipschits, Gary N. Knoppers, and Rainer Albertz. Winona Lake, IN: Eisenbrauns, 2007.

Magen, Yitzhak, and N. Carmin. *The Samaritans and the Good Samaritan.* Translated by Edward Levin. Judea and Samaria Publications. Jerusalem: Israel Antiquities Authority, 2008.

Magen, Yitzhak, Haggai Misgav, and Levana Tsfania, eds. *The Aramaic, Hebrew and Samaritan Inscriptions*. Judea and Samaria Publications. Jerusalem: Israel Antiquities Authority, 2004.

Magness, Jodi. *The Archaeology of Qumran and the Dead Sea Scrolls*. Grand Rapids, MI: Eerdmans, 2003.

Magonet, Jonathan. "Jonah, Book of." *The Anchor Yale Bible Dictionary* 3:936–42.

Malina, Bruce J., and John J. Pilch. *Social-Science Commentary on the Book of Revelation*. Minneapolis, MN: Fortress Press, 2000.

Malkin, Irad. *Returns of Odysseus: Colonization and Ethnicity*. Berkeley, CA: University of California Press, 1998.

Manville, Brook. *The Origins of Citizenship in Ancient Athens*. Princeton, NJ: Princeton University Press, 1997.

Marcus, David. *From Balaam to Jonah: Anti-prophetic Satire in the Hebrew Bible*. BJS 301. Atlanta, GA: Scholars Press, 1995.

Markner, Reinhard. "Forschungen zur Judenfrage: A Notorious Journal and Some of Its Contributors." *European Journal of Jewish Studies* 1.2 (2007): 395–415.

Martin, James D. "Ben Sira's Hymn to the Fathers: A Messianic Perspective." *OtSt* 24 (1986): 107–23.

Marttila, Marko. "The Deuteronomic Ideology and Phrasology in the Book of Baruch." Pages 321–46 in *Changes in Scripture: Rewriting and Interpreting Authoritative Traditions in the Second Temple period*. Edited by Hanne von Weissberg, Juha Pakkala, and Marko Marttila. BZAW 419. Berlin: de Gruyter, 2011.

Mason, Steve. "Josephus, Daniel, and the Flavian House." Pages 161–91 in *Josephus and the History of the Greco-Roman Period*. Edited by Morton Smith, Fausto Parente, and Joseph Sievers. Leiden: Brill, 1994.

"Jews, Judaeans, Judaizing, Judaism: Problems of Categorization in Ancient History." *JSJ* 38 (2007): 457–512.

Mayes, A. D. H. "Israel in the Pre-Monarchy Period." *VT* 23.2 (1973): 151–70.

McBride, S. Dean. "Polity of the Covenant People: The Book of Deuteronomy." *Int* 41.3 (1987): 229–44.

McConville, J. Gordon. "Ezra-Nehemiah and the Fulfillment of Prophecy." *VT* 36.2 (1986): 205–24.

"Narrative and Meaning in the Books of Kings." *Bib* 70 (1989): 31–49.

"Restoration in Deuteronomy and the Deuteronomic Literature." Pages 11–40 in *Restoration: Old Testament, Jewish and Christian Perspectives*. Edited by James M. Scott. JSJSup 72. Leiden: Brill, 2001.

Exploring the Old Testament, Volume 4: A Guide to the Prophets. Downers Grove, IL: InterVarsity Press, 2002.

McCracken, David. "Narration and Comedy in the Book of Tobit." *JBL* (1995): 401–18.

McCready, Wayne O. "The 'Day of Small Things' vs. the Latter Days." Pages 223–36 in *Israel's Apostasy and Restoration: Essays in Honor of Roland K. Harrison*. Edited by Avraham Gileadi. Grand Rapids, MI: Baker Books, 1988.

McCutcheon, Russell T. "Myth." Pages 52–71 in *A Modest Proposal on Method: Essaying the Study of Religion*. Supplements to Method and Theory in the Study of Religion 2. Leiden: Brill, 2014.

McNutt, James E. "A Very Damning Truth: Walter Grundmann, Adolf Schlatter, and Susannah Heschel's The Aryan Jesus." *HTR* 105.3 (2012): 280–301.

Melton, J. Gordon. "Spiritualization and Reaffirmation: What Really Happens When Prophecy Fails." *American Studies* 26.2 (1985): 17–29.

Mendels, Doron. *The Land of Israel as a Political Concept in Hasmonean Literature: Recourse to History in Second Century BC claims to the holy land*. TSAJ 15. Tübingen: Mohr Siebeck, 1987.

Mendelson, Alan. *Philo's Jewish Identity*. BJS 161. Atlanta, GA: Scholars Press, 1988.

Mendenhall, George E. *Law and Covenant in Israel and the Ancient Near East*. Pittsburgh, PA: Presbyterian Board of Colportage, 1954.

"Samuel's 'Broken Rîb': Deuteronomy 32." Pages 169–80 in *A Song of Power and the Power of Song: Essays on the Book of Deuteronomy*. Edited by Duane L. Christensen. Winona Lake, IN: Eisenbrauns, 1993.

Meritt, Benjamin Dean, ed. *Greek Inscriptions, 1896–1927*. Cambridge, MA: Harvard University Press, 1931.

Metso, Sarianna. "Whom Does the Term Yahad Identify?" Pages 215–35 in *Biblical Traditions in Transmission: Essays in Honour of Michael A. Knibb*. 111. Edited by Charlotte Hempel and Judith M. Lieu. JSJSup 111. 2008.

Mettinger, Tryggve N. D. *Solomonic State Officials: A Study of the Civil Government Officials of the Israelite Monarchy*. ConBOT 5. Lund: Gleerup, 1971.

Metzger, Bruce M. "The Fourth Book of Ezra." Pages 517–59 in *OTP* 1. Edited by James H. Charlesworth. Garden City, NY: Doubleday, 1983.

Meyers, Eric M. "Galilean Regionalism as a Factor in Historical Reconstruction." *BASOR* 220/221 (1976): 93–101.

"The Cultural Setting of Galilee: The Case of Regionalism and Early Judaism." *ANRW* 19.1:686–702.

"Exile and Restoration in Light of Recent Archaeology and Demographic Studies." Pages 166–73 in *Exile and Restoration Revisited: Essays on the Babylonian and Persian Period in Memory of Peter R. Ackroyd*. Edited by Gary N. Knoppers, Lester L. Grabbe, and Dierdre N. Fulton. LSTS 73. London: T&T Clark, 2009.

Middendorp, Theophil L. *Die Stellung Jesu Ben Siras zwischen Judentum und Hellenismus*. Leiden: Brill, 1973.

Middlemas, Jill A. "Going beyond the Myth of the Empty Land: A Reassessment." Pages 174–94 in *Exile and Restoration Revisited: Essays on the Babylonian and Persian Periods in Memory of Peter R. Ackroyd*. Edited by Gary N. Knoppers, Lester L. Grabbe, and Dierdre N. Fulton. LSTS 73. London: T&T Clark, 2009.

"Trito-Isaiah's Intra- and Internationalization: Identity Markers in the Second Temple period." Pages 105–25 in *Judah and the Judeans in the Achaemenid Period: Negotiating Identity in an International Context*. Edited by Oded

Lipschits, Gary N. Knoppers, and Manfred Oeming. Winona Lake, IN: Eisenbrauns, 2011.

Millar, Fergus. *The Roman Near East, 31 BC–AD 337*. Cambridge, MA: Harvard University Press, 1995.

Miller, David M. "The Messenger, the Lord, and the Coming Judgement in the Reception History of Malachi 3." *NTS* 53.1 (2007): 1–16.

"The Meaning of *Ioudaios* and Its Relationship to Other Group Labels in Ancient 'Judaism.'" *CurBR* 9.1 (2010): 98–126.

"Ethnicity Comes of Age: An Overview of Twentieth-Century Terms for *Ioudaios*." *CurBR* 10 (2012): 293–311.

"Ethnicity, Religion and the Meaning of *Ioudaios* in Ancient 'Judaism.'" *CurBR* 12.2 (2014): 216–65.

Miller, J. Maxwell, and John H. Hayes. *A History of Ancient Israel and Judah*. Philadelphia, PA: Westminster, 1986.

Modrzejewski, Joseph Mélèze. "La sanction de l'homicide en droit grec et hellénistique." Pages 3–16 in *Symposion*. Pacific Grove, CA: 1990.

"How to Be a Jew in Hellenistic Egypt." Pages 65–91 in *Diasporas in Antiquity*. Edited by Shaye J. D. Cohen and Ernst S. Frerichs. BJS 288. Atlanta, GA: Scholars Press, 1993.

The Jews of Egypt: From Ramses II to Emperor Hadrian. Princeton, NJ: Princeton University Press, 1995.

Mojola, Aloo Osotsi. "The 'Tribes' of Israel? a Bible Translator's Dilemma." *JSOT* 81 (1998): 15–29.

Montgomery, James Alan. *The Samaritans, the Earliest Jewish Sect: Their History, Theology and Literature*. Eugene, OR: Wipf & Stock, 2006.

Moo, Douglas J. *The Epistle to the Romans*. Accordance electronic ed. NICNT. Grand Rapids, MI: Eerdmans, 1996.

Moore, Carey A. *Daniel, Esther, and Jeremiah: The Additions*. AB 44. Garden City, NY: Doubleday, 1977.

Judith: A New Translation with Introduction and Commentary. AB 40. New York, NY: Doubleday, 1985.

Tobit: A New Translation with Introduction and Commentary. Accordance electronic ed. AB 40. Garden City, NY: Doubleday, 1996.

Mor, Menachem. "The Building of the Samaritan Temple and the Samaritan Governors – Again." Pages 89–108 in *Samaria, Samarians, Samaritans: Studies on Bible, History and Linguistics*. Edited by József Zsengellér. SJ 66. Berlin: de Gruyter, 2011.

Morgenstern, Julian. "The Calendar of the Book of Jubilees, Its Origin and Its Character." *VT* 5.1 (1955): 34–76.

Moule, Charles F. D. "Once More, Who Were the Hellenists?" *ExpTim* 70.4 (1959): 100–2.

Movers, Franz Carl. *Kritische Untersuchungen über die biblische Chronik*. Bonn: Habicht, 1834.

Mulder, Otto. *Simon the High Priest in Sirach 50: An Exegetical Study of the Significance of Simon the High Priest as Climax to the Praise of the Fathers in Ben Sira's Concept of the History of Israel*. Leiden: Brill, 2003.

Mulder, Otto, and Renate Egger-Wenzel. "Two Approaches: Simon the High Priest and YHWH God of Israel/God of All in Sirach 50." Pages 221–34 in *Ben Sira's God: Proceedings of the International Ben Sira Conference, Durham-Ushaw College 2001.* BZAW 321. Berlin: de Gruyter, 2002.

Mullen, E. Theodore. *Narrative History and Ethnic Boundaries: The Deuteronomistic Historian and the Creation of Israelite National Identity.* SemeiaSt. Atlanta, GA: Scholars Press, 1993.

Müller, Sabine. "Darius I and the Problems of (Re-)Conquest: Resistance, False Identities and the Impact of the Past." Pages 5–10 in *Greece, Macedon and Persia.* Edited by Timothy Howe, E. Edward Garvin, and Graham Wrightson. Oxford: Oxbow Books, 2015.

Murray, Donald F. "Dynasty, People, and the Future: The Message of Chronicles." *JSOT* 58 (1993): 71–92.

"Retribution and Revival: Theological Theory, Religious Praxis, and the Future in Chronicles." *JSOT* 88 (2000): 77–99.

"Of All the Years the Hopes – Or Fears? Jehoiachin in Babylon (2 Kings 25:27–30)." *JBL* 120.2 (2001): 245–65.

Murray, Robert. "Jews, Hebrews, and Christians: Some Needed Distinctions." *NovT* 24.3 (1982): 194–208.

Myers, Jacob M. *1 Chronicles: A New Translation with Introduction and Commentary.* AB 12. Garden City, NY: Doubleday, 1965.

Myles, Robert, and James G. Crossley. "Biblical Scholarship, Jews and Israel: On Bruce Malina, Conspiracy Theories and Ideological Contradictions." The Bible and Interpretation (2012): https://www.bibleinterp.com/opeds/myl368013.shtml

Na'aman, Nadav. "The Kingdom of Judah under Josiah." *TA* 18.1 (1991): 3–71.

Population Changes in Palestine Following Assyrian Deportations." *TA* 20.1 (1993): 104–24.

"When and How Did Jerusalem Become a Great City? The Rise of Jerusalem as Judah's Premier City in the Eighth-Seventh Centuries BCE." *BASOR* 347 (2007): 21–56.

"Saul, Benjamin and the Emergence of 'Biblical Israel' (Part 1)." *ZAW* 121.2 (2009): 211–24.

"The Israelite-Judahite Struggle for the Patrimony of Ancient Israel." *Bib* 91.1 (2010): 1–23.

Na'aman, Nadav, and Ran Zadok. "Assyrian Deportations to the Province of Samerina in the Light of Two Cuneiform Tablets from Tel Hadid." *TA* 27.2 (2000): 159–88.

Naveh, Joseph, and Yitzhak Magen. "Aramaic and Hebrew Inscriptions of the Second-Century BCE at Mount Gerizim." *'Atiqot* 32 (1997): 9–17.

Neusner, Jacob. *Genesis Rabbah: The Judaic Commentary to the Book of Genesis, A New American Translation. Vol. 1.* 3 vols. Atlanta, GA: Scholars Press, 1985.

Self-Fulfilling Prophecy: Exile and Return in the History of Judaism. Boston, MA: Beacon, 1987.

Judaism and Its Social Metaphors: Israel in the History of Jewish Thought. Cambridge: Cambridge University Press, 1989.

The Way of Torah: An Introduction to Judaism. 5th ed. Belmont, CA: Wadsworth, 1993.

"Was Rabbinic Judaism Really 'Ethnic'? A Theological Comparison between Christianity and the So-Called Particularist Religion of Israel." *Catholic Biblical Quarterly* 57.2 (1995): 281–305.

"The Premise of Paul's Ethnic Israel." Pages 1–20 in *Children of the Flesh, Children of the Promise: A Rabbi Talks with Paul.* Cleveland, OH: Pilgrim, 1995.

"Exile and Return as the History of Judaism." Pages 221–37 in *Exile: Old Testament, Jewish, and Christian Conceptions.* Edited by James M. Scott. JSJSup 56. Leiden: Brill, 1997.

"Judaism and Christianity in the Beginning: Time for a Category-Reformation?" *BBR* 8 (1998): 229–38.

"What Is 'a Judaism'?: Seeing the Dead Sea Library as the Statement of a Coherent Judaic Religious System." Pages 3–21 in *Theory of Israel.* Edited by Alan J. Avery-Peck, Jacob Neusner, and Bruce D. Chilton. HOS 56. Leiden: Brill, 2001.

Judaism When Christianity Began: A Survey of Belief and Practice. Louisville, KY: Westminster John Knox, 2002.

In the Aftermath of Catastrophe: Founding Judaism 70 to 640. MQSHR. Montreal: McGill-Queen's University Press, 2009.

Newing, Edward G. "A Rhetorical and Theological Analysis of the Hexateuch." *South East Asia Journal of Theology* 22.2 (1981): 1–15.

Newman, Judith H. "Bethulia." *NIDB* 1:449.

Newsome, J. D. "Toward a New Understanding of the Chronicler and His Purposes." *JBL* 94 (1975): 201–17.

Ngunga, Abi T. *Messianism in the Old Greek of Isaiah: An Intertextual Analysis.* FRLANT 245. Göttingen: Vandenhoeck & Ruprecht, 2012.

Nickelsburg, George W. E. *Jewish Literature between the Bible and the Mishnah.* Philadelphia, PA: Fortress, 1981.

"The Bible Rewritten and Expanded." Pages 89–156 in *Jewish Writings of the Second Temple period.* Edited by Michael E. Stone. CRINT 2. Philadelphia, PA: Fortress, 1984.

"The Search for Tobit's Mixed Ancestry. A Historical and Hermeneutical Odyssey." *RevQ* 17 (1996): 339–49.

1 Enoch: A Commentary on the Book of 1 Enoch. Hermeneia. Minneapolis, MN: Fortress, 2001.

Nickelsburg, George W. E., and Robert A Kraft. "Introduction: The Modern Study of Early Judaism." Pages 1–29 in *Early Judaism and Its Modern Interpreters.* Edited by Robert A. Kraft and George W. E. Nickelsburg. Minneapolis, MN: Fortress, 1986.

Niehoff, Maren R. "What Is in a Name? Philo's Mystical Philosophy of Language." *Jewish Studies Quarterly* 2.3 (1995): 220–52.

Philo on Jewish Identity and Culture. TSAJ 86. Tübingen: Mohr Siebeck, 2001.

Nielsen, Flemming A. J. *The Tragedy in History: Herodotus and the Deuteronomistic History.* JSOTSup 251. Sheffield: Sheffield Academic, 1997.

Niese, Benedictus. *Flavii Iosephi Opera.* Berlin: Weidmann, 1888.

Nihan, Christophe. "Ethnicity and Identity in Isaiah 56–66." Pages 67–104 in *Judah and the Judeans in the Achaemenid Period: Negotiating Identity in an International Context*. Edited by Oded Lipschits, Gary N. Knoppers, and Manfred Oeming. Winona Lake, IN: Eisenbrauns, 2011.

Nikiprowetzky, Valentin. *Le commentaire de l'Écriture chez Philon d'Alexandrie: Son caractère et sa portée; Observations philologiques*. ALGHJ 11. Leiden: Brill, 1977.

———. "Josephus and the Revolutionary Parties." Pages 216–36 in *Josephus, the Bible, and History*. Edited by Louis H. Feldman and Gohei Hata. Detroit: Wayne State University Press, 1989.

Nodet, Etienne. *A Search for the Origins of Judaism: From Joshua to the Mishnah*. Translated by E. Growley. JSOTSup 348. Sheffield: Sheffield Academic, 1997.

———. "Israelites, Samaritans, Temples, Jews." Pages 121–71 in *Samaria, Samarians, Samaritans: Studies on Bible, History and Linguistics*. Edited by József Zsengellér. SJ 66. Berlin: de Gruyter, 2011.

Nogalski, James. *Literary Precursors to the Book of the Twelve*. BZAW 217. Berlin: de Gruyter, 1993.

———. *Redactional Processes in the Book of the Twelve*. BZAW 218. Berlin: de Gruyter, 1993.

Noth, Martin. *Das System der zwölf Stämme Israels*. Stuttgart: Kohlhammer, 1930.

Nowell, Irene. "Tobit: Narrative Technique and Theology." PhD diss., The Catholic University of America, 1983.

———. "The Book of Tobit: An Ancestral Story." Pages 3–13 in *Intertextual Studies in Ben Sira and Tobit: Essays in Honor of Alexander A. Di Lella, O.E.M.* Edited by Jeremy Corley and Vincent Skemp. CBQMS 38. Washington, DC: Catholic Biblical Association of America, 2005.

O'Neill, John C. "What Is Joseph and Aseneth About?" *Hen* 16 (1994): 189–98.

Oded, Bustenay. "Observations on Methods of Assyrian Rule in Transjordania after the Palestinian Campaign of Tiglath-Pileser III." *JNES* 29.3 (1970): 177–86.

———. *Mass Deportations and Deportees in the Neo-Assyrian Empire*. Wiesbaden: Reichert, 1979.

———. "II Kings 17: Between History and Polemic." *Jewish History* 2.2 (1987): 37–50.

———. "Where Is the 'Myth of the Empty Land' to Be Found? History versus Myth." Pages 55–74 in *Judah and the Judeans in the Neo-Babylonian Period*. Edited by Oded Lipschits and Joseph Blenkinsopp. Winona Lake, IN: Eisenbrauns, 2003.

———. "Exile – The Biblical Perspectives." Pages 85–92 in *Homelands and Diasporas: Greeks, Jews and Their Migrations*. Edited by Minna Rozen. International Library of Migration Studies 2. New York, NY: Tauris, 2008.

Odorico, Marco de. *The Use of Numbers and Quantifications in the Assyrian Royal Inscriptions*. SAAS. Helsinki: Neo-Assyrian Text Corpus Project, 1995.

Oeming, Manfred. *Das wahre Israel: Die 'genealogische Vorhalle' 1 Chronik 1–9*. BWANT. Stuttgart: Kohlhammer, 1990.

"Jewish Identity in the Eastern Diaspora in Light of the Book of Tobit." Pages 545–62 in *Judah and the Judeans in the Achaemenid Period: Negotiating Identity in an International Context*. Edited by Oded Lipschits, Gary N. Knoppers, and Manfred Oeming. Winona Lake, IN: Eisenbrauns, 2011.

Olick, Jeffrey K., and Joyce Robbins. "Social Memory Studies: From 'Collective Memory' to the Historical Sociology of Mnemonic Practices." *Annual Review of Sociology* (1998): 105–40.

Olson, Daniel C. *A New Reading of the Animal Apocalypse of 1 Enoch: "All Nations Shall Be Blessed."* SVTP 24. Leiden: Brill, 2013.

Olyan, Saul M. "Purity Ideology in Ezra-Nehemiah as a Tool to Reconstitute the Community." *JSJ* 35.1 (2004): 1–16.

Ophir, Adi, and Ishay Rosen-Zvi. *Goy: Israel's Multiple Others and the Birth of the Gentile*. Oxford: Oxford University Press, 2018.

Osten-Sacken, Peter. "Walter Grundmann – Nationalsozialist, Kirchenmann und Theologe: Mit einem Ausblick auf die Zeit nach 1945." Pages 280–312 in *Das missbrauchte Evangelium: Studien zu Theorie und Praxis der Thüringer Deutschen Christen*. Edited by Peter Osten-Sacken. Berlin: Institut Kirche und Judentum, 2002.

Oster, Richard E. "Use, Misuse and Neglect of Archaeological Evidence in Some Modern Works on 1 Corinthians (1Cor 7,1–5; 8,10; 11,2–16; 12,14–26)." *ZNW* 83.1–2 (1992): 52–73.

Otzen, Benedikt. *Tobit and Judith*. GAP 11. London: Continuum, 2002.

Palmisano, Maria Carmela. *"Salvaci, Dio dell'Universo!": studio dell'eucologia di Sir 36H, 1–17*. AnBib 163. Rome: Pontifical Biblical Institute, 2006.

Pao, David W. *Acts and the Isaianic New Exodus*. WUNT 130. Tübingen: Mohr Siebeck, 2000.

Pasto, James S. "When the End Is the Beginning? Or When the Biblical Past Is the Political Present: Some Thoughts on Ancient Israel, 'Post-Exilic Judaism,' and the Politics of Biblical Scholarship." *SJOT* 12.2 (1998): 157–202.

——— "Who Owns the Jewish Past? Judaism, Judaisms, and the Writing of Jewish History." (Ph.D. diss., Cornell University, 1999).

——— "H. M. L. De Wette and the Invention of Post-Exilic Judaism: Political Historiography and Christian Allegory in Nineteenth-Century German Biblical Scholarship." Pages 33–52 in *Jews, Antiquity, and the Nineteenth-century Imagination*. Edited by Hayim Lapin and Dale B. Martin. Studies and Texts in Jewish History and Culture. College Park, MD: University Press of Maryland, 2003.

Paul, Shalom M. *Amos: A Commentary on the Book of Amos*. Accordance electronic ed. Hermeneia. Minneapolis, MN: Fortress, 1991.

Pearce, Laurie E. "New Evidence for Judeans in Babylonia." Pages 399–411 in *Judah and the Judeans in the Persian Period*. Edited by Oded Lipschits, Gary N. Knoppers, and Manfred Oeming. Winona Lake, IN: Eisenbrauns, 2006.

——— "'Judean': A Special Status in Neo-Babylonian and Achemenid Babylonia?" Pages 267–77 in *Judah and the Judeans in the Achaemenid Period: Negotiating Identity in an International Context*. Edited by Oded Lipschits, Gary N. Knoppers, and Manfred Oeming. Winona Lake, IN: Eisenbrauns, 2011.

Pearce, Sarah J. K. "Jerusalem as 'Mother-City' in the Writings of Philo of Alexandria." Pages 19–37 in *Negotiating Diaspora: Jewish Strategies in the Roman Empire*. Edited by John M. G. Barclay. London: T&T Clark, 2004.

Pearson, Birger A. "Christians and Jews in First-Century Alexandria." *HTR* 79.1/3 (1986): 206–16.

Peltonen, Kai. "A Jigsaw without a Model? The Date of Chronicles." Pages 225–73 in *Did Moses Speak Attic? Jewish History and Historiography in the Hellenistic Period*. Edited by Lester L. Grabbe. JSOTSup 37. Sheffield: Sheffield Academic, 2001.

Perdue, Leo Garrett. "Ben Sira and the Prophets." Pages 132–54 in *Intertextual Studies in Ben Sira and Tobit: Essays in Honor of Alexander A. Di Lella, O.F.M.* Edited by Jeremy Corley and Vincent Skemp. CBQMS 38. Washington, DC: Catholic Biblical Association of America, 2005.

Perlitt, Lothar. *Deuteronomium-Studien*. Tübingen: Mohr Siebeck, 1994.

Perry, Timothy Peter John. "Exile in Homeric Epic." PhD diss., University of Toronto, 2010.

Philonenko, Marc. *Les interpolations chrétiennes des Testaments des douze patriarches et les manuscrits de Quomràn*. Paris: Presses universitaires de France, 1960.

Pitkänen, Pekka. "Family Life and Ethnicity in Early Israel and in Tobit." Pages 104 in *Studies in the Book of Tobit: A Multidisciplinary Approach*. Edited by Mark R. J. Bredin. LSTS 55. London: T&T Clark, 2006.

Pitre, Brant. *Jesus, the Tribulation, and the End of the Exile: Restoration Eschatology and the Origin of the Atonement*. JSOTSup 37. Grand Rapids, MI: Baker Academic, 2005.

Plöger, Otto. *Theocracy and Eschatology*. Translated by Stanley Rudman. Oxford: Blackwell, 1968.

Pocock, J. G. A. "The Ideal of Citizenship since Classical Times." *Queen's Quarterly* 99.1 (1992): 35–55.

Poirier, John C. "The Endtime Return of Elijah and Moses at Qumran." *DSD* 10.2 (2003): 221–42.

Polzin, Robert. *Moses and the Deuteronomist: A Literary Study of the Deuteronomic History. I: Deuteronomy, Joshua, Judges*. Bloomington, IN: Indiana University Press, 1980.

——. Review of *The Sense of Biblical Narrative: Structural Analyses in the Hebrew Bible II*, by David Jobling. *Bib* 69.1 (1988): 122.

Porten, Bezalel. *Archives from Elephantine*. Berkeley, CA: University of California Press, 1968.

Porten, Bezalel, and Ada Yardeni, eds. *Textbook of Aramaic Documents from Ancient Egypt*. 4 vols. Winona Lake, IN: Eisenbrauns, 1986.

Porter, Stanley E., and Cynthia Long Westfall. "A Cord of Three Strands: Mission in Acts." Pages 108–34 in *Christian Mission: Old Testament Foundations and New Testament Developments*. McMaster New Testament Studies. Eugene, OR: Wipf and Stock, 2010.

Portier-Young, Anathea E. *Apocalypse against Empire: Theologies of Resistance in Early Judaism*. Grand Rapids, MI: Eerdmans, 2011.

Priest, John. "Testament of Moses." Pages 919–34 in *OTP* 1. Edited by James H Charlesworth. Garden City, NY: Doubleday, 1983.

Pritchard, J. B., ed. *Ancient Near Eastern Texts*. 3rd ed. Princeton, NJ: Princeton University Press, 1969.

Pucci Ben Zeev, Miriam. *Jewish Rights in the Roman World: The Greek and Roman Documents Quoted by Josephus Flavius*. TSAJ 74. Tübingen: Mohr Siebeck, 1998.

Diaspora Judaism in Turmoil, 116/117 CE: ancient sources and modern insights. Interdisciplinary Studies in Ancient Culture and Religion. Leuven: Peeters, 2005.

"The Uprisings in the Jewish Diaspora (116–117 CE)." Pages 93–104 in *The Cambridge History of Judaism, Vol 4: The Late Roman-Rabbinic Period*. Edited by Stephen T. Katz. Cambridge: Cambridge University Press, 2006.

Pummer, Reinhard. "Samaritanism in Caesarea Maritima." Pages 181–202 in *Religious Rivalries and the Struggle for Success in Caesarea Maritima*. Edited by Terence L. Donaldson. SCJ. Waterloo, ON: Wilfrid Laurier University Press, 2000.

The Samaritans in Flavius Josephus. TSAJ 129. Tübingen: Mohr Siebeck, 2009.

"Samaritanism: A Jewish Sect or an Independent Form of Yahwism?" Pages 1–24 in *Samaritans: Past and Present: Current Studies*. Edited by Menachem Mor and Fredrick V. Reiterer. SJ 53. Berlin: de Gruyter, 2010.

"Alexander und die Samaritaner nach Josephus und nach samaritanischen Quellen." Pages 157–80 in *Die Samaritaner und die Bibel: Historische und literarische Wechselwirkungen zwischen biblischen und samaritanischen Traditionen = The Samaritans and the Bible: Historical and Literary Interactions Between Biblical and Samaritan Traditions*. Edited by Jörg Frey, Ursula Schattner-Rieser, and Konrad Schmid. SJ 70. Berlin: de Gruyter, 2012.

The Samaritans. Grand Rapids, MI: Eerdmans, 2016.

Purvis, James D. "The Samaritans." Pages 591–613 in *The Hellenistic Period*. Edited by W. D. Davies and Louis Finkelstein. Cambridge: Cambridge University Press, 1989.

Qimran, Elisha. "The Nature of the Reconstructed Composite Text of 4QMMT." *SBLSym* Reading 4QMMT: New Perspectives on Qumran Law and History (1996): 9–14.

Qimron, Elisha et al. "Some Works of the Torah." Pages 187–251 in *The Dead Sea Scrolls: Hebrew, Aramaic, and Greek Texts with English Translations: Damascus Document II, Some Works of the Torah, and Related Documents*. Edited by James H. Charlesworth and Henry W. M. Rietz. PTSDSSP. Tübingen: Mohr Siebeck, 2006.

Qimron, Elisha, and Florentino García Martínez. *The Temple Scroll: A Critical Edition with Extensive Reconstructions*. Beer-Sheva: Ben-Gurion University of the Negev Press, 1996.

Qimron, Elisha, and John Strugnell. *Qumran Cave 4: V: Miqsat Ma'ase Ha-Torah*. DJD 10. Oxford: Clarendon, 1994.

Rabin, Chaim. "Hebrew and Aramaic in the First Century." Pages 1007–39 in *The Jewish People in the First Century (2)*. Edited by Menahem Stern and Shmuel Safrai. CRINT 2. Amsterdam: Assen, 1976.

Rabinowitz, Isaac. "A Reconsideration of 'Damascus' and '390 Years' in the 'Damascus' ('Zadokite') Fragments." *JBL* 73.1 (1954): 11–35.

Rad, Gerhard von. *Das Geschichtsbild des chronistischen Werkes*. BWANT 3/4. Stuttgart: Kohlhammer, 1930.

Radice, Roberto, and David T. Runia. *Philo of Alexandria: An Annotated Bibliography 1937–1986*. VCSup 8. Leiden: Brill, 1988.

Rahlfs, Alfred, ed. *Septuaginta*. Stuttgart: Deutsche Bibelgesellschaft, 2006.

Rajak, Tessa. *The Jewish Dialogue with Greece and Rome: Studies in Cultural and Social Interaction*. AGJU 48. Leiden: Brill, 2002.

Translation and Survival: The Greek Bible of the Ancient Jewish Diaspora. Oxford: Oxford University Press, 2009.

Rappaport, Uriel. "Reflections on the Origins of the Samaritans." Pages 10–19 in *Studies in Geography and History in Honour of Yehoshua Ben-Arieh*. Edited by I. Bartal and E. Reiner. Jerusalem: Magnes, 1999.

The First Book of Maccabees – Introduction, Hebrew Translation and Commentary. Jerusalem: Yad Izhak Ben-Zvi, 2004.

Ravens, David. *Luke and the Restoration of Israel*. JSNTSup 119. Sheffield: Sheffield Academic, 1995.

Ravid, Leora. "The Book of Jubilees and Its Calendar – A Reexamination." *DSD* 10.3 (2003): 371–94.

Redditt, Paul L. "Recent Research on the Book of the Twelve as One Book." *Currents in Research: Biblical Studies* 9 (2001): 47–80.

Reed, Annette Yoshiko. "*Ioudaios* Before and After 'Religion.'" *Marginalia Review of Books* (2014). http://marginalia.lareviewofbooks.org/ioudaios-reli gion-annette-yoshiko-reed/

Reed, Jonathan L. *Archaeology and the Galilean Jesus: A Re-examination of the Evidence*. Harrisburg, PA: Trinity Press International, 2002.

Regev, Eyal. "How Did the Temple Mount Fall to Pompey?" *JJS* 48 (1997): 276–89.

Reimer, David J. "Exile, Diaspora, and Old Testament Theology." *SBET* 28.1 (2010): 3–17.

Rendtorff, F. M. "Diaspora II. Evangelische." Pages 1916–20 in *Die Religion in Geschichte und Gegenwart (RGG2)*. 1. Edited by Hermann Gunkel and Leopold Zscharnack. 1. Tübingen: Mohr, 1927.

Rendtorff, Rolf. "The Image of Post-Exilic Israel in German Bible Scholarship from Wellhausen to von Rad." Pages 165–73 in *'Sha'arei Talmon': Studies in Bible, Qumran, and the Ancient Near East Presented to Shemaryahu Talmon*. Edited by M. Fishbane, Emanuel Tov, and W. W. Fields. Winona Lake, IN: Eisenbrauns, 1992.

Richardson, Peter. "Augustan-era Synagogues in Rome." Pages 17–29 in *Judaism and Christianity in First-Century Rome*. Edited by Karl Donfried and Peter Richardson. Grand Rapids, MI: Eerdmans, 1998.

Richter, Melvin, and Michaela Richter. "Introduction: Translation of Reinhart Koselleck's 'Krise' in Geschichtliche Grundbegriffe." *Journal of the History of Ideas* 67.2 (2006): 343–56.

Ricks, Stephen D. "The Prophetic Literality of Tribal Reconstruction." Pages 273–81 in *Israel's Apostasy and Restoration: Essays in Honor of Roland K. Harrison*. Edited by Avraham Gileadi. Grand Rapids, MI: Baker Books, 1988.

Ricoeur, Paul. *Time and Narrative*. Translated by Kathleen McLaughlin and David Pellauer. 3 vols. Chicago, IL: University of Chicago Press, 1984–2008.
—. *Interpretation Theory: Discourse and the Surplus of Meaning*. Fort Worth, TX: Texas Christian University Press, 1976.
—. *Lectures on Ideology and Utopia*. Edited by George H. Taylor. New York, NY: Columbia University Press, 1986.
Ridgway, David William Robertson. "Colonization, Greek." *The Oxford Classical Dictionary* 362–63.
Riesenberg, Peter. *Citizenship in the Western Tradition: Plato to Rousseu*. Chapel Hill, NC: University of North Carolina Press, 1994.
Roddy, Nicolae. "The Way It Wasn't: The Book of Judith as Anti-Hasmonean Propaganda." *Studia Hebraica* 8 (2008): 269–77.
Rodríguez, Rafael. *If You Call Yourself a Jew: Reappraising Paul's Letter to the Romans*. Eugene, OR: Cascade, 2014.
Rofé, Alexander. "Ephraimite versus Deuteronomistic History." Pages 462–74 in *Reconsidering Israel and Judah: Recent Studies on the Deuteronomistic History*. Edited by Gary N. Knoppers and J. Gordon McConville. SBTS 8. Winona Lake, IN: Eisenbrauns, 2000.
Rolfson, Vann D. "The Syro-Ephraimite War: Context, Conflict, and Consequences." *Studia Antiqua* 2.1 (2002): 87–100.
Rom-Shiloni, Dalit. "Ezekiel as the Voice of the Exiles and Constructor of Exilic Ideology." *HUCA* (2005): 1–45.
—. "From Ezekiel to Ezra-Nehemiah: Shifts of Group Identities within Babylonian Exilic Ideology." Pages 127–51 in *Judah and the Judeans in the Achaemenid Period: Negotiating Identity in an International Context*. Edited by Oded Lipschits, Gary N. Knoppers, and Manfred Oeming. Winona Lake, IN: Eisenbrauns, 2011.
Römer, Thomas. "Deuteronomy in Search of Origins." Pages 112–38 in *Reconsidering Israel and Judah: Recent Studies on the Deuteronomistic History*. Edited by Gary N. Knoppers and J. Gordon McConville. SBTS 8. Winona Lake, IN: Eisenbrauns, 2000.
Römer, Thomas. ed. *The Future of the Deuteronomistic History*. Bibliotheca Ephemeridum Theologicarum Lovaniensum 147. Leuven: Leuven University Press, 2000.
Ropes, James Hardy. *A Critical and Exegetical Commentary on the Epistle of St. James*. ICC. Edinburgh: T&T Clark, 1978.
Rosenbaum, Jonathan. "Hezekiah's Reform and the Deuteronomistic Tradition." *HTR HUCA* 72.1-2 (1979): 23–44.
Rozen, Minna. "People of the Book, People of the Sea: Mirror Images of the Soul." Pages 35–81 in *Homelands and Diasporas: Greeks, Jews and Their Migrations*. Edited by Minna Rozen. International Library of Migration Studies 2. New York, NY: Tauris, 2008.
Rudolph, Wilhelm. *Esra und Nehemiah samt 3*. HAT. Tübingen: Mohr, 1949.
Runesson, Anders. *The Origins of the Synagogue: A Socio-Historical Study*. ConBNT 37. Stockholm: Lund University Press, 2001.
Runia, David T. "Philonic Nomenclature." *SPhiloA* 6 (1994): 1–27.

Philo of Alexandria: An Annotated Bibliography 1997–2006, with Addenda for 1987–1996. VCSup 109. Leiden: Brill, 2011.

Runia, David T., and Helena Maria Keizer. *Philo of Alexandria: An Annotated Bibliography 1987–1996, with Addenda for 1937–1986.* VCSup 57. Leiden: Brill, 2000.

Rutgers, Leonard Victor. *The Hidden Heritage of Diaspora Judaism.* Contributions to Biblical Exegesis and Theology. Leuven: Peeters, 1998.

Ryle, Herbert E., and Montague R. James. *Psalms of the Pharisees, Commonly Called the Psalms of Solomon: The Text Newly Revised from All the MSS.* New York, NY: Columbia University Press, 1891.

Sáenz-Badillos, Angel. *A History of the Hebrew Language.* Cambridge: Cambridge University Press, 1993.

Safrai, Shmuel. "Relations between the Diaspora and the Land of Israel." Pages 184–215 in *The Jewish People in the First Century: Historical Geography, Political History, Social, Cultural and Religious Life and Institutions.* 1. Edited by Menahem Stern and Shmuel Safrai. CRINT 1. Philadelphia, PA: Fortress, 1974.

Saldarini, Anthony J. *Pharisees, Scribes, and Sadducees in Palestinian Society.* Wilmington, DE: Glazier, 1988.

Samkutty, Vanmelitharayil John. *The Samaritan Mission in Acts.* LNTS 328. London: T&T Clark, 2006.

Sanders, E. P. "Patterns of Religion in Paul and Rabbinic Judaism." *HTR* 66 (1973): 455–78.

———. "The Covenant as a Soteriological Category and the Nature of Salvation in Palestinian and Hellenistic Judaism." Pages 11–44 in *Jews, Greeks and Christians: Religious Cultures in Late Antiquity.* Edited by Robert G. Hamerton-Kelly. Leiden: Brill, 1976.

———. *Paul and Palestinian Judaism: A Comparison of Patterns of Religion.* Philadelphia, PA: Fortress, 1977.

———. *Jesus and Judaism.* Minneapolis, MN: Augsburg Fortress, 1985.

———. *Judaism: Practice and Belief 63 BC–66 CE.* London: SCM, 1992.

Sanders, James A. "The Exile and Canon Formation." Pages 7–37 in *Exile: Old Testament, Jewish and Christian Conceptions.* Edited by James M. Scott. JSJSup 56. Leiden: Brill, 1997.

Sandler, Adam. "The Chanukah Song." *Saturday Night Live.* Studio City, CA: NBC, 1994.

Sargent, Lyman Tower. "The Three Faces of Utopianism." *Minnesota Review* 7.3 (1967): 222–30.

———. "The Three Faces of Utopianism Revisited." *Utopian Studies* 5.1 (1994): 1–37.

Satlow, Michael L. "Defining Judaism: Accounting for 'Religions' in the Study of Religion." *JAAR* 74.4 (2006): 837–60.

———. *How the Bible Became Holy.* New Haven, CT: Yale University Press, 2014.

———. "Jew or Judaean?" Pages 165–75 in *"The One Who Sows Bountifully": Essays in Honor of Stanley K. Stowers.* Edited by Caroline Johnson Hodge, Saul M. Olyan, Daniel Ullucci, and Emma Wasserman. BJS 356. Providence, RI: BJS, 2014.

Saulnier, Christiane. "Lois romaines sur les Juifs selon Flavius Josèphe." *RB* 88.2 (1981): 161–98.

Scafuro, Adele C. "Atimia." *The Encyclopedia of Ancient History* 923.

Schalit, Abraham, ed. Josephus, Jewish Antiquities *[in Hebrew]*. 3 vols. Jerusalem: Bialik, 1944.

Schaller, Berndt. "Philon von Alexandreia und das 'Heilige Land,'" Pages 172–87 in *Das Land Israel in biblischer Zeit*. Edited by Georg Strecker. GTA 25. Göttingen: Vandenhoeck & Ruprecht, 1983.

Schiffman, Lawrence H. "The Samaritans in Tannaitic Halakhah." *JQR* 75.4 (1985): 323–50.

"Miqtsat Má asei Ha-Torah." *EDSS* 1:558–60.

"The Concept of Restoration in the Dead Sea Scrolls." Pages 203–22 in *Restoration: Old Testament, Jewish and Christian Perspectives*. Edited by James M. Scott. JSJSup 72. Leiden: Brill, 2001.

Schlatter, Adolf von. *Die Theologie des Judentums nach dem Bericht des Josefus*. Beiträge zur Förderung schriftlicher Theologie. Gütersloh: Bertelsmann, 1932.

Schmalz, Mathew N. "When Festinger Fails: Prophecy and the Watch Tower." *Religion* 24.4 (2011): 293–308.

Schmid, Konrad, and Odil Hannes Steck. "Restoration Expectations in the Prophetic Tradition of the Old Testament." Pages 41–81 in *Restoration: Old Testament, Jewish and Christian Perspectives*. Edited by James M. Scott. JSJSup 72. Leiden: Brill, 2001.

Schmitt, Armin. "Die hebräischen Textfunde zum Buch Tobit aus Qumran 4QTob^c (4Q200)." *ZAW* 113.4 (2001): 566–82.

Schnackenburg, Rudolf. "Gottes Volk in der Zerstreuung. Diaspora im Zeugnis der Bibel." Pages 321–37 in *Schriften zum Neuen Testament. Exegese in Fortschritt und Wandel*. Edited by Rudolf Schnackenburg. Munich: Kosel, 1971.

Schniedewind, William M. "The Problem with Kings: Recent Study of the Deuteronomistic History." *RelSRev* 22.1 (1996): 22–27.

"Aramaic, the Death of Written Hebrew, and Language Shift in the Persian Period." Pages 137–47 in *Margins of Writing, Origins of Cultures(2)*. Edited by Seth L. Sanders. Chicago, IL: University of Chicago Press, 2006.

Schorch, Stefan. "The Samaritan Version of Deuteronomy and the Origin of Deuteronomy." Pages 23–37 in *Samaria, Samarians, Samaritans: Studies on Bible, History and Linguistics*. Edited by József Zsengellér. SJ 66. Berlin: de Gruyter, 2011.

"The Construction of Samari(t)an Identity from the Inside and from the Outside." Pages 135–49 in *Between Cooperation and Hostility: Multiple Identities in Ancient Judaism and the Interaction with Foreign Powers*. Edited by Rainer Albertz and Jakob Wöhrle. JAJSup 11. Göttingen: Vandenhoeck & Ruprecht, 2013.

Schrader, Lutz. *Leiden und Gerechtigkeit: Studien zu Theologie und Textgeschichte des Sirachbuches*. BBET 27. Frankfurt: Lang, 1994.

Schuller, Eileen M. "4Q372 1: A Text about Joseph." *RevQ* 14 (1991): 349–76.

Schuller, Eileen M., and Moshe J. Bernstein. "4QNarrative and Poetic Composition." Pages 151–205 in *Wadi Daliyeh II: The Samaria Papyri from Wadi Daliyeh and Qumran Cave 4, XXVIII: Miscellanea, Part 2*. Edited by Douglas M. Gropp et al. DJD 28. Oxford: Clarendon, 2001.

Schwartz, Barry. "The Social Context of Commemoration: A Study in Collective Memory." *Social Forces* 61.2 (1982): 374–402.

"Social Change and Collective Memory: The Democratization of George Washington." *American Sociological Review* 56 (1991): 221–36.

"Memory as a Cultural System: Abraham Lincoln in World War II." *American Sociological Review* 61 (1996): 908–27.

Schwartz, Daniel R. "The End of the ΓΗ (Acts 1:8): Beginning or End of the Christian Vision?" *JBL* 105.4 (1986): 669–76.

"On Abraham Schalit, Herod, Josephus, the Holocaust, Horst R. Moehring, and the Study of Ancient Jewish History." *Jewish History* 2.2 (1987): 9–28.

Agrippa I: The Last King of Judaea. TSAJ 23. Tübingen: Mohr Siebeck, 1990.

Studies in the Jewish Background of Christianity. Tübingen: Mohr, 1992.

"Temple or City: What Did Hellenistic Jews See in Jerusalem." Pages 114–27 in *The Centrality of Jerusalem: Historical Perspectives*. Edited by Marcel Poorthuis and C. Safrai. Kampen: Kok Pharos, 1996.

"On Something Biblical about 2 Maccabees." Pages 223–32 in *Biblical Perspectives: Early Use and Interpretation of the Bible in Light of the Dead Sea Scrolls*. Edited by Michael E. Stone and Esther G. Chazon. STDJ 28. Leiden: Brill, 1998.

"The Other in 1 and 2 Maccabees." Pages 30–37 in *Tolerance and Intolerance in Early Judaism and Christianity*. Edited by Graham N. Stanton and Guy G. Stroumsa. Cambridge: Cambridge University Press, 1998.

"From Punishment to Program, From Program to Punishment: Josephus and the Rabbis on Exile." Pages 205–26 in *For Uriel. Studies in the History of Israel in Antiquity Presented to Professor Uriel Rappaport*. Jerusalem: Zalman Shazar Center for Jewish History, 2005.

"'Judaean' or 'Jew.'" Pages 3–27 in *Jewish Identity in the Greco-Roman World: Jüdische Identität in der griechisch-römischen Welt*. Edited by Jörg Frey and Stephanie Gripentrog. Leiden: Brill, 2007.

"Yannai and Pella, Josephus and Circumcision." *DSD* 18.3 (2011): 339–59.

"Judeans, Jews, and Their Neighbors." Pages 13–32 in *Between Cooperation and Hostility: Multiple Identities in Ancient Judaism and the Interaction with Foreign Powers*. Edited by Thomas Römer and Jakob Wöhrle. JAJSup 11. Göttingen: Vandenhoeck & Ruprecht, 2013.

Schwartz, Seth. "How Many Judaisms Were There? A Critique of Neusner and Smith on Definition and Mason and Boyarin on Categorization." *JAJ* 2.2 (2011): 208–38.

Schweitzer, Steven J. "Reading Utopia in Chronicles." PhD diss., University of Notre Dame, 2005.

"Utopia and Utopian Literary Theory: Some Preliminary Observations." Pages 13–26 in *Utopia and Dystopia in Prophetic Literature*. Edited by Ehud Ben Zvi. PFES. Göttingen: Vandenhoeck & Ruprecht, 2006.

Reading Utopia in Chronicles. JSOTSup 442. London: T&T Clark, 2007.

Scott, J. Julius. *Jewish Backgrounds of the New Testament*. Grand Rapids, MI: Baker Books, 2000.

Scott, James C. *Domination and the Arts of Resistance: Hidden Transcripts*. New Haven, CT: Yale University Press, 1990.

Scott, James M. "Paul's Use of Deuteronomic Tradition." *JBL* 112.4 (1993): 645–65.

———. "Philo and the Restoration of Israel." Pages 553–75 in *Society of Biblical Literature 1995 Seminar Papers*. Edited by Eugene H. Lovering Jr. Atlanta, GA: Scholars Press, 1996.

———. "Exile and the Self-Understanding of Diaspora Jews in the Greco-Roman Period." Pages 173–218 in *Exile: Old Testament, Jewish, and Christian Conceptions*. Edited by James M. Scott. JSJSup 56. Leiden: Brill, 1997.

———. *On Earth As in Heaven: The Restoration of Sacred Time and Sacred Space in the Book of Jubilees*. JSJSup 91. Leiden: Brill, 2005.

———. "Exile and Restoration." *DJG*, 251–58.

Seeliger, Rolf, ed. *Braune Universität: Deutsche Hochschullehrer gestern und heute; Dokumentation mit Stellungnahmen*. Munich: Seeliger, 1968.

Seeligmann, Isac Leo. "Problemen en perspectieven in het moderne Septuagintaonderzoek." *JEOL* 7 (1940): 359–90.

———. *The Septuagint Version of Isaiah and Cognate Studies*. Edited by Robert Hanhart and Hermann Spieckermann. FAT 40. Tübingen: Mohr Siebeck, 2004.

Segal, Michael. *The Book of Jubilees: Rewritten Bible, Redaction, Ideology and Theology*. JSJSup 117. Leiden: Brill, 2007.

Seibert, Eric A. *Subversive Scribes and the Solomonic Narrative a Rereading of 1 Kings 1–11*. LHBOTS 436. New York, NY: T&T Clark, 2006.

Seibert, Jakob. *Die politischen Flüchtlinge und Verbannten in der griechischen Geschichte: von d. Anfängen bis zur Unterwerfung durch d. Römer. Vol. 30*. Darmstadt: Wissenschaftliche Buchgesellschaft Abt. Verlag, 1979.

Seitz, Christopher R. *Zion's Final Destiny: The Development of the Book of Isaiah: A Reassessment of Isaiah 36–39*. Minneapolis, MN: Fortress, 1991.

Shahar, Yuval. "Imperial Religious Unification Policy and Its Decisive Consequences: Diocletian, the Jews and the Samaritans." Pages 109–19 in *Romans, Barbarians, and the Transformation of the Roman World: Cultural Interaction and the Creation of Identity in Late Antiquity*. Edited by Ralph W. Mathisen and Danuta Shanzer. Farnham: Ashgate, 2011.

Sharp, Carolyn J. *Irony and Meaning in the Hebrew Bible*. Bloomington, IN: Indiana University Press, 2008.

Shepherd, David. "Prophetaphobia: Fear and False Prophecy in Nehemiah VI." *VT* 55 (2005): 232–50.

Sherman, Phillip Michael. *Babel's Tower Translated: Genesis 11 and Ancient Jewish Interpretation*. Leiden: Brill, 2013.

Sherwin-White, A. N. *The Roman Citizenship*. Oxford: Oxford University Press, 1980.

Shochet, Azriel. "Josephus' Outlook on the Future of Israel and Its Land." Pages 43–50 in *Yerushalayim. 1*. Edited by Michael Ish-Shalom, Meir Benayahu,

Yeshayahu Press, and Azriel Shochet. 1. Jerusalem: Mosad Ha-Rav Kook, 1953.

Simon, Marcel. *St. Stephen and the Hellenists in the Primitive Church*. London: Longmans, Green, 1958.

Verus Israel: A Study of the Relations between Christians and Jews in the Roman Empire AD 135–425. Translated by H. McKeating. London: The Littman Library of Jewish Civilization, 1986.

Skehan, Patrick W., and Alexander A. Di Lella. *The Wisdom of Ben Sira: A New Translation with Notes, Introduction and Commentary*. Abhandlungen zum christlich-jüdischen Dialog 39. Garden City, NY: Doubleday, 1987.

Skemp, Vincent T. M. "ΑΔΕΛΦΟΣ and the Theme of Kinship in Tobit." *EThL* 75 (1999): 92–103.

Slenczka, Notger. "Römer 9–11 und die Frage nach der Identität Israels." Pages 463–78 in *Between Gospel and Election: Explorations in the Interpretation of Romans 9–11*. Edited by Florian Wilk, J. Ross Wagner, and Frank Schleritt. WUNT 257. Tübingen: Mohr Siebeck, 2010.

Smith, Anthony D. *The Ethnic Origins of Nations*. Oxford: Blackwell, 1986.

Smith, Barry Douglas. *Jesus' Last Passover Meal*. Lewiston, NY: Mellen, 1993.

Smith, Christian. "Living Narratives." Pages 63–94 in *Moral Believing Animals: Human Personhood and Culture*. London: Oxford University Press, 2003.

Smith, Daniel L. *The Religion of the Landless: The Social Context of the Babylonian Exile*. Bloomington, IN: Meyer-Stone, 1989.

Smith, James. *The Book of the Prophet Ezekiel: A New Interpretation*. London: SPCK, 1931.

Smith, Morton. *Palestinian Parties and Politics That Shaped the Old Testament*. New York, NY: Columbia University Press, 1971.

"The Gentiles in Judaism 125 BCE–CE 66." Pages 192–249 in *Cambridge History of Judaism, III: The Early Roman Period*. Edited by William Horbury, W. D. Davies, and John Sturdy. Cambridge: Cambridge University Press, 1999.

Smith, Ralph Lee. *Micah–Malachi*. Accordance/Thomas Nelson electronic ed. WBC 32. Nashville: Nelson, 1984.

Soderlund, Sven. *The Greek Text of Jeremiah: A Revised Hypothesis*. Sheffield: JSOT Press, 1985.

Soll, Will. "Misfortune and Exile in Tobit: The Juncture of a Fairy Tale Source and Deuteronomic Theology." *Catholic Biblical Quarterly* 51.2 (1989): 209–31.

"The Family as Scriptural and Social Construct in Tobit." Pages 166–75 in *The Function of Scripture in Early Jewish and Christian Tradition*. Edited by Craig A. Evans and Jack A. Sanders. JSNTSup 154. Sheffield: Sheffield Academic, 1998.

Spilsbury, Paul. *The Image of the Jew in Flavius Josephus' Paraphrase of the Bible*. TSAJ 69. Tübingen: Mohr Siebeck, 1998.

"Flavius Josephus on the Rise and Fall of the Roman Empire." *JTS* 54.1 (2003): 1–24.

Staples, Jason A. "What Do the Gentiles Have to Do with 'All Israel'? A Fresh Look at Romans 11:25–27." *JBL* 130.2 (2011): 371–90.

Starling, David I. *Not My People: Gentiles as Exiles in Pauline Hermeneutics.* BZNW 184. Berlin: de Gruyter, 2011.

Steck, Odil Hannes. *Israel und das gewaltsame Geschick der Propheten: Untersuchung zur Überlieferung des deuteronomistischen Geschichtsbildes im Alten Testament, Spätjudentum und Urchristentum.* WMANT 23. Neukirchen-Vluyn: Neukirchener Verlag, 1967.

———. *Das apokryphe Baruchbuch: Studien zu Rezeption und Konzentration "kanonischer" Überlieferung.* FRLANT 160. Göttingen: Vandenhoeck & Ruprecht, 1993.

———. *Das Buch Baruch, Der Brief des Jeremia, Zusätze zu Ester und Daniel.* ATD. Göttingen: Vandenhoeck & Ruprecht, 1998.

Steinweis, Alan E. *Studying the Jew: Scholarly Antisemitism in Nazi Germany.* Cambridge, MA: Harvard University Press, 2008.

Stendahl, Krister. "The Apostle Paul and the Introspective Conscience of the West." *HTR* 56.3 (1963): 199–215.

Sterling, Gregory E. "Thus Are Israel: Jewish Self-Definition in Alexandria." *SPhiloA* 7.8 (1995): 12.

Stern, Ephraim. "What Happened to the Cult Figurines? Israelite Religion Purified after the Exile." *Biblical Archaeologist Reader* 15.4 (1989): 22–29, 53.

———. *The Assyrian, Babylonian, and Persian Periods, 732–332 BCE.* ABRL. New York, NY: Doubleday, 2001.

———. "The Religious Revolution in Persian-Period Judah." Pages 199–205 in *Judah and the Judeans in the Persian Period.* Edited by Oded Lipschits and Manfred Oeming. Winona Lake, IN: Eisenbrauns, 2006.

Stern, Menahem. "The Jewish Diaspora." Pages 117–83 in *The Jewish People in the First Century: Historical Geography, Political History, Social, Cultural, and Religious Life and Institutions. Vol. 1.* Edited by Shmuel Safrai and Menahem Stern. CRINT 1. Philadelphia, PA: Fortress, 1974.

Stern, Menahem. ed. *Greek and Latin Authors on Jews and Judaism, Vol 2: From Tacitus to Simplicius.* Jerusalem: Israel Academy of Sciences and Humanities, 1980.

Sternberg, Meir. *The Poetics of Biblical Narrative: Ideological Literature and the Drama of Reading.* Bloomington, IN: Indiana University Press, 1985.

Steudel, Annette. "Melchizedek." *EDSS* 282–84.

Stevenson, Gregory M. "Communal Imagery and the Individual Lament: Exodus Typology in Psalm 77." *RestQ* 39 (1997): 215–30.

Stone, Michael E. *Fourth Ezra: A Commentary on the Book of Fourth Ezra.* Accordance electronic ed. Hermeneia 41. Minneapolis, MN: Fortress, 1990.

Stott, Katherine M. "A Comparative Study of the Exilic Gap in Ancient Israelite, Messenian and Zionist Collective Memory." Pages 41–58 in *Community Identity in Judean Historiography: Biblical and Comparative Perspectives.* Edited by Gary N. Knoppers and Kenneth A. Ristau. Winona Lake, IN: Eisenbrauns, 2009.

Strugnell, John. "MMT: Second Thoughts on a Forthcoming Edition." Pages 57–73 Edited by Eugene Ulrich and James C. VanderKam. CJAS 10. Notre Dame, IN: University of Notre Dame Press.

Stuart, Douglas K. *Hosea-Jonah.* Accordance electronic ed. WBC 31. Grand Rapids, MI: Zondervan, 1988.

Sweeney, Marvin A. "Jeremiah 30–31 and King Josiah's Program of National Restoration and Religious Reform." *ZAW* 108.4 (1996): 569–83.

Talmon, Shemaryahu. "The New Covenanters of Qumran." *Scientific American* 225.5 (1971): 72–83.

———. "'In Those Days There Was No King in Israel,'" *Imm* 5 (1974): 27–36.

———. "Waiting for the Messiah: The Spiritual Universe of the Qumran Covenanters." Pages 111–37 in *Judaisms and Their Messiahs at the Turn of the Christian Era.* Edited by Jacob Neusner, William Scott Green, and Ernest S. Frerichs. Cambridge: Cambridge University Press, 1987.

———. "The Emergence of Jewish Sectarianism in the Early Second Temple period." Pages 587–616 in *Ancient Israelite Religion: Essays in Honor of Frank Moore Cross.* Edited by Patrick D. Miller, Paul D. Hanson, and S. Dean Mcbride. Philadelphia, PA: Fortress, 1987.

———. "The Community of the Renewed Covenant: Between Judaism and Christianity." Pages 3–24 in *The Community of the Renewed Covenant: The Notre Dame Symposium on the Dead Sea Scrolls.* Edited by Eugene Ulrich and James C. VanderKam. CJAS 10. Notre Dame, IN: University of Notre Dame Press, 1994.

———. "'Exile' and 'Restoration' in the Conceptual World of Ancient Judaism." Pages 107–46 in *Restoration: Old Testament, Jewish and Christian Perspectives.* Edited by James M. Scott. JSJSup 72. Leiden: Brill, 2001.

Taylor, Joan E. *The Immerser: John the Baptist within Second Temple Judaism.* Grand Rapids, MI: Eerdmans, 1997.

Tcherikover, Victor. *Hellenistic Civilization and the Jews.* Translated by Shimon Applebaum. Peabody, MA: Hendrickson, 1999.

Testuz, Michel. *Les idées religieuses du Livre des Jubilés.* Paris: Droz, 1960.

Theissen, Gerd. *Neutestamentliche Wissenschaft vor und nach 1945: Karl Georg Kuhn und Günther Bornkamm.* Schriften der Philosophisch-historischen Klasse der Heidelberger Akademie der Wissenschaften. Heidelberg: Universitätsverlag, 2009.

Thiel, Nathan. "'Israel' and 'Jew' as Markers of Jewish Identity in Antiquity: The Problems of Insider/Outsider Classification." *JSJ* 45.1 (2014): 80–99.

Thiessen, Matthew. "The Form and Function of the Song of Moses (Deuteronomy 32:1–43)." *JBL* 123.3 (2004): 401–24.

———. "4Q372 1 and the Continuation of Joseph's Exile." *DSD* 15 (2008): 380–95.

———. *Contesting Conversion: Genealogy, Circumcision, and Identity in Ancient Judaism and Christianity.* New York, NY: Oxford University Press, 2011.

Thomas, Samuel I. *The "Mysteries" of Qumran: Mystery, Secrecy, and Esotericism in the Dead Sea Scrolls.* EJL 25. Leiden: Brill, 2009.

Thompson, Thomas L. *The Mythic Past: Biblical Archaeology and the Myth of Israel.* London: Basic Books, 1999.

Thornton, Timothy. "Anti-Samaritan Exegesis Reflected in Josephus' Retelling of Deuteronomy, Joshua, and Judges." *JTS* 47.1 (1996): 125–30.

Tiller, Patrick A. *A Commentary on the Animal Apocalypse of 1 Enoch.* EJL 4. Atlanta, GA: Scholars Press, 1993.

Tobin, Thomas H. "Philo and the Sibyl: Interpreting Philo's Eschatology." *SPhiloA* 9 (1997): 84–103.

Tobolowsky, Andrew. *The Sons of Jacob and the Sons of Herakles.* FAT 96. Tübingen: Mohr Siebeck, 2017.

"Israelite and Judahite History in Contemporary Theoretical Approaches." *CurBR* (2018): 33–58.

Tomson, Peter J. "The Names Israel and Jew in Ancient Judaism and in the New Testament." *Bijdragen: Tijdschrift voor filosophie en theologie* 47 (1986): 120–40, 266.

Torrey, Charles Cutler. *The Composition and Historical Value of Ezra-Nehemiah.* BZAW 2. Giessen: Ricker, 1896.

Tov, Emanuel. *The Septuagint Translation of Jeremiah and Baruch: A Discussion of an Early Revision of the LXX of Jeremiah 29–52 and Baruch 1:1–3:8. 8.* Cambridge, MA: Harvard University Press, 1976.

Trafton, Joseph L. "What Would David Do? Messianic Expectation and Surprise in Pss. Sol. 17." Pages 155–74 in *The Psalms of Solomon: Language, History, Theology.* Edited by Eberhard Bons and Patrick Pouchelle. EJL 40. Atlanta, GA: SBL Press, 2015.

Trebilco, Paul R. *Jewish Communities in Asia Minor.* SNTSMS 69. Cambridge: Cambridge University Press, 2006.

Tromp, Johannes. *The Assumption of Moses. A Critical Edition with Commentary.* Leiden: Brill, 1992.

"Moses, Assumption of." *EDEJ* 970–72.

Tsedaka, Benyamin. "Samaritanism-Judaism or Another Religion?" Pages 47–51 in *Jewish Sects, Religious Movements, and Political Parties: Proceedings of the Third Annual Symposium of the Philip M. and Ethel Klutznick Chair in Jewish Civilization Held on Sunday-Monday, October 14–15, 1990.* Edited by Menachem Mor. SJC. Omaha, NE: Creighton University Press, 1990.

Tuval, Michael. *From Jerusalem Priest to Roman Jew: On Josephus and the Paradigms of Ancient Judaism.* WUNT 357. Tübingen: Mohr Siebeck, 2013.

Unnik, Willem Cornelis van. *Tarsus or Jerusalem? The City of Paul's Youth.* Translated by G. Ogg. London: Epworth, 1962.

"Aramaisms in Paul." Pages 129–43 in *Sparsa Collecta: The Collected Essays of W. C. van Unnik: Part One: Evangelia, Paulina, Acta.* Edited by William Foxwell Albright, and C. S. Mann. NovTSup 29. Leiden: Brill, 1973.

Das Selbstverständnis der jüdischen Diaspora in der hellenistisch-römischen Zeit. Edited by Pieter Willem van der Horst. AGJU 17. Leiden: Brill, 1993.

Unterman, Jeremiah. *From Repentance to Redemption: Jeremiah's Thought in Transition.* JSOTSup 54. London: Continuum, 1987.

Van der Vorm-Croughs, Mirjam. *The Old Greek of Isaiah: An Analysis of Its Pluses and Minuses.* Atlanta, G: Society of Biblical Literature, 2014.

Vanderhooft, David S. "New Evidence Pertaining to the Transition from Neo-Babylonian to Achaemenid Administration in Palestine." Pages 219–35 in *Yahwism after the Exile: Perspectives on Israelite Religion in the Persian Era.* Edited by Rainer Albertz and Bob Becking. Assen: Van Gorcum, 2003.

Vanderkam, James C. "2 Maccabees 6,7a and Calendrical Change in Jerusalem." *JSJ* 12.1 (1981): 52–74.

The Book of Jubilees: A Critical Text. 2 vols. CSCO. Leuven: Peeters, 1989.

The Dead Sea Scrolls Today. Grand Rapids, MI: Eerdmans, 1994.

"Exile in Jewish Apocalyptic Literature." Pages 89–109 in *Exile: Old Testament, Jewish, and Christian Conceptions.* Edited by James M. Scott. JSJSup 56. Leiden: Brill, 1997.

"Studies in the Chronology of the Book of Jubilees." Pages 522–44 in *From Revelation to Canon: Studies in the Hebrew Bible and Second Temple Literature.* Leiden: Brill, 2002.

"Recent Scholarship on the Book of Jubilees." *CurBR* 6.3 (2008): 405–31.

Vermes, Géza. "The Symbolical Interpretation of Lebanon in the Targums: The Origin and Development of an Exegetical Tradition." *JTS* 9.1 (1958): 1–12.

"Jewish Studies and New Testament Interpretation." Pages 58–73 in *Jesus and the World of Judaism.* London: SCM, 1983.

"Josephus' Treatment of the Book of Daniel." *JJS* 42.2 (1991): 149–66.

The Complete Dead Sea Scrolls in English. London: Penguin Books, 2004.

Vleminck, Serge. "La valeur de ἀτιμία dans le droit grec ancien." *Les études classiques* 49 (1981): 251–65.

Vogelsang, Willem J. "Medes, Scythians and Persians: The Rise of Darius in a North-South Perspective." *Iranica Antiqua* 33 (1998): 195–224.

Vos, J. S. "Antijudaismus/Antisemitismus im Theologischen Wörterbuch zum Neuen Testament." *Nederlands theologisch tijdschrift* 38 (1984): 89–110.

Vries, Simon J. de. *1 Kings.* Grand Rapids, MI: Zondervan, 2003.

Wacholder, Ben Zion. "Jubilees as the Super Canon: Torah-Admonition versus Torah-Commandment." Pages 195–211 in *Legal Texts and Legal Issues: Proceedings of the Second Meeting of the International Organization for Qumran Studies, Cambridge, 1995, Published in Honour of Joseph M. Baumgarten.* Edited by Moshe J. Bernstein, Florentino García Martínez, and John Kampen. STDJ 23. Leiden: Brill, 1997.

The New Damascus Document: The Midrash on the Eschatological Torah of the Dead Sea Scrolls: Reconstruction, Translation and Commentary. STDJ 56. Leiden: Brill, 2007.

Wagner, J. Ross. *Heralds of the Good News: Isaiah and Paul in Concert in the Letter to the Romans.* Leiden: Brill, 2003.

Reading the Sealed Book: Old Greek Isaiah and the Problem of Septuagint Hermeneutics. Waco, TX: Baylor University Press, 2013.

Wahl, Thomas P. "Chronicles: The Rewriting of History." *TBT* 26 (1988): 197–202.

Waters, Guy Prentiss. *The End of Deuteronomy in the Epistles of Paul.* WUNT 221. Tübingen: Mohr Siebeck, 2006.

Watson, Francis. *Paul and the Hermeneutics of Faith.* London: T&T Clark, 2004.

Watts, James W., and Paul R. House, eds. *Forming Prophetic Literature: Essays on Isaiah and the Twelve in Honor of John DW Watts.* JSOTSup 235. Sheffield: Sheffield Academic, 1996.

Watts, John D. W. *Isaiah 1-33.* Accordance electronic. 2nd ed. WBC 24. Grand Rapids, MI: Zondervan, 2005.

Watts, Rikki E. "Consolation or Confrontation? Isaiah 40–55 and the Delay of the New Exodus." *TynBul* 41 (1990): 31–59.

Isaiah's New Exodus and Mark. Tübingen: Mohr Siebeck, 1997.

Wearne, Gareth. "4QMMT: A Letter to (Not from) the Yaḥad." Pages 99–126 in *Law, Literature, and Society in Legal Texts from Qumran.* Edited by Jutta Jokiranta and Molly Zahn. STDJ 128. Leiden: Brill, 2019.

Webb, Barry G. *The Book of Judges: An Integrated Reading.* JSOTSup 46. Sheffield: JSOT Press, 1987.

Weber, Max. *Ancient Judaism.* Translated by Hans H. Gerth, and Don Martindale. New York, NY: Free Press, 1952.

On Charisma and Institution Building. Chicago, IL: University of Chicago Press, 1968.

From Max Weber: Essays in Sociology. London: Routledge, 2009.

Weeks, Stuart. "Some Neglected Texts of Tobit: The Third Greek Version." Pages 12–42 in *Studies in the Book of Tobit: A Multidisciplinary Approach.* Edited by Mark R. J. Bredin. LSTS 55. London: T&T Clark, 2006.

"A Deuteronomic Heritage in Tobit?" Pages 389–404 in *Changes in Scripture: Rewriting and Interpreting Authoritative Traditions in the Second Temple period.* Edited by Hanne von Weissberg, Juha Pakkala, and Marko Marttila. Berlin: de Gruyter, 2011.

"Restoring the Greek Tobit." *JSJ* 44.1 (2013): 1–15.

Weeks, Stuart, Simon Gathercole, and Loren Stuckenbruck, eds. *The Book of Tobit: Texts from the Principal Ancient and Medieval Traditions. With Synopsis, Concordances, and Annotated Texts in Aramaic, Hebrew, Greek, Latin, and Syriac.* Berlin: de Gruyter, 2004.

Weinreich, Max. *Hitler's Professors: The Part of Scholarship in Germany's Crimes Against the Jewish People.* 2nd ed. New Haven, CT: Yale University Press, 1999.

Weissenberg, Hanne von. *4QMMT: Reevaluating the Text, the Function, and the Meaning of the Epilogue.* Leiden: Brill, 2009.

Weitzman, Steven. "Allusion, Artifice, and Exile in the Hymn of Tobit." *JBL* (1996): 49–61.

Song and Story in Biblical Narrative: The History of a Literary Convention in Ancient Israel. Bloomington, IN: Indiana University Press, 1997.

Wellhausen, Julius. *Prolegomena to the History of Israel.* Translated by J. S. Black, and A. Menzies. Edinburgh: Black, 1885.

"Israel und das Judentum." Pages 370–431 in *Prolegomena zur Geschichte Israels.* Berlin: Reimer, 1886.

"Das Gesetz." Pages 177–87 in *Israelitische und jüdische Geschichte.* Berlin: Reimer, 1958.

Wells, Kyle B. *Grace and Agency in Paul and Second Temple Judaism: Interpreting the Transformation of the Heart.* Leiden: Brill, 2014.

Wenham, Gordon J. *Genesis 16–50.* Accordance electronic ed. WBC 2. Grand Rapids, MI: Zondervan, 1994.

West, Mona. "Irony in the Book of Jonah: Audience Identification with the Hero." *PRSt* 11 (1984): 232–42.

Westerholm, Stephen. "Whence 'The Torah' of Second Temple Judaism." Pages 19–43 in *Law in Religious Communities in the Roman Period.* Edited by

Peter Richardson and Stephen Westerholm. Waterloo, ON: Wilfrid Laurier University Press, 1991.

Wette, W. M. L. de. "Dissertatio critica qua Deuteronomium a prioribus Pentateuchi libris diversum alius cuiusdam auctoris opus esse monstratur." PhD diss., Jena, 1805.

Biblische Dogmatik des Alten und Neuen Testaments oder kritische Darstellung der Religionslehre des Hebraismus, des Judentums und des Urchristentums. 3rd ed. Berlin: Realschulbuchhandlung, 1813.

Whaley, Ernest Boyd. "Samaria and the Samaritans in Josephus's 'Antiquities' 1–11." PhD diss., Emory University, 1989.

White, L. Michael. "The Delos Synagogue Revisited: Recent Fieldwork in the Graeco-Roman Diaspora." *HTR* 80.2 (1987): 133–60.

White Crawford, Sidnie A. "The Rewritten Bible at Qumran." Pages 173–95 in *The Hebrew Bible and Qumran.* Edited by James H. Charlesworth. North Richland Hills, TX: Bibal Press, 1998.

———. "Reading Deuteronomy in the Second Temple period." Pages 127–40 in *Reading the Present in the Qumran Library: The Perception of the Contemporary by Means of Scriptural Interpretation.* Edited by Kristin De Troyer, Armin Lange, Katie M. Goetz, and Susan Bond. SymS 30. Leiden: Brill, 2005.

Wijnsma, Uzume Z. "The Worst Revolt of the Bisitun Crisis: A Chronological Reconstruction of the Egyptian Revolt under Petubastis IV." *JNES* 77.2 (2018): 157–73.

Wilckens, Ulrich. *Der Brief an der Römer.* EKKNT VI/1. Neukirchen-Vluyn: Neukirchener Verlag, 1980.

Williams, Margaret H. "The Meaning and Function of Ioudaios in Graeco-Roman Inscriptions." *Zeitschrift für Papyrologie und Epigraphik* (1997): 249–62.

Williams, Ritva. "*BTB* Readers' Guide: Social Memory." *BTB* 41.4 (2011): 189–200.

Williamson, Hugh G. M. *Israel in the Books of Chronicles.* Cambridge: Cambridge University Press, 1977.

———. "Eschatology in Chronicles." *TynBul* 28 (1977): 115–54.

———. *Ezra-Nehemiah.* Accordance/Thomas Nelson electronic ed. WBC 16. Louisville, KY: Nelson, 1985.

———. "The Concept of Israel in Transition." Pages 141–61 in *The World of Ancient Israel: Sociological, Anthropological and Political Perspectives.* Edited by Ronald E. Clements. Cambridge: Cambridge University Press, 1989.

———. *The Book Called Isaiah: Deutero-Isaiah's Role in Composition and Redaction.* Oxford: Clarendon, 1994.

———. *Isaiah 1–5.* ICC. London: T&T Clark, 2006.

Wills, Lawrence M. "Jew, Judean, Judaism in the Ancient Period: An Alternative Argument." *JAJ* 7.2 (2016): 169–93.

Wilson, Gerald H. "The Prayer of Daniel 9: Reflection on Jeremiah 29." *JSOT* 48 (1990): 91–99.

Wilson, Stephen G. "'Jew' and Related Terms in the Ancient World." *SR* 33 (2004): 157–71.

Winston, David. *Logos and Mystical Theology in Philo of Alexandria*. Cincinnati, OH: Hebrew Union College Press, 1985.

"Review of *Das Selbstverständnis der jüdischen Diaspora in der hellenistisch-römischen Zeit*, by Willem Cornelis van Unnik." *AJSR* 20.2 (1995): 399–402.

Wolf, Werner. "Metareference across Media: The Concept, Its Transmedial Potentials and Problems, Main Forms and Functions." Pages 1–85 in *Metareference across Media: Theory and Case Studies*. Edited by Werner Wolf. SIM. Amsterdam: Rodopi, 2009.

ed. *The Metareferential Turn in Contemporary Arts and Media: Forms, Functions, Attempts at Explanation*. SIM. Amsterdam: Rodopi, 2011.

Wolff, Hans Walter. "Das Kerygma des deuteronomischen Geschichtswerks." *ZAW* 73 (1961): 171–86.

Wolfson, Harry A. *Philo: Foundations of Religious Philosophy in Judaism, Christianity, and Islam*. 2 vols. Cambridge, MA: Harvard University Press, 1947.

Woude, Adam S. van der. *Jona, Nahum*. POuT. Nijkerk: Callenbach, 1978.

Wright III, Benjamin G. *No Small Difference: Sirach's Relationship to Its Hebrew Parent Text*. Atlanta, GA: Scholars Press, 1989.

Wright "Conflicted Boundaries: Ben Sira, Sage and Seer." Pages 229–53 in *Congress Volume Helsinki 2010*. 148. Edited by Martti Nissinen. VTSup 148. BRILL: 2012.

Wright III, Benjamin G., and Claudia V. Camp. "'Who has Been Tested by Gold and Found Perfect?'" Pages 71–96 in *Praise Israel for Wisdom and Instruction: Essays on Ben Sira and Wisdom, the Letter of Aristeas and the Septuagint*. JSJSup 131. Leiden: Brill, 2008.

Wright, G. Ernest. "The Provinces of Solomon." *ErIsr* 8 (1967): 58–68.

Wright, Jacob L. *Rebuilding Identity*. BZAW 348. Walter de Gruyter, 2004.

Wright, N. T. "The Lord's Prayer as a Paradigm of Christian Prayer." Pages 132–54 in *Into God's Presence: Prayer in the New Testament*. Edited by Richard N. Longenecker. McMaster New Testament Studies. Grand Rapids, MI: Eerdmans, 2001.

"Israel's Scriptures in Paul's Narrative Theology." *Theology* 115.5 (2012): 323–29.

Wright, Robert B. "Psalms of Solomon." Pages 639–70 in *OTP* 2. Edited by James H. Charlesworth. Garden City, NY: Doubleday, 1985.

The Psalms of Solomon: A Critical Edition of the Greek Text. Jewish and Christian Texts Series. London: T&T Clark, 2007.

Wright, William A. "Note on the 'Arzareth.'" *Journal of Philology* 3 (1871): 113–14.

Yadin, Yigael. "Some Notes On: The Newly Published 'Pesharim' of Isaiah." *IEJ* 9.1 (1959): 39–42.

The Ben Sira Scroll from Masada. Jerusalem: Israel Exploration Society, 1965.

"Is the Temple Scroll a Sectarian Document?" Pages 153–69 in *Humanising America's Iconic Book*. Edited by G. Tucker and D. Knight. Chico, CA: Scholars Press, 1982.

Yonge, Charles Duke. *The Works of Philo: Complete and Unabridged*. Peabody, MA: Hendrickson, 1993.

Younger, K. Lawson. "The Deportations of the Israelites." *JBL* 117.2 (1998): 201–27.

"The Fall of Samaria in Light of Recent Research." *Catholic Biblical Quarterly* 61.3 (1999): 461–82.

Zangenberg, Jürgen. *Samareia: Antike Quellen zur Geschichte und Kultur der Samaritaner in deutscher Übersetzung*. Tübingen: Francke, 1994.

Frühes Christentum in Samarien: topographische und traditionsgeschichtliche Studien zu den Samarientexten im Johannesevangelium. TANZ. Tübingen: Francke, 1998.

Zapff, Burkard M. *Jesus Sirach 25–51*. NEchtB. Würzburg: Echter, 2010.

Zappella, Marco. "L'immagine di Israele in Sir 33(36),1–19 secondo il ms. ebraico B e la tradizione manoscritta greca. Analisi letteraria e lessicale." *RivB* 42.4 (1994): 409–46.

Zawadzki, Stefan. "Bardiya, Darius and Babylonian Usurpers in the Light of the Bisitun Inscription and Babylonian Sources." *Archäologische Mitteilungen aus Iran* 27 (1994): 127–45.

Zeitlin, Solomon. "The Names Hebrew, Jew and Israel: A Historical Study." *JQR* 43.4 (1953): 365–79.

"Did Agrippa Write a Letter to Gaius Caligula?" *New Series* 56.1 (1965): 22–31.

Zellentin, Holger. "The End of Jewish Egypt: Artapanus and the Second Exodus." Pages 27–73 in *Antiquity in Antiquity: Jewish and Christian Pasts in the Graeco-Roman World*. Edited by Gregg Gardner and Kevin Lee Osterloh. TSAJ 123. Tübingen: Mohr Siebeck, 2008.

Zertal, Adam. "The Pahwah of Samaria (Northern Israel) during the Persian Period. Types of Settlement, Economy, History and New Discoveries." *Transeu* 3 (1990): 9–30.

"The Province of Samaria (Assyrian Samerina) in the Late Iron Age (Iron Age III)." Pages 377–412 in *Judah and the Judeans in the Neo-Babylonian Period*. Edited by Oded Lipschits and Joseph Blenkinsopp. Winona Lake, IN: Eisenbrauns, 2003.

Zimmerli, Walther. "Israel im Buche Ezechiel." *VT* 8.1 (1958): 75–90.

Ezekiel I: A Commentary on the Book of the Prophet Ezekiel, Chapters 1–24. Edited by Frank Moore Cross and Klaus Baltzer. Translated by Ronald E. Clements. Accordance electronic ed. Hermeneia. Philadelphia, PA: Fortress, 1979.

Ezekiel II: A Commentary on the Book of the Prophet Ezekiel, Chapters 25–48. Accordance electronic ed. Hermeneia 26B. Philadelphia, PA: Fortress, 1979.

Zimmermann, Frank. *The Book of Tobit*. Dropsie College ed. Jewish Apocryphal Literature. New York, NY: Harper, 1958.

Zoccali, Christopher. "'And So All Israel Will Be Saved': Competing Interpretations of Romans 11.26 in Pauline Scholarship." *JSNT* 30.3 (2008): 289–318.

Whom God has Called: The Relationship of Church and Israel in Pauline Interpretation, 1920 to the Present. Eugene, OR: Pickwick, 2010.

Zsengellér, József, ed. *Samaria, Samarians, Samaritans: Studies on Bible, History and Linguistics*. SJ 66. Berlin: de Gruyter, 2011.

Zunz, L. "Dibre-Hayamim oder die Bücher der Chronik." Pages 13–36 in *Die Gottesdienstlichen Vorträge der Juden, historisch Entwickelt*. Berlin: Asher, 1832.

Index of Primary Sources

General Index

Abegg, Martin G., 266, 274, 276, 284
Abraham, 1, 6, 45, 73, 76, 92, 127, 192, 235, 300
Ackroyd, Peter R., 121
age of wrath, 141, 156, 160, 163, 168–69, 172–73, 175–77, 202, 265, 267, 286, 316, 347
Agrippa, 213, 235
Al Yahudu, 41, 148
Alexander the Great, 68, 70
Alexander, T. Desmond, 93, 120
Alexandria, 69–70, 187, 189, 195, 249, 309, 311–12
allegory, 239, 241, 245, 248, 254, 291
am haaretz See people of the land
anachronisms, 44, 58, 83, 152, 171, 294, 303, 306
anti-Judaism/anti-Semitism, 12, 29–39, 55, 72, 146, 209
Antiochus IV Epiphanes, 67, 163, 171, 223, 285, 306
apocalyptic literature, 97, 161, 164, 196, 245, 250, 316–38
apocalypticism, 95, 162, 164, 245, 250, 316
Apocrypha, 290
apoikia, 188, 191, 234, 236, 239–40, 332, *See also* diaspora
Aristobulus II, 281
ark of the covenant, 175
assembly, 156–58, 324, 347

Assyria, 51, 56, 62–63, 98, 108, 114, 122, 124, 127, 130–31, 150, 266, 271–72, 274, 299, 303–4
campaigns against Israel, 56, 62, 108, 122–23
Athens, 144–45
Atkinson, Kenneth R., 325
Attridge, Harold W., 209

Babylon, 45, 49–51, 56, 137, 150, 195, 299, 335
Baker, Cynthia M., 13, 19, 31, 347
Balaam, 220, 229, 242, 246, 254
Baltzer, Klaus, 125, 127, 129
Bar Kokhba, 42, 169, 172, 207, 221, 224, 346
Barclay, John M. G., 27, 81, 200
Barmash, Pamela, 49, 61, 109, 230, 321
basic concept, 5, 9
Bauckham, Richard J., 294–96, 301
Beattie, D. R. G., 51, 72, 78, 80, 293, 305
Beek, M. A., 32, 34–35
Benjamin, 49, 51, 92, 114, 143, 149, 153, 156, 271–72, 284, 342
Bergsma, John S., 172, 259, 262–63
Bernasconi, Rocco, 346
Berrin, Shani L., 129, 279–80, 282
Bethel, 148, 282
Bilde, Per, 220–21
Birnbaum, Ellen, 233, 253–54, 256
Bloch, Renée, 316
Blumhofer, Christopher, 21

420